PSYCHOLOGY
Its Principles and Applications

Engle/Snellgrove

HARCOURT BRACE JOVANOVICH, PUBLISHERS

Orlando   San Diego   Chicago   Dallas

AUTHORS

T.L. Engle is widely known for his many contributions to high school psychology courses. Dr. Engle has taught psychology and other subjects in high schools and also has worked with secondary school teachers for many years. He is Professor Emeritus of Psychology at Indiana University at Fort Wayne. Dr. Engle has written numerous articles for professional journals on the teaching of high school psychology and has served as chairman of several committees of the American Psychological Association on teaching psychology at the secondary school level.

Louis Snellgrove is Professor of Psychology at Lambuth College, Jackson, Tennessee. He has researched many projects and activities for the teaching of high school psychology and has been a full-time counselor to high school students. In addition, Dr. Snellgrove has been active in many APA activities related to high school psychology. He has published a number of articles on psychology and is the author of *Psychological Experiments and Demonstrations.*

CONTRIBUTORS

Dr. George M. Diekhoff, Midwestern State University, Wichita Falls, Texas
Dr. John Hensley, Midwestern State University, Wichita Falls, Texas
David K. Hogberg, Albion College, Albion, Michigan
Dr. Patricia A. Lutwack, Florida International University, Miami, Florida
Dr. Paul Wellman, Texas A&M University, College Station, Texas
Dr. Kathleen White, Boston University, Boston, Massachusetts

Acknowledgments

For permission to reprint copyrighted material, grateful acknowledgment is made to the following sources:

Academic Press, Inc.: From "Beliefs, Personality and Person Perception: A Theory of Individual Differences" by Nancy Hirschberg and Susan J. Jennings in *Journal of Research in Personality,* Vol. 14, 1980, pp. 235–248. Copyright © 1980 by Academic Press, Inc.

Academic Press, Inc. and Charles D. Spielberger: From "Test Anxiety Reduction, Learning Strategies, and Academic Performance" by Charles D. Spielberger, Hector P. Gonzalez, and Tucker Fletcher in *Cognitive and Affective Learning Strategies,* edited by Harold F. O'Neil, Jr. and Charles D. Spielberger. Copyright © 1979 by Academic Press, Inc.   *(Acknowledgments continue on page 533.)*

Printed in the United States of America

ISBN 0–15–374800–1

PSYCHOLOGY

Its Principles and Applications

NINTH EDITION

Critical Readers and Consultants

CONTENTS

UNIT 1  INTRODUCTION

Chapter 1   **A LOOK AT PSYCHOLOGY**   2

What Is Psychology?	2
What Psychologists Study	4
Psychology and Other Sciences	5
Early History of Psychology	6
Later Developments in Psychology	8
The Field of Psychology Today	11
Psychology and You	15
CASE STUDY: FOCUS ON RESEARCH	12
INTERPRETING SOURCES	17

Chapter 2   **PSYCHOLOGICAL METHODS**   21

Studying Behavior Scientifically	21
Psychological Experiments	24
Correlational Research	29
Nonscientific Approaches to Psychology	30
The Study of Parapsychology	31
CASE STUDY: FOCUS ON RESEARCH	26
INTERPRETING SOURCES	35

UNIT 2

HUMAN GROWTH AND DEVELOPMENT

Chapter **3** **HUMAN DEVELOPMENT** 42

Patterns of Development 42
Prenatal Development 44
Physical Development 45
Motor Development 46
Language Development 47
Emotional Development 52
Social Development 54
Intellectual Development 56
Moral Development 58
CASE STUDY: FOCUS ON RESEARCH 50
INTERPRETING SOURCES 61

Chapter **4** **HEREDITY AND ENVIRONMENT** 65

Inherited Characteristics 65
Some Studies of Heredity 67
Heredity and Maturation 70
Influences of the Environment 74
Heredity and Environment Interact 75
CASE STUDY: FOCUS ON RESEARCH 72
INTERPRETING SOURCES 79

Chapter **5** **BIOLOGICAL INFLUENCES ON BEHAVIOR** 84

Nervous Systems 84
The Brain 87
Glands 92
Sleep 95
Methods Used in Hypnosis 98
CASE STUDY: FOCUS ON RESEARCH 90
INTERPRETING SOURCES 101

UNIT 3

UNDERSTANDING HUMAN BEHAVIOR

Chapter **6** **UNDERSTANDING PERSONALITY** 108

The Development of Personality 108
Theories of Personality 111
Psychoanalytic Theories 111
Social Psychoanalytic Theories 114
Behavioristic Theories 118
Humanistic Theories 122
Some Criticisms of Personality Theories 125
CASE STUDY: FOCUS ON RESEARCH 120
INTERPRETING SOURCES 127

Chapter **7** **MEASURING PERSONALITY** 131

Standardized Tests 131
Ratings 133
Personality Inventories 135
Interviewing 139
Behavior Sampling 141
Projective Techniques 141
Achievement and Aptitude Tests 143
Vocational Interest Inventories 145
CASE STUDY: FOCUS ON RESEARCH 136
INTERPRETING SOURCES 149

Chapter **8** **MEASURING INTELLECTUAL ABILITY** 154

The Nature of Intelligence 154
Individual Tests of Intelligence 156
Group Tests of Intelligence 158
The Intelligence Quotient (IQ) 161
Some Uses of Intelligence Tests 166
Mental Retardation 167
Superior Intelligence 170
CASE STUDY: FOCUS ON RESEARCH 164
INTERPRETING SOURCES 173

UNIT 4

LEARNING AND THINKING

Chapter 9	PRINCIPLES OF LEARNING	180
	What Is Learning?	180
	Classical Conditioning	181
	Operant Conditioning	188
	The Role of Punishment	193
	Operant Conditioning and Programmed Learning	194
	Operant Conditioning and Biofeedback	196
	Cognitive Learning	197
	CASE STUDY: FOCUS ON RESEARCH	184
	INTERPRETING SOURCES	201

Chapter 10	LEARNING, REMEMBERING, AND FORGETTING	206
	Learning Efficiently	206
	The Process of Learning	213
	Remembering	214
	Forgetting	220
	CASE STUDY: FOCUS ON RESEARCH	218
	INTERPRETING SOURCES	223

Chapter 11	THE PROCESS OF THINKING	228
	What Is Thinking?	228
	Uncritical Thinking	230
	Creative Thinking	232
	Imagining	236
	Problem Solving	237
	CASE STUDY: FOCUS ON RESEARCH	238
	INTERPRETING SOURCES	243

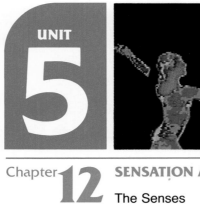

UNIT 5

PERCEPTION, EMOTIONS, AND MOTIVES

Chapter **12**

SENSATION AND PERCEPTION 252

The Senses 252
Perceptions 253
Attention 254
Vision 257
Hearing 264
Other Sense Fields 267
CASE STUDY: FOCUS ON RESEARCH 262
INTERPRETING SOURCES 271

Chapter **13**

MOTIVATION AND EMOTIONS 276

The Concept of Motivation 276
Biological Drives 277
Social Motives 279
Intrinsic Motivation versus Extrinsic Motivation 285
Emotions and Bodily Changes 285
Theories of Emotion 286
Measuring Emotional States 289
CASE STUDY: FOCUS ON RESEARCH 280
INTERPRETING SOURCES 292

ix

UNIT 6

CONFLICTS AND ADJUSTMENTS

Chapter 14 **FACING FRUSTRATION AND CONFLICT** 300

Frustration 300
Kinds of Conflicts 303
Adjustment Mechanisms 308
CASE STUDY: FOCUS ON RESEARCH 312
INTERPRETING SOURCES 320

Chapter 15 **COPING WITH STRESS** 324

The Nature of Stress 324
What Determines Stress? 326
Change as a Stressor 331
Stress Through the Life Cycle 335
Controlling Stress 336
CASE STUDY: FOCUS ON RESEARCH 328
INTERPRETING SOURCES 340

Chapter 16 **PSYCHOLOGICAL DISTURBANCES** 345

Psychological Disturbances in Our Society 345
Psychological Disorders 348
Various Approaches to Psychological Disturbances 363
CASE STUDY: FOCUS ON RESEARCH 350
INTERPRETING SOURCES 367

Chapter 17 **TREATMENT OF PSYCHOLOGICAL DISTURBANCES** 372

Medical Therapy 372
Psychotherapy 373
Behavior Therapy 376
Group Therapy 378
Mental Hospitals and Community Centers 379
The Effectiveness of Different Therapies 380
CASE STUDY: FOCUS ON RESEARCH 382
INTERPRETING SOURCES 386

UNIT 7

SOCIAL BEHAVIOR

Chapter **18** **BEHAVIOR IN SMALL GROUPS**   394

The Influence of Small Groups   394
Kinds of Small Groups   397
The Effectiveness of Small Groups   401
Belonging to Small Groups   404
Keeping Small Groups Together   405
How Group Roles Vary   407
Communication Within a Group   408
CASE STUDY: FOCUS ON RESEARCH   398
INTERPRETING SOURCES   415

Chapter **19** **SOCIAL INFLUENCE**   419

Social Attitudes   419
Changing Attitudes   420
Attribution   422
Leadership   423
The Power of Authority   426
Peer-Group Influence   430
Male and Female Roles   433
CASE STUDY: FOCUS ON RESEARCH   428
INTERPRETING SOURCES   437

Chapter **20** **SOCIAL INTERACTION**   442

Helping Others   442
Social Facilitation   452
Social Competition   453
The Effects of Competition   457
Social Cooperation   459
CASE STUDY: FOCUS ON RESEARCH   448
INTERPRETING SOURCES   463

Using Statistics   471   **Glossary**   507
Careers in Psychology   483   **Index**   523
Biographical Profiles   503

CASE STUDY: FOCUS ON RESEARCH

Chapter 1	The Remarkable Pigeon	12
Chapter 2	A Surprise at Western Electric	26
Chapter 3	The Silent World of Genie	50
Chapter 4	"You Look Just Like Me"	72
Chapter 5	A Brain Divided	90
Chapter 6	Subject See, Subject Do	120
Chapter 7	"Beware—Generalities Ahead"	136
Chapter 8	When a Test Is Not the Answer	164
Chapter 9	Fearless Albert and Fearful Peter	184
Chapter 10	"I Saw It with My Own Eyes"	218
Chapter 11	"A Penny for Your Thoughts"	238
Chapter 12	Crossing the Checkered Cliff	262
Chapter 13	Animals Need Love, Too	280
Chapter 14	Learning Not to Learn	312
Chapter 15	Type A Behavior and Your Health	328
Chapter 16	Sixteen People All in One	350
Chapter 17	You Are What You Eat	382
Chapter 18	A Minority of One	398
Chapter 19	The Power of Power	428
Chapter 20	Helping the Helpless	448

INTERPRETING SOURCES

		Author	
Chapter	1	Amedeo Giorgi	17
Chapter	2	Frank McGuigan	35
Chapter	3	Lawrence Kohlberg	61
Chapter	4	Jules Asher	79
Chapter	5	Doreen Kimura	101
Chapter	6	Nancy Hirschberg and Susan Jennings	127
Chapter	7	Melvin Marx and William Hillix	149
Chapter	8	Kevin McKean	173
Chapter	9	Farnum Gray	201
Chapter	10	Roberta Klatzky	223
Chapter	11	James Adams	243
Chapter	12	Peter Lindsay and Donald Norman	271
Chapter	13	Paul Ekman and Wallace Friesen	292
Chapter	14	C. R. Snyder	320
Chapter	15	Charles Spielberger, Hector Gonzalez, and Tucker Fletcher	340
Chapter	16	D. L. Rosenhan	367
Chapter	17	Harold Sackeim	386
Chapter	18	Marvin E. Shaw	415
Chapter	19	Neal Osherow	437
Chapter	20	Bibb Latané and John Darley	463

DEVELOPING SKILLS IN PSYCHOLOGY

Chapter 1	Identifying Data and Inferences	19
Chapter 2	Formulating Hypotheses	37
Chapter 3	Using Case Studies to Examine Psychological Concepts	63
Chapter 4	Understanding a Bar Graph	82
Chapter 5	Using the Library to Further Your Understanding	104
Chapter 6	Identifying Implicit Theories	129
Chapter 7	Classifying Information	152
Chapter 8	Reading Tables	175
Chapter 9	Diagramming Relationships	204
Chapter 10	Mastering Descriptive Statistics	226
Chapter 11	Classifying Types of Uncritical Thinking	246
Chapter 12	Using the *Psychological Abstracts*	274
Chapter 13	Keeping a Behavioral Record	295
Chapter 14	Content Analysis of Literary Materials	322
Chapter 15	Creating a Stress Scale	343
Chapter 16	Generating Alternative Interpretations	370
Chapter 17	Using the *Citation Index*	389
Chapter 18	Achieving Reliability	418
Chapter 19	Understanding Attitudes and Behavior	440
Chapter 20	Designing an Experiment	465

USING THE SKILLS OF A PSYCHOLOGIST

Unit 1	Evaluating Evidence	39
Unit 2	Interpreting Data	105
Unit 3	Evaluating Test Validity	177
Unit 4	Shaping Behavior Through Conditioning	249
Unit 5	Identifying Emotions	297
Unit 6	Learning How Values Affect Behavior	391
Unit 7	Studying Group Behavior	467

CAREERS
IN PSYCHOLOGY

Becoming a Psychologist   483
Experimental Psychologist   484
Developmental Psychologist   485
Rehabilitation Counselor   486
Special Education Teacher   487
Writer/Editor   488
Personnel Manager   489
School Psychologist   490
Educational Psychologist   491
Teacher   492
College Professor   493
Occupational Therapist   494
Marriage/Family Counselor   495
Guidance Counselor   496
Industrial Psychologist   497
Psychiatric Nurse   498
Clinical Psychologist   499
Salesperson   500
Probation or Parole Officer   501
Social Psychologist   502

INTRODUCTION

Chapter 1   A LOOK AT PSYCHOLOGY
Chapter 2   PSYCHOLOGICAL METHODS

Chapter 1

A LOOK AT PSYCHOLOGY

Chapter Focus

This chapter presents:
- **a definition of psychology**
- **the relationship of psychology to the other sciences**
- **a brief history of psychological thought**

"If you eat your spinach, you'll grow up to be big and strong."

"Mmm, I wish *I* had liver for dinner."

"Now open the hangar and let the airplane in."

No doubt, you've heard these and similar expressions during a baby's feeding time. The parent uses "psychology" in an attempt to get the child to eat. Very often one of these strategies works, and the child passively finishes the meal. If not, the parent might try a different approach—or a different type of food.

Parents are not the only ones who use "psychology." Suppose, for example, you are scheduled to help your parents clean the house. You had fully intended to keep the commitment, but a spurt of good weather, just right for a baseball game, has given you second thoughts. To solve this dilemma you might make your younger sister a deal. If she fills in for you at home, she can borrow some of your records.

Or suppose you are planning to play tennis this afternoon. Your opponent is a better player, although somewhat smaller. To help you win you might try to create a powerful image and "outpsych" your opponent.

These examples tell us how ordinary people view psychology. But how do psychologists define psychology? This chapter will examine what psychology is all about.

What Is Psychology?

Not all researchers think of psychology in exactly the same way. For one thing, as you will see, psychology is a relatively new science and has not yet established a standard definition accepted by all. In addition, there are many branches of psychology, each approaching the subject somewhat differently. Just as the approaches differ, the definitions differ. Nevertheless, before you can study psychology, you must have a working definition of the term.

Despite their differences, most researchers would agree that **psychology** is the science that deals with the behavior and thinking of organisms. ("Psychology" comes from the Greek words *psyche* and *logos*. *Psyche* means "mind" or "soul" and *logos* means "study of.") This definition contains four important words that must be examined—science, behavior, thinking, and organism.

Science. A *science* is a branch of study that is based on systematically conducted research. Such research is undertaken in order to prove or disprove ideas about what we think we know. Scientists conduct research by collecting information, or data, in an organized fashion. That is, they do not just collect a fact here and a fact there, but instead follow strict procedures.

Suppose a student wants to conduct research on how the reading scores at Midland High School compare with the national average. The student overhears a friend talk about some low reading scores and concludes that all of Midland's scores must be lower than those in the rest of the country.

Was the student gathering information scientifically? Definitely not. The student did not have any sound data on which to base conclusions. An acceptable way of conducting the research would have been to talk to knowledgeable people at the school, check primary sources such as newspapers and statistical studies, and analyze the information carefully and without any bias. Only proper research methods yield sound results.

Behavior and thinking. The second important term in the definition of psychology is behavior. In psychology, *behavior* refers to those activities of people or animals that can be observed directly or measured by special techniques.

Many kinds of behavior can be observed directly, such as eating, talking, or running around the room. Other kinds of behavior cannot be measured so easily. For example, how might a teacher measure what you have learned in your history course? The instructor can't tell just by looking at you. Perhaps the teacher will give you a test—one way of finding out what you have learned.

Throughout his baseball career, slugger Reggie Jackson "outpsyched" many an opposing pitcher with his home-run swing. Other athletes also have used what they consider to be "psychology" to defeat their opponents.

Psychologists often wish to learn about our emotional behavior. This display of affection between a mother and child might be of interest to a psychologist.

Much more complicated measuring techniques may be necessary to study such behaviors as emotions. Some emotions result in directly observable behavior, such as crying when we are sad or shouting when we are angry. However, some emotions can be measured only by using complicated devices. An emotion such as anxiety, for example, might be measured through changes in heartbeat or blood pressure. These changes can be measured only with special machines.

Thinking refers to unobservable activity by which a person or animal reorganizes past experiences through the use of symbols and concepts. It can be studied only through observable behavior or through tests or physiological changes, such as heart rate. For example, suppose you are asked to rearrange the furniture in your classroom to increase the interaction among the students. You propose placing all chairs in a circle because all students then will be facing one another. Your behavior suggests that you gave some thought to the situation. Actually, the process of thinking is much more complex than is implied here. Thinking will be discussed in more detail in Chapter 11.

Organism. An *organism* is any living person or animal. Although psychologists are primarily interested in human beings, they may study chimpanzees, pigeons, rats, or other animals. One reason for studying animals is that many experiments cannot be performed on human beings.

For example, suppose researchers wanted to learn what would happen to babies who were deprived of proper care. The scientists would certainly not try to find out by taking human babies away from their parents. Such an experiment, however, has been performed with monkeys, and the results have greatly expanded our knowledge of infant development. Research suggests, for instance, that there is a bond between infants and the major caretaker, who is usually the mother.

What Psychologists Study

So far you have learned that psychology is the science that deals with the behavior and thinking of organisms. In studying behavior and thinking, psychologists focus on both common and unusual activities.

Psychology and everyday life. Psychologists are interested in many day-to-day behaviors. For example, a psychologist might focus on a behavior as common as eating. Do people eat because they are hungry or because it is "lunchtime"? What role might stress play in a person's eating habits? Psychologists have also studied such behaviors as sleep, speech patterns, and our ability to remember. In doing so, they have learned about behaviors we take for granted.

In addition, psychologists have studied certain everyday situations. Suppose, for example, that you go to a job interview. What role would your appearance, your sex, or your age play? How might the distance you sit from the interviewer affect the way the person reacts to you?

Or suppose you are invited to a party. Why might one person act like the life of the party, while another spends the evening sitting alone in a quiet corner? Why might one guest hear a baby cry above the noise of the crowd, while another seems not to hear a person talking just a few feet away? These are only a few of the situations that interest psychologists.

Psychology and "abnormal" behavior. Although much of psychology is concerned with our everyday lives, some psychologists study what is commonly referred to as "abnormal" behavior. For example, a psychologist might try to find out why a person went berserk and shot several people, or why a seemingly content individual took an overdose of drugs. However, this area of concern is only a small part of the varied subject matter of psychology.

In studying "abnormal" behavior psychologists first try to diagnose the problem, which includes determining the cause. Was the berserk attacker fired from a job earlier in the week? Did the person have marital problems? Had the person ever shown other signs of disturbed behavior? Based on what the psychologist finds out, the psychologist tries to help the person. There are currently many different ways of treating such behavior disturbances.

Psychology and Other Sciences

In studying the various aspects of behavior, psychologists often draw on the findings of many other sciences. Other scientists, in turn, make use of psychological knowledge. In what ways is psychology related to other sciences?

Psychology and physics, chemistry, and biology. Psychology has gained a great deal from the physical and biological sciences. From physics, psychology has borrowed a number of instruments for measuring bodily changes. Many psychology laboratories today have complex and expensive electronic

equipment. For example, some labs make use of electronic tubes and electron optics.

From chemistry, psychology has learned much about how the body's chemistry relates to mood, performance, and personality disturbance. In addition, chemists have developed a number of medications useful in the treatment of psychological disorders.

Biologists have provided psychology with information about the sense organs, the nervous system, and our glands. Moreover, they have uncovered a wealth of information about the brain—the basis for human behavior. Biology has also contributed greatly to our understanding of heredity. The characteristics we inherit from our parents partially influence the type of people we become.

Unlike in physics, chemistry, and biology, however, the focus of psychology is always on *behavior*. Psychologists study the various activities, or behavior, of an organism.

Listening to music is a typical part of everyday life for many teen-agers. Although we may take such behavior for granted, psychologists may find it very revealing.

Psychology and anthropology and sociology. Other sciences also are concerned with behavior, but in a slightly different way. **Anthropology** is the study of the culture, or way of life, of people in all parts of the world. Anthropologists provide psychologists with valuable information on how people learn and how they are affected by their surroundings. For example, in her studies of three tribes in New Guinea during the 1930's, anthropologist Margaret Mead found strong evidence that our male and female roles are culturally determined rather than biologically determined.

Sociology is the study of human groups. It is the science most closely related to many areas of psychology. The chief difference, however, is that sociologists focus primarily on the behavior of groups while psychologists focus primarily on the behavior of the individual. Sociologists usually conduct research within their own culture. Some topics studied by sociologists are family life, urban and rural living, shifts in population growth, crime, and voting trends. Sociologists use their research as the basis for information made available to psychologists.

Sociology and psychology overlap in an area known as social psychology. **Social psychology** is concerned with the effects of groups on the individual and with how individuals think about other people. For example, a social psychologist might study how leadership patterns emerge in a group and affect group behavior.

Early History of Psychology

From the scope of its subject matter you might think that the science of psychology has existed for hundreds of years. Actually, psychology has existed for only about a century. Before that time, people speculated about human behavior, offering to explain it through various reasoning processes. However, they did not begin to study behavior scientifically until the late 1800's.

The earliest developments. To people in the Stone Age, life must have been mystifying indeed. What made the body alive and then left it at death? What happened to the body during sleep or unconsciousness?

Our early ancestors may have tried to explain these phenomena by suggesting that the body was inhabited by spirits of various kinds. These spirits were thought to be responsible not only for life itself but for various kinds of behavior as well. For example, a person who behaved abnormally was thought to be possessed by evil spirits.

The logical treatment for abnormal behavior was to help the evil spirits escape. Consequently, Stone Age people sometimes chipped a hole in the skull of the afflicted person. This crude method, which we know about from archeological evidence, usually resulted in the death of the person on whom it was practiced. We say "usually," though, because some of these people actually survived!

Fortunately, this "treatment" did not gain overwhelming support, although it was practiced in some societies as late as the Middle Ages. However, the ancient belief in good and evil spirits persisted. In many of the world's cultures, in fact, it continues today.

The ancient Egyptians. The ancient Egyptians took a different approach to human behavior. They believed that inside each person was an even smaller person called Ka who was responsible for behavior. Eventually the question arose as to who controlled Ka. The answer was "Ka number two," who was even smaller than Ka. This line of reasoning was used up to Ka number seven. At this point it stopped, because the number seven was sacred to the Egyptians and was not to be questioned.

What evidence did the Egyptians use to prove Ka existed? Just look into the eye of someone and you will see a little person peering out at you!

The ancient Greeks. Much of ancient Greek thought concerning behavior stemmed from philosophy. The philosopher Plato be-

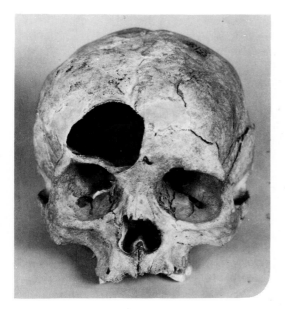

By drilling a hole in the skull, our Stone Age ancestors hoped to release evil spirits from afflicted individuals. This victim may not have been one of the lucky survivors.

lieved that the mind and body are two distinct elements, with the mind having a life of its own both before birth and after death. Plato's student Aristotle, however, took an opposing view. He argued that mind and body are related and act as one unit. According to Aristotle, one could not exist without the other.

A major contribution to psychological thought was based largely on the work of Hippocrates, who has been called "the father of medicine." According to Hippocrates, abnormal behavior was not caused by evil spirits. Rather, it had natural causes. These might be internal, such as disease or a chemical imbalance within the body, or they might be external, such as a head injury.

One of Hippocrates' important "discoveries" was that the body contains four vital fluids called "humors," each corresponding to a force of nature (fire, water, earth, and air). These humors were blood, phlegm, black bile, and yellow bile. According to Hippocrates, an imbalance among these humors produced a particular type of personality. A person whose body contained excess blood was warmhearted, but might suffer from rapid shifts of mood. Someone with too much phlegm would be phlegmatic—sluggish and apathetic. If too much black bile was present, the person would be melancholic, or sad. And if there was too much yellow bile, the person would be choleric, or aggressive and irritable.

Although many of Hippocrates' theories were primitive, his theory that body chemistry affects behavior was a major breakthrough. Modern medicine is still exploring the connection between body chemistry and "mental" problems—a connection that Hippocrates identified more than 2,000 years ago.

The Middle Ages. During the Middle Ages the achievements of the Greeks were largely forgotten in Western Europe. The Middle Ages saw a striking revival of the idea that behavior could be explained by the actions of good and evil spirits. Those who behaved abnormally were considered to be possessed by demons.

Many of these unlucky people were made to withstand the rites of exorcism. These were rituals that were intended to drive the demons out of the body. Sometimes these rites were harsh, and the victim was whipped, starved, or immersed in hot water. Although this treatment was cruel, it did not usually result in death. Such a fate was reserved for the "witches" of the period, many of whom were burned at the stake.

The 1600's and 1700's. With the rise of modern science in Europe in the 1600's, speculation began again about the biological foundations of behavior. The French philosopher Descartes, for example, proposed that the mind and the body interact. According to Descartes, each influenced the other although neither controlled the other. The ideas of Aristotle and Hippocrates surfaced once more.

Not all developments were this promising, though. The development of phrenology was a step backward. Phrenology was a false sci-

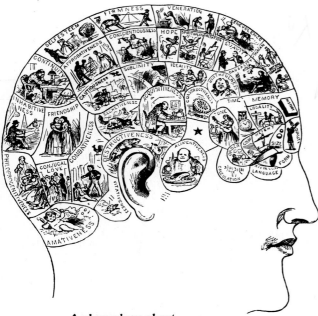

A phrenology chart.

ence, based purely on unfounded theories, that dates from the late 1700's. Phrenologists believed that they could read people's personality and character by feeling the bumps on their heads. This was possible, phrenologists thought, because the brain was made up of a number of "faculties." Each faculty had a given location on the skull. Thus, a person whose "faculty" for friendship or destructiveness was particularly well developed would have a prominent bump in the appropriate place.

We now know that bumps on the head have nothing to do with personality. Yet the belief in phrenology persisted into the 1800's.

Later Developments in Psychology

Despite the popularity of phrenology, true scientific developments were taking place throughout the 1800's. During this period, physicists were discovering the nature of the atom. Biologists were revealing new information about cells. Still other scientists were proposing theories about the nature of be-

havior. Let's take a brief look at some of these theories. More detailed information about personality theories will be given in Chapter 6.

Wundt's structuralism. Psychology is usually said to have begun in 1879, when Wilhelm Wundt set up the first psychology laboratory at the University of Leipzig in Germany. In actuality, Wundt was a professor of physiology, but his interest lay in studying human behavior.

Wundt sought to learn about human consciousness. However, he was faced with a problem. He could not put the human mind under a microscope. Consequently he had to develop a different technique, which consisted of two aspects. The first aspect was introspection—a process by which people closely examine their own thoughts. The second aspect was experimentation. Experiments involve carefully controlled procedures and are the basis of scientific research.

Because Wundt studied the structure of human consciousness, his approach came to be known as **structuralism.** Wundt is best known, however, for turning the study of behavior into a science.

The functionalism of William James. Up until the late 1800's, psychology was based mostly on German thought. Americans traveled to Wundt's laboratory in Leipzig, where they studied under this respected scholar. They then returned to the United States to apply the knowledge they had acquired. Harvard professor William James, however, changed all that. He developed a new branch of psychology in this country.

James approached the study of human behavior from a different perspective than did Wundt. James believed that studying the structure of the mind was far less important than studying how the mind works. The proper emphasis of psychology, as James saw it, should be how the human mind functions in helping us adapt to our surroundings. Because of the importance that James placed on how the mind functions, his approach became known as **functionalism.**

WILHELM WUNDT

WILLIAM JAMES

SIGMUND FREUD

Freud and the psychoanalytic school. If your mental image of psychology includes a bearded psychiatrist listening to a patient describe some innermost thoughts and dreams while reclining on a couch, it is probably because of the ideas of Sigmund Freud. Sigmund Freud began his career as a physician in the late 1800's in Austria. While treating some of his patients, he noticed that some were suffering from certain disabling illnesses, such as paralysis, for which no physical cause could be found. This discovery greatly perplexed Freud and ultimately led to the development of psychoanalysis.

Psychoanalysis is based on the idea that human behavior is greatly influenced by feelings and wishes that are buried deep inside a person. Consequently, people are unaware of them. In fact, many times these thoughts contradict those of which they are aware. This situation often produces severe inner conflicts in people.

A young man with a paralyzed right arm, for example, might be unconsciously enraged at his father. Deep down he might wish to strike at his father, although on the surface both father and son get along quite well. This conflict has disabled the son's arm and keeps the young man from hitting his father.

The cure for such a problem, Freud thought, was to make the person aware of these unconscious feelings. Once the person recognized the unconscious feelings and discovered their source, the disability usually would vanish. The process of bringing unconscious feelings to the surface is called ***psychoanalysis.***

Freud first attempted to help his patients by hypnotizing them. Later he turned to the method known as free association. In this technique the patient is asked to say the first things that come to mind, regardless of whether they seem to make sense. For example, somebody who fears water might be asked to free-associate with the word "water." The first word that comes to mind might be "drown."

Freud also used dream analysis to get at a patient's unconscious feelings. He reasoned that dreams often serve as a means of fulfilling our unconscious wishes. For example, a shy student might dream of being outgoing. An assembly-line automobile worker might dream of becoming a famous creative artist. Therefore, analyzing the person's dreams might reveal some deep-rooted unconscious desires.

Freud believed that all human beings — not just the psychologically troubled — were influenced by their unconscious wishes and desires. As a result, he applied his theory of behavior to everyone.

The behaviorists. Many early psychologists relied on introspection as a means of studying behavior. To John B. Watson, a psychologist in the early 1900's, this was a serious error. Because the mind could not be seen, Watson argued, it could not be measured. Therefore even the most carefully prepared introspective report did not constitute scientific evidence. What did make up the subject matter of psychology? According to Watson, observable behavior should be the focus of study. Because of Watson's views, this approach is called **behaviorism.**

The behaviorists believe that our surroundings are very important in determining our personalities. From infancy on, our behavior is shaped—that is, we are rewarded for some kinds of behavior and punished for others. For example, if you study hard for a test, you may receive a good grade. Or, in contrast, if you stay out past your parents' curfew, you may be "grounded" for a week. To the behaviorists, it is the sum total of these rewards and punishments that have made us what we are.

An important implication of behaviorism is that our behavior is totally determined by our surroundings. According to a strict behaviorist, there is no such thing as free will, so we are not responsible for our actions. For example, according to a strict behaviorist,

a criminal did not choose a life of crime. Rather, given the way the person was shaped, the individual could have become nothing else. In fact, Watson asserted that he could take a normal, healthy infant and, given control of the environment, turn that child into just about anything—a doctor, a lawyer, or even a thief.

The behaviorist approach is still an important one in modern psychology. Its best known representative today is B. F. Skinner. Skinner revised and expanded Watson's theories in a number of books and articles.

Another important behaviorist is Albert Bandura. Bandura believes that behavior is learned mostly through observation and imitation. We learn, he argues, by watching and imitating models. Models are people that serve as examples of how to behave.

Gestalt psychology. At about the same time that behaviorism was taking shape in the United States, another branch of psychology arose in Germany. This was **Gestalt psychology.** (Gestalt is the German word for "form" or "shape.")

While behaviorists focus on learning and observed behavior, Gestalt psychologists study how people use the five senses to extract information from the environment. Gestalt psychologists believe that the overall

JOHN B. WATSON

B. F. SKINNER

ALBERT BANDURA

Through shaping, even tigers can learn to behave like kittens. This photographer, though, took no chances and shot the picture through the fence.

form, shape, or pattern of things is determined by how people perceive or interpret a series of separate sensations. Their study focuses on the everyday perceptions of people. For example, how do people determine distance or perceive motion?

Gestalt psychologists stress that the whole is more important than the individual parts that make it up. For example, we are able to identify the pattern of a particular song because of the relationship of the notes, or parts, to each other. The song may be heard in any key, but our perception of the pattern, or whole, is not changed. If the notes are rearranged, we perceive a different pattern, or a different song.

An understanding of how a series of still pictures becomes a motion picture illustrates the principle of Gestalt psychology. For example, each individual frame of a motion picture is a still photograph. When these frames are shown in rapid succession, however, you no longer see still photographs but

objects and people in motion. According to Gestaltists, then, a movie is more than just a series of still photographs; and the whole complex picture of everyday human behavior is more than the parts that make it up.

The Field of Psychology Today

The brief descriptions of five approaches to psychological thought may leave you wondering. Which are right? Which have been proved correct? Which have been discarded?

As you consider the different theories, remember that psychology is a young science that goes back little more than a hundred years. One reason that several theories are still being discussed and disputed is that we simply don't know enough yet to prove or disprove any theory completely and more work is needed.

Text continues on page 14.

Case Study: Focus on Research

THE REMARKABLE PIGEON

Would you believe that pigeons can bowl, play table tennis, and play the piano? Perhaps they can't do so in the way that we might, but they have been taught these skills nonetheless. Through a series of shaping procedures, psychologist B. F. Skinner and other researchers have taught pigeons some very humanlike behaviors.

The bowling experiment grew out of a World War II project that Skinner and a colleague were working on in 1943. The roof above their makeshift laboratory on the top floor of a flour mill happened to serve as home to large flocks of pigeons. Easily caught, these birds made convenient subjects for experiments. One day, to relieve the tension of their more serious research, Skinner and his fellow researcher decided to teach a pigeon how to bowl.

Earlier, Skinner and his colleague had taught the pigeon to respond to an auto-matic grain dispenser. Whenever the dispenser made a certain sound and the pigeon turned toward the machine, the bird was promptly rewarded with some grain. This set the pattern for rewarding other favorable behaviors.

Now the researchers aimed to teach the pigeon to knock down a set of toy pins at the other end of a miniature alley. Using its beak, the pigeon was to send a small wooden ball careening down the alley in the direction of the pins. With the grain dispenser fully loaded, Skinner placed the ball in the pigeon's "bowling alley" and prepared to reward the bird as soon as the first "roll" took place. To the surprise of the researchers, no such behavior occurred.

The researchers soon grew tired of waiting. They decided to reward any response that was a step in the right direction. Thus as soon as the pigeon looked at the ball—although accidentally—it was given some grain. The next reward occurred as soon as the pigeon took a step closer to the ball. Then the pigeon received some grain after it came *very* close to the ball. Next it had to touch the ball before receiving any food.

By rewarding a series of behaviors—each one closer to the desired final outcome—Skinner was soon able to achieve his goal. Within a short period, the bird acted like a champion bowler! Today any good animal trainer can teach a pigeon to bowl in less than two hours.

In another experiment, Skinner taught two pigeons to play table tennis. The pigeons were placed on opposite sides of a small table and were conditioned to swat a ball back and forth between them. When one missed the ball, the ball dropped into a trough. This triggered a grain dispenser to

Parrots, as well as pigeons, can be trained easily to perform various humanlike tasks. This parrot has been trained to "count" to four with blocks.

reward the victor with some grain. The loser, however, often did not accept defeat graciously. Skinner had to place a wire shield between the two players because the loser sometimes tried to attack its opponent.

In a more serious project, Skinner trained a group of pigeons to guide missiles that might be used to attack enemy targets during World War II. The method was relatively simple. Skinner had trained the birds to peck at a target that appeared on a screen. In an actual mission the pigeons would be mounted in the nose of a missile and would peck at the image of a real target—for example, a railroad station. This pecking would trigger a guidance system. As soon as the missile started straying from its intended target, the pigeons' pecking behavior would activate the system and bring the missile back on course.

However, despite repeated displays of the pigeons' abilities, the project was never given serious consideration by government scientists. They refused to believe that a pigeon could be trusted to carry out such a crucial assignment.

Skinner was a pioneer in demonstrating how the behavior of pigeons and other animals can be easily shaped. Other researchers, however, also carried out some fascinating projects. In one experiment psychologist Thom Verhave trained pigeons to serve as quality-control inspectors in a pharmaceutical (prescription drug) company. These pigeons were able to identify defective capsules at an accuracy rate of 99 percent within one week of daily training. (See pages 189–190 for a more detailed description of this project.) Like Skinner's missile project, though, this one was never put into actual practice.

Each of these experiments is an example of a research project in psychology. Although all of these projects involved only pigeons, plentiful research has also been carried out with other animals and with people. (Of course, there are guidelines that researchers must follow. These are discussed on page 28.)

Throughout the rest of this book you will read about some of these research studies. Like this research feature, all will appear on beige-tinted pages and will fall at appropriate places in the book. There will be one research feature in each chapter. By reading these features, you will become part of the exciting world of psychological research.

SOURCE: B. F. Skinner, "Reinforcement Today," *American Psychologist*, 1958, *13*, 94–99; B. F. Skinner, "Pigeons in a Pelican," *American Psychologist*, 1960, *15*, 28–37; Thom Verhave, "The Pigeon as a Quality-Control Inspector," *American Psychologist*, 1966, *21*, 109–115.

"Keep your eye on the ball" would be good advice to these players in their game of table tennis.

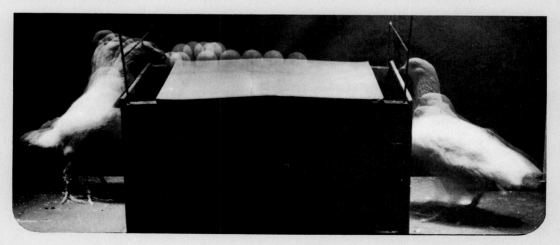

Because of the way our thought processes work, many of us would conclude that this boy's sheep has just won a prize at a fair. Cognitive psychologists study how we process information.

Contributions of each approach. A good way to look at the competing approaches is to consider the contributions of each. To Wundt and the structuralists, we owe the beginnings of a scientific approach to the study of psychology. James and the functionalists reminded us that we must study how the mind works if we are to understand behavior.

Freud introduced us to a buried part of our nature, the unconscious. Focusing on the unconscious, he offered us a new way of interpreting behavior.

Watson and the behaviorists greatly expanded our knowledge of how people learn. In addition, they reminded us of the importance of our surroundings and encouraged the use of well-designed experimental methods.

Finally, the Gestalt psychologists urged us to consider behavior in context rather than in isolation. This enables us to see the whole picture.

Of these viewpoints, psychoanalysis, behaviorism, and Gestalt psychology are still prominent today, although in revised versions. The others are no longer important as theoretical approaches. Instead, their contributions have been accepted into the body of psychology as a whole. And the very early approaches—the belief in Ka, the "humors" theory, and phrenology—have just about been dismissed completely.

The five psychological approaches discussed here are not the only important ways of looking at human behavior. In the mid-1900's, many other branches of psychology developed, often in response to earlier views. Three important branches are cognitive psychology, existential psychology, and humanistic psychology.

Cognitive psychology. Cognitive psychology developed in response to behaviorist theories on learning and to new discoveries about how the brain functions. According to cognitive psychologists, the behaviorists oversimplified the process of learning. Instead of focusing on rewards and punishments, *cognitive psychology* focuses on how people perceive, store, and interpret information.

For example, consider the following passage: "Mary heard the ice-cream truck coming down the street. She remembered her birthday money and ran into the house." Most of us would conclude that Mary wants ice cream and that she is going to buy some. Yet nowhere does the passage say this. We draw such conclusions because of how we process information. Cognitive psychologists are interested in the way we use our knowledge to fill in gaps to create new thoughts.

Cognitive psychologists also study how thought processes develop over time. For example, they might examine how your thought processes as a ten-year-old differed from what they are today. Other cognitive psychologists study the connections between thought and feeling. In other words, they look at how our patterns of thinking can help make us feel good or bad.

Existential psychology. A branch of psychology that stresses the importance of individual choice in determining human behavior is *existential psychology.* This branch was a reaction to the ideas of both the behaviorists and the psychoanalysts. Representatives of those two branches believed that behavior is largely determined by events in childhood. Existentialists, however, believe that people have free will. An adult's behavior is not simply determined by events that happened many years earlier. Existentialists, then, believe that behavior is determined by a combination of previous events and the choice of the individual.

Humanistic psychology. *Humanistic psychology* is the study of how people try to achieve their maximum potential, or "self-actualization," through health and self-growth. Humanistic psychology resembles both Gestalt psychology and existential psychology. Like the Gestaltists, humanists argue that people are more than just the sum of their parts. And like the existentialists, humanists believe that people have free will and can control their own behavior.

Current views. Most psychologists today do not take any one approach to the study of behavior, but instead take an eclectic, or combined, approach. They might agree with some of the behaviorists' views, but they may find others unsuitable. They may support some psychoanalytic theories but disregard others. Many times, the problem they are trying to solve helps determine the approach they decide to take. For example, Sigmund Freud proposed several explanations for understanding the significance of people's dreams. In a problem concerning dream interpretation, a psychologist may turn to psychoanalytic theories. Yet the same psychologist might turn to behaviorism when studying why some children frequently disrupt their class in school.

At the same time, psychologists may seek new explanations for difficult concepts. They may propose new theories that seem to further our understanding of human behavior. This is how psychology grew from its small beginnings to its current position.

Psychology and You

As you can see, psychology is a new and exciting field, growing and changing in response to new developments. As such it offers people many opportunities to become a part of it.

For adults, there are many rewarding careers dealing with different areas of psychology. For example, people who enjoy working with teen-agers might be interested in becoming adolescent psychologists. Or people who like to help individuals with personal problems might consider a career in clinical psychology. There are still other careers that make use of psychology, although in an indirect way. Teaching, writing, and research are examples of such careers.

Psychology offers many career opportunities to those who enjoy helping others. People who choose service careers often find them very rewarding.

You may be interested in learning about some of the possible careers in psychology. In the appendix material, you will find features that focus on specific careers. Some of the careers that have been profiled include a developmental psychologist, an experimental psychologist, a social psychologist, an industrial psychologist, an occupational therapist, a rehabilitation counselor, a teacher, a salesperson, and a guidance counselor. These career features try to shed some light on the broad spectrum of opportunities available to people with an interest in studying behavior.

You may also wish to learn more about yourselves. What makes you do the things you do? Can you learn to remember more things? Why do you react as you do when you are frightened? The chapters that follow present an overview of the different aspects of behavior. Although the chapters cannot provide definite answers, they will give you some insight into behavior. That's what psychology is all about.

Summary

Psychology is the science that deals with the behavior and thinking of organisms. Psychologists study many different aspects of behavior, ranging from everyday behaviors such as eating and sleeping, to abnormal behavior such as why people kill others.

Psychology has drawn on the findings of many other sciences, including sociology. In fact, psychology and sociology overlap in an area known as social psychology.

Psychology, as a science, has existed for only about a hundred years. Before that time, people tried to explain behavior through various reasoning processes. But it wasn't until Wilhelm Wundt founded his laboratory in 1879 that psychology gained its scientific foundations.

Wundt's structuralism was an attempt to study the structure of human consciousness based on introspection and experimentation. This school of thought was soon followed by the functionalism of William James. James believed that the proper emphasis of psychology should be how the mind functions in helping us adapt to our surroundings.

Sigmund Freud developed the psychoanalytic approach to understanding behavior. It is based on our unconscious wishes and desires. Through such processes as hypnosis, free association, and dream interpretation, Freud was able to get at his patients' unconcious feelings.

Behaviorism is based on the study of observable and measurable behavior. Behaviorists believe that the shaping of behavior is based on rewards and punishment. According to the behaviorists, there is no such thing as free will. John B. Watson and B. F. Skinner are two important behaviorists.

The Gestalt psychologists stress the concept of the whole. They believe that the overall form, shape, or pattern of things is determined by how people perceive or interpret a series of separate sensations.

Each of these approaches has contributed to our understanding of human behavior. In addition, there have been other approaches put forth, most notably cognitive psychology, existential psychology, and humanistic psychology.

In recognition of psychology's 100th anniversary in 1979, the American Psychological Association brought together a group of America's most eminent psychologists to discuss developments in psychology during the preceding century. The following excerpt is from *A Century of Psychology as Science.* In an address given by Amedeo Giorgi, it is argued that psychology is so diversified and fragmented that it is difficult to conceive of it as a single discipline. As you read the excerpt, think about whether you agree or disagree with this assessment.

It is clear to most astute observers of the field that psychology's disciplinary status is ambiguous at best and chaotic at worst.... Its precise meaning and its place among the other sciences are still to be determined in a manner acceptable to the majority of psychologists. Throughout its history, psychology has been described as a natural science, a human science, two or more sciences, as intrinsically nonscientific—and other things too numerous to mention. Every decade of its history has been a questioning of psychology's status and a demand that it be conceived as other than it was.... I think the ambiguous status of psychology as a discipline can be demonstrated equally convincingly ... by quoting two evaluations of psychology's status that ... appeared one hundred years apart....

In 1879, the very year of the alleged founding of psychology, G. H. Lewes ... wrote: ["] In every science we define the object and scope of the search, the motive of the search, and the means whereby the aim may be reached.... A glance at the literature of (psychology) discloses the utmost discordance on these cardinal points . . . . ["]

In 1979...J. R. Kantor wrote: "It is quite apparent that in spite of all the historical efforts to make psychology a science, and the ambition of psychologists to convert psychology to a science, this discipline cannot fully qualify as a natural science.... Many persons still regard it as a problem whether psychology is an authentic science or at best only a profession."

The fact, I think, that establishes the point I want to make is that one could easily reverse the dates of these two descriptions and find that they are equally applicable. Both make the claim that psychology should be a natural science, and both find it wanting. Moreover, no sense of progress is evident when one compares the two assessments....

Psychology's crisis is not contemporary but perennial. We did not have an early and adequate coherence that we lost over time; we never were coherent.... While from time to time there has been agreement with respect to a label—study of mind, consciousness, psyche, experience, or behavior—a common in-depth understanding of each of those terms was never achieved....

Simply calling psychology the science of behavior, or of experience, or both, will no longer do if one cannot, in turn, say what behavior and experience are....

I believe that psychology's disciplinary status cannot be solidified until we clarify the meaning of psychology, however difficult that may be. Once we know in depth what we mean by psychology ... we should be able to discover how to approach [psychology] systematically.... I do not believe that is yet a historical theoretical scientific achievement....

Source Review

1. What do you think J. R. Kantor meant when he questioned "whether psychology is an authentic science or at best only a profession"?

2. Having read the excerpt, do you agree that there is no such thing as a single psychology? Can you think of anything that all psychologists share in common?

CHAPTER 1

REVIEWING TERMS

psychology
science
behavior
thinking
organism
anthropology

sociology
social psychology
structuralism
functionalism
psychoanalysis
behaviorism

Gestalt psychology
cognitive psychology
existential psychology
humanistic psychology

CHECKING FACTS

1. Why do psychologists define psychology in different ways?

2. How do researchers study behavior?

3. Describe the subject matter of psychology. Give some examples of what psychologists might be interested in.

4. In what ways is psychology related to the other sciences?

5. Describe the early developments concerning human behavior in the Stone Age and ancient Egypt.

6. How did Hippocrates contribute to the development of psychological thought?

7. Why is Wundt considered the founder of psychology? Describe his approach.

8. How does functionalism differ from structuralism?

9. What contributions did Freud make to the study of human behavior? Describe Freud's views.

10. According to the behaviorists, what determines personality? What role does free will play?

11. What do Gestalt psychologists believe about perception?

12. Describe the contributions made by each approach to psychology.

13. What are some of the new branches of psychology? Discuss the main ideas of each.

APPLYING YOUR KNOWLEDGE

1. Look through your local newspaper or a magazine for statements that appear to be based on scientific research. (Advertisements might be particularly good for this assignment.) Then analyze the statements closely to see if they were based on carefully collected data or on personal opinions.

2. Select an organism, human or otherwise, and observe its behavior for five minutes. Take notes on as many details as possible, focusing on actions that you might ordinarily overlook. How does detailed observation increase our understanding of behavior? Which of our common behaviors might be better understood with careful observation?

3. Suppose a friend or a classmate strongly believed that behavior is controlled by "Ka." How would you prove that "Ka"

doesn't exist? You and another student might try acting out this situation. You will find that your task is more difficult than you think.

4. Over the course of a school day, keep track of the way your behavior is shaped. For example, did one of your teachers acknowledge a correct answer in class? Did someone comment on your clothes? Based on your observations, do you agree that behavior is determined solely by rewards and punishments? What counter arguments might you propose?

5. Prepare a timeline that traces the development of psychology. After you have finished, study the timeline to see how each event may have been caused or influenced by the event that preceded it. Did psychology develop in a logical fashion? Explain.

THINKING CRITICALLY ABOUT PSYCHOLOGY

1. **Interpreting Ideas** Psychologists use animals in their experiments quite often. Do the results obtained from such studies apply also to human beings? Why or why not?

2. **Forming Opinions** Do you think that psychology is as "true" a science as chemistry, physics, or biology? Explain.

3. **Debating Ideas** Some people might argue that psychology is based mostly on common sense. Do you agree?

4. **Analyzing Ideas** Why do you think psychology as a science took so long to develop?

5. **Evaluating Ideas** Why might people believe in such false sciences as phrenology? What other false sciences can you name?

6. **Drawing Conclusions** What direction do you think psychology will take in the next ten years? Explain your answer.

DEVELOPING SKILLS IN PSYCHOLOGY

Identifying Data and Inferences

Data are the basic facts with which scientists work. Scientists use the data they collect to derive *inferences,* which are tentative conclusions or generalizations that go beyond the data.

When scientists disagree about something, it is more likely to be about inferences than about data. For example, there is ample data that little boys tend to behave more aggressively than little girls in almost every society in the world, and that they have done so throughout history. Some psychologists infer from these data that the greater aggressiveness of males is biologically determined.

Other psychologists disagree with this interpretation of the data. They argue that males have always been rewarded for aggressiveness more than females have. These psychologists reject the inference that we can do nothing about human aggressiveness because of its biological basis. Both groups of psychologists try to back up their inferences by showing how the data support their view.

Conduct library research to collect data on the percentages of psychologists in different fields and settings. What kinds of inferences might you draw about the general popularity of different fields in psychology? What kinds of inferences might you draw about the predominant interests of people who go into psychology?

READING FURTHER ABOUT PSYCHOLOGY

American Psychological Association, *Careers in Psychology,* Washington D.C., 1986. Discusses the nature of psychology, what psychologists do, where they work, and the various fields of study in psychology.

Bruner, Jerome, *In Search of Mind,* Harper & Row, New York, 1984. An autobiographical inquiry that explores the author's own experiences in the field of psychology. Also looks at the men and women who contributed to the growth of psychology over the past 50 years.

Bugelski, Bergen R., and Graziano, Anthony M., *The Handbook of Practical Psychology,* Prentice-Hall, Englewood Cliffs, N.J., 1980. Discusses psychological concepts used in the study of mental disorders, emotional disturbances, intelligence, personality, memory, and so on. A general guide to over 500 psychological problems.

Hearnshaw, L. S., *The Shaping of Modern Psychology,* Routledge & Kegan Paul Inc., New York, 1987. Discusses the historical development of psychology, medical and social influences on the field, and the application of these influences on modern psychology.

McNamara, J. Regis, editor, *Critical Issues, Developments and Trends in Professional Psychology,* Praeger, New York, 1984. Focuses on the remarkable changes that the field of psychology has undergone in the United States over the past decade.

Miller, Jonathan, *States of Mind,* Pantheon, New York, 1983. In a series of 15 interviews, the author gives a representative view of the current state of psychology.

Reed, Jeffrey G., and Baxter, Pam M., *Library Use: A Handbook for Psychology,* American Psychological Association, Washington, D.C., 1983. A manual for those new to the field of psychology. Discusses the process involved in selecting a research topic and provides introductory, how-to-use coverage of library sources. Contains carefully labeled illustrations of actual resource materials.

Smith, Samuel, *Ideas of the Great Psychologists,* Harper & Row, New York, 1983. A compact reference work that describes the ideas of almost all of the major contributors to psychological thought.

Wertheimer, Michael, *A Brief History of Psychology,* Third Edition, Holt, Rinehart and Winston, New York, 1986. A concise yet complete overview of the history of psychology. This easy-to-read volume includes new material reflecting the contributions by women to the field and the use of computers in psychology.

Chapter 2

PSYCHOLOGICAL METHODS

Chapter Focus

This chapter presents:

- **the various methods psychologists use to study behavior scientifically**
- **the procedures and problems of psychological experiments**
- **some nonscientific research methods**

A commercial flashes on the TV screen. The announcer boasts that children who use one brand of toothpaste have fewer cavities.

Does this mean that the toothpaste advertised prevents cavities? Of course, the advertiser would like you to draw that conclusion. But let's look at this claim more closely to see how you may be misled. For one thing, you might note that the basis for comparison is unclear. Do these children have fewer cavities than children who don't brush their teeth at all? Than children who don't use toothpaste? Or than children who use a different brand?

Also, even if there appears to be a relationship between a brand of toothpaste and a decrease in tooth decay, you can't be certain that one *causes* the other. Perhaps these children drink plenty of milk. Or perhaps they don't eat cake and candy. These other factors may be more influential than the toothpaste used.

From this example you can see why people can easily misinterpret data, or information. Psychologists are aware of this tendency and try to analyze their data scientifically. In this chapter we will examine the methods that psychologists use.

Studying Behavior Scientifically

When studying behavior scientifically, researchers keep in mind five guidelines. First, the behavior being studied must be measurable. That is, changes in behavior must be able to be detected by the human eye or other measuring devices. Second, the methods and data must be objective. In other words, the opinions of the experimenters must enter into the gathering and interpreting of data as little as possible. Third, the procedures must be repeatable. Other individuals who wish to do the same experiment or expand upon the data must be able to do so.

Fourth, scientists must be able to communicate the results of their experiment to others. They often do this at scientific meetings or through articles in professional journals. After all, what good would the data be if no one but the experimenter knew about them or could understand them? Finally experimenters must use an organized and systematic approach in gathering data. This means that they must follow an orderly arrangement of procedures.

A number of scientific methods and techniques have these five characteristics. We will look at some that are especially suited to studying behavior.

Natural observation. This method consists of observing and recording the behavior of organisms in their natural environment. We can learn about how individuals adjust to social situations by observing them and their companions at informal social gatherings. We can find out about people's attitudes by listening to their conversation.

Natural observation quite often includes the use of tape recorders, motion pictures, and other ways of recording data. It provides a record of activities. It has the disadvantage of giving little or no information about why or how behavior occurs. However, it does provide a description of the way organisms behave in their surroundings. Later, ideas about the reasons for the behavior can be checked in a laboratory.

Directed observation. This method involves observing behavior under controlled conditions in an experimental or a laboratory setting. For example, a psychologist using this method might plan to observe how children react to specific toys. Children might then be brought into a laboratory to be observed. All details, no matter how trivial, would be recorded in shorthand, by a camera, or by some other device.

Although this method allows for the control of events and behaviors, some people object to the data obtained. They claim that taking an organism from its natural environment may change the behavior being measured. Another objection is that people are biased in their observations. Of course, this applies to other methods as well. But researchers using this method try to record their data objectively.

The case-study method. Psychologists, social workers, and psychiatrists often use the case-study method. They try to get objective descriptions of the background forces that may have influenced an individual's development. The case record includes information on family background, home life, neighborhood activities, experiences at school, health, and so on. This method is based on the idea that the more we know about individuals, the better we will be able to understand and help them.

The case-study method is very useful in some psychological work. But it has certain limitations. For instance, the information usually comes from parents, teachers, and other associates of the individual being studied. Without meaning to, these people may give partial and biased reports rather than the impartial and objective reports that psychologists need.

Interviews. In psychology, sociology, and other fields, data are often obtained through interviews. Perhaps you have been interviewed by your teacher or guidance counselor. Certainly you have been interviewed if you have ever applied for a job. Public opinion researchers conduct interviews to determine attitudes toward certain products or to predict voting trends. Psychologists use interviews for such purposes as putting together an individual's case record or studying prejudices in groups.

The value of data from an interview depends on how well the interviewer has been trained for the job. For instance, good interviewers are careful to establish rapport—that is, a relaxed and cooperative relationship—with the person being interviewed. They plan in advance what questions they are going to ask and the general order in which they will ask them. Nevertheless, they keep the interview flexible enough so that both parties can bring up topics not on the list of questions. The skilled interviewer can add to the data by observing gestures and expressions, or noting topics that the person being interviewed tries to avoid.

The entire interview may be tape-recorded. Interviewers can then play it back for further consideration. They may call in other trained interviewers to hear and evaluate the entire recorded interview.

The interview method is widely used. But

it has drawbacks. One is the problem of getting rid of the personal prejudices of the interviewer. Another is the difficulty of expressing the results of an interview in exact terms. A person may be recorded as being "favorable" toward a group. But how favorable— 100 percent? 50 percent? This sort of vagueness rules out the exact measurement that is necessary in all scientific work.

Despite these shortcomings, interviews conducted by well-trained people can provide valuable data. Also, it is possible to train individuals to reduce errors in observing behavior during an interview. One common error is the tendency of the interviewer to rate people more favorably when they are similar to the interviewer. Using videotaped interviews and training interviewers to be aware of such errors helps reduce this tendency in interviewing.

The questionnaire method. This method consists of giving a list of questions on some subject to a selected group of individuals. Occasionally, the questions are asked directly in an interview. The questions are not a test with right or wrong answers. Rather, they are designed to gather facts about the individuals or to get their opinions. The answers to the questions can be treated statistically.

There are disadvantages to the questionnaire method. Individuals answering a questionnaire may give inaccurate replies. If they don't like the questions, they may decide to give false responses. Often, investigators don't receive replies from 100 percent of the people to whom they send questionnaires. Frequently, less than 50 percent reply. And those who do reply may not represent the group being studied very well. But despite these limitations, a well-formed questionnaire sent to carefully selected groups can give useful information about trends in behavior.

Tests and similar methods of measurement. Psychologists have devoted much time to developing tests to measure intellectual ability. They have designed aptitude

1. How many courses are you taking this semester?
   ___ one   ___ four
   ___ two   ___ five
   ___ three   ___ other

2. Which of these courses are electives?
   ___ psychology   ___ history
   ___ government   ___ economics
   ___ sociology   ___ other

3. Why did you choose the elective(s) you did?
   (Check as many as apply.)
   ___ You were interested in the subject.
   ___ It was the only course that fit into your program.
   ___ You liked the teacher.
   ___ Your friends were taking the course.
   ___ Other

A good questionnaire should be clear, free of bias, and related to what the researcher wishes to find out. This chart contains sample questions from a questionnaire on your course load this semester.

tests, which help predict what individuals are likely to accomplish if they receive training in a given field. Psychologists also have techniques for measuring attitudes toward social problems. And they have measuring devices for basic vocational interests and personality characteristics. You are no doubt familiar with achievement tests, which measure how well you have mastered certain subject matter, such as math or history.

Tests and similar methods of measurement are valuable in psychology. They give more objective data than interviews and questionnaires. They give results that can be expressed in statistical terms. Often an individual's score can be compared with scores for large groups. Nevertheless, tests must be used with care. Some people think a psychologist can give them a few tests and then tell them exactly what college to attend, what job to take, and which person to marry. This is not the case. Even with the most expert interpreter, test results do not give full and final answers to individual problems. They should be used only as a means to an end. Test results are but one source of important data. They are only one aspect of studying the behavior of an organism.

Psychological Experiments

The method that psychologists use most is the experimental method. Perhaps you think of experiments as activities carried out in laboratories containing dials, meters, rows and rows of bottles, glass tubing, and so on. Some experiments require such equipment. But many worthwhile experiments can be carried out in the classroom with the aid of simple apparatus. The method, rather than the amount of equipment, determines the value of the work. The experimental method permits control over conditions and provides psychologists with relatively accurate measurement of behaviors.

Setting up an experiment. An experiment usually begins with a hypothesis. Simply stated, a **hypothesis** is a tentative assumption or an educated guess that is often based on some previous research. It is sometimes stated in an *If-then* form. For example, the following might be a hypothesis: *"If people are rewarded, then they will become more productive."*

A hypothesis always states a relationship between two or more variables. A **variable** is any condition or behavior that can change in amount or in quality. In the hypothesis above, the variables are rewards and people's degree of productivity.

In experiments, researchers want to test the effect of one variable on another. Thus, a hypothesis usually contains two types of variables—an independent variable and a depen-

In the experimental method, some psychologists prefer using animals as their subjects. It is usually much easier to control the conditions under which the experiment takes place if animals are used.

dent variable. The *independent variable* is controlled and manipulated by the experimenter to determine how it affects the dependent variable. Ideally, it causes any changes that result. The *dependent variable*, in contrast, changes in response to the independent variable.

In the above example the degree of productivity, the dependent variable, changes in response to whether or not people are rewarded, the independent variable. An easy way to remember the distinction is to think of the dependent variable as *depending on* the independent variable.

Conducting an experiment. Suppose a psychologist wanted to conduct an experiment on the effect of a limited amount of sleep on students' examination grades. The hypothesis might be: "If the sleep of students is limited the night before an exam, then their exam grades will be lower than they would be otherwise." In an experiment to test this hypothesis, the psychologist must make certain that lower grades are not caused by factors other than lack of sleep, such as differences in age or sex. One way of doing this is to match two groups of students for these characteristics. Another way would be to randomly assign students to one of two groups. By *random* we mean that each student would have an equal chance of being assigned to either group. For example, a researcher might assign, say, every tenth student out of a listing of all students in a school to one group and every twelfth student to the second group.

In either case, the psychologist might then instruct one group of students to get at least eight hours of sleep the night before the exam. The other group might be instructed to get only four hours of sleep. The experiment would thus investigate the effect of a particular condition (a limited amount of sleep the night before an exam). Psychologists call the group in which the condition under study is present (in this case, the group that gets little sleep) the *experimental group.* The group in which the condition is not present (the group that gets an average amount of sleep) is called the *control group.*

The amount of sleep is the factor being varied. It is the variable acting on the students. Therefore, amount of sleep is the independent variable in the experiment. Lower exam grades are, according to the hypothesis, a result of limited sleep and a response to the independent variable. Therefore, examination grades are the dependent variable.

After giving the experimental and control groups the same examinations, the psychologist would study the grades and compare the performance of the two groups. If the students in the experimental group received lower grades than those in the control group, the hypothesis would be supported.

In the experimental method, and in the other research methods as well, researchers construct theories with the information they gather. A *theory* is simply a general principle, based on information, to explain what has been learned. Other scientists might then test these theories and either build on them or prove them inaccurate.

The subjects in an experiment. In psychology, a *subject* is the organism, human or animal, participating in an experiment. The subject's responses are the dependent variable in the experiment. Although psychologists are interested mainly in human behavior, they do much work with animals.

There are certain advantages to using animals as subjects. The behavior of animals can be controlled to an extent not possible with human beings. A rat, for example, can be raised from birth in a cage. A record can be kept of what happens to it. The rat can then be used in a learning experiment, with the experimenter having a good idea of what it has already learned. Human beings, on the other hand, have many experiences that cannot be controlled or even recorded by an experimenter. And these experiences may influence experimental data.

There is another advantage to using animals as subjects. Many animals have fairly short life spans and reproduce at rapid rates. Thus, a psychologist can study the behavior of several generations within a relatively short period of time.

Text continues on page 28.

Case Study: Focus on Research

A SURPRISE AT WESTERN ELECTRIC

Do people change their behavior when they know they are taking part in an experiment? Does the mere presence of an experimenter influence the way people act? Some researchers found out the hard way that the answers to both questions appear to be "yes."

The year was 1927. The place was the Hawthorne plant of the Western Electric Company in Chicago. Managers at this factory, which manufactured telephones, were interested in increasing worker productivity. To do so effectively, they called on the services of industrial psychologists.

Industrial psychology was a young science at this time, but it had begun making inroads into performance at the workplace. For example, researchers knew that working conditions affected productivity. However,

These three women formed part of the group that was studied. The group's productivity remained high despite many negative changes in their work environment.

they were less certain about precise relationships. Which conditions would achieve what effects? What was the best way of getting workers to maximize their output? Western Electric wanted answers to such specific questions.

The researchers who were called in had their work cut out for them. Previous tests on the effect of artificial light on the workers had proved inconclusive. Now the company wanted definite answers and turned to a new research team.

The new group of researchers had ideas about which improvements in the working environment would increase employee output. To test their hypothesis, they planned to observe the effects of various changes in working conditions (independent variables) on productivity (dependent variable).

First the researchers selected a small group of young women—five operators who assembled telephone relays. They measured the women's output under normal working conditions. They then isolated the five subjects in a test control room, where the workers were supervised by a trained observer. During the next two years working conditions were altered several times, each time favorably.

One change was to form the workers into a separate group for computing piecework earnings. In other words, each was now to be paid as a member of a group of five rather than of a hundred, as before. In addition, work breaks of varying lengths and at different times of the day were established. Moreover, the workday was shortened and the workweek was cut by the elimination of a Saturday morning shift.

In each case the results were positive. Regardless of the change that was instituted, productivity increased. The researchers seemed to prove their hypothesis.

An important part of research, however, is to make sure that no other variables contribute to the final outcome. That is, it is important to be certain that no extraneous factors, or variables, cause the dependent variable to vary. Consequently, the researchers decided to return to the original conditions. (The only exception was that the size of the group was kept at five, so it could still be studied easily.) If improved conditions increased productivity, they reasoned that a resumption of the former pattern should decrease it.

A surprising thing happened, though. Week after week, the subjects continued to assemble telephone relays at the same high rate. No matter what the researchers did, productivity remained high.

The researchers were at a loss to explain this odd occurrence. Finally, the answer was provided by the team's director, Elton Mayo, a professor of industrial research at Harvard. The important factor, he said, was not the independent variables introduced by the researchers. Instead it was the feeling of the subjects themselves that they were special.

Ever since the Western Electric experiments, researchers have been alerted to what they call the "Hawthorne effect." This is the impact that being part of an experiment has on the subjects. It often acts as an extraneous variable, causing the dependent variable to vary. It also often biases the outcome of an experiment by interfering with the results. Consequently, it is something researchers now try to avoid by using such devices as hidden cameras and tape recorders.

Recently, however, some researchers have questioned the existence of a Hawthorne effect. They claim that output may have increased mostly because the workers became more skilled at their tasks. In addition, in the test situation the subjects frequently received feedback on their performance. This feedback may have encouraged them to produce even more. Nevertheless, the Hawthorne effect is still an important factor to consider when analyzing the results of an experiment.

SOURCE: F. J. Roethlisberger and William J. Dickson, *Management and the Worker*, Cambridge, Mass.: Harvard University Press, 1939; Berkeley Rice, "The Hawthorne Defect: Persistence of a Flawed Theory," *Psychology Today*, February 1982, pp. 70–74.

Researchers are now aware that a feeling of being special can affect people's productivity on the job.

A third advantage is that some experiments can be performed with animals but not with people. These would include experiments involving brain or other surgery or the use of certain drugs.

Psychologists study animals to get clues to human behavior. However, they are careful to avoid **anthropomorphism** — attributing human characteristics to nonhuman beings. For example, we see a dog "begging" for a bone. When the dog barks, we may say that it is asking for the bone. When it buries the bone, we may be tempted to say that it is thinking, "I'm not hungry now, so I'll bury it in this hole to keep the dog next door from running off with it." Thinking in terms of words and complete sentences is a human characteristic. There is no evidence that animals think in this way. It is inaccurate to attribute human characteristics to them. But we can learn much about human behavior by observing the behavior of animals.

Protecting subjects. The American Psychological Association (APA) has established guidelines for using animals as subjects in experiments. All animals must be acquired and treated according to local laws. Animals must be given a comfortable environment. Every care must be taken to ensure this environment. The only exception is when discomfort is a necessary part of the experiment. Any use of animals by students must be done under the direction of a qualified teacher.

The APA also has a set of guidelines for conducting research with human subjects. Personal information collected must be kept confidential. The experimenter must protect the subject from psychological and physical harm. This includes the right of the subject to withdraw from the experiment at any time. Also, the experimenter must inform the subject of the real nature of the experiment after the experiment is over, if the subject was not aware at the beginning. There should be an agreement between the experimenter and the subject stating the responsibilities of each. If undesirable results do arise, the experimenter is responsible for removing or correcting these results.

Problems in using the experimental method. Like the other methods, the experimental method has certain shortcomings. One of the problems is that subjects, realizing that they are participating in an experiment, may change their ordinary behavior. For example, if you walked up to someone and said, "Please count out loud from one to fifty," do you think the person would do it? But suppose you said, "I am doing an experiment as part of my course in psychology. Please count out loud from one to fifty." Do you think that there would be any difference in the amount of cooperation? The knowledge that the person is to participate in an experiment would probably influence the person's behavior.

Another problem is the selection of individuals to participate in studies. Too often, people are selected for an experiment simply because they are easily available. For example, college students are taking a course and the professor needs some subjects. But such subjects may not be very representative of the population as a whole.

This problem is related to a third one, that of generalizing from results. Suppose an experiment is performed on college psychology students. Would the results apply to high school psychology students? Do the results of an experiment on rats also apply to people?

A fourth problem is the possibility that the opinions of the experimenters will influence the experiment. As in other methods, experimenters may allow their opinions to influence their selection and treatment of subjects or their interpretation of the results.

A final problem is the protection of the privacy of subjects. Some experiments will be meaningful only if the subjects don't realize that they are participants. But is this an invasion of privacy? This is a difficult question. To help provide an answer, the APA developed its guidelines for treating subjects in experiments.

Regardless of the problems associated with the experimental method, this research technique remains in wide use because it permits control over conditions and provides accurate data for psychologists.

Subjects in scientific experiments sometimes change their behavior if they know they are being observed.

Correlational Research

In addition to experiments, psychologists also conduct correlational research. This method permits psychologists to investigate the relationship between two variables. Unlike experimental research, in which the independent variable is controlled by the experimenter, correlational research permits psychologists to study data over which they have little control. For example, in studies of the effect of heat on aggressive behavior in people, the researcher has no control over the independent variable since temperature changes.

Psychologists use correlational research to describe the relationship between one variable and another variable. A **correlation,** then, refers to the consistent relationship between two sets of events or variables.

Correlations also allow psychologists to make predictions. For example, intelligence is often correlated to academic success. Although some very intelligent people do not make good grades, most people who make good grades are intelligent people. The accuracy of predictions is determined by the strength of the correlations.

Positive correlations. Correlations can tell us several different things. When changes in events or variables move in a similar direction, a **positive correlation** occurs. For example, research has shown that there is a positive correlation between cigarette smoking and diseases such as lung cancer and emphysema.

A positive correlation between cigarette smoking and lung disease means that there will be a greater incidence of lung disease among groups of smokers than among groups of nonsmokers. It is important to note, however, that this correlation does not enable the researcher to predict which specific individuals will suffer from lung disease. Thus, correlational research applies primarily to group predictions and does not always provide proof that smoking always causes lung disease in every individual. What researchers have proven through correlational research is that people who smoke have a significantly higher risk of being affected by lung disease than people who do not smoke.

As you have learned, correlational research may indeed result in definite cause-and-effect relationships between variables. However, in some instances the relationship between variables may be attributed to coincidence. For example, if you wear a favorite sweater each time you take a test, and you get a good grade on each test, then you may think of your favorite sweater as a symbol of good luck. Even though you realize that the clothing is not really the cause of good grades, if the clothing makes you feel your best, then perhaps your test score is higher because of your increased self-confidence. The correlation between wearing your favorite sweater and good test scores would be just a coincidence.

Negative correlations. A *negative correlation* exists when changes in events or variables move in opposite directions. For example, there is a negative correlation between the age of people and the amount of sleep they require. An infant requires many hours of sleep because infancy is a period of rapid growth and development. Similarly, the number of hours of sleep young children and

adolescents need is greater than the number of hours of sleep most adults need. As adults grow older, the number of hours they need for sleep gradually decreases. Thus, a negative correlation exists because one variable (age) increases while the other variable (sleep) decreases.

Now that you have learned about scientific methods used by psychologists, you might be interested in some of the less scientific approaches to psychology. We will examine a few in the following pages.

Nonscientific Approaches to Psychology

The term "psychologist" refers to an individual with professional standards and scientific

This student is demonstrating the positive and negative correlations between two sets of variables.

training from a recognized college or university. In addition, a psychologist must meet certain qualifications and obtain a license from the state in order to practice. Unfortunately, there are some people who call themselves psychologists but who are not qualified to use that title.

Some people work around the fringes of psychology. They appeal to individuals who want advice about personal problems. Their methods are by no means scientific. They often promise quick diagnosis, advice, and therapy. Phrenologists, for example, claim that they can tell you all about yourself by examining the bumps on your head. Astrologers, who study the positions of the stars, and numerologists, who look at the letters in your name, also make such claims. Their "treatment" may consist of nothing more than telling you to think, "I am a success," or "I am happy."

That these individuals tell troubled persons exactly what to do indicates that they are not professionally trained. Trained psychologists help troubled people develop insight into their own problems and guide them in working out their own solutions.

Anyone who wants to consult a psychologist should not hesitate to ask about his or her qualifications. The well-trained psychologist will be glad to give this information. Others will try to bluff and avoid giving direct answers. Or they may claim to have training, but the education they report may be inadequate.

The Study of Parapsychology

Can someone actually bend a key simply by "willing" it to happen? Is it possible to "know" that a friend has been in an accident before you have heard the news? There are some well-qualified psychologists who are very much interested in such events. They study these and other related subjects, which fall under the category of parapsychology.

Parapsychology. The prefix "para-" means "to the side of" or "beyond." *Parapsychology* is concerned with psychological phenomena that are to the side of, or go beyond, the main area of psychological knowledge and interest.

One of the areas that particularly interests parapsychologists is psychokinesis. *Psychokinesis (PK)* is the study of experiences in which the thought of an individual is said to influence the performance of some physical object or event. For example, one psychic (a person said to be in touch with forces beyond the physical world) has performed such feats as fixing broken watches after briefly handling them. Some of the broken watches started running again!

Not all such performances, however, are actually examples of psychokinesis. One

Text continues on page 33.

Uri Geller, a psychic, appears to make a metal fork bend simply by looking at it.

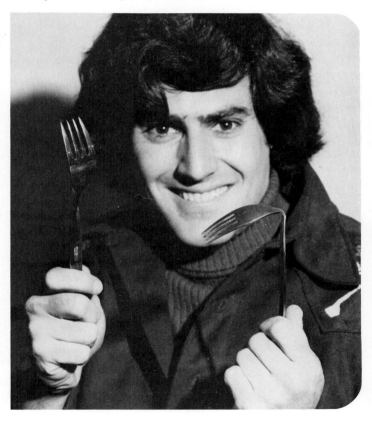

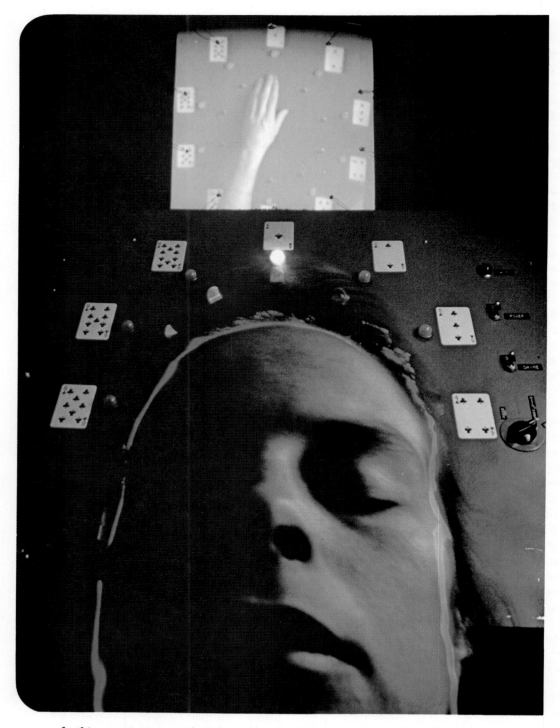

In this experiment on telepathy, a "sender" in another room is told in advance which light will go on. The sender tries to relay this information mentally to the subject (above). The subject chooses a card. Then the previously selected light is turned on and compared with the subject's choice.

group of college students decided to check on the psychic's performance. They stopped strangers on the street and asked them for broken watches. After the students handled these watches for only about five minutes, 57 percent of them started running. This seemed to be an example of psychokinesis. But there is another explanation. A jeweler has reported that over half of the watches brought in for repairs have gummed oil inside them. Holding a watch warms the oil enough to start the watch. Hence, many psychologists dispute the merits of psychokinesis.

The other major area of parapsychology is that of extrasensory perception. **Extrasensory perception (ESP)** investigates experiences in which knowledge appears to be gained independently of the known senses. "Extrasensory" literally means "outside the senses" or "apart from the senses."

Telepathy. One of the areas of extrasensory perception that many people find interesting is "mind reading," or telepathy. **Telepathy** has been defined as the transfer of thought from one person to another without the use of the senses. Usually we communicate our thoughts by either vocal sounds or written words. In telepathy, thoughts are believed to be transmitted without using any of the senses.

Telepathy can be studied in the laboratory. So far, scientific studies have not produced conclusive evidence to support telepathy. Some experiments have shown that what is often assumed to be extrasensory communication of thought is really communication through the senses. That is, people who believe in telepathy quite often pick up signals through their senses, such as seeing and hearing another person.

A psychic came to visit a class of psychology majors. The students sat in a half-circle, where the psychic could see each one. The psychic told one male student that he had a problem with his parents. The student immediately changed his position in the chair and asked, "How did you know?" The psychic then stated that there had been a problem with his father. This was correct. But how unusual is it for a male to have a problem with his father? Suppose the psychic had been blindfolded. Would he have been able to determine so easily which student had had a problem? Or did he get clues for his answers by watching the behavior of the student?

Telepathy or coincidence? Consider this example. Friends, living far apart, have not seen or written to each other for years. Suddenly they write to each other on the same date. Is this long-distance telepathy? Possibly both had just watched a television program or read a newspaper article that reminded them of each other. The timing of the letter writing could also be due to chance alone. Out of the tens of thousands who actually write letters, it is likely that two people will do so at the same time simply by chance.

The writing of the two letters on the same date seems so unusual to the friends that they tell everyone about it. As a result, people remember this story. They ignore the other thousands of letters that were written on different dates. They also ignore the thousands of friends who are separated, think of each other often, yet never write.

What do psychologists think of ESP? Extrasensory perception is an unsolved problem of science. At one time, some members of the American Psychological Association were asked to indicate whether they believed extrasensory perception was an established fact. The majority regarded the investigation of ESP as a "legitimate scientific undertaking." They were open-minded about the possibility that ESP might prove to be a fact. But only a small percentage of them believed that enough accurate evidence was available to say that it was a fact now.

There are a number of reasons that many psychologists have doubts about extrasensory perception. First of all, the data on ESP are easily faked. Second, not many of the ESP experiments have been repeated to see if the results are the same. In fact, some of the results of ESP experiments do not agree. Finally, there is a tendency to be wary about very unusual phenomena.

Drawing by W. Miller, © 1977, *The New Yorker Magazine, Inc.*

Most of the studies of extrasensory perception have been made by individuals who are not psychologists. Although much scattered research is being done, very few trained psychologists are investigating ESP. There is a need for well-trained men and women to do studies using the best of modern methods. Only after much research can we determine if extrasensory perception and psychokinesis can be understood in scientific terms.

The addition of fresh data and new ideas keeps the field of psychology exciting and challenging. Perhaps you will be one of those people who contribute to the findings of psychology.

Summary

Psychologists use various methods when studying behavior. These include natural observation, directed observation, the case-study method, interviews, the questionnaire method, and testing. The most frequently used method, however, is the experimental method. This method allows the researcher to control conditions and draw conclusions on the effect of one variable on another.

The experiment has certain procedures and components. It usually begins with a hypothesis, which is a tentative assumption or an educated guess. A hypothesis always states a relationship between two or more variables. Two types of variables usually found in hypotheses are independent variables and dependent variables.

When conducting an experiment, psychologists test a hypothesis on various subjects. The subjects may be animals or human beings, depending on the experiment. There are certain advantages to using animals as subjects. Their behavior can be controlled, they have shorter life spans, and they can be used in experiments that cannot be conducted with people. There are, however,

guidelines that regulate the use of animals (as well as people) in research.

Like all research methods, the experimental method has certain limitations. Subjects may change their behavior if they know they are being studied. Subjects are not always selected at random. It is often difficult to generalize from the results. There is a danger of experimenter bias. Finally, the protection of the privacy of subjects sometimes presents a problem.

The correlational research method permits psychologists to investigate the relationship between one variable and another. Correlations allow psychologists to make predictions. The accuracy of these predictions is limited by the strength of the correlations. Although coincidence may play a role in the relationship between variables, psychologists can sometimes use correlational research to suggest cause and effect.

Parapsychology falls outside the main body of psychological thought. Yet some people are very much interested in this subject. Parapsychologists focus on such areas as psychokinesis, ESP, and telepathy.

In the following excerpt from *Experimental Psychology: A Methodological Approach,* experimental psychologist Frank McGuigan discusses the importance of definitions in psychological research. The author points out that unless terms are defined in ways that make them observable and measurable—in other words, unless terms have operational definitions—they cannot be studied experimentally. As you study the reading, think about how operational definitions for terms apply to scientific research.

In our everyday research we . . . formulate a problem that we seek to solve and then a hypothesis that is a potential solution to the problem. . . . We then observe a sample of those events in our effort to collect data and confront the hypothesis with those observations. Next, we test the hypothesis, a process by which we conclude that the hypothesis is confirmed (supported) by the data or disconfirmed (not supported). . . .

There are two specific criteria in order for a hypothesis to be tested (and thus to be confirmed or disconfirmed):

1. Do all of the variables contained in the hypothesis actually refer to . . . observable events?
2. Is the hypothesis formulated in such a way that it is possible to relate it to . . . observable events?

If all of the events referred to in the hypothesis are publicly observable, then the first criterion is satisfied. Ghosts, for instance, are not typically considered to be reliably observable by people in general, so that problems formulated about ghosts are unsolvable and corresponding hypotheses about them are untestable. Then, if a hypothesis is well formed in accordance with our rules of language, and if we can unambiguously specify how we might relate the hypothesis to . . . observable events in order to render a confirmed-disconfirmed decision, then our second criterion is satisfied. . . . It is, in fact, often difficult for us to sift out statements that are testable from those that are untestable by applying the above criteria to testability. . . . Since the proper formulation of, and solution to a problem is basic to the conduct of an experiment, it is essential that the experimenter be agile in formulating solvable problems and testable hypotheses.

First, let us consider some problems that are obviously unsolvable as they are formulated. . . . How, for instance, can one answer such questions as "What's the matter with his (her, my, your) mind?" "How does the mind work?" "Is it possible to change human nature?" and so forth. . . .

One of the main reasons that such problems as those considered above are unsolvable as they have been stated is that many of the terms have been imported from everyday language. Our common language is replete with ambiguities as well as with multiple definitions for any given word. . . .

The importance of adequate definitions in science cannot be too strongly emphasized. The main functions of good definitions are: (1) to clarify the phenomenon under investigation; and (2) to allow us to communicate with each other in an unambiguous manner. These functions are accomplished by *operationally defining* the . . . terms with which the scientist deals.

Source Review

1. What two criteria does the author list as being necessary in order for a hypothesis to be tested?

2. Why does the author consider the question "How does the mind work?" to be unsolvable?

REVIEWING TERMS

hypothesis	control group	negative correlation
variable	theory	parapsychology
independent variable	subject	psychokinesis (PK)
dependent variable	anthropomorphism	extrasensory
random	correlation	perception (ESP)
experimental group	positive correlation	telepathy

CHECKING FACTS

1. What are the five guidelines that researchers keep in mind when studying behavior scientifically?

2. Identify the various methods that psychologists use to study behavior and discuss the advantages and disadvantages of each.

3. Which method do psychologists use most frequently? Why?

4. Explain the role of the hypothesis and variables in an experiment. How do an independent variable and a dependent variable differ?

5. Why does a researcher use an experimental group and a control group when conducting research?

6. Why are animals often used as subjects in experiments?

7. What are some of the guidelines that have been established for protecting subjects in an experiment?

8. Describe some of the problems involved in using the experimental method of research.

9. How does correlational research differ from experimental research?

10. What role does correlational research play in helping psychologists to make predictions?

11. Explain why not all demonstrations of psychokinesis are true examples of this phenomenon.

12. How do psychologists view extrasensory perception and telepathy?

APPLYING YOUR KNOWLEDGE

1. Research some specific behavior in your school using the method of natural observation. You might study the behavior of teen-agers in the cafeteria during lunch. Do students eat mostly alone or in groups? Do they eat leisurely or rush through lunch? What seems to be the main topic of conversation? Carefully record your observations and summarize them in a short report.

2. As a class, or on your own, develop a ten-item questionnaire to investigate music preferences of adolescents. Consult with your teacher to make sure that the questions are clear and focus on

what you are trying to learn. Then distribute the questionnaire to several teenagers not taking this course. (If you are working as a class, each student can be responsible for one or two respondents.) Analyze your results and discuss them in class.

3. With the permission of the teacher, divide the class into groups of about five or six students. Have one student in each group take the part of a talk-show host and the others the roles of panelists. The group leader should interview the others about their plans for the future.

4. Imagine that you are a researcher with unlimited time and money. List the five most interesting psychological questions that you would like to try to answer. Select one and write it in the form of a hypothesis. How might you go about researching the topic?

5. Using the information in the text on conducting an experiment, design an experiment that you would like to perform in school. In detail list your hypothesis and your proposed research procedures, and identify the dependent and independent variables. Make sure to include provisions for protecting your subjects. With the approval and guidance of your teacher, you might like to conduct your experiment and present the findings to the school newspaper for publication.

THINKING CRITICALLY ABOUT PSYCHOLOGY

1. **Interpreting Ideas**   Why must the procedures of an experiment be repeatable?

2. **Forming Opinions**   When might natural observation be considered an invasion of privacy?

3. **Summarizing Ideas**   Who should decide what is harmful and what is not harmful to subjects in an experiment?

4. **Evaluating Ideas**   How do you decide whether the possible harm for subjects in an experiment is greater or less than the possible gain for society from this experiment?

5. **Debating Ideas**   Should people who work around the fringes of psychology be allowed to practice their profession? Why or why not?

6. **Gathering Information**   Do you know anyone who claims to have had an experience that might fit under the heading of parapsychology? If so, what evidence was there that it took place? Is there any other explanation for what happened?

DEVELOPING SKILLS IN PSYCHOLOGY

Formulating Hypotheses
Scientific studies typically are designed to test a hypothesis. As noted in this chapter, a hypothesis is a tentative prediction about the relationship between two or more variables. Psychologists test hypotheses such as,

"Children will behave more aggressively if they see others being aggressive than if they do not observe aggressiveness in others."

"People will evaluate the creativity of a story less favorably if they think the author is a woman than if they think the author is a man."

"People are more likely to become sick if

they have recently experienced a lot of stress than if they have not been undergoing stress."

In the first example, the independent variable is children's exposure to aggression in others and the dependent variable is the children's own aggressive behavior. In the second example, the independent variable is the information that an author is a man or a woman. The dependent variable is evalua-tions of creativity. What are the variables in the third example?

Try to derive hypotheses of your own connecting each of the following pairs of variables:

1. Number of hours since eating/Amount of food consumed;

2. Number of hours spent studying alone/ Degree of interest in seeing friends.

READING FURTHER ABOUT PSYCHOLOGY

Bachrach, Arthur J., *Psychological Research: An Introduction,* Fourth Edition, Random House, New York, 1981. An excellent, nontechnical introduction to the scientific method, with an emphasis on psychological research.

Harriman, Philip L., *Handbook of Psychological Terms,* Littlefield, Adams & Company, Totowa, New Jersey, 1968. An excellent reference for students of psychology.

Hoover, Kenneth R., *The Elements of Social Scientific Thinking,* Third Edition, St. Martin's Press, New York, 1984. A short, readable introduction to the research process. Excellent for beginning students.

Kunda, Ziva, and Nesbett, Richard E., "The Psychometrics of Everyday Life," *Cognitive Psychology,* 18 (April 1986): 195–224. Discusses research on people's ability to assess everyday correlations and the degree of consistency that characterizes social behavior from occasion to occasion.

Lorenz, Konrad, *King Solomon's Ring,* Harper & Row, New York, 1979. This book, written by one of the world's leading ethologists, provides a thorough glimpse into animal behavior through the process of natural observation.

Notterman, Joseph M., *Forms of Psychological Inquiry,* Columbia University Press, New York, 1985. A distinguished expert in experimental psychology provides a clear and integrated account of the ways in which people have viewed themselves psychologically from ancient times to the present.

Using the Skills of a Psychologist

Unit 1 Evaluating Evidence

One of the most important skills a psychologist uses is evaluating evidence–the ability to gather information and to determine its significance. Evaluation and analysis provide structure and credibility to the study of psychology. In the following skill lesson, you will learn more about the steps psychologists use to evaluate experimental and correlational research.

Select an article from a newspaper or a periodical that focuses on research concerning some aspect of behavior. Read the article and answer the following questions. It is important to note that some of the questions may not apply to the article you have selected.

1. Identify the following:

   (a) Hypothesis being tested
   (b) Basis or rationale for the hypothesis
   (c) Independent variable(s)
   (d) Dependent variable(s)
   (e) Control procedures or groups
   (f) Results
   (g) Conclusion
   (h) Extent to which the research findings can be generalized

2. Could you possibly attribute the reported results to something other than the independent variable?

3. What further questions arise as a result of the reported findings?

4. How much time do you think it required for the investigators to carry out the reported research?

5. Do you *believe* the results of the investigation? Why or why not?

6. What factors may have led up to the study being conducted? What factors are more important now than they may have been at an earlier date? Do these factors explain why the study was not conducted earlier?

7. Is there a better way or a better procedure that the investigator(s) could have used? For example, did the investigator(s) do a real experiment or was this a study based on relationships between events that already had taken place?

Now that you have answered these questions, you can apply the skill of evaluating evidence in another way. As you have studied in this unit, psychologists also evaluate evidence through correlational research.

While experimental research may provide conclusions about cause-and-effect relationships, correlational research focuses on the relationship between one variable and another. For example, correlational research could indicate that there is a relationship between two variables such as frustration and aggression. It might be found that people who are frustrated tend to be aggressive. However, does that also mean that frustration causes aggression? People who exhibit aggressive behavior may become frustrated for many different reasons. Perhaps they are perceived as difficult people because they are frustrated and their aggression is a result of not feeling accepted. As you can see, it is difficult to determine a direct cause-and-effect relationship. What can be shown is that there is a relationship between frustration and aggression.

Now that you have seen how a psychologist may evaluate different kinds of evidence, review the article you selected for this assignment. Choose several specific examples from your article and classify them as experimental evidence or correlational evidence. Does the article focus primarily on an experiment, or is the emphasis upon events used for correlational research?

REVIEWING THE UNIT

1. Why do psychologists study abnormal behavior?

2. How does psychology differ from physics, chemistry, and biology?

3. Why does the experimental method of research remain in wide use?

4. Why do many psychologists dispute the merits of psychokinesis?

CONNECTING IDEAS

1. **Applying Ideas** How do anthropologists, sociologists, and social psychologists help us to understand more about psychology?

2. **Drawing Conclusions** How do you think early psychologists may have been viewed by other people who lived at that time? How does that apply to people who have new ideas today?

3. **Evaluating Ideas** How did psychology develop from its beginnings to its current standing as a science? How may new ideas in psychology serve our society in the future?

4. **Synthesizing Ideas** How did advancement in scientific research methods contribute to advancement in the study of psychology?

PRACTICING RESEARCH SKILLS

Organize into small groups. Each group should consult with the teacher and select a widely available product as a research topic. Each group should then conduct library research on the development of this product from its origin to the present.

Each group should then present its findings to the class. The first part of the presentation should focus on the data obtained through research. The second part of the presentation should be in the form of a commercial advertising the product. Following each presentation, members of the class should discuss the correlation between the data and the psychology observed in the presentation of the commercial.

FINDING OUT MORE

You may wish to contact the following organizations for additional information about the material in this unit.

American Association for the Advancement of Science (AAAS)
1333 H St. N.W.
Washington, D.C. 20005

Society of Experimental Psychologists
Department of Psychology
UCLA
Los Angeles, California 90024

National Science Foundation
1800 G St., N.W.
Washington, D.C. 20550

Unit 2

HUMAN GROWTH AND DEVELOPMENT

Chapter 3   HUMAN DEVELOPMENT
Chapter 4   HEREDITY AND ENVIRONMENT
Chapter 5   BIOLOGICAL INFLUENCES ON BEHAVIOR

Chapter 3

HUMAN DEVELOPMENT

Chapter Focus

This chapter presents:
- **some patterns and principles that characterize development**
- **the various forms of development**
- **an overview of how development progresses from infancy through old age**

"When I was your age. . . ." How many times have you heard your parents use this expression? It's hard to imagine them *ever* being twelve, or fifteen, or eighteen.

Similarly, how many times have you been asked, "What will you be doing ten years from now?" Do you try to imagine what you will look like at age twenty-five or thirty? Or do you picture yourself the way you look now?

Most of us tend to think of everything in the present. Yet we know that our parents were once teen-agers just as we know that someday we will be adults. We know this because everybody passes through the stages of development in a certain order. In this chapter we will explore the concept of development, including its patterns and the various areas of development.

Patterns of Development

Although we all experience development, we do not all experience it at the same rate. Some children, for example, may walk at one year of age, while others may not take their first steps until they are fifteen months old. Still others may not walk for another month or so. Yet individual rates of development usually fit into a pattern that is similar for most people.

Some general principles of development. Perhaps the most important single principle is that *development follows a predictable pattern*. One predictable pattern occurs in the early physical development of infants. In babies, development spreads downward from the head to the feet. If you ever have the opportunity to observe infants, you will notice that they develop control of their eyes first. Then they learn to turn their heads. Then their trunks. Finally they gain control over their legs and can walk. In babies, development also proceeds outward from the central part of the body to the wrists and fingers.

Another principle of development is that *the individual first develops general responses and then proceeds to specific responses*. Very young babies trying to reach for a toy seem to use their entire bodies. A few months afterward, the same babies use more specific parts of their bodies to reach the toy. Later on, they will use only those parts of their bodies actually needed to obtain the toy.

A third characteristic of development is that *it is a lifelong continuous process.* The expression "stages of development" suggests that developmental tasks have a definite starting and stopping point. But there is no one point at which a task suddenly appears or disappears. The term "stage of development" is used for convenience only.

A fourth principle of development is that *each stage has unique features.* Each stage is expressed differently, depending on the society and the period of development involved. For instance, the rebellion period of adolescence is a feature of our own society and culture. It does not take place in most other societies.

A final characteristic is that *early development can be more important than later development.* This is because many crucial behaviors, including walking and talking, take place during a child's early years.

Critical periods. Some psychologists believe that **critical periods** are another important aspect of development. These are the time periods during which an individual can learn specific behaviors most easily. Before or after these periods, learning these behaviors is more difficult. For example, many psychologists believe that the most critical period for learning language is from birth to age six. If individuals do not learn any language before age twelve, they are limited in their ability to do so later on.

Recently, some researchers have noted that the first few hours after birth are critical for a bonding, or attachment, between mother and child. These researchers believe such an attachment is critical for later adequate emotional development of the child. However, other researchers disagree. They argue that adopted children, often deprived of this bonding experience, also tend to develop normally. These psychologists use the term **sensitive period** rather than critical period. To them an attachment and other stimula-

Look closely at these baby pictures. In what ways do they suggest that each state of development has unique features?

tion from the environment is important. Yet a lack of such stimulation is not necessarily critical, unless prolonged or severe.

How do psychologists study development? One way that psychologists learn about behavior and development is through modern methods of observation. They observe individuals and keep careful records. From these records, they can determine patterns of behavior.

Psychologists may study the behavior and development of an individual by using the *longitudinal method.* This involves selecting several individuals and studying the development of their behavior over a considerable period of time. In some longitudinal studies, individuals are observed from birth to adulthood. However, the method has the following limitations: (1) It is time-consuming. (2) It can be very expensive. (3) Keeping in touch with the same group over a period of time can be a problem. Some individuals may move to another location during the study. (4) The individuals chosen for study may not be typical of their age group. Nevertheless, the longitudinal method has the important advantage of providing psychologists with information about specific changes in behavior and development.

The *cross-sectional method* selects people of different ages in order to study groups of various age levels at the same time. For example, groups of three-, four-, and five-year-olds can be selected and studied at the same time. This method has the advantage of reducing the amount of time necessary for the study. Again, however, the groups selected may not be typical of their age levels. Also, because members of the groups grow up at different times, it is difficult to know whether differences are due to different maturity levels or background experiences.

Prenatal Development

Many people think of development as beginning at birth. However, *prenatal development*—the development that takes place before birth—is equally important. It is the process by which in nine months a single cell develops into a highly complex human being of over 800 billion cells!

Development begins at conception, when the father's sperm meets the mother's egg. At this point the fertilized egg consists of just a single cell that is scarcely visible to the human eye. Almost immediately, though, that cell begins dividing and certain processes get underway.

Although the individuals in this class photograph are approximately the same age, there is a great deal of variation in their heights. Within certain general patterns of physical development, there are vast individual differences.

By the end of the first month, the heart has begun to develop. By the end of the second month, the various systems—respiratory, digestive, and nervous systems—also have begun to develop. By the end of the third month, the fetus, as it is now called, is approximately ten centimeters (four inches) in length.

By the middle of the fourth month, the pattern for all biological systems has been set. The remaining time is spent in refining these patterns and in growing. At the end of the sixth month, the fetus has a chance to survive if born prematurely. By about nine months after conception, the fetus is ready to start life as a fully developed infant.

Physical Development

Physical development is the growth of an individual's body. As you can imagine, it has a considerable effect on a person's behavior.

The development of height and weight. The two most common examples of an individual's physical growth are height and weight. Both height and weight have a developmental pattern of increasing in spurts. In both cases, the greatest percentage of growth is in the earliest stages.

The greatest rate of growth in height for both sexes takes place during the preschool years. Tremendous growth occurs during the first year, when the average increase is 50 percent. At the end of the third year, the average person is half as tall as he or she will be as an adult. By the fifth year a person is twice as tall as at birth.

Girls grow faster in height than boys until about age thirteen. Then the average male passes the female. By adulthood, the average male will be some 10 or 13 centimeters (4 or 5 inches) taller than the average female.

The largest percentage increase in weight also occurs during the first five years of life. By age five the average person will weigh about five times what that person weighed at birth. During the next seven years, a person's weight will more than double.

During adulthood, the individual will gain weight. As the person approaches the middle-age period, extra fat may gather. Later, however, as individuals reach old age, they will lose weight. This is mostly because of a loss of body fluids and the various chemical changes associated with advanced age.

The effect of physical development on personality. There are some general relationships between body development and personality traits. Remember, however, that they don't apply to all individuals. An early-maturing male is one who develops physically faster than other males of his own age. As a group, early-maturing males tend to feel more self-confident and independent. A late-maturing male is one who develops more slowly than the average for his age. These males may have a more difficult time in adjusting. For example, they lack the physical strength of the average male until they reach maturity. Thus, as adolescents they may be unable to participate in some games and sports that require strength and power, such as football. They may be less popular with their classmates, which in turn may affect their social development.

Psychological differences between early- and late-maturing females aren't nearly as great as for males. In the junior high school years, both early- and late-maturing females usually have more prestige than average-maturing females and participate more as leaders in school activities. Nevertheless, late-maturing females may view themselves as less adequate and may have somewhat poorer relationships with parents and people of their own age.

The attitude and behavior of parents, brothers and sisters, friends, and teachers will greatly influence people's attitudes toward their own physical development. Probably the most important single factor, though, is the individual's own attitude toward his or her development. If a very short person feels inferior, this may affect his or her participation with others. Or the person may try too hard to overcome a feeling of being inferior. Having a good attitude about yourself is very important.

Motor Development

Motor development is development of control over the muscles of the body. It is a very important area in the total development of an individual. It is related to good physical and mental health. By joining in games and activities, a person gets the exercise and practice necessary for better physical development and motor coordination. Motor development is related to making social contacts. Learning to walk and run allows an individual to increase the number of people, events, and situations that he or she encounters. Motor development is also related to a person's self-image. It contributes to the individual's growing awareness of being awkward or coordinated, dependent or independent.

Motor development in a baby. Motor development in the head region takes place at a very rapid rate after birth. Newborn babies not even a day old can track a triangle with their eyes. In addition, infants just two weeks old were able to repeat certain facial gestures made by researchers. When researchers stuck out their tongues, the babies responded with similar gestures. When the experimenters opened their mouths, the babies did likewise. It has also been shown that infants two months old can adjust the focus of their eyes.

Since physical development proceeds from the head downward, the trunk area develops next. After babies have learned to control their head movements, they can learn to turn over completely. Learning to turn over is a gradual response. Babies first turn over from their side to their back. Then they turn from back to side. Eventually they succeed in making a complete turn.

Physical development also proceeds from the body's center to the arms and hands. Babies will make some general responses to an object put in front of them by the second month. They can see the object before they have the coordination to reach it. They can't grasp objects until the fourth month or pick up objects until the ninth month.

Most individuals are physically ready to walk between nine and fifteen months of age. They usually progress through a crawling, creeping, pulling-up, and standing-alone stage before actually walking. Most babies walk within one month after they reach the standing-alone stage.

Motor development in childhood, adolescence, and old age. Motor development in early and late childhood increases more slowly than in the period immediately after birth. But it does continue to increase. Some people think that during adolescence individuals are awkward and clumsy. On the contrary, many studies have shown that motor coordination increases considerably during this period. The appearance of awkwardness in adolescence often seems to be the result of adolescents' lack of assurance toward themselves and their abilities. It arises from the self-concept rather than from lack of motor control. During adolescence the individual tries out various new patterns of behavior and sometimes may give the appearance of lacking coordination.

The development of an individual's motor abilities generally increases until about the early to middle twenties. There is a slight decline until the age of fifty, and more of a decline to age sixty-five. After that, it becomes considerably more rapid.

However, not all older adults experience such a decline. It has been shown, for example, that given enough time, older adults in good physical health can perform various tasks just about as well as younger persons can. What has declined is their speed, not their ability to complete a task.

Hand-eye coordination. Must organisms be able to see their arms and hands before they can learn to reach for something? To find out, psychologists performed an experiment with monkeys. One group was raised with a shield placed below their heads. The monkeys could freely move their arms and hands, but they could not actually see them. Another group was raised under similar conditions. But these monkeys could see their hands and arms through a glass shield.

Each monkey was trained to reach for a string that pulled a piece of candy close enough to eat. Being unable to see their arms and hands from birth did affect the experimental group of monkeys. They seemed to reach for the string as if they were blind. And once they found it, their hands fumbled with it rather than grasping it firmly. The other group of monkeys reached for the string rather easily.

Human beings who were born blind and later gained their sight have shown similar behavior in learning to reach for objects. It seems that we need to see our arm and hand movements for these movements to develop satisfactorily.

Language Development

People must use accepted adult language to be approved by society. This doesn't mean that everyone must agree on all language usage. For example, there are distinct differences in our society in the pronunciation of words. Have you ever visited a different part of the United States and heard the same words pronounced differently? Sometimes even the words themselves are different. For example, certain vocational groups, such as doctors, lawyers, mechanics, and electricians, each have their own "language."

Nevertheless, language has certain common features that everyone uses. All languages have vocabulary. The English language is made up of tens of thousands of words. If you have studied a second language, you know that rules of grammar must be followed. All languages have certain rules for the sound and arrangement of words. Finally, all languages consist of sounds or symbols that have specific meanings. Think of the word "music." The meanings you associate with this word may differ slightly from someone else's associations. But there will still be some common meanings. You may think of rock-and-roll, and someone else may think of opera. But you both will be referring to an arrangement of sounds or tones.

Jazz pianist Eubie Blake, who lived to be one hundred, still played the piano in his nineties. Here, at ninety-eight, he accepts an honorary degree from Fisk University.

Do animals have a language? Animals have the ability to communicate with one another. For example, honeybees perform a dance to communicate to other honeybees where they can find nectar in relation to the hive. Apes can make sounds indicating such things as danger and food. But animals don't use a spoken language.

Psychologists have tried to teach chimpanzees to speak. A number of psychologists have raised chimpanzees in their homes and treated them very much like human children. One chimpanzee, Gua, never learned to speak. Another, named Vicki, learned to make only four sounds that could be recognized as English words. It appears that animals cannot speak our language with any ease because they don't have the vocal structures needed to make the sounds of human speech.

However, recent attempts to teach chimpanzees to learn symbols associated with English words have been successful. A female chimpanzee named Washoe was taught to use the American sign language

Although a chimpanzee cannot speak the English language, it can learn to communicate with people. It can use other forms of language, such as gestures, to carry on a conversation with a human being.

(the sign language used by deaf people in the United States and Canada). After three years of training, she had learned to make 85 signs. At the age of five years, she could make 160 signs. Once she learned the signs, she could communicate with her trainer in new ways by combining signs. For example, she learned the sign for "dirty." When she became angry with her trainer, she could make the signs for "Roger dirty."

Another chimpanzee named Sarah has learned to communicate using small pieces of plastic. Each piece, varying in color and shape, stands for a word. Sarah has learned to arrange the pieces of plastic to make simple sentences. Each time Sarah used a plastic word correctly, she was rewarded. So far she has learned about 130 such words.

In still another study, a female chimpanzee called Lana has been taught to use a typewriter attached to a computer. Each key on the typewriter, when Lana strikes it, makes a symbol on a screen in front of her. Lana has even learned to correct herself when she uses the wrong order of symbols to form a sentence.

However, several questions have recently been raised about whether chimpanzees actually learn a language the way people do. For example, there is no evidence to suggest that animals understand grammar. Some researchers argue that the animals simply repeat symbols without understanding their relationship. Much still remains to be discovered about how animals learn a language.

Language development in human beings. *Language development* involves using symbols to communicate. One psychologist has divided language development into four stages. Stage 1 covers the ages from birth to about three weeks. It includes the first cries, coughings, and gurgles of the infant. Stage 2 goes from three weeks to about five months of age. During this stage, babies' cries vary in both their length and their tone. In Stage 3, which covers from five months to about one year of age, babies produce babbling sounds, which are similar to vowels. Stage 4, from one year on, is the language period. It is in this stage that the formal parts of language usage develop.

The growth of vocabulary is one of the most amazing changes in language development. Most babies produce their first words by about one year of age. From fifteen to eighteen months, the child uses a vocabulary of about two dozen words. From eighteen to twenty-four months, children begin to use simple two-word sentences, such as "Mommy gone." At two years of age children have a vocabulary of about 275 words. But only one year later, their vocabulary has grown to nearly 1,000 words. By the time they are four years old, most children have mastered the basic rules of grammar. At six years of age, the average child understands the meaning of about 8,000 words and can correctly use approximately 4,000 words. By twenty years of age, the average person understands about 50,000 words and can use about 10,000 words. How does an individual, who at birth knows none of these words or rules of grammar, eventually come to pronounce, combine, and understand these words?

Some explanations for how children learn language. In earlier days, people who studied language development emphasized the importance of rewards in learning language. For example, a baby may make a sound, such as "dada," by chance. If the father interprets this as "daddy," he may reward the baby by picking up and kissing the baby. This would increase the chance that the baby would make the same sound again.

Reward does play a role in the development of language. But it does not fully explain how we acquire language. For one thing, children learn more than just particular words, pronunciations, and combinations of words. Long before the school years, children acquire ways of expressing themselves without being specifically taught or rewarded for them. There are billions of sentences in the English language that contain only 20 words. A person cannot learn that number of sentences simply by imitating the words or being rewarded for each sentence. Language development is not just repeating words because we have heard them before. Previous experience does not explain behavior that occurs for the first time.

Also, studies have shown that parents reward the proper pronunciation of statements more often than the correct grammatical structure of language. For example, if a child points to a rubber ball and says, "That a ball," parents are likely to agree. However, if the child says, "That a all," parents are likely to correct the pronunciation. The parents are more likely to correct words that are mispronounced than they are to correct bad grammar.

If we are not taught all the rules of grammar, then how do we acquire such aspects of language? Some psychologists continue to emphasize the role of learning in language development. Others believe that infants are born with the ability to develop their own rules for using language.

Studies of the development of infants have found that infants in different countries make sounds that are very similar. For example, American infants make sounds that are suitable for learning French or German. Chinese infants make sounds that are appropriate to English. However, as infants grow, they begin to make those sounds that are found mainly in their own culture. This suggests that learning plays an important role in language development. On the other hand, even deaf children make the same sounds as children with normal hearing. This suggests that innate biological factors also play a role in language development.

Children differ in the rate at which they learn a language. But there is evidence that all children go through a similar order in learning the meaning of words and developing rules. This holds true across various

Text continues on page 52.

THE SILENT WORLD OF GENIE

Until recently, many psychologists firmly believed that there is a critical period of language development. If a child did not acquire language between the ages of two and twelve, they argued, the child might be locked into a world of silence or, at best, incoherent utterances. The case of Genie, however, has cast some doubts on this theory. At the same time it has given its supporters some new ammunition.

When Genie's case came to the attention of social workers in 1970, Genie was thirteen. Unable to stand up straight or to speak, and suffering from severe malnutrition, she was sent to a children's hospital for tests. It was while she was there that her pitiful background became known.

Genie had been reared in almost total isolation, confined to a room beginning at the age of twenty months. Her father, a man of violent rages, hated children and could

The "Wild Child of France" was a predecessor to Genie. Found in the woods in the 1700's, he was unable to speak. This photo was taken from Truffaut's film The Wild Child.

not stand noise. Her mother, slowly going blind and threatened with harm by Genie's father, was kept from the child as much as possible.

Every day in Genie's life followed a similar pattern. During the day she was strapped to a potty in a harness that her father had made for her. At night, if she was not forgotten, she was wrapped in a kind of straitjacket and placed in a crib covered with wire mesh. She was fed by an older brother, mostly baby food and milk. Frequently, she went hungry. (She weighed only fifty-nine pounds when she was admitted to the hospital.)

Genie never had the opportunity to develop language during her confinement. Her brother, fearful of their father, often fed her silently. When her brother and father did choose to communicate, they adopted strange doglike behavior toward her—growling and barking but never speaking. If Genie tried to speak, call out, or cry, she was severely punished for making noise.

Finally, at the age of thirteen, Genie escaped from the prison that was her home. After a heated argument with her husband, Genie's mother fled, taking Genie with her. They went to a welfare office to apply for public assistance. It was there that the social worker noticed that Genie required a great deal more. The worker notified her supervisor, who in turn notified the police. The puzzle surrounding Genie's life then began to unravel.

When Genie was freed, she had almost everything to learn about being human—how to stand, how to walk, how to wear clothes, even how to cry. And of course she had to learn language—how to understand it and how to speak it. Psychologists were among those who helped her, first at a rehabilitation center and then in a foster home. They had many questions. Could someone of Genie's age learn language? Would she learn it the way that normal children do?

The answer to the first question was "yes." In a few months, through constant exposure to new objects, Genie learned many words. She could even put them together in very simple, awkward sentences. She could tell about the past ("Father hit Genie big stick") and describe emotions in the present ("Genie happy").

Genie's language development, though, was unlike that of normal children in many ways. For one thing, it was slow. Most children learn the basic rules of grammar in about two years. After four years, Genie's grammar was still primitive.

There were other deficiencies as well. Genie seemed unable to learn any pronoun but "I," to use pitch to emphasize words, or to distinguish between active and passive verb forms. After years of training, she could not spontaneously ask "who, what, why, or where" questions, something that normal children master at an early age. She also spoke mostly about objects. Whereas most children begin talking about relations between people and about actions, she spoke only about the quality of things (for example, "black shoe").

Genie's accomplishments and difficulties have contributed much to our knowledge about language development. She has shown that a certain degree of language mastery is possible after the age of twelve. This feat has placed doubts on the theory that after about age twelve the brain is fully organized and cannot readapt to learning a first language. Yet her limitations have suggested that there might indeed be a critical period after which complete mastery is impossible, or much more difficult. (Genie's upbringing, though, may have played a much greater role than her age in her lack of language development.)

Thus, despite our newly acquired knowledge, we still have a long way to go before we can fully understand how people learn language. Unfortunately, it is through the abuses suffered by such children as Genie that we often gain insight into this complex process.

SOURCE: Maya Pines, "The Civilizing of Genie," *Psychology Today*, September 1981, pp. 28–34; Susan Curtiss, *Genie: A Psycholinguistic Study of a Modern-Day "Wild Child,"* New York: Academic Press, 1976.

Most people learn language by listening to those around them. Deaf people, though, must rely on others to teach them every sound.

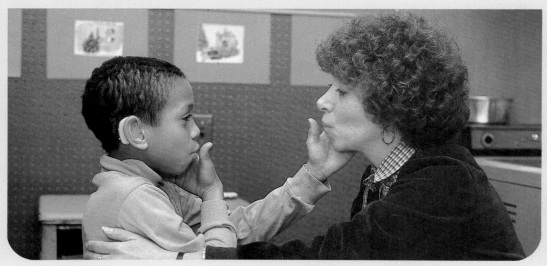

CASE STUDY: FOCUS ON RESEARCH

languages, thus also suggesting a biological explanation. So far, psychologists disagree as to whether language is mostly learned or mostly biologically determined.

Emotional Development

Emotional development refers to the individual's awareness and expression of an affective (emotional) experience. The kinds of emotions we feel play a large part in how we get along with others and how well we get along with ourselves. A person who experiences mostly unpleasant emotions is likely to be an unhappy person. Those people whose emotions are mostly pleasant will lead relatively happy lives.

Just as important as the kinds of emotions that people feel is the way in which they handle their emotions. Two individuals can experience the same emotion. However, one may handle it in an acceptable fashion, and the other may not. For example, one person may become angry and express this anger in words. Another person may become angry and smash a window, throw things, or perform some other unsuitable act to express the anger.

What emotions are present at birth?
No specific emotions can be determined in the newborn infant. There is only a general state of excitement. Newborn infants do seem to respond to differences in sound, however. One study investigated whether one-day-old

This chart shows at approximately what age certain emotions are thought to appear. It covers the first two years of life.

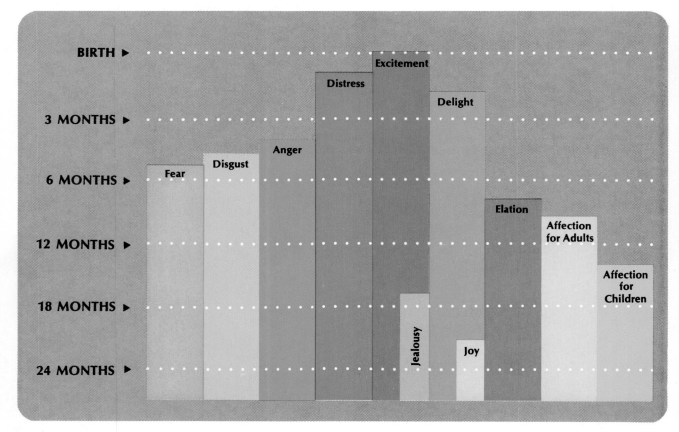

infants could tell the difference between the cry of another newborn infant, and an infant's cry created by a computer, and silence. Infants who heard the real cry joined in more frequently than infants in the other two groups. Thus, even one-day-old babies may be able to tell the difference between a real cry of another baby and a computer cry.

The emotions of distress and delight show up in infants shortly after birth. Although distress appears a little earlier than delight, both are present by the end of the third month. Distress is characterized by muscular tension and crying. Delight is shown by muscular relaxation and smiling. Fear, disgust, and anger appear by the sixth month. By the end of the first year, elation (high spirits) and affection are present.

How can psychologists determine that an infant is feeling an emotion? Consider the case of "stranger anxiety." Psychologists know that children often fear strangers at about eight months of age. Several methods were used to determine this. They found that at the age of five months an infant's heart rate slows down when a stranger appears. But the rate of the heartbeat of an eight- or nine-month-old infant increases when a stranger appears. If nine-month-old infants are given a free choice, they prefer not to be in the presence of a stranger. Also, when they can press a lever to see either their mother or a stranger, they press the lever more quickly to see their mother.

How does emotional behavior change with age? When young children become angry, they usually show openly aggressive or hostile behavior. As they grow older, they soon learn that this type of behavior is not socially acceptable. They then begin to hide it. Or they may turn to pouting.

In middle age, individuals become less aggressive and hostile. The change is more noticeable in the later years of life. This may occur partly because people then are considerably less able to defend themselves physically.

In later life the emotions associated with distress, such as grief, self-pity, and bore-

Not all people express their emotions in the same way. Although many of these people are experiencing the same emotions at this celebration, their faces do not show this.

dom, seem to take on a more personal character. Emotions become more related to ourselves as individuals and less involved with the social world around us.

However, some of the emotions expressed by older people are brought about by their reactions to the outside world. On the one hand, society believes that the elderly have fulfilled their societal obligations. As a result, it encourages them to rest and relax. Yet, on the other hand, it is forcing the elderly into a life of uselessness. Faced with this conflict, some elderly people spend their later years angry, bored, and depressed. Of course, when the separation is voluntary, the elderly more easily accept their new role. But very often the separation is not a matter of choice.

Fear as a common emotion. Everyone experiences love, anxiety, worry, anger, or jealousy. Different people show varying amounts of these emotions at different times.

Another common emotion is fear.

There is usually a pattern of fears that changes with the different stages of life. Young infants seem to fear nothing until they reach the stage where they can recognize possible dangers. Young children often fear such things as strange people, unfamiliar animals and objects, and the dark. Older children have conquered many of these fears because of their increased understanding of the environment around them. However, they may have developed other fears as substitutes.

As children grow older, they begin to develop fears involving social situations. They also fear things they cannot understand at the time, such as thunder and lightning and death. High school students develop a fear of failing courses, or being "different." As adults, people begin to fear such things as a loss of security. In old age there is an increase in the fear of losing a job, financial problems, and death.

Social Development

Social development involves learning to act and live in a society as a member of that society. Sometimes it means learning to control your impulses. At other times it requires doing things that you may not like. Social development occurs through associations with other people. From others we learn social habits, customs, what is right and wrong in that society, and how to influence and get along with people.

When does social behavior appear? There is some evidence that social behavior begins almost from the moment of birth. Newborn infants seem to respond to facelike objects, even if they have never seen a human face. This was determined by using four models of human heads. One model mask looked like an average human face. Another had the facial features slightly mixed up. A third had them completely mixed up. And a fourth model mask had no features at all. The infants were presented with these

masks three to twenty-seven minutes after birth. The more the model mask looked like a human face, the more the infants followed it with eye and head movements. It appears that newborn infants enter the world ready to respond to a human face.

When the average baby is about two months old, the baby will cry when an adult leaves and smile when the person returns. Children under one year of age will pay attention to the presence of another child. Yet they usually don't interact with two children at the same time until about thirty months of age.

During the preschool years children seem to interact with adults in three stages: (1) dependence, (2) resistance, and (3) cooperation. Children accept their dependence on adults early in life. Then, at about two years of age, they reach a stage of resistance. They rebel against adult standards. This is sometimes called the "I, me, mine" or "Let me do it!" stage. At this time children begin to realize that they are separate individuals with certain rights and privileges. It can be a very confusing time of life for children. They must learn that although they do have rights, they also must have limits placed on their behavior. In the third stage children become more cooperative and friendly as they begin to accept the limits put on them.

Social changes during the early school years. As children enter school, they run into conflicting ideas and attitudes more often than in the past. Meeting new people, getting an education, and being away from home each day bring about confusing situations for children. At about this point, children begin to adopt the standards of their age group.

Around the age of eight, children start to choose members of their own sex as playmates. Between this age level and adolescence, the two sexes often remain somewhat separate in our society.

Some characteristics of the social behavior of adolescents. The adolescent period is the time when the individual grows

It is common for both girls and boys of this age to associate with others of their own sex rather than with members of the opposite sex. At a later stage in their social development, they begin to spend more time with people of the other sex.

out of childhood into adulthood. Adolescents often strive to be independent from the home. They may rebel over minor things, such as how late they can stay out at night. Parents often fail to recognize their teenager's growing need for independence. Adolescents often fail to recognize that their parents are trying to protect them. When neither parent nor offspring recognizes the other's point of view, both experience frustration.

One of the most characteristic social developments during this period is an increasing interest in members of the opposite sex. Generally, the individual passes through a hero-worship stage, then the so-called puppy-love stage, and finally the more intense romantic-love stage.

The first stage occurs in the early teens. It involves a strong attraction toward someone of the same or opposite sex. It is based on a great admiration of the person. This person, who is usually older, may be a movie or television star, athletic hero, singer, or a successful person in some other area.

Individuals move out of this stage into the puppy-love stage during junior high school and early senior high school years. The affection then turns to a member of the opposite sex close to the individual's own age.

The last stage, romantic love, starts in late adolescence. It is a more intense, stable, and mature affection. The person's interest in other members of the opposite sex decreases as attention focuses mainly on one individual.

Characteristics of social development in adulthood and old age. The years after the teens to the late sixties are usually filled with getting additional education, finding and keeping a job, getting married, and raising a family.

With marriage comes the responsibility of a spouse and a family. Marriage often means the end of membership in some earlier social groups. But it also usually leads to interacting with new groups, such as other married couples of about the same age.

As people approach old age, they experience changes in their physiological, emotional, and intellectual development. People who work may begin to fear losing their jobs and having to retire. Some people prepare themselves for retirement by learning new things and developing hobbies. People who participate in intellectual, social, and physical activities throughout their adult years tend to age more successfully than those who are inactive.

Many wives outlive their husbands by several years. This can make old age a lonely time for many women. On the other hand, people who continue their social relationships into old age often gain a great deal of satisfaction during these years.

Intellectual Development

Intellectual development is the development of an individual's mental abilities. For many years our knowledge of intellectual development was based mainly on the results of scores on intelligence tests. In fact, intellectual development was thought of as the increase and decrease of the traits and abilities that make up an individual's intelligence.

However, the Swiss psychologist Jean Piaget (1896–1980) provided another way of studying the development of intelligence, reasoning, and thinking. While administering an intelligence test to children, he became interested in the reasons children gave for responding as they did. He believed that the reasons were more important than whether the children's answers were right or wrong.

Piaget began conducting studies of children's intellectual development using this approach. He found that intellectual development can be divided into four stages or periods. Although the periods of development have age ranges associated with them, these are only rough guidelines. They are not specific ages at which a person will develop the stated abilities. Piaget said that the order of the stages will hold true for all children, regardless of the culture in which they are reared. However, the age at which an individual starts or ends a stage will vary, depending on the environment, abilities, and socioeconomic position of the person.

Piaget called these four stages of intellectual development the sensory-motor, preoperational, concrete-operational, and formal-operational periods.

Sensory-motor period (birth to about two years). During the *sensory-motor period,* children use their senses and various muscular movements to interact with the environment. They begin to realize that they can bring about changes in their surroundings. For example, a child might reach for a mobile in an attempt to make it move.

By making things happen, children develop an appreciation of cause and effect. The mobile moves because they touched it. A toy rattles because they shake it. However, this understanding is limited. Children at this stage do not realize that a toy squeaks because of something inside it.

Children do, however, develop a sense that objects continue to exist, even if they can't see them. At about nine months of age children will search for a toy that has been hidden under a blanket. Before this period, the expression "out of sight, out of mind" would more appropriately describe their behavior. A child would lose interest in a toy instead of looking for it.

Preoperational period (about two to seven years). During this period children become more than just "sensory-motor" organisms. They learn to use symbols and, more importantly, language. For example, children will know the meaning of the word "ball" without having a ball in front of them.

In the **preoperational period,** children's thinking lacks organization and is still self-centered. They don't realize that there are viewpoints besides their own. In an interesting study, Piaget showed a child a large model of three mountains. The child was allowed to walk around each mountain. Each mountain had familiar objects on it. Then the child stood on one side of a mountain, and the experimenter stood on the side of another mountain. The experimenter asked the child to explain what the experimenter was looking at. In reply, the child described what the *child* was looking at.

During this period the child also tends to attribute human characteristics to objects. For example, the child might say, "The house looks tired," or "The tree feels old." And the child appears to believe that the house is tired and the tree feels old. However, children can differentiate between living and nonliving things. Part of the problem stems from their inability to explain things in any other way.

Concrete-operational period (about seven to eleven years). The period when children begin to think logically and realize that quantities remain the same although their shape may change is the **concrete-operational period.** Before this stage, children decide if things are equal by how they appear. Suppose, for instance, a five-year-old is shown two rows of marbles. Each row has the same number of marbles. However, one row is longer because there is more space between each marble. If you ask the five-year-old which row has the most marbles, the child will pick the row that is longer. A child in the concrete-operational stage, however, recognizes that the number of marbles in the two rows is equal.

Similarly, a young child may watch you pour the same amount of water into a tall, narrow glass and into a short, wide glass. When asked which glass has more water, the young child will choose the taller glass. A child in the concrete-operational period, however, understands that the amount of water in both glasses is equal.

This child shows preoperational thinking. She notes that two wide containers have the same amount of liquid. Yet when the liquid from one wide container is poured into a narrow, high container, she thinks that the high container has more liquid.

Formal-operational period (about eleven years and older). Even though people in the *formal-operational period* are no longer self-centered, they are still concerned with their own problems. However, now they begin to try combining various possibilities in solving a problem. They then drop the combinations that don't solve the problem. In other words, they can experiment with cause and effect until they discover the causes of events. The formal-operational individual can grasp very abstract principles. For example, suppose you ask what is wrong with the statement, "John's feet are so big that he has to put his shoes on before he puts on his socks." A child in an earlier stage may say that the statement is wrong because no one can have feet that big. The formal-operational individual points out that it is wrong because it is not logical. John isn't going to put his socks on over his shoes.

This information about Piaget's theories is merely one sample. Piaget made great strides in promoting research in the area of how a child thinks. In addition, his approach to studying intellectual development has had a tremendous influence on the study of all areas of development.

Yet Piaget's theories have not gone without criticism. For example, some researchers have found that formal operations are found in only about 30 to 40 percent of adolescents and adults in the United States. Also, they are found more often among those who have taken science courses, or who have learned about scientific procedures. They seem almost absent in many nonliterate cultures. Even Piaget, in his later years, admitted that formal operations may not appear in some societies, and that training can strongly influence performance.

Moral Development

Just as we go through stages of physical, motor, emotional, social, and intellectual growth, some people think that we also go through stages of moral development. *Moral development* means that an individual de-

velops the knowledge of what is right and wrong.

Lawrence Kohlberg (1927–), a developmental psychologist, believes that there are six stages of moral development, each more complex than the one before it. These stages occur in the same order for everyone, although moral development may stop at any stage.

Measuring moral development. How do you measure moral development? One way is to present individuals with situations that involve a "moral dilemma." In a moral dilemma, individuals must decide which is the "right" way to behave in these predicaments.

For example, in his studies Kohlberg uses a story that involves a man whose wife is dying of cancer. A local druggist has some medicine that will cure the dying woman, but is charging more than the husband can afford. The druggist refuses to lower the price or give him credit. Desperate, the husband breaks into the store and steals the medicine for his wife.

Individuals are then asked to respond to such questions as, "Should the husband have stolen the medicine?" They are also asked to give reasons for their responses. These reasons are more important to Kohlberg than the actual "yes" or "no" responses. Based on the reasoning behind the responses, Kohlberg has outlined his six stages of moral development. As you might expect, each is characterized by different reasoning.

The six stages of moral development. In Stage 1, children base their answers to a moral dilemma on avoiding punishment. They decide what is right or wrong by whether the behavior will be punished. For example, in the case of the whether-or-not-to-steal dilemma, children may answer, "If he lets his wife die, he will get into trouble." Or, "He will be sent to jail if he steals the drug."

In Stage 2, children make moral judgments according to what behavior will benefit them, bring them rewards, or cause someone to return a favor. An example of an answer in this stage would be, "If he gets caught, he can give the drug back so he would not get much of a jail sentence."

In Stage 3, people make moral decisions based on what will please or help others and avoid their disapproval. People in this stage are concerned with what others want and think. A typical answer would be, "People will praise the husband for saving his wife's life." Or, "He should not steal the drug because it would disgrace his family."

Stage 4 involves a respect for authority and one's duty as a citizen. Moral judgments are determined by what the society says is right and wrong behavior. For example, "He should not steal the drug because stealing is against the law."

In Stage 5, people make moral decisions based on the welfare of the community and the rights of others. One answer might be, "The druggist has no right to charge such a high price for the medicine."

In Stage 6, people decide on the basis of their own principles of justice. If the husband stole the drug, he would condemn himself for stealing. If he did not steal the drug, he would condemn himself for allowing his wife to die.

In Stages 5 and 6, individuals have more fully developed their own standards of morality than at previous stages. Stage 5 recognizes that different societies or groups have different viewpoints of what is right or wrong. In Stage 6, individuals recognize that there are universal points of view on which all societies should agree. For example, it is generally accepted that all persons in every society should have some rights.

Criticisms of Kohlberg's theory. Not all psychologists agree with Kohlberg. Those who disagree point out that moral development may not occur automatically in stages. It may depend on the home environment within which the child is raised, a child's association with parents, and whether the child has been rewarded or punished for certain behavior. In addition, there is some question as to whether moral reasoning is the same as moral behavior. That is, individuals may say they will do something when presented with a story involving a moral dilemma. However, they actually might not do what they say they would.

The decision of whether or not to cheat in a game is based on a knowledge of right and wrong.

Summary

There are various kinds of development that all people undergo. Prenatal development is the development that occurs before birth. This is an important process during which people acquire many of the characteristics that make them human.

Physical development has a great effect on people's behavior. Height and weight are two important aspects of physical development. The rate at which people develop physically may influence their attitudes and social adjustment.

Motor development is related to control over muscles of the body. In babies, motor development takes place very rapidly, as infants systematically gain control over their bodies. After infancy, however, motor development increases more slowly. In fact, motor development tends to decline after the middle twenties.

There have been various attempts to explain language development in human beings. Some people argue that learning accounts for much of language development. Other researchers stress the role of biological factors.

Emotional development affects the way people relate to themselves and others. Our emotions change with age as we relate in varying ways to other people and our environment. Some common emotions include fear, love, anxiety, worry, anger, and jealousy.

Social development occurs through interactions with other people. There is evidence that it begins almost with birth. Then as we grow and develop in other ways, our social relationships change to fit our changing needs and environment.

Jean Piaget greatly increased our knowledge of intellectual development. After studying many children, he concluded that intellectual development takes place in four stages. These are the sensory-motor, pre-operational, concrete-operational, and formal-operational periods. Each occurs within a different age span and is characterized by certain unique behaviors.

Lawrence Kohlberg theorizes that people go through various stages of moral development. These stages are based on ways of handling moral dilemmas. Kohlberg identifies six stages, but believes that not all people reach the highest level. Each stage represents a different way of thinking about moral problems.

INTERPRETING SOURCES

In this reading, from "Moral Stages and Moralization," developmental psychologist Lawrence Kohlberg discusses some of the factors that influence the development of moral reasoning. As you read this excerpt, think about how parents might try to promote their children's moral development.

Moral development depends upon stimulation ... the kind that comes from social interaction and from moral decision-making, moral dialogue, and moral interaction. . . . We have found that attainment of a moral stage requires cognitive development, but cognitive development will not directly lead to moral development. On the other hand, an absence of cognitive stimulation necessary for developing formal logical reasoning may be important in explaining ceilings on moral level. . . .

Of more importance than factors related to stimulation of cognitive stage are factors of general social experience and stimulation, which we call *role-taking opportunities*. . . .

Although moral judgments entail role-taking—putting oneself in the place of the various people involved in a moral conflict—attainment of a given role-taking stage ... is a necessary but not a sufficient condition for moral development. . . . Role-taking level, then is a bridge between logical or cognitive level and moral level; it is one's level of social cognition.

In understanding the effects of social environment on moral development, then, we must consider that environment's provision of role-taking opportunities to the child. Variations in role-taking opportunities exist in terms of the child's relation to his [or her] family, his [or her] peer group, his [or her] school, and his [or her] social status [in] the larger economic and political structure of the society.

With regard to the family, the disposition of parents to allow or encourage dialogue on value issues is one of the clearest determinants of moral stage advance in children. . . . Such an exchange of viewpoints and attitudes is part of what we term "role-taking opportunities." With regard to peer groups, children high in peer participation are more advanced in moral stage than are those who are low. With regard to status in the larger society ... the higher an individual child's participation in a social group or institution, the more opportunities he [or she] has to take the social perspectives of others. . . .

A notion that a higher-stage environment stimulates moral development is an obvious extension of experimental findings ... that adolescents tend to assimilate moral reasoning above their own, while they reject reasoning below their own. The concept of exposure to a higher stage need not be limited to a stage of reasoning, however; it may also include exposures to moral action and to institutional arrangements. What the moral atmosphere studies ... show is that individuals respond to a composite of moral reasoning, moral action, and institutionalized rules as a relatively unified whole in relation to their own moral stage.

Source Review

1. What does the author mean when he describes role-taking opportunities as "a bridge between logical or cognitive level and moral level"?

2. What characteristics of one's family tend to promote higher moral development? Why?

3. Why do children who are high in peer-group and social participation show higher levels of moral reasoning than children who are low in peer-group participation?

4. How does the moral level of one's social environment influence one's own moral development?

CHAPTER 3

REVIEWING TERMS

critical period
sensitive period
longitudinal method
cross-sectional method
prenatal development
physical development

motor development
language development
emotional development
social development
intellectual development
sensory-motor period

preoperational period
concrete-operational
   period
formal-operational period
moral development

CHECKING FACTS

1. Describe some of the general principles of development.

2. What is a critical period in development? How does it differ from a sensitive period?

3. What is prenatal development? Describe the nine-month process during which we develop before birth.

4. Discuss how physical development influences personality both for males and females.

5. Describe motor development in a baby. How does it compare with motor development in childhood, adolescence, and old age?

6. Explain how chimpanzees have been taught to communicate. Why do some psychologists believe they cannot learn to speak a language?

7. What are some of the different explanations for how children learn language?

8. How does emotional behavior change with age? Why are some elderly people angry, bored, and depressed?

9. Discuss social development in adolescence, adulthood, and old age.

10. Describe the four stages of intellectual development that Piaget identified. What are some criticisms of Piaget's theories?

11. Describe the six stages of moral development that Kohlberg proposes. What are some criticisms of Kohlberg's theory?

APPLYING YOUR KNOWLEDGE

1. If family members do not object, bring in some baby pictures that were taken of you or your brothers and sisters up to about two years of age. Sort them by age, and compare them with photos brought in by other students. Or you might wish to bring in one of your elementary school class photos showing all of your classmates. Do the pictures support the statement that not all people develop at the same rate? Explain your answer.

2. Imagine that you have been asked to prepare a film on the development that takes place during a child's first five years of life. Prepare a brief description of the behaviors you hope to illustrate and the ages at which they occur.

3. To show how emotional behavior changes with age, divide the class into five groups. The first group should represent ages one and two, the second ages five and six, the third adolescence, the fourth middle age, and the fifth old age. One member of each group should then volunteer to imitate the behavior of a person who is denied a favorite food. The other group members can coach the performer. How accurate do you think the performances were?

4. Create a moral dilemma and write six statements that illustrate each of the stages of moral reasoning. Do your class-mates agree with your statements? Explain.

5. Assume that you have discovered a twelve-year-old who has been reared by wolves since shortly after birth. Describe the procedures you would use in helping the person develop appropriate social behavior. How would you teach the person your language?

6. Ask a five-year-old, a ten-year-old, and a fifteen-year-old where dreams come from. The descriptions will illustrate how thinking and reasoning change with age.

THINKING CRITICALLY ABOUT PSYCHOLOGY

1. **Evaluating Ideas** Sometimes we hear it said that a particular person "never really grew up." What does this mean?

2. **Interpreting Ideas** How well do you think you could tell the difference between the cries of babies born in different countries? Explain.

3. **Drawing Conclusions** How would a society or culture function if there were no means of communication between members of that society?

4. **Classifying Ideas** Which of our emotions do you think are inborn and which are learned? Explain.

5. **Analyzing Ideas** Suppose that you are a parent and one of your children has a "temper tantrum." How would you handle such behavior?

DEVELOPING SKILLS IN PSYCHOLOGY

Using Case Studies to Examine Psychological Concepts

Case studies are intensive examinations of individual children or adults. Sometimes psychologists conduct case studies to examine hypotheses about human behavior in one individual of special interest. Often they report on their case studies to illustrate principles related to their theories about behavior.

This chapter's discussion of Genie is a good example of a case study. It allows us to make inferences about the role of experience in human development. Listed on the following page are some competing inferences that have been made about children. Look at the case study on pages 50–51 and decide what data either support or contradict each statement.

1. Children will never develop language if they do not acquire it between the ages of two and twelve.

2. Language is biologically built into all human organisms as a result of evolu-tion, rather than being a product of experience.

3. Children learn language by imitating others and being rewarded for their efforts.

READING FURTHER ABOUT PSYCHOLOGY

Csikszentmihalyi, Mihaly, and Larson, Reed, *Being Adolescent,* Basic Books, New York, 1984. This book is the result of a creative study that recorded teen-agers' spontaneous thoughts and feelings. The responses of the teen-agers reveal a great deal about how experiences influence human development.

Erikson, Erik H., *Childhood and Society,* Revised Edition, W. W. Norton, New York, 1964. Erikson's classic work describing his theory and perspective on human development. This book is both readable and intellectually stimulating.

Flavell, John H., *Cognitive Development,* Second Edition, Prentice-Hall, Englewood Cliffs, N.J., 1985. One of the most prominent authorities on cognitive development presents an easy-to-understand introduction to Piaget's theories.

Gardner, Howard, *Artful Scribbles,* Basic Books, New York, 1982. In this instructive book, a noted cognitive psychologist explores the vital links between children's art and their emotional, social, and mental development.

Lidz, Theodore, *The Person: His and Her Development Throughout the Life Cycle,* Basic Books, New York, 1983. One of the definitive sources for psychological theories on human development.

Miller, Patricia H., *Theories of Developmental Psychology,* W. H. Freeman, New York, 1983. The author describes six quite different approaches to the study of developmental psychology.

Sheehy, Gail, *Passages: Predictable Crises of Adult Life,* Bantam, New York, 1977. Describes the processes of change from adolescence through late adulthood. The book is filled with case histories illustrating the author's views on adult development.

Chapter 4

HEREDITY AND ENVIRONMENT

Chapter Focus

This chapter presents:
- **a discussion of how heredity affects development**
- **the effects of the environment on development**
- **the interaction between heredity and environment**

"He has his father's eyes."

"She has her mother's sense of humor."

No doubt many of you have heard similar expressions. How true are they? Are you solely the product of the characteristics you inherit from your parents? Or do other factors influence your development as well?

Actually, both heredity and environment determine the person you become. **Heredity** —all the characteristics transmitted from parents to children before birth—may give you your father's eyes, your mother's nose, and so on. But **environment**—all the surrounding forces that affect your life—may determine such characteristics as an interest in music or sports.

Which factor, then—heredity or environment—determines a characteristic such as shyness? Perhaps both. You may inherit your shyness from one of your parents. At the same time, though, you may be shy because of certain childhood experiences.

Most of our behavior is determined by both heredity and environment. Moreover, both these factors start having an effect as soon as the first human cell is formed. In this chapter we will examine these two powerful forces.

Inherited Characteristics

Each person originally begins as a single cell. From that one cell each person develops into a unique individual. Brothers and sisters may look somewhat alike. They may have the same color hair and eyes. Yet each person has a unique inheritance. How does inheritance take place?

Chromosomes and genes. Almost all of the cells of the body contain tiny rod-shaped bodies called **chromosomes.** Each human cell normally contains 46 chromosomes. These chromosomes are in pairs. We get 23 chromosomes from the father's sperm and 23 chromosomes from the mother's egg. The fertilized egg then contains 46 chromosomes, or 23 pairs.

In other species, however, the number of chromosomes in each cell is different. For example, the crayfish has 100 pairs. The moth has 31 pairs. Even in human beings the number of chromosomes occasionally differs from the usual 46. About 95 percent of all children with Down's syndrome have 47 chromosomes. This extra chromosome often can result in various abnormalities in these children. Children with Down's syndrome tend to have broad faces, slanting eyelids, and low intellectual ability. Chromosomes often explain the presence of some physical irregularities at birth.

Each chromosome is composed of many smaller units called *genes.* Genes are responsible for transmitting inherited traits from parents to children. In human beings there are probably at least a thousand genes in each of the 46 chromosomes. Within each gene is a chemical called **DNA** (deoxyribonucleic acid). DNA gives special "building instructions" for the development of different parts of the human body. For example, there are at least 150 different genes whose DNA gives instructions for the development of the brain alone. We know this because there are 150 genes that produce different kinds of mental retardation. If the in-

This is a single gene. It is from one of the bacteria sometimes found in the human intestine. (It is not a human gene.)

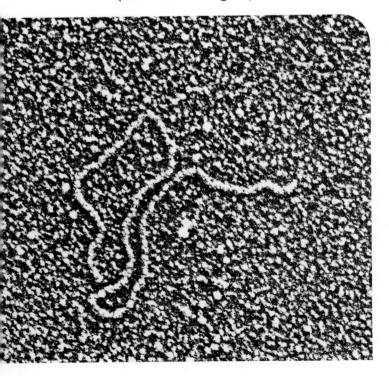

structions are not obeyed — if there is a defective gene — such results as low intellectual ability, a deformed arm, unusual shortness, or even death may occur.

Just how genes provide the "building instructions" for development is still a biochemical mystery. But scientists are making giant strides forward. In recent years they have been able to transplant the genetic materials of one cell into the cells of an entirely different species. In the future it may be possible to correct inherited irregularities in people.

Dominant and recessive genes. Another feature of genes is their dominance or recessiveness. A **dominant gene** is one that determines if an individual will show a particular characteristic or trait controlled by that gene, such as brown eyes. The characteristic will appear if either one parent or both parents have that gene. Some examples of traits determined by dominant genes are freckles, dimples, and curly hair.

A **recessive gene** is one that determines a characteristic or trait only if the gene on the matching chromosome is also recessive. Blue eyes are recessive. To have a blue-eyed child, then, both parents must have a recessive gene for blue eyes. If the gene matched to a recessive one is dominant, the effects of the recessive gene will not show. They will be masked, or hidden. Two examples of recessive gene characteristics are baldness and straight hair.

To summarize, if the pair of genes that children receive from their parents differs, the one that always wins out is dominant. The one that doesn't show is recessive.

Each mother and each father has genes that can operate in several million different ways. The genes of both can operate, then, in an almost limitless number of ways. So unless you are an identical twin, probably no other person in the world has — or ever had — your particular genetic makeup.

Where do your inherited characteristics come from? Do you inherit characteristics from your parents or from remote ancestors?

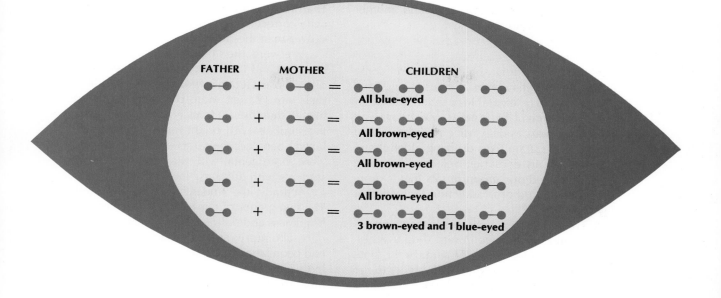

FATHER   MOTHER   CHILDREN

All blue-eyed

All brown-eyed

All brown-eyed

All brown-eyed

3 brown-eyed and 1 blue-eyed

If you have brown eyes, what possible combinations of genes for eye color might your parents have? What are the combinations if your eyes are blue?

Strictly speaking, you do not inherit tallness, eye color, or any other specific trait from your parents. Parents merely pass on to their children some genetic makeup that they received from their parents. Their parents had passed on a genetic makeup from their parents, and so on. The genes within the chromosomes within the reproductive cells are not changed by the individual carrying them. Instead, parents transmit to their children, unchanged, genes that they have inherited from their own parents.

A characteristic acquired by parents themselves and not present in earlier generations is not transmitted by heredity. A husband and wife may spend years studying music. Yet their children won't know one note from another unless they are taught, just as other children whose parents are not musicians are taught. In one scientific study, a biologist cut off the tails of mice for twenty generations. Yet each new litter of mice appeared with full-length tails. For generations, Chinese girls in certain families had their feet bound. But each baby in these families was born with normal feet.

If you look like your mother or your father, it is because you both have a common ancestry. Children inherit characteristics from their parents only in the sense that the parents are the immediate carriers of the characteristics of their ancestors.

Some Studies of Heredity

Much of our information about heredity comes from experiments with animals. We can breed animals selectively. That is, we can conduct genetic studies on animals to find out if genes are responsible for a particular behavior. By breeding animals as if there were a dominant gene or a recessive gene for the behavior, that behavior should change. For example, suppose we think that attraction to light is inherited. If it is, we should be able to selectively breed animals so that one strain will be attracted to light and another strain attracted to the dark.

The results of animal experiments. Selective breeding has produced some changes in behavior in animals. Dogs have been bred to be excitable or quiet. The excitable dogs might be used as watchdogs and the quiet ones as pets. Mice have been bred so that one strain likes drinking alcohol and another strain does not. Selective breeding has produced one group of rats that is more inclined toward drug addiction than another group.

There have also been experiments on heredity and intelligence in rats. One psychologist taught 142 rats to run a maze for food. The rats differed greatly in their ability to run the maze. Some seemed more intelligent than others. The ones with the best maze records were then bred with one another. Those average in ability were bred with other average rats. And those lowest in ability mated with other "dull" rats. This was continued for several generations of rats. What do you think were the results? Actually, the bright rats produced mostly bright rats. The dull rats produced mainly dull rats. And the average rats mainly produced rats with average maze-running ability.

This experiment is very impressive. But the data must be interpreted with caution. Further experiments with the two strains of rats showed that the bright rats were much more active than the dull rats. Perhaps what was transmitted from one generation to the next was something other than a general intellectual ability. Furthermore, one study suggested that differences in intelligence were due not to heredity but to the bias of the experimenter. There may not have been enough control of the experimental conditions and collection of data.

In a college psychology class, students were told about the experiment just described. Then half of the students were given a dull strain of rats, and half were given a bright strain of rats. The rats were trained to run a maze. The rats from the dull group had an average of 1.5 daily correct responses. The rats from the bright group averaged 2.3 daily correct responses. Also, the dull rats ran slower than the bright rats.

Afterward, the students were asked to rate their rats and their own attitudes toward the rats. Those students with bright rats rated their rats smarter, more pleasant, and more likable than the students with dull rats. Also, the students with bright rats were more relaxed, handled their rats more often, and were more gentle with their rats than those students with dull rats.

Actually, the students had been misled. The two groups of rats had not been bred for brightness and dullness. They were just ordinary laboratory rats of the same strain. They had been labeled as dull or bright at random. In this instance, the differences in maze-running ability were due to environmental factors, such as the students' treatment of their rats, rather than to heredity.

This experiment does not rule out the possibility that brightness or dullness is inherited. There is considerable evidence that learning capacities are inherited to some extent. But it does suggest that we need further careful experimentation on the subject.

Studies of human families. What are the roles of heredity and environment in human beings? For example, are some forms of psychological disturbances inherited? One psychological disorder that psychologists have been studying is schizophrenia. Symptoms of this disorder are loss of contact with reality, withdrawal, and disturbances of emotions. How can we determine whether or not schizophrenia is inherited?

Earlier studies were based on the belief that the more similar people were in genetic makeup, the more likely they would be to have a similar disorder. For example, *identical twins* come from a single fertilized egg. They have the same genetic makeup. Therefore, if an identical twin develops schizophrenia, the other twin would be very likely to develop the disorder. If this disorder were due only to genetics, the other twin would develop schizophrenia 100 percent of the

Because identical twins have the same heredity, they are always of the same sex. It is very rare for two sets of such twins to be born in one family.

time. The chances of the other twin also getting schizophrenia are high. They can vary from 24 percent to 85 percent. But it does not happen 100 percent of the time.

It is true that the more similar the genetic makeup of two people, the more likely one is to develop schizophrenia if the other person does so. Thus a brother and sister would be more likely to develop schizophrenia than two first cousins because the genetic makeup of brothers and sisters is more similar. However, it is also true that brothers and sisters have a more similar environment than first cousins do. How much of a factor is the environment in the development of schizophrenia? To find out, psychologists have studied children who were separated from their parents and the influence of the family environment at birth. They found that children of schizophrenic mothers who were

raised in foster homes had a higher probability of showing schizophrenia than children of normal parents who were reared in foster homes.

Thus there is evidence that schizophrenia has some genetic connections. But the present data don't identify exactly what is inherited. If genetic factors alone were responsible for schizophrenia, the data should be much more consistent.

Genetic counseling. In recent years it has become more common for adults to seek advice on having children when they suspect a problem—a defect—in their genetic makeup. Some types of hereditary defects can be determined before a child is conceived. This can be done by looking at the family history of the marriage partners or by analyzing their chromosomes. Even after the child is on the way, tests are available to detect some disorders.

Heredity and Maturation

A discussion of heredity must include mention of a particular inherited process—maturation. **Maturation** consists of patterns of individual growth that appear more or less automatically as an individual gets older, if the environment provides a necessary amount of support. For example, a child automatically begins to crawl at a particular stage of development. The infant is not taught this behavior.

Different organisms inherit different rates of maturation. Eight-week-old puppies, for example, can run about, eat from a dish, and do most of the things they will do as grown dogs. Eight-week-old human babies, on the other hand, are still quite helpless. They could not survive if they were not cared for. As a result of heredity, dogs mature more rapidly than human beings.

Maturation and learning in animals. An experiment was done with salamanders to find out if their ability to swim was learned or was the result of maturation. A large number of salamander eggs was divided into two groups. The first group served as the control group. The eggs of this group were placed in ordinary water. They were permitted to develop as they normally would in nature. The second group of eggs served as the experimental group. These eggs were placed in a drug solution. The solution didn't interfere with the normal processes of growth. But it did paralyze the animals so that they could not move.

The control group developed the usual swimming ability. After the salamanders in the control group had been swimming for five days, the salamanders in the experimental group were taken out of the drug solution and placed in ordinary water. Within thirty minutes they were swimming about with as much ease as those in the control group, which had had five days' practice. Apparently the development of a salamander's ability to swim depends on maturation rather than on practice or learning.

Maturation and human learning. Experiments on maturation and learning often use identical twins as subjects. Identical twins have the same heredity. Therefore, whatever differences appear in them must be due to the influence of the environment. **Fraternal twins** are children who merely happen to be born at the same time. Their heredity is no more alike than other children of the same parents.

The following experiment involved comparing the ability of identical twin girls to climb stairs. At the age of forty-six weeks, one of the twin girls was given an opportunity to climb a set of stairs. She did not climb any of them. She was then given training in going up stairs. After four weeks of training, she was climbing the stairs without help.

The other twin was not given any experience with stairs until she was fifty-three weeks old. In her first test at this age, she climbed the stairs unaided in 45 seconds. After two weeks of training, she was climbing stairs better than her twin, who had received many more weeks of training. Clearly, in this case, maturation was more important than environmental experiences in enabling the children to climb stairs.

Another study, which did not use identical twins, also explored the relationship between maturation and learning. This study compared two groups of Hopi Indian babies to determine whether walking was a learned process or the result of maturation.

The first group of infants was raised in the traditional Hopi way. That is, the babies were strapped to cradle boards for much of the first nine months of their lives. Because of this confinement, they had little chance to exercise their muscles and few opportunities to prepare themselves for walking.

The second group, however, was allowed to move about freely. The infants were allowed to creep, crawl, stand, and grasp for

These are fraternal twins. They are born at the same time but do not have the same genetic makeup. Such twins can be of the same sex or different sexes.

nearby objects. They were free to behave in much the same way as children that age normally do.

How do you think the two groups compared? Which group do you think walked first? In this study, the researchers found that both groups began walking at almost exactly the same age. Although infants in the first group were deprived of various pre-walking experiences, they, too, were able to take their first steps when they reached the proper stage of development.

From this study it appears that walking results mostly from the hereditary process of maturation. What role, then, might the environment play in walking and other kinds of motor development?

Actually, the environment plays an important role in development. For example, proper nutrition helps children reach their maturation potential, while poor nutrition can severely hinder development. Such substances as lead-based paint might also retard development.

Does maturation guarantee learning? When children reach a certain age, will they suddenly be able to read without training? No, they won't. Do all children mature into being ready to read at the same age? Once again, the answer is no. Some children are ready to read at an earlier age than other children because of their more rapid biological growth rate. Also, environmental forces play a part. Children growing up in a home where there is a good deal of reading and other broadening experiences usually want to learn to read at an earlier age than children in surroundings where reading is neglected and experiences are limited. Learning to read, then, is influenced partly by maturation and partly by environmental influences.

In general, human learning is not a matter of maturation alone. Learning takes place faster when it is keyed to the person's degree of maturation. Children can learn to read and perform other mental and physical tasks most efficiently if they are given instruction when they reach the proper degree of maturation.

Text continues on page 74.

Case Study: Focus on Research

"YOU LOOK JUST LIKE ME"

Imagine discovering after thirty-nine years that you have an identical twin who not only looks like you but may act like you as well. That is just what happened to two men named Jim. Separated at the age of one month and adopted as babies by two different Ohio families, the twins had finally located each other through courthouse records thirty-nine years later.

Hearing about the reunion, psychologist Thomas Bouchard began a project in Minneapolis known as the Minnesota Study of Twins Reared Apart. As part of this study, he conducted six days of physical and psychological tests on his subjects, trying to determine similarities and differences. The results were surprising.

The Jim twins, as they looked in Bouchard's laboratory.

Of course, the twins looked alike. But the similarities went much further than that. Both men had identical pulse rates, blood pressure, and sleep patterns. Both had suffered from the same severe headaches since the age of eighteen—and described the pain in a similar manner. Both had been indifferent students, liked to work in their basement workshops, and enjoyed stock-car racing. They drove the same make of car, smoked the same brand of cigarettes, and drank the same kind of beer. They even vacationed at the same three-block beach on Florida's Gulf coast.

They also had the same name, and thus received the nickname of the "Jim twins." In addition, each married a Linda, divorced her, and married a Betty. One had a son named James Alan; the other had a son named James Allan. Each had once owned a dog called Toy.

The "Jim twins" were only one of several sets of twins assembled and studied by Bouchard. Another set of twins in this research project—two Englishwomen who met for the first time on the flight to Minneapolis—both showed up wearing exactly seven rings each. One had named her children Richard Andrew and Catherine Louise. The other's son and daughter were named Andrew Richard and Karen Louise.

The most remarkable pair, however, were two men born in Trinidad. One, reared as a Jew by his father, spent part of his youth on an Israeli kibbutz and eventually moved to the United States. The other was reared as a Nazi and a Catholic by his grandmother in Germany. Despite radically different environments, they displayed many similarities when they met in Minneapolis. They had similar eyeglasses and mustaches, wore two-pocket shirts with epaulets, read magazines from back to front, and tended to shout at their wives.

In undertaking his study, Bouchard was looking for individual differences—evidence of how the environment shapes personality. Instead he found what he called "amazing similarities." When referring to the "Jim twins," one of Bouchard's researchers noted, "They were like bookends."

Bouchard's study also may help researchers investigate the age-old question: How much of our behavior is influenced by heredity and how much by environment? Since identical twins have exactly the same genetic makeup, and these twins have been reared in different households, behavioral similarities might be attributed to heredity, and differences to the environment.

What does Bouchard conclude from his study? So far his sample is small—under 100 sets of twins—and the results have not been completely analyzed. Yet certain tentative statements have been made. In the case of the Trinidad twins, the similarities suggest that children's personalities are not necessarily shaped by the sex of those who rear

them. Although one twin was reared by a male and the other by a female, both displayed remarkably similar characteristics.

In addition, some of the resemblances suggest that certain combinations of genes may result in certain preferences. This does not mean that there is a specific gene for choice of eyeglasses or deciding to wear seven rings. Rather, certain genes might combine to produce pretty hands. This trait in turn might prompt a fondness for rings. The verdict is not yet in, but the evidence is convincing.

Not all people are convinced, however, and for good reasons. For one thing, despite the similarities, the twins also exhibited numerous differences. These differences were played down while the similarities were emphasized. In addition, the sample is in no way representative. Thus, much remains to be learned before any definite conclusions can be drawn.

SOURCE: Constance Holden, "Twins Reunited," *Science 80,* November 1980, pp. 55–59; Rochelle Distelheim, "The Mysteries of Identical Twins," *McCall's,* January 1981, pp. 68+; Constance Holden, "Identical Twins Reared Apart," *Science,* 1980, *207,* 1323–1327.

This set of twins shares some information with a researcher. Researchers were amazed at the similarities exhibited by all of the twins.

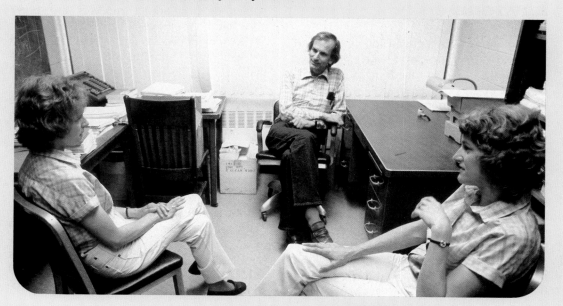

It is important for a pregnant woman to take care of herself. Her health affects the health of the unborn infant.

Influences of the Environment

The environment affects an individual from the moment of conception (when the sperm fertilizes the egg). For nine months after conception, the child lives in the limited environment of the mother's body. Perhaps it seems strange to you that we include influences during those nine months before birth under the heading of environment. This environment, however, is very important in the development of a child.

Some maternal influences. There is a common superstition that the thoughts of a pregnant woman affect the unborn baby that she is carrying in her body. It is said that if the mother reads good literature, the child will have literary ability. Or if the mother reads crime stories and sees crime films, the child is likely to become a criminal. Such ideas are groundless. Scientists know that there is no connection between the nervous system of the mother and the nervous system of the child developing in her body.

The blood of the mother does not flow through the veins of the child. But some things do pass from the mother to the child. Disease germs, such as those of diphtheria, typhoid, and syphilis, may succeed in passing from the body of the mother to the body of the child. Suppose the mother is unusually worried or has a severe emotional shock. Some scientists believe that the chemicals formed in the mother's body as a result of this worry or shock may be carried to her unborn child. Also, there is evidence that if the mother is a cigarette smoker, her baby may be underweight and smaller than average.

The use of alcohol, even when consumed in moderation, also can produce abnormalities. About 40 percent of infants born to alcoholic mothers suffer from physical abnormalities and mild mental retardation. Certain drugs taken by the mother also can cause defects in the child. One of the most famous examples involved the drug called Thalidomide. Mothers taking the drug often gave birth to children who had no arms, or no legs, or very small limbs. Also, babies of drug-addict mothers are born addicted themselves.

Such influences as these are due to environment, not to heredity. They can affect the child during the nine months before birth. Heredity, on the other hand, is complete at conception.

The influence of malnutrition. Malnutrition during pregnancy can have undesirable influences on the later development of the offspring. If the mother is severely undernourished during pregnancy, the child may be born with a reduced number of brain cells. A protein deficiency in the mother can affect the intellectual growth of the child. It may cause a lack of protein in the unborn child. And protein is responsible for the development of memory.

Malnutrition affects the development of unborn children in other ways as well. One study found that the offspring of undernourished human mothers were, at birth, 15 percent smaller in body weight than children from healthy mothers. Furthermore, some of their organs were unusually small.

Influences of the environment after birth. Malnutrition after birth also has serious effects. It affects both development and behavior. Recent studies indicate that the earlier malnutrition occurs, the greater the effect. Children with malnutrition during the first year of life tend to score lower on intelligence tests than children who had an adequate diet early in life. They tend to be especially retarded in language development.

Malnutrition before two years of age has been linked with some behavioral problems. In one study, mothers were asked about the social relations, maturity, and activity levels of sons who had experienced malnourishment before they were two years old. In general, the mothers stated that their sons' behavior was backward, withdrawn, or unsocial. The mothers also believed that these sons were less liked by their brothers and sisters and were unhappy in school. However, perhaps the feelings of the mothers influenced the behavior of their sons. For example, if a mother believes that her son is backward, the mother may treat the son as backward. This can cause the son to act in a backward way.

What can be done about the effect of malnutrition on children? Giving vitamins to malnourished pregnant mothers has reduced the effects of malnutrition on their children. In one research study, mothers from a nutritionally poor environment took special vitamins during pregnancy. The children they bore scored eight points higher on intelligence tests than the children of mothers from a similar nutritional environment who received no vitamins.

But what about the children born of malnourished mothers who did not receive a vitamin-enriched diet during pregnancy? Can we improve the intellectual ability of malnourished children by giving them more nutritious food?

One study gave nutritional therapy to four groups of children. The children were all between two and ten years of age. One group consisted of well-nourished but intellectually retarded children. A second group consisted of well-nourished and intellectually normal children. A dietary improvement for these two well-nourished groups produced little change in their intellectual ability. The third group consisted of malnourished and intellectually retarded children. The fourth group was made up of malnourished but intellectually normal children. After a period of dietary improvement, the malnourished retarded children gained ten points on intelligence-test scores. The malnourished normal children gained eighteen points. Nutritional therapy did make a difference.

But prevention is better and more certain than cure. Something can be done to prevent malnutrition. What can you do to help improve our environment so that there is enough nourishing food for everyone?

Heredity and Environment Interact

Over the years psychologists have conducted studies in which they have tried to answer the question, "Which is more important, heredity or environment?" Today, psychologists concentrate more on finding answers to the questions "How do heredity and environment interact?" and "What is the contribution of each?"

The interaction of heredity and environment in an animal experiment. This experiment used rats that had been bred for brightness and dullness over 13 generations. The bright and dull rats that resulted were raised under three different environmental conditions: restricted, neutral, and enriched.

For the restricted environment, cages were covered with wire mesh and contained only food and water. The neutral environment consisted of the usual rat cages, from which the rats could observe activities in the laboratory. The cages with an enriched environment contained marbles, bells, swings, mirrors, tunnels, and other small objects. Half of the rats placed in each environment were bright, and half were dull. The rats were kept in their environments for forty days after weaning. Then all of the rats were tested in a maze. A record was kept of how many errors each made. The more errors they made, the lower their learning ability. The results are shown in the graph on this page.

You can see that in the restricted and enriched environments, the performances of the bright and dull rats were quite similar. Also, both bright and dull rats made many more errors in the restricted environment than in the enriched environment. These data suggest that any hereditary differences between the bright and dull rats were overshadowed by environmental influences. It was only in the neutral environment that heredity seemed to play a major role. Here the bright rats made considerably fewer errors than the dull rats. In general, heredity factors were of greatest importance when the environmental influence was neither overwhelmingly positive nor negative. If we wanted to develop a society of bright rats, we would need either to breed them for brightness or provide them with an enriched environment.

What is the role of heredity in determining intellectual ability? We can't carry out experiments like the one just described with children. But we can learn something about the interaction of heredity and environment in human beings through studies of twins.

If intellectual ability is inherited, then identical twins should be more alike in intellectual ability than brothers and sisters of the same parents. Many studies have found this to be the case. However, some of these studies have not taken into account certain environmental factors. Identical twins reared in the same home have a more similar environment than brothers and sisters in the same home. Identical twins often wear similar clothes, have more friends in common, and are somewhat closer to each other than typical brothers and sisters.

What happens when identical twins are reared apart in very different environments? If the environment were totally responsible for intelligence, then identical twins raised in different environments would be no more alike than any two people reared in different environments. However, identical twins reared apart do show more similarity in intelligence-test scores than two people chosen at random. Therefore, heredity seems to play some role in determining scores on intelligence tests. Estimates on how much of a role heredity plays range from about 20 percent to more than 80 percent. At present we don't have enough accurate data to be able to give a more exact answer.

What environmental factors affect intelligence-test scores? Suppose you were locked in a closet for the first sixteen years of your life. Your experiences would be ex-

The number of errors made by rats raised under three different environmental conditions.

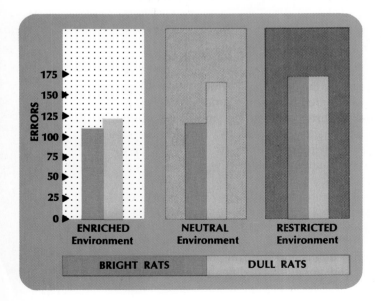

tremely limited. Then, on your sixteenth birthday, the closet door is opened, and you are given an intelligence test. What would you know?

Studies suggest that children who grow up with limited experiences and little intellectual stimulation do less well on intelligence tests. But there are many other factors that influence scores on intelligence tests. For example, both the sex and the race of the tester can influence scores. Even the attitudes of testers toward the person taking the test can affect scores.

Another important factor is the cultural background of the children. Children from certain cultural backgrounds often have not come in contact with many of the items being tested for. As a result, they tend to score lower than children who are familiar with these items.

To stress this point, a researcher created the "Dove Counterbalance General Intelligence Test." This test includes questions on such topics as the amount of time needed to cook chitlings (hog intestines) and the place where the "Hully Gully" (a dance) originated. Children from certain cultural backgrounds often score high on this test. However, children from various other cultural backgrounds might do quite poorly.

In addition, it has been suggested that lower-class children put forth less effort when taking intelligence tests. They see the tests as punishment, and fear that the exams will present them in a bad light. Frequently they just race through the tests, trying to finish them as quickly as possible. They use little care in choosing their answers. As a result, their scores are often notably lower.

Can changes in the environment raise intelligence-test scores? The following is a study of 26 children in an orphanage. Conditions in this particular orphanage were unsatisfactory. There was overcrowding. Those in charge were not trained for the work. Play and study equipment was lacking or was very poor. And the children received very little individual attention. On entering the orphanage, all the children had intelligence-test scores of 80 or above. The average was 90. After these children had lived in this undesirable environment for less than two years, their average score dropped sixteen points.

Would taking children out of an orphanage raise their intellectual levels? One group of infants was removed from an orphanage and raised by attendants and the mentally retarded women in an institution. They gave considerable care, attention, and love to the infants. On intelligence tests given later, these children scored an average of about thirty points higher than a control group of infants that had been left in the orphanage. Twenty years later they were still higher in intellectual ability than the orphanage group. Half of them even attended college for a year or more.

To further test the effects of environment on intelligence-test scores, psychologists developed an enrichment program for children growing up in culturally limited environments. A group of black boys fifteen months old with culturally limited environments were given special tutoring for almost two years. The boys were tutored for one hour a day, five days a week. They were talked with and read to. They were given experiences with books and puzzles. They went on special trips and walks. And they received help with their emotional or behavioral problems. A control group of similar age, background, and intelligence did not receive any tutoring.

At the close of the study, the average score of the tutored boys was higher than the average score of the boys in the control group. When the tutoring stopped, the scores of the tutored group went down somewhat. But they were still higher after tutoring than those of the control group. The data suggest the value of a stimulating environment in developing intellectual ability.

How do heredity and environment interact? In most cases it is impossible to separate completely the effects of heredity and environment. Heredity may increase the chances that a person will develop a particular disorder. But the environment may determine whether or not the disorder ever appears. Diabetes is a condition in which the sugar level in the blood is too high due to a lack of insulin. Diabetes is inherited. Yet in studies of identical twins, only a small percentage of both twins develops diabetes when one twin has it. How could this be? Perhaps the other twin carries the gene for diabetes, but because of diet never develops the condition.

As a result of their studies of twins, some psychologists believe that physical characteristics are least likely to be affected by the environment. Intelligence, as measured by tests, is more likely to be affected. Education and achievement are still more apt to be influenced by the environment. And personality is most likely to be affected.

However, the important question today is not *which* behaviors are influenced by heredity and *which* by environment. The question is *how* such behaviors are influenced. It is not enough to know that height and intelligence are affected by heredity. We need to know how they are affected. We need to find out more about how an inherited trait interacts with the environment to produce behavior.

Summary

Two factors that influence the development of an individual are heredity and environment. Both start having an effect as soon as the first cell is formed. Moreover, both influence most of our behavior.

Our inherited characteristics are transmitted by chromosomes and genes. Every human cell normally contains 46 chromosomes, which in turn contain at least a thousand genes each. Genes provide the building blocks for development and may be dominant or recessive.

Maturation is a process that is entwined with heredity. It occurs when an organism is ready for a particular change. Studies have shown that both animals and human beings develop certain behaviors through maturation rather than learning.

The environment is the other factor that affects an individual's development. The environment starts exerting its influence at conception, as the child begins to develop inside the mother's body. Some maternal factors that may negatively affect the health of an unborn child are cigarettes, alcohol, and certain drugs. Malnutrition during this time can be particularly harmful. A poor diet after birth can also seriously affect the child.

Both heredity and environment interact in many instances. Intelligence is a major area in which both factors play important roles.

INTERPRETING SOURCES

Human development is determined by the interaction of heredity and environment. In the following excerpt from "Born to be Shy?" (*Psychology Today*, April 1987), Jules Asher discusses the genetic and learned basis of shyness.

We've all met shy toddlers—the ones who cling to their parents and only reluctantly venture into an unfamiliar room. . . . Parents of such children are likely to say they've always been on the timid side. . . .

Harvard University psychologist Jerome Kagan has found this in his long-term studies of human infant development, and psychologist Stephen Suomi, of the National Institutes of Health, has seen the same thing in his developmental studies of monkeys. . . .

In 1979, Kagan and psychologists J. Steven Reznick and Nancy Snidman started to follow the development of extremely inhibited and uninhibited children. . . .

These [shy] children, in addition to their continuing timidity, show a pattern of excessive physiological responses to mildly stressful situations that wouldn't faze their easygoing peers. Their unusually intense physical responses to mental stress—which include more dilated pupils and faster and more stable heartbeats—indicate that their sympathetic nervous system is revved up. . . .

While Kagan was conducting his early studies of child development in the 1950s and 1960s, psychologist Harry Harlow . . . was doing his own classical research on infant monkeys' reactions to separation from their mothers. Harlow showed that while some baby monkeys became depressed, others emerged relatively unscathed. In the 1960s and 1970s, Suomi, working with Harlow, zeroed in on the depression-prone monkeys—the ones he would later identify as "uptight"—and found that they had behavioral and physiological characteristics closely resembling those of Kagan's timid children. . . .

During infancy, under the stress of brief separations, they became less playful and showed the . . . unusually high and stable heart rate seen in Kagan's shy toddlers. . . .

Suomi has found that uptight monkeys, like Kagan's shy children, do not often outgrow their abnormal physiological response to stress. . . .

The extreme timidity of Suomi's simians and of Kagan's kids seems to have a genetic foundation, the researchers agree. . . . For example, Suomi found that siblings and half-siblings . . . are more likely to react similarly to stress than are unrelated monkeys.

Evidence that humans may have a special biological predisposition for extreme shyness comes from the studies of behavioral geneticists Robert Plomin of Pennsylvania State University and David Rows of the University of Oklahoma, who found that identical twin pairs are particularly prone to react alike to strangers.

What does this predisposition mean for the babies who inherit such a legacy? . . . Suomi's current work suggests that, under the right circumstances, being born uptight need not be a social handicap. . . .

[Kagan] advises parents of very shy children to recognize their problem early; protect them from as much stress as possible and help them learn coping skills. . . . In the case of inborn shyness, biology clearly sets the stage, but learning helps to write the script.

Source Review

1. How do extremely shy children react to novel situations and mild stress?

2. What does Kagan recommend to parents of shy children?

3. How might one summarize the relative importance of heredity and environment in determining shyness?

CHAPTER 4

REVIEWING TERMS

heredity
environment
chromosome
gene

DNA (deoxyribo-
nucleic acid)
dominant gene
recessive gene

identical twins
maturation
fraternal twins

CHECKING FACTS

1. What is the difference between heredity and environment? Which factor determines most of our behavior?

2. What is the relationship between chromosomes and genes? What functions do genes serve?

3. How do dominant genes differ from recessive genes? Give an example of a dominant and a recessive characteristic.

4. Do you inherit characteristics from your parents or from remote ancestors? Explain your answer.

5. What do animal experiments tell us about the influence that heredity has on behavior?

6. Why do scientists use identical twins when studying the effects of heredity?

7. Describe the relationship between maturation and learning in human beings. Are both processes necessary for complete development to occur? Explain.

8. How does the environment inside the body of a mother-to-be influence the development of the unborn child? What substances can harm the child?

9. Discuss how malnutrition affects development both before and after birth. What can be done to counter the effects of malnutrition in children?

10. What environmental factors affect intelligence-test scores? How can changes in the environment raise such scores?

11. Why is it difficult to separate the effects of heredity and environment on development?

APPLYING YOUR KNOWLEDGE

1. Make a list of some of the physical characteristics that you and your brothers and sisters may have inherited from your parents. Which parent do you take after more? How about your brothers and sisters?

2. With your parents' permission, bring in some photographs of your parents that were taken when they were children.

Have your teacher tape them to the chalkboard in front of the room without identifying any of the pictures. How many students can you correctly match up with their parents?

3. Look through your school library or local library for information on identical twins who have been reared apart. Try to find out as much as possible about the

personality and habits of each twin. Then prepare a report that discusses the roles that heredity and environment each may have played in the twins' development. If a set of these twins lives in your area, you might invite them to address your class.

4. A group of students should contact a social agency that deals with parenthood or child care, and gather some information on the following topics: proper prenatal care, genetic counseling, and methods of promoting intellectual development in infants through early environmental stimulation. If possible, students might invite a representative from one of these agencies to speak to the class.

5. Assume you have been given the task of providing an "ideal" environment for the next generation of children. Organize into small groups. Identify some problems associated with the task, discuss possible solutions, and develop a plan for carrying out the assignment. Present your ideas to the class.

6. Hold a debate in class. Have one team provide evidence of how the environment is the major influence in the development of the individual. The other team should show how heredity is of primary importance in influencing the development of a person. The debate can be made more interesting if team members take the side that they don't agree with.

THINKING CRITICALLY ABOUT PSYCHOLOGY

1. **Forming Opinions** What changes in society might occur if we could presently control, through genetic changes, all types of human behavior? Would this necessarily be desirable?

2. **Debating Ideas** Should we attempt, through legislation, to reduce the number of children born to parents of limited intellectual ability? Or should we attempt to provide a richer environment for whatever children are born to parents of limited intellectual ability?

3. **Applying Ideas** What would you do to improve our environment so that human beings born a hundred years from now will be superior to human beings living today?

4. **Classifying Ideas** Suppose that someday you want to adopt a child five or six years of age. Which factor would you give greater consideration to: the child's heredity, or the child's early home or institutional care? Why?

5. **Synthesizing Ideas** Some people believe that researchers should not use animals in experiments. How would research on heredity be affected if researchers could not experiment with animals?

6. **Analyzing Ideas** A few researchers have argued that some criminals have an extra chromosome, which may have contributed to their criminal tendencies. Do you think that living in an enriched environment might help them change their behavior? Explain your answer.

7. **Comparing Ideas** Should genetic counseling be required for all people thinking of having children? Explain. What are the advantages and disadvantages that genetic counseling offers?

8. **Researching Ideas** What social programs can be instituted to prevent malnutrition in children and pregnant women? Do you think the benefits of these programs would outweigh the costs? Explain.

DEVELOPING SKILLS IN PSYCHOLOGY

Understanding a Bar Graph

Scientists use many devices to summarize information and present it clearly and succinctly. This chapter contains an example of a *bar graph*, which in this case illustrates the number of errors made by rats raised under three different environmental conditions.

Bar graphs use bars to represent information. They have titles to tell you what information they contain, and labels on the side and bottom to help clarify the information being presented in each bar. In the bar graph on page 76, one color is used to represent rats bred to be bright and another color is used to represent rats bred to be dull. At the left-hand margin you see a guide to the number of errors made by rats. At the bottom you see labels indicating whether the rats being tested were from an enriched, neutral, or restricted environment.

Study the bar graph on page 76 and then answer the following questions. Under what environmental conditions was there the greatest discrepancy in errors of bright and dull rats? Approximately how big was the discrepancy? That is, judging from the marginal guide, approximately how many more errors were made by the dull than by the bright rats in the condition that produced the greatest discrepancy? When dull rats were raised in an enriched setting, how did their performance compare with that of dull rats raised in the other two settings?

READING FURTHER ABOUT PSYCHOLOGY

Bank, Stephen P., and Kahn, Michael D., *The Sibling Bond*, Basic Books, New York, 1982. Discusses the powerful emotional connections between brothers and sisters.

Ernst, Cecile, and Angst, Jules, *Birth Order: Its Influences on Personality*, Springer-Verlag, New York, 1983. Examines the research on the psychological effects of birth order with topics ranging from possible birth order influences on occupation through socialization and personality.

Farber, Susan, *Identical Twins Reared Apart*, Basic Books, New York, 1981. All available records of monozygotic twins who were separated at birth were researched to provide the basis of this book.

Fausto-Sterling, Anne, *Myths of Gender: Biological Theories About Women and Men*, Basic Books, New York, 1986. Discusses whether men and women think, feel, and behave differently because of biological differences.

Lewontin, Richard C., Rose, Steven, and Kamin, Leon J., *Not in Our Genes: Biology, Ideology, and Human Nature*, Pantheon, New York, 1984. A geneticist, a psychologist, and a neurobiologist discuss the beliefs of those who claim that we are only what our biological makeup allows us to be.

Mead, Margaret, *New Lives for Old: Cultural Transformation, Manus, 1928–1953*, Greenwood Press, Westport, Conn., 1980. A well-known and respected anthropologist describes the cultural effects of environmental changes on a tribal society.

Oakley, Ann, *Sex, Gender and Society*, Gower Publishing Co., Brookfield, Vt., 1985. A discussion of the origins of sex differences and the extent to which these differences are biologically or culturally determined.

Osherson, Samuel, *Finding Our Fathers: The Unfinished Business of Manhood,* Free Press, New York, 1986. Explores how men's early and ongoing relationships with their fathers may affect their own identities and their subsequent relationships with wives, children, friends, and bosses. Discusses how current situations may rekindle feelings of loss unresolved since childhood.

Rossi, Alice S., ''Gender and Parenthood,'' *American Sociological Review,* 1984, Vol. 49, pp. 1–19. A thought-provoking analysis of the biological roots of gender differences.

Tavris, Carol, and Wade, Carole, *The Longest War: Sex Differences in Perspective,* Second Edition, Harcourt Brace Jovanovich, San Diego, Calif., 1984. A review of various approaches to the study of gender roles and cultural inequalities.

Watson, Peter, *Twins: An Uncanny Relationship,* Harvard University Press, Cambridge, Mass., 1984. An easy-to-read book by a leading psychologist who suggests such human traits as certain fears and appreciation of beauty are genetically determined.

Wilson, Edward O., *Biophilia: The Human Bond to Other Species,* Harvard University Press, Cambridge, Mass., 1984. A fascinating book by a leading psychobiologist who argues that even such human traits as fear of snakes, sense of beauty, and use of religious symbolism are influenced by genetic inheritance.

Chapter 5

BIOLOGICAL INFLUENCES ON BEHAVIOR

Chapter Focus

This chapter presents:

- **how the nervous systems work**
- **the role of the brain in behavior**
- **a discussion of glands and their influence on bodily activity**
- **the effect of sleep on behavior**
- **methods used in hypnosis**

A final exam, a road test, an oral report, a job interview. What do they all have in common? For one thing, they are all tests. A final exam tests your understanding of the semester's work. A road test measures your driving ability. An oral report tests your ability to present a topic to your classmates. A job interview tests your ability to convince a prospective employer to hire you.

What other characteristics do these four items share? Try to remember your feelings right before each of these important events. Was your stomach upset? Your heart pounding? Your legs shaky? Did you feel jittery inside?

You've probably experienced several of these symptoms at one time or another. Whenever you become nervous or upset, you may find that your body reacts in a number of ways. This is because the human body is very complex, and whatever affects one part affects all others. A troubling thought, therefore, may produce a headache or an upset stomach. An argument with a friend might cause someone to break out in a rash. Similarly, a physical disorder might produce certain changes in a person's behavior. For example, an imbalance of hormones can cause a person to become irritable. Or a genetic defect might be responsible for a type of mental retardation.

In this chapter we will take a look at how the body works. By examining various biological processes, you may gain an understanding of the relationship between biology and behavior.

Nervous Systems

The human nervous systems regulate the body's activities. Therefore, they regulate behavior. Imagine what life would be like without nervous systems. You would not be able to see, hear, smell, or use any of your senses. Neither would you be able to walk, think, laugh, cry, become hungry or thirsty, speak, or even remember anything from one minute to the next. Would you even be alive?

The central and peripheral nervous systems. We can divide the nerve structure of the body into two main divisions—the central nervous system and the peripheral nervous system. The **central nervous system** is made up of the brain and the spinal cord.

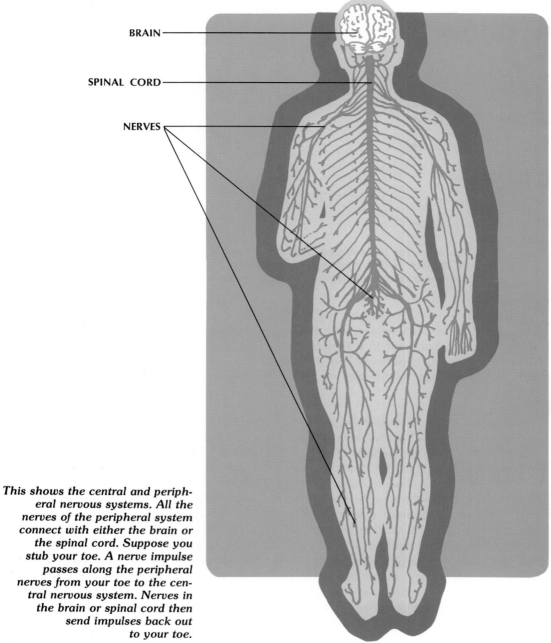

BRAIN

SPINAL CORD

NERVES

This shows the central and peripheral nervous systems. All the nerves of the peripheral system connect with either the brain or the spinal cord. Suppose you stub your toe. A nerve impulse passes along the peripheral nerves from your toe to the central nervous system. Nerves in the brain or spinal cord then send impulses back out to your toe.

The **peripheral nervous system** consists of nerve fibers running to and from the central nervous system. It connects the fingers, toes, ears, heart, lungs, stomach, and so on, with the brain or spinal cord. The central and peripheral nervous systems act as connecting and coordinating systems between the sense organs and the muscles and glands. Nerve impulses carry messages from the sensory receptors to the central nervous system and then back out to control the muscles or organs. You start to unscrew a hot light bulb. A

```
AXON
```

CELL BODY

END BRANCHES

SYNAPSE

DENDRITES

All neurons are fiber-shaped cells with a cell body, dendrites at one end, and an axon, which extends to the other end. The point at which the axon of one neuron makes contact with another neuron is called a synapse.

message is carried to a reflex center in the spinal cord and back out to a muscle. Instantly you jerk your hand away from the hot bulb. When the message reaches the brain, you feel pain.

The neuron. How do nerve impulses work? Nerve impulses travel across nerve cells. A nerve cell is called a **neuron.** There are billions of neurons in the human body.

Neurons can be classified according to their function. There are sensory neurons and motor neurons. A **sensory neuron** receives and carries sensory information, such as seeing, hearing, tasting, and smelling. Sensory neurons conduct impulses only *toward* the brain or spinal cord. A **motor neuron** is involved in motor activities, such as running, jumping, or writing. Motor neurons conduct impulses *from* the brain or spinal cord to muscles and glands. Most behaviors involve both sensory neurons and motor neurons.

A neuron is made up of four basic parts. The **dendrites** are those parts of a neuron that receive the nerve impulses. Dendrites look like the branches of a tree. They branch out from the cell body of a neuron. The **cell body** contains the neuron's chromosomes and genes. It also provides the energy for the neuron's activities. The nerve impulse travels

from the dendrites to the cell body and then down the length of the axon. The **axon** is the fiber part of the neuron—the part that sends messages to other neurons.

The point at which two neurons meet is called the **synapse.** There is no physical connection between neurons, only a chemical connection. A nerve impulse travels to the end of one neuron. Then, at the synapse, a chemical substance from the first neuron causes the second neuron to set off its own impulse. A nerve impulse is a very small, very fast electric charge. It travels at a speed from 3 to 117 meters (10 to 390 feet) per second. The passage of nerve impulses through our nervous system enables us to do many things—to taste, learn, ride a bicycle, or play the piano.

The autonomic nervous system. A part of the central and peripheral nervous systems regulates the activities of the vital organs. We call the part of the nervous systems that performs this function the **autonomic nervous system.** It acts somewhat independently of the central nervous system, but not entirely. Usually we aren't aware of its activities. It regulates the activity of those organs necessary for life and reproduction. These include the lungs, the stomach, the intestines, the heart, the liver, the eliminative organs, and the reproductive organs.

Generally, we cannot voluntarily control the activities regulated by the autonomic nervous system. We don't control the digestion of our food, for example. However, we can regulate a few activities, such as breathing, for a short period of time. And we can control several activities performed by the autonomic nervous system through certain learning procedures and meditation.

The Brain

The brain is an important part of the central nervous system. It plays an essential role in human behavior.

How can scientists determine the role of the brain in behavior? Scientists today use five main techniques to study the relationship of the brain to behavior. One technique involves stimulating specific areas of the brain. This can be done by placing small electrodes (conductors of electricity) in the brain. The scientist then passes a very weak electrical current through these areas of the brain and notes the effect on behavior. For example, scientists can cause rats to eat or drink by sending an electrical current through one part of their brain. Scientists can also stimulate the brain by injecting drugs through tiny tubes placed in a particular area of the brain.

Another technique for studying the relationship between the functioning of the brain and behavior involves brain lesions. A **brain lesion** refers to a part of the brain that has been destroyed through surgery, accident, or disease. With animals, the experimenter may destroy specific parts of the brain and study the effects on behavior. With human subjects, the scientist can study only those cases in which brain surgery is necessary for medical reasons. Or they can study cases where there has been a brain-damaging accident, or where disease has destroyed part of the brain.

A third technique for the study of the relationship between brain activity and behavior involves recording the activity of the brain. One common method is the use of the **EEG.** These initials refer to an instrument called an **electroencephalograph.** It is used to record a person's brain wave pattern on a chart. Electrodes from the EEG can be placed on a person's scalp. The instrument then makes a recording of the electrochemical changes, which indicate brain activity. The recordings change as the activity of the individual changes. The record is different when people sleep and when they are awake. It changes when they start out balancing their checkbook and then try to remember the name of a popular song.

A fourth procedure involves studying nerves connected to the brain. When a section of the brain decays or loses its function, nerves connected to that part of the brain may also decay. By tracing the decayed nerve, scientists sometimes can determine which part of the brain is associated with that nerve. For example, imagine that because of an accident, a person loses control of the left arm. Then, years later, that person requires brain surgery for other medical reasons. During the surgery, if decayed nerves are found, their location could indicate what area of the brain controls left arm movements.

The fifth method used in relating the brain to behavior is biochemical studies. This can involve a chemical analysis of normal brains in healthy people. It can consist of analyzing small slices of brain tissue, which are obtained during necessary medical surgery. Or it can mean analyzing some chemical substances found in the brain. For example, a particular chemical substance has been found in greater amounts in the brains of rats raised in an enriched environment than in the brains of rats raised in a limited environment. This substance has also been related to learning. Therefore, there may be a relationship between learning and the organism's type of environment early in life.

The brain and the computer. Both the computer and the human brain can receive

BIOLOGICAL INFLUENCES
ON BEHAVIOR

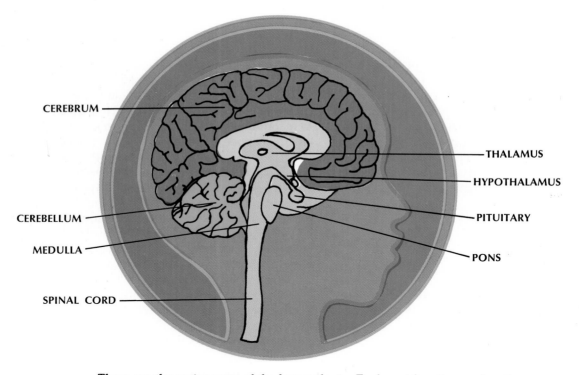

These are the major parts of the human brain. Each part has its own functions. At the same time, the separate parts work closely with one another. For example, the cerebellum, which controls the coordination of our muscle movements, works together with the spinal cord when we walk.

information, store it, and send out information. However, there are many differences between the brain and the most complex computer now in existence. Computers are much, much faster than the human brain. On the other hand, a computer that would include the same parts or functions as a human brain would weigh about 9 million kilograms (10,000 tons)! And the amount of energy necessary to run this computer would be enormous.

The brain receives several million inputs at any given time. Computers today can receive inputs only one at a time. It is as if the brain were a large number of computers connected together so that many inputs can be handled at one time.

How does the brain process information? The basic operations of the brain are genetically determined. That is, the procedure for responding to some stimuli coming

from the environment is inherited. Information is carried to the brain by neurons. A nerve cell receives the information, or the nerve impulse, on its dendrites. The information is sent to the axon. Whether or not it continues to another neuron depends on a number of factors.

These factors can be compared to people waiting to take a ferry boat to the other side of a river. Whether the nerve impulse will be accepted at the synapse is similar to the people arranging with the ferry-boat owner for the cost of the trip. Acceptance is related to the amount of chemicals for transmitting the impulse—the amount of money the people and owner agree on. It is also related to the availability of the receiving neuron—or whether there is room available on the ferry. It depends on the previous state of the synapse—or the condition of the ferry from previous use. And finally, it is based on the possibilities of changing conditions—if it's

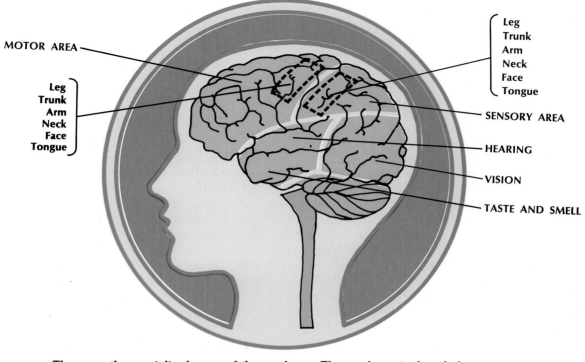

MOTOR AREA

Leg
Trunk
Arm
Neck
Face
Tongue

Leg
Trunk
Arm
Neck
Face
Tongue

SENSORY AREA

HEARING

VISION

TASTE AND SMELL

These are the specialized areas of the cerebrum. The cerebrum is the whole upper part of the brain and is covered by the cerebral cortex. As you can see, certain areas of the cerebral cortex control specific sensory and motor functions. These include seeing, hearing, speech, and arm motions.

going to be rough weather, the trip might cost more.

All of this activity takes place in fractions of a second. It is repeated from one neuron to another for each stimulus or tiny bit of behavior. The brain consists of 10 to 12 billion neurons that receive, pass on, and coordinate these nerve impulses.

What type of information does the brain receive? This is determined by the specific nerve pathway carrying the impulse. For example, if the information travels on the optic (visual) nerve, you would have a visual experience. If the auditory (hearing) nerve is stimulated, you would hear something. We don't know exactly how these nerve impulses are changed into seeing or hearing, however.

Is certain information processed in specific parts of the brain? The highest brain center in humans is the ***cerebral cortex.*** It is a thick layer of gray-colored neurons just under the skull. The cerebral cortex is divided into areas. Some areas are related to sensory processes, such as vision and hearing. Other areas are related to motor activities, such as walking.

In addition, neurons within certain areas of the brain have specific functions. If a very mild electric current stimulates one particular spot in the brain, the toes will move. Stimulating another spot produces movement of the neck, and so on.

Although some areas of the cerebral cortex are related to particular processes, nearly three-fourths of it has no known specific function. The processes of thinking seem to be spread over much of the cerebral cortex. Parts of the cortex may be destroyed without a loss of general intellectual ability. General intelligence tests have been given to individuals both before and after brain surgery. In most cases the tests did not show a loss of intellectual ability.

Text continues on page 92.

Case Study: Focus on Research

A BRAIN DIVIDED

Human beings have only one stomach, one heart, and one brain, . . . right? Not exactly. The cerebral cortex, the most advanced part of the brain, might be thought of as two structures, connected by a band of fibers called the corpus callosum. Each structure, or hemisphere, performs different tasks and is responsible for different functions.

The right side of the body is controlled by the left hemisphere of the cortex, and vice versa. Thus the hand movements of right-handed people are controlled by the left hemisphere and those of left-handed people by the right hemisphere. Similarly, everything perceived on the right is processed by the left hemisphere. Whatever is received in one hemisphere is quickly transmitted to

This drawing shows the two hemispheres of the brain. The corpus callosum, the band of fibers that connects the two halves, is set off by the black-and-white area.

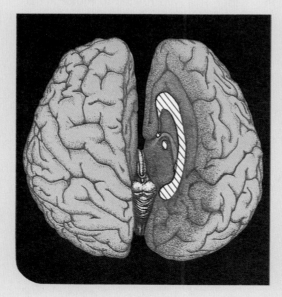

the other across the corpus callosum. Thus, we see a single visual world rather than two half-worlds.

The two hemispheres not only control opposite sides of the body, but also seem to differ in function. The left hemisphere is apparently responsible for language and logical thought. The right hemisphere seems to be concerned more with spatial relations, perception, and fantasy.

How do scientists know all this? In some pioneering experiments, researchers have studied the behavior of patients who have had their corpus callosum severed through surgery. This operation, sometimes performed on patients with severe epilepsy, prevents seizures from traveling across both hemispheres. It also produces a split brain, with each hemisphere functioning more or less independently.

In the everyday world, people with split brains function with little difficulty. This is because full communication between the two parts of the brain is not necessary in most processes. For instance, split-brain subjects can see what a normal person does by moving their eyes so that both hemispheres perceive an image. In some situations, however, the effects of split-brain surgery can be quite dramatic.

In one experiment researcher Roger Sperry (who won a Nobel Prize for his work) flashed the word "heart" across the center of a screen. The "he" was shown to the left part of the visual field, the "art" to the right. When asked to *say* what they had seen, the subjects answered "art." This is because speech is controlled by the left hemisphere, where the "art" was processed. However, when they were told to *point* with the *left hand* to one of two cards—"he" or "art"—

to identify what they had just seen, the subjects always chose the card with "he." In this case, the right hemisphere—which controls the left side of the body—prevailed.

In another experiment, a split-brain subject was asked to focus his eyes on the middle of a screen. The word "nut" was flashed on the left part of the screen for just a tenth of a second, leaving him no time to shift his eyes. Thus the word registered only in the right hemisphere. The subject was then asked to select from a group of objects the one just referred to on the screen. He could do this—with his left hand—because his right hemisphere both processed the word and controlled his left hand. What he could *not* do was name the object aloud. The left hemisphere, which controls language, did not "see" the word.

One of Sperry's subjects was asked to arrange some wooden blocks into a certain pattern. This involves spatial relations, which is traditionally a right hemisphere task. If the subject was told to use just his right hand, he was unable to complete the assignment. It was only when he was allowed to use both hands that he was able to arrange the blocks correctly. And while he was completing the assignment, the left hand knocked the right hand out of the way several times to prevent it from interfering!

It would be a mistake to assume that *all* language involves only the left hemisphere or that *all* spatial relations engage only the right. When a brain is damaged on one side, as in the case of a brain stroke, the other side frequently takes over and does its work. Neither hemisphere has exclusive control over any one task.

In fact, experiments on normal people indicate that we use one hemisphere or the other depending on how we want to process material, not on the material itself. For example, on a test involving spatial tasks—selecting an arc to match a circle—some subjects handled the problem in an analytic, or left-brain, way. Thus while split-brain research is fascinating, we must consider the brain as a whole in helping us live our lives as full human beings.

SOURCE: R. W. Sperry, "Hemisphere Deconnection and Unity in Conscious Awareness," *Scientific American*, 1964, 210, 42–52; Robert Ornstein, "The Split and the Whole Brain," *Human Nature*, 1978, 1, 76–83.

A researcher conducts tests on a "split-brain" subject. While the subject sees the word "cup" with one hemisphere, he might not be able to identify the word in ways that involve the other hemisphere.

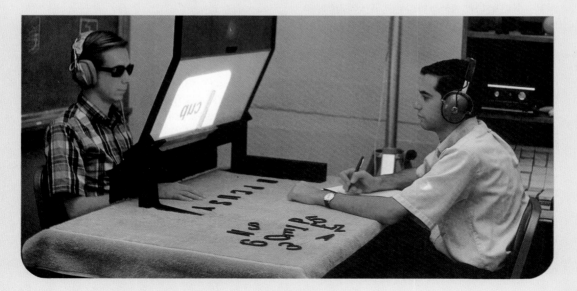

CASE STUDY:
FOCUS ON RESEARCH

Does the size of the brain affect intelligence? On the average, the brains of adult men weigh 1,360 grams (48 ounces). The brains of adult women weigh about 1,247 grams (44 ounces). From this scientific fact, some people have jumped to the conclusion that men must be more intelligent than women. However, many studies of intellectual ability show that on the average, women are just as intelligent as men. The brain of a woman tends to weigh less than the brain of a man, just as the average weight of women is less than the average weight of men.

Are the brains of very intelligent people heavier than the brains of mentally retarded people? The heaviest brain ever found was that of a retarded individual. The lightest brain ever recorded was also that of a retarded person. Individuals differ in the size of their brains. But size in itself is not a measure of an individual's intellectual ability.

How can someone "look" at the brain as it works? For years surgeons have been able to examine the *structure* of the human brain during necessary brain surgery. They have been able to do so because during an operation parts of the brain are exposed.

It has also been possible to see the brain's structure on X-rays. In this case the various components are visible on a photographic plate. In neither case, though, were people looking at how the brain *functions*. They were not watching the brain perform its many activities.

In recent years this situation has changed. It has now become possible to "look" at the brain as it works. One technique that has been developed to accomplish this task is called **positron-emission tomography,** or **PET.**

To understand how this technique works, you must know a little about how the brain functions. Like the rest of the body, the brain runs on glucose, a type of sugar. As the different parts of the brain become more active, they need more glucose to carry out their tasks. Additional glucose is then used by each of these parts.

During a PET scan, a person is given a small amount of radioactive glucose, which can then be monitored on a machine. When a specific part of the brain becomes active, the glucose travels to that site. The machine detects this through the actions of positrons, or radioactive particles. For example, if a person is shown a picture, the machine will show that glucose has traveled to the occipital lobes. If a person listens to music, the machine will show that activity is occurring in the temporal lobes.

The PET scan has so far had tremendous value for researchers. It can presently be used to locate sites of brain tumors and epileptic seizures. In addition, it has been used to identify defects in the heart and other organs.

In the future, though, the PET scan may serve other functions as well. Psychologists hope that it might be used to diagnose and investigate abnormal behaviors. Although at present the data are tentative, there is some evidence that the brains of individuals who behave abnormally are different from those of other individuals. For example, research has shown that schizophrenics have a low level of activity in their frontal lobes. This part of the brain is partially responsible for emotional control. Perhaps in the near future, the PET scan will be used routinely to help psychologists in their work.

Glands

Quite a bit of our bodily activity is related to our glands. Our glands determine our growth, our energy level, our moods, and many other reactions. There are two kinds of glands in the body—duct glands and ductless glands.

Duct glands (or exocrine glands). **Duct glands** empty their contents through small openings, or ducts, onto the surface of the body or into body cavities. They do not send their products directly into the bloodstream. One example of duct glands are your sweat glands, which you notice on a warm day or

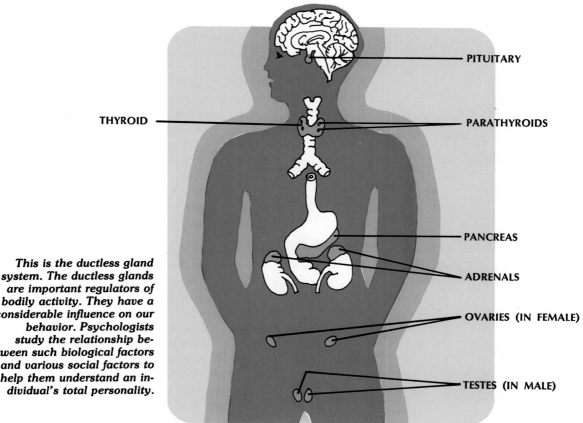

PITUITARY

THYROID

PARATHYROIDS

PANCREAS

ADRENALS

OVARIES (IN FEMALE)

TESTES (IN MALE)

This is the ductless gland system. The ductless glands are important regulators of bodily activity. They have a considerable influence on our behavior. Psychologists study the relationship between such biological factors and various social factors to help them understand an individual's total personality.

when you exercise. Whenever you get a tiny object in your eye, you become aware of your tear glands. When you put food in your mouth, or sometimes when you just think about food, the salivary glands pour saliva into your mouth. After food is swallowed, the contents of other duct glands are poured into the stomach and intestine so the food can be digested.

Ductless glands (or endocrine glands). Although the duct glands are important, psychologists are more interested in the ductless glands. **Ductless glands** have no openings or ducts through which they can pour their contents. They empty their products directly into the bloodstream. The chemical substances that they release into the bloodstream are *hormones*. We will examine the effects on our behavior of four of the ductless

glands—the thyroid, the pituitary, the adrenals, and the gonads.

The thyroid gland. Located in the neck in front of the windpipe, the **thyroid gland** produces the hormone that regulates the speed of chemical reactions and the rate of growth. The thyroid gland can become underactive. If the underactivity starts in infancy, *cretinism* results. The cretin is dwarfed, with a thickset body. The legs are short and bowed, the feet and hands are stubby, the hair is coarse, and the skin is yellow.

Sometimes there is overactivity of the thyroid gland. In this case, individuals are very restless and excitable, have difficulty in sleeping, tend to be irritable, and seem to work with untiring energy. The thyroid gland may become very enlarged, producing a condition called *goiter.*

One function of the pituitary gland is to regulate bodily growth. An overactive pituitary gland results in giantism.

The pituitary gland. Psychologists call the **pituitary gland,** which is attached to the underside of the brain, the "master gland" because it controls outputs from the other endocrine glands. Part of this gland controls the amount of bodily growth. If there is over-activity of the gland in childhood, *giantism* results. There is a record of one young man who at the age of nineteen years was 259 centimeters (8 feet 6 inches) tall. And he was still growing at the rate of 5 centimeters (2 inches) a year. He weighed 197 kilograms (435 pounds) and wore size 36 shoes. For a time he played basketball. "But it's too easy," he said. "I'd stand down near the net, someone would throw me the ball, and I'd drop it in. I don't think the other teams liked it much." At birth he was of normal size. A pituitary condition produced his great height. A skillful surgeon can remove some of the extra glandular substance and so prevent giantism if the pituitary condition is discovered early.

In a case of underactivity of part of the pituitary gland in childhood, the individual becomes a dwarf or midget. Unlike cretins, many dwarfs and midgets have well-proportioned or reasonably well-proportioned bodies. Giving pituitary extract to such a child can do much to bring about normal growth. In one case a very thin, underdeveloped eighteen-year-old boy was treated with pituitary extract. He had not grown for eight years. Yet within four and a half months after treatment began he had grown 5 centimeters (2 inches) taller.

The adrenal gland. Located just above each kidney is a small gland called the **adrenal gland.** It consists of two parts. Each part produces different hormones.

One psychologist tells the story of a young woman who was a musician. She was very fond of her piano. It was a heavy piano, which she could not move. Whenever she wanted to dust behind the piano, she had to have someone move it for her. One day the house caught fire. No one else was at home. It seemed that her piano was going to burn. In her excitement, she moved the piano across the room and out the door to safety. Had she been pretending when she required someone to move the piano for her on cleaning days? No. Because of the excitement and fear of the fire, she was able to do something that she actually could not do under normal conditions. Activity of the adrenal glands was in part responsible for the change.

When a person is experiencing anger or fear—or perhaps even uneasiness before giving a speech—one part of the adrenal gland becomes quite active. As it releases its hormone, called *adrenalin,* into the bloodstream, a number of changes take place in the body. The heartbeat increases. The stomach stops digesting. The pupils of the eyes become wider. The person may perspire freely. Feelings of tiredness disappear. Breathing is speeded up. All these bodily changes help prepare an individual for short-time emergency activity.

The hormone *cortisone,* produced by the other part of the adrenal gland, helps the individual fight infection. It also seems to play an important part in preparing a person for long-continued muscular activity. If the amount of the hormone produced is very small, blood circulation slows, sexual development lessens, and the individual becomes weak. Death follows, unless the hormone is given artificially.

If the adrenal gland produces too much cortisone, the individual shows increased sexual development, regardless of how young the person is. Too much cortisone may also produce masculine characteristics in a woman.

The gonads. The glands called **gonads** supply the sperm and egg cells for reproduction. In addition, they produce hormones that affect the personality development of the individual. Although the sex hormones are present in childhood, production of the hormones increases during adolescence. This brings about the development of the biologically mature man and woman. The behavior of a male horse that has had its gonads removed is quite different from that of a stallion. If the gonads are removed from female animals, male characteristics often develop. Human beings, however, are much less influenced by hormone levels than are the lower animals.

Thus, particular glands produce particular effects on individuals. But remember that the glands interact with one another. Furthermore, the glands are only part of the total individual. Social factors as well as physiological factors are important in development.

Has our changing environment affected glandular activity? To study the effects of environment on glands, one psychologist compared his laboratory Norway rats with wild Norway rats trapped in alleys and yards. His lab rats had been interbred for over thirty-six years. The psychologist came to these conclusions: (1) The adrenal glands in lab rats are smaller and less effective than in wild rats. (2) The thyroid glands are less active in lab rats than in wild rats. (3) The gonads develop earlier, function with greater regularity, and cause a much greater fertility in lab rats than in wild rats. He also found that the brains of lab rats weigh less than the brains of wild rats.

The psychologist who reported this comparison raises the question, ''To what extent has civilization brought about changes in human beings similar to those produced in the laboratory rat?'' He points out that great physical energy is usually not needed today. In many ways, people now live in a very ''soft'' environment. The psychologist concluded his report with the questions, ''Where are we going? What is our destiny?''

Sleep

One final biological influence that we will consider is the effect of sleep on behavior. The amount of sleep we get each night, a change in sleeping schedules, and dreaming all influence our behavior.

How important is sleep? In many cases, production in an industrial plant tends to be low on Monday. By Tuesday or Wednesday, workers seem to be ''warmed up.'' Production is at its highest for the week. One possibility is that Friday, Saturday, and Sunday nights may be spent in long and tiring entertainment. The resulting loss of sleep shows up in lower production on Monday.

Various tests indicate that loss of sleep is followed by poorer performance. It is true that very motivated people can do surprisingly well after long periods of staying awake. But they are able to do so only by using up a great amount of energy.

People can lose sleep in two ways. They may go without any sleep for a long period. Or they may sleep much less than usual for a period of several nights. In one experiment, subjects were kept awake continuously for 72 hours. They were under medical care during this dangerous experiment. Even so, some fainted at the end of the experiment. In another part of the experiment, subjects reduced the amount of their sleep from about 8 hours to about 5 hours a night for five nights. In both cases, the subjects were given tests before and after the periods of no sleep or reduced sleep. Intelligence-test scores dropped 24.5 percent following a period of 72 hours without sleep. However, the scores dropped only 14.9 percent following five nights with only 5 hours' sleep each night. How much the individual swayed forward and backward when trying to stand still was also measured. After 72 hours without sleep, there was a 51.8 percent loss in control of bodily swaying. After five nights of 5 hours' sleep each, there was a loss of only 6.1 percent.

The amount of sleep a person needs varies with age. It also varies from individual to individual. But suppose it is absolutely impossible to get normal amounts of sleep. Studies have shown that it is better to take a number of short naps than to use all available sleeping time in one period. Other studies have found that performance drops in the early afternoon. One way of improving performance is to take a nap about halfway through the waking period.

Does changing your sleep schedule affect your behavior? Several studies have indicated that changing your sleep schedule can have some negative effects on behavior. For one study, subjects were asked to record when they went to bed, how long they slept, and when they got up. They reported sleeping about 10 hours each night. Then they moved into the lab. When they got used to sleeping in the lab, their sleep cycles were changed. The subjects slept as usual, were awakened three hours early, or three hours late. Other times they went to bed three hours earlier or three hours later than usual.

They were tested at different times during the day following each change in their sleep schedule. After sleeping longer than usual, shorter than usual, or changing the times they went to sleep or awoke, subjects scored lower on a task that required close attention. The subjects had less energy in the mornings. They were more tired about noon of each day. And they were less lively in the evenings. The researchers concluded that a regular sleep schedule may be as important for performing well as the amount of sleep you get.

The different stages of sleep. At one time, EEG records alone were used to determine whether subjects were asleep and how deeply they were sleeping. Today, psychologists use an electroencephalograph together with several other methods to determine the depth of sleep. One method uses noises of different loudnesses. It assumes that the louder the noise needed to awaken subjects, the deeper their sleep. Other methods may use pressure or electrical shock. Sometimes, though, as a result of using different methods, research studies may produce what appear to be contrasting results.

The EEG and new research methods have helped psychologists learn more about sleep in the last twenty years than they found out during all the time before then. They now know that sleep occurs in cycles. The pattern of sleep varies for the same individual from one night to the next. It also varies from one individual to another. But there is a general pattern that involves going from light sleep to deeper sleep.

There are five stages of sleep. The first four stages are known as non-rapid eye movement or NREM sleep. The fifth stage is known as REM, or rapid eye movement sleep. As individuals fall asleep, they progress rapidly through the different stages. They reach Stage 4 in about 45 minutes. After spending about 15 to 20 minutes in Stage 4, the pattern of Stage 1 reappears, but because the individual does not wake up and experiences rapid eye movements, it is called Stage 5. Then, a second cycle of these stages begins. Most individuals have at least four or five cycles each night. With each cycle, the individual spends less and less time in deep sleep and more and more time in lighter sleep. By studying sleep cycles, researchers have also learned when dreams occur.

How do we know when a subject is dreaming? REM sleep is the lightest sleep, according to EEG records. It is the stage at which subjects often have **rapid eye movements (REMs).** REMs seem to indicate that an individual is dreaming. Some people say that they don't dream. But if they are awakened when they are having rapid eye movements, they do report dreaming. On the other hand, individuals who are awakened while not having rapid eye movements rarely report dreaming. This fifth stage of sleep is called **paradoxical sleep.** It is paradoxical because EEG recordings show a light sleep as in Stage 1. Yet when individuals are having REMs, they are harder to arouse, indicating deeper sleep.

Dreams may last from a few minutes to more than an hour. The average dream period lasts about 25 minutes. This finding is contrary to beliefs held by some psychologists only a few years ago. At that time, dreams were thought to last only a few seconds. It is a good example of how new evidence changes ideas and concepts.

Do dreams change with age? To answer this question, psychologists studied two groups of children for five years. One group began the study at ages three and four, and were eight and nine years old at the end of the experiment. The other group of subjects were nine and ten years old at the beginning, and fourteen and fifteen years of age at the end. The children were volunteers. They slept in the lab several nights each year for five years. What did the researchers learn about children's dreams?

The children who were three and four years old dreamed mainly of animals and home. By ages five and six, their dreams had doubled in length and involved many activities and feelings. Girls' dreams were mostly of pleasant things. Also, girls assumed more active roles in their dreams. The boys reported more unpleasant dreams. And they took more passive roles in their own dreams. By ages seven and eight, the boys' unpleasant dreams had almost disappeared.

At ages nine and ten, there was a definite

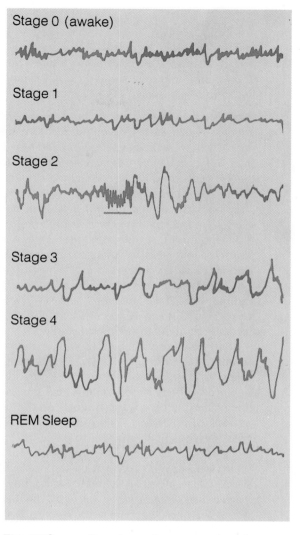

Stage 0 (awake)

Stage 1

Stage 2

Stage 3

Stage 4

REM Sleep

This EEG recording shows the progression of an individual through the five stages of sleep. Notice that the waves produced during REM sleep, Stage 5, are very similar to the waves produced during Stage 1.

increase in dreams involving school settings and the happiness of the dreamer. Dreams about animals had decreased. By the age of eleven and twelve, girls and boys dreamed mostly about people their own age. Fewer of their dreams involved feelings of sadness. Boys and girls were about equal in having dreams that involved motor activities. But the dreams of boys contained more aggressive content than the dreams of girls. At ages thirteen and fourteen, there was an increase in dreams in which people were angry. However, dreams of this nature are quite common during adolescence and do not usually indicate psychological disturbances.

Are dreams necessary? In one experiment, subjects were prevented from dreaming. They were awakened during REMs. It was found that when they were allowed to sleep undisturbed, they dreamed longer. Sometimes they dreamed twice as long as they normally would dream. It is as if they were trying to catch up on their dreaming.

In addition, people who are prevented from dreaming show changes in behavior during their waking hours. They may become more irritable, have trouble concentrating, and have memory lapses. These changes disappear, however, when the subjects are allowed to sleep undisturbed.

Perhaps you are wondering whether these results were due to people's sleep being disturbed rather than their dreams being disturbed. Experimenters investigated this possibility by waking subjects up during periods of no REMs. This produced no increase in dreams or changes in behavior.

If a particular small section of a cat's brain is removed, the cat shows no REM sleep. Cats can sleep without REMs, however. After several days the cats behave strangely. They become very active. They stare in one direction for unusual lengths of time. Some of them show increased eating. In some of the cats, normal REM sleep returns. But in cases where REM does not return, the cats become increasingly active until they eventually die.

The evidence today indicates that dreams seem necessary for sleep. Also, probably everyone does dream—even though some people may not remember their dreams. Have you ever gone for a long period of time without sleeping and dreaming? What changes in your reactions did you notice? Theorists have suggested that physical restoration occurs during the first four stages of sleep, and psychological restoration takes place during the fifth stage of sleep.

Methods Used in Hypnosis

Some areas of psychology attract both real scientists and unqualified people. Hypnosis is one of these areas. Hypnosis is not a major field of interest to most psychologists. But it is an accepted area of scientific study.

What is hypnosis? *Hypnosis* is an unusual state of consciousness that has some features in common with sleep. Perhaps you can remember what you feel like when you are about to fall asleep or about to wake up. You are aware of what is going on around you. And you find it difficult to fall either into a deep sleep or to wake up completely. People who have been hypnotized sometimes report that the experience is similar to going to sleep.

Hypnosis is not the same as sleep, however. People who are hypnotized are usually very open to suggestion. They understand what is said to them and are able to carry out simple directions. People in normal sleep, on the other hand, are usually open to little, if any, suggestion. And generally they are not aware of what is going on around them.

How is hypnosis produced? There is no certain formula to follow in producing a state of hypnosis. Some psychologists use one technique, some use another.

One instrument used to hypnotize someone is a flashing light. The light flashes at a specific rate per minute, while the subject stares steadily at it. It tends to make the subject more relaxed and sleepy and therefore more open to being hypnotized. The presence of the flashing light also gives the subject something to focus on.

Other methods for producing hypnosis include the use of sounds or objects, such as a pencil, to which subjects direct their attention. Still other methods involve no mechanical aid of any kind. They rely on the spoken word, encouraging the subject to concentrate on a specific thought.

All the techniques involve the narrowing of attention so that subjects are aware only of what the hypnotist is saying to them. As their attention is narrowed, subjects have less resistance to the hypnotist's suggestions. The suggestions can also be placed on a phonograph record or a tape recording. The hypnotist does not even need to be present during the process of producing a hypnotic state.

Most people can be hypnotized if they are willing, allow enough time, and cooperate in the process. Subjects must be able to concentrate on what the hypnotist says and does. Very young children, for instance, who usually cannot concentrate for very long, are not good subjects.

How do people react under hypnosis?

Suppose you are hypnotized. You are then given the suggestion that you will not feel pain when a pin is jabbed into your finger. The result is that you don't flinch or show any sign of pain when the pin goes into your finger. Or the hypnotist can tell you that you are going to be stuck with a pin and that it will hurt. If the hypnotist then touches you with a finger, you will jump and show all the signs of having experienced pain. Hypnotized people can't tell the difference between suggested pain and real physical pain.

Adult subjects under hypnosis can often recall facts from far back in their experience. They may be able to remember the name of the person who sat in front of them in the first grade in school. Subjects can, in some cases, give the license number of a car they owned or drove five or six years earlier, although in a normal waking state they may not even know the license number of their present car. However, people who are hypnotized cannot recall facts they have never known or facts they know only slightly. A psychologist demonstrating hypnotism once asked a woman whom he had hypnotized, "What was the license number on your car five years ago?" She seemed disturbed and did not answer for a minute. Finally she said, "I didn't have a car five years ago."

People who are hypnotized tend to stop making their own plans. They seem to wait for the hypnotist to tell them what to do. Their attention becomes directed toward what the hypnotist tells them to focus on. Also, subjects often can't remember what happened during the hypnotic state if the hypnotist has told them not to remember.

Some practical uses of hypnosis.

Doctors have used hypnosis in treating patients with painful illnesses and severe burns. For some patients, hypnosis reduces suffering and discomfort. For others, it gets rid of pain entirely. In one study, patients who had been in pain for many years were taught self-hypnosis techniques. They reported experiencing less daily pain. And they were able to participate in more activities.

In some surgical cases, hypnosis has been used successfully instead of a chemical anesthetic. Appendectomies have been performed with no anesthetic other than hypnosis. Also, some dentists have hypnotized patients and then removed a tooth—and the patients reported no pain.

Hypnosis may also be used in treating certain kinds of psychological disturbances. Many people have unreasonable fears that interfere with their lives. Such fears may have begun in early childhood. Under hypnosis, a person may recall the circumstances that originally produced a particular fear. And hypnosis has been used to change certain undesirable behavior, such as smoking.

Lost articles have been found and information has been recalled through the use of hypnosis. People may have forgotten where they left such valuables as diamond rings. After being hypnotized, they may remember exactly where they placed them.

Because of all these uses of hypnosis, and because hypnosis helps to give insight into behavior, research continues in this area. However, students should not carry out scientific experiments involving hypnosis. The use of hypnosis should be left to professionals. Some states even have legal restrictions concerning the use of hypnosis.

Summary

Biological factors greatly influence human behavior. The human nervous systems are one of the most influential factors.

The nerve structure of the body is made up of the central nervous system and the peripheral nervous system. The central nervous system is comprised of the brain and the spinal cord. The peripheral nervous system consists of nerve fibers that connect the various parts of the body with the central nervous system.

The brain plays an essential role in behavior. Scientists can study this role by stimulating specific areas of the brain, by examining the effects of brain lesions, by using EEG's, by studying nerves connected to the brain, and by doing biochemical studies. A new way of studying the brain is the PET scan. Scientists have also determined that certain areas of the brain have specific functions. However, it seems that the process of thinking is spread throughout the brain.

Glands are another biological factor that influences behavior. Glands affect your moods and your growth, among other things. Psychologists are interested mostly in the ductless glands. Four important ductless glands are the thyroid, the pituitary, the adrenals, and the gonads.

Your behavior is also influenced by sleep. Loss of sleep reduces your performance level. Changing your sleep schedule can affect behavior, too. The recurring sleep cycle contains five stages of sleep. Stages one through four are each deeper than the preceding stage.

Dreams are an important and probably necessary part of sleep. Dreams differ with age and between males and females. It seems that everyone dreams, although some people seldom remember their dreams.

Although not used as frequently as many other research methods, hypnosis is used by some psychologists in their work. Under hypnosis a subject is brought into an unusual state of consciousness. While in this state, subjects are very open to suggestion. Hypnosis has some practical uses. Psychologists use it to reduce pain and to treat some behavior disorders. They may even use it to help locate lost articles.

INTERPRETING SOURCES

In this excerpt from "Male Brain, Female Brain: The Hidden Difference" (*Psychology Today*, November 1985), Doreen Kimura discusses some of the differences in how the two brain hemispheres function in males and females.

The notion that men's and women's brains are differently organized began to take hold in earnest ... with the work of psychologist Herbert Lansdell, who studied neurosurgical patients. Others before him had found that, in general, removing the brain's left temporal lobe interfered with verbal skill, while removing the right impaired nonverbal skills. Lansdell found that although such injuries caused a similar overall pattern of impairment in women and men, women were less severely affected than men....

Studies of both brain-damaged and normal people revealed that while men and women tend to use one hemisphere more than the other for certain verbal tasks, such as recognizing spoken or seen words, women seem to rely less strongly on a single hemisphere than men do....

These findings led to what seemed to be an obvious conclusion: Certain thinking skills are more lateralized—more dependent on one hemisphere—in the male brain than in the female. Or, putting the comparison the other way, women's brains are more diffusely organized than men's....

The problem with viewing men's brains as more lateralized than women's was that it left a lot of questions unanswered. Why, for example, are women more often right-handed than men? ... And why was there no evidence that speech disorders occur more often in women following right-hemisphere brain damage, as one would expect if they, unlike men, depended on both hemispheres for speech?

In the course of looking at how damage to specific regions of one hemisphere affects speech and related functions, I came across some unexpected findings....

I was looking at people whose brain damage was restricted to either the front (anterior) or back (posterior) sections of the brain. I found that left-hemisphere damage could cause aphasia [language disorder] in both men and women, but different sites within that hemisphere were involved in the two sexes.... Women, however, were much less likely than men to become aphasic after restricted posterior damage....

This seemed to suggest that the brain areas involved in women's speech are, if anything, more localized than in men, at least in the left hemisphere....

What's more, the right hemisphere does not seem to contribute to speech any more in women than in men. Reviewing ... cases with damage restricted to the right hemisphere, we found that aphasic disorders after such damage are very rare ... and there is absolutely no difference between men and women in this respect....

Our findings that basic speech functions are quite focally organized in women mean that we have to give up the idea that women's brains are generally more diffusely organized than men's. But this could still be true, if not for speech, at least for other functions.

We have, in fact, found . . . [that] defining words and using them appropriately . . . [does] seem to be more bilaterally organized in women than in men....

In short, we are finding that, depending on the particular intellectual functions we're studying, women's brains may be more, less, or equally diffusely organized compared with men's. No single rule holds for all aspects of thinking.

Source Review

1. Which of the hemispheres is more verbal and which is more nonverbal?

2. What are the usual effects of verbal skills when the right hemisphere is damaged?

REVIEWING TERMS

central nervous system
peripheral nervous system
neuron
sensory neuron
motor neuron
dendrite
cell body
axon
synapse

autonomic nervous system
brain lesion
electroencephalograph
    (EEG)
cerebral cortex
positron-emission
    tomography (PET)
duct gland
ductless gland

thyroid gland
pituitary gland
adrenal gland
gonads
REMs (rapid eye
    movements)
paradoxical sleep
hypnosis

CHECKING FACTS

1. Distinguish between the central nervous system and the peripheral nervous system. What are the primary functions of these nervous systems?

2. Describe the parts of a neuron. How do nerve impulses travel between neurons?

3. What is the autonomic nervous system?

4. What five techniques do scientists use to determine the role of the brain in behavior?

5. Do certain areas of the brain process specific information? Explain.

6. How does the PET scan allow researchers to "look" at the brain?

7. Describe the duct glands and the ductless glands. Give an example of each.

8. What does the pituitary gland regulate? What happens if this gland is overactive? What happens if it is underactive?

9. What functions are performed by each part of the adrenal gland?

10. How does loss of sleep affect performance?

11. Describe the sleep process. What happens if REM sleep is disturbed?

12. How do dreams change with age? Are dreams necessary? Explain.

13. Describe the techniques that are used to produce hypnosis. How do people react under hypnosis?

14. What are some practical uses of hypnosis?

APPLYING YOUR KNOWLEDGE

1. In a simple drawing, show the path that a nerve impulse takes to and from the brain after a person touches a hot saucepan. Label each part of your drawing.

2. Conduct a panel discussion on the pros and cons of altering human behavior through psychosurgery. For example, should brain surgery be performed on individuals who commit crimes because of brain disorders? You should do library research beforehand, so that your answers will be based on facts and not just personal opinions.

3. Make a list of various activities that you think can best be performed by the human brain. Make a second list containing those activities that the computer can best perform. Is there any activity that you think a computer will never be able to do? Why?

4. The left hemisphere of the brain is responsible for skills involving logic, math, and verbal reasoning. The right hemisphere controls intuitive thought, art, music, and creativity. Try to determine whether you are "right brained" or "left brained" by making a list of your favorite classes, hobbies, social activities, and special talents. Draw a picture of a brain and place each item in the appropriate hemisphere. Then count the number of items you have included in each half. The half with the most items shows your tendency.

5. Which of your eyes is dominant—the left one or the right one? To find out, perform the following simple experiment. With both eyes open, hold up one finger at arm's length in front of you. Stare at that finger for a moment. Then close first your left eye and then your right eye, leaving the other eye open. Notice that in one case what you see with one eye matches what you see with both. That is, your finger will not appear to have "moved" from a center point to the right or the left. The "matching" eye is your dominant eye.

6. To understand the complexity of human thought, take a simple behavior like writing your name and analyze every step or process necessary to complete the task. Remember that each of these steps occurs in a fraction of a second.

7. Invite a computer expert to speak to your class on how the popular TV video games work. Is there a connection between how the computer handles such an activity and how the human brain works?

8. For at least one week, and perhaps two weeks, keep an account of how long you sleep during each 24-hour period. Include the approximate time that you go to sleep and wake up. Compare your average sleeping and waking time with that of other class members. Do you tend to sleep more on specific days? Are there any differences in your behavior on the days in which you've had less sleep?

THINKING CRITICALLY ABOUT PSYCHOLOGY

1. **Applying Ideas**   Imagine that human behavior could be changed chemically in any way you wish (nerve impulses could be slowed down, the functioning of your glands could change, and so on). What changes would you wish for?

2. **Evaluating Ideas**   Suppose a bridge had to be designed to span a body of water larger than any ever crossed before. Would you choose to have it designed by a leading engineer or by a computer? Why?

3. **Analyzing Ideas**   What ethical problems might be present if psychologists used PET scans routinely?

4. **Forming Opinions**   If you could dream about anything you wished, what would you choose to dream about? What do you think these dreams might indicate about you?

5. **Correlating Ideas**   Why might a person's dreams differ from his or her waking experiences? What might a person's dreams reveal about that person?

DEVELOPING SKILLS IN PSYCHOLOGY

Using the Library to Further Your Understanding

This psychology text is like all other introductory textbooks—it introduces you to a subject by providing a general overview of the field. It cannot provide in-depth coverage of all the current research and knowledge within all the different psychological specializations. Whole textbooks have been written on the brain. Others have been written on sleep and dreaming. Obviously not all the information from these books can be condensed into one introductory chapter. Fortunately, you have your library as a source of additional information.

In this chapter, it is noted that different *functions* (jobs, processes) are associated with each of the structures of the brain, such as the cerebral cortex and the hypothalamus.

Go to the library to learn what these specific functions are. Try looking in the card catalog, the *Reader's Guide to Periodicals,* and a current encyclopedia under the heading "brain." Once you have found the information, make a list showing what functions are associated with each structure. Then answer these questions:

1. Which part of the brain is most closely associated with thinking and problem solving?

2. Which part of the brain seems most important to the process of sleeping and waking?

3. Which part helps you maintain your balance when walking?

READING FURTHER ABOUT PSYCHOLOGY

Blakeslee, Thomas R., *The Right Brain: A New Understanding of the Unconscious Mind and Its Creative Powers,* Doubleday, New York, 1980. A work devoted to the powers of the right hemisphere of the brain. Includes discussions of creativity, thinking, language development, gender and left-handedness, and the effects of right-brain damage.

Crichton, Michael, *The Terminal Man,* Avon Books, New York, 1982. A fictional account of a man whose brain is connected to a computer.

Dement, William C., *Some Must Watch While Some Must Sleep,* W. W. Norton, New York, 1978. A scientifically sound and often humorous review of sleep and dreaming.

Hartmann, Ernest, *The Nightmare: The Psychology and Biology of Terrifying Dreams,* Basic Books, New York, 1985. Psychologists have long been captivated by dreams and nightmares. What causes these frightening dreams? What do they mean? Why do some people have more nightmares than others? The author, a noted sleep researcher, presents a comprehensive analysis that answers these and other questions.

Ornstein, Robert, and Thompson, Richard F., *The Amazing Brain,* Houghton Mifflin, Boston, 1984. An illustrated overview of the operations of the human brain.

Restak, Richard, *The Brain,* Bantam, New York, 1985. Teaches the basics about the brain and describes several interesting brain abnormalities, such as separated hemispheres, in humans. Based on the PBS series.

Using the Skills of a Psychologist

Unit 2 Interpreting Data

Interpreting data—the mass of measured, factual materials about large groups—is one of the most important skills psychologists use. This important process serves as a foundation for many kinds of psychological studies.

Data may be collected in a variety of ways. One method of gathering data, for example, is through experiments. Once data is obtained, it must be organized in a way that will help the researcher support or disprove the hypothesis. Data may appear in the form of statistics in charts, tables, or graphs; recorded observations; or mathematical computations. Once data is organized in a form that suits the purpose of the investigator(s), it must be interpreted.

Turn to page 97 in the text and examine the chart illustrating EEG recordings during the five stages of sleep. Notice that the brain waves are actually very tiny, but their peaks occur frequently. Psychologists call this pattern a low-amplitude, high-frequency EEG. As you relax, your EEG pattern changes, the waves are bigger (higher amplitude), but occur less frequently (lower frequency). For example, when you enter light sleep, they become bigger and slower. In deep sleep, as in Stage four, the waves are relatively large, but they take a longer time to reach their peak amplitudes.

Through the interpretation of EEG recordings, psychologists have been able to identify the five stages of sleep and to learn more about the nature of sleep.

Now that you have learned more about interpreting data, organize into small groups. With your teacher's approval, select a research topic that would require the interpretation of data. Using research methods appropriate for the topic, gather data and then organize it in a way most useful to your study. For example, the survey method may be more appropriate for the study of your research topic than the experimental method. If this is the case, construct a survey. Remember that a survey may be conducted through interviewing or by using a questionnaire. Use specific questions that provide for all possible answers, but note that specific answers are easier to record.

After you have conducted the research, tally the results. Then, organize the data in the form of a chart, a graph, or other illustration that is useful. You now have a visual picture of the results of your survey. The last step in the process is to interpret the data in order to form a conclusion.

Putting the visual image into words will help you to learn more about interpreting data. In a brief paragraph, describe the visual picture you have created. Classify the data and summarize the primary characteristics of your visual picture. For example, did you use a chart with columns showing various categories of statistics? Was a line graph or a bar graph showing percentages more useful for your research purposes? Did you use more than one illustration? What concepts does your visual picture illustrate? Have you transferred the data accurately?

Before drawing a conclusion, remember that data may be obtained and interpreted in different ways—some more valid than others. Data obtained from a group of people selected at random, for example, may be very different from data obtained from a group of people not selected at random.

Once you have interpreted the data, share your findings with the class. Are the results of your research surprising? Why or why not? Do you believe that the research method you used was valid? Do you think that a different research method would result in the same conclusion? Support your answer with specific examples.

REVIEW

REVIEWING THE UNIT

1. What is the most important principle of development?

2. What are the two most common examples of an individual's physical growth?

3. What abnormalities appear in most people who have 47 chromosomes?

4. What chemical substances do the ductless glands release into the bloodstream?

CONNECTING IDEAS

1. **Correlating Ideas** How does the interaction between heredity and environment affect intellectual development?

2. **Drawing Conclusions** From your study of Chapters 4 and 5, what general conclusion could you draw about the effects of heredity, environment, and biological processes on an individual's mental health?

3. **Synthesizing Ideas** How do the biological processes that affect physical development also affect the personality of an individual?

4. **Seeing Relationships** How may language development affect an intelligence-test score? How valid, then, is a certain score on a specific intelligence test?

PRACTICING RESEARCH SKILLS

Organize into small groups. Each group should conduct library research on a separate topic concerning the differences in the developmental patterns of humans and selected lower animals. Research topics may include prenatal development, patterns of physical development, motor development, and how selected species of animals relate to other individuals of the same species. Members of each group should then present their findings to the class. Discussion may also include the following questions.

1. Do certain animals demonstrate elements of personality?

2. Do these animals communicate with other individuals of the same species?

3. Do animals exhibit "body language"? Cite specific examples.

4. Does the physical size of the animal and/or the size of the animal's brain indicate the level of intelligence observed?

FINDING OUT MORE

You may wish to contact the following organizations for additional information about the material in this unit.

Basic Research, Inc. (BRINC)
#5 Old Chimney Rd.
P.O. Box 864
Huntsville, Alabama 35801

Sleep Research Society (SRS)
Department of Psychiatry
University of California
La Jolla, California 92093

The Psychological Corporation
555 Academic Ct.
San Antonio, Texas 78204–0952

UNDERSTANDING HUMAN BEHAVIOR

Chapter 6   UNDERSTANDING PERSONALITY
Chapter 7   MEASURING PERSONALITY
Chapter 8   MEASURING INTELLECTUAL ABILITY

Chapter 6

UNDERSTANDING PERSONALITY

Chapter Focus

This chapter presents:
- **some factors that influence the development of personality**
- **an overview of the various major personality theories**
- **some criticisms of each theory of personality**

"Last one home is a rotten egg!"

"Tag, you're it!"

Remember when you used to play these games after school? Chances are that you've outgrown such pastimes. You've changed dramatically over the years.

Yet in many ways you have probably remained the same. If you were shy as a child, most likely you are still somewhat timid. If you were outgoing, you still probably approach situations boldly. These similarities in your behavior over a long period of time help to define the term "personality."

Many psychologists define **personality** as the sum total of an individual's relatively consistent, organized, and unique thoughts and reactions to the environment. "Relatively consistent" means that the way we behave today is similar to the way we will behave tomorrow, or the way we have behaved in the past. In addition, the behaviors are "organized." That is, they are related to, and interact with, one another. Finally, the behaviors are "unique," in that no two people behave in exactly the same way.

In this chapter we will examine the concept of personality. We will look at how personality develops and the factors that help

shape it. We will also study the various theories used to explain it.

The Development of Personality

How does personality develop? How do our patterns of behavior build up? There are no simple answers to these questions. Personality is very complex. Many factors, such as intellectual ability, heredity, and social factors, influence its development. Since we discuss these elements in other chapters, we will focus on some additional factors here.

Early childhood. The early years of life are very important to the development of personality. Even during the first few weeks of life, infants differ in their behavior. At that age, such differences are mainly biologically determined. For example, some infants cry more than others. Some are active. Others are more passive.

During the first six months of life, behavior starts to become individualized as the infant reacts to food, clothing, light, dark, and so on. Through interactions with the environment, the infant is developing that complex pattern called personality.

Some researchers believe that personality patterns established in the early years of a child's life remain throughout life. For example, an aggressive child will become an aggressive adult. However, other researchers disagree. They argue that personality undergoes many changes as people develop. Thus, a person may be aggressive as a child but passive as an adult. Still other researchers believe that personality goes through alternate phases marked by changes and stability. The periods of change, they argue, provide a chance for personal growth.

The influence of the home. In America the home plays a major role in the development of personality. This is because many foundations of personality are laid down early in life. And most of the child's early life is spent in the home.

Different home environments produce different personalities. Some parents constantly tell their children what they must not do, rather than showing them what they should do. The child may react by becoming rebellious, or withdrawing from contacts with other people, or living in a world of daydreams. Some parents make nearly all the decisions for their children. Others give children an opportunity to make decisions for themselves. They might let the child choose what clothes to wear each day, or whether to have oatmeal or corn flakes for breakfast. In this way, the child develops a personality that includes the experience of making decisions.

Affection in the home also influences the personality development of children. If there is affection in the home, children feel free to tell their problems to their parents. Parents are interested in and recognize the work and play of their children. There is mutual sharing of some activities in the family. There is evidence that children who experience a great deal of affection in their family relations tend to be responsible and honest in their social relationships.

The attitudes of the parents and the activities that family members share affect the personality development of the children.

The influence of birth order. Does the order in which a child is born into a family affect the child's personality? Psychological studies have failed to show that birth order establishes a *biological* effect on the kind of personality that a child develops. However, the birth order of children in a family does alter the circumstances under which children are reared. Thus it has a *social* effect.

One study compared the mother's care of the first-born with her care of the second-born child. Observations of the mother-infant interactions began when the first-born and the second-born infants each were about three months old. The following results were

UNDERSTANDING
PERSONALITY

Personality must be evaluated in terms of the society in which it is found. These Japanese schoolchildren are being taught the value of conformity.

found: (1) Mothers spent less time in social activities and caretaking with their second-born than with their first-born child. (2) There was less maternal treatment toward the second-born when that child was female and had an older sister. (3) There was little decrease in motherly attention for the male second-born who had an older sister.

In addition to maternal treatment, there are other ways in which the experiences differ for children of different birth positions. For example, the first-born child is an only child for some period of time. The second-born child is reared from birth with a sibling (brother or sister). Such differing circumstances do contribute to differing personality patterns. One study has indicated that the older child in a two-child family tends to be serious, shy, and oriented toward adults. The younger child tends to be cheerful, easygoing, and less studious than the older sibling.

Other studies have shown a relationship between birth order in a family and certain other variables. For example, famous people are more likely to have been first-born, or the eldest, children. Also, a larger percentage of first-born children are likely to go to college. An even larger percentage will go on to grad-uate school. Both male and female first-born tend to be more socially conforming than later-born children. And first-born females, when afraid, desire the company of others more strongly than do later-born females.

The influence of society. A *society* is a large group of people who share common traits, customs, or ways of behaving. Children learn about their society first through their home life. Then, as they grow older, they have more and more social contacts outside the home. Their personality development is shaped by their contacts in school, in religious activities, and in playing with children in the neighborhood. Through their home and social contacts, they gradually learn what is expected of them as members of the society in which they live. The social group in which children are reared will help them learn ways of behaving that are accepted by their society. To understand an individual's behavior, we must also understand the society in which he or she is reared.

Perhaps we can get a good idea of how much a society influences personality by looking at some ways in which societies may differ from one another. In some societies of the world, such as the Balinese, orthodox Hindu, and Hopi Indians, we don't find the striving for financial success that is characteristic of many people in the United States. In some societies, an individual's lifework is determined by the occupational group into which the person is born. (If your father is a farmer, you will be a farmer.) Societies may also differ in their stress on individual achievement, the rights of the individual, education, marriage, and wealth. The types of achievement stressed, and how much emphasis a particular society puts on them, help determine the personalities of the members.

There are also differences among social groups within a society. The standards of these social groups can influence personality development. For instance, a member of a gang may adopt the standards and values of the gang. These values may differ from the values of the society as a whole.

To summarize, personality is influenced by the home in which we are reared, the social groups to which we belong, and the society in which we are raised. If you had been brought up in a different society and a different geographical setting, you would probably have a different personality.

Theories of Personality

Over the years, as psychologists have studied personality, they have developed a number of theories to explain its nature. Before examining these, however, let's look at some factors involved in forming personality theories.

Developing theories of personality. Some of those who have formed personality theories have been viewed as rebels. They developed theories that were contrary to the popular beliefs of their day. While most psychologists early in this century were concerned with laboratory experiments and small bits of behavior, personality theorists were concerned with the adjustment of the whole person. Personality theorists were interested in what caused personal problems

and how people could adjust better. In addition, the early personality theorists emphasized motivation—the "why" of behavior.

Today, most psychologists use one of two approaches. They may take the **molecular approach,** which means they are explaining behavior in terms of tiny, very specific units, such as nerve impulses. Or they may take the **molar approach,** which is concerned with larger, more general units of behavior, and the influence of your goals and expectations on behavior.

Personality theorists differ in their general approach to explaining behavior. They also differ in how much (if at all) they emphasize such factors as the following: (1) The role of goals. (2) The effects of reward and punishment. (3) The role of learning. (4) The influence of heredity. (5) The importance of early childhood experiences. (6) How unique behavior is. (7) The role of the environment. Perhaps you can see that developing a theory of personality is not a simple job.

Judging personality theories. Once a personality theory is developed, the next step is to evaluate it. First, a theory should be clearly and precisely stated so that others understand the ideas, terms, and principles involved. Second, a theory can be judged on how closely it fits the data. How well does it explain behaviors that can be observed and measured? Third, a theory must be able to predict behavior accurately. Fourth, all things being equal, the simpler a theory the better. Finally, we can judge a theory by how much research it produces. If a theory causes others to think about new ideas and test them, then it has been worthwhile.

Psychoanalytic Theories

Psychoanalytic theories of personality stem from the work of Sigmund Freud. Freud was perhaps the first and certainly one of the most influential people to form a theory of personality. Although many of the ideas and principles that he developed are not used by psychologists today, his ideas have had a major impact on the development of psychology.

Sigmund Freud (1856-1939). One of Freud's most important contributions is his view of the unconscious. Before Freud, psychologists had focused their attention on the conscious level of people's minds. The **conscious** level contains those thoughts that we are aware of at any given moment—such as what you are thinking about at this instant. According to Freud, the **unconscious** level contains the desires, wishes, needs, and impulses that we are not aware of under normal circumstances. Freud compared the human mind to an iceberg. The part of the iceberg that we can see is similar to the conscious level of our minds. By far the largest part of the iceberg is below the surface of the water, similar to our unconscious. In Freud's view, the unconscious level, the part that we are not aware of, plays the major role in determining our behavior.

The id, ego, and superego. Freud also stated that personality is composed of three systems—the id, ego, and superego. The **id** is the original system of personality. It is present at birth. The id becomes the energy source for the other two systems. It is completely unconscious and has no direct contact with the environment. The id acts according to the **pleasure principle,** which means that it seeks to keep the level of tension low by obtaining pleasure.

The **ego,** on the other hand, is primarily conscious. It involves learned ways of behaving. It plays a middle role between the desires of the id and the realities of the outside world. The ego operates on the basis of the **reality principle.** It finds appropriate ways for the person to satisfy needs. If an individ-

SIGMUND
FREUD

Suppose this person decides to go to the game. How do you think her id, ego, and superego would react?

ual is thirsty, for instance, the id might urge the person to drink large amounts of whatever is available. The ego would develop a plan to find a satisfactory liquid and would encourage drinking only an appropriate amount. It would recognize the social needs as well as the physiological needs.

The **superego** refers to the moral aspects of the personality. It represents those values and ideals that are established by society and learned by the individual. Our superego tells us what is right and wrong. It tries to prevent id impulses from being expressed, since most id impulses are socially unacceptable. It tries to persuade the ego to adopt moralistic goals in place of realistic ones. And it strives for perfection rather than for pleasure or for realistic thinking.

How do these three systems interact? First, in order to have the systems function together, there must be some kind of energy. According to Freud, most of the energy in our personality comes from the id. It is changed and used in different ways by the ego and superego.

Since the system contains only a limited amount of energy, the three parts of the system compete with one another for their share. If one part of the system gains control of most of the energy, the other two parts become weaker and cannot carry out all their functions. For example, if the id keeps the major share of the energy, the individual tends to act on impulse and wants immediate rewards. If the ego has the main control, the person is very realistic. If the superego gains primary control, the individual becomes extremely moralistic.

Studying the unconscious. Since the id operates at the unconscious level, how can we know what it does? How can we discover what goes on in the unconscious? Certainly we can't just ask the person, because people aren't aware of what's happening at this level.

Freud solved this problem in several ways. At first he used hypnosis to help individuals recall childhood experiences that were no longer in their conscious awareness. Then he discovered the technique of **free association,** in which individuals say whatever comes into their consciousness. Freud found that the associations they made indicated the structure and development of their personality. Freud also believed that dreams were expressions of the unconscious. Dreams revealed a person's unconscious desires or needs. By studying an individual for several years using these methods, Freud was able to understand what went on in the person's unconscious.

Carl Jung (1875-1961). Jung was a personal friend and a follower of Freud for seven years. Then Jung broke away to form his own approach to psychoanalysis, called Analytical Psychology. He and Freud stopped writing to each other and never saw each other again.

One reason for the break in friendship was their differing views of what determines human behavior. Freud emphasized early childhood experiences. Jung, on the other hand, believed that human behavior is also determined by goals. We strive toward the goal of developing and pulling together all parts of our personality. In addition, Jung stressed the influence of our ancestral past in determining our behavior. According to Jung, we inherit from our ancestors such things as an interest in magic, heroes, and power.

The unconscious. Freud and Jung did agree, however, on the importance of the unconscious. Jung divided the unconscious into the personal unconscious and the collective unconscious. The **personal unconscious** consists of experiences that were once conscious but have since been forgotten. For instance, no doubt you were taught how to use a fork and spoon as a child, but you may no longer remember that experience.

The most influential region, however, is the **collective unconscious.** It contains all the memories from our ancestors. The collective unconscious is universal. It is the same for everyone. For example, we are all born

CARL JUNG

with a tendency to be afraid of the dark. According to Jung, this is because in ancient days our ancestors experienced dangers in the dark that might harm them.

Introversion and extraversion. Jung also believed that our personalities include two major attitudes: *introversion* and **extraversion.** Introverted people respond mainly to internally oriented stimuli, such as their own ideas and inner thoughts. Extraverted people respond mainly to external stimuli, such as social situations and ideas from others.

Psychologists have made up lists of activities, interests, and attitudes that reflect introversion and extraversion. Among the traits considered characteristic of introversion are: feeling hurt easily, daydreaming frequently, blushing often, and keeping in the background on social occasions. Also, suffering from stage fright, worrying over possible misfortune, being unable to make decisions, showing great concern over what others think of you, and being extremely careful of personal property.

Traits considered characteristic of extraversion include: not feeling hurt easily, seldom daydreaming, making friends easily, being the "life of the party," not worrying a great deal, and laughing frequently and easily. Other traits are preferring oral reports rather than written reports, accepting orders from others as a matter of course, preferring work involving social contacts rather than many details, and being a good loser.

Although both attitudes are present in every personality, one attitude is usually uppermost. According to Jung, most people are either primarily introverted or primarily extraverted.

Social Psychoanalytic Theories

Freud and Jung thought that forces inside the person determined personality. Other theorists have considered this a narrow view of personality. While using some of Freud's psychoanalytic ideas, these theorists take a broader viewpoint, developing theories that emphasize forces outside the person. They stress the social and cultural influences on personality. Some of these theorists are Alfred Adler, Erich Fromm, Karen Horney, Harry Stack Sullivan, and Erik Erikson.

Alfred Adler (1870-1937). Adler was also closely associated with Freud. Like Jung, he then began to develop theories opposed to those of Freud. He separated from Freud and started his own group. His views became known as Individual Psychology.

Adler differed from Freud by emphasizing that people are primarily social creatures. They are motivated chiefly by social interests. In addition, people are mainly conscious beings. Adler stressed the importance of conscious awareness rather than the role of the unconscious.

In Adler's view, people strive to be perfect. They may have feelings of inferiority because of their imperfections or incompleteness. Such inferiority feelings drive people to try to improve and to be superior. Superiority means the total completion of the personality.

Adler's most important idea is the **creative self.** The creative self is what makes people strive toward complete fulfillment. It causes them to create both the goals to be reached and the means of reaching them. Thus each person is unique. And each person takes an active part in forming his or her own personality.

Erich Fromm (1900–1981). Fromm wrote a great deal about how human society affects the individual. He noted that as people have gained more freedom through the ages, they have felt more and more isolated. A slave, for instance, belonged to someone. When slaves gained their freedom from their masters, they sometimes experienced a feeling of loneliness and isolation. Similarly, as children grow up and become separated from their parents, they begin to feel isolated.

How can we solve this problem? Fromm saw two possibilities. We can subject our-

ALFRED ADLER

ERICH FROMM

selves to authority and conform to the rules of society. In this case, we become slaves all over again. Or we can make use of our freedom to join others in love and work. In this case, we develop a better and more civilized society.

According to Fromm, our personalities are shaped by the interaction between our basic needs and the opportunities in the society for fulfilling them. Fromm described five specific needs. The need for *relatedness* comes about because human beings have been separated from nature. In place of our ties with nature, we create our own relations with other people. The need for *transcendence* is a need to go beyond our original animal nature — to become creative. The need to *belong* is a desire to feel part of the world around us — to feel a closeness with other people. The need for *identity* is a striving to be a unique person. We each want to be recognized as an individual who is different from the other people around us. Finally, we have a need to have a *frame of reference,* a way to view life, to look at our own actions, and to understand the world around us.

No society has yet met all of these needs. Therefore, we have had to compromise between our inner needs and the requirements of the society. A society, to preserve itself, requires that we obey its rules. Instead of conformity, Fromm would have liked to see a society in which every person has an equal opportunity to become a full human being.

Karen Horney (1885-1952). Horney disagreed with Freud regarding the amount of our personality that is inborn and determined by biology. Freud believed that people were governed by their innate desires, drives, and impulses. Horney, on the other hand, emphasized the social relationship between young children and their parents.

In analyzing how individuals become disturbed, Horney looked for problems in the parent-child relationship. She found that basic anxiety arises because children feel alone and isolated and helpless. A number of situations can produce this anxiety. The parents may reject the child. They may act inconsistently toward the child. They may not respect the child's needs and rights. They may not give warmth and protection. The result is a strong need for security on the part of the child.

An insecure child may develop many different ways of behaving to handle these feelings of isolation and helplessness. Children may become hostile and seek revenge against those who have mistreated them. They may become overly submissive in trying to win back the lost love. They may develop self-pity to gain sympathy. If the attempts to gain love fail, the child may then seek power over others. This makes the child feel less helpless.

KAREN HORNEY

Here the father shows love and affection. Karen Horney believed that psychological disturbances occur when the child's needs for love and security are not met.

Horney thought that everyone has inner conflicts. They become a problem for an individual when they cause great anxiety and lead to unsuccessful solutions. The person may be in conflict because of a need to be both independent of people and loved by them. A person might deal with this conflict by recognizing only one of these needs and denying the other.

115

To Horney, such conflicts are not built into an individual. They are the result of interaction with social conditions. Therefore conflicts can be resolved, since both the individual's personality and the social conditions can change.

Harry Stack Sullivan (1892-1949). Sullivan believed that the individual's personality does not and cannot exist apart from relationships with other people. From the day we are born until the day we die, we are members of a social group. Even if we eventually become stranded on an island with no one around, we would still have memories of our social relationships. For Sullivan, there is no personality except in terms of interpersonal relationships. To understand personality, we must study the situation and the relationships.

Sullivan focused on three processes that occur in interpersonal relationships. The first, *dynamism,* is the smallest unit that can be studied about the individual. It is a pattern of behavior that occurs over and over again. For example, we may consistently look down after eye contact with another person. A dynamism is similar to a habit. It is meant to help fulfill a person's basic needs.

A second process Sullivan studied is *personification.* This is the image that people have of themselves or of another person. It is a kind of picture we carry around with us. It involves attitudes, feelings, and ideas that grow out of experiences. These personifications of other people may or may not be accurate. Yet they still affect our reactions to those around us. For instance, suppose a child has a personification of his or her father as caring and concerned. The child may then include these qualities in a personification of male teachers and all other men in positions of authority.

The third process that Sullivan associated with personality is *cognitive processes.* These consist of ways of thinking. They include fleeting sensations and images that have no meaning for the individual, as in the early months of life. They also include using symbols, such as words and numbers, in some logical way. This enables people to communicate with one another, and thus to have interpersonal relationships.

According to Sullivan, then, we know about the personality of an individual through the dynamisms, personifications, and cognitive processes that the person uses in his or her relationships with others.

Erik Erikson (1902-1982). Erikson divided personality development into eight stages. In each stage the individual meets and must solve a major crisis, or problem. If the crisis is not solved, the individual is less able to solve crises at later stages. (However, at a later stage the person might solve an earlier crisis and continue developing favorably.) It is as if society gives its members "tests" in the form of crises to make sure they develop socially as they grow up. As people attempt to solve each major crisis, they learn ways of dealing with society. They develop a particular feeling or personality characteristic that is associated with each stage.

The first stage, according to Erikson, occurs during the first year of life. This stage involves the crisis of establishing a feeling of basic trust or mistrust. For example, mothers are quite often separated from their infants. If an infant feels hungry and the mother returns to feed it, the infant is likely to develop a feeling of trust. If the mother returns to feed the infant only some of the time, the infant may develop a feeling of mistrust of the mother and the environment in general.

Erikson's second stage occurs between the second and third years of life. At this stage, children face the crisis of achieving individuality. They strive for control over muscular activities, including control of the bladder. If such control is developed, children experience a feeling of autonomy—a feeling of being self-governing. If children don't gain this control over their behavior, they develop a feeling of shame and doubt.

In the third stage, which occurs during ages four and five, a child faces the crisis of being attracted to the opposite-sex parent. The crisis is solved as the child channels these feelings into socially acceptable behavior. The child also learns initiative as he or she becomes involved in activities and social relations. If this does not happen, the child develops guilt.

The fourth stage covers ages six through eleven, which make up the early school years. During this stage, the child acquires the ability to learn and to work hard. Erikson calls this ability "industry." If children do not properly develop this ability, they may experience failure in school. As a result, they may develop feelings of inferiority.

The fifth stage occurs during adolescence. At this time the individual must solve the crisis of "Who am I?" "Where am I going in life?" It is a crisis of identity. The individual looks to the peer group and to role models to develop a plan for the future. Individuals who do not successfully solve this crisis may develop feelings of role confusion.

The sixth stage occurs during young adulthood. During this period people face the crisis of intimacy. Once young adults determine their own roles and an awareness of self, they move toward sharing themselves with others. Or else they find themselves isolated from others.

The seventh stage occurs during middle adulthood. Individuals at this stage develop the feeling that they are productive—that they are accomplishing something worthwhile. This includes being responsible for the next generation. If they don't develop this feeling, they may feel that they aren't getting anywhere. They become preoccupied with themselves. Erikson calls this crisis "generativity versus stagnation."

The final period occurs during late adulthood. When people reach this final stage, they can develop either a sense of integrity or of despair. People who believe their life has been full and "together" develop feelings of integrity. In looking back over their growth and development, they feel they've

According to Erikson, adolescence is a time of identity crisis. The peer group often provides social support.

UNDERSTANDING
PERSONALITY

STAGE	AGE	CRISIS
One	Birth–1	Trust vs. Mistrust
Two	2–3	Autonomy vs. Shame and Doubt
Three	4–5	Initiative vs. Guilt
Four	6–11	Industry vs. Inferiority
Five	Adolescence	Identity vs. Role Confusion
Six	Young Adulthood	Intimacy vs. Isolation
Seven	Middle Adulthood	Generativity vs. Stagnation
Eight	Late Adulthood	Integrity vs. Despair

The eight stages of development, according to Erikson.

been successful. Those who fail to develop this feeling may despair, thinking that their life has been unfulfilled. They regard their life as a series of disappointments.

These, then, are Erikson's eight stages of development. Erikson never meant that a person experiences either the feeling related to each crisis or its opposite at any one stage. Rather, it is the degree to which we experience the various opposite feelings that influences our development at each stage. Underlying all these stages of development are the general tendencies to develop a strong identity and to master the environment.

Behavioristic Theories

The personality theories we've discussed so far have not emphasized the processes involved in learning behavior. This is what behaviorists attempt to do. They investigate the role of learning in the development of personality. In particular, they examine the conditions and situations that affect the learning of behavior. We will consider two

such theorists—B. F. Skinner and Albert Bandura.

B. F. Skinner (1904-   ). Skinner defines personality in terms of behavior. To find out how personality develops, he studies what conditions produce specific behaviors. He looks for relationships between causes (environmental factors) and effects (the responses to the environmental factors).

Skinner does not take into account factors *within* a person to explain behavior. He analyzes only external events — which can be measured.

To understand Skinner's point of view, you might think of studying a human being as you would a box you've just found on the street. The box has all sorts of levers, buttons, and switches on the outside. The box won't open, no matter what you do. So you can't see what connections exist inside it. However, by pushing levers on the outside, you may find that when one lever is pushed down, another one always goes up. You may eventually work out many relationships between the levers, buttons, and switches — without ever knowing what is happening inside the box.

. F. SKINNER

118

From his studies, Skinner has found certain rules or principles that explain behavior. One of these is the principle of **reinforcement.** When a behavior is reinforced, or rewarded, the chances of that behavior occurring again increase. If the behavior is not rewarded, the chances of the behavior occurring again decrease. Suppose a child asks a parent politely for a piece of candy and receives it. The next time the child asks, the parent also gives the child candy. As the parent continues to reinforce the child's behavior of asking for candy, the chances become greater that the asking behavior will occur again. Or, on the other hand, suppose the parent does not give the child candy when the child asks for it. In this way the parent can reduce the chances that the child's asking behavior will occur again.

Another way in which the environment can reduce the chances of a behavior occurring is by punishment. Suppose each time the child asks for candy, the child is spanked. To avoid being spanked, the child is likely to stop asking for candy. Skinner does not place emphasis on weakening a behavior by **punishment,** however. Instead, he emphasizes strengthening desirable behavior by rewarding it.

Albert Bandura (1925-   ). Bandura's explanations of learned behavior and personality development differ from Skinner's in two ways. First, Bandura limits his explanations mainly to social behavior, such as aggression. Skinner, on the other hand, seeks explanations that apply to many kinds of behavior. Second, Bandura believes that new behavior is learned mostly through observation and imitation. After this learning occurs through observing and imitating, the newly learned behavior continues because it is reinforced. For instance, children see their parents hug each other. Children imitate this behavior. When they hug their mother or father, the parent may smile. This sign of approval reinforces the hugging behavior and encourages children to do it again.

According to Bandura, we learn by watching and imitating a **model,** or a person

According to Bandura, we learn much of our behavior from watching and imitating the actions of others.

whom we use as an example of how to behave. For instance, watching other people being kind and generous can teach us to be kind and generous. The following experiment shows the effects of a model on first-grade children. The children were divided into groups. The first group saw a model share some candy with other children. The second group watched the model just play games with other children. Then both groups of first-grade children were given an equal amount of candy. The first group, which had seen the model sharing, shared much more of their candy with other children than did the second group.

What can be done to increase the

ALBERT BANDURA

Text continues on page 122.

119

UNDERSTANDING PERSONALITY

Case Study: Focus on Research

SUBJECT SEE, SUBJECT DO

No one who has watched a small child "drive" a car like Mommy or Daddy can doubt the importance of imitation in human behavior. Without models, we would find it extremely difficult to develop a tennis backhand, master such crafts as knitting or sewing, or learn the latest dance steps.

At the same time, imitation might also be responsible for producing undesirable behavior, such as aggression. At least, that is what psychologist Albert Bandura would argue, based on studies he has conducted.

Aggression can be defined as hostile behavior with the intent to do harm. While some psychologists argue that such behavior is inborn and grows out of anger or frustration, Bandura believes that "aggressive behavior is learned through essentially the same processes as those regulating the acquisition of any other form of behavior." In other words, he would say, people learn aggressive behavior by watching other individuals and through rewards and punishments.

In one of his experiments, Bandura divided a number of nursery school children into five groups. One group watched a man or woman punch, kick, and verbally abuse a big plastic doll. A second group saw a film of the same activity. A third group witnessed similar behavior, but with the aggressor disguised as a cartoon cat. Groups four and five were control groups. That is, one group saw no modeling activity at all, while the other group saw models acting only in a calm, nonaggressive way.

All five groups of children were then taken to a room full of toys, where they could play freely. Observers noted that children who had watched aggressive models tended to imitate their behavior in both actions and words. The live model brought forth the most aggressive behavior, the cartoon cat the least. Although neither control group acted very aggressively, the one that had watched the nonaggressive model displayed the least amount of hostility of all five groups.

Bandura showed that children who watched aggressive models were more likely to be aggressive themselves.

In variations of this experiment, Bandura had three groups of children watch a film of aggressive behavior. In one case, the model was punished. In the second, the model was rewarded. In the third, there were no consequences. As might be expected, the children in the first group exhibited less aggression than did those in the other two groups. But when all three groups of children were *themselves* rewarded for copying the aggressive behavior they saw, the rates of aggression were high for everyone. All three groups learned aggressive behavior by observing the model. But it was the expectations of reward or punishment that determined whether they would display this aggression.

Bandura's studies of aggression have lent support to people who feel that there is too much violence on television. A follow-up study, however, showed that when a parent or other adult was present to explain the content of the TV programs, the children's level of aggression did not rise significantly.

Another series of Bandura's modeling experiments has been used to help people conquer fears. In one study, Bandura and his researchers worked with adolescents and adults who were terrified of snakes. Many of them were so fearful that they avoided almost every outdoor activity, from gardening to hiking.

Again, Bandura divided his subjects into groups. One group watched a film of children and adults approaching, touching, and holding a large snake. The second group worked directly with experimenters, who handled a snake without fear and gradually persuaded subjects to imitate their behavior. A third group, following the procedure known as desensitization, paired snake fantasies with relaxation techniques. The fourth group was a control group.

All of the subjects then took a closely supervised test that moved through a range of behaviors: approaching a snake, touching it, removing it from its cage, holding it close to the face, and finally holding it in the lap. The group that had worked directly with the researchers and live snakes showed the best results. Fear of snakes was eliminated in 92 percent of these subjects. The group that saw the film showed substantial improvement, the desensitization group less. The control group exhibited no change at all.

A follow-up study a month later indicated that the changes had remained in effect. The subjects who had been helped could now hike, camp, and enjoy the outdoors. Some were even working with their children and friends to help them overcome the same fear. As a result of this experiment, these people were able to lead fuller lives.

SOURCE: Albert Bandura, *Principles of Behavior Modification,* New York: Holt, Rinehart & Winston, 1966; Albert Bandura, *Aggression: A Social Learning Analysis,* Englewood Cliffs, N.J.: Prentice-Hall, 1973.

Through procedures that include first holding rubber snakes and then viewing live snakes through a glass, people can overcome a fear of snakes.

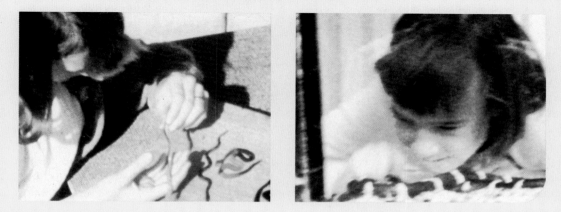

*"Like this— see? You've got to get
your back into it."*

Drawing by Garrett Price, © 1942, 1972, *The New Yorker Magazine, Inc.*

desires and impulses that push us in certain directions. Humanistic theories, on the other hand, imply an active drive of the individual toward health, growth, and creativity. Humanistic psychologists believe that human nature is basically good. They stress that it is the environment, not our inner nature, that causes people to develop violent or destructive tendencies.

Abraham Maslow (1908-1970). Maslow explained personality and human behavior in terms of motivation. According to him, people act as they do because they are motivated by certain needs. Maslow has listed seven such needs that rule our behavior. He arranged these needs in a specific order, or hierarchy, as shown on page 123. The need on the bottom has to be satisfied before a person can become fully involved in satisfying the need at the next level. For example, physiological needs must be met before a person becomes active in satisfying safety needs.

What did Maslow mean by physiological needs? By safety needs? The lowest level of needs, the physiological needs, refer to things our bodies require for survival, such as food, water, air, and rest. If these basic needs are not satisfied—if we are hungry, for instance—we are not apt to be motivated by the next level, or safety needs. Safety needs refer to our desire for security. They are satisfied as we learn how to avoid situations in which dangers may occur. The third level, love and belongingness needs, is a desire for affectionate relationships with other people and for having a place in a group.

Once people have their need for love and belonging satisfied, they are interested in moving to the next level. They want to fulfill their need for self-esteem. They seek recognition as a worthwhile person. They develop a feeling of confidence.

If their need for an awareness of self-worth is met, they then attempt to satisfy their needs to know and understand. These needs can be observed more in some people than in others. Some individuals are curious and have a need to explore and to acquire

chances that learning by observing and imitating a model will take place? For one thing, imitative behavior is more likely to occur if the observer sees the model being rewarded or knows the model will be rewarded for the behavior. The observer is also more likely to imitate the model if he or she has been rewarded in the past for showing the same behavior as the model. Observers who believe themselves similar to the models are more likely to imitate them.

Punishment also has an effect on imitative behavior. Observers who see a model being punished are less likely to imitate the model's behavior. However, the effects of punishment are not as predictable as the effects of reward.

Humanistic Theories

The special feature of humanistic personality theories is that they emphasize the positive aspects of human growth. The Freudian theory of personality implies that we have

ABRAHAM MASLOW

122

more knowledge. People with a need to know and understand often also have a need to organize, analyze, and look for relationships.

The next level consists of a desire for beauty, or aesthetic needs. These needs may be accompanied by needs for truth, perfection, and justice. Not all people, not even a majority, show aesthetic needs.

Those who do show and meet their aesthetic needs can strive for self-actualization. **Self-actualization** needs are fulfilled by developing abilities that are as yet undeveloped. People in this level try new things in order to grow into the people they can become. The following are characteristics of self-actualized people. They accept themselves and others as they are. They have a good sense of humor. They are creative. They are concerned for the welfare of others. They look at life objectively. Finally, they are problem-centered rather than self-centered.

According to Maslow, the top three needs reflect growth motivation. Once the lower four needs—the physiological through esteem needs—are satisfied, the growth needs can become active. The bottom four needs "push" an individual in certain directions for need fulfillment. The growth needs—the top three—"pull" the person toward their fulfillment.

Carl Rogers (1902-1987). Like Maslow, Rogers believed that each person has the possibility for being self-actualized. In addition, all individuals determine their own personality and whether or not they become self-actualized. People are free to choose to be themselves. They can decide to develop their own identity rather than let themselves be shaped by the demands and expectations of others.

In Rogers' view, an important part of the development of personality is an individual's self-concept. **Self-concept** is a system of attitudes that people have toward themselves, with all the emotions and feelings associated with these attitudes. It becomes evident when children begin to see themselves as being separate from their surroundings. They develop an awareness of "I" or "me." A per-

CARL ROGERS

Maslow's hierarchy of needs.

SELF-ACTUALIZATION NEEDS

AESTHETIC NEEDS

NEEDS TO KNOW AND UNDERSTAND

ESTEEM NEEDS

LOVE AND BELONGINGNESS NEEDS

SAFETY NEEDS

PHYSIOLOGICAL NEEDS

son's self-concept is shown by statements like, "I want . . . ," "I feel that . . . ," and "I am. . . ."

People have a strong tendency to behave in ways that will support or agree with their self-concept. For example, suppose people believe "I am very honest." Then they will tend to act in ways they believe honest people act. If they think honest people don't cheat, they won't do so. For to cheat would create a conflict between their behavior and this part of their self-concept. Imagine that you are taking an exam and the teacher leaves the room. You have a chance to look on someone else's paper. If you believe that you are an honest person and that honest people don't look at someone else's paper, you will not do so. But suppose you think that honest people sometimes cheat, under special circumstances. You know that you must pass this exam or fail the course. Then you might cheat.

What happens when there is a conflict between what you think is true about yourself—your self-concept—and reality? Assume that you believe you are very good at repairing small electrical appliances. But the truth is that you really are not good at repair-ing such items. Whenever there is a conflict between your self-concept and reality, you must do something about it. If you attempt repairs and fail, you might place the blame on having inferior tools. You might claim that someone else distracted you while you tried to work. You would look for some explana-tion. Or you might change your self-concept to be closer to the facts.

However, suppose you believe that you are good at learning mathematics, and you are. In this case, there is agreement between reality and your self-concept. The more agreement there is between what you think is true and what is true, the better adjusted you are. Rogers states that all individuals strive to develop more agreement between their self-concept and reality.

Once a self-concept is in agreement with reality, should it ever change? The answer is yes. Imagine that at the age of eighteen you believe you are a very fast runner—and you are. What would happen if at the age of eighty you still believed that you were as fast a runner as you were at eighteen? As we grow up and change physically and psycho-logically, our self-concept must also change. Our personalities develop as we strive for

You do not have a conflict if your self-concept includes the belief that you have mechan-ical ability and you usually can find solu-tions to mechanical problems.

complete adjustment between our behavior and our beliefs.

We've now examined some of the major theories of personality. We've looked at psychoanalytic theories, social psychoanalytic theories, behavioristic theories, and humanistic theories. Is there any way to decide which is the best one?

Some Criticisms of Personality Theories

Each of the theories of personality that we have just discussed has certain shortcomings. No single personality theory is accepted by all psychologists. Do you agree with one of these theories? With none of them? Or do you accept various parts of different theories? Before deciding, you may want to consider some of the criticisms that have been made of these different theories.

Psychoanalytic theories. Freudian theory has been criticized because Freud accepted at face value what his patients told him. He did not check on the accuracy of their statements. Also, Freud never made clear the processes he used to reach conclusions about patients. He did not record his method of analysis. Nor did he test his theories under controlled conditions. As a result, psychologists have found it extremely difficult to repeat Freud's procedures in order to support his findings. Finally, Freud looked at behavior after it had occurred and then explained it. Today, psychologists emphasize predicting behavior that will occur in the future.

Social psychoanalytic theories. These theories, which emphasize the importance of the social environment, have been criticized as being too idealistic. Such theories suggest that if we just improved the social environment, we would have fewer problems. Yet we have been trying to do this for thousands of years. We've succeeded only in creating imperfect social systems, in which violence, crime, and wars still occur. Another criticism of such theories is that they fail to state exactly how society molds its members. For example, exactly how do we learn to be members of a society? What specific role does learning play in the development of members within a society?

Behavioristic theories. These theorists are criticized mainly for examining behavior in small bits and for not relating these isolated behaviors to one another in some meaningful way. They are also criticized for putting too much emphasis on environmental forces in the shaping of personality. To some psychologists, this outlook makes humans seem like puppets whose strings are pulled by the environment. There is another problem. What is a reward to one individual is not necessarily a reward for others. Nor is punishment the same for everyone. Therefore, we must find out what is a reward and what is punishment for each individual. This would be extremely difficult, if not impossible. Today, most psychologists are not strict behaviorists. However, behaviorist theories have made significant contributions to modern psychology.

Humanistic theories. Criticisms of the humanistic approach center around the subjective terms used in such theories. Many of the ideas involved in this approach cannot be tested easily. Also, critics take issue with the humanistic view that you can understand an individual's behavior best by using the person's own frame of reference. The problem is that only the specific individual can ever really know how he or she perceives the world. And sometimes individuals may not even be aware of how they interpret a situation. Finally, critics of Maslow say there is no evidence that human needs are organized in a hierarchy of levels.

You are now familiar with some theories that psychologists have put forth to explain personality. You also know some of the criticisms of these theories. What ideas do you have about how personality develops?

Summary

Personality refers to the sum total of an individual's relatively consistent, organized, and unique thoughts and reactions to the environment. Among the many factors that influence personality are early childhood experiences, the home environment, birth order, and society.

Various theories have been proposed to explain the nature of personality. They differ in general approach as well as how much they emphasize goals, rewards and punishment, learning, heredity, early childhood experiences, the uniqueness of behavior, and the environment.

Psychoanalytic theories stress the role of internal forces in determining personality. Freud and Jung are two important representatives of this point of view.

Social psychoanalysts partially agree with this viewpoint. However, they take a broader view, stressing the role of forces outside the person. Adler, Fromm, Horney, Sullivan, and Erikson each have proposed theories with this emphasis.

Behavioristic theories emphasize the role of learning in the development of personality. Skinner argues that what people learn through rewards and punishment determines behavior. Bandura also believes that personality results from learning. But he believes this learning takes place mostly through the observation and imitation of the behavior of people he calls models.

The humanists emphasize the active role of the individual in determining personality. They argue that people strive to maximize their potential. Maslow and Rogers are two prominent humanists.

Each of the various theories tries to explain personality. Yet each has certain shortcomings. As a result, no single theory is accepted by all psychologists.

INTERPRETING SOURCES

In this excerpt from an article in *Journal of Research in Personality* (Vol. 14, 1980), Nancy Hirschberg and Susan Jennings discuss the "individual differences" theory of person-ality. According to the authors, how we see other people gives us insight in regard to our own personalities.

Personality has been characterized recently not as the study of the traits people possess but rather as the study of the beliefs people hold.... The notion is that the beliefs we hold about the personality of other people are a clue to what we are like....

In particular, Hirschberg's theory of individual differences [assumes] that people will pay attention to those aspects of their interpersonal environment that correspond to prominent personality characteristics of the persons themselves.... For example, if I am exceptionally wealthy, I will tend to discriminate among other people along the dimension of wealth rather than along other dimensions such as intelligence or wit. Thus, a given personality dimension will be more [important] to people who think they possess a high degree of that personality trait....

A study of face perception ... indicated that subjects attended to those aspects of a face, as portrayed in a photograph, that corresponded to prominent characteristics of the subjects' own face, such as attractiveness. And a study of the prediction of intelligence ... found that people paid attention to the type of intelligence that they themselves possessed. For example, people high on mechanical aptitude weighted that variable in their estimates of other persons' intelligence, while people high on spatial reasoning were more apt to weight spatial reasoning in their appraisal of the intelligence of other people....

It is interesting to speculate about the possible reasons for the individual difference hypothe-sis. The fact that we attend to aspects of our interpersonal environment corresponding to what we think are central, important, or superor-dinate aspects of our own personality may rest on a general concern about personality charac-teristics on which we think we are deviant, or extreme.... But why should this be?

One explanation of this phenomenon is found in an analysis of pride.... If one possesses a characteristic that he [or she] esteems, or is proud of, it follows that one values that charac-teristic. Being proud of, say, having a lot of money entails that we think it is a good thing to have money. And if we think having money makes people esteemable, we would discrimi-nate among other people in terms of how much money they possess....

One can reason that if we have a personality characteristic (or think we have a characteristic), we deem that characteristic as good since we like to think well of ourselves. And if the present conceptual analysis is correct, it would follow that we would discriminate among others with respect to that characteristic....

Another explanation of the individual differ-ence hypothesis is that we discriminate among others with respect to characteristics which we think will fulfill our own needs.... In either case it would be important to know whether our evalua-tion of the importance of a trait we believe we possess or simply the belief that we possess the trait determines the individual difference phenomenon.

Source Review

1. According to the authors, what character-istics in others are we most likely to be attentive to?

2. What makes a particular personality trait especially important in how you see your-self and others?

CHAPTER 6

REVIEWING TERMS

personality
society
molecular approach
molar approach
conscious
unconscious
id
pleasure principle
ego

reality principle
superego
free association
personal unconscious
collective unconscious
introversion
extraversion
creative self
dynamism

personification
cognitive process
reinforcement
punishment
model
self-actualization
self-concept

CHECKING FACTS

1. What are some factors that influence the development of personality? Show how each operates.

2. Whose ideas are generally considered to form the basis of psychoanalytic theories? According to this person, which level of our mind plays the major role in determining personality?

3. What are the three systems that compose personality, according to Freud? Explain how each acts, and how they interact.

4. According to Jung, how do introverted people and extraverted people differ? Give some traits of each.

5. How do Adler's views on personality differ from those of Freud? What did Adler mean by the "creative self"?

6. Describe the personality theories proposed by Fromm, Horney, and Sullivan. How do they differ?

7. What are the eight stages of personality development, according to Erikson?

8. Discuss Skinner's views on the development of personality.

9. According to Bandura, how do we learn? In what two ways does this viewpoint differ from Skinner's?

10. What special feature distinguishes humanistic personality theories from other theories? Explain Maslow's hierarchy of needs.

11. Describe some criticisms of the various personality theories.

APPLYING YOUR KNOWLEDGE

1. Sometimes authors seem to "write themselves into their work." Write down your impressions of the personality of some author whose works you have studied in an English course. You might choose an author like Ernest Hemingway, Emily Dickinson, Edgar Allan Poe, F. Scott Fitzgerald, or Willa Cather. Then check biographical material to learn to what extent that author has included his or her own experiences in the writings.

2. Bring to class a picture of a food that you think best describes your personality. Explain why you chose that food.

3. Research the family history of a famous person. Students should focus on family size, birth order, childhood experiences, and any other significant events that may have influenced the person's development. How might the person's childhood background have affected his or her adult personality and accomplishments? Discuss your findings in class.

4. Interview a foreign-born student about the similarities and differences between his or her culture and ours. How might such factors as family structure, home life, and social attitudes influence the development of personality?

5. Divide the class into four groups with each group representing a different view of personality (psychoanalytic, social psychoanalytic, behavioristic, and humanistic). Within each group, members should choose to represent specific theorists (such as Sigmund Freud, Carl Jung, etc.). Then hold a debate on which theory seems to explain more about personality. You might wish to do library research to strengthen your arguments.

6. Watch some Saturday morning children's shows and observe the kinds of role models that are presented. How might these role models affect the personality of young viewers?

THINKING CRITICALLY ABOUT PSYCHOLOGY

1. **Classifying Ideas** Suppose you had to decide which behaviors are "desirable" for all members of a society. How would you go about determining such behaviors? What specific behaviors would you include in a listing?

2. **Evaluating Ideas** In competitions such as those to select a "Miss" city, state, or America, personality as well as appearance and achievement is considered. Suppose you were one of the judges in such a contest. How would you evaluate the personality of each contestant?

3. **Forming Opinions** What would the world be like if everyone's personality were exactly the same? What influence,

if any, would this situation have on the development of personality theory?

4. **Interpreting Ideas** Suppose you were blindfolded and were introduced to five strangers. Then you were given an opportunity to talk with each one on a specific topic. How well do you think you could evaluate their personalities on the basis of voice quality alone? What clues (other than speech) to an individual's personality do you get from face-to-face contact?

5. **Applying Ideas** If you had your choice—and to some extent you do—would you prefer to be primarily introverted or primarily extraverted? Why?

DEVELOPING SKILLS IN PSYCHOLOGY

Identifying Implicit Theories

It has been argued that every psychologist has either an implicit or an explicit theory of human nature. Sometimes researchers tell you what theoretical framework guides their

CHAPTER REVIEW

studies. Other times they may discuss previous research concerning a problem but not tell you what theory underlies their data-collection efforts. Knowing a psychologist's theoretical orientation can help you understand why he or she chose to study a particular problem in a particular way. Use the material in this chapter to identify the implicit personality theories underlying each of the following studies:

1. Following an earthquake, a researcher asks subjects to report on their dreams. The hypothesis is that the dreams will contain symbolic images representing unconscious fears of death and destruction.

2. To test the hypothesis that children will be more generous with their toys if they observe an adult being generous, an experimenter stages a situation in which children see adults exchanging vegetables from their gardens.

3. To learn how teen-agers deal with issues of identity development, a researcher interviews them about their goals and their conflicts.

READING FURTHER ABOUT PSYCHOLOGY

Appignanesi, Richard, and Zarate, Oscar, *Freud for Beginners,* Pantheon, New York, 1979. An introduction to Freud, written as a documentary "comic book," that gives a thorough review of Freud's theory of personality.

Bandura, Albert, *Social Learning Theory,* Prentice-Hall, Englewood Cliffs, N.J., 1977. A review of social learning, one of the major orientations in personality theory today. Focuses on personality as shaped by rewards and punishments.

Corriere, Richard, and McGrady, Patrick, *Life Zones,* William Morrow, New York, 1986. Teaches readers how to gain control over their personalities and lead more fulfilling and successful lives. The authors view personality as a flexible system that can be changed.

Hall, Calvin S., and Lindzey, Gardner, *Theories of Personality,* Third Edition, John Wiley & Sons, New York, 1978. A classic book that introduces personality theory. Each of the current theories is analyzed in terms of structure, dynamics, development, and characteristic research.

Moriarty, David, editor, *The Loss of Loved Ones: The Effects of a Death in the Family on Personality Development,* Warren H. Green, St. Louis, Mo., 1983. Examines early loss as a factor influencing personality development. This book is based on case material drawn from a state mental institution.

MEASURING PERSONALITY

Chapter Focus

This chapter presents:

- **the characteristics of standardized tests**
- **the various methods used to measure personality**
- **some of the methods used to measure abilities and interests**

"People with round, soft bodies are friendly and carefree. Those with square, muscular bodies are active, impulsive, and energetic. Those who are thin and delicate tend to be shy and introverted." Does this sound strange? Perhaps. However, back in the 1940's a psychologist developed a classification system that linked body type with personality.

Throughout history people have tried various methods to measure personality. The position of the stars, bumps on the head, lines on the hand, and handwriting analysis all have been used as telltale signs of what people really are like. However, all of these measures have been shown to have little merit.

Today, psychologists often use tests to measure personality. In this chapter we will examine different psychological tests and see how they are used.

Standardized Tests

To measure a person's characteristic behavior as accurately as possible, psychologists often use standardized tests. A **standardized test** is one that can be given, scored, and interpreted the same way by different people. Suppose you want to find out what your classmates know about theories of personality. You might give them a standardized test on personality theories. In this case, you would give, score, and interpret the test in the same way that others would if they gave the same test to students in another city or state.

Suppose you make up an objective test, such as a multiple-choice type. It could be given and scored by different people in the same way. However, the results of your test probably would not be interpreted in the same way by different people. For example, others might not give the same letter grades to your classmates' scores as you would. Therefore, it would not be a standardized test.

The norm group. To help you interpret your scores, a standardized test has a set of scores to which you can compare your individual or group scores. A comparison set of scores on a standardized test is provided by a **norm group**. The norm group consists of a group of people similar to those who will take the test

How do you evaluate someone else's personality? What factors do you consider when deciding what another person is like?

later on. The scores of these people are arranged according to how many scored on the test at different levels. You can then see whether your scores are high or low by comparing them to those of the norm group.

Reliability and validity. The two major characteristics of a standardized test are reliability and validity. **Reliability** is the degree to which your score on a test will have the same, or about the same, position or rank each time you take that test. Suppose you took a particular test for the first time and got the highest possible score. If you got the highest score each time you took the test, the test would have reliability. However, if the second time you took the test you got the lowest score, it would not have reliability. Of course, reliability of tests is not established on the basis of how one person scores on a test. It depends on many people. If all the people taking the test maintain their same ranks or positions on the test every time they take it, the test would have perfect reliability. Actually, no tests, including standardized tests, have perfect reliability. But the more reliable they are, the better the tests.

There are other ways of establishing reliability aside from taking the same test twice. A test can be split in two, and each half can be given separately. Or two different but approximately equal forms of a test can be given. If people score about the same on the two forms, the test is reliable.

A second characteristic of a standardized test is validity. **Validity** means that the test measures what it is supposed to measure. For instance, a test may be called an intelligence test. But it may measure something other than intellectual ability. Or suppose you are given a standardized test as the final exam of your psychology course. You read through the questions. They are all on sociology. Would it be a valid test of your achievement in the psychology course?

A test can have perfect reliability without having any validity. Consider the following example. Suppose you took an exam on this chapter in Greek. Assume that you cannot read Greek and do not guess any of the answers correctly. Your score would be zero. Suppose you take the same test a year later. Again, you would score zero—the same score you made the first time. The test would be reliable. But would it measure your knowledge of this chapter? Of course not. So it would not be valid.

A test cannot be valid unless it is reliable. In other words, a test that is not reliable cannot be valid. Suppose you and all your friends estimate someone's height. All the estimates are different. Therefore, the "test" is not reliable. Since there is no agreement among all the raters, the "test" cannot be valid, either.

Tests may be valid and reliable for one age level but not another. A test on concepts in this chapter may be reliable and valid for senior high school students. The same test probably would not be reliable or valid if given to elementary school children—even if they had been able to study the chapter.

A number of factors affect the reliability of tests. The major factor is the number of items on the test. Generally, the more items on the test, the more reliable it will be. There is a larger sample of items to measure whatever is being measured. Another factor is the emotional state of the person taking the test. If you are upset when you take a test, does this influence your score? Might you miss some items that you would otherwise have answered correctly? Other factors that influence your test scores include how clearly directions are presented, how answers are to be marked, the type of test, and the physical surroundings, such as the noise level.

There are also other aspects of validity. For example, the purpose of an aptitude test is accurate prediction. The test questions are designed to measure abilities that are broader and more difficult to measure than one specific area of subject matter. These tests are useful in helping people to identify skills and predict success in many specific occupations.

We will now examine a number of different techniques that psychologists use to measure personality. As you read about each form, try to decide whether or not it is a standardized test.

Ratings

Rating refers to assigning a rank or a score to an individual, based on a more-or-less subjective impression of that person. This method is often used in businesses and schools.

Executives may be asked to rate the salespeople in their division on personality traits that relate to their work, such as friendliness and honesty. Managers in industry may rate the people working under them on certain aspects of their personalities. And in many schools, the development of desirable student personalities is recognized as being important. It is much easier to measure ability in math or history than it is to measure personality patterns. Although subjective, teachers sometimes rate their students on selected personality traits. They may do so by using one of the following methods.

The ranking method of rating. There are a number of techniques for rating. One is known as the **ranking method.** In using this technique, the raters assign numbers, beginning with 1, to the persons they are rating. Suppose you are trying to find the most polite person in the class. If you are one of the raters, you would assign a number to each member of the class. Suppose you decide from your knowledge of the behavior of Henry Fisk that Henry is the most polite person in the class. Then you would assign the number 1 to Henry. If you think Maria Jones is the next most polite person in the class, you would assign her the number 2, and so forth.

This technique is easy to use if you write the name of each person on a separate slip. Then you can sort and re-sort the slips until you have them in what you believe to be the correct order. You would arrange them from highest to lowest, according to your judgment. Then combine your ratings with those of the other judges. Each individual's rating on a trait is the average of all the judges' scores on that trait. Such a technique can be used only where the group to be rated is fairly small.

A graphic rating scale. Another rating technique makes use of a **graphic rating scale.** For each trait considered, a line is drawn. The line is divided into a number of sections—usually five or seven. Under each section is written a rating. Possible ratings

POOR   **BELOW**   **AVERAGE**   **GOOD**   **EXCELLENT**
                      AVERAGE

could be Poor, Below Average, Average, Good, and Excellent, as shown at the top of this page. The rater simply puts a check mark in the section above the rating that best describes the person. Suppose you were going to rate a person on leadership. You would put a check mark in the section that most accurately describes the person's ability as a leader.

What dangers are there in rating? It helps to be aware of the following whenever you are called on to rate others on traits of personality.

First, be careful of **overrating.** There is a tendency for people to give overly high ratings to most persons on most traits. In general, the most often used rating should be the one in the middle. But raters tend to judge people slightly above average on many traits.

Second, be careful of the **halo effect.** Psychologists use the term "halo effect" to describe the tendency to rate a person high on all traits because of one trait or a favorable general impression. The term also describes the tendency to rate people low on all traits because they make an unfavorable general impression. For example, it is difficult to rate salespeople on specific personality traits without being influenced by their sales records. A person who has been bringing in large orders is very apt to be rated high on all personality traits. A person who has a poor sales record is very apt to be rated low on all personality traits. Such high and low ratings may be justified. However, if the sales records were to change, the ratings might be quite different.

Such a halo effect can be overcome, in part, by rating all individuals on one trait before going on to the next trait. For example, you could rate all salespeople on initiative, then rate all of them on dependability, and so forth. By concentrating on one trait at a time, you can make more accurate judgments.

Be careful also of a third error, the **stereotype.** We tend to apply to an individual the judgments we have previously formed of the person's racial, national, or social group. For example, suppose we have formed a stereotyped judgment of the Japanese. If we meet a Japanese person, we would assume that the person "runs true to type." If we attempt to rate the individual, we would do so in terms of our prejudices and biases toward all Japanese rather than on the basis of the individual's personal characteristics. But suppose we stop and investigate. We are likely to find that the person does not fit our stereotyped idea of Japanese people. Knowing of the error of the stereotype, a rater can be on guard against it.

There is another aspect of stereotyping to be guarded against in rating—the error of the **pigeonhole.** We should be careful not to categorize—to pigeonhole—people into a certain type. We should not rate individuals as the blond type or the brunette type, as the good type or the bad type. To do so introduces an error in our judgment.

Finally, there is the danger that when we rate another person, we may attribute either our own characteristics, or their opposites, to the person. If we are very thrifty, we rate the person as being either very thrifty or else very wasteful. If we are very neat in dress, we are likely to regard the person as similar to ourselves or very sloppy.

Rating is not a perfect measure of personality. But if the raters are trained in rating and if the technique is carefully developed, it is very useful. The main requirement is that those who do the rating must observe and know the individuals they are rating. Sometimes it is impossible to find enough judges who know the individuals to be rated and who are willing to take the time and effort necessary to rate them. How can psychologists get a measure of personality in such cases? The following method was devised for this situation.

Personality Inventories

The word "inventory" means literally "to find out." A **personality inventory** is designed to find out about various aspects of personality or the general adjustment of individuals to their environment. Inventories are based on a sampling. That is, from all the habits of action and thought that a person can have, as many as 100 to 200 habits may be selected. These represent a cross section of what all of the person's habits are like.

The use of inventories to measure personality stems from studies made during World War I. The hundreds of thousands of men who entered the United States Army in 1917-18 differed greatly in their total personality patterns. Some fit into army life easily.

Others adjusted with some, but not too much, difficulty. Still others found it almost impossible to adjust to the army and the war. It was necessary to find out which men would make good front-line fighters and which ones would not.

A committee of psychologists went to work to devise a method for measuring personality on a large scale. The committee made up a list of 116 questions. For example: "Can you stand pain quietly?" "Can you stand the sight of blood?" All questions were to be answered yes or no. The committee devised a scoring key to measure answers and obtain a score for each individual.

After the war, the list was adapted for civilian use. Schools and businesses took up the inventory method.

How are inventories made up and scored? Inventories were first developed as group measures of personality. More recently, some personality inventories have been developed to give to one individual at a

Text continues on page 138.

We sometimes stereotype people. We assume that everyone in a group has similar characteristics, when actually each person in the group is quite different.

Case Study: Focus on Research

"BEWARE—GENERALITIES AHEAD"

Are you among the millions of Americans who read their horoscopes every day? Do you know people who get a little anxious because their horoscope says that they will have a bad day? In a sense, a horoscope is like a personality inventory. Both of them have similar limitations.

One of the greatest limitations of personality inventories is that they may not provide an accurate assessment of someone's personality. Rather, the statements in an evaluation may be so general that they may apply to everyone. This does not mean that people do not believe in them. On the contrary, because of the universal acceptance of these evaluations, people are more likely to rely on them.

In an experiment he performed with the 39 students in one of his psychology classes, psychologist Bertram Forer demonstrated

Fortune-tellers often claim to have unusual powers that enable them to make predictions. Most, though, speak only in broad generalities that would apply to almost anyone.

our tendency to accept blindly someone else's judgments of us. First Forer gave the students a personality test he called the Diagnostic Interest Blank (DIB), which he constructed specifically for this experiment. The students were asked to check off their responses to questions dealing with hobbies, secret hopes, and so on. Then, based on the answers they received, experimenters worked out personality evaluations for the students.

What the students did not know, however, was that the researchers prepared one general evaluation for the entire class. Instead of receiving an individual assessment of his or her personality, each student—unknown to the student and to the 38 others—was presented with the same assessment, consisting of the following list of 13 items:

1. You have a great need for other people to like you and admire you.

2. You have a tendency to be critical of yourself.

3. You have a great deal of unused capacity which you have not turned to your advantage.

4. While you have some personality weaknesses, you are generally able to compensate for them.

5. Your sexual adjustment has presented problems for you.

6. Disciplined and self-controlled outside, you tend to be worrisome and insecure inside.

7. At times you have serious doubts as to whether you have made the right decision or done the right thing.

8. You prefer a certain amount of change and variety and become dissatisfied when hemmed in by restrictions and limitations.

9. You pride yourself as an independent thinker and do not accept others' statements without satisfactory proof.

10. You have found it unwise to be too frank in revealing yourself to others.

11. At times you are extraverted, affable, sociable, while at other times you are introverted, wary, reserved.

12. Some of your aspirations tend to be pretty unrealistic.

13. Security is one of your major goals in life.

After reading their evaluations, the students were asked to rate the accuracy of these assessments on a scale from 0 (poor) to 5 (perfect). Forer then had them turn in their ratings. With this formality out of the way, the professor next asked for a show of hands. How many thought the personality test had done a good job? Almost all hands went up.

Now was the chance for Forer to make his point. He read the first item and asked who had received a similar inventory statement. All hands went up. Suddenly, heads turned and embarrassed laughter swept the room. The students realized they had been tricked.

The phenomenon Forer was demonstrating has sometimes been called the "Barnum effect." The phrase refers to a quip attributed to showman P. T. Barnum: "There's a sucker born every minute." It shows how readily we accept generalized, universally applicable statements as accurate descriptions of our own personality traits. We also tend to accept these evaluations because of the aura of mystery surrounding them. We believe we are presenting parts of ourselves that only others can interpret. We tend to put our faith in the tester's ability to interpret the true meaning of our answers.

Forer's experiment not only revealed a major pitfall in relying on personality tests. It also showed how our memories work to protect our self-esteem. Three weeks after the test, Forer claimed to have lost the students' ratings of the personality sketches. He asked them to give their judgments again. When Forer compared earlier and later ratings, he found, not surprisingly, that more students "remembered" giving lower ratings than they actually had. Feeling foolish about having been taken in, they reconstructed the past in order to put themselves in a better light.

SOURCE: B. R. Forer, "The Fallacy of Personal Validation: A Classroom Demonstration of Gullibility," *Journal of Abnormal and Social Psychology*, 1949, *44*, 118–123.

Some people cannot get through the day without consulting their horoscopes. Others seek out spiritual readers for advice.

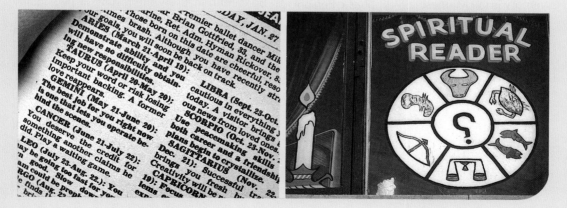

1. I am a good mixer.

2. I usually feel that life is worthwhile.

3. I see things or animals or people around me that others do not see.

4. Everything tastes the same.

5. I am greatly bothered by forgetting where I put things.

6. I frequently ask people for advice.

7. I like to let people know where I stand on things.

These are some sample items from the Minnesota Multiphasic Personality Inventory. Individuals taking this inventory would mark each statement either "True" or "False" on the answer sheet.

a. I daydream a lot.

b. I am afraid that I am losing my mind.

c. Most of the time I am happy.

d. Many people seem to like me.

e. My head frequently hurts.

One problem with the inventory method is that the individual can purposely bias the results of an inventory. People who feel that an answer of "True" is socially unacceptable may answer "False." One way to overcome this problem is to include "lie" questions. If the answers to these questions are not consistent with the large majority of other answers, they indicate that the person taking the test is lying. The examiner then knows that it is best to be suspicious of the scores on other parts of the inventory. The MMPI uses this device.

Another device for detecting people who give answers on the basis of what is socially acceptable is called the forced-choice format. It is used in the Edwards Personal Preference Schedule. In this inventory, the individual has to choose between two statements that are favorable or two statements that are unfavorable. For example, the person may be asked to choose between the following:

a. I sometimes feel that I want to hurt others.

b. I feel inferior to others.

Some cautions in using personality inventories. Even trained psychologists must be careful in using the results of personality inventories. We might assume that an individual who scores high on some aspect, such as conformity, will behave in that way in actual situations. However, a number of studies have shown that this is not always true. College students were given an inventory to measure conformity. Later, they were placed in an experimental situation designed to put them under social pressure to conform. Their behavior showed little relationship to the scores they had made on the inventory.

When considering scores on inventories,

time. Psychologists find individually administered inventories more valuable than group-administered inventories for the study of personality.

An example of a widely used group inventory is the Minnesota Multiphasic Personality Inventory (MMPI). It was originally developed to distinguish between "normal" people and nine separate groups of disturbed patients in a mental hospital. Each of the nine groups showed a particular pattern of responses to the items. One form of the inventory is now used to identify levels of depression.

The MMPI contains about 550 items. Each item is answered as either "True" or "False." The kind of items used on the MMPI include:

remember that they are not like the scores on school tests. They do not represent right or wrong. They merely indicate the trend of the individual's habits of action and thought. Inventories are of value in helping us understand one personality as compared with the personalities of others. But they are not examinations on which there is a passing or failing grade.

Furthermore, inventories are measures of habits. And habits can be changed. We are not born with fixed personalities. Recent research has shown that important changes in habits and attitudes may continue to occur in the adult years of life. Such changes may even mean the difference between a personality that is pleasing and one that is not.

Scores on an inventory are of value only if the individuals have answered the questions frankly and honestly. Even then, especially if they stop to think about their answers very long, individuals may indicate the kind of personality they would like to have. If the inventory is to have meaning, their responses must indicate the kind of personality they have at the time.

There is also the problem that some items on inventories are interpreted in different ways by different people. On one inventory, college students were asked to check items that showed desirable behavior. Later, it was found that some students interpreted desirable to mean what *other* people think is desirable. Other students answered according to what behavior *they* thought would be most desirable.

Another limitation of the inventory approach to measuring personality is that some traits, such as passive and aggressive, only describe behavior. They do not explain it. Human behavior is influenced by many factors. Paying attention to only one trait does not allow psychologists to predict behavior.

For all these reasons, it is best not to use standardized inventory data alone to understand personality. Personality inventories should always be used with other related information about the person. And they should be interpreted by a trained and qualified psychologist.

Interviewing

Sometimes *interviewing* is used as a technique for measuring personality. Many employers and personnel managers believe that they can size up an applicant for a job very quickly through a personal interview. They certainly can learn something about an individual's personality from an interview. However, such a general sizing up may not give a valid impression of the individual's personality.

Why is interviewing not always a valid measure? Earlier we mentioned certain precautions to be taken in rating individuals. We need to take these same precautions when interviewing. The following experiment shows that interviewing is not always a valid way of evaluating personality.

Twelve sales managers were asked to interview 57 applicants for sales positions. These sales managers were accustomed to interviewing people and selecting those whose personalities seemed best suited for selling. Each sales manager interviewed each one of the 57 applicants. Then, without consulting anyone, the sales manager ranked the applicants in order of desirability for sales positions. If the manager believed an applicant to be the best prospect, the applicant received a rank of 1. The applicant judged to be the next best received a rank of 2, and so on down to a rank of 57.

Then the rankings of the sales managers were compared. There were many differences. For example, one applicant had been given the following rankings: 1, 2, 6, 9, 10, 16, 20, 21, 26, 28, 53, 57. One of the sales managers had thought this person the best prospect, and another the worst prospect—on the basis of the interview. Thus, one applicant might be judged very desirable by some sales managers, very undesirable by other sales managers, and intermediate in desirability by still others. As you can see, this way of sizing up people, even by these experienced interviewers, did not give consistent results.

Some interviewers use a standardized list of questions to collect information.

How has interviewing been improved?
The main problem with interviewing was that so much depended on the judgment of the interviewer. Psychologists have found that judgments made after interviews become more valid if they also include other techniques for measuring personality, such as inventories and rating scales.

The interviewer may use a list of questions. In a well-conducted interview, these questions may be answered more frankly and honestly than if they were to be answered in written form. The interviewer can explain questions not fully understood. The person being interviewed can give more complete replies.

Interviewers may also use a rating scale. They can record their estimate of the degree to which the individual being interviewed has certain traits of personality. The rating scale is used during the interview or immedi-

ately following it. Judgments recorded while they are fresh are often better than those based on memory of past impressions.

Another procedure that produces more valid measures is to have several interviewers speak to an individual and then pool their findings. Also, it is helpful to recheck interviews. Rechecking is possible through the use of tape-recording equipment. Tape recordings of interviews can by played back later. Interviewers can correct any wrong first impressions. Or they can note any points they missed during the original interview.

As commonly used (by personnel managers, for example), interviewing is not a scientific attempt to measure personality. Interviewing by scientific methods is another matter. Interviews by well-trained interviewers who use modern techniques may measure personality as well as, or even better than, ratings or inventories.

Behavior Sampling

Behavior sampling is quite different from the three techniques just described. In this method, no one is asked about another person. Nor do people answer questions about themselves. Instead, in **behavior sampling,** actual behavior is measured or recorded. To measure a personality characteristic, the psychologist sets up a sample situation in which the person may display this characteristic. To measure the trait of leadership, the psychologist can create a situation in which the individual has a chance to show an ability to lead. Some indication of how much a person may lie can be determined by counting the lies the person tells in a given number of answers to questions.

How behavior sampling works. Suppose we wanted to measure the characteristic of cheating. We could measure cheating in schoolwork by setting up an experimental situation in which students can cheat if they wish to do so. One method is to have the teacher give a test on some subject. The teacher then collects the papers and makes a record of each person's right and wrong answers. (The papers are scored without marking them in any way.) The next day the teacher returns the papers to the class. The students are asked to score their own papers. They are told that the teacher will collect them and record the marks in the grade book. Perhaps the teacher leaves the room for a few minutes, to give the students a chance to cheat. The student-scored papers are then collected. Any differences between the scores the students set down when marking the papers and the scores recorded earlier are a measure of cheating.

Behavior sampling can be used to help predict how a person will react in a situation similar to the one being tested. One police academy found behavior sampling useful for training police officers. The academy set up situations that represented a police patrol and a missing-person investigation. How the individuals reacted in these two situations was found to predict future success in police work.

Caution is needed in interpreting behavior samplings. Behavior samplings are valuable in the scientific measurement of personality. But they must not be interpreted too broadly. Psychologists strive for samplings that represent a person's behavior— that is, whether the person would behave similarly in a similar situation. But we can't assume that because a trait is shown in one situation, it will necessarily be shown in all situations. Students who cheat in schoolwork may not cheat in athletic contests. However, such traits are usually representative enough of the person that behavior samplings can be of considerable value in studying personality.

Projective Techniques

Projection is the process whereby people attribute elements in their own personalities to other people or objects. It is mainly the undesirable elements of our personalities that we tend to project. For example, the individual who is dishonest tends to project this trait onto the personalities of others. The person might say, "Pat is so dishonest," or, "Everybody is dishonest." Usually people are not aware that they are projecting their own characteristics onto others. People who say that everyone is dishonest don't realize that they are seeing their own dishonesty in others.

Inkblot tests. Place several drops of ink on a sheet of paper. Fold the paper in half. The ink will blot and give an irregular but symmetrical design. What does the design look like to you? Show your inkblot to several friends. Ask them to tell you what they see. You will probably find that different people interpret the inkblot in quite different ways. A person who has had a lot of experience with animals may see some kind of animal. A person who has studied designing may see a basic pattern for wallpaper in the same inkblot. What people see in the inkblot depends to some extent on their own abilities and experiences. What they see is, in reality, a projection of their own thoughts.

A Swiss psychiatrist, Hermann Rorschach, developed an inkblot test that some psychologists find very useful in studying personality. Individuals whose personality patterns are being studied are shown a series of ten standardized blots, one at a time. They are asked to describe the things and ideas that each inkblot suggests to them.

The giving and scoring of this test are fairly standardized. But interpreting the responses is not completely standardized. Two psychologists often disagree on their interpretation of the same record of responses. The lack of agreement among interpreters has caused some psychologists to question

One of the projective techniques that psychologists use to study personality is the standardized inkblot.

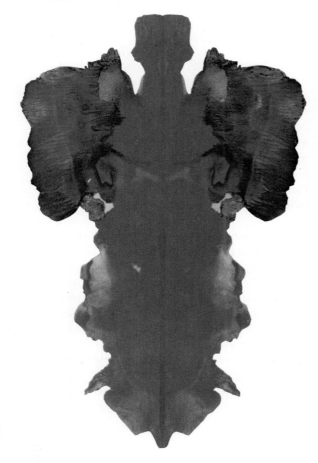

the low validity and reliability of this test for evaluating personality.

One attempt to use the projective technique and at the same time provide an objective comparison of scores is the Holtzman Inkblot Test. It uses 45 inkblots. An unlimited number of responses are allowed on the Rorschach test. On the Holtzman test, the subject is allowed only one per card. And the response is scored more objectively. The score of the individual can be compared directly with the responses of one or more norm groups. For example, the score of a college student can be compared with those of other college students.

Other projective techniques. Some techniques involve the use of pictures and stories. Psychologists may use a series of rather vague pictures involving persons, animals, and objects. They ask their subjects to tell stories suggested by the pictures. Sometimes the psychologist merely begins telling a story without a picture and then asks the subject to complete the story. The themes of these stories and the characters involved are thought to reveal a great deal about the subject's personality. For example, suppose a young boy tells a story in which the hero is so small that he has difficulty in defending himself. Yet he suddenly learns how to fight and goes about knocking down boys twice his size. The psychologist would have reason to believe that the teller of this story feels inferior. In his story, the boy was projecting his feeling of inferiority onto the hero. Also, he was expressing his own desire to be superior.

Sometimes children are given toys to play with as they wish. While they are playing, a psychologist observes indications of their personality. For example, suppose a child builds a house with a fence around it. The child says, "This is my house, and I'm building a high fence around it so other kids can't come in and bother me." The psychologist will have reason to think that the child has some fear of other children and wants to be protected.

Another projective technique has individuals draw pictures and tell the stories behind

One projective technique has subjects create a story about pictures presented to them. What story can you make up about this picture? Who are the people? What are they doing?

the pictures. In other cases, the individual is given a background picture, such as a living room, a forest, an attic, a schoolroom, or a street scene. These pictures contain no people. The individual is given cutout figures of men, women, and children, of some objects, of animals, and so on. The person is then asked to place these figures on the background pictures and tell the stories of the pictures. Finger painting has also been used as a projective technique. Or the first part of sentences may be given, and the individual is asked to complete the sentences. Whatever the specific technique, all projective techniques give subjects a great deal of freedom in expressing themselves.

What cautions must be considered in using and interpreting projective tests? Of all the tests given by trained psychologists, projective tests are perhaps the most difficult to administer, score, and interpret. For example, it usually takes at least one year of graduate school training to qualify for administering and interpreting the Rorschach test.

Another problem is that sometimes projective tests are scored and interpreted in different ways by different psychologists. As yet, there is no universal agreement about the interpretation of specific responses on some projective tests.

Achievement and Aptitude Tests

By now you have probably had experience in taking achievement tests. And you may also have taken an aptitude test. How do they differ?

What sort of items would you put on a test so that you could find out if a person is likely to be a good attorney?

Achievement tests. An *achievement test* measures how much knowledge a person can report in a particular subject matter area. For example, an achievement test in psychology would measure how much you have learned about psychology—after having studied the subject. Some sample items might include the following (the asterisk indicates the correct answer):

1. Psychology is defined as "the study of the _____ of living organisms."
   a. instincts
   * **b.** behavior
   c. habits
   d. reflexes

2. Reliability of a test means that the test:
   a. measures what it is supposed to measure.
   b. is expensive.
   * **c.** gives consistent results.
   d. adequately covers the area it is supposed to cover.

3. The individual who started psychoanalysis is:
   a. Skinner
   b. Horney
   c. Jung
   * **d.** Freud

Achievement tests cover such school subjects as history, math, chemistry, physics, biology, psychology, sociology, Spanish, French, and economics. One purpose of achievement tests in schools is to determine the strong and weak areas of students. Achievement tests can spot a student's strong areas, which might be used for advanced placement. By identifying weak areas, teachers can provide additional help where it is most needed.

Aptitude tests. Psychologists have developed tests, known as *aptitude tests,* that help individuals judge if they are likely to succeed at a particular activity or skill. Aptitude tests do not provide a magic score that will tell people exactly what kind of work they should do. But these tests often give information that can help them arrive at such a decision.

A person's score on an aptitude test can be compared with the scores of others who have taken the same test and have gone on to training or work experience in the given field. For example, people applying for admission to a hospital school of nursing can take a nursing aptitude test. Their scores can be compared with the scores of others who have taken the test and then successfully completed the required years of training. In one study of student nurses, it was found that all those who made a score of 130 or above on a nursing test graduated in the upper two-thirds of their class. No one with a score below 80 graduated in the upper two-thirds of the class. This particular aptitude test was a very good indicator of the likelihood of succeeding in nurses' training.

The most frequently used test for admission to the study of veterinary medicine is the Veterinary Aptitude Test. The results of this test are used to help evaluate students who plan to study veterinary medicine. The test consists of five different areas: Reading Comprehension, Quantitative Ability, Biology, Chemistry, and Study-Reading. In Reading Comprehension, applicants are given a paragraph of reading material. They are tested on how well they can interpret the information in the paragraph. Quantitative Ability is measured by questions that involve math and algebra. The Biology and Chemistry sections test a person's abilities and knowledge in these subjects. And the Study-Reading section involves reading some material within a given time limit. Then the material is removed, and the person must answer questions from memory.

The person taking a mechanical aptitude test may be asked to do some matching. In one column there may be pictures of a hammer, a wrench, and a saw. In a second column are pictures of a board, a nail, and a nut. The person is expected to match the hammer with the nail, the wrench with the nut, and the saw with the board. A mechanical aptitude test may also contain a series of pictures of pulleys with belts connecting them. The person has to indicate the direction of the pulleys and the speed of the second pulley compared to the first pulley. Some mechanical aptitude tests use actual tools.

Distinguishing between achievement tests and aptitude tests. The difference between the two types of tests may seem very clear at first. But the distinction is not always clear-cut. Achievement tests imply a gathering of knowledge about some subject. Aptitude tests suggest an innate ability in some area. However, some aptitude tests do rely on past knowledge. For example, consider the Scholastic Aptitude Test (SAT). It is divided into two parts: Verbal and Quantitative. The SAT is called an aptitude test. Yet the questions rely a great deal on past knowledge in verbal areas and mathematics. So this test actually measures, to some degree, previous knowledge in these areas. But the test is designed to predict success of high school seniors in college. For this reason it falls into the category of an aptitude test.

Another factor is involved in distinguishing between achievement and aptitude tests. The more you know about a subject, the more difficult it becomes to make up an aptitude test for you in that area. And the easier it becomes to make up an achievement test. For example, it would be very difficult to give an aptitude test in math to people who have a Ph.D. in mathematics. This is because the amount of math yet to be learned is not so large. On the other hand, it would be easier to make up an achievement test in math for those people. There would be a great deal of past knowledge in mathematics from which to select items. Thus, the higher up the "educational ladder" people go, the more difficult it becomes to make up a test for them that distinguishes between aptitude and achievement.

Vocational Interest Inventories

There is a definite relationship between success in a given kind of work and interests that are commonly associated with that type of work. **Vocational interest inventories** help individuals determine if their interests are similar to the interests of people in specific occupations. While personality inventories measure an individual's habits of thought and action, vocational interest inventories are designed to indicate the person's work interests.

One widely used interest inventory is the Kuder Preference Record — Vocational. It requires about 45 minutes to take. Individuals indicate on each item which one of three activities they like most and which one they like least. For example, they might be asked which of the following three activities they like most and which they like least:

a. collecting autographs
b. collecting coins
c. collecting butterflies

The results can be scored to indicate the strength of an individual's interests in each of ten vocational areas: outdoor work, mechanical work, computation, science, persuasion, art, literary work, music, social service, and clerical work. Individuals can then determine how their interests compare with the interests of others in a certain area or areas.

Another widely used instrument to measure interests is the Strong-Campbell Interest Inventory. For this test, the patterns of scores of individuals in specific occupations were analyzed. Then their interests were put together with their occupational groups. The result is that individuals who answer items on the Strong-Campbell Interest Inventory are comparing their interests with the interests of people who have been successful in particular occupational groups. For example, a person giving answers similar to those given by psychologists would have interests that are similar to those of successful psychologists. However, a lack of similar interests is not a guarantee that a person would be unhappy in a particular vocation. Nor does great interest guarantee that a person would be successful in that field. Success and happiness in a specific occupation depend on many other factors as well.

The Strong-Campbell Interest Inventory has one possible disadvantage for society. It tends to encourage individuals who are similar to those already in an occupation to enter that occupational group. This means that people with other characteristics are less likely to enter that occupation. Suppose an occupation has members who are aggressive and outgoing. The Strong-Campbell Interest Inventory tends to select similar individuals, people who are aggressive and outgoing. It does not add members to the occupational group who do not have these characteristics. Thus it may limit the variety of personality traits in that group.

Do your interests change? As a rule, things liked best by people when they are young will be liked more and more with increasing age. And those things disliked by individuals when they are young tend to be disliked more and more as they grow older.

However, new interests may develop through experience. After learning about a particular subject or occupation, for example, you may find that you have become very interested in it.

How accurate are vocational interest inventories? Sometimes people take a vocational interest inventory and are dissatisfied with the results. They say that the inventory does not agree with what they think they would like to do. Actually, interest inventory scores do not always relate closely to short-term interests and achievement. But inventory scores do tend to be closely related when interests and achievement are measured over a considerable period of time. In any case, scores on an interest inventory are arrived at by scientific and standardized procedures, as opposed to personal opinions about interests. And in the long run they are usually more accurate.

Can a person purposely swing the results of an interest inventory toward or away from specific areas? Actually, you can bias the results of some inventories. Suppose you want to score high in social service to prove that you are interested in other human beings and that you should enter this occupation. You can decide to give answers that don't truly reflect your interests. This, however, doesn't allow you to make the best use of the inventory. The inventory tries to collect as much valid information as possible about a person's interests. Giving false information only limits the usefulness of the results for the individual.

A new approach in measuring personality. In the past, most measures of personality emphasized studying the differences among individuals. An individual's score on a standardized test, for example, is interpreted by comparing it to the scores of other people.

Perhaps you enjoy working in the garden, growing plants. But will this interest continue into your adult life? Actually, the majority of your present interests usually do stay with you throughout your life.

A new approach focuses on what is called person-centered psychology. It involves studying individuals in relation to their own lives, such as the specific environment in which they live. For example, individuals might be asked to select the particular conditions of the situation to be measured. This is because in everyday life we often select the conditions and situations to which we subject ourselves. To a large degree we choose our friends, what courses we will take in school, what we spend our money for, with whom we will spend our time, and the foods we will eat.

In one experiment, college students were asked to rate how consistent they were in two behaviors—friendliness and conscientiousness. In general, those students who rated themselves as consistent in these two behaviors were consistent. Those who identified themselves as varying and inconsistent did vary more. Thus the subjects were personally asked about their own behavior. And they were generally correct. These results seem to indicate that people may know and understand more about their own behavior than many psychologists have been assuming.

MEASURING
PERSONALITY

Summary

Psychologists often use standardized tests to measure behavior. Two important characteristics of standardized tests are reliability and validity. Reliability refers to the degree of consistency from one performance to the next, or between parts of a test. Validity means that a test measures what it is supposed to measure. Tests can be reliable without being valid, but they cannot be valid unless they are reliable.

Rating is another method of measuring behavior. The ranking method and a graphic rating scale are two techniques for rating. There are, however, certain dangers in rating. These include the tendency to overrate, the halo effect, the stereotype, the pigeonhole, and the tendency to judge another person by our own characteristics.

Personality inventories are used to find out about various aspects of personality or the general adjustment of individuals to their environment. Inventories can measure personality on a large scale, but they have certain shortcomings. People completing the inventory can purposely bias results. They also may behave differently in actual situations or may misinterpret questions. Moreover, inventories by themselves do not always enable psychologists to predict behavior accurately. However, they are helpful when used along with other techniques.

Interviews are sometimes used to measure personality. Because interviews depend mostly on the judgment of the interviewer, various steps have been taken to increase their validity.

In behavior sampling, actual behavior is measured or recorded. This technique is used to help predict behavior. Researchers must be careful, though, about generalizing from the results.

Researchers sometimes use projective techniques to measure personality. Inkblot tests and tests involving pictures and stories are some of the techniques they use. Of all the tests given by psychologists, projective tests are perhaps the most difficult to administer, score, and interpret.

Achievement tests and aptitude tests are used to measure acquired knowledge and potential ability in various subject areas. These two tests may overlap in several respects. Vocational interest inventories are used to indicate a person's work interests. These tests tend to be valid when used over a considerable period of time.

In this excerpt from *Systems and Theories in Psychology,* psychologists Melvin Marx and William Hillix describe somatotyping, a method of assessing personality. William Sheldon developed this method.

William H. Sheldon . . . [was] a trained physician, as his theoretical efforts to relate behavioral and body components might indicate. . . .

Sheldon's writing has been characterized by concern for the identification of, and relationships between, structural [body types] and temperamental factors, particularly as applied to the problem of delinquency. . . .

Sheldon's system is a modern version of statements running back at least as far as Hippocrates, who believed that there were associations between body fluids and temperaments. . . . [This] has probably also contributed to [Sheldon's] difficulty in getting a completely open-minded hearing from American psychologists. Hippocrates and his [ill-natured] temperaments are all too easy to laugh at, and some of this attitude toward humors has generalized to Sheldon. . . .

An important difference exists between [Sheldon's] work and earlier theorizing. . . . Sheldon has recognized that any given individual is marked by some *degree* of each type and thus is in this sense always a blend of types rather than a pure type. . . .

The obtained data fall into three categories of body types: endomorphy, mesomorphy, and ectomorphy. . . .

The endomorph tends to be soft, fleshy, and round; the mesomorph is square, tough, muscular, dense, and athletic; the ectomorph is tall, thin, fragile, and small-boned. . . .

Three components of temperament correspond, according to Sheldon, to the three components of the physique: visceratonia, somatotonia, and cerebrotonia. The visceratonic individual loves comfort, food, and affection, and is good-natured. The somatotonic person is active, vigorous, and aggressive. The cerebrotonic individual is a bookish, sensitive, shy individual who withdraws from social contacts.

If we assume that there are such identifiable components of [body types] and of personality, are the two related or not? Sheldon . . . found a remarkably high correlation between the components that one would expect to find associated: endomorphy-visceratonia; mesomorphy-somatotonia; and ectomorphy-cerebrotonia. . . . However, other experimenters generally find that the correlations are lower than those obtained by Sheldon. . . .

Sheldon has also been attacked on the grounds that he assumes that genetic, strictly biological factors account for the observed correlations. If Sheldon really maintained that these direct biological influences were *the* reason for the correlations, he would be open to attack. He does not; he recognizes, as do his detractors, that different cultural expectations or differential rewards related to different body builds might account for the observed personality differences. . . .

A major asset of Sheldon's theory is that it has kept public the fact that there is some type of relationship between physique and temperament; at the present time, however, we cannot ascertain its direction. Does the physique direct the temperament, or does the temperament determine the physique; or, more logically, is it a two-way process?

Source Review

1. How does Sheldon's view of personality differ from earlier theories?

2. What major question about Sheldon's theory remains today?

CHAPTER 7

REVIEWING TERMS

standardized test
norm group
reliability
validity
rating
ranking method
graphic rating scale

overrating
halo effect
stereotype
pigeonhole
personality inventory
interviewing
behavior sampling

projection
achievement test
aptitude test
vocational interest
    inventory

CHECKING FACTS

1. What is a standardized test? What is the major advantage of such a test?

2. How are reliability and validity related?

3. How is the ranking method used to measure personality? How is the graphic rating scale used?

4. Explain five of the dangers involved in rating people.

5. How are personality inventories made up and scored?

6. What are some cautions that must be taken in using the results of personality inventories?

7. Why is interviewing not always a valid measure of personality? In what ways has interviewing been improved?

8. What is the major shortcoming of behavior sampling?

9. How are inkblot tests used to measure personality? Are they always valid? Explain.

10. Describe some of the other projective techniques used by psychologists. What cautions must be taken when using these techniques?

11. What is the difference between an achievement test and an aptitude test? How do they overlap?

12. What is the purpose of vocational interest inventories? How accurate are they?

APPLYING YOUR KNOWLEDGE

1. In class, select a specific trait, such as shyness. List various behaviors that describe or illustrate that particular trait. Then compare your list to the behavior lists of other students. Explain why personality inventories need to be standardized.

2. One night this week watch your usual television programs. Only this time pay attention to how the *halo effect, stereotyping,* and *pigeonholing* are used to shape the personalities of the major characters. Use your observations as the basis for a class discussion.

3. Divide the class into four groups. Have each group create a personality inventory that can be used to select one of the following: (a) the best Santa Claus for a department store, (b) the next President of the United States, (c) an Olympic athlete, and (d) an astronaut. Fill out each other's questionnaires and return them to the appropriate groups. Each group can then meet to analyze the responses and select the person best qualified to fill each position. Discuss the various aspects of personality that were measured in each inventory and how each "winner" was chosen.

4. Create ten inkblots of your own by placing several drops of ink on a sheet of paper and folding the paper in half.

When you open it, a symmetrical shape will appear. Look at each inkblot and write down the first thing that comes to mind. Do you think your responses reveal anything about your personality? Your teacher might photocopy a few of these inkblots and distribute them to the entire class. How do interpretations differ among students?

5. Make up a list of about ten questions that you believe would measure some aptitude, such as for music, art, science, or foreign languages. Consult several people who have the ability related to your items. Ask them if they think that your items accurately measure what they are supposed to measure.

THINKING CRITICALLY ABOUT PSYCHOLOGY

1. **Interpreting Ideas** Why would it be an advantage to compare your scores on tests to your previous scores, rather than comparing your scores only to those of other people?

2. **Supporting an Opinion** Suppose a psychologist asked your permission to measure your personality and indicated that he or she would use only one measuring instrument. Which one would you prefer—an inkblot test, a personality inventory, an interview, a rating scale, or a behavior sampling? Give some reasons for your answer. (Actually, a psychologist would not be willing to evaluate your personality on the basis of just one such measuring instrument.)

3. **Identifying Ideas** What are some of the conditions that could affect your scores on a test? How would they affect scores?

4. **Forming an Opinion** Suppose a psychologist gave you some vocational aptitude tests and also some vocational interest tests. In which set of scores would you place the greater confidence? Why?

5. **Understanding Ideas** Sometimes two tests that are supposed to be measuring the same things result in quite different scores for the same person. What are some reasons that could cause this?

6. **Applying Ideas** Standardized tests have been widely used in many areas of life. Suppose all of them had perfect validity and reliability. How might you use such tests to improve your life?

7. **Classifying Ideas** If you were interviewing someone, or rating that person according to some scale, what types of errors should you guard against? How would you go about avoiding these errors?

8. **Summarizing Ideas** On interest and personality tests, it is sometimes easy to answer some questions dishonestly. Why do you think people would knowingly bias their answers?

DEVELOPING SKILLS IN PSYCHOLOGY

Classifying Information

Classification is the process by which we examine a set of apparently different elements and then group them into classes on the basis of some sort of commonality. For example, in the last chapter, theories of personality were grouped into four classes—psychoanalytic, social psychoanalytic, behavioristic, and humanistic. This is not the only classification system that can be used with these theories. Some experts on personality like to classify all the theories into three types—clinical, humanistic, and behavioristic. Different scientists classify the same sets of information in different ways to highlight different common qualities or characteristics that they see as important.

To gain some experience in classifying, go through this chapter and try classifying as many tests as possible in two ways:

1. a group designed to yield a numerical score and a group designed to yield a more descriptive picture of personality functioning;

2. a group of measures that subjects can complete and even score themselves and a group that requires the presence of an examiner and/or scorer.

READING FURTHER ABOUT PSYCHOLOGY

American Psychological Association, *American Psychologist,* "Testing: Concepts, Policy, Practice, and Research," Vol. 36, 1981. The entire issue of this journal is devoted to psychological testing.

Anastasi, Anne, *Psychological Testing,* Fifth Edition, Macmillan, New York, 1982. One of the great names in the psychological testing field looks at many different psychological measurements.

Buros, Oscar K., editor, *The Ninth Mental Measurements Yearbook,* Second Edition, Gryphon Press, Highland Park, N.J., 1985. The complete reference for all psychological tests published. Includes descriptions and critical reviews of each measure.

Cronbach, Lee J., *Essentials of Psychological Testing,* Fourth Edition, Harper & Row, New York, 1984. A general review of individual differences and psychological testing. A considerable amount of the material is devoted exclusively to personality assessment.

Eysenck, Hans, and Wilson, Glenn, *Know Your Own Personality,* Penguin, New York, 1976. A guide to help readers see themselves as others do, in an objective light. Actual tests and questionnaires are given with explanations on how to score and interpret them.

Jackson, Douglas N., and Messick, Samuel, *Problems in Human Assessment,* Krieger, New York, 1978. A sophisticated and comprehensive review of historical information on human assessment. Provides an in-depth understanding of psychological measurement and human assessment.

Levin, Meyer, *Compulsion,* Arbor House, New York, 1984. A novel about the Leopold-Loeb murder trial, one of the first trials in which psychological test data were used as part of the defense.

Lundberg, Norman D., *Personality Assessment,* Prentice-Hall, Englewood Cliffs, N.J., 1977. An overview of the different methods used in personality assessment. Discusses interviewing and observing, behavioral techniques, and assessment of cognitive abilities.

Semeomoff, Boris, *Projective Techniques,* John Wiley & Sons, New York, 1976. An explanation of projective techniques used to measure personality. Provides understandable definitions of measurement terms.

Tyler, Leona E., *Individual Differences: Abilities and Motivational Directions,* Prentice-Hall, Englewood Cliffs, N.J., 1974. A simple, straightforward account of what psychologists have learned about individual differences and how to assess them.

Zucker, Robert A., Aronoff, Joel, and Rabin, A. I., *Personality and the Prediction of Behavior,* Academic Press, Orlando, Fla., 1984. A sophisticated analysis of the problems involved in predicting behavior from personality.

Chapter 8

MEASURING INTELLECTUAL ABILITY

Chapter Focus

This chapter presents:
- **the concept of intelligence**
- **the characteristics of individual and group intelligence tests**
- **the meaning of IQ**
- **a discussion of mental retardation and superior intelligence**

How long must tripe be cooked before it is ready to be eaten? Where would you find lapsang souchong? What is the proper way to prepare plantains? What are bok choy and lychees?

No doubt many of you are unable to answer all these questions. This does not mean that you are not intelligent. Rather, you may have grown up in a culture that did not contain these articles.

Intelligence is a difficult concept to measure. What is considered intelligence in one culture may not be considered so in another. For example, to a Pygmy the ability to hunt might be the most prized sign of intelligence. In many other cultures, hunting is less important and therefore a less often used measure.

Moreover, the way one person within a culture defines intelligence may differ from another person's definition within the same culture. For example, an educator may view intelligence as the ability of a person to learn. A biologist may focus on the ability of an organism to adapt to the environment. A computer operator may stress the ability to process information.

In this chapter we will discuss the concept of intelligence. We also will explore various ways in which intelligence can be measured.

The Nature of Intelligence

We can see that there are many definitions of intelligence. However, most of them have certain common elements. Most include such aspects as the ability to learn, to understand and deal with people and things, and to adapt to the environment. We might define **intelligence,** then, as the ability of an organism to adapt to the new as well as the old situations in the environment. Individuals are intelligent to the extent that they can adjust to situations quickly and successfully. They adjust on the basis of their past learning and their present grasp of the problems they find. They use their present knowledge and past experience to come up with new solutions.

How many factors make up intelligence? Some psychologists have broken down intelligence into a number of factors.

154

One psychologist, L. L. Thurstone, has classified the ways of being intelligent into seven main factors. He identified the following seven primary abilities:

1. Space factor — the ability to visualize flat figures and objects in three dimensions, and to see the relationships of forms.

2. Number factor — the ability to do numerical tasks and arithmetic problems.

3. Verbal comprehension factor — the ability to understand words and to interpret verbal passages.

4. Verbal fluency factor — the ability to express yourself orally or in writing, to think of appropriate words rapidly.

5. Memory factor — the ability to recall learned materials, to remember facts of all kinds with ease.

6. Reasoning factor — the ability to figure out a general rule on the basis of presented data.

7. Perceptual factor — the ability to grasp visual details and determine similarities and differences between pictures.

Originally, some psychologists thought that these seven primary factors were independent of one another. It seemed that each factor was a separate, basic element of intelligence. However, it is now thought that a general intellectual ability contributes to performance on subtests.

A second major theory that separates intelligence into factors was developed by the psychologist J. P. Guilford. Guilford's model of intelligence consists of 120 separate factors. A person can vary in ability for each factor, having high intellectual ability for some and low ability for others.

Guilford has broadened the concept of intelligence by including creative and imaginative thinking in his model. In this type of thinking, the individual is to give the widest possible range of answers. For example, one question might be, "What uses can you think of for a straight pin?" An answer might include, "To hold two items together, to bend

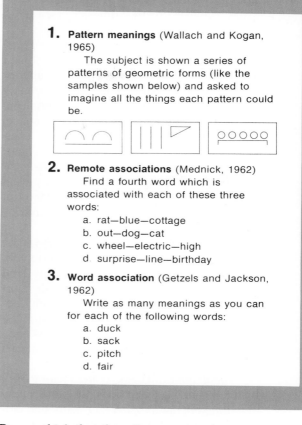

1. Pattern meanings (Wallach and Kogan, 1965)

The subject is shown a series of patterns of geometric forms (like the samples shown below) and asked to imagine all the things each pattern could be.

2. Remote associations (Mednick, 1962)

Find a fourth word which is associated with each of these three words:
a. rat—blue—cottage
b. out—dog—cat
c. wheel—electric—high
d. surprise—line—birthday

3. Word association (Getzels and Jackson, 1962)

Write as many meanings as you can for each of the following words:
a. duck
b. sack
c. pitch
d. fair

Do you think that these items are good measures of creativity? What other items might you include in a test of creative thinking?

it and use as a fish hook, to clean in small cracks," and so on. By designing tests for this kind of thinking, Guilford has increased our understanding of the range of intellectual abilities.

How can we apply factor theories of intelligence? Some people have always assumed that a child who is bright in some ways must be bright in all ways. Or they've assumed that a child who is slow in one area will be slow in all areas. Actually, a child may be high in one factor of intelligence, yet low in another. For example, some children can do well in arts and crafts but have great difficulty in other subjects because they can't read efficiently. Eventually, teachers may be able to fit their methods of teaching to each child's ability in the different factors of intelligence.

Knowledge of factors of intelligence may be valuable to young people in selecting a vocation. For example, students of superior ability in the verbal factors would probably do well to consider writing or journalism. Students superior in the visualizing (space) and reasoning factors might consider engineering or work in the physical sciences. However, in our present state of knowledge there are no tests that can tell a young person exactly what vocation to choose. Many of the factors involved cannot be measured by present tests.

Another advantage in recognizing the various factors in intelligence has to do with personality development. Some children may fail in schoolwork, become discouraged, and develop feelings of inferiority because they are forced to try to succeed in the wrong area. Instead, they can be given a chance to excel in the area of their greatest ability.

The major drawback to any factor theory of intelligence is that it does not explain how the different factors interact with one another. There is also the possibility that a general factor exists—a general intellectual ability. Perhaps the best position for those involved in education is to assume that possibly every intellectual factor can be developed by learning.

Individual Tests of Intelligence

Measurement is a very important part of scientific study. Psychologists have spent many years devising tests to measure intelligence.

How did intelligence tests originate? There were a number of attempts to develop measures of general intelligence before a really workable test was devised. Intelligence tests in the form used today were first developed in 1905 by Alfred Binet, a French psy-

Alfred Binet (above) decided that abilities should be measured by tasks that require reasoning and problem solving.

chologist. Faced with the task of identifying those children who could not benefit from regular schooling, Binet and his assistant, psychologist Theodore Simon, developed their test. This test consisted of 30 tasks to be performed by children. These were simple tasks that the children would know from their everyday experiences without formal teaching.

Binet and Simon made several important revisions of this test. In them they arranged the tasks in groups from age three to adulthood. But first they had to select the tasks to be assigned to each age group. To do this, they tested a large number of children on all tasks on their list. If at least half of the children at a given age passed a task, the task was considered to be correctly placed for that age. For example, they found that about

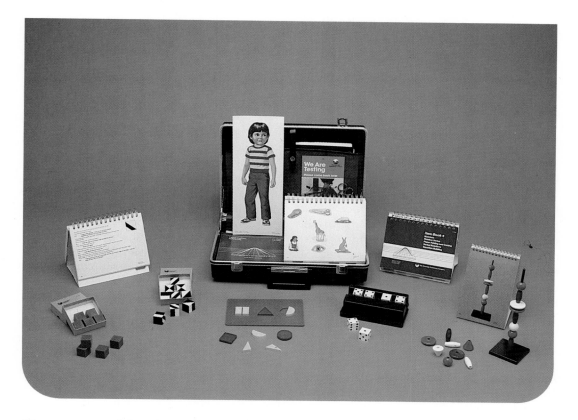

These are some of the test materials for giving the Stanford-Binet Intelligence Scale to children. These materials are helpful when testing young children who have not yet developed many language skills.

one-half of all five-year-olds could count four coins. Most four-year-olds could not do so. And the task was too easy for most children six years of age. Therefore, they concluded that the task was suitable for testing five-year-olds.

Some individual intelligence tests for Americans. American psychologists soon became very interested in the work of Binet. They began using the Binet-Simon tests with American children. These tests were translated from French into English and adjusted to fit the conditions of American life.

One American psychologist who became involved in the problem of measuring intelligence was Lewis M. Terman of Stanford University. In 1916 he published the Stanford-Binet Intelligence Test. This test con-

sisted of 90 items arranged by years. It covered a range from three years of age to superior-adult ability. The test has been used a great deal in schools and psychological clinics in America. Revisions of it are known as the Revised Stanford-Binet. It now covers a range starting at two years of age.

The type of items found on the Revised Stanford-Binet might be like the following:

a. A series of numbers to repeat, such as 9 - 1 - 6 - 3 - 2. (auditory memory)

b. A picture of a car, desk, chair, or coin to identify. (picture vocabulary)

c. A story told aloud, which involves figuring out why it is "silly." For instance, "The police officer rode the fire truck to put out the criminal." (verbal reasoning)

d. Problems in math to work out, such as: 3 + 3 + 6 divided by 4 = ? (mathematical ability)

e. A drawing to look at for five seconds and then draw from memory. (visual memory)

Three other individual tests of intelligence are widely used in the United States. They are the Wechsler Preschool and Primary Scale of Intelligence (WPPSI), the Wechsler Intelligence Scale for Children—Revised (WISC-R), and the Wechsler Adult Intelligence Scale—Revised (WAIS-R). All are composed of two parts. There is one section on verbal activity and one on performance. A measure of intellectual ability is obtained for each part separately. The total score is then based on a combined score of the two parts. The WPPSI is designed to measure the intelligence of individuals from four to six and a half years of age. The WISC-R is used with individuals from six and a half to sixteen and a half years of age. And the WAIS-R measures individuals who are sixteen years of age and older.

On the Revised Stanford-Binet, items measuring different factors (such as verbal and numerical ability) are mixed together within any single age grouping. On the Wechsler tests, all similar items are under one heading. They are arranged in an order starting with easy questions and going to very difficult ones. For example, on one part of the WAIS-R, people are asked to repeat a series of numbers. If they correctly repeat a series, they are given the next longest series. This continues until they miss two series of the same length in a row. Examples might be:

a. 1 - 9 - 2
6 - 4 - 7

b. 8 - 5 - 3 - 9
1 - 6 - 4 - 7

c. 3 - 5 - 1 - 2 - 9
2 - 6 - 9 - 5 - 8

Items on the WAIS-R that estimate mathematical ability might be like these:

a. How much is 5¢ plus 33¢?

b. What is the square root of 49?

c. 10 is what percent of 50?

Culture-fair tests of intelligence. Sometimes psychologists want to measure the intelligence of someone who has a different cultural background. Or someone who doesn't speak the English language. Or an infant who is too young to know the language. Performance tests, sometimes known as nonverbal tests, are also designed to be given to these people. One type of performance test involves picture completion. In the picture-completion test, certain details have been left out. The person must select the parts that will complete the picture.

Another type of performance test measures auditory memory. Testing auditory memory is especially useful for measuring individuals who do not speak English. It requires little or no verbal instruction by the person giving it. For example, the examiner can tap on a desk three times with a pencil as the subject listens and watches. Then the examiner hands the pencil to the subject. The subject repeats the same number of taps. Then the examiner repeats the tap but lengthens the number of digits presented. For example, the examiner may tap three times, pause, then tap two more times (3 - 2).

It should be noted, however, that these tests measure only nonverbal aspects of intelligence. Because of their limitations, these tests are not used as sole measures of intellectual ability. Rather, they are used together with various other tests.

Group Tests of Intelligence

All the measuring devices mentioned so far have been individual tests. The examiner gives the test to one individual at a time. This presents certain limitations on the number of people who can be tested.

These are army recruits taking an intelligence test during World War I. Group IQ tests are routinely used today in schools, employment offices, and the military.

During World War I, the army was faced with the problem of testing the intelligence of many thousands of men. In the rush of war, there was not enough time to give individual tests to all the men. A group of psychologists was called together to develop group tests of intelligence. In all, 1,726,966 enlisted men and officers were tested during World War I. The foundation had been laid. Work in group intelligence testing has continued ever since.

Some group tests of intelligence. One of the most frequently used group intelligence tests is the California Test of Mental Maturity (CTMM). The CTMM is divided into a language section and a nonlanguage section. The language section consists of subtests of number problems, verbal comprehension, and delayed recall. The nonlanguage section includes such subtests as Opposites and Similarities. The Opposites subtest presents an object, such as a new article of clothing. It then asks individuals to find something in a group of pictures that is the opposite of the new clothing—in this case, an old article of clothing. The Similarities subtest presents an object and asks individuals to pick out an ob-

ject that is similar to it from a group of pictures.

Another widely used group intelligence test, especially in schools, is the Otis-Lennon Mental Ability Test. There are no subtests on the Otis-Lennon test. Items that measure different factors associated with intelligence are mixed together. The Otis-Lennon emphasizes verbal aspects of intelligence. But there are items that measure other factors, such as numerical ability. Some examples of the types of items on the Otis-Lennon test are: (The asterisks indicate the correct answers.)

1. If you were walking north, turned left, and then turned left again, you would be headed:
   (a) north   (b) east   *(c) south   (d) west

2. Jim is taller than Bob. Jane is shorter than Bob. Susie is shorter than Jane. The shortest person is:
   (a) Jim   (b) Bob   *(c) Susie   (d) Jane

3. If you have $1.10 and buy a dozen pencils at 3 for 25¢, how much would you have left?
   (a) $1.00   *(b) 10¢   (c) 25¢   (d) 75¢

MEASURING INTELLECTUAL ABILITY

4. What is the last digit in the series:
  1   5   2   4?
  *(a) 3   (b) 2   (c) 1   (d) none of these

The use of group intelligence tests in school. Group intelligence tests for school use have certain advantages over individual intelligence tests. There are not enough trained psychologists available to give each child an individual test. Also, the cost per student would be too high for most schools. Group intelligence tests can be given and scored by administrators and teachers who are already salaried employees of the school system. A large number of children can be tested at one time. And their papers can be scored easily, often by a machine.

A drawback of the group test is that it may not give as valid a measure of a child's intellectual ability as individual intelligence tests. Children may be emotionally upset or not feeling well when the test is given. They may not understand the directions. Or they may not be motivated to do their best. In some cases, children have achieved high scores because they have managed to copy from the papers of other children! The trained psychologist giving an individual test can help avoid such conditions.

Thus, from the practical point of view of the school, group intelligence tests have many advantages. From the point of view of the individual child who needs guidance and assistance, these tests have some disadvantages.

No psychologist claims that any test, whether an individual or group test, is a perfect measure of general intelligence or of any factor in intelligence. But tests are accurate enough to give a numerical score that is a close estimate of a child's academic ability. Such tests, along with other information, enable a teacher, counselor, or psychologist to help a student in school.

These are three items from a group intelligence test for elementary schoolchildren in grades one through three. In example No. 1, the children are told to mark the answer space under the one item that is different in some way from the other three. In No. 2, they are instructed to mark the space under the square that has a colored circle inside it and a white star above it. In No. 3, they are to answer: the bird nest is to the bird as the dog house is to what?

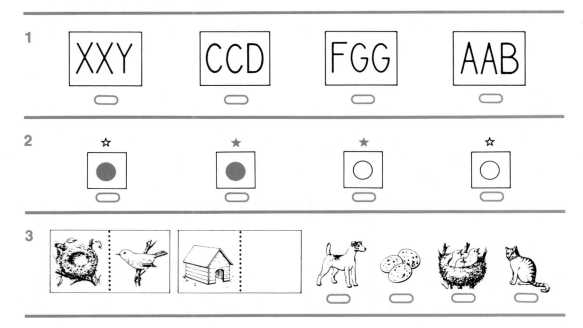

Schools can use group tests to help judge if a child is ready to start school. This is one of the most valid uses of such tests.

The Intelligence Quotient (IQ)

One mathematical measure of intelligence is the intelligence quotient, or IQ. An *intelligence quotient* is the ratio between a person's mental age and that person's chronological age. An individual's *mental age* is an estimate of a person's level of mental functioning, as indicated by scores on a standardized test of intelligence. It is determined by what questions the individual answers correctly on an intelligence test. A certain number of months of mental age are given for correct answers. If an individual has a mental age of ten years, it means that he or she is functioning as well as the average person who is ten years of age.

A person's *chronological age* is the number of years, months, and days since the person was born. By comparing mental age with chronological age, it is possible to de-termine a person's IQ by the following formula:

$$IQ = \frac{\text{Mental Age (MA)}}{\text{Chronological Age (CA)}} \times 100$$

Mental age shows the present level of intellectual functioning. It does not indicate whether a person has high, average, or low intelligence. If you heard that Johnny has an MA of fourteen years, you could not say whether his intelligence was high, average, or low. You would merely know that he can do what the average fourteen-year-old can do. However, if you are told a person's IQ, you can say whether the person is progressing faster, slower, or about average for his or her chronological age.

The meaning of IQ. If an individual can do less on an intelligence test than the average person of the same chronological age, the individual has an IQ below 100. If the individ-

MEASURING INTELLECTUAL ABILITY

ual can do more than the average person of the same chronological age, the individual has an IQ above 100.

The concept of IQ is often helpful in measuring the intellectual ability of children. As a measure of adult ability, however, it is more subject to errors. One problem is that chronological age continues to change, but mental age becomes fairly stable during adult years. Therefore, the method of computing IQ just described is no longer used for adults. It assumes that both chronological age and mental age as measured by tests are continuing to grow.

Psychologists have since improved their methods of computing the IQ. One method is the **deviation IQ.** It is used on the Wechsler tests, and also now on the Revised Stanford-Binet. This method of computing an IQ compares a person's ability with others of the person's own chronological age. The score on a test for a given individual is compared to the average score of a large number of persons who represent that particular age group. The deviation IQ score tells how far above or below a person's score is from the average score for the person's age group.

Does deviation IQ remain the same? The deviation IQ of an individual tends to remain about the same throughout the person's life. If a person takes an intelligence test at age twenty, chances are that the person will show a similar deviation IQ at age thirty. In the majority of cases, the score does not vary by more than about four points either way from year to year.

One psychologist has developed the concepts of fluid intelligence and crystallized intelligence to explain patterns of intelligence. **Fluid intelligence** consists of those aspects of intelligence that are mostly inherited. These aspects are determined at birth and do not change. Taking a reaction-time test would require using fluid intelligence. **Crystallized intelligence,** in contrast, is made up of those parts of intelligence that are mostly acquired through interaction with the environment. This kind of intelligence can increase or decrease, depending on a person's experiences. A vocabulary test requires the use of crystallized intelligence.

As we get older our fluid intelligence tends to decline. However, our crystallized intelligence tends to increase as we have more and more experiences. Very often, this increase offsets the decline, and our deviation IQ remains the same.

Of course, our intelligence-test scores sometimes can change. We have spoken of the group tests of intellectual ability that were given during World War I (p. 159). Thirty years after they had taken one of the army tests, a group of 127 men took the same test again. The results showed that they had increased their scores over the period of thirty years. These were college-trained men. But there is some evidence that even retarded individuals can improve in intelligence-test scores as they grow older if they live in a challenging environment.

There is even evidence that a change in motivation of a person taking an intelligence test can produce some change in IQ. One scientist says that students are not likely to try as hard on a test conducted merely for research. He found a difference when students' acceptance at some school or university depended on their intelligence-test score. The score may rise ten IQ points higher than when the student takes the same test for a research study.

Some problems in determining the stability of IQ. One problem is that no one intelligence test covers all age groups. Tests for the different age groups involved, from infants to elderly persons, measure IQ somewhat differently. Therefore, we can expect that scores will differ from one test to another.

Even suppose one test were available for all age groups. There would still be the problem of testing over a long time. It takes many years to test the same individuals. If you first test individuals at one month of age and continue to test them until they are seventy years of age, it would take seventy years to complete the study. During this time some of the individuals would die. Also, it would be difficult to keep track of them over the seventy-year span.

Finally, there are many factors that can cause changes in scores on intelligence tests. Any of the following can affect scores on intelligence tests: emotional changes, interests, motivation, educational level, and medical problems, such as brain injuries.

IQ ranges. Sometimes psychologists give descriptive terms to IQ ranges. One such classification (by Wechsler) appears on this page. In this classification, IQ's from 90 to 109 are described as average. Nearly half of all individuals tested have IQ's in this range. It is not indicated in this table, but we know that about one-third of all persons tested have IQ's between 100 and 115. Also, about one-third have IQ's between 85 and 100.

DESCRIPTIVE CLASSIFICATION OF INTELLIGENCE QUOTIENTS

IQ	Description
130 and above	Very superior
120-129	Superior
110-119	Bright normal
90-109	Average
80-89	Dull normal
70-79	Borderline
Below 70	Mentally retarded

We must be very cautious in using a classification of IQ's. Classification ranges are not fixed. Psychologists do not agree on the descriptive terms to be used. Furthermore, the IQ is, at best, a rough measure of intelligence. How can we say that an individual with an IQ of 110 is of high average

Text continues on page 166.

Along with personal interests, an individual's level of intelligence often influences the choice of career.

Case Study: Focus on Research

WHEN A TEST IS NOT THE ANSWER

At one time or another you may have been asked to take an intelligence test. Pencil poised, you probably filled in the boxes as instructed. Yet you could not help wondering, "What if I fail?" "How important is this test?"

Unfortunately, some people rely too much on IQ tests. As a result, a student's performance on a particular test may be used to chart the student's course throughout school. The student may then be placed in a slower (or faster) class and may be asked to take certain courses that will affect his or her chances of going to college.

This does not mean that IQ tests are not useful. They do provide a fairly accurate

Research has shown that teachers' expectations may affect how well students do in school. Students thought of as "bright" or as "dull" may indeed live up to these labels.

measure of a person's potential in school. This, in turn, helps schools evaluate student needs. Yet reliance solely on IQ scores can be misleading and even detrimental to students. This is because IQ tests do not take into account other factors that may affect test scores and achievement. One such factor is teacher expectation.

Psychologists Robert Rosenthal and Lenore Jacobson investigated the relationship between teacher expectation and student performance. They hypothesized that the expectations of teachers might very well affect their pupils' achievement. Teachers who expected more from students would get more; those who expected less would get just that.

Rosenthal and Jacobson set up an experiment in a California grade school. In the spring they had teachers give an intelligence test to some 370 students. (The teachers administered the test but did not grade it.) The following fall, teachers of every class were given a list on which from one to nine children had been singled out. These students, said the psychologists, were children "who would show unusual academic development during the coming school year," as predicted by the test scores. They made up 20 percent of the total taking the test.

In reality, these "magic" children—also known as "spurters" or "bloomers"—had been chosen simply at random. There was no evidence that they would develop more quickly, or slowly, than any of the other students. The only characteristic that distinguished them from the rest of the students was the teacher's belief that they would succeed.

At the end of the school year, all the children were again given the intelligence test. Everyone showed gains, but the "bloomers" registered the greatest improvement—an average of 12 points, as compared to 8 points for the control group. The discrepancy was most pronounced in first and second graders. In this group "spurters" made gains of up to about 27 points and 17 points, respectively.

Several reasons were given for this, all suggesting that younger children are more likely than older children to be influenced by teachers. For one thing, younger children are more easily "molded" by teachers and are therefore easier to change. In addition, younger children are less likely to have established bad reputations. This enables teachers to believe that these children are really capable of "blooming." Moreover, the teachers at the lower grades may be different from those at other levels and may be more likely to influence student performance.

There was also substantial improvement among Mexican-American youngsters compared to other ethnic groups. This finding suggests that racial prejudice may have adversely affected their earlier performance.

Or it is possible that over time these children gradually adapted and adjusted to their new culture.

The results of this experiment indicate that schoolroom situations may well affect intelligence scores. When teachers expect children to excel, they do so. But the experiment did not show how teachers actually influenced their "bloomers." Rosenthal and Jacobson speculate that they probably watched them more closely and thus responded more quickly with positive reinforcement. They may also have communicated their expectations through facial expressions, posture, and gestures.

The Rosenthal-Jacobson experiment certainly does not dismiss intelligence testing as invalid. But it does serve as a warning that the results should not be interpreted too rigidly. The most technical-looking numbers may be influenced by something as simple as an encouraging smile.

SOURCE: Robert Rosenthal, *Experimenter Effects in Behavioral Research,* New York: Appleton-Century-Crofts, 1966; R. Rosenthal and L. Jacobson, *Pygmalion in the Classroom,* New York: Holt, Rinehart & Winston, 1968.

By reinforcing correct or incorrect answers, teachers may influence a student's later performance.

intelligence, while a person with an IQ of 109 is only of average intelligence? Such a strict classification of intellectual abilities ignores social factors, such as home, school, and community. These factors are not measured well by present intelligence tests. And this strict classification ignores the fact that an individual's test scores may vary somewhat from one testing to another.

Measures of intelligence are valuable. But much harm can be done by classifying individuals on the basis of such measures alone. Many elements besides IQ contribute to success and happiness.

Some Uses of Intelligence Tests

The development of intelligence tests led some people to think that we now had a way for fitting everyone into a suitable place in life. Actually, human beings are far too complex for us to use any one procedure in arranging their lives. Yet many sound suggestions can be made for school and adult living on the basis of intelligence tests.

How schools use intelligence tests. Schools can use the results of a general intelligence test to predict the length of time that individuals will need to master a unit of study. Such test results also can be used to predict how much help the person will need in the early stages of study. In addition, the results are useful for predicting the person's final level of learning, and the time and amount of help that person will need in later units of study. However, any predictions of school success that are made should never be based on a single intelligence-test score, especially a score that comes from a group test.

Sometimes psychologists are asked to advise parents and teachers about the educational possibilities of particular children. The psychologist is likely to use an intelligence test for background information. It would be difficult, for example, for children with IQ's below 50 to do first-grade work satisfactorily in traditional schools.

Psychologists also might use intelligence tests to help students performing below their expected level of achievement. For example, suppose an "A" student is receiving straight "C's" or a "C" student is getting all "F's." The psychologist, knowing the student's potential, might work with the person to improve school performance.

What is the relationship between IQ and school grades? In the elementary school, psychologists have found a close relationship between achievement in classwork and intelligence-test scores. Thus, by giving an intelligence test early in a school year, a teacher can predict with considerable accuracy the quality of work the child will be able to do. Teachers recognize, of course, that factors other than intelligence are involved in schoolwork.

Prediction of school achievement from intelligence-test scores is less certain at the high school level than at the elementary school level. There are two reasons for this. One is that students of low intelligence may drop out of school at the first opportunity. As a result, there is less range in intellectual ability among high school students. Thus, it is harder to distinguish between them. It is harder to predict that one will do better than another.

A second reason for the lower relationship in predicting school achievement at the high school level is that more factors are involved in high school achievement. In elementary schools, the subjects studied are much the same for everyone. But high school students have some opportunity to choose the subjects they wish to study. Therefore, interest plays a greater part in determining achievement than it does at the elementary level. Also, if high school students spend a great deal of time on their social life, school success may not be very closely related to their intellectual ability. Or if they have jobs that take time away from their studies, the relationship between school success and intelligence may be less.

At the college level, the relationship between achievement in classwork and intelligence-test scores is even smaller. The college group is more similar in intellectual ability than the high school group. Also, college students have much more freedom than high school students. And students differ in the way they respond to the stress of college examinations. Some students get poor grades mostly because of stress. All these factors tend to reduce the relationship between intellectual ability and school achievement. However, IQ is still one of the best predictors of academic success.

Intelligence tests have proved to be valuable in helping teachers and administrators guide students. In some cases, too much confidence has been placed in the score on a single test. Sometimes teachers and administrators don't recognize the importance of elements other than intellectual ability in influencing school success. But when properly used, intelligence tests are one of the major contributions of psychologists to the work of the schools.

What is the relationship between intelligence and occupations? Studies have shown a relationship between intelligence and occupational success. Generally, the more prestige an occupation has and the more education required for it, the higher the intelligence-test scores of the people in that occupation. You might wonder, however, if intelligent people happen to choose such occupations, or if such occupations require more intelligence. It is probably a combination of both. It takes more education to become a brain surgeon than it does to sweep floors. A person with graduate training and a high IQ could choose to sweep floors. But that person would probably not be happy sweeping floors as a lifetime occupation.

There is a relationship between the kind of work that people can do successfully and their ability as measured by intelligence tests. Yet many elements other than general intelligence are involved in success in any vocation. Individuals may be well below the test-score average for a given vocation. But if they are motivated and able to work hard, they can be successful.

Mental Retardation

It has been estimated that more than 2 percent of the population of the United States is mentally retarded. Some are being cared for and trained in special institutions for the retarded. Still others are in prisons, hospitals, and social welfare institutions. However, the great majority of mentally retarded individuals are not institutionalized.

How do we know if a person is mentally retarded? IQ has been an often used measure. Usually anyone with an IQ below 70 has been considered retarded. Today, however, psychologists try to avoid classifying persons as retarded on the basis of IQ alone. Some psychologists suggest that social factors, such as the person's ability to adapt to the environment, should be used instead of IQ. But the ability to adapt cannot be used as the only factor, either. We would not classify all murderers as retarded, for instance. But we can use IQ in combination with other factors, including social factors, to determine mental retardation.

There are four commonly described levels of **mental retardation: profound, severe, moderate,** and **mild.** People have social contacts with mildly retarded persons nearly every day without recognizing them as retarded.

Profoundly and severely retarded persons. Today, efforts are being made to take care of some of these individuals outside of institutions. But most are cared for in special institutions. They make up only a small portion of all mentally retarded persons. Some are so low in intellectual ability that they cannot understand the simplest statements or utter single words. Often they cannot wash and dress themselves. Some cannot eat and drink or take care of other bodily needs without help. They do not know how to avoid the ordinary dangers of life, such as speeding cars.

Profoundly retarded persons—those individuals whose IQ's are below 20—show almost no response to their environment. As adults, severely retarded persons, with IQ's between about 20 and 34, have an intellectual ability similar to that of a normal three-year-old child. When they are twenty or twenty-five years of age, they can do no better on an intelligence test than a child who is just learning to talk well.

Moderately retarded persons. Moderately retarded people have more ability to adjust to life than severely and profoundly retarded individuals. But they cannot respond to the teaching of ordinary school subjects. In special schools, they can learn to take care of themselves to a certain extent. They can learn to avoid the common dangers of life as well as feed, dress, and wash themselves. They can also help in the work of the institution. They can make beds, set tables, help in a laundry, and perform other simple routine tasks. But they must have someone watch over them all the time, telling them how and when to do these activities.

After a period of training, some are able to return to their homes. They still need someone to supervise their activities. They may help with tasks in the home or do other useful work under supervision. But they seldom can be entirely self-supporting.

Moderately retarded individuals have IQ's ranging from about 35 to 49. As adults, their mental ages range from about four to seven years. More individuals are moderately retarded than are severely retarded. But this group is still only a small percentage of all mentally retarded persons.

Mildly retarded persons. People who have IQ's ranging from about 50 to 69 are usually considered mildly retarded. The great majority of all mentally retarded persons are in this group. Many of them are not in institutions but live in the community. The mental ages of adults who are mildly retarded are usually between eight and twelve years.

Mildly retarded children cannot progress normally in school. In special upgraded

Many individuals who are mildly retarded can learn basic skills that may enable them to hold jobs in the community.

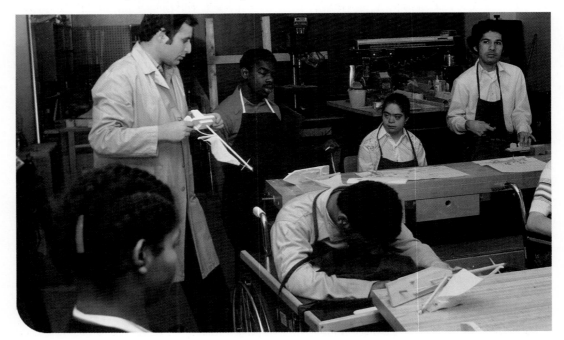

classes, and with time and effort, they may learn to read, write, and do simple arithmetic problems. Ordinarily, they do not progress much beyond the level of the third grade, no matter how long they remain in school. However, mildly retarded persons can take their places in society as self-supporting citizens. Some, for instance, can earn a living as farm workers or day laborers.

Why are some mildly retarded individuals placed in institutions while others are not? Much depends on emotional stability. Some mildly retarded persons have calm temperaments. They can get along successfully with other people and are able to work. Other mildly retarded individuals are easily upset and have trouble interacting with people. They require a lot of support from those around them. If their surroundings cannot be supportive enough, these individuals are often placed in institutions.

What can mentally retarded persons learn? In recent years, educators have become more aware of the possibilities of teaching the mentally retarded.

Classes for mildly retarded individuals deal mainly with programs emphasizing social skills, the use of money, and developing simple occupational skills. Such classes are designed for the mentally retarded who are educable. These persons can learn some of the simple processes involved in such subjects as reading and arithmetic.

Classes for the moderately retarded have more limited objectives. As adults, these persons can be taught to take care of themselves and to work in unskilled or semiskilled occupations with supervision.

The severely retarded can be taught, as adults, to maintain some self-care under constant supervision. That is, they are trainable.

The profoundly retarded may develop some motor and speech abilities. But they cannot care for themselves. They need complete supervision, even in adult life.

Today, more emphasis is being placed on developing new programs that use principles of learning to enable mentally retarded persons to become active, productive members of society. Many programs help such persons care for themselves and, if possible, obtain work in various service occupations. Some products today are made entirely by mentally retarded persons. When they are employed, retarded individuals usually have excellent attendance and production records.

What causes mental retardation? Why are millions of Americans mentally retarded? At the present time there are more than 150 known or suspected causes of mental retardation. Yet it is very difficult—and sometimes impossible—to determine the exact cause in a particular case. Mental retardation, especially at the severe and moderate levels, may appear in any family. There may not be any known cases of it in the family history. But some forms of mental retardation do run in families. Many scientists believe that heredity is the basic factor in causing some mental retardation.

Other causes involve environmental factors. Injury before, during, or shortly after birth is responsible for some cases of retardation. Poisonous substances, such as carbon monoxide and lead, may bring about brain damage in an unborn child. Biochemical factors, genetic-chromosomal factors, and premature birth may cause other cases of mental retardation. Children with Down's syndrome, for instance, have 47 rather than the normal 46 chromosomes. Their IQ's are most often in the severely and moderately retarded ranges. If a mother develops an infection such as measles early in her pregnancy, she might have a retarded child. After birth, severe early malnutrition can affect a child's intelligence. Such children are retarded in language development, perception, and memory. Nevertheless, despite all these possible causes, often the specific cause of mental retardation is unknown.

Can mental retardation be cured? Much can be done through training retarded persons. Retarded adolescents have even been trained to teach younger retarded children. In such cases, the younger children improved in their eating and dressing skills.

And the retarded adolescents showed a decrease in their rebellious and difficult behavior.

At present there is no known way of curing those who have serious brain damage. Drugs, individual psychotherapy, and special education programs are useful in helping the mentally retarded make a better adjustment in their social life. Mentally retarded individuals need support and understanding, just as other people do. But these procedures do not cure the disorder. Administering the hormone thyroxin has sometimes produced considerable improvement in a specific type of mental retardation (cretinism). Also, surgery has been used to treat hydrocephalus, a condition in which an abnormal amount of fluid in the cavities of the brain results in a very large head. Vitamin therapy has improved the mental functioning of children who suffer from malnutrition. In those cases where a treatment exists, early diagnosis is very important if treatment is to be of the most value.

Superior Intelligence

Psychologists do not agree on what the term "superior intelligence" means. People of superior intelligence are above average, just as the mentally retarded are below the average. Sometimes IQ is used to classify intellectual superiority. The term **gifted** is still often applied to those with IQ's of 140 or higher. Some psychologists prefer to define superior intelligence in terms of behavior. According to this viewpoint, the key term is productivity. A gifted person is anyone who produces a great amount of work that influences many people over a long period of time.

Prodigies. Gifted people tend to be bright in many areas. However, sometimes people display a very high degree of mastery in a particular area, such as chess. These people are known as **prodigies.** A prodigy at chess, though, would probably not also be a prodigy in music. Prodigies are rarely found across several disciplines.

One example of a young prodigy is Dylana Jenson. She started taking violin lessons at the age of three. At the age of twelve she was a solo artist with the New York Philharmonic. At sixteen, she had made over 50 appearances with leading symphony orchestras in the United States, Latin America, and Europe.

Some other young prodigies include Galileo, who made his basic discovery of the pendulum movement at the age of seventeen. Edmund Halley, after whom a comet was named, made several major planetary discoveries while still in his teens. Credit for developing the concepts that led to the invention of television belongs to a person who was only fifteen years of age.

Characteristics of gifted persons. Gifted persons usually stand out academically from the average of their age group. For instance, half of the gifted have learned how to read before they enter school. About three-fourths of gifted students in the eighth grade make scores on achievement tests that are equal to or higher than those of the average twelfth grader. Also, the top 10 percent of all high school seniors score higher than the bottom 10 percent of all college seniors on tests that measure knowledge of subject matter.

Gifted people also have a number of psychological and social characteristics. They are usually leaders in high school. They become less self-centered much earlier than others in their age group. They become more interested in the problems of society earlier than their peers. From the fifth grade through high school, they have a greater feeling of social commitment than the average person of their age. In general, gifted people are better adjusted than the average. They have a lower rate of suicide and a lower divorce rate. And they develop career plans earlier than the average. Giftedness is not limited to a single area or field, although some gifted persons may become focused on only a few areas. But even then, their interest in other areas is much wider and stronger than that of others of their age group.

The most famous single research project

ever performed with gifted individuals began in 1921. At that time, Lewis M. Terman and other psychologists began a study of 1,528 children of very superior intelligence. Even today these people are still being studied. The results have helped correct some of the misunderstandings about gifted persons. Children of very superior intelligence are popularly supposed to be physically inferior, "bookish," a bit peculiar, and superior in only one subject. Instead, this study found that on the average, gifted persons are taller, physically healthier, stronger, have greater lung capacity, and weigh more at birth than the average person. Their schoolwork tends to be superior in all subjects of study rather than in just one subject. Superior children read on a wide range of topics. As a rule, their social interests are normal, and their fellow students and friends don't think they are peculiar.

Terman kept in touch with individuals of this gifted group and found that they continued to be superior as they grew older. Many of them entered the professions. They went far in formal education. Forty-eight percent of the men and 27 percent of the women obtained academic degrees beyond the bachelor's degree. They wrote books and magazine articles. They made good, or at least comfortable, salaries.

Terman's study has received substantial criticism, though. For one thing, Terman chose all his subjects from California. His sample may not have been representative of the entire population. Also, there was a social-class bias. About one-third of his subjects were from professional families. Because of their social standing, they may have had a better than average opportunity for education. Their education, in turn, may have helped them enter and advance in their career. Based on this information, some researchers have suggested that family background—not *only* IQ—contributed to success.

Marie Curie was a person of superior intelligence. She received the Nobel prize for the discovery of radium.

In addition, some researchers have noted that although many of Terman's subjects were successful, none have yet become famous or made any creative contributions. Therefore, they contend, Terman measured only certain aspects of intelligence.

Do you know any gifted individuals? Which characteristics do they have?

Summary

The definition of intelligence often depends on who is doing the defining. Many psychologists would agree, however, that intelligence involves the ability to adapt to both old and new situations.

Some psychologists have broken down intelligence into a number of factors. Recognizing the various factors may help people in choosing a vocation and in maximizing personality development. The major drawback to factor theories, though, is that they don't explain how the various factors interact with one another.

Measuring intelligence is important to researchers. The first workable intelligence test was devised by Alfred Binet and his assistant in 1905. An American adaptation was subsequently developed by Lewis Terman in 1916. Revisions of this test are still being used today. There are also various performance, or nonverbal, tests in use.

Group tests of intelligence were developed during World War I. Group intelligence tests enable many individuals to be tested at the same time. They are also much less expensive to administer than individual tests. In addition, they can be given and scored by persons who aren't thoroughly trained in testing procedures. A major drawback is that they may not give as valid a measure as individual intelligence tests.

The intelligence quotient is a mathematical measure of intelligence. Intelligence tends to remain the same throughout life, but IQ test scores can change in either direction. Psychologists give descriptive ranges to IQ's, with scores of between 90 and 109 being average. However, psychologists disagree on exact classifications.

Intelligence tests are used in schools to predict how long it will take students to master a unit of study. They also provide psychologists with background information about a child's educational possibilities. Moreover they might help educators identify students performing below their potential. IQ scores can be used more accurately to predict achievement at the elementary school level than later on.

Mental retardation affects more than 2 percent of the population. There are four levels of retardation: mild, moderate, severe, and profound. Mildly retarded individuals can learn social and simple occupational skills. Learning abilities at the other levels are more limited. There are various causes of mental retardation but no known cures for the vast majority of retarded people.

Some people in our population have superior intelligence. Gifted people are usually considered to be those with IQ's of 140 or higher, who are bright in many areas. Gifted individuals are usually leaders in high school, have more social concern, and develop career plans earlier. Although subject to substantial criticism, Terman's study of the gifted is the most famous ever performed.

In this excerpt from *Current* (January 1986), Kevin McKean considers the issue of racial and national differences in measured intelligence.

The lesson that there's more to intelligence than IQ is one that most people learn the hard way at one time or another. Everyone has known people with low IQs who get along in the world famously, and others with high IQs who never amount to much....

Defenders of IQ, like Hans Eysenck of the University of London, point to its eight-decade record of service: "There's an indisputable body of scientific evidence showing that IQ tests do reflect actual cognitive abilities...."

Critics counter that IQ's many flaws render it useless. "The assumption that intelligence can be measured as a single number is just a twentieth-century version of craniometry," says biologist and author Stephen Jay Gould, referring to the nineteenth-century "science" that claimed a man's intelligence could be determined by measuring his head....

The modern conception of intelligence has its roots around the turn of the century when... French psychologist Alfred Binet in 1905 published the first modern IQ-like test....

Binet's test was taken up enthusiastically by American psychologists, chief among them Stanford's Lewis Terman.... While Binet meant his test simply as an educational tool, Terman had broad ambitions for wide-spread testing of adults....

Terman's dream of mass testing was quickly realized. A Harvard psychologist named Robert Yerkes persuaded the Army to examine some 1.75 million recruits during World War I.... The test's authors were dismayed by the low scores, but encouraged that the racial and national break-down suited the prejudices of the day....

[Psychologist] Arthur Jensen . . . believes that it's genes, not culture or environment, that do the most to determine intelligence. Specifically, Jensen argues that ... there are sharp biological limits set at birth on an individual's intellectual capacity; and that there may also be clear-cut differences in average intellectual potential among races and nationalities....

Jensen's critics regard this kind of talk as meaningless. "To say that because [some] children *don't* do well on IQ tests they *can't* do well is extraordinarily simple-minded," says Sandra Scarr, chairman of the psychology department at the University of Virginia....

Others add that tests designed for one culture are notoriously faulty when applied to another. A classic example is the study by Joseph Glick of Liberia's Kpelle tribesmen. Glick, of the City University of New York, asked the tribesmen to sort a series of objects in a sensible order. To his consternation they insisted on grouping them by function (placing a potato with a hoe, for example) rather than by taxonomy (which would place the potato with other foods). By Western standards, it was an inferior style of sorting. But when Glick demonstrated the "right" answer, one of the tribesmen remarked that only a stupid person would sort things that way. Thereafter, when Glick asked tribesmen to sort the items the way a *stupid* person would, they sorted them taxonomically without difficulty.

Source Review

1. Who developed the first modernistic test of intelligence?
2. How did the psychologists who administered intelligence tests to World War I soldiers react to the results?
3. In addition to genetics, what other factors might influence IQ?

REVIEWING TERMS

intelligence
intelligence quotient (IQ)
mental age
chronological age
deviation IQ
fluid intelligence

crystallized intelligence
mental retardation
profound retardation
severe retardation
moderate retardation
mild retardation

gifted
prodigy

CHECKING FACTS

1. What is the generally accepted definition of intelligence?

2. What are some advantages of recognizing the various factors of intelligence? What is the major drawback of factor theories?

3. Describe the first intelligence test. How did Binet and Simon select the tasks to be assigned to each group?

4. Why might psychologists use culture-fair tests? Describe some performance tasks characteristic of culture-fair tests.

5. What are some advantages of group intelligence tests? What are some of their disadvantages?

6. What is the intelligence quotient, and what does it indicate?

7. Does intelligence remain the same throughout a person's life? Explain.

8. How might schools use intelligence tests?

9. What is the relationship between IQ and school grades at the elementary level, the high school level, and the college level?

10. What are the four levels of mental retardation? Describe the characteristics of people at each level.

11. Discuss some of the causes of mental retardation. Can mental retardation be cured?

12. What is meant by "gifted"? Describe some of the characteristics of gifted people.

APPLYING YOUR KNOWLEDGE

1. Each student in the class should provide a definition of intelligence. (Do not base your answers on the textbook.) What common ideas emerge? Can you see why some psychologists have difficulty agreeing on a satisfactory definition of intelligence?

2. Read the biography of a famous person. What psychological or social qualities

that indicate high intelligence does the person have? Can you think of a good way of predicting superior intellectual performance in people?

3. In the 1960's a black psychologist constructed a "culture-bound" intelligence test to show that traditional tests might be biased against certain groups of people. (For example, many students would

not know where the Hully-Gully originated. This was one of the questions on the test.) Using this idea, create a culture-bound intelligence test that focuses on the knowledge and skills needed for being successful as a teenager. Administer the test to some non-teen-agers to see how well they do. How might the opinions of the dominant culture affect the definition of intelligence?

4. Hold a debate to explore the statement: "Superior intelligence in childhood leads to superior intelligence in adulthood." Both sides should do library research to gain support for their arguments.

5. Did you know that Albert Einstein was four years old before he could speak and seven before he could read? Beethoven's music teacher said that, "As a composer, he is hopeless." Thomas Edison's boyhood teacher thought he was not intelligent enough to learn. Look into the biographies of these "gifted" individuals to see how slow beginnings can lead to striking success stories. What characteristics in these people's backgrounds hinted that these individuals would later excel? Do you know of any other people who did not excel in childhood but who made extraordinary gains as adults?

THINKING CRITICALLY ABOUT PSYCHOLOGY

1. **Debating Ideas** Should employers be required to give intelligence tests to job applicants? Would this be an invasion of an applicant's right to privacy? Explain.

2. **Applying Ideas** Imagine that you are a psychologist living with members of a tribe, say, deep in the jungles of South America or in the bush section of Australia. You wish to measure their intellectual ability. What kind of test would you use? What questions would you include?

3. **Drawing Conclusions** Suppose every-

one in the world had the same IQ. How would societies be different from the way they are today?

4. **Summarizing Ideas** With improved nutrition and improved social conditions, do you think that mental retardation would disappear from our society? Why or why not?

5. **Forming an Opinion** As schools develop better methods for teaching children of superior intellectual ability, do you think that the number of gifted people will increase?

DEVELOPING SKILLS IN PSYCHOLOGY

Reading Tables

Scientists often summarize information in tables, which are useful ways of presenting data and other items in a concise, visually descriptive fashion.

This chapter has a table providing a descriptive classification of intelligence quotients. This table is easy to read because it has only two columns. It could be expanded to include additional columns—indicating, for example, the percentages of the population falling into each IQ level.

To read a table, you note the title and column headings to see what information is being given. Then you read the information across each line. In this chapter's table, how many IQ levels are presented? What description is used for people at the highest level of IQ? What is the IQ level of people who are called "mentally retarded" on the basis of their test performance?

READING FURTHER ABOUT PSYCHOLOGY

Dickman, Irving, and Gordon, Sol, *One Miracle at a Time,* Simon & Schuster, New York, 1985. Presents advice to parents on how to get help for a retarded child. Taken from the experiences of parents with retarded children.

Fancher, Raymond E., *The Intelligence Men,* W. W. Norton, New York, 1985. Discusses the controversy surrounding the matter of IQ determination. Introduces some of the people who have been influential in the field of human intelligence testing.

Galbraith, Judy, *The Gifted Kids' Survival Guide,* Free Spirit, Minneapolis, Minn., 1984. Provides motivation and support for the intellectually gifted, who often find themselves facing special demands at home and at school.

Gardner, Howard, *Frames of Mind: The Theory of Multiple Intelligence,* Basic Books, New York, 1985. The author challenges conventional notions of intelligence and argues that intelligence is made up of a number of different factors.

Grosswirth, Marvin, and Salny, Abbie, *The Mensa Think-Smart Book,* Harper & Row, New York, 1985. A collection of brain busters compiled by members of Mensa, the internationally famous high-IQ society.

Owen, David, *None of the Above: Behind the Myth of Scholastic Aptitude,* Houghton Mifflin, Boston, 1985. The author examines the historical development of mental measurement.

Phillips, John L., *Piaget's Theory: A Primer,* W. H. Freeman, San Francisco, Calif., 1981. A review of Piaget's work and theory on intellectual development.

Using the Skills of a Psychologist

Unit 3 Evaluating Test Validity

Evaluating test validity is one of the skills psychologists use to assess a person's personality. In order to understand more about this process, it may be helpful to learn how other types of tests may be evaluated and to consider some of the factors that may determine their validity.

There are several ways to evaluate a test's validity. One way to measure validity is to determine whether the test is measuring what it was designed to measure. Say, for example, that a person applies for a job as a secretary. One of the skills required of a secretary is fast and accurate typing. Employers determine the typing speed and accuracy of job applicants by giving them a typing test. All applicants are given the same material to type within a certain amount of time. The tests are then scored by the amount of material the applicants are able to type in the given amount of time and by the number of errors they make. This is a valid test of typing skills because it directly measures the ability to type quickly and accurately.

Another way to measure the validity of a test is to determine how well it predicts the behavior it was designed to test. For example, college entrance examinations are designed to predict how well students will do academically in their future college courses. One way to test the validity of these examinations is to compare college students' grades with their scores on the entrance examinations. Those students who received high scores on the entrance examinations probably will be making high grades in their college courses.

Another way to evaluate test validity is to give several tests examining the same ability or personality trait and then compare the scores. For example, people who apply for a driver's license for the first time must take two tests: a pencil-and-paper test and an actual driving test. The pencil-and-paper test is designed to measure the person's knowledge about road signs, the rules of driving, and safety precautions while on the road. If the person receives a passing score on the pencil-and-paper test, the driving test is then given to evaluate how well the applicant can apply this knowledge to actual driving conditions. An evaluator scores the applicant on driving ability, safety, and courtesy. These two tests are used in combination to determine if the applicant has the knowledge and ability to be a good driver. An applicant who fails one or both of these tests will not be given a driver's license.

From time to time issues of popular magazines include short tests that readers can take on such personality or social traits as "Are You Assertive?" or "Are You Trustworthy?" or "Do You Use Your Time Effectively?" These tests usually include questions about real-life situations and ask readers to choose the answer that most applies to them. When the test is completed, answers are scored and tallied. The final score is then supposed to give readers an idea of how assertive they are or how trustworthy they are or how well they use their time.

With the approval of your teacher, locate one of these tests for members of the class to read, complete, and score. While you are working on the test, think about what you have just read concerning the ways in which a test's validity is evaluated. Do you think the items on the test really measure the trait they were designed to measure? How well does your final score go along with your image of yourself on that trait? Compare your final score with the ways in which you have behaved in actual situations calling for that trait. Does your score match your real-life behavior? Can your score predict how you will behave in future situations?

REVIEWING THE UNIT

1. How are personality theories judged?

2. What is the main requirement for a rating scale to be a valid assessment of a person's personality?

3. How does the "Barnum effect" describe how people may view their own personality traits?

4. How do interests change with age?

5. Why is intelligence difficult to measure?

6. What is the relationship between intelligence and occupations?

CONNECTING IDEAS

1. **Seeing Relationships** What correlation, if any, could be made between a person's basic personality and that individual's performance on standardized tests?

2. **Interpreting Ideas** Once a self-concept is in agreement with reality, should it ever change? Why or why not?

3. **Applying Ideas** In what way is the new approach that focuses on person-centered psychology especially applicable to people of our society in the 1980's?

4. **Analyzing Ideas** How might intelligence factors determine personality?

PRACTICING RESEARCH SKILLS

Each student should use materials available at home or in the classroom to create a display of things you consider to be especially interesting or beautiful. Each display should be approved by your teacher and may include items such as photographs, art, written exhibits such as poetry, or auditory exhibits such as tape recordings.

Think about the things that are meaningful to you in terms of visual or auditory expression. For example, do you enjoy the sound of noise in a city, the pounding surf, or the quiet breeze through trees? Do you find beauty in the face of a child, or reflected through the eyes of an older person?

Each person in the class should select one item from his or her display to present to the class. You will see that your interests reveal a lot about your personality. You will also see how unique each individual is and how people define beauty in different ways.

FINDING OUT MORE

You may wish to contact the following organization for additional information about the material in this unit.

Society for Personality Assessment
866 Amelia Ct., N.E.
St. Petersburg, Florida 33702

Unit 4

LEARNING AND THINKING

Chapter 9 PRINCIPLES OF LEARNING
Chapter 10 LEARNING, REMEMBERING, AND FORGETTING
Chapter 11 THE PROCESS OF THINKING

Chapter 9

PRINCIPLES OF LEARNING

Chapter Focus

This chapter presents:

- **the roles of classical and operant conditioning in learning**
- **the relationship between operant conditioning and punishment, programmed learning, and biofeedback**
- **the cognitive approach to learning**

You walk into the kitchen and the smell of freshly baked cookies suddenly fills the air. Your mouth starts watering. It's hard to believe you felt full just a few minutes earlier.

Does this scene sound familiar? Probably many of you have had similar experiences. Just the sight or smell of one of your favorite foods makes your mouth water.

What, you may wonder, has this got to do with psychology? Psychology isn't about the foods you eat. Or is it? Actually, many of your food likes and dislikes depend on learning. You learn to associate certain foods with pleasant feelings. For example, a hamburger might remind you of a barbecue at a friend's house. Television advertisers take advantage of this fact all the time.

You also learn to avoid many foods because of past experiences. You skip the rolls because you've put on a pound or two lately. You pass up the hot sauce because it once upset your stomach.

Most other behaviors are also learned. You learn to recognize when others need help and how you can help them. You learn how to adjust your actions to function well with members of a team. You learn, too, to love other people. Unless the process of learning takes place, none of these behaviors would be possible.

In this chapter we will focus on how learning occurs. Learning about learning can give you insight into many of your life experiences.

What Is Learning?

You have been learning all your life. You will continue to learn for the rest of your life. Learning is not just what you do in school. You learn from friends, movies, television, newspapers, and jobs. Before you started school, you were learning in your home and while playing with other children.

Learning refers to rather lasting changes in behavior that occur as a result of practice or other past experience. Learning usually involves acquiring the ability to do something that you haven't done before. Or it may mean the ability to use already acquired reactions in new and different ways. Some learning involves acquiring and making use of facts. Some involves acquiring and using certain skills.

Not all behavior has to be learned. Some behavior—like blinking your eyes when a puff of air strikes them—occurs automatically. Such automatic behavior, which does not require previous experience or practice, is called a **reflex.**

Still other unlearned behavior is mainly the result of physical growth and development. For example, as babies grow and develop, they are able to crawl. People then say, "The baby has learned to crawl." But what they really mean is that the child's nerves and muscles have developed to a point where crawling is possible. In early adolescence a boy's voice changes. This is a result of the growth of his vocal cords. Such changes are due to physical growth and development rather than to learning.

In this chapter the term "learning" refers to changes in behavior that are not the result of reflexes and are not primarily due to physical growth.

Classical Conditioning

Animals as well as people may feel their mouths water at the sight or smell of a tasty bit of food. Ivan Pavlov (1849-1936), a Russian scientist, observed this mouth-watering behavior when he fed the dogs in his laboratory. He decided to follow up his observation by studying salivation (mouth watering) under controlled experimental conditions. Pavlov designed an apparatus that held the dog in a desired position. A tube attached to the dog's cheek near one of the salivary glands drained off the saliva. It permitted accurate measurement of the flow. The apparatus was in a soundproof room. There was a one-way-vision screen between the experimenter and the dog. This allowed the experimenter to see the dog, although the dog could not see the experimenter.

How classical conditioning works. Powdered meat was placed in the mouth of the hungry dog. As usual, the dog's saliva flowed. The flow of saliva became known as the **unconditioned response (UCR).** This is the response that occurs normally, with no learning necessary. Pavlov called the meat the **unconditioned stimulus (UCS).** It is the normal, unlearned agent for causing salivation.

Next, the experimenter sounded a bell just before he gave meat to the dog. He sounded the bell and presented the meat immediately afterward several more times. Then he sounded the bell without presenting the meat. He found that the dog's saliva flowed anyway. The dog had been conditioned to salivate at the sound of a bell. The sound of the bell had become a **conditioned stimulus (CS).** The salivation at the sound had become a **conditioned response (CR).** A new association had been formed.

This is what classical conditioning is all about. **Classical conditioning** refers to a learning situation in which a certain stimulus brings forth a response that it did not previously evoke. It results from combining this stimulus (in Pavlov's experiment, the bell) for a number of trials with a stimulus that normally did bring forth the response (the meat). To make this definition clearer, let's consider other examples of classical conditioning.

Other conditioning experiments. It is easy to demonstrate classical conditioning. Picture several subjects seated with one arm

The apparatus Pavlov used in his experiments in classical conditioning. Food could be placed in the bowl by remote control. The dog's salivation was recorded automatically.

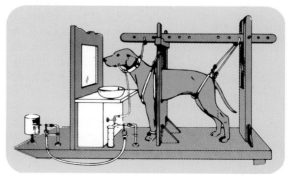

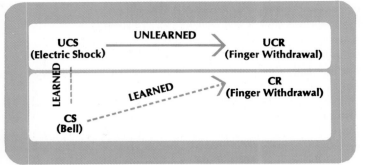

| UCS (Electric Shock) | UNLEARNED → | UCR (Finger Withdrawal) |

In classical conditioning, the UCR occurs without learning. However, the associations between the UCS and the CS, and between the CS and the CR, are learned.

resting on a table. Electrodes are attached so that these people can receive a safe but noticeable shock through their hands and fingers. When they get a shock, they normally jerk their fingers away without having to learn to do so.

At the beginning of the experiment, the subjects hear a bell. They don't jerk their fingers because they have no reason to give such a response. Then the bell is rung, and a shock is given almost at the same time. This bell-followed-by-shock routine is repeated a number of times. The subjects always respond with a finger jerk. Next, although the subjects don't know what is going to happen, they hear the bell ring but do not receive a shock. Again, they jerk their fingers. Conditioning has taken place.

Take a look at the diagram on this page. The unconditioned stimulus (UCS) is a stimulus—such as electric shock—that normally brings forth an unconditioned response (UCR)—the finger jerk. That is, the UCR is an unlearned response. Then the conditioned stimulus (CS)—the bell—is associated with the UCS. It eventually evokes a conditioned response (CR)—the finger jerk. The CR is similar to the UCR but is usually weaker in strength. The dotted lines indicate the connections that are learned.

Even bodily functions that we are not normally aware of can be conditioned. For example, if you stick your left hand in a container of cold water, the blood vessels will draw together, or constrict. This is to help prevent heat loss from the body. Suppose you ring a bell and then stick your hand in the cold water. Your blood vessels will constrict. Repeat this often enough, and eventually the sound of the bell alone will cause your blood vessels to constrict.

A practical application of the principle of classical conditioning is the use of the electrically charged wire fence for keeping livestock in a pasture. A fence with a few strands of charged wire will serve as well as a much higher, stronger, and more expensive fence. Animals that touch the charged wire receive a harmless but unpleasant shock. In some cases, even one experience of shock will condition an animal against trying to pass under, through, or over the fence. The expense of the conditioning is slight. Current is used only during those seconds when animals touch the fence. Soon all the animals become so well conditioned that they won't go near the fence.

Counter-conditioning. Another practical application is a procedure that is called **counter-conditioning.** It consists of conditioning the stimulus to a different response. It is usually used to get rid of certain learned, undesirable behaviors, such as alcoholism. Individuals may be given a drug that produces nausea when they taste alcohol. Later, when they desire alcohol, they associate the feeling of nausea with alcohol and avoid drinking. Counter-conditioning is also used to reduce fear and anxiety.

When an organism is taught to avoid a stimulus, it is called **avoidance conditioning.** For example, suppose you want to teach a rat not to go to the part of its cage that has a grid floor. Through the grid floor electric shocks can be given. Every time the rat stands on the grid floor, it gets an electric shock. Soon the rat is conditioned to avoid that part of its cage completely.

Counter-conditioning has been criticized for treating the symptoms of the undesirable behavior rather than the underlying causes. When used together with treatment of underlying causes, this method has more success. This is especially true when the desirable new behavior is rewarded.

Consider, for example, the following study. Overweight subjects were divided into an experimental group and a control group. The subjects in the experimental group were asked to list the foods they most desired, such as pies, cakes, candies, and doughnuts. The subjects then handled each food, thought about each, and finally smelled it. Immediately after smelling the food, subjects placed gas masks over their faces. An unpleasant odor was blown into the mask. All subjects in the experimental group lost weight during conditioning. Nearly one year later, they still had an average weight loss of more than 4 kilograms (9 pounds). Subjects in the control group had gained an average of .45 kilograms (1 pound). The study also involved rewarding the subjects in the experimental group. The experimenter talked at length with the subjects about weight reduction, listened to their problems, insisted that they lose weight, and praised them as their weight decreased. The success of the experimental group was the result of using the counter-conditioning procedures along with rewarding the desirable behavior of losing weight.

Extinction and spontaneous recovery.

What do you suppose would happen if a conditioned stimulus (CS) were presented a number of times alone, without the unconditioned stimulus (UCS)? What happens is that the learner eventually stops responding to the CS. This process is called **extinction.** Let's go back to the example of Pavlov's dog. Suppose the bell is sounded but no meat is presented. The conditioned response— salivating at the sound of the bell—may last for a while. But if the bell is rung a number of times and no meat follows, the conditioned response (salivating) will be weakened. Soon it will no longer occur. Extinction will have taken place.

Some conditioned responses are difficult to extinguish. A CR of fear, for instance, may continue even though the original object or

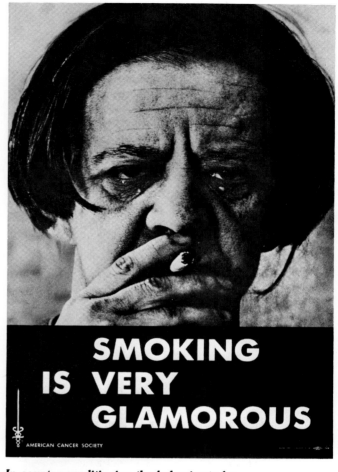

SMOKING IS VERY GLAMOROUS

AMERICAN CANCER SOCIETY

In counter-conditioning the behavior to be avoided is associated with something undesirable.

situation (the UCS) may not have been present for years. One study found that fifteen years after their last war experience, sailors still responded more than the average person to a rapidly sounding gong. This was a signal used in the navy to announce battle stations.

Suppose there is a rest period after extinction. Then the conditioned stimulus is given. The conditioned response will probably reappear. The reappearance of the conditioned response without reinforcement after a period of extinction is known as **spontaneous recovery.** Both extinction and spontaneous recovery are illustrated in the diagram on

Text continues on page 186.

183

PRINCIPLES OF LEARNING

Case Study: Focus on Research

FEARLESS ALBERT AND FEARFUL PETER

One of the most famous laboratory subjects of all time was little Albert. As a toddler, he lived for a few months at a children's home connected with Johns Hopkins University in Baltimore. During this period he was the focus of an important experiment conducted by psychologist John B. Watson.

Watson believed that the environment—rather than inborn tendencies—determines most of people's behavior. In other words, he thought that behavior is learned rather than inherited. According to Watson, a child was born with a blank slate upon which just about anything could be written. Watson argued that he could take any healthy infant and, given the opportunity, could readily mold the child into anything he chose—a

While Albert learned to fear a rat, and Peter had a fear of rabbits, fortunately this child has no fear of her pet cat. Such fears often come from conditioning.

doctor, a lawyer, a carpenter, a beggar, and even a thief.

Watson was also greatly influenced by Pavlov's discovery that classical conditioning could be used to produce such simple physical behaviors as salivation in animals. Pairing these two ideas, he wondered whether classical conditioning could be used to affect more complex behaviors such as emotions.

Watson and his associate, Rosalie Rayner, decided to test this notion using the emotion of fear. As their subject, they selected Albert—the son of an employee of the children's home—because he seemed fearless. Watson described him as "a child with a stolid and phlegmatic disposition."

While at play, little Albert happily touched and petted a white rat. He had no fear of the animal. But, like most children, he responded with fright to loud noises—in this case the sound of a hammer hitting a steel bar behind his head.

Now classical conditioning was introduced into the experiment. Whenever Albert touched the rat, Watson beat on the steel bar. After just seven pairings of noise and rat, Albert had learned to fear the animal.

In technical terms, the unconditioned stimulus of noise had first led to the unconditioned response of fear. By the end of the experiment, a conditioned stimulus—the white rat—was producing fear as a conditioned response. In fact Albert was afraid not only of white rats, but generalized his fear to include white rabbits, a white fur coat, and the experimenter's white hair.

Watson and Rayner planned to decondition Albert so that he would not go through life with this irrational fear. Unfortunately, his mother left the home, taking Albert with her, on the day this phase of the work was to start. (The two dropped out of sight and could never again be located by psychologists.)

Not long afterward, however, a student of Watson's, Mary Cover Jones, was confronted with a similar situation. Three-year-old Peter, a bright child, was normal in all respects except that he feared white furry objects, including rats, rabbits, feathers, and fur coats. It was not known how his fear originated, but it was thought to have developed through conditioning, just like Albert's. Why not attempt deconditioning on him?

Since Peter's most extreme reactions were caused by a white rabbit, Jones concentrated on this animal. First, she brought Peter and three other children (all unafraid of animals) to her laboratory each day for a play period. During that time Peter watched Jones and the other children fearlessly play with a white rabbit. However, despite this demonstration, Peter was not convinced that the animal was harmless.

Next, Jones tried more direct conditioning. She paired the rabbit with a stimulus that was pleasurable to Peter—eating. Whenever Peter munched on some food, the psychologist made sure a caged rabbit was in the room. At first, the rabbit was kept in a far corner of the room. As days passed, the rabbit's cage was gradually moved closer and closer to Peter. Then the animal was allowed to roam freely—eventually even sitting on Peter's lap while he casually enjoyed his meals.

At the end of several months, Peter's fear of rabbits had vanished completely. The rabbit became the youngster's constant companion, as he carried it about, petted it, and even let it nibble at his fingers. Gone too were his fears of related objects. Albert, wherever he was, might still be troubled, causing us to question the ethical implications of this experiment. (Today guidelines set up by the American Psychological Association try to protect subjects from harmful effects of experiments.) But Peter fortunately had been cured.

SOURCE: J. B. Watson and R. Rayner, "Conditioned Emotional Reactions," *Journal of Experimental Psychology*, 1920, *3*, 1–4; M. C. Jones, "A Laboratory Study of Fear: The Case of Peter," *Journal of Genetic Psychology*, 1924, *31*, 308–315.

Even Santa Claus cannot calm these frightened youngsters. Perhaps an earlier experience caused them to fear this jolly old man.

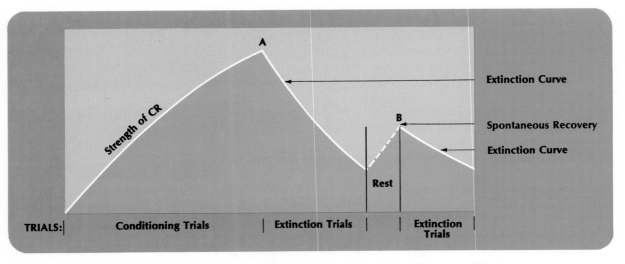

This diagram shows that the conditioned response increases during conditioning trials and decreases during extinction trials. However, after a rest period, spontaneous recovery occurs — the CR returns although it is not reinforced.

this page. At point A in the conditioning, the conditioned stimulus (CS) is presented without the unconditioned stimulus (UCS). As the CS is continually presented without the UCS, the strength of the CR will begin to decrease. This would be the beginning of the extinction period. Then, at point B, after a period of time, the CS is presented to the subject. When this occurs, the CR will again appear in the subject's behavior as spontaneous recovery. For example, consider a rat conditioned to press a lever for food. After a rest period, the rat will begin pushing the lever again, even though it receives no food.

Reinforcement. In Chapter 6 we defined reinforcement as a process that increases the chances of a certain behavior occurring again. In classical conditioning, ***reinforcement*** is the procedure of presenting the unconditioned stimulus immediately after the conditioned stimulus. For example, shock (the unconditioned stimulus) strengthens the tendency for the finger-jerk response to be made. The UCS of shock thereby increases the chances that the finger-jerk (CR) behavior will occur again when the bell (CS) is rung.

In real life, ***intermittent reinforcement,*** or occasional rather than continuous rein-

forcement, is given. Once a conditioned response has been established, it will continue to occur even when there is only occasional reinforcement with the unconditioned stimulus. Subjects may no longer jerk their fingers after the bell has been sounded a number of times without the accompanying shock. But they will begin jerking their fingers again as soon as the bell and shock are paired one or more times. In fact, there is evidence that intermittent reinforcement produces more lasting behavior than occurs with 100 percent reinforcement.

Generalization. It might seem that learning in everyday situations would require a huge number of different conditioning experiences. In a way this is true. But generalization helps. Suppose that a conditioned response to a certain stimulus has been established. Other similar stimuli will also bring about that response. That is, there will be ***generalization.***

We know from experience that we perspire under severe emotional strain. In one experiment, individuals were given a fairly severe electric shock. They perspired in response to the shock. The electric shock (UCS) was then paired with a tone of a certain pitch (CS). Conditioning took place. The subjects perspired to that particular tone even when the shock was not given. Next, the particular tone was replaced by tones slightly higher and slightly lower while no shock was administered. The conditioned response of perspiration continued. Generalization had occurred.

Then tones further and further from the original tone were introduced. The skin response of perspiration was brought on by these tones. But the reactions were less strong than those for the original tone. This experiment suggested that the greater the similarity between stimuli, the greater the generalization between them.

Some of the fears of children may be due to generalization. For example, a child may be beaten by a bully at school, during which time the child's heartbeat increases. The sight of the bully may then become a conditioned stimulus that increases heartbeat. Later on, generalization may take place, and the child's heartbeat may speed up at the sight of someone who looks like the bully.

Discrimination. Generalization, then, is a tendency to respond to all stimuli of a similar kind in the same way. **Discrimination,** on the other hand, is a tendency to respond to a particular stimulus in one way and to respond to similar stimuli in another way. Discrimination is established by reinforcing the desired response but withholding reinforcement for the generalized responses. In this way, these other responses are extinguished.

For example, we can condition a dog to salivate at the sound of a tone. If we present a tone that is somewhat different from the original tone, the dog will salivate to it. This is an example of generalization. Now, however, we present food (reinforcement) whenever the first tone is sounded. We do not present food when the second tone is sounded. The dog will soon salivate to the first tone only. This is discrimination.

Babies learn to respond by saying "Daddy" at the sight of their fathers. For a while there is likely to be amusing generalization as they apply the term to any man

A child learns to discriminate between two similar stimuli, a "c" and an "o," in writing the letters of the alphabet.

they see. However, parents usually reinforce (with some expression of pleasure) the response "Daddy" only when babies apply it to their fathers. It is not reinforced for other men. Soon there is discrimination. The term "Daddy" is applied only to the father.

Perhaps you have noticed that extinction, spontaneous recovery, generalization, discrimination, and acquiring a response are all done by providing or by withholding reinforcement for the response. The point at which reinforcement is given is an important aspect of the classical conditioning process.

Operant Conditioning

Suppose you want to train your dog to come when you whistle. The first time you try whistling, the dog comes running to you. You quickly give it a dog biscuit. This type of learning is called operant conditioning. The word "operant" is used because the organism's response in some way operates on the environment. For example, the dog's response (running to the person who whistled) operated on the environment. It resulted in the person giving the dog a biscuit. Suppose the dog had not responded to the whistle. We would say that the dog has not learned to respond to that particular stimulus. **Operant conditioning** may be defined as the strengthening of a stimulus-response relationship by following the response with a reinforcement.

What are some differences between classical and operant conditioning? An illustration will help to make clear the distinction between classical and operant conditioning. In a laboratory a dog has elec-

trodes attached to one of its feet. Whenever the current is turned on, the dog receives a shock (UCS). It then lifts its foot (UCR). Next, a bell is sounded (CS) each time the dog is shocked. The dog is soon conditioned to lift its foot (CR) when the bell is sounded, even though it is not shocked. This is a case of classical conditioning.

The contemporary psychologist B. F. Skinner has done a great deal of work on operant conditioning. For animal experiments he developed a box, as shown on this page. One side of the box contains a bar with a food cup below. When a hungry rat is placed in the box, the rat will begin to explore. In the course of its wandering, it may push the bar by accident. The box is designed so that whenever the bar is pressed, a pellet of food falls into the cup. After a few such experiences of pressing the bar and receiving food, the hungry rat is conditioned to press the bar in order to get food. It operates on the environment to bring about a desired result. This is operant conditioning.

Many of the same principles that apply to classical conditioning also apply to operant conditioning. But there are important differences. One difference is that in operant conditioning the subject takes a more active role in the procedure. The rat in the Skinner experiment is an operator, not just a salivator or foot raiser. Another difference is that in classical conditioning the unconditioned stimulus, such as an electric shock, is specifically known. In operant conditioning the unconditioned stimulus is not known. Its existence is assumed. For example, in operant conditioning, when a rat presses a lever to obtain food, the unconditioned stimulus is assumed to be hunger. A third difference is that in classical conditioning the reinforcer is the unconditioned stimulus. It occurs *before* the response. In operant conditioning the reinforcer occurs *after* the response and as a result of the response. The following experiment will illustrate this difference.

Operant conditioning with animals. How would you teach a pigeon to make complete turns in a clockwise direction?

Skinner designed this apparatus for animal experiments in operant conditioning. When the animal presses the lever, food appears.

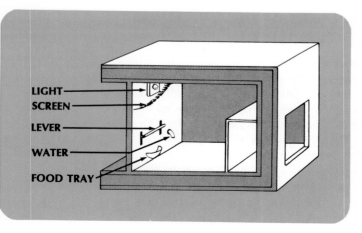

LIGHT
SCREEN
LEVER
WATER
FOOD TRAY

Making complete clockwise turns is not part of a pigeon's ordinary behavior. Skinner, however, found a way. He placed the pigeon in the conditioning box. At first the pigeon merely wandered about. But in a relatively short time it learned that it could get grain in the food tray. (This box had no lever.)

Then the psychologist began training the pigeon. In the course of its movements, the pigeon chanced to turn a few degrees in a clockwise direction. Immediately, the psychologist reinforced this behavior with some grain. Each time the pigeon turned a bit more in a clockwise direction, the movement was reinforced. The pigeon received grain for a quarter-turn, for between a quarter- and a half-turn, and so on, to a complete clockwise turn. Soon the pigeon was regularly making clockwise turns to get food.

This procedure, in which the experimenter rewards the organism each time it makes a response that approximates (is close to) the desired response, is called **shaping**. On future trials each response must be more like the desired response for reinforcement to occur. Reinforcement follows only the desired response.

To summarize, during classical conditioning the order of events is stimulus-reinforcement-response. To ensure that the response occurs, reinforcement is given before each response. Pavlov's dog receives meat before it salivates. During operant conditioning the order is stimulus-response-reinforcement. Reinforcement follows the response. And it follows only a correct response. The pigeon receives grain only for turning clockwise.

Animals can be trained to do any number of tasks through the use of operant conditioning procedures. Psychologists simply reinforce the desired response and extinguish all others by withholding reinforcement. Two psychologists once trained a hen to play a five-note tune on a small piano. They provided reinforcement in the form of grain for desired responses as they occurred in correct order. They presented no grain for undesired behavior.

Operant conditioning has even been used to teach pigeons to select the rejects among drug capsules. (Rejects were capsules with a double cap or a rough edge.) The pigeons viewed the capsules from behind a

The differences between classical and operant conditioning.

	CLASSICAL CONDITIONING Stimulus → Reinforcement → Response	OPERANT CONDITIONING Stimulus → Response → Reinforcement
ORDER OF EVENTS	Reinforcement is given before the response and helps cause the response.	Reinforcement follows a correct response.
ROLE OF SUBJECT	Subject is passive and reacts only when a stimulus is introduced.	Subject is active and operates on the environment.
AWARENESS OF STIMULUS	The specific unconditioned stimulus is known.	The specific unconditioned stimulus is unknown.

glass window. They rejected capsules by pecking on the glass. They were reinforced only when they correctly selected a reject. During the training period, rejects had been mixed in with acceptable capsules and placed on an endless conveyor belt. The pigeons were able to differentiate between acceptable and unacceptable capsules on a 99 percent-correct basis within one week of daily training. (This was only an experiment. The pigeons were never actually used by the drug company to sort capsules.) This experiment, as well as those in which pigeons were taught to bowl and guide missiles, is described in the research feature for Chapter 1 (pages 12-13).

It should be noted, however, that the desired behavior must be within an animal's capabilities. For example, no amount of conditioning can teach a pigeon how to recite a poem. Nor can fish be trained to ride a bicycle.

Using operant conditioning with human beings. Operant conditioning, like classical conditioning, is not limited to animals. Reinforcing desired responses is a standard procedure in teaching, for instance. In one experiment, subjects were asked to make up sentences. Each sentence had to contain a pronoun and a verb. The experimenter provided reinforcement by saying "Good" whenever a sentence contained the pronouns "I" or "we." The production of sentences containing other pronouns was not reinforced. In the course of 80 trials, there was a steady increase in the number of sentences containing "I" and "we." In a control group of subjects, to whom no reinforcement was given, there was no increase.

In another experiment, a psychologist and a subject carried on an informal conversation. Occasionally the subject used a sentence beginning with "I think," "I believe," or a similar expression. The psychologist reinforced it by saying, "You're right" or by expressing agreement in some other way. No reinforcement was given for other sentences. The record showed a steady increase in the number of sentences beginning with "I

think" and similar expressions. Heads of committees and leaders of discussion groups often use this technique to encourage discussion.

Extinction and spontaneous recovery. In classical conditioning, extinction takes place if the conditioned stimulus is repeated without the unconditioned stimulus. Similarly, a learned response in operant conditioning can be extinguished by withholding reinforcement. A pigeon that has been conditioned to make clockwise turns stops doing so if it no longer gets food whenever it makes such a turn. As in classical conditioning, spontaneous recovery will also occur. The extinguished response of clockwise turns will reappear spontaneously when, after a period of time, the pigeon is again placed in the box.

We have mentioned the experiment in which subjects were conditioned to express their opinions by reinforcing all statements beginning with "I think," "I believe," and so on. In a later part of the experiment, no reinforcement was given following such statements. That is, the experimenter simply said nothing when such sentences were used. There was a marked drop in the number of sentences beginning with "I think" and the like. The head of a committee or discussion group might use this technique to quiet some members of the group who are taking too much of the group's time for their personal opinions. Spontaneous recovery can be seen in these cases, too. It occurs when the group meets once more and some of the same people again begin talking too much.

Reinforcement. Reinforcement may be either positive or negative. **Positive reinforcement** strengthens a response by its presentation, as in the case of giving the pigeon some grain. Operant conditioning tends to rely mostly on positive reinforcement. **Negative reinforcement** strengthens a response by its absence, as in the absence of an electrical shock. Negative reinforcement can be considered a form of reverse reward. Removing the reinforcer often increases the probability of an unpleasant response.

This child is receiving positive reinforcement from the teacher for completing a classroom assignment. Giving gold stars to young children who perform well in school can have a strong effect on their learning.

One aspect of reinforcement is the amount of time between performance of the correct response and reinforcement of that response. Generally, the shorter the time in receiving a reward after a correct response, the more likely it is that an organism will learn that response. Even a delay of 15 seconds between performance and reinforcement will have an effect on the learning of a response. This would mean, for instance, that students performing correctly at school should receive immediate and frequent rewards, especially at early grade levels. As individuals become older, they are better able to accept and learn from delayed rewards.

Another important aspect of reinforcement is how frequently a correct response is reinforced. Reinforcement may be given each time a correct response occurs. This generally results in fast learning of a response. However, in real-life situations we are not usually rewarded after every correct response.

Intermittent reinforcement. Animals and people continue to perform many acts even when there is only intermittent reinforcement. The gambler continues to put money in the slot machine or to play the roulette wheel even though such behavior is reinforced by winning only a small part of the time.

A pigeon can be conditioned to peck at a disk to get food. After conditioning, the pigeon does not have to get food every time it pecks at the disk in order for it to continue pecking. In one experiment a pigeon was rewarded with food only 12 times an hour (about every five minutes). Yet it pecked at the disk about 6,000 times an hour. Some

191

pigeons have been kept pecking at a disk several thousand times with only one reinforcement of food. There is evidence that human beings, too, perform faster and over longer periods under intermittent reinforcement than under constant reinforcement.

Knowledge of intermittent reinforcement can assist a person in breaking some habits and developing others. *Habits* are tendencies toward a particular behavior that have become relatively fixed by repeated performance. Take, for instance, the habit of smoking. This behavior has usually been reinforced so many times that extinction may be difficult. Suppose a person wishes to stop smoking but decides to start out by smoking only once a day. Knowledge of the effects of intermittent reinforcement suggests that it is better to stop smoking completely than to be reinforced by occasional smoking.

Intermittent reinforcement can be given on several types of schedules. The two basic types are ratio and interval. In **ratio schedules,** the reinforcement depends on the number of correct responses between reinforcements. A **fixed-ratio schedule** means that the organism is reinforced for a fixed number of responses, such as for every fifth correct response. A **variable-ratio schedule** means that the number of responses between reinforcements varies. A pigeon might be reinforced after its first response, then after its third, then its seventh, its sixteenth, and so on.

In **interval schedules,** reinforcement is determined by the time between responses. A **fixed-interval schedule** means that the response of the organism is reinforced after a fixed time period. In this schedule, the organism might receive reinforcement every two minutes—assuming that within the two-minute period a correct response has been made. If the organism has not made a correct response at the end of the two-minute period, reinforcement is withheld until a correct response is made. Reinforcement is given again after the next two-minute period. In a **variable-interval schedule,** the time between reinforcements varies throughout the conditioning procedures.

Suppose you use a fixed schedule (either ratio or interval) in one experiment. And you use a variable schedule (either ratio or interval) in another similar experiment. In which situation do you think the learned response would continue longer after reinforcement is stopped? If reinforcement is withdrawn, the behavior will usually continue longer when learned under a variable schedule than when learned under a fixed one. The subject is never sure when reinforcement is coming and so keeps showing the behavior, expecting reinforcement.

Secondary reinforcement. Instead of being a direct reward, reinforcement can have a secondary stage. A **secondary reinforcement** is a stimulus that has been associated with something that satisfies a need. As a result, the stimulus comes to act as a reward by itself. Money is a good example of a secondary reinforcer. To maintain a family, individuals must provide food, clothing, and shelter. However, when they work they don't earn these items directly. Instead they earn money, which they can then use to buy these necessities.

The following experiment provides another example of secondary reinforcement. First, chimpanzees were conditioned to do certain work, such as moving a lever, to earn raisins. Then they were required to do work to get poker chips. The chimpanzees were conditioned to trade poker chips for raisins. In one test, three of the four chimpanzees worked as hard for poker chips as they did for raisins. The poker chips alone had no direct value to the chimpanzees. They had acquired a secondary reinforcement value, similar to that of money for humans.

Later, the experimenters tried giving the chimpanzees poker chips before beginning a session. During the session the animals could earn still more chips by working at the machines. The amount of work they did was much less. One chimpanzee ordinarily worked for about 20 chips at a single work session. When it was given 30 chips before beginning the work session, however, the chimpanzee would work for only about three

This chimpanzee is working for poker chips, a secondary reinforcement, which it inserts into the "Chimp-o-mat" to obtain food.

chips. The "handout" seemed to lessen the value of the secondary reinforcement.

Generalization and discrimination. These procedures occur in operant conditioning as well as in classical conditioning. In the experiment just mentioned, the chimpanzees learned that a poker chip of one color was good for a raisin. Afterward, they would work for poker chips of another color. This was generalization. Then a chip of a certain color was regularly reinforced with food. A chip of another color was not reinforced with food. Discrimination developed. The chimpanzees learned not to work for chips that could not be used to obtain food.

One scientist has been able to teach animals to discriminate without making any errors during a part of the experiment. First the psychologist taught pigeons to discriminate between red and green circles. Here they did make mistakes. After they had learned to distinguish between the two col-

ors, vertical lines were placed in the red circle, and horizontal lines in the green circle. The pigeons were reinforced when they selected the correct color, which they had already learned. The colors in the circles were gradually faded away. This left only the vertical and horizontal lines. The pigeons were able to discriminate between the lines without making any mistakes. Such learning with no errors tends to be stable over a long period of time. Similar techniques have been used to teach mentally retarded people to make discriminations that were once thought to be impossible for them.

The Role of Punishment

Punishment consists of providing a negative stimulus after the behavior has occurred. Punishment for doing what is considered undesirable is our traditional method for training children and adults as well as animals. We may punish the dog that does not obey a command. Parents may punish small children for picking up breakable objects and throwing them on the floor. Society punishes adults with fines if they drive too fast.

Punishment seems to help animals and people learn acceptable behavior. However, some research suggests that the negative effects of punishment outweigh its benefits. Consider the following situation.

A mother and father punish their children whenever the youngsters misbehave. They believe that punishment is the best way to teach the children acceptable behavior.

The children, however, view the situation very differently. Ordinarily, the parents tend to ignore them. When the children are punished, though, they receive attention from the parents. This attention is seen as a greater reward than they would get from behaving properly. It also outweighs the consequences that result when they misbehave. As a result, the children misbehave as often as possible.

193

There is also evidence that children who receive excessive punishment tend to inflict punishment on others. People who were mistreated as children are more likely to mistreat their own offspring.

In addition, punishment identifies only behaviors that are not acceptable. For example, a child might learn through punishment that it is wrong to touch a hot stove. But would the child know that it is all right to go near the stove when it is *not* hot?

Because of these drawbacks, some researchers suggest that we might do better in many cases to reward desired behavior. Nevertheless, the fear of punishment is an important factor in our lives. People who feel their skin begin to scorch from the sun often seek a shady spot to avoid becoming sunburned. Drivers of speeding cars usually slow down when they see a police officer because of the fear of punishment. Furthermore, mild punishment can be useful to a child if it helps the child learn to be cautious about such things as fire, hot water, and traffic.

Operant Conditioning and Programmed Learning

Programmed learning is an instruction method that uses the operant conditioning techniques of presenting an organism with stimuli. The organism responds and receives reinforcement for a correct response. Programmed learning helps the subject respond correctly by providing material to be learned in small amounts and in a specific order. It also gives immediate knowledge of results.

How is programmed learning presented? Subject matter is presented to the learner in a series of small steps, or *frames.* Each of the frames contains material that requires an active response, either by answering a question or completing a statement. Learners find out immediately whether or not they have given a correct response. If their response is correct, it is immediately reinforced by the knowledge that they are right.

The frames of programmed materials are arranged so that students are not likely to make many errors. If they do make an error, they discover it immediately and so do not go on in the wrong direction. They spend their time learning what they should learn rather than unlearning what they stumbled onto by error.

There are two basic ways to arrange programmed material. One is a linear program. The other is a branching program. In the **linear program** the individual moves step by step in a line through the material. Individuals keep to the sequence whether their answers are right or wrong. In the **branching program,** students are given another sequence, depending on their answer. If they respond correctly, they are presented with the next question. If they do exceptionally well, they may be given an opportunity to skip some material. But if they make an error, they will be branched off into some extra material on the subject that they answered incorrectly. For example, suppose a child learning to read has trouble with the word "church" in a sentence. The child may be shown a picture of a church. If the child still cannot read the word, another branch of instructional material will appear.

Teaching machines and programmed books. Teaching machines are educational devices designed to present programmed material to the learner. In the hand-operated machines, a question is asked or an incomplete sentence is presented in a window of the machine. The learner writes the answer beside it. By means of a lever, the correct answer is then moved into view. If the answer given is correct, the learner can go on to new material.

If the teaching machine is a computer, it sends out instructions on a screen, on paper, or through earphones. The student responds on a special typewriter or writes on the screen with a special pen. Each response determines which item in the lesson sequence will be presented next.

transfer	**1.** It is important that the knowledge and abilities developed through school experiences *transfer* to similar situations you will meet later in life. For example, we want typing skill developed in school to _____ to typing skill on the job.
transfer	**2.** We might ask whether learning one language influences the learning of a second language, or whether studying traffic regulations contributes to driving skill. Any investigation of the *effects of previous learning on later learning* (or performance) is a study of _____.
previous later (or synonyms)	**3.** Studies of transfer investigate the effects of _____ learning on _____ learning or performance.
negative	**4.** If learning Task 1 aids the learning of Task 2, we say that the transfer effect is *positive*. On the other hand, if learning Task 1 interferes with the learning of Task 2, we say that the transfer effect is _____.
positive negative	**5.** If learning one language helps in the learning of a second language, the *transfer effect* is _____. If batting left-handed interferes with learning to bat right-handed, then the transfer effect would be described as _____.

This is part of a programmed unit on learning. To use it, you would cover the answer column on the left. After filling in the blanks in each frame, you would uncover the answer for that item to see if you responded correctly.

In programmed books, there are a number of frames on each page. The correct response to each frame is covered until after the student has made a response. The student can then receive immediate reinforcement by uncovering the correct response. A programmed book is designed to encourage the student to learn by breaking the process down into simple steps and reinforcing the correct response at each step. The book, however, cannot force the student to learn. This is also true of teaching machines.

Some advantages of programmed materials. Teaching machines and programmed books can free teachers from time-consuming routine work. The programmed materials also are able to teach very efficiently. They permit learners to progress at their own speed. In addition, as we mentioned earlier, programmed materials provide learners with immediate reinforcement, or rewards.

Learners who are physically handicapped may move awkwardly and respond very slowly. Others may become impatient with them. Programmed books and teaching machines cannot become impatient, no matter how slowly the learner responds.

In industry each new employee has to learn many facts. The military services also have a great deal of technical material that must be taught in a time-saving and efficient manner. Programmed books and machines are part of the answer to efficient learning of much new material.

Operant Conditioning and Biofeedback

Psychologists once thought that classical conditioning was concerned with involuntary responses (related to the autonomic nervous system), such as a rise in blood pressure or an increase in salivation. They thought that operant conditioning was concerned with voluntary behavior (involving the central nervous system), such as pressing a lever.

However, today we know that operant conditioning procedures can involve some responses that are controlled by the autonomic nervous system. *Biofeedback* is the process of learning to voluntarily regulate

This machine provides feedback and the subject learns to control the brain's alpha waves.

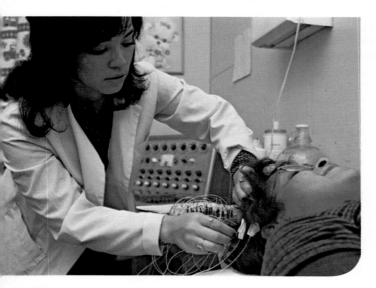

bodily responses. It occurs through feedback (knowledge of results) of information about a particular physiological response.

Biofeedback training. The original biofeedback experiments were carried out on rats. When the rats increased a specific biological function, such as heart rate, they were rewarded. They were never punished if they did not respond. Eventually the rats were able to increase the bodily function. In other experiments, animals were taught to change their salivation, blood pressure, and stomach contractions. One group of rats was taught to blush (raise their blood pressure) in the left ear, but not in the right ear.

Eventually the question arose, "Can humans learn to control physiological functions normally regulated by the autonomic nervous system?" The answer has turned out to be yes. The procedures used in biofeedback training of humans are basically the same, regardless of the bodily function being controlled. Suppose the bodily function to be learned is a decrease in blood pressure. Small changes in blood pressure can be measured by an electronic instrument and indicated to the subject by a sound or light. Subjects are given the goal of decreasing their blood pressure. Their rewards are achieving this goal and receiving feedback.

In one study, subjects were taught a technique to relieve severe headaches. Their goal was to learn to relax muscles associated with headaches. When the subjects reached their goal, a clicking sound was heard. The further they went beyond their goal, the faster the clicking became. Human subjects have been taught not only to relax muscles, but also to lower their heart rate, lessen the secretion of stomach acids that may produce ulcers, and reduce the temperature in the palm of their hands.

Some practical uses of biofeedback. Operant conditioning techniques have proved useful in controlling a number of physiological functions. If you have frequent and severe headaches, you can learn to reduce the frequency of such headaches. Individuals who tend to have high blood pressure can learn to control and lower their blood pressure. This should reduce their chances of having a heart attack or stroke.

There is also some indication that biofeedback procedures can be used successfully with overactive children. One child was so overactive that he cried in ordinary schoolroom situations. He could not sit still and take tests. He was constantly moving about in the classroom. The procedure consisted of using an instrument that measured the muscle tension in his forehead. As muscle tension increased, a tone sounded. The child was asked to try to keep the tone off as much as possible. By the fifth session he had learned to reduce his muscle tension by over two-thirds. Even seven months later, he was still using this learned control. His scores on tests had improved. And there was a tremendous increase in his self-confidence.

Cognitive Learning

So far we've examined learning by conditioning. In classical conditioning, an individual learns a response by having it paired with a specific stimulus. In operant conditioning, the individual learns a response because that response is reinforced after it is made.

However, some psychologists believe that learning is not solely a matter of conditioning. They stress *cognitive learning*—a process that involves organizing information, making comparisons, and forming associations. The result is new information. When the new information is stored in our memory, learning has taken place.

Some characteristics of the cognitive approach. Cognitive psychologists view learning as a process of organization. When you look at a friend, you do not simply see the individual features of your friend's face. You organize all of the features in some way. This organization of all the individual stimuli allows you to recognize your friend.

The cognitive approach also emphasizes that learning is not a passive process. Rather, we actively do something with stimuli that results in learning. As you look at the words on this page, you compare them with previous memories and experiences. You do not react just to print on the page. You arrange the printed marks so they have meaning to you in terms of your past experiences.

Learning is guided by past and present rewards and experiences. But it is also related to expectations of future happenings. For example, your learning about psychology is guided by the past rewards you've received in learning about this field. But it is also affected by what you expect to occur in the future. Your learning is affected, for instance, if you expect to use your knowledge of psychology to help prepare you for a major in psychology in college.

One of the earliest psychologists to develop the cognitive approach to behavior was E. C. Tolman. According to Tolman, an organism explores and discovers that certain events or situations lead to certain other events. For example, you learn that the ringing of the last bell at the end of the school day will lead to your leaving school. Through such experiences, the organism learns the "lay of the land." When the organism learns the makeup of the environment, it is then able to find its way around in it. The organism forms what Tolman called a *cognitive map.* Just as you might look at a map of a town or city to discover how to get somewhere, you can use the cognitive map to make your way from one point to another. Your cognitive map consists of your past experiences, your own particular style of behaving, your knowledge, and the various meanings you attach to things in your environment. A rat uses its cognitive map to learn a maze. The rat discovers that if it turns right at a certain point, right again at the next point, then left, and so on, it will eventually arrive at a food dish. If one route is blocked toward the goal, the rat will take another route. Similarly, wouldn't you take another route home if the streets that you usually take were blocked?

A good example of the cognitive approach is learning by insight. Insight is another way—in addition to conditioning—that an individual learns a particular response.

What is insight? To the psychologist, *insight* is the relatively sudden change in one's perception of a problem that results in the solution of the problem. It is not a blind, chance hitting upon a solution. It is based on past experience. The insight appears to come quickly after a period of little or no progress. But actually the individual may see a number of minor relationships before having the final insight into the problem.

An animal experiment on insight. One psychologist placed fruit beyond a chimpanzee's reach outside its cage. Within the cage were two bamboo sticks. Neither of them was long enough to reach the fruit. The chimpanzee nevertheless tried first one stick and then the other. It even pushed one stick with the other toward the fruit but could not rake in the fruit. It then seemed to give up in its attempt to solve the problem.

Later, while playing with the sticks, the chimpanzee happened to hold one so that it came into a straight line with the other. The chimpanzee pushed the thinner stick into a hole in the end of the thicker stick. Now there was a new relationship or pattern. Instead of two short sticks that could not be used to reach the fruit, there was one long stick. The chimpanzee jumped up, ran to the side of the cage, and used this long stick to rake in the fruit.

This successful bit of behavior was reinforced by the reward of eating the fruit. Thus we could say that the chimpanzee would be conditioned to repeat its efforts. The basic learning, however, depended on the animal solving its own problem, after a considerable time, by insight.

Some examples of human insight. A similar experiment was carried out with children of preschool age. In one case a toy was placed outside a child's playpen, where the child could not reach it. Some children spent a great deal of time trying to reach the toy with their hands, although there was a stick

Here the chimpanzee is faced with the problem of reaching the bananas.

in plain sight in the pen. Other children seemed to spend some time sizing up the situation. Then they would pick up the stick and rake in the toy.

Have you ever had insight into some problem—maybe a problem in a mathematics course? Perhaps you worked long and hard on the problem. You used methods you had learned previously. There were many trials that were not reinforced by the satisfaction of finding a solution. Then, perhaps rather suddenly, you saw a relationship that you had not seen before. The whole problem became clear. Maybe you said, "Aha, I see it! How simple! How could I have missed seeing the solution in the first place?" The answer is that you had not reached the point of insight into the problem. Sometimes insight is called the "Aha" experience.

What causes the learner to have insight? Learning by insight appears to be sudden. Yet the learner is not starting from scratch. The subject has had some past experience with the tools involved in the problem. The chimpanzee and the children had had previous experiences with sticks. The student has had past experience with mathematical pro-

The chimpanzee has insight. It begins to pile up the crates beneath the fruit, climbs onto the top crate, and grabs the bananas.

cesses and principles. Also, the subjects have had the experience of making several incorrect attempts. They have therefore already ruled out some possibilities.

This brings up an important difference between insightful learning and many cases of conditioning. When a situation is worked out through insight, learners are often aware of steps in their thinking. In conditioning, on the other hand, learners are hardly likely to recall saying to themselves, "I see a light. The light is associated with a shock. I will jerk my finger to avoid a shock."

Human subjects can be asked about their thinking experiences. But with animals we have to depend on observable behavior. By using special instruments and techniques, we can record and observe animal behavior that might not be noticed otherwise. In one experiment, rats were faced with a row of four doors. They had to learn to choose the one door that would lead them to food. One door was white, one medium gray, one light gray, and one black. The food was always behind the white door. During the trials the experimenter was able to count the number of times that each rat looked back and forth from one door to another. A casual observer

might have said that the rat learned suddenly to go to the white door without any trial-and-error experience. The experiment suggests, however, that the rats were looking at the gray and black doors in place of trying them.

Insight, then, is not something that comes "out of the blue." For example, students would be unsuccessful if they came to a math exam unprepared, expecting to solve the problems by insight. To have insight, they need previous experience with the material covered in the course.

Perhaps at this point you are wondering, "Which of these learning theories is the right one?" The answer is, "No one theory of learning is *the* correct one." No single learning theory explains all of the different kinds of learning that occur. All studies of learning today are based to some degree on learning theories set up in the past. Perhaps it is somewhat like building a house. No one tool can be used to build a house. For each stage there is a particular tool that is most useful, such as a hammer, a screwdriver, or a saw. Each tool contributes something to the development of the house. Similarly, each learning theory adds to our knowledge of the process of learning.

199

PRINCIPLES OF LEARNING

Summary

Learning refers to rather lasting changes in behavior that occur as a result of practice or other past experience. Most of our behavior is learned, although some behavior is the result of reflexes or growth and development.

Classical conditioning is a learning process developed by Pavlov. In classical conditioning a conditioned stimulus is paired with an unconditioned stimulus to bring forth a response usually associated only with the unconditioned stimulus.

An important practical application of classical conditioning is counter-conditioning. In this process a stimulus is conditioned to a different response. Counter-conditioning is usually used to get rid of certain learned, undesirable behavior.

When a conditioned stimulus is presented several times without the unconditioned stimulus, extinction takes place. During extinction, the conditioned response no longer occurs. It may reappear, however, during a period of spontaneous recovery.

Two other important processes related to learning are generalization and discrimination. Generalization helps us apply what we learn in one situation to similar situations. Discrimination, in contrast, causes us to respond to a particular stimulus in one way and to similar stimuli in another way.

Operant conditioning is a learning process in which behaviors are followed by rewards or punishments. This strengthens the stimulus-response relationship.

Operant conditioning differs from classical conditioning in several ways. In operant conditioning a subject takes a more active role in the process. In addition, in operant conditioning the unconditioned stimulus is not known, whereas it is known in classical conditioning. Moreover, in operant conditioning the reinforcer occurs after the response. In classical conditioning it occurs before.

Reinforcement is an important part of operant conditioning. It may be positive or negative, but it is usually positive. Two important aspects of reinforcement are the amount of time between correct performance and reinforcement and the frequency of reinforcement. Most responses are reinforced only intermittently. Four patterns that may be followed are the fixed-ratio schedule, the variable-ratio schedule, the fixed-interval schedule, and the variable-interval schedule.

Punishment consists of providing a negative stimulus after a behavior has occurred. Research suggests that the negative effects of punishment might outweigh its benefits.

Programmed learning uses the principles of operant conditioning to transmit knowledge. Programmed procedures can free teachers from time-consuming work and permit students to work at their own speed.

Biofeedback is another procedure that is related to operant conditioning. Biofeedback has been used to control such physiological functions as headaches and high blood pressure.

Some researchers take the cognitive approach to explain learning. This approach sees learning as a process of organization. It also views learning as an active process which is guided by experiences. Learning by insight is one example of the cognitive approach.

INTERPRETING SOURCES

In the following excerpt from "Little Brother Is Changing You" (*Psychology Today*, March 1974), Farnum Gray describes the work of Paul Graubard (a school district consultant) and Harry Rosenberg (a school district Director of Special Education) in training junior high school students to use operant conditioning procedures. Their goal was to help students shape the behavior of their teachers. As you study this reading, consider how you might apply the techniques described to deal more effectively with your teachers, friends, and family members.

Jess's eighth-grade teachers at Visalia, California, found him frightening. Only 14 years old, he already weighed a powerful 185 pounds. . . .

Inevitably, Jess's teachers agreed that he was an incorrigible, and placed him in a class for those with behavioral problems. Had they known that he had begun secret preparations to change *their* behavior, they would have been shocked.

His math teacher was one of the first to encounter his new technique. Jess asked for help with a problem, and when she had finished her explanation, he looked her in the eye and said, "You really help me learn when you're nice to me. . . ." Suddenly Jess was consistently making such statements to all of his teachers. . . .

Some teachers gave credit for Jess's dramatic turnaround to a special teacher and his rather mysterious class. They naturally assumed that he had done something to change Jess and his "incorrigible" classmates.

Rather than change them, the teacher had trained the students to become behavior engineers. . . .

Behavior engineering involves the systematic use of consequences to strengthen some behaviors and to weaken others. Jess, for example, rewarded teachers with smiles and comments when they behaved as he wanted; when they were harsh, he turned away. . . .

Stressing the idea that the program was a scientific experiment, the special teacher required each student to keep accurate records.

During the experiment, they were to record daily the number of both positive and negative contacts with their clients. . . .

While the students quickly learned to score negative behavior, they were seldom able to recognize positive behavior in their teacher-clients. . . . [Rosenberg] speculated that students were unable to recognize positive teacher behavior because they were accustomed to failure and negative treatment.

The students learned to identify positive teacher behavior accurately by role playing and by studying videotapes. . . .

Rosenberg and Graubard taught the students various reinforcements to use in shaping their teachers' behavior. . . .

When he explained the project to teachers afterwards, two or three . . . admitted that they had become more positive toward their engineers. It is interesting to note, however, that most teachers tended to think of the project as having changed the *children* rather than themselves. . . .

The crucial goal of the project was to instill within the student a feeling of power, the ability to control the controllers. . . . As a result of their training . . . the students reported feeling more power in their relationships with their teachers and the school than ever before. And with that feeling of power came a new feeling of self-confidence.

Source Review

1. What is behavior engineering? Give an example.

2. In what way was Jess using behavior engineering?

CHAPTER 9

REVIEW

REVIEWING TERMS

learning
reflex
unconditioned
  response (UCR)
unconditioned
  stimulus (UCS)
conditioned
  stimulus (CS)
conditioned
  response (CR)
classical conditioning
counter-conditioning
avoidance conditioning
extinction
spontaneous recovery

reinforcement
intermittent
  reinforcement
generalization
discrimination
operant conditioning
shaping
positive
  reinforcement
negative
  reinforcement
ratio schedule
fixed-ratio schedule
variable-ratio schedule
interval schedule

fixed-interval
  schedule
variable-interval
  schedule
secondary
  reinforcement
punishment
programmed learning
frame
linear program
branching program
biofeedback
cognitive learning
cognitive map
insight

CHECKING FACTS

1. What is meant when it is said that not all behavior is learned?

2. Identify the various components of classical conditioning and explain how this process works. Give an example of classical conditioning.

3. How are counter-conditioning and avoidance conditioning used?

4. Describe the process of extinction.

5. How do generalization and discrimination affect learning?

6. How does operant conditioning differ from classical conditioning?

7. How are animals taught certain unique behaviors?

8. Describe the different types of schedules that are used with intermittent reinforcement.

9. Explain why the negative effects of punishment may outweigh its benefits. What do researchers suggest as an alternative?

10. Describe how programmed learning materials are presented. What are some advantages of programmed learning?

11. Can you think of any disadvantages of programmed learning?

12. What are teaching machines?

13. How does biofeedback help people to control physiological functions? What are some practical uses of biofeedback?

14. Describe some characteristics of the cognitive approach to learning.

15. What is the basis of insight?

APPLYING YOUR KNOWLEDGE

1. Try this classical conditioning experiment on a group of friends or family members. During a group discussion, tap a pencil or your finger on a table loudly three times and say, "Shh! I think I heard something." Do this three or four times. Each time the group should quiet down for a moment and soon return to the conversation. Then make the tapping noise again, this time without saying anything. How did the group respond? How might you "decondition" the subjects?

2. Using discarded magazine photographs and slogans, create a poster or bulletin board display that uses counter-conditioning to teach the avoidance of various undesirable behaviors. You might focus on such behaviors as smoking, drug abuse, and driving while intoxicated.

3. Most people would argue that dogs, cats, and other family pets cannot think. Use Skinner's theory on learning to explain how animal behaviors that seem to involve thought have really been learned through rewards and punishments.

4. Assume you are a psychologist who has been asked to "cure" an irrational fear of taking tests. Using counter-conditioning, explain how you would accomplish this task. You might wish to act out the situation in front of the class.

5. Teachers often use verbal statements or other actions as reinforcers. The reinforcement may be either positive or negative. For example, one teacher might remark, "That's a good paper." Another might say, "Don't come to class late again without a very good excuse." Over a period of several days, make a list of statements and actions made by teachers that would illustrate principles of reinforcement. (Do not include the names of the teachers on any such list.) See if you can also note what effect the teachers' reinforcement has on the behavior of the other person or persons involved.

6. Assume that you wish to teach some animal a complex behavior, such as training a dog to turn a somersault. Break this behavior down into small units. Then describe how you would teach this animal to perform the behavior, using the method of shaping. Include what you would use as a reward, how it would be given, and if you would use punishment as part of the training.

THINKING CRITICALLY ABOUT PSYCHOLOGY

1. **Selecting Information** Assume that you have the necessary qualifications and are employed as a teacher of learning theory at a university. Which theory would you choose to explain how organisms learn? Why would you choose this particular theory and not some other theory?

2. **Explaining Ideas** Consider the following statement: "The more past experiences a person has, and the wider the variety of such experiences, the easier it will be for that person to learn." Would you agree or disagree with this statement? Why or why not?

3. **Forming an Opinion** Do you think social scientists should use principles of operant conditioning to try to shape the behavior of large masses of our population? If so, who should decide what behaviors to reinforce? How would such behavior shaping be done?

4. **Identifying Preferences** How would you like to attend a school where all of the teaching is done by teaching machines? What would you like about it and what would you dislike?

5. **Applying Ideas** What do you think is the most efficient method of learning? Why? Support your answer with specific examples.

DEVELOPING SKILLS IN PSYCHOLOGY

Diagramming Relationships

Like tables and graphs, diagrams can be a useful way of presenting information concisely. Diagrams can be particularly valuable in explaining relationships.

Turn to page 182 and examine the diagram illustrating the relationships among stimuli and responses in classical conditioning. For purposes of illustration, the sample UCS (unconditioned stimulus) is an electric shock, the CS (conditioned stimulus) is a bell, and the response in both cases is finger withdrawal. Note that the arrows indicate which portions of the set of relationships are unlearned and which portion is learned.

This diagram is quite general—that is, it can be used to describe a wide variety of classical conditioning situations. Change the diagram so that the sample stimuli and responses are the ones involved in Pavlov's conditioning of a hungry dog. Then change it again to illustrate the counter-conditioning described in the study of obese subjects. Note that in each case, all you need to do is relabel the UCS, UCR, CS, and CR. Finally, see if you can think of a way to diagram the relationships among stimuli and responses in the case of extinction.

READING FURTHER ABOUT PSYCHOLOGY

Danskin, David G., and Crow, Mark A., *Biofeedback: An Introduction and Guide,* Mayfield, Palo Alto, Calif., 1981. Examines the therapeutic claims of biofeedback. Indicates for what health problems biofeedback is best suited and who it can best help.

Henderson, Robert, editor, *Learning in Animals,* Van Nostrand Reinhold, New York, 1982. A collection of papers written by some of the most renowned scholars in the field of learning, including Charles Darwin and B. F. Skinner.

Huxley, Aldous, *Brave New World* and *Brave New World Revisited,* Harper & Row, New York, 1965. Two set-in-the-future novels that examine the implications and consequences of behavior control for an entire society.

Montessori, Maria, *The Secret of Childhood,* Ballantine, New York, 1982. Describes the development of the Montessori method of education, which is based on the idea that children have a spontaneous urge to learn. The book is filled with an array of educational materials and techniques.

Moore, T. William, Manning, Sidney A., and Smith, Wendell I., *Conditioning and Instrumental Learning: A Program for Self Instruction,* McGraw-Hill, New York, 1977. An introductory look at classical conditioning, including reinforcement, extinction, and discrimination.

Patterson, Francine, and Linden, Eugene, *The Education of Koko,* Holt, Rinehart and Winston, New York, 1981. The story of a young psychology graduate student who used behavioral principles to teach a baby gorilla to communicate.

Pryor, Karen, *Don't Shoot the Dog,* Simon & Schuster, New York, 1984. Demonstrates the practical applications of positive reinforcement in a variety of situations.

Skinner, B. F., *Walden Two,* Macmillan, New York, 1976. A fictional description of a modern utopia based on operant conditioning principles.

Whaley, Donald L., and Malott, Richard, *Elementary Principles of Behavior,* Prentice-Hall, Englewood Cliffs, N.J., 1971. An easy-to-read introduction to learning processes, including conditioning, the method of successive approximation, contingent reinforcement, and stimulus withdrawal.

Chapter 10

LEARNING, REMEMBERING, AND FORGETTING

Chapter Focus

This chapter presents:

- **some factors that may increase your capacity to learn**
- **a look at the process of learning**
- **a discussion of how memory works**
- **some explanations of why people forget**

''My very educated mother just served us nine pickles.''

Nonsense? Not really. The first letters of the nine words represent the order of the planets from the sun. Beginning with the planet closest to the sun, the planets are situated as follows: Mercury, Venus, Earth, Mars, Jupiter, Saturn, Uranus, Neptune, and Pluto.

You probably would have had trouble remembering this fact without some sort of memory device. Yet such devices are only a small part of the process of remembering. In this chapter we will explore this complex process as well as the related processes of learning and forgetting. By studying about learning, remembering, and forgetting, perhaps you will be able to influence how well you learn and how much you remember.

Learning Efficiently

Learning is something you do, not something that is done to you. Knowing how the following factors affect learning may help you to do it better.

1. TRANSFER

Will studying French help you learn Spanish? Will learning in one field transfer to other fields? People once thought that the mind was like a muscle. If used often enough, it would become stronger. They also believed that transfer between subjects occurred quite easily.

Today, however, psychologists no longer hold either viewpoint. They don't believe there are faculties of the mind that can be developed by exercise. Nor do they believe that learning one language automatically makes learning another language easier.

However, transfer is an important factor in learning. We can define **transfer** as the effect of previous learning on later learning, or later performance. Improvement in a given bit of learning as a result of earlier learning is called **positive transfer.** When earlier learning interferes with the learning of new material, **negative transfer** takes place.

Experienced typists know that there is some slight difficulty in changing from one kind of typewriter to another. For example, if they change from an electric to a manual typewriter, there may be some negative transfer. On the other hand, there is also a great deal of positive transfer. Individuals do not have to learn the entire skill of typing each time they change typewriters.

Why is positive transfer important? We can see the importance of positive transfer if we review the topic of generalization. For instance, chimpanzees that have learned to work for a poker chip of one color will work for chips of other colors. A child who has learned to write with a pencil on paper can also write with chalk on a chalkboard. Generalization of this kind saves much time in learning.

Schools do not claim that the way to learn Spanish is to study French and hope for positive transfer. The way to learn Spanish is to study that language. For practical reasons, however, schools encourage transfer whenever it can be useful. For example, technical schools usually cannot afford the kind of equipment found in industrial plants. Therefore they use less costly equipment to teach principles, and trust that there will be positive transfer. People learning to drive a car cannot be permitted to go out on the highway in heavy traffic for their first experience. In some driver-training courses, they are seated in a carlike apparatus. They watch a film taken from a car in actual highway operation. In the safety of their simulated car, they learn what to do under different conditions. They have a chance to judge their own correct and incorrect performances. Later this training transfers to actual automobile operation.

How can the amount of transfer be increased? Many studies show that learning in one situation will transfer to other situations. But we cannot assume that transfer will occur automatically from one field to another. We must make an effort to achieve such transfer.

Training must include both theory and practice. Laboratory courses are designed to promote transfer from theories to everyday life situations. Medical students are given ac-

A child who can ride a tricycle can make a positive transfer of the knowledge of how to use the pedals and handlebars when he starts learning how to ride a two-wheel bike.

tual practical experience with people who are ill. Dental students are required to apply their knowledge to persons needing dental care.

A student's attitude toward transfer is very important. Some transfer will take place without an active effort on your part. But it is much more likely to occur if you do something to bring it about. One way to use learning time efficiently is to look for similarities in various courses, such as in history and literature. Also, look for applications outside of school. For instance, you can make use of information learned in an economics course in your activities as a consumer. Apply the prin-

LEARNING, REMEMBERING, AND FORGETTING

ciples learned in one situation to other situations.

In the future, positive transfer will probably become more important in the educational process. There is a constant increase in the contents of various courses, such as biology, chemistry, physics, and psychology. It is becoming more and more difficult for any one teacher to try to teach all the information in any one course. Therefore, what an individual learns in one course will have to transfer and relate to other courses to a greater extent than happens today. For example, the use of scientific methods as a way of discovering information can transfer to many different courses.

2. MEANINGFULNESS

Meaningful material is much easier to learn than nonsense. Here are several suggestions about the relationship of meaningfulness to learning subjects in school.

The greater the variety of experiences you have, the easier future learning will be. That is, the more basic information you have, the more meaning you will find in each new chapter or book or course. When the basic principles and rules in a subject field are understood, new material in that field will be relatively easy to learn. On the other hand, if you ignore the early lessons in a mathematics course, you are likely to run into difficulty later on. Mathematical formulas can be little more than nonsense material if basic principles are not understood.

It is relatively easy to learn material when you understand the "why" of that material. Also, material that can be applied is easier to learn than material that is theoretical. Often teachers can help students see some use or application for what seems to be purely theoretical material.

3. FEEDBACK

At times, humans and animals seem to learn in spite of unfavorable learning conditions. But they learn more efficiently under favorable conditions. One favorable condition is to have **feedback,** or knowledge of the results of the learning effort. Feedback can act as a reward for behavioral changes in the right direction.

Feedback techniques have been used in many learning situations. For example, they have even been used to help correct poor posture. A feedback device is strapped to an individual's back. It makes a sound as soon as improper posture occurs. In this way, individuals get immediate feedback and can change their posture.

The principle of feedback functions in social situations in our daily lives. For example, we constantly notice how other people react toward us. We consider the feedback. We may then change our own behavior toward them.

In school, you can make use of the principle that knowledge of the results aids learning when you take an exam. You can look up the information after handing in an exam to see which questions you answered correctly. For best results, you should find out the correct and incorrect answers as soon as possible after the completion of an examination. One experiment, conducted over an entire semester, used freshman students in a college chemistry course. Some students checked the answers to short tests as soon as they handed in their papers. Other students did not have knowledge of results until the next meeting of the class. The students who had immediate feedback made considerably higher grades on the final examination.

4. MASSED VERSUS DISTRIBUTED PRACTICE

Massed practice refers to the running together of practice sessions during which material is being learned. **Distributed practice** refers to a type of practice in which the sessions are separated by rest periods.

Which kind of practice is more efficient? At one time it was thought that distributed practice was more efficient in most cases than massed practice. Modern research has indicated that the answer is not so simple. It is complicated by such factors as the following. In massed practice, tiredness may reduce efficiency. In distributed practice, forgetting is likely to occur between sessions. In massed practice, the person may become bored. On the other hand, the person may become bored if a learning task stretches over too long a period of time because practice is spaced. Probably the best answer is that the efficiency of massed and distributed practice depends on the type of learning task involved.

Much experimental work has been done on practice in learning motor skills, such as throwing a ball or dancing. In general, in learning a motor skill, performance is better under conditions of distributed practice, particularly during the early stages of learning. For simple tasks, too, distributed practice is usually more effective than massed practice.

For more complex learning, however, results are different. In one experiment, subjects were required to learn certain nonsense material. The subjects were divided into six groups. Three groups learned under conditions of massed practice. The other three groups learned under conditions of distributed practice. Three tasks of increasing difficulty were assigned to each group. For both the massed and distributed practice groups, the number of trials required to master the tasks increased as the complexity of the problem increased. Also, the difference between massed and distributed practice groups decreased as the task became more complex. There is further evidence that in complex learning, where seeing relationships is important, massed learning may be better than distributed learning.

When to use massed and when to use distributed practice. In general, for learning that involves mostly motor skill, such as typing, some form of distributed practice is best. This is especially true during the early periods of practice. (At later stages, more massed practice may be desirable.) Distributed practice also is better for learning material that requires making responses in a specific order, as in memorizing a poem.

When responses are independent of each other, as in a vocabulary list, the superiority of distributed practice is less certain. As learning becomes more complex, and includes ideas and principles, the advantage of distributed over massed practice becomes less. In fact, the best procedure is massed practice at first, followed by distributed practice.

5. WHOLE LEARNING VERSUS PART LEARNING

Students have to memorize a certain amount of material. The music student must memorize long passages of music to play in a concert. A person who studies acting must memorize many speeches. The student in a

Is it more effective to learn a new song on the clarinet in one long session (massed practice), or in several shorter sessions (distributed practice)?

chemistry course may be required to memorize formulas. Foreign language vocabulary usually must be memorized.

Perhaps you've wondered, "Should I try to learn this material as a whole? Or should I learn it part by part and then combine the parts into a whole?" At one time, psychologists felt that it was more efficient to learn material as a whole. But more recent evidence suggests that the answer is not so clear-cut. Whether the whole method is superior to the part method seems to be related to the general intellectual ability of the learner. There is evidence that the whole method is more efficient for children of superior intellectual ability than for children of normal ability. Also, the more a learner uses the whole method, the more effective it becomes for that person. If the learner is using distributed practice, the whole method seems to be superior to the part method.

Should you use whole or part learning? You will need to determine for yourself which method—whole or part—is better for you. And you cannot depend on your general impression. You will have to test out both methods with a variety of courses. Keep track of the time you spend. Try to check your learning by seeing how much you remember and what grades you get.

Most students find that they learn meaningful passages more efficiently by the whole method than by the part method. On the other hand, disconnected material, such as vocabulary words, probably can be learned at least as well by the part method.

The part method has the advantage of reinforcing learning at frequent intervals. You can feel that you are making progress. However, the part method involves the additional task of eventually putting the parts together to make a whole.

For greatest learning efficiency, the whole and part methods may be combined. In many learning situations, it is probably best to begin with the whole method. You can then use the part method with the difficult sections. This way you don't have to spend time going over material you already

know well. At the end of your study session, you should return briefly to the whole method to review and to check on your learning.

6. MNEMONIC DEVICES

Sometimes the use of memory aids, or **mnemonic devices**—such as catchwords, jingles, and formulas—helps you recall particular facts. For instance, as we noted earlier, such a device can help you remember the order of the planets from the sun. Or, the following rhyme may help you remember when Columbus landed in America.

> In fourteen hundred ninety-two
> Columbus sailed the ocean blue.

Then there is the story of the pupil who wrote 1493 on the exam because

> In fourteen hundred ninety-three
> Columbus sailed the deep blue sea.

It is always possible to make such mistakes when we depend on mnemonic devices. Nevertheless, mnemonic devices can be of some value in learning simple facts and organizing the information to be remembered. For example, mnemonic devices can be used to learn foreign languages. Suppose you want to learn new words in a foreign language. First you associate the foreign word with an English word that sounds like the foreign word. Then you link the two words by forming a mental image of the association. For example, the Russian word *zvonok* means "bell." It is pronounced "zvahn-oak." So you might imagine a swan under an oak tree with bells on it. In an experiment in learning Russian, the group that used this method recalled 72 percent of the items on an exam. The control group recalled only 46 percent.

Another use of mnemonic devices is known as the **loci method.** This method works by relating the items to be remembered to a list of locations. You first establish a list of locations that are familiar to you. This might include places that you pass when you walk from your kitchen out the front door to

Suppose you need to remember what to buy at the supermarket. First you select a familiar route, such as the route from your bedroom to the kitchen. Then you associate items on the grocery list with locations along the route.

a nearby building. Then you mentally attach items to be remembered to each of the locations. Suppose you wanted to remember a grocery list that included ice cream and potatoes. You might imagine the ice cream on the kitchen counter. You might see a bag of potatoes hanging from the front door. You would attach other items on the list to other locations on your walk. In one experiment, students were given a total of 100 words to remember. One group of students used the loci method. The other group was left to use whatever procedures it wished. At the end of the sessions, the loci group was able to remember 72 out of 100 items. The control group recalled only 28 out of 100 words.

Thus, mnemonic devices can be a useful tool for remembering certain kinds of data. Be careful, however, not to spend too much time on developing and using mnemonic

devices and not enough time on understanding what is being learned.

7. OVERLEARNING

Suppose you have to memorize a poem, a speech, or a vocabulary list. You study until you can close your book and recite the material without a mistake. Why study more? There is evidence that materials learned to the level of a single perfect recitation are forgotten more rapidly than materials that are studied more thoroughly through **overlearning.** Suppose you study only to the point of being able to recite the material perfectly one time. You will probably find that you can no longer repeat it perfectly by the day of the exam.

In a classic experiment on overlearning, adults were asked to learn lists consisting of

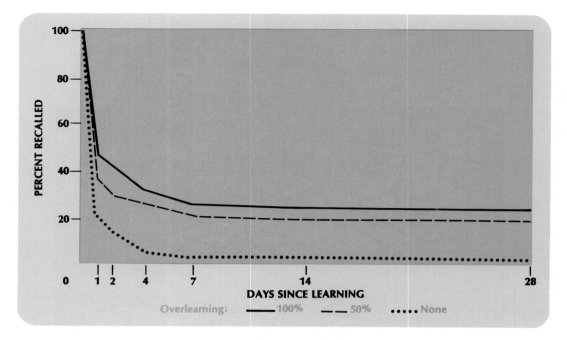

Here you can see the amount of retention following 100 percent overlearning, 50 percent overlearning, and no overlearning in one experiment. How much overlearning do you think you should do?

12 nouns of one syllable each. Some of the lists were repeated until the subject had learned them well enough to repeat them once without error. These particular lists were studied no further. For other lists, the subject went on with the repetitions to the extent of 50 percent overlearning. For example, if four repetitions had been required to make one repetition without errors, the subject went on to a total of six repetitions. For still other lists, the subject went on to the extent of 100 percent overlearning. If it took four repetitions to make a repetition without errors, the subject went on to a total of eight repetitions. Learning was measured at intervals over a period of 28 days.

The results of this experiment are shown in the graph on this page. You can see that overlearning results in an increase in what is remembered, especially over longer periods of time. Note also, however, that the returns are less for considerable overlearning. There is less difference between 50 percent over-

learning and 100 percent overlearning than there is between no overlearning and 50 percent overlearning. The advantages are even less at 200 percent.

8. CHUNKING

Another method that we use to help us learn is chunking. **Chunking** is the combining or grouping of information into related units.

For example, suppose you are asked to memorize this list of words: cat, dog, fish, yard, house, tree, ball, bat, and toy. You might find the task easier if you grouped these words into the following chunks:

cat	yard	ball
dog	house	bat
fish	tree	toy

The items in each chunk are related.

Another instance of chunking can be seen in the following example. Which is easier to learn—the number 7672676 or the word "popcorn"? Most likely you would say the word "popcorn." This is because you see it as an entire familiar chunk. The number consists of seven isolated bits of information, although each digit corresponds to a letter of the word "popcorn" on a telephone dial. Until the whole number takes on meaning, you see it as seven chunks.

The Process of Learning

We have been considering specific techniques involved in learning. Now let's look at the entire process of learning a set of facts or a skill. How fast should that process be? Should we expect to improve at a steady rate until we achieve mastery?

Graphs of learning. Graphs can show us how learning progresses. Suppose we could measure the process of learning a skill or set of facts from the very beginning to at least a fair degree of mastery. The graph of our data would probably show an S-shaped curve, as indicated on this page. Learning progress is generally very slow at first. Then it speeds up. And finally it slows down.

Graphs of learning data for an individual are usually irregular. One day we may not have as good a record as on a previous day. Perhaps the learning process itself is irregular. Or perhaps the irregularity comes from not being able to measure all that is really taking place as a person learns.

Sometimes people become discouraged because they slow up in a given learning process. They may be slowing up because they are nearing the end of the total learning process. They may have reached a fair degree of mastery. On the other hand, the slowing up may be just a stage.

Plateaus. Occasionally there are one or more plateaus in a learning graph. A *plateau* is a period of little or no apparent progress in learning. There is measurable learning both before it and after it. A plateau occurs more

often in learning a complex skill than in learning a simple skill.

At one time, psychologists conducted a study of workers learning a particular industrial job. They found that the productivity of the workers rose rapidly and steadily for the first ten weeks of the job. This learning was followed by a ten-week plateau. After the plateau there was a further rise in skill, but at a slower rate.

If you ever learned to type, do you think data on your progress might have shown a plateau? People who learn to ski often feel that they go through a plateau period. Might you have a plateau while learning to play a musical instrument?

Why does a plateau occur? There are a number of possible explanations. A plateau is likely to occur when the learner becomes bored. Beginning typing students are quite enthusiastic. They are on their way to learning a very useful skill. Their motivation is high. In time, however, the novelty wears off. They become discouraged. They lose interest. And their progress levels off. In this situation, a short period of no practice may be helpful. The learner may return to the original practice material with renewed enthusiasm and leave the plateau.

This is an S-shaped curve — the typical shape of a learning curve. It shows the progress from starting to learn a skill to mastering it.

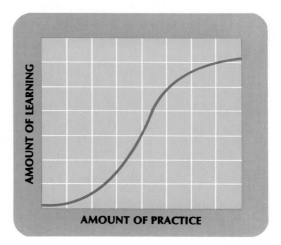

AMOUNT OF LEARNING

AMOUNT OF PRACTICE

213

A plateau may occur when the learner has to discover a better work method. For example, some people learn to type by the hunt-and-peck system. They may achieve considerable speed with this system. But they don't become excellent and efficient typists. To become good typists, they must change to the touch system. A plateau may occur while the change is being made. As they acquire skill in the touch system, they leave the plateau.

Lessons from a skilled teacher may help an individual leave a plateau. Suppose your progress in learning to play a musical instrument has leveled off. A music teacher might help by instructing you to change the position of your hands or the angle of the mouthpiece.

A plateau may appear because the learner has not understood earlier material.

In learning to play soccer, people sometimes reach a plateau. Such plateaus, though, may disappear through practice or the help of a skilled teacher.

Learners leave the plateau as soon as they master this earlier material.

When the learner becomes tense, a plateau may occur. Knowing that a plateau is only temporary and that further progress will come may relieve the tension. It may help the learner rise above the plateau.

Also, the plateau may not represent an actual lack of improvement. The learning curve does level off temporarily. But if we could measure the learning process more accurately, we might find that progress is steady. The plateau might disappear.

Remembering

Included in our discussion of learning has been the idea of remembering. We learn with the thought that at some future time we will be able to recall what we've learned. Quite a bit of experimental work has been done on **retention**—on what is retained or remembered. There are a number of different methods for measuring retention. We will consider three basic methods here.

The method of relearning. The method of **relearning** can be illustrated by a classic experiment of the German psychologist Hermann Ebbinghaus. He wanted to avoid the effects of previous experiences. So he introduced the use of nonsense syllables (meaningless syllables, such as *lar* or *ral*) in his experiments on learning. Serving as his own subject, he memorized lists of nonsense syllables. He recorded the amount of time it took him to learn each list until he could make two errorless recitations. Following various intervals, he relearned the lists. He again kept a record of the time required. The difference between the time needed for the original learning and the time needed for relearning was a measure of retention. The table on page 215 shows the percent of material recalled after varying elapsed times. Note, however, that there is greater retention for meaningful material.

Other experiments also have indicated that material once learned can be relearned with less effort than material not learned before. This is true even when the original learning occurred early in life and a long time elapsed between learning and relearning. A psychologist read selected passages of Greek to his child when the child was between fifteen and thirty-six months of age. When the child was eight and a half years old, and again when he was fourteen years old, he had to memorize these same passages as well as new Greek passages of equal length and difficulty. At age eight and a half, 27 percent fewer repetitions were required for the passages heard in infancy. By the age of fourteen, the saving was reduced to 8 percent. Yet there was some retention for what was obviously nonsense material to the young child.

Perhaps you have studied a foreign language in high school. Later, in college or while traveling, you may need to read, write, or speak this language. At first it may seem that you have completely forgotten your high school language training. Yet it takes much less time to relearn vocabulary than to learn the same amount of vocabulary in a language you've never studied.

The method of recall. In the *recall* method of studying retention, individuals are asked to reproduce certain material that they have learned in the past. For example, subjects may be asked to learn a list of nonsense syllables or words. Later, their retention is measured by giving them the first syllable or word. They are to respond with the rest of the list.

Another method of measuring recall involves anticipation. The syllables or words are shown on a machine, one at a time, at intervals of a few seconds. Then they are presented again, in the same order. During the interval between showings, the subject tries to anticipate what the next syllable or word will be. Usually the series is repeated, until the subject can correctly predict the next syllable or word for the entire list.

All students have a great deal of experience with the recall method. For instance, essay questions on an exam measure reten-

INTERVAL BETWEEN LEARNING AND RELEARNING	PERCENT RETAINED
None (immediate recall)	100
20 minutes	58
1 hour	44
9 hours	36
24 hours	34
2 days	28
6 days	25
31 days	21

The retention of lists of nonsense syllables, as measured by Ebbinghaus.

tion by the method of recall. You are asked to reproduce in some form material that you've learned in the past, without having any of the data before you.

The method of recognition. Suppose, following an essay exam, you talk over the questions and answers with some of your classmates. Perhaps there was one question that you found particularly difficult. Your friends mention the answer they gave. You recognize immediately that their answer represents what you had learned. That is, you use the method of *recognition.*

Usually, objective questions are used to measure retention by the method of recognition. An objective test may contain a question such as the following:

1. The strengthening of a stimulus-response association by following the response with a reinforcing stimulus is a definition of what kind of conditioning?
(a) classical   (b) Pavlovian   (c) operant
(d) none of these

Isn't it easier to recognize the correct response to this question than to have to recall the answer to the question, "How do we define operant conditioning?"

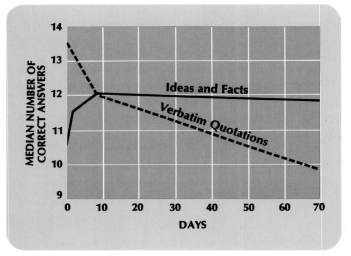

How does the retention of general ideas compare with the retention of exact words?

Are ideas or exact words easier to remember? Sometimes students try to memorize word for word the material in their textbooks. Later, they may find that they cannot recall material studied in this way. Psychologists have found that long-time retention is greater for ideas than for memorized statements.

In one study, students were required to recognize the correctness or incorrectness of statements on the basis of a passage they had read previously. Some of the statements were worded exactly as they had been in the passage. Others were worded differently, although expressing the same general idea as the original passage. Retention was measured at various intervals over a period of seventy days. The results are shown in the graph on this page.

As you can see, there was actually a rise in retention of essential ideas and facts for a number of days following the reading of the passage. This rise occurred even though retention of essential ideas was lower at first than word-for-word retention. Some loss followed the rise in retention of essential ideas. But this loss was slight compared with the loss for word-for-word retention.

Apply the results of this experiment to your own studying. Do you merely try to memorize what the book says? Or do you focus on understanding the meaning of what you read?

Do you remember what you hear while you are asleep? It has been estimated that in a normal lifetime a person spends approximately twenty-three years sleeping. If some of this time could be used for learning purposes, total learning could be greatly increased. A few research reports suggest that people can remember some of what they hear while in light sleep. In one study, subjects were told that they would hear paired Russian-English words while they slept. None of the subjects had any knowledge of Russian. The probability of a subject correctly guessing the paired words was zero. The average recall after five nights of sleep was 13 percent.

It appears that there may be slight retention of what is heard during a light stage of sleep. However, individuals who spend their time learning while awake will learn much more than those who try to learn when asleep. No learning at all occurs during deep sleep, so you should not expect to learn psychology by having your textbook read to you while you sleep!

Does sleep after learning help retention? Experiments have shown that learning followed by rest is retained better than learning followed by an activity. We usually seem to rest most completely when we sleep. Therefore, is retention of learning followed by sleep better than retention of learning followed by waking activity?

To answer this question, six subjects were tested 24, 48, 72, and 96 hours after the original learning. There was more retention of learning in the sessions followed by sleep. Other experiments indicate that details of organized material are remembered better if the learning is followed by sleep rather than by waking activity. But important items are retained about as well when the person stays awake after learning them.

How does memory work? Memory is much more complex than was originally believed. In the past, studies tended to view memory as a stimulus-response behavior. A particular stimulus occurs. A response is made to it. You "remember" the connection made between them. Thus, when the stimulus occurs again, the same response will follow.

In recent years, psychologists have adopted a somewhat different approach to studying memory. This approach may be divided into four processes: encoding, rehearsal, storage, and retrieval. *Encoding* involves changing data from one system of communication to another. Encoding begins with a physical stimulus, such as the words on this page. You somehow change this stimulus from a sensory input (visual in this case) to a form that can be handled by your memory system. Suppose you look up a telephone number and want to remember it to use in the future. First you must encode the number.

Rehearsal involves repeating or practicing information. For example, suppose you look up the call number of a library book. You would repeat the number to yourself until you can get to the correct shelf. This rehearsal is necessary to prevent you from forgetting the information.

Storage means that the encoded and rehearsed information is kept in your memory system. Without storage, of course, there would be no memory.

Retrieval refers to the process by which you can recall the information stored in your memory system. No one knows for certain how much information the memory system can store. But it is probably at least hundreds of thousands of varied bits of information.

Sensory registers, short-term memory, and long-term memory. One model suggests that there are three parts to memory. These are sensory registers, short-term memory, and long-term memory. *Sensory registers* are a type of memory in which information is stored momentarily. In fact, sensory registers last only about a quarter of a second. During that time, information is either encoded or lost.

Information that gets encoded enters short-term memory. *Short-term memory* (STM) is a type of memory that lasts anywhere from a few seconds to about half a minute. While the information is in STM, it can be recalled perfectly. For it to stay there, though, it must be rehearsed.

Short-term memory has a limited capacity. In addition, it constantly receives

Text continues on page 220.

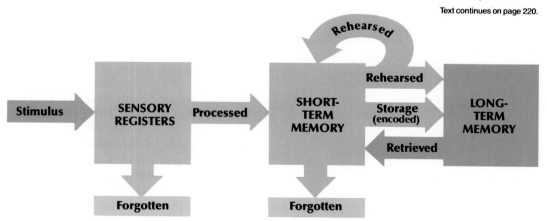

Stimuli from the outside world enter the sensory registers. Those that are encoded enter short-term memory. Here some remain as long as they are rehearsed. Those that are not rehearsed are forgotten. Still others that are needed for future use are rehearsed and coded for storage in long-term memory. When needed, they can be retrieved.

Case Study: Focus on Research

"I SAW IT WITH MY OWN EYES"

Have you ever been in the following situation? You and a friend both witness an event and start discussing it. However, the more you talk, the more your accounts seem to differ.

This sort of thing happens quite often, since what we see is not necessarily what we remember. Although people place a great deal of value on eyewitness reports, studies have shown that our memories often are quite unreliable.

In one study researcher Robert Buckhout and his associates staged a mock assault in a classroom at California State University. While the class was in session, a stranger suddenly burst into the room and headed straight for the professor. The man began

Although many people may have witnessed this car crash, their accounts of the crash may differ greatly. What we see is not necessarily what we remember.

shouting and swinging his fists. After being pushed away, the intruder left as quickly as he appeared.

Although this event was far from commonplace, it seemed not to make much of an impact on the victim or the witnesses. Only a few weeks after the incident, a majority of the class was unable to identify the assailant correctly. After being shown six photographs from which to choose, a striking 60 percent of the class—including the professor himself—selected the wrong man. Almost half picked a person who was in the room at the time, but who was an innocent bystander.

Psychologist Elizabeth Loftus also investigated the reliability of people's memory. One hypothesis that she tested was whether leading questions—those whose form or content suggested certain answers—would influence a person's recall of an event. For example, would "When did you stop fighting with your brothers or sisters?" prompt a different answer than "Did you ever fight with your brothers or sisters?"

In one study Loftus and her assistants showed a hundred students a short film depicting a five-car collision. They then asked the viewers to answer a 22-item questionnaire about the film. Three of the questions focused on items that did not appear in the film, such as broken headlights. Half of the subjects were asked a neutral question: "Did you see a broken headlight?" The other half were asked a leading question: "Did you see the broken headlight?" The only difference between the two questions was the substitution of *the* for *a*.

On the average, 15 percent of the group that was asked a leading question recalled that they had seen a nonexistent item. In contrast, only 7 percent of the neutral group claimed to have observed something that did not exist. The groups also differed in the percentage of "don't know" answers. Such answers occurred more than twice as often among the neutral group as among the group that was asked the leading questions.

In another experiment, Loftus tested subjects' reactions to different verbs. She asked one group, "About how fast were the cars going when they hit each other?" Other groups were asked the same question except that the words *smashed, collided, bumped,* or *contacted* were used instead of *hit.* She found that answers differed, depending on which verb was used. Subjects who saw the word *smashed* gave the highest estimates of speed. Those who had questions with *contacted* gave the lowest. Responses for *collided, bumped,* and *hit* fell in between, ranging from high to low.

In a variation of this experiment, subjects were given the same question with the verb *hit* or *smashed.* As before, those who saw the word *smashed* guessed a higher speed. Then a week later subjects were asked whether they had seen any broken glass in the film. (In actuality, there was none.) Twice as many of the group whose questions contained *smashed* answered yes. Thus those who remembered more dangerous speeds also filled in their recollection of the accident with appropriate details.

Why do answers vary so drastically? Why do we see things that aren't there? One reason for such distortion is the nature of the process of recall. When asked to describe an event, we do not simply retrieve a memory and read off what we've stored. Instead, we reconstruct the event, using not only our original perception, but information from various other sources as well. For example, an unusual incident from our childhood is commonly remembered not simply through our own eyes, but also as we have heard it described by our parents or other relatives.

Studies like these reveal how complex the process of remembering can be. The next time you hear someone say, "I saw it with my own eyes," you may indeed wonder if every detail is correct.

SOURCE: R. Buckhout, "Psychology of the Eyewitness," in P. G. Zimbardo and F. L. Ruch, *Psychology and Life,* 9th ed., Glenview, Ill.: Scott, Foresman, 1977; Elizabeth Loftus, "The Incredible Eyewitness," *Psychology Today,* December 1974, pp. 116–119.

Juries often rely on eyewitness testimony to help them reach a verdict. Eyewitnesses, though, may have faulty recollection of an event.

new information from the senses. Therefore it must either encode all this information, or the information is forgotten.

Information that will be used in the future can be kept in long-term memory. **Long-term memory** (LTM) is a more-or-less permanent type of memory storage. It is like a large storage room. The question then is, "Why is it difficult to recall some information from LTM?" One possible answer is that some information never reaches LTM (although we may think it has). Another possibility is the lack of a stimulus by which the individual can locate the information properly once it is stored in LTM. It is one thing to store information away. It is another thing to find it at a later time—especially when it can be filed under many different headings.

Forgetting

There are a number of theories that attempt to explain why we forget. We will examine five of these theories: (1) elapse of time, (2) inattention, (3) retroactive inhibition, (4) proactive inhibition, and (5) motivated forgetting.

1. Elapse of time. This theory assumes that when we learn, a **memory trace** is laid down in the nervous system, and especially in the brain. Learning causes a physical change in the brain and nervous system. This memory trace fades and disappears over time.

To date there is little evidence to support this belief. One argument against this theory is that some apparently "lost" material is later remembered. There is a record of one man who, at the age of ninety, suddenly recalled a poem of eight lines that he had learned at the age of fifteen. He could not remember having heard the poem again during the interval of seventy-five years.

2. Inattention. Another explanation for some forgetting is that we sometimes don't pay attention when we are supposed to be learning. For example, we are introduced to someone. Unless we are paying close atten-

tion, it is sometimes very difficult, if not impossible, to recall the person's name after a few seconds. The name has not been encoded for storage in long-term memory.

3. Retroactive inhibition. The theory that new learning may interfere with old learning is called **retroactive inhibition.** For example, in one experiment subjects were required to learn a list of nonsense syllables (List A). Next, they learned a different list of nonsense syllables (List B). Then they were required to recall List A. A control group learned only the syllables on List A. The control group was able to recall more of List A than the experimental group. The control group had no new learning to interfere with their memory of List A. (This is why sleep after learning helps. It prevents this inhibition.)

Other studies suggest that retroactive inhibition is greatest when the original learning is followed by the learning of very similar material. There is less interference if the new learning is quite different from the original learning.

4. Proactive inhibition. Proactive inhibition is similar to retroactive inhibition, except that the order of the interference of learning material is turned around. That is, **proactive inhibition** is the interference of old learning with new learning. In one experiment, subjects first learned List A and then List B. Then they were asked to recall List B. A control group showed that the earlier learning of List A interfered with the recall of List B.

Actually, evidence has shown that experience with learning lists does improve the learning of new lists. But it also shows that past experience in learning such lists interferes with the recall of lists or information of a similar nature. Such interference is considerably less, though, when the material learned is meaningful. Also, overlearning can reduce the amount of interference.

5. Motivated forgetting. An important aspect of forgetting is the individual's motives.

One instance in which an individual is motivated to forget is **repression.** Repression is an unconscious process by which we make memories unavailable to recall. The reason is usually that we become uncomfortable when we do recall them. Such memories are not lost because of an organic decay or time lapse. For under hypnosis these memories can be recalled. In one experiment, subjects were hypnotized. They were told that upon waking they would not be able to remember certain critical words suggested to them while under hypnosis. When the subjects awoke, hints were given to them. But they could not remember the critical words. To prove that these words were not permanently forgotten, the subjects had also been told, while under hypnosis, that they would remember the words when given permission to do so. When the subjects received verbal permission to remember, they did recall all of the repressed words.

No single belief or theory can answer all questions related to forgetting. At present we must use a number of different approaches to explain why we forget. All the approaches agree, however, that forgetting—like learning—is an active process, not a passive one.

Summary

There are several factors that can help you learn efficiently. These include transfer, making material more meaningful, feedback, the use of massed and distributed practice, deciding when to use whole and part learning, mnemonic devices, overlearning, and chunking. Used correctly, each of these factors can make learning easier.

Learning typically progresses in the shape of an S-shaped curve. Learning starts out slowly, then speeds up, and finally slows down. There also may be one or more plateaus in a learning curve.

Three basic methods for measuring retention are relearning, recall, and recognition. In the relearning method, the difference between the time required for the original learning and the time needed for relearning is a measure of retention. In the method of recall, people are asked to reproduce material that they have learned in the past without having it available. With recognition, several choices are provided, but people must recognize the correct answer.

Studies have shown that it is more efficient to memorize ideas rather than word-for-word quotations. They have also shown that learning while asleep is not a very good way of learning material. However, there is an increase in retention if sleep follows learning.

Memory involves four processes: encoding, rehearsal, storage, and retrieval. In order to remember data, first you must encode it. Then you must repeat or practice it. Next it is stored in your memory system. And, finally, you can retrieve the information when you need it.

One model suggests that there are three parts to memory: sensory registers, short-term memory, and long-term memory. Sensory registers last only about a quarter of a second, during which time information is either encoded or lost. Material that is encoded enters short-term memory, which lasts for about 30 seconds or less without rehearsal. If this material is to be used in the future, it is encoded and rehearsed for storage in long-term memory.

There are many theories that try to explain why we forget. Five important theories are elapse of time, inattention, retroactive inhibition, proactive inhibition, and motivated forgetting.

In *Human Memory: Structures and Processes*, psychologist and memory expert Roberta Klatzky discusses the levels-of-processing theory of memory. According to this theory, the more we think about the meaning of something, the better we will remember it later. Have you ever been unable to remember something that you know you read? Was it because you did not pay enough attention to the meaning of the reading?

An incoming stimulus can be processed in many different ways (or levels), and . . . these various manners of processing can be viewed as forming a dimension called depth (or level) of processing. The processing of a stimulus is roughly divided into three broad domains: physical, acoustic, and semantic. These domains are best illustrated by considering the ways in which a single item, a word, can be processed. First, it can be processed at a physical, or perceptual level—in terms of its appearance. The word *train*, for example, can be encoded as a string of lower-case (small) letters of a certain typeface. Second, the word can be processed in terms of its acoustic properties—how it sounds. *Train* rhymes with *pain* and begins with a sound like that beginning the word *trill*. Third, the meaningful attributes of the word can be processed. *Train* can be represented as a vehicle of transportation, related to car and bus.

Not only can these types of processing be isolated, but they can also be ordered in terms of the depth, or elaborateness, of analysis they involve. It seems intuitively reasonable to say that processing the physical form of a word takes place at a more superficial, or shallow, level than processing its sound, and that processing sound, in turn, occurs at a more shallow level than processing meaning. Thus, the three domains can be ordered, with physical processing at the shallowest level, acoustic processing intermediate, and semantic processing deepest. . . .

The levels-of-processing theory relates these distinctions among types of processing to memory by a very straightforward assumption: Deeper processing leads to better memory. It is as if the act of processing an item leaves behind it traces that are stored and can be retrieved later. The deeper these traces, the better the memory. However, the details of this assumption have been modified since the theory was first described in a paper by Craik and Lockhart (1972). For example, Craik and Lockhart initially assumed that the three domains of processing—physical, acoustic, and semantic—formed a continuum, so that . . . semantic processing could be reached only after . . . acoustic processing. However, later descriptions of the model . . . changed the continuity assumption, [stating] only that the three domains could be ordered in depth and not that each ran continuously into the next. . . .

It is good to keep in mind that no matter what theory you may accept—and this statement goes beyond arguments about models of memory—it is a theory. As such, it is to be taken not as a rigid proclamation or literal description but as a useful tool for describing and explaining events.

Source Review

1. What is meant by "shallow" and "deep" processing? Give an example of each.

2. What are the effects of deep processing on memory? How has this assumption been modified?

3. What are the three levels of processing that Craik and Lockhart described?

4. Do the three levels of processing form a continuum? That is, does one level of processing flow smoothly into the next?

REVIEWING TERMS

transfer
positive transfer
negative transfer
feedback
massed practice
distributed practice
mnemonic device
loci method
overlearning

chunking
plateau
retention
relearning
recall
recognition
encoding
rehearsal
storage

retrieval
sensory register
short-term memory (STM)
long-term memory (LTM)
memory trace
retroactive inhibition
proactive inhibition
repression

CHECKING FACTS

1. How might transfer help you learn? How might it interfere with the learning of new material?

2. What roles do meaningfulness and feedback play in learning?

3. When is it most advantageous to use massed practice? When should distributed practice be used? When is whole learning most effective? When is part learning most effective?

4. Give an example of a mnemonic device. How might mnemonic devices help you learn? What precaution should be taken?

5. What effect does overlearning have on learning? How can chunking help us learn?

6. Describe how learning of skills progresses.

7. When does a plateau usually occur? Why might plateaus occur?

8. Name three basic methods for measuring retention. Explain how each method works.

9. Explain each of the four processes that make up memory.

10. What happens when information enters sensory registers?

11. Describe short-term memory.

12. How does retroactive inhibition affect learning? How does proactive inhibition interfere with the learning process?

APPLYING YOUR KNOWLEDGE

1. Make a list of the courses you have taken that have provided positive and negative transfer for you in school so far. Which classes might you expect to transfer positively to later college courses or job situations? Are there any classes that you think might transfer to life situations, such as marriage?

2. Write a ten-word sentence on an index card. Next, take ten different words and write them in any order on another card.

Then select someone who has not taken or is not taking this course. Show the person the card with the ten randomly written words for ten seconds. Afterward, ask the person to write down as many words as he or she can remember. Next, present the card with the words in sentence form for ten seconds and ask the person to write down these words. On which list did the person remember more words? Why?

3. The next time you go shopping, try using the loci method of memory in place of a shopping list. How efficient was your memory?

4. Take fifteen minutes during class to perform the following experiment. Organize into two groups. One group should memorize the following list of twenty words using any method except chunking, while the other half uses chunking. Each student in the "chunking" group can use chunks of his or her choice. Then after the allotted time has elapsed, have students write down their lists. Which group has a better showing?

desk	pocket	sofa	leg
banana	grapes	sock	shirt
doctor	thumb	bricklayer	pilot
mouse	hair	fish	apple
chair	alligator	cow	lamp

5. Studies have shown that the first and last pieces of information presented in a series tend to be remembered, while the middle items are more often forgotten. You can test this phenomenon by giving a friend a list of 15 words to memorize and write down in order. Check over his or her list for accuracy. Did the middle third contain more incorrect entries than the first and last groups?

Applying this phenomenon to your own study habits, you might place the more difficult subjects at the beginning and end of your study period, with the easier materials in the middle. What effect did this method of learning have?

6. Take 50 small index cards and number them from 1 to 50. Divide a tabletop in half by placing a small board or a piece of string down the middle so that there is a right side and a left side. Next, shuffle the cards thoroughly. Hand the cards to a subject. Tell the person to place all even-numbered cards on the right side of the table and all odd-numbered cards on the left side as fast as possible without making any mistakes. If the person places a card on the wrong side, it must be replaced on the correct side. Time the person to see how fast he or she can correctly place all cards on the table. Repeat this same procedure at least ten times or until there is no further decrease in time for three trials in a row. This is Procedure 1.

For Procedure 2, have the person reverse the order of placing the cards on the table. Even-numbered cards go on the left side and odd-numbered cards on the right side. What happens to the time it takes to place the cards?

For Procedure 3, have the person repeat the first procedure (even-numbered cards go on the right and odd-numbered cards on the left), using the same number of attempts. Compare the learning during Procedure 1 and Procedure 3. Which took less time? Did the reverse placement in the second procedure affect the placement in the third procedure? If so, how?

THINKING CRITICALLY ABOUT PSYCHOLOGY

1. **Evaluating Ideas** Assume that you decide to learn Chinese, and you know someone who can instruct you. How much transfer do you think there would be from English to Chinese? Do you think there would be more or less transfer from English to Chinese than from English to French? Why?

2. **Interpreting Ideas** Suppose all transfer

in learning were positive. How would this affect what is taught in schools? What if transfer were all negative? How would this change what is taught in schools?

3. **Expressing Opinions** Do you think that exams help make school learning more efficient for the student? Which kinds of exam questions do you think should be given? Why?

4. **Analyzing Ideas** Suppose you want to learn to play a musical instrument, such as the piano. Do you think it would be better to learn by "ear" or by learning to read the music? Why?

5. **Forming an Opinion** Suppose you could take a pill that would let you learn anything you wish. Would you miss the enjoyment of learning on your own? What other disadvantages might such a procedure have?

6. **Debating Ideas** Do you think people can take steps to prevent them from forgetting anything? Why or why not? How might their efforts interfere with their ability to learn new material?

7. **Classifying Ideas** Which factor in the chapter would you say is the most important for helping you learn more efficiently? Why?

DEVELOPING SKILLS IN PSYCHOLOGY

Mastering Descriptive Statistics

Psychologists use a number of statistics to describe performance on a particular task. These statistics are the mean, the median, and the mode.

You probably are familiar with the mean already. The mean is the arithmetic average of a group of scores. You calculate it by adding up a set of scores and then dividing by the number of scores in the set. If your grades on psychology quizzes were 90, 95, 85, 80, and 95, your mean grade would be 89. (Note that while this grade captures your average performance, it is not a grade that you actually received on any test, and that it is pulled down by the one low 80.)

In this chapter's figure on retention of general ideas versus exact words, a different type of score is mentioned—the median. This score is the middle score. To determine the median score in a series, one simply arranges them from lowest to highest and chooses the score that falls right in the middle. If we rank order the scores presented previously (80, 85, 90, 95, 95), then the median is 90. Half of the scores are above 90 and half of them are below 90.

Finally, another way of looking at performance is simply to identify the score that occurs most often. We call this score the mode, and in our grades example, the mode (or modal score) is 95. The score of 95 occurred most often in the set.

Determine the mean, median, and mode in the following set: 80, 80, 85, 90, 95, 95, 95.

READING FURTHER ABOUT PSYCHOLOGY

Kellet, Michael, *High Intensity Memory Power,* Sterling, New York, 1986. Describes the physiological aspects of memory. Gives a clear account of what memory is.

Lorayne, Harry, *Page a Minute Memory Book,* Ballantine, New York, 1986. A detailed description of memory, with examples of different systems that can help the reader learn to concentrate and remember names and numbers.

Minninger, Joan, *Total Recall,* Pocket Books, New York, 1984. A comprehensive book that discusses the historical evolution of memory theories, including the current stage theory of memory, memory blocks, and memory enhancements. Includes a brief overview of the brain.

Norman, Donald A., *Learning and Memory,* W. H. Freeman, San Francisco, Calif., 1982. Describes the process of learning, modes of learning, and memory. Written for a general audience.

Schulman, Steven, "Facing the Invisible Handicap," *Psychology Today,* 20:2, February, 1986. Deals with the unrecognized learning disabilities that trouble millions of adults. Includes accounts of several famous people with learning disabilities.

Weinland, James D., *How to Improve Your Memory,* Harper & Row, New York, 1986. Describes time-tested memory devices, many of which are used by professional memory experts to remember names, faces, dates, events, and other useful information.

Chapter 11

THE PROCESS OF THINKING

Chapter Focus

This chapter presents:
- a definition of thinking and the components of thinking
- the shortcomings of uncritical thinking
- a discussion of creative thinking
- a discussion of imagining
- a description of problem solving

Suppose you are asked to draw the figure below without taking your pen from the paper. You also cannot trace over any line twice. Can you perform this task?

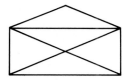

Given enough time, many of you will be able to complete the assignment. (If not, the solution is on page 247.) Perhaps you will reach a solution by trial and error, but you might also solve the problem by thinking.

The ability to think is one of your most valuable assets. It enables you to solve problems, to reason, and to plan for the future. Without this ability, you could carry out very few important tasks. In this chapter we will examine this crucial process.

What Is Thinking?

Perhaps you have a problem. You want to find a solution. You might say to yourself, "If I try method A, I'll run into difficulty W. If I try method B, I'll run into difficulty X. Will I run into difficulty if I use method C? Ah— that's the method that will solve the problem." In other words, you use previous experience to find a solution for the problem. You are engaged in the process of thinking.

Thinking is not easily and directly observable. But it can often be assumed from behavior that is observable. If we watch children solve a puzzle, we can observe their movements. From these movements we determine that they are thinking. Or we can use very delicate instruments to detect the tiny muscular movements of the speech apparatus that often occur during thinking. Or we can use other instruments to measure changes in brain wave patterns.

Thinking implies more than just perception by the individual. It is more than simply becoming aware of objects, qualities, or relationships through our sense organs. It depends on past experience as well. And it implies the use of symbols. We may define **thinking,** then, as unobservable activity by which a person or animal reorganizes past experiences through the use of symbols and concepts. What do we mean by symbols and concepts?

Symbols. Suppose you are attending a basketball game at the West Side High School. You notice several students wearing red and white ribbons. Since you know that red and white are the colors of the high school, you think, "They go to West Side High School." The red and white ribbon is a symbol representing that school — its teams, student body, teachers, and building. A **symbol,** then, is an object, act, or sound that stands for something else. Flags, pins, colors, and badges often serve as symbols for organizations. Gestures, diagrams, pictures, and numbers may serve as symbols in our thinking.

Letters and the words they form are symbols. On a white page you see the black marks MOUNTAIN. These marks mean something to you. Arranged as they are, they have become a symbol for a raised part of the earth's surface. On another white page you see a black mark, ⊥. This mark probably has no meaning for you, unless you know Chinese symbols, or ideographs. The ideograph ⊥ stands for a mountain. To those of us who read English the printed word or symbol MOUNTAIN has more meaning.

We recognize the symbol MOUNTAIN rather than ⊥ because our past experience has taught us printed words rather than ideographs. If we see that a bolt needs tightening, we think of the word or symbol "wrench." (We might also think of an image of a wrench. Images, too, are symbols.) Our past experience tells us that we need the object for which "wrench" is the symbol. Thus, thinking about what we are to do involves making use of our past experience to work out a solution to a current problem.

Concepts. In thinking, we also tend to classify objects and to group them in some way. We do this through concepts. A **concept** is the meaning we attach to the qualities or characteristics that different objects, situations, or events have in common. In forming a concept, we think of similarities and groupings. We associate them with a word or other symbol that can thereafter be used to describe other similar objects, situations, or events. Take, for example, the concept of

"house." We have never seen all possible shapes and sizes of houses. But if we were traveling through the countryside and saw hundreds of houses, we could correctly identify each structure as a house.

To form concepts, we must know similarities. But we must also be able to discriminate, or know the differences between objects, events, or situations. If we did not discriminate between structures, for instance, we might identify all buildings as houses.

How do we form concepts? One psychologist, working with human subjects, presented them with material similar to the figure on this page. He asked them to identify the characteristics that distinguished *dax* from non-*dax*. Then they were to define the nonsense syllable *dax*.

What do you think "dax" are?

All of these figures are DAX

None of these figures are DAX

THE PROCESS OF
THINKING

What does *dax* mean? Did you note that all the figures in the top circle on page 229 are similar in certain respects? Are all the figures at the bottom similar in some ways to those at the top, but at the same time different in at least one important respect? In this experiment, many subjects could correctly identify figures that are *dax*. But often they could not express the principle in words. Did you state your concept in words? Did you spend most of your time looking at the figures at the top or the figures at the bottom? In the experiment the subjects learned much more from studying the positive examples at the top than from studying the negative examples at the bottom. (*Dax* are circles having one dot inside and one outside.)

This experiment may give the impression that developing concepts is a quick and simple experience. On the contrary, we develop and even change many of our concepts over days, months, and years. In forming concepts, it is important to have wide and varied experiences. Sometimes high school and college students become too narrow in their training. They take only courses that seem to have immediate, practical value. They avoid courses that will give them experiences in a wide variety of situations. Over a lifetime we must learn thousands of concepts. These should include broad as well as specialized concepts.

The development of thinking. Perhaps the most complete study of the process of thinking in children was that done by the Swiss psychologist Jean Piaget. He believed that the development of thinking depends on children's interactions with their environment. Piaget described two processes by which we interact with our environment—assimilation and accommodation. *Assimilation* refers to the way we take in new experiences and relate them to our existing cognitive structure. It is a means of handling a new situation on the basis of past experiences. *Accommodation* refers to the way we change our cognitive structure to adapt to each new experience. Through accommodation we adapt to an ever-changing environment. Thus our cognitive structure changes to become a truer representation of "reality."

Each of us is constantly involved in acting on the world around us. At the same time, the world around us is constantly acting upon us. We must learn to react to the world around us in ways that help us to adapt to it. Piaget believed that this constant interaction between the individual and the world is an attempt to bring about a state of balance through the processes of assimilation and accommodation.

Uncritical Thinking

Humans are very proud of their ability to think. Yet when they compare some of their thought processes with mature thinking, humans are far less proud. The concepts developed in childhood are egocentric, or self-centered. Children tend to think of themselves as the center of the world. However, this self-centered thinking does not have the same meaning as when used by adults. It is more the result of children's inability to view the world through a larger frame of reference.

As we become more mature, we learn to understand other viewpoints. But our thinking often is still limited. We may feel sure that we go to the best school. Or that the political party to which we don't belong is totally corrupt. Or that our family is the best in the neighborhood. These are all examples of uncritical thinking.

Instead, we could think critically about schools, political parties, and families. We could analyze them and find both good and bad features. Yet all too often we don't bother. It is frequently easier to accept incomplete information than to examine an issue more thoroughly. Our friends may think the same way, too. As long as we associate only with people who have the same values as we do, we are likely to continue our uncritical thinking. In the following examples of uncritical thinking in our society, consider what the risks of such thinking might be.

"All-or-nothing" thinking. Popular fiction, movies, television, and other mass media may encourage us to go all out one way or the other in our thinking. The child watching a thrilling television program is apt to think that there are just two kinds of people in the world: the good guys and the bad guys. The child may not realize that goodness and badness are relative. The bad guys have some good characteristics, and the good guys have some bad characteristics.

As individuals get older, they become interested in romantic stories, movies, and television programs. They may come to believe that they must be either completely in love or not in love at all. This belief seems to be easier than thinking about friendships in general and seeing romance in the framework of general social relationships.

Many individuals tend to think that they have either good jobs or bad jobs. This "all-or-nothing" thinking is easier than considering their jobs in light of what other jobs offer and what sort of job they can reasonably hope to get.

Confusing coincidence with cause. Sometimes events seem to go together. There is a spell of cold, wet weather, and a large number of people have head colds. We often jump to the conclusion that the cold weather caused the colds. We assume that because two things occur together, one has caused the other. But this is not a scientific conclusion unless we have screened out all other causes. We would also need to know how many people actually had colds before and after the bad weather. We cannot assume that because B is found with A, A caused B. Both A and B might be related to or caused by C. For example, statistics indicate that church weddings are less likely to be followed by divorce than weddings not performed in churches. Would our divorce problem therefore be lessened by requiring all couples to be married in churches? If we examine the issue critically, we find that

In uncritical thinking, we accept the word of a rock singer when he promotes a particular kind of camera, even though he is not a photographer.

other factors are involved. Persons who have fairly stable home backgrounds and religious beliefs tend to marry in a church. Stable home backgrounds and religious beliefs often contribute to lasting marriages.

Delusions. Perhaps the most extreme examples of uncritical thinking are found in the delusions of mentally ill persons. A *delusion* is a false belief that continues despite evidence to the contrary. Persons with delusions may insist that they are great generals who are being held prisoner in a concentration camp. It can be pointed out to them that they

THE PROCESS OF
THINKING

have no military records. Also, the hospital in which they find themselves has none of the characteristics of a concentration camp. Yet they continue to think of themselves as great generals being punished by the enemy. They are incapable of critical thinking.

Anyone can have a delusion. Students sometimes insist that they are brilliant but that all the teachers "have it in for them." They may have done poorly on objective, standardized tests in which no teacher judgments were involved. Teachers may have asked them to come in for personal help. But they ignore this evidence and continue with their uncritical thinking.

Creative Thinking

Sometimes schools are criticized for not producing students who can do truly creative thinking. Actually, it has been estimated that of all the people who have lived throughout history, only about two in a million have become truly distinguished for their creative thinking. We cannot all achieve great artistic and scientific creativity. But most of us are capable of some creative thinking. Schoolwork often calls for creativity.

In *creative thinking,* people strive to discover new solutions to problems or to find new ways of artistic expression that are socially beneficial. They try to discover new and better means of achieving goals. Their thinking produces something that is new for society, or at least for themselves. For contrast, consider "do-it-yourself" kits. We buy the parts, we follow the directions, and behold—we have made a radio or a piece of furniture. Perhaps we buy a numbered canvas and a set of numbered bottles of paint, and we paint a picture. Such activities may be fun and serve a purpose. But they do not give us the opportunity to do creative thinking.

The steps in creative thinking. In various courses you may be assigned to write papers. In laboratory or shop courses you may be asked to design new apparatus or tools. Later, you may have a job that requires some creative thinking. Many individuals have found that the following four steps are helpful to all creative thinking.

1. Preparation. Preparation in creative thinking may be a very long process. It may require weeks, months, or years. Albert Einstein, the famous scientist, wrote his highly creative treatise on the theory of relativity in a few weeks. But he had spent seven years in

Many people have been hit on the head by apples. But it was Isaac Newton who, through creative thinking, made use of this experience to develop the theory of gravity.

232

preparation for the writing. Such extended study is not possible in all creative work. But preparation does mean enough time for a "soaking-up" process. During this time, individuals read widely. They may attend lectures. They talk with others interested in their problem. They strive to find the most useful and productive way to define the problem. They often find it useful to keep a card index of notes and lists of references. Undoubtedly, they will follow some blind leads. For they will have such a mass of material that they can easily become confused. Such confusion, however, should not be discouraging. It seems to be a normal part of the process of creative thinking.

2. "Sitting on" the problem. After collecting many facts and opinions during the stage of preparation, creative thinkers may put their work aside for a while. They have their equipment at hand. And they have at least a rough map of the road they are following. But before continuing on their journey, they take time to allow their thinking to settle. During this period, although the individuals may not work consciously on their problem, they may find themselves thinking about it at odd times.

This stage applies to schoolwork. Students often leave the writing of term papers and other creative work until it is nearly time to hand in the assignment. They don't complete the preparation stage early enough to allow time for their thinking to settle. The absence of this step may cause their reports to be little more than a jumble of facts and opinions. The results represent only the preparation stage of the creative process.

3. Inspiration. This step involves a rather sudden solution to the problem already studied. Individuals may not be able to trace the steps by which they reached their solution. But their inspiration has followed preparation and "sitting on" the problem. There is a dropping out of unrelated material. They see new relationships. Often the new ideas come very rapidly. Although it is still difficult, thinking becomes enjoyable as the goal is neared.

Students may put off all preparation of a report until the last minute, hoping to have a sudden inspiration. But they may be disappointed, for many researchers believe that creative thinking follows a logical sequence. Thus, the first two steps are necessary before inspiration can occur.

4. Verification and revision. It is often tempting to stop with the step of inspiration. More work is needed, however. In scientific thinking, for example, the inspiration may have been incorrect or only partly correct. Objective data are necessary to determine the correctness of the inspiration. Scientists have to go to their laboratory and verify their hypothesis or theory by experimentation. They have to add to their observations. They may need to read further about the thinking of others along similar lines and then revise their thinking a number of times. Painters and writers also need to check and recheck their work to be sure that they've achieved the artistic effect they wanted. They are very likely to make at least minor changes as a result of this verification process.

The four steps that seem to be necessary for creative thinking are difficult steps. But those who follow them can look forward to the reward of knowing that they have achieved something truly worthwhile.

Does brainstorming help creative thinking? *Brainstorming* is a method of thinking in which individuals attempt to solve problems by expressing all the possible solutions they can, without stopping to evaluate them. In the following experiment, two groups of college students were matched on the basis of grades, age, and sex. Brainstorming instructions were given to the first group: "You are to list all the ideas that come to your mind, without judging them in any way. Forget about the quality of the ideas entirely. We will count only quantity on this task. Express any idea that comes to your mind. As you go along, you may combine or modify any of the ideas that you have already listed in order to produce additional ideas. Remember that quantity and freedom of expression without evaluation are the key points."

To the second group the instructions

Brainstorming can be an effective way of developing creative ideas and solutions to problems.

were: "You are to list all the good ideas you can think up. Your score will be the total number of good ideas. Don't put down any idea unless you feel it is a good one."

The results showed that many more ideas of good quality were produced under the brainstorming instructions. Why? The subjects in the experiment suggested that in much of our thinking, we tend to hold back ideas because we fear criticism by others or even by ourselves. Brainstorming seems to reduce this fear. It thereby encourages more ideas, including better ideas. However, because we still may tend to hold back somewhat, some experts believe that brainstorming alone is sometimes more effective than brainstorming in a group.

Some characteristics of a creative person. From experimental data, psychologists know that some individuals are more creative than others. This being the case, do creative individuals have any behavior characteristics in common?

Several different studies have shown that creative individuals are more flexible and more willing to analyze their own impulses than most people. They have a sense of humor. They are independent in both thought and action. They prefer the complex to the ordinary. They show originality and unusualness in solving problems. They prefer to work for self-enjoyment rather than for money or outside rewards. And they see themselves as thorough and responsible individuals who don't like detailed work or conforming to rules.

The most frequently used method to study creativity is to locate individuals who are considered the most creative in their occupation and then determine the characteristics of such persons. One objection to this method is that it overlooks those who may be very creative but are not leaders in their field. For example, an individual may be very creative at repairing things around the house. The person may repair clocks or lawn mowers successfully by making use of parts from other objects that most people wouldn't think of using.

Is intelligence a major aspect of creativity? There is a positive relationship between the two. That is, some people who are creative score high on intelligence tests. But individuals with high intellectual ability are not necessarily creative. In fact, the relationship between creativity and intelligence is very small for people with high IQ's. It seems that motivation and personality are more important than intelligence in influencing creativity among individuals with high intellectual ability. Nevertheless, a basic level of intelligence seems to be necessary for creativity. There is very limited creativity in a school for retarded individuals.

Creative individuals tend to have the characteristics described here. But we cannot assume that a specific individual is creative or not creative on the basis of these characteristics alone. A person who possesses the characteristics described is not automatically creative. Nor does a lack of such characteristics guarantee that the person is not creative.

What conditions help develop creativity? The following procedures can be used to promote creativity: First, providing a rich and varied environment that stimulates thinking. Second, encouraging spontaneity and originality once they appear in the individual. Third, keeping the environment fairly unstructured so that the person is allowed to think freely. For example, creativity is promoted in a school situation by having some homework assignments that allow students to devise different and perhaps better ways of doing the work. Fourth, providing recognition for creativity, not only from parents and teachers, but from the community as a whole. And fifth, recognizing the readiness for creativity, so that it can be developed. Creativity is not always encouraged in our society. Yet the society needs creative people and their contributions.

How do you measure creativity? There are a number of ways to measure creativity. Most of them present the individual with an undefined stimulus, such as a blurred picture. Individuals are asked to do as many dif-

One way of encouraging creativity is to have children develop and present skits. They can act out situations and find solutions on their own.

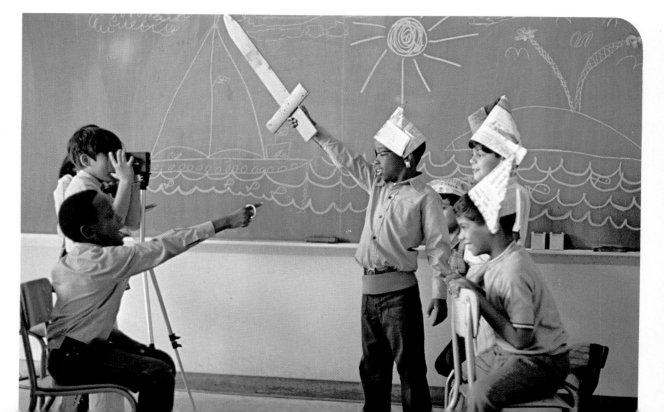

ferent things with it, or associate as many different ideas with it, as they can. The following are a few examples of procedures that are presently being used to measure creativity.

1. Incomplete figures test. Individuals are given a sheet of paper containing several meaningless lines, such as half of a circle or a straight line. They are asked to "make something no one else in class will think of." Each figure is scored for flexibility, originality, and the amount of detail.

2. The circles task. Three dozen small circles are printed on a sheet of paper. Subjects are asked to make drawings using each circle as the main element of a drawing.

3. Consequences. This test might ask such questions as: "What would happen if all water in the world were solid instead of liquid?" "What would happen if all the continents on earth were one great land mass with no water between them?" "What would happen if trees and bushes were made of lead?"

4. Imaginative stories. In a 20-minute period, subjects are asked to write stories about animals or people who show strange behavior.

Most of the tests that measure creativity are scored in terms of the originality of the subject's responses, the number of meaningful responses, the amount of detail, and the flexibility of the responses. To promote consistency in scoring these tests, sample-type answers are often provided. This gives the persons scoring the test a standard of comparison to which they can compare the responses of their subjects.

Imagining

Can you picture how the breakfast table looked this morning? Can you recall the sound of a friend's voice? Such images occur in normal thinking. Psychologists have determined that most, if not all, people are capable of some imagery.

Eidetic images. Particularly lifelike and detailed images are called *eidetic images.* An eidetic image is so vivid that it almost seems like a sensory experience. The person with eidetic imagery is popularly said to have a "photographic mind."

Studies of eidetic imagery are often conducted by showing a picture to subjects for a short length of time, such as 30 seconds or less. Then the picture is removed. The subject is asked to report on the details. The picture may contain an unusual word or a word in a foreign language. The subject with clear eidetic imagery will be able to spell the word both forward and backward. Why? The person can "see" it.

One psychologist tells of a law student suspected of cheating on an exam. The student's answer to one question was a word-for-word reproduction of the law case given in the textbook. The student said that he had been able to recall such a clear image of the textbook page that he could reproduce it on the exam. The faculty decided to test the student. He was given a page of unfamiliar material and permitted to study it for five minutes. At the end of that time the material was taken away. He was asked to reproduce it. He did so — writing some 400 words without a single error. Even punctuation was exactly the same.

How useful is eidetic imagery? Eidetic imagery might be useful for examinations. But having such imagery does not guarantee superior intellectual ability. In fact, there is some evidence that the highest and most abstract kind of thinking does not make use of visual imagery. As you have grown older and turned to more abstract thinking, you probably have less vivid imagery than you had as a child. Research has shown that eidetic imagery seems to be more common in children than in adults.

Imagination. Most of us do not have eidetic imagery, but we still use imagination. That is, we create images based on what we have experienced. Psychologically speaking, *imagination* is the reproduction and reorganization of past experiences into some present pattern of ideas.

Many times our images stem from a dissatisfaction with the way things are. For example, a poor child might imagine living in wealthy surroundings. Or a discontented writer might imagine life as a teacher.

Even when we try to create an exact mental image of something with which we are familiar, very often our image differs from reality. For example, picture the cover of your psychology book. Now try to describe the cover exactly. You will find that your mental image differs from the actual book cover. This is because your brain created an image of the way it sees the cover, not of the way the cover actually is.

Problem Solving

Suppose you find yourself faced with trying to reach a goal. Something prevents you from reaching that goal. You have a problem.

Text continues on page 240.

Marc Chagall's paintings illustrate the effects of imagination. They show a fanciful restructuring of elements in some original way.

Marc Chagall, "Paris Through the Window," 1913; *The Solomon R. Guggenheim Museum,* New York, Robert E. Mates and Susan Lazarus Collection

Case Study: Focus on Research

"A PENNY FOR YOUR THOUGHTS"

The kind of thinking you have been reading about in this chapter is what might be called thinking with a purpose. It is directed thinking—thinking aimed at solving a problem or reaching a correct decision. However, there is another kind of thinking that occupies much of our time. It is known as daydreaming.

Daydreaming is undirected thinking. It is a process of wakeful fantasizing, usually pleasurable. Most of us daydream, letting our thoughts roam freely, although we may feel guilty about it. And—most important—daydreaming may even be beneficial to our health. In some situations daydreaming can help us work through our problems.

Most of us daydream at one time or another. Research has shown that daydreaming in moderation may be beneficial, enabling us to cope with life's difficult situations.

How do psychologists study daydreaming? In one simple study, four graduate students wanted to find out what thoughts pass through people's heads in the course of their normal daily activities. They set up tables at two locations in New York City, each table carrying the sign "a penny for your thoughts."

All in all, 187 people stopped for their penny and wrote down what they were thinking. At one location, people were most involved in thoughts on their immediate environment—for example, how nice the city was. The next category contained thoughts on work—current projects and not wanting to go back to the office that afternoon, to name a few. This was followed by thoughts of love.

At the second location, a less fashionable area, thoughts on material concerns such as money headed the list. Thoughts on future plans were second, and those on love were third.

Overall, more women than men had thoughts on work. A possible explanation, according to the researchers, might have been the nature of their jobs. Perhaps the women's jobs were less interesting than the men's, and they dreaded going back to the same dull routine.

Other, more extensive research studies on daydreaming have been done by Jerome L. Singer of Yale University. For his early studies he devised a questionnaire containing a number of simple fantasies. Among them were "I have my own yacht and plan a cruise of the Eastern seaboard" and "I suddenly find I can fly, to the amazement of passersby." People were to check off whether they had had such a daydream and when.

After testing some 500 subjects—most of them members of the middle class—Singer reported a number of findings. One was that men and women daydream with the same frequency. Another was that men fantasize more about heroic deeds, women more about clothes. Daydreaming, Singer says, reaches its peak in mid-adolescence and then tapers off, although most people fantasize throughout their lives.

Other research done or supervised by Singer revealed still more about who daydreams and what they fantasize about. One study indicated that only and firstborn children are more apt to daydream than are children in the middle of large families.

A comparison of blind with sighted children showed that blind children tend to fantasize in terms of sound and movement. In addition, they daydream about situations close to home. A blind child, for instance, will daydream about a trip to a local supermarket. A sighted child will fantasize about taking off in a rocket ship or on a flying carpet. Blind children, so dependent on others for help, also are more likely to develop make-believe companions.

Why do we daydream? Freud believed that we do so to reduce drives, such as that of aggression. Singer disagrees. To demonstrate his view, he deliberately induced anxiety in subjects by scheduling a surprise exam. Then he assigned one group a distracting task, and allowed another group to daydream. At the end of the allotted period, those subjects who were allowed to daydream showed more anxiety than the others. (Some people would argue, however, that it was simple relaxation and not daydreaming that brought about the increase in anxiety.)

Daydreaming probably serves a number of functions. It restores feelings of self-esteem. If we are turned down for a job, we may imagine ourselves to be the successful president of a giant corporation. In addition, daydreaming may compensate for racial or other discrimination. People who are the victims of discrimination can daydream about being heroes. Daydreaming also entertains us, helps us plan for the future, and allows us to change our moods. All in all, daydreaming—in moderation—is one way of helping us cope with life's challenges.

SOURCE: Jerome L. Singer, ''The Importance of Daydreaming,'' *Psychology Today*, April 1968, pp. 19–26; Jeffrey S. Shaw, Frances Francois, Hadassa Filler, and Vincenza Sciarillo, ''The Thoughts of Persons in an Urban Environment,'' *Journal of Social Psychology*, 1981, *115*, 293–294.

Oh, to be in this tropical paradise! While this may not be possible for many of us in reality, it is a possibility in our daydreams.

Perhaps at some point you've had difficulty in understanding a psychological term or concept presented in this course. If your goal is to understand such things, you've faced a problem. If you are on your way to school one morning and the car that you are in breaks down, you have a problem. Life is constantly full of problems.

Studying problem solving. There are three basic approaches to studying problem solving. Some psychologists emphasize studying the processes involved in problem solving. They would investigate what influences it, the various stages involved, and the emotions that accompany it. A second way is to study individual differences. Psychologists using this approach would investigate how people differ in their method of solving problems. What are the characteristics of those who solve problems rather easily as compared to those who do not? A third approach is to study the various ways in which problem-solving abilities can be developed or promoted.

How can this person tie the ends of both strings together with the aid of a pliers? One solution is discussed on this page.

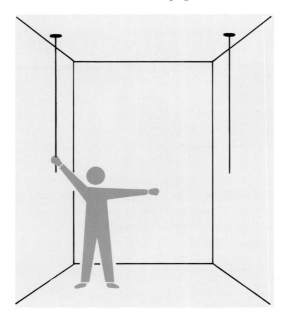

Problem-solving situations have certain common characteristics. Each problem-solving task involves a goal that the person is trying to reach. Past habits alone are not enough to solve the problem. Problem solving also involves the process of thinking. The thinking may be either logical or nonlogical.

Consider the following study of problem solving. Two strings hang down from the ceiling. They are so far apart that you cannot hold the end of one and touch the end of the other. In the room are several small objects, including a pair of pliers. The problem is to tie the ends of the strings together. Before you read further, try to solve this problem. If you do not solve it in a few minutes, return to your reading.

If you were unable to solve the problem, perhaps this hint will help. In the original study, the experimenter walked around the room and "accidentally" hit one string so that it began to swing. Can you now solve the problem? If you don't solve it in a minute or two, continue reading for a second hint.

The second hint given by the experimenter was to hand the subject a pair of pliers. He then said, "With this pair of pliers and nothing else in the room, there is a way of solving the problem." Do you know how to solve the problem now? You tie the pliers onto the end of one string and swing it. While the pliers and string are swinging back and forth toward the other string, you hold onto the other string. When the pliers on the string swing toward you, grab them, untie the pliers, and tie the two strings together.

What factors affect our ability to solve problems? A number of studies have been done on the factors that influence the development of problem-solving abilities.

One factor involves our way of using past experiences. Past experiences can be of help in solving problems. They can also prevent us from solving problems. Generally, the more past experiences we have, and the more varied they are, the easier it will be to solve problems in the future. However, if we have developed a set way of behaving or thinking, this will interfere with problem solving. For example, we may become focused on approaching the solving of different problems in the same way. This lack of flexibility may hinder us in solving problems. In the problem about the two strings and the pliers, suppose we thought only of the main function of a pair of pliers. We would not be likely to see them as anything but a tool for gripping small objects. It would be more difficult, then, to realize that they can also be used to make a pendulum. This factor of becoming focused, or fixated, on only one function of something—like a pair of pliers—is called **functional fixedness.**

Another factor that helps determine how individuals solve problems is the instructions given to them. For example, suppose an experimenter instructs subjects to "think." This will actually cause them to take longer to solve the problem.

Did the hints in the problem about the strings and pliers help you to solve that problem? If so, then this would illustrate another factor that influences problem solving. If individuals are given hints to the solution of a problem, often they will be able to solve the problem faster.

Either too much or too little motivation can hinder problem solving. If individuals have too little motivation, then they will not keep trying to find the solution. However, too much motivation can also prevent the individual from reaching a solution. The individual may concentrate on the goal to be achieved rather than on finding a solution to the problem. Have you ever been emotionally upset when taking an exam because you just *had* to make a good grade? Being upset, did you then have difficulty in supplying the answers to the exam?

Probably the most important single factor in solving problems is flexibility in thinking. It is sometimes called **divergent thinking.** This is a form of thinking in which a person looks for many ideas or solutions to a problem. Such a person does not fixate on just one possible solution to a problem. Rather the person thinks of many possible solutions. The diagram on this page shows how divergent thinking works.

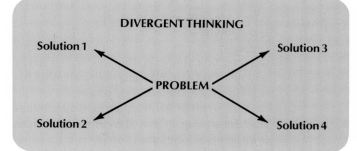

In divergent thinking, people consider various solutions to a problem. People then eliminate any incorrect solutions as necessary.

To solve the following problem, you need to be flexible in your thinking. The problem is: "On a piece of paper, draw a complete circle with a dot in the center without lifting your pen or pencil from the paper. There can be no line connecting the dot to any part of the circle." The end result should look like this:

(The solution is on page 247.)

Reasoning. An important part of problem solving is reasoning. **Reasoning** is the ability to comprehend or think in an orderly and rational way. Reasoning also involves using past experience in a new manner. For example, suppose you go shopping in a new supermarket. Knowing how items are arranged in another store might help you locate things in this one.

Inductive and deductive reasoning. Reasoning is often described in terms of two types—inductive reasoning and deductive reasoning. **Inductive reasoning** moves from specific cases to general principles. The thinker discovers common characteristics in otherwise separate and unique events. For example, suppose you wanted to study the relation between little sleep and low exam grades. You've noticed that if you are tired when you come to an exam, you seem to score low grades on it, even though you are prepared. You might reason inductively from the specific cases of getting low scores when you are tired to the general principle that insufficient sleep causes low scores.

On the other hand, you might use **deductive reasoning.** Here the thinking moves from general principles to specific cases or consequences. You might begin with the general principle that people who are tired are less efficient than are those who are not tired. You might then deduce that in the specific cases where students are tired, they will not perform well on exams, even when prepared for them.

In our daily problem solving, we seldom use only the inductive or only the deductive method. We change from one form to the other and back again many times as we think through our problems.

Summary

Thinking is one of our most valuable assets. Two important components of thinking are symbols and concepts. Symbols are objects, acts, or sounds that stand for something else and that help us reorganize our past experiences. Concepts also help us classify and group objects.

Uncritical thinking is a way of thinking that is often limited in scope and does not consider all available information. Some common instances of uncritical thinking include using "all-or-nothing" thinking, confusing coincidence with cause, and creating delusions.

Most people are capable of some creative thinking. The four steps involved in creative thinking are preparation, "sitting on" a problem, inspiration, and verification and revision. There is also evidence that brainstorming helps creative thinking.

Creative people share several behavior characteristics. They are more flexible, have a sense of humor, are independent, prefer the complex, show originality, prefer to work for self-enjoyment, and dislike rules. There are various ways to promote creativity, as well as various methods of measuring it.

Most people use imagination as a part of thinking. They reproduce and reorganize past experiences into some present pattern of ideas. Some, in fact, even have "photographic minds." These people use eidetic imagery. Eidetic imagery does not guarantee superior ability, but it may be useful.

Problem solving is an important aspect of thinking. Various factors affect our problem-solving abilities. These include our ways of using past experiences, the instructions given to us, motivation, and flexibility in thinking. Inductive and deductive reasoning are also an important part of problem solving.

INTERPRETING SOURCES

If a problem is not seen clearly, solving it is almost impossible. In this excerpt from *Conceptual Blockbusting,* engineer James Adams discusses some obstacles to perceiving problems.

Perceptual blocks are obstacles that prevent the problem-solver from clearly perceiving either the problem itself or the information needed to solve the problem. Perhaps the best way of helping you overcome perceptual blocks is to talk about some common and specific ones.

One: Seeing What You Expect to See—Stereotyping

Stereotyping and labeling are extremely . . . effective perceptual blocks. You simply cannot see clearly if you are controlled by preconceptions. . . .

Once a label . . . has been applied, people are less likely to notice the actual qualities or attributes of what is being labeled.

Two: Difficulty in Isolating the Problem

Problems we face may be similarly obscured by either inadequate clues or misleading information. . . . If the problem is not properly isolated, it will not be properly solved. . . .

Is your problem really a bad tank of gas? . . . Or is your problem a living situation that makes you overly dependent upon a car? Problem statements are often liberally laced with answers. . . .

Three: Tendency to Delimit the Problem Area Too Closely

Just as a solution is sensitive to the proper isolation of the problem, it is also sensitive to proper delimitation (constraints). In general, the more broadly the problem can be stated, the more room is available for conceptualization. . . .

Four: Inability to See the Problem from Various Viewpoints

It is often difficult to see a problem from the viewpoint of all of the interests and parties involved. . . . Certainly in a problem between two people, the ability to see the problem from the other's point of view is extremely important. . . .

Five: Saturation

If the mind recorded all inputs . . . our conscious mind would be very full indeed. Many extremely familiar inputs are not recorded in a way that allows their simple recall. . . .

Very few people can [draw an ordinary telephone dial, putting the letters and numbers in their proper locations]. . . . The mind does not hold on to the locations of all the details of a phone dial, since it does not have to. If the letters and numbers were not marked on the phone, the mind would store the information for easy recall. . . .

Six: Failure to Utilize All Sensory Inputs

Problem-solvers need all the help they can get. They should therefore be careful not to neglect any sensory inputs. An engineer working on an acoustics problem for a concert hall, for instance, should not get so carried away with his theoretical analysis that he neglects to . . . listen to the quality of [the] sound.

Source Review

1. How does the author define perceptual blocks?

2. What are six of the common perceptual blocks? How can an awareness of these blocks help you to solve more of your problems successfully?

REVIEW

REVIEWING TERMS

thinking
symbol
concept
assimilation
accommodation

delusion
creative thinking
brainstorming
eidetic image
imagination

functional fixedness
divergent thinking
reasoning
inductive reasoning
deductive reasoning

CHECKING FACTS

1. How is thinking measured?

2. Why do some people recognize some symbols but not others?

3. How do people form concepts?

4. Give some examples to illustrate the risks of uncritical thinking.

5. Describe the four basic steps involved in creative thinking.

6. Does brainstorming help creative thinking? Explain why or why not.

7. What are some characteristics of creative people? What role does intelligence play in creativity?

8. Describe some procedures that can be used to promote creativity. How can we estimate creativity?

9. Discuss whether or not eidetic imagery is useful.

10. Why do we create images?

11. How do psychologists study problem solving? What do problem-solving situations have in common?

12. Describe some of the factors that influence our problem-solving abilities. How does functional fixedness compare with divergent thinking?

13. Differentiate between inductive and deductive reasoning, and give examples of each.

APPLYING YOUR KNOWLEDGE

1. Read a newspaper editorial and analyze it. You might choose an editorial that discusses some political problem. On the whole, how would you rate the editorial? Is there any evidence of uncritical thinking? Give some examples.

2. Are you a creative thinker? To find out, try to solve each of the following problems creatively. Remember to be flexible and open to unique approaches:

(a) Design a system for dropping an uncooked egg from a height of 3 meters (10 feet) onto a carpeted floor, without it breaking. (Don't try out your system!)

(b) Create a robot for ten dollars or less that will move across the floor, pick up a piece of paper, and drop it into a wastebasket.

3. Try to come up with as many answers as

possible to the following questions. You might wish to work in small groups, with each group tackling only one problem.

(a) What uses can you find for a pair of nail clippers?

(b) In what ways are a spoon and a car alike?

(c) What would happen if tomorrow morning all the bricks in the world turned into hamburgers?

(d) How might you find a needle in a haystack?

How many of your answers involved critical thinking? How many involved creative thinking? Perhaps as a class, you might wish to brainstorm for awhile.

4. To see how functional fixedness interferes with learning, try solving the following problem: How can you mount a candle vertically on a wall if all you have is the candle, a piece of string, some thumb tacks, and an empty box of matches? Refer to page 248 for the solution.

5. Talk out loud to yourself as you try to solve the following problem. If possible, use a tape recorder to record what you say. You will need six sticks (such as matchsticks) of the same length. The problem is:

"How can you make four triangles with equal sides out of six sticks of equal length?" Work on the problem for ten minutes. If you have not solved the problem in that time, turn to page 248 for the solution.

Next, replay your tape recorder and listen to what you said while you tried to solve the problem. What approaches did you take in attempting to solve it?

Did you seem to have flexibility in thinking about solutions to this problem?

6. Imagery might help you improve your memory. To see how this works, carry out the following activity. First, memorize these rhyming pairs and create a vivid image of each object: one-sun, two-shoe, three-tree, four-door, five-hive, six-sticks, seven-heaven, eight-gate, nine-vine, ten-hen. Now, take a list of ten common object names and, one at a time, pair them with each of the original images, creating a completely new image. For example, if the word "truck" is the first word on your list, you might imagine a truck riding along a highway with suns for wheels. Continue until you have created ten pairs of images. Then, to recall the words, think of the original numbered images, and the test words should come to mind. How well did you do? How could you use this memory device in other classes?

7. Organize into small groups. Each group should create a plan for making a million dollars. Each student should write down his or her ideas. The groups should then exchange their plans and critically evaluate each other's plans for flaws.

8. Make a list of some problems that you will be facing in the next week. Then consider the following: (1) Do your problems seem to group themselves in specific areas? (2) What can you do to reduce the number and different kinds of problems? (3) What kinds of solutions do you have for these problems? (4) What other approaches might you take to finding solutions?

THINKING CRITICALLY ABOUT PSYCHOLOGY

1. **Forming an Opinion** To what extent do you think politicians make their appeals through critical thinking?

2. **Applying Ideas** If you were a teacher, how would you go about getting students to think instead of just memorizing facts? What kinds of thinking would you emphasize the most?

3. **Summarizing Ideas** Can individuals really think in more than one language? What evidence do you have for your answer?

4. **Evaluating Ideas** Which of the following contribute the most to society: Creative persons? Those who can solve problems? Those who can reason very well? Explain your answer.

5. **Classifying Ideas** How many symbols can you think of for the word "house"? To what extent do you think the values of a society determine the number of symbols the society has for particular objects?

DEVELOPING SKILLS IN PSYCHOLOGY

Classifying Types of Uncritical Thinking

Suppose you read in a popular magazine that a psychologist has reported evidence indicating that men are more creative than women. For example, suppose the psychologist's research showed that more patents were awarded to men than to women within a particular time period. The author of the magazine article goes on to conclude that if women cannot get patents as often as men, then women must be less capable of completing creative endeavors. The author suggests that such evidence means that there are good reasons to exclude women from advanced training programs in science and mathematics because it would be wasteful to invest in their training. It is suggested that these people will never be able to make creative use of their knowledge, and may never make contributions to their field of specialization.

What types of uncritical thinking would the author be demonstrating by making assertions such as these? Use your critical thinking skills to support the argument that in addition to "all-or-nothing" thinking, the author would be guilty of confusing coincidence with cause. For example, make the argument that even if fewer patents have been awarded to women than to men, the reason for this difference is not necessarily because women are less creative. Support your presentation with facts.

READING FURTHER ABOUT PSYCHOLOGY

Adams, James L., *Conceptual Blockbusting: A Guide to Better Ideas,* Addison-Wesley, Reading, Mass., 1986. Considers various mental blocks and suggests ways to overcome them through creative problem solving.

Berger, Melvin, *Mind Control,* Crowell, New York, 1985. Provides a good introduction to the diverse forms of mind control.

Clark, Ronald W., *Einstein: The Life and Times,* Avon Books, New York, 1984. Presents the human side of the brilliant man who was also known as "the absent-minded professor."

Gardner, Howard, *Art, Mind, and Brain: A Cognitive Approach to Creativity,* Basic Books, New York, 1982. Combines insights from a wide range of psychological areas to examine the human creative process as a whole.

Hampden-Turner, Charles, *Maps of the Mind,* Macmillan, New York, 1982. A collection of work by some of the world's foremost psychologists. Describes various concepts of the human mind.

Harrison, Allen, and Bramson, Robert M., *Styles of Thinking: Strategies for Asking Questions, Making Decisions, and Solving Problems,* Doubleday, New York, 1982. Provides useful techniques to assist the reader in becoming a more adaptable and versatile problem solver.

Perkins, D. N., *The Mind's Best Work,* Harvard University Press, Cambridge, Mass., 1983. A book about creativity that is amply filled with illustrations and exercises.

Roach, Marion, *Another Name for Madness,* Houghton Mifflin, Boston, 1985. A highly personal account of a young woman's suffering as she witnesses her mother's degeneration from Alzheimer's disease.

Solution to problem on page 228.

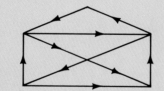

start here

Solution to problem on page 241. Draw the top half of the circle on a piece of paper. Fold the lower half of the paper over so that it fits where you have stopped drawing. Then continue drawing on the *folded* part of the paper, going across to the middle of the circle. Move from the folded paper to make the dot in the circle. Return to the folded paper. Continue your line on the folded paper to the point on the circle where you had left off drawing it. Unfold the paper and draw the lower part of the circle.

Solution to problem on page 245.

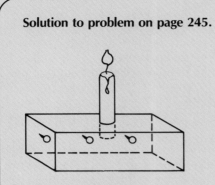

(String is unnecessary.)

Solution to problem on page 245. Lay three sticks on a table so they form a triangle with equal sides. Then stand the other three upright, so that one end of each is in a corner of the triangle on the table and the other ends of each are touching. Now you have one triangle flat on the table and three upright triangles. In working on this problem, did you think only of trying to lay the sticks flat on the table? If you did not try a third dimension, why do you suppose you didn't think of this solution?

Using the Skills of a Psychologist

Unit 4 Shaping Behavior Through Conditioning

As you read in Chapter 9, many behaviors are learned through conditioning. For example, many of you are familiar with the school bell used to dismiss classes. Watch your classmates the next time this bell rings and see how quickly everyone gathers their things to leave. Students are so conditioned to associating this bell with the end of class that many will make motions to leave even though the teacher is still talking! This is behavior learned through conditioning.

Psychologist B. F. Skinner is well known for his theory of operant conditioning. According to this theory, operant behaviors are learned when the desired responses are rewarded or reinforced and the undesired responses are either punished or ignored.

Operant conditioning has many useful applications. For example, many years before Skinner's theory was proposed, a teacher named Anne Sullivan taught young Helen Keller, born both deaf and blind, to finger spell using the principles of operant conditioning. Sullivan would place an object in Helen's hand and finger spell the name of the object in her other hand. She would then guide Helen's fingers to spell the name of the object. Every time Helen correctly spelled the object, Sullivan would reinforce her behavior with a piece of cake. She would give no cake if Helen spelled the word incorrectly. Eventually Helen learned to give the responses quickly and accurately.

This is only one example of the teacher's work with Helen Keller. Anne Sullivan actually devoted years of her life to teaching Helen Keller. Through much trial and error, she taught her student the desire to learn about all aspects of life. Helen Keller went on to become a writer and lecturer known worldwide at a time when other children born with her handicaps were institutionalized and forgotten. The unwritten techniques of operant conditioning used by Sullivan with Helen marked a great teacher and were dramatized in a play about their early years together, called The Miracle Worker.

Today, as you know, animals are often used in movies and television shows. Trainers use conditioning techniques to teach their animals to behave in certain ways. Those of you who have a cat or dog for a pet can try this at home. The first thing you will have to do is establish a conditioned response to some neutral stimulus that you can control. A sound such as clapping your hands twice will do, but make sure you choose a sound the pet doesn't hear often or its conditioned response will be quickly extinguished. Now, wait until your pet comes in for its usual meal. To condition its response, you must give the neutral stimulus, the two hand claps, immediately before you present the unconditioned stimulus (the food). Every time you give the pet its usual meal or a special treat, clap your hands twice before presenting the food.

After about a week you can begin to reinforce the conditioning. Every time your pet walks toward you, clap your hands twice and then pet it and talk to it, or give it some special tidbit of food. You are reinforcing the pet's association between hand clapping and walking toward you, so only reward the pet when it walks directly toward you. Do this for about five days. Then, wait until your pet is resting somewhere and get a special treat ready for it. Clap your hands twice and you will see your pet get up and come over to you. Write a report about your procedures to present to the class.

Students who do not have pets at home may, with the teacher's permission, conduct library research on the conditioning techniques used by professional animal trainers.

REVIEW

REVIEWING THE UNIT

1. Is any one correct theory of learning *the* correct one? Why or why not?

2. What are the five theories that attempt to explain why we forget?

3. Is forgetting an active process or a passive process?

4. Why is coincidence often confused with cause?

5. How may daydreaming in moderation be beneficial?

6. What is probably the most important single factor in solving problems?

CONNECTING IDEAS

1. **Seeing Relationships** What is the relationship between learning and thinking?

2. **Analyzing Ideas** What role does meaningfulness play in the memory process?

3. **Correlating Ideas** In what way might overlearning limit creative thinking?

4. **Contrasting Ideas** Why is it important to recognize patterns that lead to uncritical thinking?

PRACTICING RESEARCH SKILLS

1. Review the definition of shaping on page 189. With your teacher's approval, select a research project that uses operational conditioning. After you have read about the project, analyze the information and describe any shaping methods that were used. Then write a paragraph that explains why shaping was or was not an important factor in the research.

2. Advertisers often use mnemonic devices such as catchwords and jingles to help people associate these devices with specific products. With your teacher's approval, look at several advertisements and television commercials for selected foods or household products. Identify the mnemonic devices. Was the advertisement primarily auditory, visual, or a combination of both? What imagery was used to make the product appealing to consumers? Did time or place affect your interest? For example, if the commercial was advertising pizza, would it be more important to you before you had eaten an evening meal? Would your perception of the commercial be different if you saw it before breakfast?

FINDING OUT MORE

You may wish to contact the following organization for additional information about the material in this unit.

University of Minnesota
Center for Research in Human Learning
205 Elliott
Minneapolis, MN 55455

Unit 5

PERCEPTION, EMOTIONS, AND MOTIVES

Chapter 12 SENSATION AND PERCEPTION

Chapter 13 MOTIVATION AND EMOTIONS

Chapter 12

SENSATION AND PERCEPTION

Chapter Focus

This chapter presents:

- **the relationship between sensation and perception**
- **an overview of attention**
- **a detailed look at the senses of vision and hearing**
- **a brief discussion of the other senses**

Read the sentence below aloud. How many "f's" are there in the sentence?

Finished files are the result of years of scientific study combined with the experience of many years.

How many did you count? Three? If that's your answer, then you had better count again.

Actually, there are six "f's" in the sentence. The words "finished," "files," and "scientific" each contain one "f." In addition, there is an "f" in each of the three "of's." Chances are that these are the ones you missed.

Nothing is wrong with your eyesight, although you might not be convinced. It's just a case of your eyes playing tricks on you. More exactly, your visual sensation differed from your perception.

Sensation and perception are two important concepts in psychology. **Sensation** refers to the arousal of a sense organ by something in the environment. In this case your eyes were aroused by the writing on this page. **Perception** refers to the interpretation of this sensation. Thus, you may have seen six "f's" but perceived only three.

The reasons for this phenomenon are quite complex. Stated simply, though, you were expecting to find "f's" that sounded like "f's." Since the "f" in "of" sounds like a "v," you may have passed right over it three times.

In this chapter you will learn more about sensation and perception. You will also learn about the various sense fields. Your understanding will help increase your awareness of the world around you.

The Senses

Perhaps you have been told that humans have five senses: those of seeing, hearing, touch, smell, and taste. But there are also others, such as the skin senses and bodily movement senses.

A person's senses are able to respond to very low amounts of stimulation. For example, most people are so sensitive to light that they can see the glare of a match at a distance of about 48 kilometers (30 miles) on a clear dark night. In a quiet room they can hear the ticking of a small clock at a distance of even 6 meters (20 feet). The sense of touch is such that people can feel the wing of a fly falling on their cheek. They can smell a single drop of perfume when it is spread through a six-room apartment. And taste is so sensitive that individuals can detect a teaspoon of sugar stirred into 7.5 liters (2 gallons) of water.

Thresholds. In studying the senses, psychologists use the concept of **absolute threshold.** This is the minimum amount of a stimulus that a subject can detect. It is, for instance, the lowest intensity of a sound that a person can hear.

In some studies, it is important to know how much a stimulus must be changed before the subject is aware of the change. The amount of change necessary for a subject to notice it is known as a **difference threshold.** The difference threshold is the amount of change necessary to detect a just-noticeable difference 50 percent of the time.

Psychologists use the concept of **just-noticeable difference** to determine the ability of an individual to distinguish between two stimuli. A single stimulus, such as a violin note, is presented to a subject. Then it is changed by a very small amount. The smallest amount of change in the stimulus that is necessary in order for the subject to be able to detect it is called the just-noticeable difference.

Perceptions

We have said that perception refers to the way in which we interpret a sensation. Perceptions are not simply the mirrored images of the world around us. There are several reasons for this. One reason is that we are not able to sense everything in the world around us. For example, we cannot hear the high-frequency sounds that bats hear. A second reason is that we sometimes perceive stimuli that do not exist in our physical environment. Our dreams, for example, are not part of the outside world. The third reason is that our expectations influence our perceptual experiences. A woman is talking on the phone and expects her baby to cry. Her expectations might cause her to hear the cry, although the baby is in the next room.

Our perceptions are also based on changes in sensations. For example, look at the figure below. Your perception is based on changes of the stimuli that make up the figure, as well as changes in outside stimuli. In other words, the contrasting edges enable you to perceive the triangles. Without such changes, your world would be simply a "oneness."

Subliminal perception. Stimuli may be so weak that we are not aware of the sensations

Perception involves the interpretation of a sensation. The inner triangles are usually perceived as being of different sizes. The particular colors of the background triangles cause the viewer to interpret one inner triangle as being larger than the other. Actually, the two inner triangles are exactly the same size.

they are arousing. But our perception of them may influence our thought or behavior. This perception of sensation aroused by stimuli that are too weak for an individual to report is called **subliminal perception.**

Psychologists studied subliminal perception for many years. The general public became interested in it several years ago because of a report. The report claimed that such phrases as "Eat Popcorn" and "Drink Cola X" had been flashed on the screen during a movie. As a result, the report said, popcorn sales at the theater increased 50 percent and sales of the soft drink increased 18 percent. It claimed that the phrases were flashed on the screen for only 1/3000 second, so the audience was not aware of seeing them. But because of the rise in sales, it was thought that the members of the audience had perceived them.

Some advertising executives immediately thought that this report might open up a whole new field for their efforts. Other people were quite alarmed by the report. They feared that subliminal stimulation might be used to control society. For instance, elections might be controlled by one political party flashing "Vote Republican" or "Vote Democratic" on the television screen for subliminal lengths of time.

There are many variables that affect successful subliminal stimulation. There is the strength of the stimulation itself. There is the speed at which the stimulus is given. The nature of the stimulation immediately after the subliminal stimulation is a factor. So is the general train of thought of the viewer at the time. And the number of times that an individual is exposed to the stimulus makes a difference.

In general, psychologists today seriously question whether subliminal stimulation can be effective in influencing behavior. Stimulation that we are aware of is certainly more effective in influencing behavior than subliminal stimulation is. At any rate, much more research is needed before we can say for sure how effective subliminal stimulation might be.

Attention

We are always surrounded by stimuli. It is impossible to react to all of them at any given moment. If we did, we would be so overwhelmed with sensations that we couldn't process very much. Therefore, we become selective. Only certain stimuli gain our attention. For example, as you read this page, stop for a moment. Concentrate on the different stimuli around you, such as sounds. Were you aware of all these stimuli before you stopped to focus on them? **Attention** is the process of focusing your perception on a limited number of stimuli.

In this case, you purposely decided to pay attention to stimuli. But sometimes stimuli just break in on you. Suppose someone nearby mentions your name while you are talking to another person. You will probably become aware that your name has been spoken and will pay attention to what that speaker is saying. What factors make us pay attention to stimuli? We can divide these factors into those related to the stimulus and those related to the individual.

The stimuli. There are several major characteristics of stimuli that make us pay attention to them: intensity, size, contrast, movement, changes, novelty, and repetition. Any of these characteristics, or a combination of them, will result in our paying more attention to one specific stimulus than to others.

Manufacturers of such goods as soap, pens, and processed food are very concerned with making us aware of their particular product. They try to make use of these characteristics to draw our attention to their product and away from competing products. For instance, they use strong and eye-catching colors for their product or packaging.

On submarines, it is often necessary to gain everyone's attention immediately. One method is to do the unexpected. For example, an important announcement might begin with a recorded *female* voice saying, "Now hear this" several times.

What part of this picture catches your attention first? Why?

The individual. Another factor that influences reaction to a stimulus is the condition of the individual at that time. For example, suppose you are hungry and looking for a place to eat. The lighted sign of a restaurant on a dark road is much more likely to draw your attention than if you are not hungry.

The needs, attitudes, expectations, motives, and past experiences of a person play a large role in determining which stimuli that person will pay attention to. A person interested in birds will pay more attention to the sound of birds on a camping trip than the person who doesn't care about birds. Have you ever looked through a book trying to locate a specific picture or diagram? Usually you will pass over many other illustrations but will give immediate attention to the correct one.

Maintaining attention. Not only is gaining our attention important. Maintaining that attention is also important. Once our attention is focused on a particular stimulus, the stimu-lus characteristics can be used to hold our attention. We hear a siren and pay attention to it for a moment. Our attention is more likely to continue if the sound of the siren changes in pitch and loudness.

Can we pay attention to two stimuli presented at the same time? To find out, we can present two different messages to a subject through earphones. One message is fed into the left ear, and another message is fed into the right ear. The experimenter asks the subject to pay attention to the message being received by, say, the left ear. Afterward, the experimenter can check on the subject's attention by asking the person to repeat the message he or she was paying attention to, as well as the message that was fed into the other ear. How much the subject remembers has a lot to do with how difficult and how familiar each message is. In general, there is some recall of the unattended message. But it is much, much less than the recall of the attended one.

Text continues on page 257.

Colors produced by light waves may be arranged according to the length of the light waves, as in the solar spectrum above. The violets are the shortest wave lengths and the reds are the longest. The solar spectrum results when sunlight is sent through a prism. The colors of the spectrum are in the same order as you see in a rainbow.

Colors may also be arranged around the circumference of a circle to form a color wheel, as shown below. When color light waves are arranged in a circle, those colors opposite each other, known as complementary colors, will mix into a neutral gray.

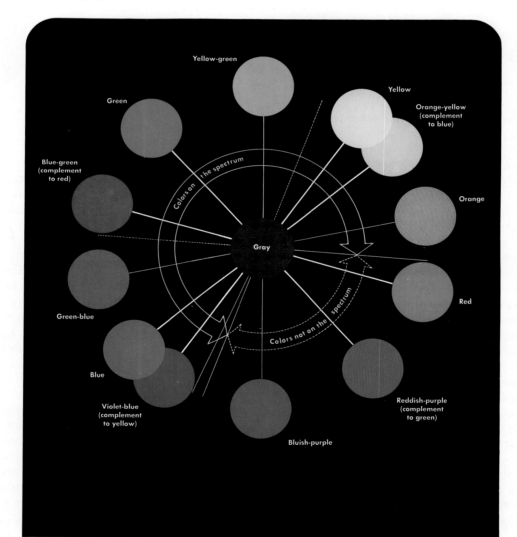

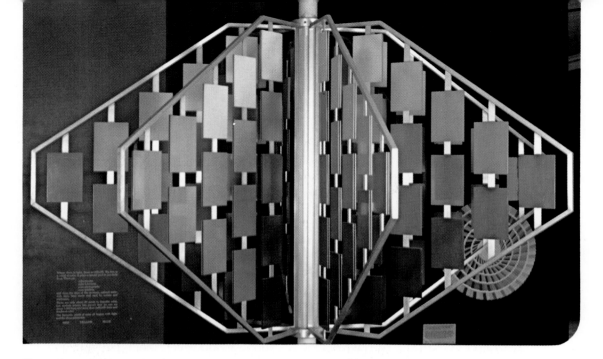

The color solid — or color cone — above illustrates the three dimensions of color: hue, brightness (from top to bottom), and saturation (from the outside to the inside). A vertical slice from the color solid for the hue red shows the brightness range vertically, from light at the top to dark at the bottom. And it gives the saturation range horizontally, running from "pure" red on the outside to gray at the center.

Vision

Vision is a major area of human sensation and perception. We will discuss such aspects of vision as what color is, how we perceive depth, and how optical illusions occur.

The physical nature of color. Three basic terms are used in describing colors. These are hue, brightness, and saturation.

Hue refers to the quality of redness, blueness, yellowness, or greenness that differentiates one color from another. It is what most people commonly call color. Sunlight can be broken up into different hues, as in a rainbow, for example.

The complete arrangement of hues that can be seen by the human eye is called the *visible spectrum.* It is arranged according to the length of the light waves that make it up. The spectrum has violet on one end and

red on the other. A picture of the visible spectrum is shown on page 256.

In the spectrum, violet shades off into blue, which shades into green, and then yellow, orange, and red. However, there are no sharp dividing lines between the colors in the visible spectrum. Instead, the colors blend into one another. As many as 150 distinct hues can be observed. These hues can also be thought of as arranged around a circle. This circle is illustrated on the opposite page.

Brightness refers to the sensation of lightness or darkness of any color or gray. Note in the picture of the color solid on this page that the vertical axis runs from white at the top to black at the bottom. Between the black and white poles of a color solid are shades of gray. As hues approach white at the top of the color solid, they become lighter and lighter. The lighter the color, the brighter it is. You can see how red (on the

257

left) increases in brightness—becomes lighter —as it moves up toward white at the top of the axis. It decreases in brightness—becomes darker—as it moves down toward black at the bottom of the axis.

Saturation refers to the pureness of a hue. It refers to the degree to which a hue differs from a gray of the same brightness. Look again at the picture of the color solid. Note how saturation is shown on it. As a hue runs from the outermost point on the color solid toward the center, it loses its pureness and becomes grayer. We say that it has become less saturated. Notice how red decreases in its amount of redness, or saturation, as it approaches the center.

Consider the following example of saturation. You shorten a pair of jeans. You save the extra material to use as patches. The jeans wear out at the knees. You take out the scraps of cloth you had saved to patch with. But the scraps no longer match the jeans. The jeans have been exposed to sunlight and washing, and they've faded. The material that was packed away in the dark is as dark as when new. In technical terms, the faded jeans are less saturated than the scraps.

Color combinations. Colors that are opposite each other on the color circle are *complementary colors.* (Look at the color wheel on page 256.) When mixed together, they give gray. Does this seem strange? Would you mix blue and yellow paint to form gray? Of course, that would give green paint. But mixing paint is different from mixing light. In this discussion of color, we are mixing lights, not paint pigments. To mix light, disks of different-colored paper are placed on a wheel, and the wheel is turned rapidly. Or different-colored lights are projected on the same area on a screen.

Suppose two colors on the color circle are mixed together but are not opposite each other. The resulting hue will be between the two hues. The hue will be closest to whichever color has the larger proportion in the mixture. As an example, if you were to mix yellow and red, the result would be orange. If yellow made up 60 percent of the mixture

and red 40 percent, the saturation would be more yellow than red.

In many cases, we want to use two colors together, as in school colors or ads or clothes. As a rule, a combination of two colors is pleasing if the colors are complementary. Blue and an orange-yellow would make pleasing school colors. What about red and blue-green, or bluish-purple and yellow-green? If three colors are to be combined, a simple rule can be followed: Pick three colors that are of equal distance on the color wheel. A triangle of equal sides placed in the circle will give you a pleasing combination of three colors.

Saturation is a factor in choosing pleasing color combinations. As a rule, red and yellow are said to be too close together on the color wheel to give a pleasing combination. Suppose, however, both the red and the yellow are of very weak saturation. They are pastel tints. Then they may give a pleasing effect when used together. But such rules are only true in general. Colors that please one person may not be liked by someone else.

There are many practical applications of color. For instance, color may determine how often a room is used. One company had its cafeteria decorated in light blue, a favorite color of many Americans. But the employees complained that the room was cold. Many insisted that they needed to wear their coats while eating. The thermometer showed that the room was at a comfortable temperature. Then the company decided to have the room trimmed in orange and to put orange slipcovers on the chairs. The employees stopped complaining of the cold. They no longer wore coats while eating. Yet the thermometer indicated that the temperature was the same as before.

Colorblindness. Perhaps you have assumed that any person who is not completely blind can see colors as well as other people. Actually, this is not true. There are some people who cannot distinguish all the colors that most of us can. Such people are said to have *colorblindness.* More strictly speaking, they are color-weak, or color-deficient.

Text continues on page 260.

258

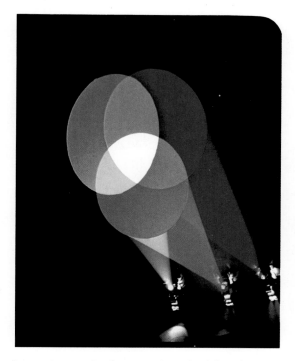

In a mixture of color wave lengths (above), the lights of two noncomplementary colors can be combined to produce a third color. For instance, red and green fuse into yellow. The three colors overlap in the middle to make white.

In a mixture of color pigments (above), pigments or color filters are used. Here yellow and blue produce green. (Such a mixture of color wave lengths would produce gray.) The three primary colors overlap in the center to make black.

The mixing of color light waves can be studied by putting discs of several different colors on the shaft of a small electric motor (right), and rotating them. As the speed of the rotation is increased, the colors seem to blend into one. Sometimes they look gray and sometimes a hue, depending on what colors the discs are. These yellow and blue discs would merge into gray.

259

We perceive parallel lines, such as the sides of a highway, as coming together in the distance. This is called linear perspective.

Two common kinds of colorblindness are total colorblindness and red-green colorblindness. To the totally colorblind person, the world appears like a black-and-white snapshot or an uncolored film. But very few people are totally colorblind. Those people who are only red-green colorblind can still distinguish blue and yellow. To the red-green colorblind person, a scene all in blue and yellow would appear just the same as to someone who is not colorblind. Red and green, however, would appear to the person as a dull yellow-gray. Interestingly enough, there are a few individuals who are colorblind in one eye but have normal color vision in the other eye.

Colorblindness is inherited. About 8 percent of men are colorblind to some extent. Almost no women are colorblind. Yet colorblindness is inherited through the female side of the family. Thus, a colorblind man will have a daughter who has normal vision, but his daughter's son may be colorblind.

How do we perceive distance and depth? We can perceive depth as well as length and width when we use only one eye. But our perception of depth is improved by looking at any object with both eyes. Using both eyes gives us some idea of the depth of an object because we have two images. However, this holds true only for objects that are less than 9 meters (30 feet) away.

One of the ways in which we perceive distance and depth is with the movements of our eye muscles. Certain muscles cause the lens of the eyes to become flatter as an object moves into the distance. They cause the lens to bulge outward when the object comes close. You can easily perform a little experiment involving movement of eye muscles. Hold a finger at arm's length. Move it slowly toward your nose. Your pupils will come closer together, or converge. This way of perceiving distance is called *convergence.*

Another way we perceive distance is based on the relative position of objects. Suppose one object blocks the view of another. We then assume that the object blocking the view is closer than the one behind it.

We also use movement to determine distance and depth. If we move, those objects near us seem to move past us. Those at a distance seem to remain still or to move by us much more slowly. For example, when you are riding in a car, the edge of the road seems to go by very fast. Objects in the distance seem to stand still or to move very slowly.

We may also judge distance through texture gradient. **Texture gradient** is the amount of detail perceived in an object. The more detail we perceive, the closer the object appears to be.

Other aids are linear and atmospheric perspective. In **linear perspective,** the farther away objects are, the closer together they appear to be. For example, railroad tracks seem to meet in the distance. Telephone poles seem to get closer together the more distant they are. In **atmospheric perspective,** objects that are blurred or hazy from smoke or dust in the air appear to be farther away than objects that can be seen clearly.

Another way to judge distance and size involves using standards or familiar objects. Suppose a close friend of yours is standing beside a stranger. You know the height of your friend. Your guess of the stranger's height will probably be much closer to the actual height than if the stranger were standing alone. You have a standard by which to compare heights. If you are unfamiliar with an object and have no standard of comparison near it, it is very difficult to judge its size or distance accurately. For example, it would be very difficult to guess the distance or size of a wire if the sky were the only background and there were no other objects around.

What happens if our world becomes visually changed, or distorted? Can we adjust to such a world? Apparently we can. In a classic experiment, a researcher wore a special set of goggles so that the world appeared upside down to him. He wore these goggles at all times. The first few days were confusing. But the researcher eventually adapted to this distorted view of the world.

He adjusted so well that he learned to ski and ride a bicycle while wearing the goggles. When he took the goggles off, he had to spend several days in confusion while readjusting to the real world.

In another experiment, subjects sat in front of a glass-top table. The glass top was covered so the subjects could not see underneath it. Across from them were several objects. They were asked to point to each of the objects by extending a hand underneath the covered glass tabletop. This procedure established that each subject was very accurate in pointing to the objects. In the second part of the experiment, subjects wore special goggles that visually moved each object four degrees to their right. The cloth was removed from the tabletop. They practiced pointing to the objects. Although they were off-target at the beginning, they quickly learned to make the necessary corrections.

There was also a third part to the experiment. The goggles were removed. Subjects then pointed to the objects with the hand they used while wearing the goggles. They were off-target by four degrees at first, although they again learned to point correctly. However, with the other hand they were able to point accurately from the start. The experimenters concluded that adapting to the visual distortion involved only the hand used when wearing the goggles.

Optical illusions. Sometimes we make mistakes in our perceptions. A false visual perception is called an **optical illusion.**

Look at the two figures on this page. Are the horizontal lines equal in length, or is one longer than the other? Actually, the length of these two lines is the same. But we perceive one as longer than the other. Why? A possible explanation is that we do not limit our attention to the horizontal lines themselves. Instead, we look at the entire figures. One

Text continues on page 264.

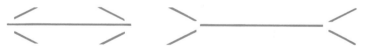

Case Study: Focus on Research

CROSSING THE CHECKERED CLIFF

One of the most important abilities in our daily lives is the ability to perceive depth—the distance between one object and another. Imagine what life would be like if we couldn't determine the drop from the sidewalk to the street whenever we stepped off a curb. Or how could we possibly drive a car if we couldn't tell the distance between us and other cars on the road? Clearly, the perception of depth is an important quality, although we usually take it for granted.

A basic issue in much of psychology is the extent to which behaviors are inborn or learned. Our ability to perceive depth has been the subject of several such arguments. Many people have assumed that since babies are protected from falls until they are "old

Animals as well as human infants feared crossing over to the "deep" side of the platform. This kitten stopped right at the drop-off point.

enough to know better," then avoiding dangerous heights is learned behavior. Yet other species seem to avoid drops instinctively and not through learning. In these instances it seems that this kind of depth perception is innate.

Psychologists Eleanor Gibson and Richard Walk decided to explore the question of whether depth perception is inborn or learned by means of a special device they called a visual cliff. It consisted of a rectangular table-like platform raised about a meter, or a yard, above the floor. It was entirely covered by a sheet of heavy glass. Over half of the platform's surface, directly under the glass, was a piece of checkered linoleum. Through the other half of the platform the same kind of linoleum could be seen, but laid directly on the floor. The effect was one of a sharp drop-off from the seemingly "shallow" surface to the "deep" side.

Gibson and Walk wanted to see how and at what stage of their development different species reacted to the visual cliff. Among the animals they tested were chicks, lambs, kittens, puppies, turtles, and rats. Their procedure was to place the animal at the dividing line between the "shallow" and the "deep" sides and then observe the direction in which the animal moved.

The chickens, lambs, kittens, and puppies almost without exception avoided the deep half of the platform. All of these animals showed this behavior as soon as they could walk. For the chicks and lambs this was almost immediately after birth. For the kittens and puppies this was at a few weeks of age.

Because of their natural environment, the turtles were expected to choose the deep side. (The deep side more closely resembled

262

the water they were used to.) The majority, however, turned to the shallow side. Perhaps the turtles, too, feared falling off the cliff.

The rats were the only animals that responded differently. Rats spend much of their time in darkness and rely mainly on their whiskers to give them clues as to their whereabouts. Thus, since they could still feel the glass with their whiskers, the deep side presented no problems. As a result most chose the deep side of the cliff.

Gibson and Walk also tested a number of human infants between the ages of six and fourteen months. This is the age when children crawl. A pinwheel toy was placed at each end of the platform. The child's mother would play with the toy and call her baby first from one end, then from the other. Of the 36 children tested, 27 moved away from the middle toward the shallow side. Only three chose to crawl across the deep side. Many of those who refused to do so cried as they gazed at their mothers. Some of them even reached out and patted the glass. But, although they could feel that the glass was solid, they refused to risk the crossing.

Interestingly enough, some children, while facing the shallow side, backed onto the deep side inadvertently. (When children are learning to crawl, they often go in reverse when they mean to go forward.) Yet even after having tested the deep side without realizing it, they still refused to crawl across it when they could see it.

As a result of their research, Gibson and Walk concluded that, if survival depends on it, a species will develop depth perception, as soon as it can move about. In fact, other researchers found that infants even too young to crawl discriminated between the deep and shallow sides of the cliff. When on the deep side their heart rates changed drastically, indicating their fear of falling. The capacity to recognize depth apparently does not depend on learning. Instead it seems to be one of an organism's inborn capabilities.

SOURCE: E. J. Gibson and R. D. Walk, "The Visual Cliff," *Scientific American*, 1960, 202, 64–71; Richard D. Walk and Eleanor J. Gibson, "A Comparative and Analytical Study of Visual Depth Perception," *Psychological Monographs*, 1961, 75, no. 15.

Many important tasks involve depth perception. Imagine what it would be like to drive a car without this valuable ability.

entire figure is longer than the other. We interpret this to mean that one horizontal line is longer than the other.

Can we make practical use of optical illusions? There are many practical applications of illusions. We choose much of our clothing to give impressions that do not exactly agree with actuality. A person who wishes to look less tall can wear clothing in which the lines run horizontally. A person who wishes to look taller can select clothes in which the lines run vertically. Light-colored clothing tends to produce the illusion that a person is sturdier and larger than is actually the case. Dark clothing tends to give the impression that a person is smaller.

Ordinary movie and television pictures are optical illusions. They are a series of still pictures shown on the screen with a very brief amount of time between them. The rate at which each picture is flicked on and off the screen is so rapid that you don't perceive the separate pictures. You experience the illusion of motion.

Advertisers often use the illusion of motion to attract our attention. For example, you may have seen a neon sign of a dog running. First the dog is shown with its legs in one position. Then the light in these legs is turned off. The light in another set of legs is turned on. The dog appears to be running. But of course it's an optical illusion.

Perception patterns. In addition to the factors discussed so far, there are several other factors that influence our perception. One such factor is *proximity.* We tend to group together objects that are close together. For example, look at the following drawing:

● ●　　● ●　　● ●

Do you see six dots or three groups of dots? Most likely you will see three groups because of how the dots are organized.

Another factor is *similarity.* We tend to group together objects that resemble each other. Thus, in the following drawing we are likely to perceive a pattern.

△ △ △ △ △
□ □ □ □ □
○ ○ ○ ○ ○

A third factor is *closure.* Our brain fills in the gaps to make an object seem complete. For example, you would recognize the first three letters of the alphabet, although this drawing is incomplete:

A B C

Each of these factors helps make our perception predictable.

Hearing

Vision and hearing are the two most important senses we have. We can see in only one direction at a time. But we can hear sounds coming from all directions. Being able to hear sounds from different directions makes hearing one of our best warning systems of possible danger. We hear a car horn and look to see if there is some danger. Parents hear their baby cry and go to see if the baby needs anything. People scream to let us know that they are in danger so we can help them.

What do we hear? What we hear is known as sound. Sound may be discussed in terms of pitch, loudness, and timbre.

Some sounds are of high pitch, others of low pitch. We can distinguish between the pitch of a flute and the pitch of a trombone. **Pitch** is determined by the rate, or frequency, of vibration of the sound wave. The greater the frequency of vibration, the higher the pitch. The lesser the frequency of vibration, the lower the pitch. A sound with a clearly marked pitch is called a *tone.*

Sound can carry through such substances as water and metal. But most sound waves that we hear travel through the air. We cannot hear all the vibrations that reach our ears. We are limited to those from about 20 to about 20,000 hertz (vibrations per second). Some individuals cannot hear sounds above

15,000 or 16,000 hertz. As people grow older, the upper pitch of the tones they hear is not so high as the highest pitch they could hear in their youth. (There is some evidence that the hearing of older Americans and Europeans is reduced partly because of the culture in which they live. Tests for the hearing of people in a tribal culture indicate that these individuals tend not to lose their hearing for higher frequencies as much as Americans and Europeans do.)

What do animals hear? It depends on the animal. Dogs can hear sounds above 25,000 hertz. Bats are able to hear sounds of 40,000 to 50,000 hertz. But turtles' ears are very sensitive only to waves ranging from about 100 to 700 hertz. They cannot normally hear above 3,000 hertz.

The **loudness** of a tone is determined mainly by the height, or amplitude, of the vibrations of the sound wave. The greater the amplitude of the waves, the louder the sound.

Suppose you are blindfolded. You hear middle C produced by a violin, a trumpet, and a human voice. Suppose, too, that the three sounds are of exactly the same pitch. Could you distinguish the sources of the three sounds?

The three sounds differ in timbre. **Timbre** is the distinctive quality of tones. It depends mainly on the overtone pattern of the sound waves. The human voice, most musical instruments, and other sources of sound give off overtones, or higher tones, as well as their basic tone. For example, a tone is played on a violin. You hear not only the fundamental tone but also a number of overtones. The human voice is very rich in overtones. If it weren't for the differing overtones in the voices of our friends, we couldn't tell one voice from another. Each of us has a characteristic voice sound pattern that usually identifies us, even if we try to change it.

Does hearing tell us anything about space? Having two eyes gives us some information about space perception. Having two ears separated by the width of the head also helps us in perceiving space. Sounds from

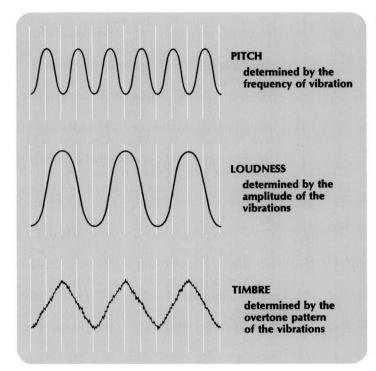

PITCH
determined by the frequency of vibration

LOUDNESS
determined by the amplitude of the vibrations

TIMBRE
determined by the overtone pattern of the vibrations

This shows some of the properties of the sounds we hear. Pitch is represented by the frequency of the sound waves. Loudness is shown by the height of the waves. Timbre is shown by the complexity of the wave pattern.

one side or the other reach our two ears at different times. The difference is less than .001 of a second. Yet it enables us to perceive the direction of sounds in space. Sounds coming from one side or the other are louder in the ear closer to the source of sound.

Another factor in space perception is that the timbre of tones in the two ears is different. In going around the head from one ear to the other, tones lose some of their overtones. This indicates direction in space.

The problem of noise. Noise, like music, is caused by vibrations in the air. But noises usually produce unpleasant experiences, whereas music usually produces pleasant experiences. The sensation of noise is frequently stimulated by sound waves of irregular and unrelated frequencies. In other words, noise has no clearly defined pitch.

Noise is a serious problem for humans, especially in thickly settled communities. Some cities have campaigns to reduce noise pollution. Police action may be brought against people who insist on playing their radios, televisions, records, or tapes at full blast during all hours of the day and night. There is even some evidence that damage to hearing may result from repeated exposure to extremely loud music or noise. When auditory cells are killed, a person becomes partially deaf.

Noise is especially annoying when it is unexpected, when it spreads, when it seems unnecessary, and when it indicates broken mechanical equipment. Irregular sounds are more annoying than steady ones. High-pitched sounds tend to be more annoying than low-pitched sounds. Loud sounds often produce changes in blood pressure, pulse rate, perspiration, breathing, and muscle tension.

The problem of noise has received increasing attention in recent years. In a study of this problem, subjects were asked to read dials on a machine. During this task, the experimenters created quite a bit of noise. The noises included shouting, ringing bells, using office machines, moving furniture, and playing loud music. Surprisingly, the subjects actually seemed to do better at reading the dials during this noise. Other subjects, who heard the same noises but had no task to perform,

responded with a feeling of weakness. Afterward, the subjects who had worked the dials were given puzzles that had no solution. Many of them showed less endurance and more frustration than before. It appears that noise may increase efficiency at a task to some degree. But there may be some aftereffects of noise. The noise may cause some undesirable behavior changes.

Deafness. There are varying degrees and kinds of deafness. Some people are tone-deaf. They can hear sounds, but they can't distinguish between pitches. If they hear two notes on the piano, they can't tell which note is higher. They can appreciate the rhythm in music. But they can't appreciate the melody. Obviously, such people could not become great musicians. And it is almost impossible for them to acquire the correct tones in a foreign language.

The word "deafness" usually refers to the condition of people who are "hard of hearing." These people cannot detect faint sounds that can be heard easily by people with normal hearing ability. Such deafness may be for the whole range of pitch. Or it may be limited to particular parts of the total range of sounds. Older people often cannot hear either high-pitched or low-pitched sounds.

At one time, the hearing of over a million people was tested. It was found that one person out of 25 had difficulty hearing people on the stage in auditoriums. One in 125 had

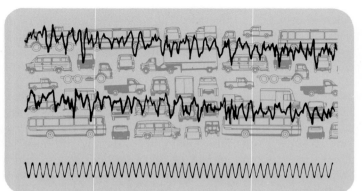

The top and middle lines are the sound waves of street noises. The bottom line is a pure tone. Do you react differently to the sounds of loud traffic noises and piano notes?

Psychologists are interested in the effects on our hearing of spending hours in a room surrounded by extremely loud noises. They might study, for instance, the effects of very loud music at discotheques.

trouble hearing in a face-to-face conversation. One in 400 had difficulty hearing over the telephone.

People who are hard of hearing can do the same kinds of work as anyone else, and they can also concentrate on their work without being bothered by the noise around them. For social contacts, they can use modern hearing devices. With the microelectronic circuits available today, hearing devices can hardly be seen and are very effective. Deaf people communicate best by using American Sign Language. This language involves movements and gestures with the arms, hands, and fingers. Each movement or gesture has meaning, just like words.

Other Sense Fields

We will not describe other sense fields in detail. But a few comments about other senses may encourage you to read more about them.

Smell. Of course, we have a sense of smell, although it is not as keen as in some animals. A good bloodhound, for example, can trace a person for a long distance by the faint odor remaining on the trail.

Our sense of smell comes from receptors in the upper part of the nose. There have been various attempts to classify the odors that we sense. One classification suggests that there are seven basic odors: camphor-like, musky, flowery, pepperminty, ether-like, pungent (sharp), and putrid (rotten). Most people consider some of these odors to be pleasing and others displeasing. Another classification system suggests only four primary odors: acid (sour), burnt, fragrant (sweet), and caprylic (rancid). These odors are substances in the air. They must actually touch the smell receptors in your nose to produce a smell sensation.

Taste. For most people, taste is mainly a way of getting enjoyment from the environment. Taste is related to the sense of smell. Much of the taste of food is really the smell of that food. You have probably noticed that when you have a cold, your appreciation of taste is much poorer.

A substance must be in liquid form to be tasted. The liquid is supplied either by the substance itself or by your saliva. Wipe the surface of your tongue dry with a clean cloth. Then place a lump of sugar or salt on the tip of the tongue. You won't be able to taste it

This is what human taste buds look like. Each little bump on our tongue contains about 245 taste buds.

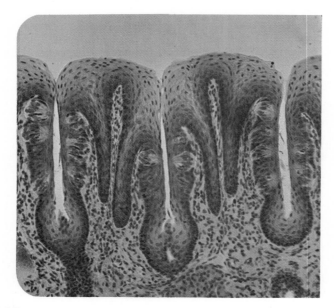

until enough saliva forms to produce a solution of sugar or salt. This seeps down to the taste buds below the surface of the tongue. **Taste buds** are the receptors on the tongue for the sensation of taste.

Adults have about 10,000 taste buds. The number gets smaller with age, however. So older people are less responsive than children to different tastes. Taste buds are located mainly on the top and sides of the tongue. They can be divided into four classes: sweet, sour, bitter, and salty. That is, there are four primary taste sensations. Taste buds at the tip of the tongue are especially sensitive to sweet solutions. Those along the sides are particularly sensitive to sour solutions. Those at the back of the tongue are sensitive to bitter solutions. Taste buds sensitive to salt solutions are located on the tip and sides of the tongue.

Taste buds are made up of taste cells. Each taste cell is replaced every seven days. So if you "burn" your tongue drinking a scalding-hot liquid, the damaged taste cells are quickly replaced.

Our ideas and expectations about taste can influence what tastes we perceive. In one experiment, a group of subjects ate what normally would have been a delicious meal. However, tinted lights were used so that the meat looked green, the milk appeared to be blue, and the potatoes were red. Many of the subjects felt ill while eating the meal. Some stated that the food "just didn't taste right."

The skin senses. There are four kinds of skin receptors. They are sensitive to cold, warmth, pain, or pressure. You can easily demonstrate these skin senses. For example, you can touch a number of points on your skin with a nail (not very sharp) that has been placed in cold water for a while. As some spots are touched, a sensation of cold will be produced. Other spots will merely yield a pressure sensation. Certain spots respond to low and high temperatures, but not to intermediate temperatures. (An intermediate temperature is the approximate temperature of the skin under normal conditions.) There are only four primary skin sensations. But our

In doing finger painting, children are using the skin senses. In particular, they are using the skin receptors for pressure.

daily experiences of touch are always complex. Experiences such as tickle, smoothness, roughness, and wetness involve combinations of the primary skin sensations.

The sense of pressure is especially valuable to a blind person. Blind people are able to read by their sense of pressure. They move their fingers across a page of Braille (a system of raised dots).

The following experiment used chimpanzees to investigate the relationship between the sense of pressure and vision. The chimpanzees were supposed to match the feel of an object with the sight of another object. They could reach through a slot and feel two objects that they could not see. Above the slot was a visible object exactly like one of the objects they were feeling. The chimpanzees were able to match the object they felt with the one they saw. Humans can also perform this same task. Thus, there appears to be some kind of neural connection between vision and the sense of touch.

Kinesthetic sense. The ***kinesthetic sense,*** or the muscle, tendon, and joint sense, is important in determining body movement and position. People can determine the position of parts of their body without the use of their eyes. You can easily prove this. Have someone put your arm in some position while you are blindfolded or have your eyes closed. You will have no trouble in recognizing the position in which your arm has been placed.

Equilibrium. The sense of *equilibrium* tells individuals where their body is in space. It is governed by the inner ear (part of our hearing system). It is used to aid us in keeping our body position. It is this sense that, when disturbed, produces "motion sickness."

These, then, are some of the factors within ourselves, as well as in the environment, that influence our perceptions. By being more aware of these factors, you may be able to observe and report on your own perceptions more objectively.

Summary

Sensation refers to the arousal of a sense organ by something in the environment. Perception is the interpretation of a sensation. An interesting type of perception is subliminal perception. At one point, people were afraid that subliminal perception would be used to control society. Today, however, psychologists generally do not believe it can influence behavior.

People can pay attention only to certain stimuli. Sometimes certain characteristics of stimuli draw our attention. These include intensity, size, contrast, movement, changes, novelty, and repetition. The condition of an individual, however, might also affect his or her reactions to a stimulus.

Vision is perhaps our most important sense. Three terms are used in describing color, an important part of our world. These are hue, brightness, and saturation. Hue refers to the quality of a particular color, brightness refers to the sensation of lightness or darkness, and saturation refers to the pureness of hue. All colors can be arranged on a color circle, with complementary colors opposite each other.

Colorblindness describes the inability of some people to distinguish certain colors. Two common forms of colorblindness are total colorblindness and red-green colorblindness. Colorblindness is inherited.

There are various cues to help us perceive depth. Our eye muscles move as objects come close or move farther away. We also rely on the relative position of objects, as well as the movement of objects. In addition, we use texture gradient, linear perspective, and atmospheric perspective. Moreover, we often base our judgments on familiar objects.

Sometimes we make faulty perceptual judgments. False visual perceptions are known as optical illusions.

For most people, hearing is the second most important sense. Sound determines what we hear. As with color, there are three terms that are used to categorize sound: pitch, loudness, and timbre. Pitch refers to the highness or lowness of a sound, loudness is the intensity of a sound, and timbre refers to the distinctive quality of tones. Not all people, however, hear all sounds. Deafness usually refers to a condition of people who are hard of hearing.

The other sense fields include smell, taste, the skin senses, the kinesthetic sense, and equilibrium. They also help influence our perceptions.

INTERPRETING SOURCES

In *Human Information Processing,* psychologists Peter Lindsay and Donald Norman describe how context and our expectations influence the way we perceive the world.

Their suggestion is that we tend to see what we expect to see. These expectations, they argue, stem largely from the context within which things appear.

A large part of the interpretation of sensory data is provided by the knowledge of what the signal must be, rather than from information contained in the signal itself. This extra information comes from the *context* of the sensory event. Context is the overall environment in which experiences are embedded. You know many things about the material you are reading, in addition to the actual patterns of letters on this page. You know that it is written in English, that it is discussing psychology in general, and the psychology of [perception] in particular. Moreover, you probably learned quite a bit about the style of writing, so that as your eyes travel over the page, you are able to make good predictions the words which you expect to see. These predictions are good enough to make you automatically fill in the missing "about" or "of" in the previous sentence, or, equivalently, not even notice its absence. The enormous amount of information that is accumulated and routinely used to understand the events, we call the context of those events....

A number of experimental techniques have been used to demonstrate the effects of context on the perceptual analysis of incoming signals. In one example, ... subjects listened to a string of words like **socks, some, brought, wet, who.** The words were mixed with noise so that each individual word could be correctly identified only about 50% of the time. In a second test, the words were then rearranged, so they appeared in a meaningful order—**who, brought, some, wet, socks,** and again the subjects attempted to identify them. When the words were spoken in a grammatical order, the recognition performance of the subjects improved dramatically.... It was the context that produced such a dramatically improved accuracy in ... perception....

We do not know exactly what mechanisms [underlie] the use of contextual information, but we do know that context plays a major role in our perceptions. It supplies the rules underlying the construction of our perceptual world, tells us what to expect, and gives plausible interpretations of what we are perceiving....

Expectations ... play a major role in [perception]. Our memory system maintains a record of past experiences, a general knowledge about the organization and format of the events we experience, and knowledge about the structure of language....

Processing starts with general knowledge of the events that are being experienced and with specific expectations generated by this knowledge.... These expectations guide the stages of analysis at all levels, from getting the language analyzing system alerted (if the input is expected to be language), ... to directing the attention of the system to the details of the particular events....

Here we have a [system] that continuously constructs and revises expectations about what it is perceiving as it proceeds to interpret a sensory message. It does not rely exclusively either on its own internal models or on the evidence of its senses. But the two sources of information must match before it concludes it has successfully interpreted the incoming signal.

Source Review

1. What do the authors mean by "context"?

2. What role does context play in our perceptions?

3. Due to the role of expectations in perception, why may it be difficult to spot errors when you proofread your own papers?

CHAPTER 12

REVIEW

REVIEWING TERMS

sensation
perception
absolute threshold
difference threshold
just-noticeable difference
subliminal perception
attention
hue
visible spectrum
brightness

saturation
complementary colors
colorblindness
convergence
texture gradient
linear perspective
atmospheric perspective
optical illusion
proximity
similarity

closure
pitch
tone
loudness
timbre
taste buds
kinesthetic sense
equilibrium

CHECKING FACTS

1. How does sensation differ from perception?

2. Describe the concepts of absolute threshold, difference threshold, and just-noticeable difference.

3. Why are perceptions not simply the mirrored images of the world around us?

4. What variables affect subliminal stimulation? How effective do psychologists consider subliminal stimulation?

5. What factors make us pay attention to stimuli? Describe some characteristics of each factor.

6. Explain what is meant by hue, brightness, and saturation.

7. What is colorblindness? Describe two kinds of colorblindness.

8. Describe some of the ways in which we perceive distance and depth.

9. What are the three factors that enter into our perception of sound? Explain each factor.

10. How does noise affect our behavior?

11. Describe how our sense of taste works.

APPLYING YOUR KNOWLEDGE

1. To illustrate absolute threshold and just-noticeable difference, try the following activity. Find a room in which the lighting is controlled by a variable dial, or dimmer, rather than by an on/off switch. Turn off the light and darken the room completely. Then gradually turn up the light until you first notice it. The exact point at which you notice the visual stimulus is your *absolute threshold*. To illustrate the *just-noticeable difference*, keep turning up the light until you perceive a second change in the level of light in the room.

If you do not have access to a room with a variable dial you might perform this experiment with a bowl of water instead.

Start out with a bowl of water at room temperature. Then either raise or lower the temperature gradually. The first noticeable change—the perception of the stimulus—would be the absolute threshold. The just-noticeable difference would be the difference between the temperature of the absolute threshold and the second noticeable change.

2. To understand how past experience can influence perception, read the following statement aloud:

A BIRD IN THE
THE HAND IS WORTHLESS.

Did you notice that the word "the" appeared both at the end of the first line and at the beginning of the second line? Chances are you didn't because from your past experience your brain ignores the second "the," which it is not accustomed to reading.

3. Look at the figure below for a few minutes. Do you see only black shapes or is there a hidden word?

You may have difficulty seeing the word because the boundaries are not clearly defined. If this is the case, place a strip of dark paper along the top and bottom edges. The word should then appear.

4. During a free moment, sit quietly in a room and write down everything you sense. Circle the items on your list that usually go unnoticed. Why do you think your brain filters out those items and pays selective attention to other things?

5. To experience how the different color receptor cells in your eye work, draw an American flag on a piece of paper, but color the stripes green and black and the stars black against a yellow background. Then stare for one minute at the star in the lower right-hand corner. When the time has elapsed, move your eyes and look at a blank white wall or a white piece of paper. Do you see an image of the flag? How does the flag appear? What you are seeing is an afterimage. It occurs when the original colors are replaced by their complementary colors. (See the color wheel on page 256.)

6. Have you ever had difficulty seeing objects when you first entered a darkened movie theater, but found that later you could see them without difficulty? Your eyes had become adapted to the dim lighting. You can easily demonstrate visual adaptation to different amounts of light by closing one eye for about 10 to 15 minutes before entering a dimly lit room. When you enter the room, keep your eye closed for a minute longer. The room will appear dark when you use the eye that you kept open. Then open your closed eye, and close the one that you kept open. Can you see more clearly?

7. Everyone has a blind spot. That is, all people have a point at which they have no vision. To find the blind spot in your visual field, try the following activity.

Hold the book at arm's length. Close your left eye and look at the smiling face. Now slowly move the book toward you until the frowning face disappears completely from your field of vision. This point demonstrates your blind spot.

8. To demonstrate body adaptation to temperature, place three bowls in a row. Pour very warm but not scalding water in one bowl. Pour very cold water in another bowl, and water at about body temperature in the third bowl. Place and keep one hand in the bowl of very warm

water and the other in the bowl of cold water for several minutes. Then put both hands in the water that is at body temperature. Does this water feel warm to one hand and cold to the other? Keep both hands in this body-temperature water for several minutes. What happens?

THINKING CRITICALLY ABOUT PSYCHOLOGY

1. **Debating Ideas** If subliminal perception of stimuli were known to be an effective way of changing our behavior, would you be for or against its use? Why?

2. **Classifying Ideas** In your own experience, under what conditions does time fly and when does time drag? What senses are involved in your perception of time when it seems to pass quickly or very slowly?

3. **Comparing Ideas** If you ever go to the moon or some planet, how will your sensory experiences there probably differ from those you have had on earth?

4. **Relating Ideas** If air, water, and noise pollution keep on increasing, how do you think our senses may be affected in the future?

5. **Analyzing Ideas** Which of your senses do you consider to be the most important to you (the one you would least like to lose)? Why? Which one is the least important to you? Why?

DEVELOPING SKILLS IN PSYCHOLOGY

Using the *Psychological Abstracts*

When psychologists are designing their studies, they must read the current literature related to their topic to see what other psychologists have discovered in recent years. They need to know what other studies have been conducted, what methods were used, and what findings emerged from the studies. Psychologists do not use textbooks to gain information—they turn instead to the scholarly research journals.

One way to find out what is available in the research journals is to use the *Psychological Abstracts*. This valuable resource guide is published monthly and contains both subject and author indexes, as well as brief abstracts (summaries) of recent publications.

To learn how to use the *Psychological Abstracts,* go to the library and look at some current volumes to see what has been learned about *depth perception*. Start by looking for the heading "Depth Perception" in the Brief Subject Index, which is located at the back of each monthly issue. You should see a list of entry numbers, which correspond to the numbered abstracts that can be found in that issue. Included with each abstract is full bibliographic information to help you locate the publication that was abstracted. Try to find at least six recent research studies on depth perception and decide what progress in understanding has been made since the work of Eleanor Gibson.

READING FURTHER ABOUT PSYCHOLOGY

Geldard, Frank A., *The Human Senses,* Second Edition, John Wiley & Sons, New York, 1972. A classic in the area of the human senses. Includes information about the sensory apparatus and about the functions of each of the human senses.

Gibson, William, *The Miracle Worker,* Alfred A. Knopf, New York, 1957. The extraordinary story of how Helen Keller, born blind and deaf, learned to communicate with the world.

Rezen, Susan V., and Hausman, Carl, *Coping with Hearing Loss: A Guide for Adults and Their Families,* Dembner Books, New York, 1986. An informative, sympathetic guide that deals with the social and psychological aspects of hearing loss, as well as the physical facts.

Rivlin, Robert, and Gravelle, Karen, *Deciphering the Senses: The Expanding World of Human Perception,* Simon & Schuster, New York, 1984. Written for the general reader, this book is an up-to-date look at perception.

Rothenberg, Marie, and White, Mel, *David,* Berkley Publishing Group, New York, 1986. Brutally burned by his father, a small boy maintains his courage through agonizing pain and severe sensory and perceptual damage.

Stearner, S. Phyllis, *Able Scientists—Disabled Persons: Careers in the Sciences,* Foundation for Science & the Handicapped, Clarendon Hills, Ill., 1984. The author, herself a disabled person, profiles 27 individuals with disabilities ranging from blindness and deafness to impaired mobility.

Chapter 13

MOTIVATION AND EMOTIONS

Chapter Focus

This chapter presents:

- **a description of motivation**
- **a look at drives and motives**
- **a discussion of emotions and the theories that attempt to explain them**
- **ways in which emotions are measured**

Suppose you planned to meet a friend for lunch. You've already been waiting half an hour, and you are very hungry. You try to telephone your friend but there is no answer. Angry, you head home.

Why might such a situation be of interest to a psychologist? What behavior patterns occurred? Actually, two important processes took place. First, you felt hunger, which, psychologically speaking, you were motivated to satisfy. *Motivation* causes us to try to satisfy our needs and achieve our goals. Second, you displayed your anger. Anger is an *emotion,* one of many that you express in your daily life.

In this chapter we will examine these two processes. We will see how they influence one another and affect our behavior.

The Concept of Motivation

In the field of psychology, "motivation" has a very specific meaning. **Motivation** refers to the activating of behavior that satisfies our needs and leads toward goals. It is a driving force that sets us in motion. Psychologists who study motivation investigate what influences people to behave in one way instead of another. Motivation helps explain why a particular behavior begins, what direction it takes, and why it persists.

The specific expectations that cause a person to strive toward a goal are called **motives.** For example, suppose you take a part-time job after school. What might your motives be? Perhaps you expect to earn enough money to buy a stereo. Or perhaps you think the work experience will help you get a job after graduation. Your expectations are your motives.

How can you know that a motive is operating within an organism? You cannot see, hear, or use any of your senses to determine its presence. Psychologists assume the presence of motives from observing the behaviors of organisms. For example, two individuals work at the same task on an assembly line, but the quality of one person's work is much higher. From this difference, you assume that the one who works harder is more motivated. Two important kinds of motives that we will study are those that are biologically based and those that are learned.

Biological Drives

One source of motivated behavior studied by psychologists is biological drives. A **drive** can be defined as a physiological condition that activates behavior toward a goal. A drive arouses the organism and produces an increase in general activity level. The activity then becomes specific as it is directed toward a goal to reduce the drive. Suppose you are cold. You start to shiver. At this point you act—you are motivated to find and put on some warm clothes. Two other biological drives that motivate people are hunger and thirst.

The hunger drive. If you have gone without eating for any considerable period of time, you know what an effective drive hunger can be. But do you know how the hunger drive works? How, for instance, do you know when you are hungry? Some people might answer, "Because my stomach feels empty," or "Because my stomach growls." And there is some evidence that awareness of hunger is associated with our stomachs. In one experiment, rats were able to feed themselves by injecting food directly into their own stomachs. In a short time, the rats regulated their own feeding schedules just as normal rats do. Their stomachs determined how much food they gave themselves.

But factors other than the stomach also influence our hunger drive. Studies with men whose stomachs have been removed surgically for health reasons indicate that they, too, feel hungry. In addition, studies show that the brain plays an important role in hunger. For example, if an area near a rat's hypothalamus is destroyed, the rat will stop eating and starve to death. If an area within the hypothalamus is destroyed, the animal will overeat. Apparently, the region of the brain called the hypothalamus is also involved in regulating food intake.

What else might influence our hunger drive? What about environmental factors? Consider the environmental factor of time. Do we feel hungry because the clock says it's the hour at which we usually eat? In one ex-periment, subjects were both overweight people and those of average weight for their age group. The room in which the experiment was taking place had a clock that was rigged to go either fast or slow. Each subject arrived at 5:00 P.M. and remained in the room half an hour, doing psychological tests. The experimenter returned to the room exactly 30 minutes later (at 5:30 P.M.), nibbling on a cracker. The subjects were told that they could eat as many crackers as they wished while they finished the test they were doing.

For some subjects, the rigged clock showed 6:05 P.M. For others, it showed 5:20 P.M. The results indicated that overweight subjects ate almost twice as many crackers when the clock showed 6:05 as when the clock showed 5:20. For the average-weight subjects, exactly the opposite was true—they ate less at 6:05. A typical saying among the average-weight subjects was, "I don't want to spoil my dinner by eating." Thus, the eating behavior of both groups of subjects appeared to be influenced mainly by the external, environmental factor of time (although in opposite ways) rather than by internal, physiological factors.

Another external factor that motivates us to eat is the taste of food. The sight or smell of food also can arouse hunger. This is so even when we have just finished a meal and have no physiological need to eat.

The thirst drive. The thirst drive is also an effective motivator. The physiological condition of thirst motivates us to drink. But what is this condition? How do we know when we are thirsty? One answer is, "When my mouth and throat feel dry." But if this were all that was involved in feeling thirsty, then we could solve the problem by simply chewing gum to produce more saliva. And we would need only a few swallows of water to wet our mouth and throat. Yet we often drink far more than one or two swallows.

In studies of thirst, animals have been trained to press a lever and inject water directly into their stomachs. Such animals regulate their water needs very well. And no water passes through their mouth and throat.

Exercise can make you feel thirsty because the body loses water through perspiration. These marathon runners probably feel very thirsty.

So there must be some other control systems that regulate their intake of water.

Two basic physiological conditions seem to start an individual drinking water. One is the concentration of a chemical, such as salt, in the cells of the body and the blood. Apparently, there are cells in the hypothalamus that detect any change in water content in the body caused by salt. Although it has not been proven, the same mechanism may be responsible for causing you to feel thirsty when you exercise or have a fever. Exercise or a fever produces a loss of water in the body, which increases the salt concentration. A second condition for starting to drink water is a decrease in the total amount of fluid in the body. For example, people become quite thirsty when they lose a lot of blood.

Biological drives are a powerful motivating force. They lead us to act in ways that keep us alive and healthy. But biological drives do not explain many of the motives we have as human beings. For example, a young man in college joins a fraternity. He has chosen to eat and sleep at the fraternity house. He certainly could have satisfied these biological drives by eating and sleeping in a dorm or at home. Why do some people choose to see a science fiction movie and others go to see a love story? Why do some people participate in sports while others prefer to be spectators? Such behaviors are often determined by social motives.

Social Motives

We acquire some motives from our interactions with the people around us. The goals we set for ourselves and the outcomes we expect are influenced by our society. Such motives are learned rather than biological. Some social motives found in our society are the motives for achievement, exploration, approval, order, recognition, certainty, and attachment.

One of the problems involved in considering social motives is determining how the present expected outcomes originated. Adults often have different motives than they had as children. Another problem is how to classify the various motives. There are some 18,000 words in the English language that describe different characteristics of humans. How should we classify human motives into a system?

The achievement motive. One of the social motives that psychologists have studied most is the need for achievement. This motive can be defined as the desire to succeed at meeting high standards of performance.

There is a test for measuring the achievement motive in human beings. The subject is presented with a series of drawings and is asked to describe the pictures, one at a time. The subject identifies the person or persons in the picture, what led up to whatever is happening, what is presently happening, and the eventual outcome. The subject's re-

sponses are then scored in terms of achievement themes. Suppose, for example, you see a picture of a person reading a book. Would you describe the person as reading for pleasure? Or would you say the person was studying to do well on an exam?

We know some of the characteristics of people who score high in achievement motivation. Such individuals often have parents who rewarded them for being independent at an early age. When given a difficult problem to solve, those high in achievement motive work much longer than those low in achievement motive. They make higher grades in high school and college than others of equal intelligence. They are more willing to take moderate chances in a gambling situation. Thus, people with a high achievement motive work longer and harder toward goals, persist more in their efforts, and usually are

Text continues on page 282.

Abe Lincoln is shown here studying at night by the light of the fire. He was strongly motivated to achieve his goals.

Case Study: Focus on Research

ANIMALS NEED LOVE, TOO

One of our most basic needs is the need for affection. Without some contact with other human beings we would not develop normally. The need for affection, however, does not seem to apply only to people. Studies have shown that animals, too, require love and affection. Beginning in the 1950's, psychologists Harry and Margaret Harlow carried out a series of important tests with monkeys, pointing out the affectional needs of animals.

The Harlows stumbled on their first findings by accident. Trying to produce a group of disease-free young monkeys, they

With one hand clutching a cloth surrogate and its thumb in its mouth, this monkey clings to its "mother" for security. Most monkeys showed similar behavior.

isolated each of 56 infants in a wire cage shortly after birth. The infant monkeys could see and hear the other monkeys, but they could not engage in any physical contact with one another. Nor were the infants "mothered," as monkeys usually are after they are born.

In a sense, the researchers achieved their goal. The animals were indeed physically healthy. However, they gradually showed signs of severe emotional disturbance. They would sit in a corner for hours just staring into space. Some clutched their heads in their hands and rocked back and forth. Others, when approached, would fly into frenzies of rage, tearing at themselves with such force that they sometimes needed medical care.

When the female "motherless" monkeys themselves became mothers, they still displayed abnormal behavior. They ignored their offspring and sometimes even attacked them brutally. Some of the infants had to be removed from the cages because of the mothers' refusal to feed them. In fact, had these infants not been raised in a laboratory environment, they would probably not have survived.

In another stage of their study the Harlows explored how monkeys would develop when raised with surrogate, or substitute, mothers. The researchers constructed two types of artificial surrogates. One type consisted simply of a wire mesh cylinder with a wooden head on top. The other type was made up of cozier figures covered with terry cloth.

When infant monkeys had a choice of surrogates, they always spent more time clinging to the cloth figure. This was true even if the wire mother was the only surrogate that contained a bottle of milk. The monkey would feed as necessary and then return to the softer figure to snuggle up. The researchers dismissed the idea that this snuggling stemmed from a need for physical warmth, since the floors of the cages were warmed by a heating pad.

Monkeys reared with surrogate mothers did seem to develop an adequate sense of security. They were able to cope with new or unfamiliar situations—if the surrogate was present. For example, if a mechanical teddy bear was brought into the room the infants, at first terrified, would cling to the cloth monkey for security. Then, reassured, they would turn to look boldly at the toy animal. They sometimes even left the surrogate for a few moments to approach the previous source of fear.

In other respects, though, these monkeys were disturbed. They were unable to form the usual relationships with other monkeys. Consequently, both mating and maternal behavior were quite abnormal.

Another series of experiments focused on monkeys' relationships with their peers — monkey companions their own age. The Harlows observed play groups composed of young monkeys of various deprived types: those reared with brutal "motherless" mothers, those reared with surrogates, and those reared alone. In all cases, the monkeys were slower than normal animals to adopt typical play behavior. Monkeys reared in isolation were especially likely to spend their time clinging to one partner. However, the study showed that the interaction between infants may in some ways compensate for a lack of contact with a parent.

The role of contact with others cannot be stressed enough. It seems that from almost the moment of birth, we need contact with others to adjust properly.

SOURCE: Harry Harlow, "Love in Infant Monkeys," *Scientific American,* 1959, *201,* 68–74; Harry F. and Margaret K. Harlow, "Social Deprivation in Monkeys," *Scientific American,* 1962, *207,* 137–146; Harry F. and Margaret K. Harlow, "Learning To Love," *American Scientist,* 1966, *54,* 244–272.

Most monkeys turned to the wire "mothers" only for milk. This monkey tries to get the best of both worlds.

A strong achievement motive has produced many women of excellence. Here we see Amy Eilberg, the first female conservative rabbi (top left); Helen Hayes, actress (top right); Barbara Gardner Proctor, founder and Chief Executive Officer of a large advertising company (bottom left); and Rosalyn Yalow, Nobel prize winner in medicine (bottom right).

more successful in life than people who score low in achievement motivation.

Achievement motivation in women. Women are equal to men in intellectual ability. But in the past, they have not contributed as much as men in the fields of science, the humanities, and the arts. In addition, fewer women have risen to the top of their profession, business, or trade. Why has this been so? Is it a lack of a need for achievement, a lack of opportunity, or perhaps both?

One researcher, Matina Horner, has suggested that females have a "fear of success." In her study, both male and female subjects were asked to make up a story based on the following sentence: "After first-term finals, Anne finds herself at the top of her medical school class." However, for the male subjects, the name "John" was used instead of the name "Anne." About two-thirds of the female subjects in this study wrote stories reflecting fear of success. Only about one-tenth of the male subjects avoided success in their stories. Horner concluded that women may have a motive to avoid success.

More recent studies have found the fear of success higher in males than the earlier studies. It is possible that the more recent findings reflect changes in the roles of males and females now occurring in our culture.

Several other explanations have been presented to account for Matina Horner's findings. One theory is that females and males still primarily see the role of the female as the one who stays home and looks after the children. Therefore, women may feel less self-confident than men in pursuing a career. The majority of studies show that in elementary school and high school, there is not much difference in feelings of self-confidence between males and females. In some studies, the lack of self-confidence in females does not appear until the college level. As expectations of what women and men can achieve become more equal in our society, perhaps this difference in self-confidence will disappear.

Another theory is that males have a greater achievement motive because traditionally they have been rewarded more frequently, and perhaps with better rewards, than females in the same types of jobs. But this, too, may change as the working situation for women continues to improve and women are rewarded in their jobs as frequently as men.

There are also other ways in which the achievement motive is expressed for women. Many women direct their expectations for achievement toward a different goal. Their rewards come from being successful in their roles as homemaker and mother.

The exploratory motive. Have you ever watched young children with a new toy? Have you seen animals at a zoo exploring some strange or new object in their cage? These are examples of the exploratory, or curiosity, motive.

This motive has been illustrated by scientists. We know that a rat or a monkey will learn a maze, although the only reward it receives is a chance to explore another maze. One experimenter tried putting a puzzle together and letting a monkey take it apart again. The experimenter wanted to know how long the monkey would continue this behavior. After ten hours, the experimenter thought that the motive had been tested enough, but the monkey wanted to keep on going!

In another experiment, a monkey was put into a cage that had two doors. On the inside of one door was a blue card. On the inside of the other door was a yellow card. The door

with the yellow card was always locked. But the door with the blue card could be opened just by pushing on it from the inside. The monkey learned to push open the correct door, although its only reward was a chance to look out into a laboratory for 30 seconds. To make certain that the monkey was pushing the correct door each time, the blue card was moved back and forth from one door to the other. In one study of this type, the monkeys opened doors for 57 days. It seems that monkeys have a strong motive to explore visually.

Later, the experimenters tried to determine if monkeys found certain kinds of visual stimuli more attractive than others. By opening the correct door, the monkey could see another monkey, or a small electric train running on a track, or fresh fruit, or monkey food, or just an empty room. The experimenters then counted the number of times the monkey opened the correct door for each of the visual stimuli. They found that the monkey responded most frequently when another monkey was seen. The toy train ran a close second, food was third, and the empty room was last.

The exploratory motive is also a strong motive in human beings. It is responsible in large part for men and women exploring caves, climbing mountains, and going to the moon. It continues to motivate people to venture into strange and unknown places.

The approval motive. Approval from others, especially from our peers and those we think highly of, is a very important motivating force. Of course, some people have a greater need for approval than others. But in general we like people who like us and make us feel good.

Do we generally like people better if they say only nice things about us? In one experiment, subjects in small groups heard a person (who was assisting the experimenter) talking about them. The first group of subjects heard the person make only nice, flattering remarks about them. A second group of subjects heard the person make only negative, unflattering remarks about them. A third group heard remarks that were at first negative, followed by a gradual change to nice ones. A fourth group heard nice remarks that gradually changed to negative ones. The subjects were then asked to rate to what extent, if any, they liked the person. Before reading any further, stop and decide which group you think liked the person the most and write your answer on a piece of scrap paper.

It may surprise you to learn that the subjects rated the person most liked as the one who first made negative comments about them and gradually changed to positive remarks. The second most liked person was the one who said only nice things about the subjects. Again, you might be surprised to learn that the third most liked person was the one who made only negative comments about the subjects. The least liked person was the one who began with nice remarks and ended with negative ones.

The authors of this study suggest that the early unflattering remarks may have helped to establish a feeling of sincerity, making the nice comments more rewarding to the subjects. And perhaps the subjects felt that the person who said only nice things was too flattering and not sincere at all. The subjects who heard positive remarks first and then negative ones may have felt some loss of self-esteem. All four situations produced some liking of the person.

Some later studies have not found evidence quite as strong as this one. It seems as if our decision to like or dislike another person is not quite this easy to determine. Also, the context or situation in which we find ourselves is a factor in whether or not we like another person. Generally, we tend to like those people who give us social approval and rewards and to dislike those who cause us a loss of self-esteem.

Do you tend to be motivated to do things for people who approve of you?

Intrinsic Motivation Versus Extrinsic Motivation

Do you have a hobby? Do you enjoy going for a walk in the woods? Do you enjoy some sport, such as swimming, basketball, or golf? Why do you engage in such activities? Do you get paid for them? Or do you engage in them just for fun?

If you engage in activities simply because you enjoy doing them, then you have intrinsic motivation. *Intrinsic motivation* can be defined as motivation that comes from within. It is motivation that comes from a person rather than from the environment. In contrast, *extrinsic motivation* is motivation that comes about because of some external reward. This reward might be money for mowing the lawn or social approval for doing community work.

Intrinsic motivation is more likely to encourage behaviors to continue for longer periods of time. If a behavior is extrinsically motivated, it is likely to stop when the reward ends. You might not study for a test next week if you knew that your score wouldn't count toward your final grade. Or you might give up babysitting if you weren't trying to earn money toward your college education. If a behavior is intrinsically motivated, however, it will probably continue as long as the motivation remains.

Are there ways to increase intrinsic motivation? The answer is yes. One way is to avoid situations that promote extrinsic motivation. This is because the external reward can become more important than the activity itself. If a student receives money for getting a good grade, the money could become more important than what the student learned to get the grade. (Grades, too, are external rewards. Getting a particular grade could become more important than learning the material.)

Most people are both intrinsically and extrinsically motivated. You might get personal satisfaction from a part-time job as well as a salary and praise from your co-workers. It is important to remember, though, that not only are you motivated by many different forces. You too can provide extrinsic motivation for other people.

Emotions and Bodily Changes

Motivation is a cause of your behavior. You are hungry, so you eat. You are motivated to succeed in school, so you do all your homework and study hard for tests. You want to learn how to play the piano, so you practice as often as possible.

One concept that is closely related to motivation is emotion. An *emotion* is a complex state of awareness that involves bodily activity. It is a way of expressing your feelings. Joy, anger, fear, and sadness are emotions we express in our daily lives.

Emotions can have various effects on our behavior. Some emotions act to increase a particular behavior. For example, if someone is afraid of failing a road test, this fear may cause the person to practice driving longer. Emotions can also interfere with behavior. A person can become so frustrated and angry when trying to repair a car that he or she may just give up in disgust.

Emotions are accompanied by bodily changes. Think about some intense emotional experience you've had recently. Did your heart pound so loudly that you thought others could hear it? Did you feel shaky? Did your stomach feel as if it were "tied in knots"? These are only a few ways of describing the many bodily, or physiological, changes that occur with different emotions.

Do these bodily changes have a function? Suppose you are about to take an important test, or you have to tell your parents about a special problem. Your face may become flushed, and your mouth may feel very dry. These are bodily changes that accompany fear. Your face becomes flushed because more blood is being pumped to it. Your mouth feels dry because your salivary glands stopped working for a short time—perhaps to save vital fluids in the body for more important functions.

Thus, there is often an explanation for why the physiological changes take place during emotional experiences. Imagine that something has just happened to make you angry. You feel your heart beating faster. This speeding up of your heart rate and blood pressure increases the oxygen supply to the brain so you can think faster. Another bodily change related to emotions is an increase in the blood sugar level. This provides more energy for such things as running or fighting. Also, blood clotting occurs more easily. It helps prevent loss of blood in case of an injury. Another bodily change that often occurs is the slowing of the digestive processes. This allows more blood to be available for other bodily functions, such as thinking and running.

How do we know that emotions affect digestion? Psychologists have studied what happens to the normal digestive processes of animals under emotion-producing situations. For example, a cat may be placed under a fluoroscope (a machine by which the cat's stomach movements can be seen on a fluorescent screen). Before being placed on the machine, the cat is given food that shows up on the fluoroscope. Under normal conditions, churning movements of the stomach take place. Then a dog is brought into the room and allowed to bark at the cat. The cat seems to be having an emotional experience. Its fur stands on end, it arches its back, it spits. The fluoroscope shows that the churning movements of its stomach stop. Even after the dog is taken from the room, the churning movements usually don't begin again for about 15 minutes.

Psychologists have also found that the emotions of uncertainty and fear may cause ulcers in the digestive system of animals. One experiment used two groups of rats. Every time a light was turned on, the rats in one group received an electric shock. But when a buzzer was sounded, they were never shocked. The other group of rats was treated differently. Half the number of times when the light was turned on, the animals were shocked. And half the time when the buzzer sounded, they were shocked. Both groups received the same total amount of light, buzzer, and shock. For rats of the first group, the shock was predictable. They learned when it was going to occur. For the rats in the second group, the shock was unpredictable. They never knew when it was going to occur. This second group developed considerably more ulcers than the first group. Their emotional state brought about more bodily changes.

What parts of the body contribute to emotional behavior? Emotional states involve the entire body. We know that the autonomic nervous system (which regulates our internal organs), the glands, and the viscera (stomach, lungs, heart, and other internal organs) are involved in emotional experiences. For instance, our glands send out hormones that regulate our behavior. A part of the brain called the hypothalamus also affects emotional states. The cerebral cortex is involved, too. By thinking about our emotional experiences, we make them last longer. On the other hand, the cerebral cortex can also reduce the intensity of emotional expressions. When the cerebral cortex is removed in animals, emotional states become more intense than before surgery. Thus, many parts of the body produce the widespread physiological changes that occur in emotional behavior.

Theories of Emotion

You are walking alone one night on a dark and lonely street. Suddenly, you hear footsteps behind you. You think it might be someone about to attack you. Do you become afraid first and then start to run? Or do you start to run and then become aware that you are afraid?

The James-Lange theory. The *James-Lange theory* of emotion states that you

Our emotions involve many bodily changes, such as different facial expressions, voice changes, muscle tensions, and glandular reactions.

are afraid because you run. Running causes bodily actions to occur, and then you become aware of your fear. You aren't aware of a specific emotion until after you've reacted. According to this theory, emotions are the awareness of bodily changes.

This theory was proposed in the 1890's by William James and Carl Lange. James emphasized visceral reactions (of the heart,

lungs, intestines) as being most important in emotional experiences. Lange emphasized vascular reactions (of the blood vessels) as being central to emotional experiences. But both stressed that the physiological changes occur first and the emotion follows.

Certain objections to the James-Lange theory began to emerge in the 1900's. It was found that when visceral organs are separated from the central nervous system (brain and spinal cord) by surgery, emotional behavior does not change very much. Also, if emotions are dependent on physiological changes, then there should be a different physiological state for each emotion. But in many cases, bodily reactions do not differ greatly from one emotion to another. A person whose heart suddenly begins to beat faster may be either afraid or in love.

The Cannon-Bard theory. In the late 1920's, a new theory emphasized one part of the brain, the hypothalamus, as the center of emotional experience. According to the **Cannon-Bard theory,** the awareness of an emotion and the bodily changes occur at the same time. An environmental stimulus

Household mishaps can produce the emotions of fear and guilt in a young child. Reassurance from a parent helps to soothe these emotions.

causes the hypothalamus to send messages to the nervous system that result in physiological changes. At the same time, messages to the cerebral cortex part of the brain bring about feelings of emotion.

Which of these theories is correct? This is an extremely difficult question to answer. How do you find out if physiological changes occur before, or at the same time as, emotions? An emotional state can be started by some internal stimulus. It is then difficult to determine exactly when such a stimulus occurred. Also, bodily changes and emotions often interact with each other. Trying to pin down which is cause and which is effect is not so easy. For example, you feel fear of being attacked. Your awareness of the fear increases your bodily reactions. Your increased bodily reactions cause you to feel as if you are more afraid, and so on.

More recently, a different explanation for emotional experience has been suggested. This theory emphasizes the cognitive factors associated with emotions.

The cognitive theory of emotions. When we're asked to describe an emotion, we usually don't describe bodily reactions associated with the emotion. Instead, we describe the external situation or object that caused the emotion, such as an accident or a beautiful sunset. The external stimulus sets off certain physiological reactions and sensations. Then we label these sensations, depending on our memories, expectations, thoughts, and associations. Thus, the **cognitive theory of emotion** emphasizes the mental processes involved in our emotional experiences.

A number of experiments have tested the role of labeling and interpretation in an emotional experience. One study investigated whether subjects who were misinformed about their physiological responses would be influenced more easily in how they interpreted their physiological reactions.

First, subjects were given an adrenalin-like drug. This drug causes certain physiological reactions to occur, such as an increase in heart rate and blood pressure. One group of subjects was given accurate information about the physiological changes they would experience. A second group was told nothing about bodily reactions. And a third group was misinformed—they were told to expect numbness, itching, and a headache.

After taking the drug, the subjects waited for it to take effect. Each subject was met in a room, one at a time, by another student, who actually was working with the experimenter. With half of the subjects in each group, the student acted very happy, flying paper airplanes and laughing. With the other half of the subjects, the student acted in an angry and hostile way.

All subjects were then requested to complete a questionnaire, reporting their feelings of happiness and anger. Subjects who knew the true effects of the drug reported being neither happy nor angry as a result of the student's behavior. However, those who were in the room when the student played a happy role reported feeling happy. Those who saw the student in an angry mood reported feeling angry. The individuals in these two groups were aware of their bodily changes but didn't know what caused them. They reported feeling happiness or anger, depending on the social situation and their interpretation of that situation.

The experimenters concluded that interpretation of physiological reactions is important in an emotional experience. When people don't know what is causing their physiological reactions, the situation influences how they label the emotion they feel. However, more recent studies have not found as strong a relationship between physiological reactions and environmental factors.

Measuring Emotional States

How do scientists go about studying emotions? It is difficult to produce genuine emotional states in the laboratory. An experimenter may say to a subject, "Be afraid now." To cooperate in the experiment, the subject may try to be afraid. But the person is

How do scientists measure emotional states, such as the feelings of these two people?

not actually afraid. On the other hand, scientists cannot be present with their measuring instruments when someone is having a narrow escape from an accident on the highway. A man and woman cannot be connected with scientific instruments while one sincerely proposes marriage to the other.

But some laboratory situations can be set up in which a person experiences an emotional state. In these cases, the subject must be unprepared for what happens. An unexpected event takes place, such as a loud foghorn blast behind the subject's back. Then the subject's physiological reactions are measured.

What physiological responses do scientists measure? One response is breathing. During an emotional experience, people often change their breathing pattern. They may gasp and hold their breath at a critical moment in an exciting movie, for example. In the laboratory, specially designed instruments record breathing rate and pattern. In one experiment, subjects sat in front of these recording instruments. Suddenly a car horn blasted. The instruments showed that the subjects held their breath very briefly and then began breathing faster and more deeply.

Another physiological reaction that scientists measure in order to understand emotions is heartbeat. Have you ever had a narrow escape and, after the danger had passed, noticed how rapidly your heart was beating? In the laboratory, the rate and strength of the heartbeat is measured by a sensitive electronic instrument called an electrocardiograph.

Measuring skin changes. In an emotion-producing situation, a person may have "goose flesh," turn pale, experience a feeling of either warmth or coldness, or have a tingling sensation in the skin. Psychologists measure such skin changes under emotion-producing conditions by a technique known as the *galvanic skin response,* or **GSR.** In this technique, two electrodes (electricity conductors) are pressed against the skin. One electrode may be placed on the left hand and the other on the right. Then a very weak electric current (2 to 3½ volts) is passed through the body. More resistance to the passage of this current occurs under some conditions than under others. When a person is asleep, resistance is great. Right after a great deal of exercise, resistance is much less. Under emotional excitement, the amount of resistance to the passage of an electric current is reduced, due partly to increased sweat secretion.

Measuring the pupil of the eye. This is another method used in measuring physiological changes during emotion. An instrument has been developed that records the changes in the pupil of a subject as stimuli are presented. The pupil of the eye enlarges when a person receives a pleasant stimulus. It gets smaller when the person receives an un-

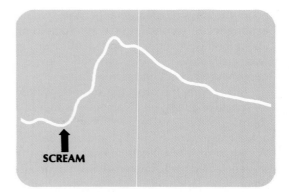

This is the record of a galvanic skin response after an emotion-producing scream.

pleasant stimulus. We can show a person a series of pictures of various situations. By observing the subject's pupil, we can determine which pictures cause a pleasant emotion and which cause an unpleasant emotion in the subject.

This method has a distinct advantage over the galvanic skin response and most other physiological measures of emotion. The pupil gets smaller and larger according to specific emotions—unpleasant and pleasant. Most other physiological measures indicate only that an emotion has occurred.

The polygraph. The most widely known device for measuring emotional states is the *polygraph.* It is commonly known as the "lie detector." Telling a lie is an emotional experience for most people. The polygraph measures some of the physiological changes that take place in an individual under the emotional stress of lying.

The polygraph measures four basic physiological factors: blood pressure, pulse rate, breathing, and the galvanic skin response. Blood pressure seems to be an especially sensitive indicator of the emotional state produced by lying. It will usually rise under the emotional stress of lying. The rate and pattern of breathing, too, are often changed when a person tells a lie. Under normal conditions, breathing in takes about half as long as breathing out. When a person tells a lie, the person takes more time to breathe out.

How accurate is the polygraph? Can criminals practice so that their blood pressure, rate of heartbeat, and breathing will not change when they tell a lie? A person can learn to control specific physiological reactions, such as breathing rate. But a person cannot control all the physiological reactions associated with lie detection so that these reactions remain normal. And the mere fact that individuals hold their breath or breathe abnormally would lead to the suspicion that they are trying to hide a lie.

The reliability of interpreting the results of polygraphs ranges from an estimated 75 percent to 99 percent. Laboratory tests involving staged crimes usually report from 70 percent to 85 percent accuracy in detecting the guilty person.

One problem is that there are no standardized procedures for interpreting the results of polygraph records. However, the professional operator almost never arrives at the final conclusion on the basis of the records alone. The operator pays attention to the behavior of the person before, during, and after the test. In addition, other professional operators, who have no knowledge of the person or the circumstance, are asked to read and interpret the record.

Nevertheless, there is a subjective aspect to the interpretation of "lie detector" tests. The results usually are not admitted as evidence in court, unless both parties in a controversy agree that they can be used.

We've seen, then, that emotions aren't simple. They involve a wide range of physiological changes. They also seem to involve a cognitive process that interprets the changes. Nevertheless, although human emotions are complex, psychologists have devised ways to measure certain emotional states.

Summary

Motivation helps explain why we behave the way we do. Biological drives are an important source of motivated behavior. Two biological drives that are of special interest to psychologists are the hunger drive and the thirst drive.

Various factors influence our hunger drive. The stomach, the brain, and environmental factors help determine when we feel hungry. Several factors also determine when we are thirsty. These include the concentration of chemicals in the blood and the level of fluid in the body.

Among the important social motives that affect our behavior are the achievement motive, the exploratory motive, and the approval motive. Studies have shown that women show less of a need to succeed. However, recent social changes may be making this difference less distinct.

People are motivated both from within and by external rewards. Intrinsic motivation, or motivation from within, is more likely to cause behaviors to continue for longer periods of time. Behavior that is extrinsically motivated is likely to stop when the reward ends.

There are several theories that attempt to explain emotions. The James-Lange theory argues that emotions are the awareness of bodily changes. For example, you run and then become aware you are afraid. The Cannon-Bard theory takes a different viewpoint. According to this theory, you become aware of an emotion at the same time that bodily changes occur. The cognitive theory takes still a different approach. It stresses that our mental processes are involved in our emotional experiences.

Scientists study emotions by measuring different physiological changes that take place, including skin changes and changes in the pupils of the eyes. In addition, they often use the polygraph to measure blood pressure, pulse rate, breathing, and the galvanic skin response.

Paul Ekman is a prominent researcher in the area of facial expressions, body language, and emotions. In the following excerpt from "Detecting Deception from the Body or Face" (*Journal of Personality and Social Psy-* *chology*, 1974, Vol. 29, No. 3), he and Wallace Friesen discuss an application of this research—detection of deception from facial expressions and body language.

Recent interest in body movement and facial expression among behavioral scientists . . . stems in part from the belief that nonverbal behavior reveals how people feel, even when they wish to conceal their feelings. The idea that nonverbal expressions of emotion are not as easily censored or disguised as the content of speech is an old one. . . . Despite this long history, there have been no data to support such claims, nor has there been . . . [any] explanation of how nonverbal behavior might escape efforts to censor interpersonal communication.

Ekman and Friesen reasoned that . . . most individuals in Western culture grow up subject to more commentary, instruction, and reinforcement on their facial activity than on their body movement during conversation. This history of greater social reinforcement for facial behavior than for body behavior . . . results in greater awareness of ongoing facial activity. . . . Although people could lie with the body as with the face, Ekman and Friesen claimed they do so less frequently. . . .

Ekman and Friesen reasoned that as a result of the greater focus on the face than the body, when people attempt to conceal actual feelings and to simulate emotions not felt, they disguise the face more than the body. . . . Through careful monitoring, attempts are made to inhibit, interrupt, or mask facial expressions of actual feelings. With more or less skill, attempts are made to convincingly simulate facial expressions and feelings not experienced. Although the body could be similarly disguised, people usually fail to do so. . . . The body, however, usually more truthfully reveals to the observer either how the person actually feels (leakage) or the fact that something is amiss (deception clues). This difference between face and body would be limited, however, to situations in which the person is engaged in deception. When there is no deception, when communication is frank, then there should be little difference in the information provided from the face and body. . . .

The proposition that the face more than the body is subject to control and disguise during deception [has been] partially . . . supported. When asked what behavior they should control when deceiving, subjects mentioned the face more often than the body. When deceptive behavior was judged and observers had seen an example of each subject's honest behavior which was so identified, judgments of the body were more accurate than of the face. Comparing facial behavior during deception with an example of honest facial behavior did not yield accurate judgments . . . presumably because the subjects disguised their facial behavior during deception to appear honest. Comparing body behavior during deception with an example of honest body behavior did yield accurate judgments . . . presumably because the subjects did not disguise their body behavior during deception.

Source Review

1. Are "leakage" and "deception" more likely to appear in body movements or in facial expressions?

2. When subjects are asked which behaviors they should control when lying, what do they say?

REVIEW

REVIEWING TERMS

motivation
motive
drive
intrinsic motivation
extrinsic motivation

emotion
James-Lange theory
Cannon-Bard theory
cognitive theory of
emotion

galvanic skin response
(GSR)
polygraph

CHECKING FACTS

1. What does motivation help explain?

2. Discuss the various factors that can affect the hunger drive.

3. What two physiological conditions seem to determine thirst? Give an example of each.

4. How does the achievement motive differ in men and women? How has this difference been explained?

5. Give some evidence of how the exploratory motive operates in animals. To what extent does it influence human behavior?

6. How does the approval motive influence behavior? Do we like people better if they say only nice things about us? Explain.

7. Which is a stronger factor in encouraging behaviors to continue—intrinsic motivation or extrinsic motivation? Explain. In what ways can intrinsic motivation be increased?

8. Name some common emotions.

9. Discuss some of the bodily changes that take place during emotional experiences. What purpose do they serve?

10. How can researchers tell that emotions affect digestion?

11. How does the James-Lange theory differ from the Cannon-Bard theory?

12. What approach does the cognitive theory of emotion take?

13. Describe some of the ways in which scientists measure emotions.

APPLYING YOUR KNOWLEDGE

1. While watching television, listening to the radio, or reading a magazine, look for ways in which advertisers use images, sounds, associations, and other hidden cues to motivate consumers to buy their products. Write down your observations. Use your findings as the basis for a class discussion. Or instead you may wish to create advertisements

that highlight each of these motivating factors. You can use your ads as the theme for a bulletin board display.

2. Prepare a questionnaire that compares the achievement motivation of male and female high school students. Include questions on education, career, and personal goals. Then administer your ques-

tionnaire to an equal number of male and female students, making sure to tell them not to include their names. Analyze your results. How does the achievement motivation of male and female students compare? How can you explain the results? How do your findings compare with those reported in the text?

3. Place a black box with a flip top lid in the school cafeteria. Place the label *What's Inside?* above it. Leave the box there for two days, while you observe the behavior of students who pass by. How many students look inside the box? How does this number compare with the number who saw the box but walked right by it? What do your observations say about the curiosity motive in people?

4. In order to conduct a class experiment to see how emotions affect the body, select another student in the class. One person should act as the experimenter and the other person should act as the subject. First, the experimenter should practice taking the pulse of the subject. This may take a few minutes. After this task has been mastered, the experimenter should take the subject's pulse again, this time recording the measurement. The teacher should then read an emotionally charged story or article to the class. When the teacher is finished, have the experimenter take the subject's pulse

rate once more, again recording the findings. How do the two figures compare for each pair? For the class as a whole?

5. Using magazines or newspapers, clip out ten photographs of people that express different emotions. Ask several people to tell you which emotion is expressed in each photo. Do your subjects all give the same answers? What other information might help determine what emotion a person is feeling?

6. To simulate how a polygraph measures emotional states, take the pulse of a friend at 30-second intervals as you ask the person a series of routine questions about his or her age, address, favorite class, and so on. Let your friend know that you want him or her to lie at three points during the questioning. Did the pulse rate change during the "lie" responses?

7. To see how the eye responds to emotional states, create a list of 20 words and read them slowly to a friend sitting across from you. Fifteen of the words should be neutral (e.g., house, car, and book) and five should be more emotionally charged (e.g., love, blood, and prison). Carefully watch for variations in the size of the subject's pupil each time an emotional word is read. Later, ask the subject if he or she felt any physical reaction to any of the words.

THINKING CRITICALLY ABOUT PSYCHOLOGY

1. **Using Creative Thinking** Assume that you could instantly create within yourself any motive that would last as long as you wished. What motive would you create, and why? Which motives would you create in all people if you could do the same? Why?

2. **Seeing Relationships** Suppose all of our needs were always satisfied. How would this change people's behavior?

3. **Classifying Ideas** In which kinds of behavior would there be changes if only external motivation were possible?

4. **Summarizing Ideas** What adaptive or survival functions do emotions serve, if any?

5. **Forming an Opinion** What do you think the world would be like if everyone had exactly the same emotions at exactly the same time?

6. **Debating Ideas** Suppose you were a lawyer defending a client. Would you be willing to stand by the results of a polygraph? Why or why not?

DEVELOPING SKILLS IN PSYCHOLOGY

Keeping a Behavioral Record

Psychologists typically differentiate between the what and the why of behavior—between what we do and why we do it. One assumption is that people are often unaware of the motives that underlie their behavior.

Clearly it would be difficult for people to explain why they do what they do if they were not aware of all their own behaviors. In order to become more aware of the complexity of your own behavior, write down everything you do in one morning, starting with the time you wake up. Be prepared for the fact that your list probably will be very long. Your behavioral record should include one column to record the time of day and one column to record the specific behavior. You will be surprised by the number of things that you do during one morning. You will also be surprised by the number of passive behaviors you can identify. For example, you may realize that you were daydreaming or looking out the window when you should have been studying or paying attention in class.

Once you have completed your behavioral record for the morning, try to analyze the motivation underlying each behavior. For example, why do you brush your teeth, dress in a certain way, or eat or skip breakfast? Once you have considered the motives for each behavior, classify them as intrinsic, extrinsic, or a combination of both. Be sure to justify your answer.

READING FURTHER ABOUT PSYCHOLOGY

Burns, David D., *Intimate Connections,* William Morrow, New York, 1984. Examines loneliness and human relationships. Presents theoretical concepts as well as self-help checklists and worksheets.

Buscaglia, Leo, *Living, Loving and Learning,* Fawcett, New York, 1983. The latest in a series of informative and amusing lectures discussing possibly our most important yet puzzling emotion—love.

Clance, Pauline R., *The Imposter Phenomenon,* Bantam, New York, 1986. Discusses the stress and changes that come about as we strive for success and the resulting motivation to develop our personalities.

Cousins, Norman, *Anatomy of an Illness,* Bantam, New York, 1981. A personal account of how one man mobilized his own natural resources of positive emotions to defeat a serious illness.

Donahue, Phil, *The Human Animal,* Simon & Schuster, New York, 1985. Who are we? What motivates us to behave the way we do? Why do we feel the way we do? Can we change? These questions are explored by famous talk show host, Phil Donahue.

Hazleton, Lesley, *Right to Feel Bad: Coming to Terms with Normal Depression,* Doubleday, New York, 1984. A psychiatrist offers new perspectives on depression. Drawing on the writings of Freud, Jung, and others, the author offers a comforting approach to coping with normal depression in everyday life.

Iacocca, Lee, and Novak, William, *Iacocca: An Autobiography,* Bantam, New York, 1986. The motivations underlying the achievement of a ''self-made man'' are explored in this candid autobiography by the president of The Chrysler Corporation.

Packard, Vance, *The Hidden Persuaders,* Revised Edition, Pocket Books, New York, 1981. Presents insights into the ways in which advertisers motivate consumers to buy various products.

Warren, Neil Clark, *Make Anger Your Ally: Harnessing Our Most Baffling Emotion,* Doubleday, New York, 1983. A how-to book for turning the negative and usually destructive emotion of anger into a positive force.

Using the Skills of a Psychologist

Unit 5 Identifying Emotions

As you learned in Chapter 13, emotions are complex states of awareness that involve bodily activity. The emotions of joy, anger, sadness, frustration, and so on are the means through which we express our feelings. These feelings are accompanied by physiological changes. For example, experiencing fear will make the heart rate increase, the mouth feel dry, and the blood sugar level go up. The body reacts immediately to the emotion.

One way in which human beings show their emotions is with facial expressions. Facial expressions are a means of communication understood throughout the world. People from many cultures around the world who are shown photographs of individuals with different facial expressions are easily able to identify the emotions of anger, surprise, happiness, disgust, and sadness.

Identifying emotions expressed through facial features is one of the skills that psychologists and counselors use to understand and help their clients. These professionals pay very close attention to facial features as a cue to underlying emotions. For example, a high school counselor talks to a boy who is having trouble concentrating in his classes. When the counselor asks the boy about his relationship with his parents, the boy replies that he gets along very well with his parents and that there are no problems in this area at all. However, as the boy talks about his relationship with his parents, his facial features show anger. This alerts the counselor to the fact that there is a discrepancy between what the boy says and what he feels. The counselor can then work toward pinpointing the sources of anger the boy is feeling and help him understand and work through these feelings.

The ability to identify emotions can also help you to become a more effective communicator. Paying attention to the facial features of people who are speaking to you can help you understand the emotions underlying their communication. Sometimes there is a discrepancy between what people say and what they feel. For example, your best friend tells you that her family is moving across the country. She tells you in glowing terms about how wonderful the weather is there, how good the school system is, and how excited she is about the possibility of meeting new and different people. She sounds very excited and happy about the move. But you can see an expression of sadness on her face. Understanding that your friend is also feeling sad about leaving her old friends and surroundings can lead to a more meaningful discussion between you about the negative and positive aspects of the move. You become more effective communicators.

To become better at identifying emotions through facial expressions, try this exercise. Focus on six common emotions: fear, anger, joy, sadness, disgust, and surprise. Using old newspapers and discarded magazines, find and clip photographs of people whose facial expressions show these emotions. Choose at least two photographs for each of the six different emotions. Use the context of the story or the caption accompanying the photograph to help you correctly identify each emotion. Assemble these photographs on a poster board and write the identifying emotions on the back.

With the approval of your teacher, have some of the students go one at a time to the front of the class. The student should point to each of the photographs on his or her poster board while the class writes down which emotion they think the photograph is expressing. When this is completed, the student should identify the emotion he or she chose for each photograph.

REVIEW

REVIEWING THE UNIT

1. What determines whether the combination of two colors is pleasing?

2. How does a person acquire colorblindness?

3. What is tone deafness?

4. Where does our sense of smell come from?

5. What sensations are detected by the four kinds of skin sensors?

6. List three examples of social motives.

7. What four physiological factors does the polygraph measure?

8. What is the polygraph's range of reliability in terms of accuracy?

CONNECTING IDEAS

1. **Seeing Relationships**   What is the relationship between taste and smell?

2. **Summarizing Ideas**   What form must a substance be in to be tasted?

3. **Evaluating Ideas**   Why does measuring the pupil of the eye have a distinct advantage over most other physiological measures of emotion?

PRACTICING RESEARCH SKILLS

From discarded magazines, clip pictures of family rooms, kitchens, and dining areas that you find particularly attractive. Arrange the pictures in a collage on a sheet of poster board. Then conduct library research on the relationship between color and mood.

What conclusions can you draw about the relationship between color and mood? Why do you think certain colors may be more appealing to some people than to others? Can you identify any patterns in the use of color? For example, are certain colors used primarily for contemporary settings?

Are other colors more likely to be used in traditional settings? What color combinations can you identify? Does the use of a certain group of colors have a specific purpose, such as making a small room appear larger than it actually is?

Now think about the role that color plays in the choices that you make. For example, if you prefer bold primary colors in a room, do you also prefer bold primary colors in clothes? Finally, think about what color preference indicates about each individual's personality, style, and unique qualities.

FINDING OUT MORE

You may wish to contact the following organizations for additional information about the material in this unit.

Vision Education Foundation (VEF)
11 N. Montgomery
Memphis, TN 38104

Ohio State University Center for
  Study of Motivation
Room 122 Ramseyor Hall
Columbus, OH 43210

Unit 6

CONFLICTS AND ADJUSTMENTS

Chapter 14 FACING FRUSTRATION AND CONFLICT
Chapter 15 COPING WITH STRESS
Chapter 16 PSYCHOLOGICAL DISTURBANCES
Chapter 17 TREATMENT OF PSYCHOLOGICAL DISTURBANCES

Chapter 14

FACING FRUSTRATION AND CONFLICT

Chapter Focus

This chapter presents:

- **some ways in which frustration affects our lives**
- **the different kinds of conflicts we often face**
- **the adjustment mechanisms we use to cope with frustration and conflict**

You have a history test first period and the bus is late. Annoyed, you start racing to school. You run only one block, when a sign suddenly stops you in your tracks: "Street closed because of repairs." You finally arrive at school but encounter a note on the classroom door: "Test moved to Room 123." Once again you get into high gear and dash down the hall to Room 123. After settling into your seat, you find that your pen is out of ink.

Have you ever had a day like this when everything seemed to go wrong? Fortunately, most days aren't this bad. Yet *frustration* is a normal part of daily life. In this chapter we will examine frustration, the conflicts that often cause it, and the adjustment mechanisms that we sometimes use to help us cope.

Frustration

People are said to be frustrated whenever any of their goal-directed activities are slowed up, made difficult, or become impossible. In our complex society, most people experience many frustrating situations. None of us can always have what we want when we want it. Each of us develops certain patterns of responding to frustrating situations.

What are some reactions to a frustrating situation? One classic study examined how frustration affects the behavior of preschool children. The children were invited to enter a room. In the room were toys with some parts missing. The children played with these toys, however, and seemed to enjoy themselves. During this time, skilled observers rated the children on their reactions as they played. The children were then allowed to enter the other side of the room. It had been blocked from view by a screen. In this side of the room, the children found much more attractive and interesting toys. They were allowed to play with these toys for a short period of time. Then they had to go back to the other side of the room. They were separated from the new toys by a wire screen. They could now see the new toys but could not reach them because of the physical barrier. The only toys they could now play with were the toys with parts missing. The children experienced frustration.

Observers again rated the children on

their play. The level of positive activity was now much lower for the children as a group. Some of the children attacked the wire screen. Others asked for help from adults. Some tried to leave the room. Others showed very childish behavior, such as whining like younger children. On the other hand, a few of the children went from destructive to constructive play. These are some of the ways in which individuals may react to a frustrating situation.

What are some frustrating situations?

There are many kinds of frustrating situations. Our physical environment often places obstacles in our path as we work toward goals. Suppose you're going to have a very full and energetic day tomorrow. You decide to go to bed early and get plenty of sleep. But the neighbors have a big party that lasts far into the night. The noise makes it impossible for you to sleep. Or suppose you've planned a picnic for a week, but on the big day it rains. Perhaps you're in a hurry to get to a football game, but heavy traffic allows you only to inch along. No doubt you can think of many other examples.

Frustration also may come from social regulations. Perhaps you would like to take a particular course, but school regulations forbid it. You may wish to get a full-time job and make enough money to buy a car, more clothes, or a television set of your own. But social pressure says that you should remain in school. Maybe you would like to get married now and establish a home of your own, but social pressures and economic factors prevent you. Or perhaps you would like to travel and have many new experiences, but parents, school, and financial problems keep you at home.

Frustration can result from personal limitations, too. A boy or girl who wants to go out for track can't run fast enough to make the team. Someone who wants to be a fashion model does not meet the required standards. A student wants to attend a certain college with very high entrance requirements and limited enrollment. But the student doesn't have the grades to compete successfully with other applicants.

Students have to face many frustrating situations. There may be difficulties in learning that prevent you from achieving certain goals

Drawing by S. Gross, © 1974, *The New Yorker Magazine, Inc.*

FACING FRUSTRATION
AND CONFLICT

in school. There may be circumstances that keep you from being popular. Perhaps there are physical handicaps that limit your activities. There may be environmental factors that hinder you.

Frustration tolerance. *Frustration tolerance* is the ability of an individual to deal with frustration without becoming maladjusted or overly upset. When a turtle meets a situation that it can't cope with, it withdraws into its shell. When people face a frustrating situation, they may also withdraw. They may not be able to tolerate the frustration. On the other hand, well-adjusted people accept frustration as one of the realities of life. They may have to readjust their goals and their plans for achieving these goals. But they don't feel that everything is hopeless. They may begin by tolerating little frustrations without becoming upset. Frustrating situations don't seem so frustrating when you realize that they're quite normal.

It is also true that a person's frustration tolerance is not the same in every situation. Someone may be able to tolerate frustration well in most situations. But the same person may have trouble tolerating frustration whenever, say, authority figures are involved.

What increases the strength of the frustration? A number of factors are related to the intensity of the frustration. One factor is the motive. The stronger the motive for something, the more intense the frustration at not getting it. If an animal were not fed for 36 hours, it would be more frustrated than if it went without food for 24 hours. Suppose you want to graduate from school so that you can continue your education or get married or get a job. Your failure to graduate would be more frustrating than if you only wanted to get out of school. The more reasons you have for graduating from school, the more frustrated you would be if you did not graduate.

The type of barrier also influences the intensity of frustration. If you can overcome the barrier rather easily, then the amount of frustration is not so great. But if the barrier is such that you have to strive very hard to overcome it, then the frustration is more intense. For example, you have a date for Saturday night and have only $2.00 to spend. The frustration might be intense if you had planned to spend quite a bit of money on the date. But if you need only a few dollars and can borrow some from a friend for a few days, then the frustration will not be as great.

The different ways of reaching a goal are also important. If you have only one or two ways of reaching some blocked goal, the amount of frustration is likely to be rather large. If you have many different ways of reaching a goal, and only one way is blocked, then the amount of frustration will be less. Suppose a boy has been going out with one girl and she starts to date someone else. Then he finds there are several other girls who are as much fun to be with as she is. If his goal is to go out with someone who is fun to be with, then the frustration at losing the first girl will be less intense.

When frustrating events occur one after the other in relatively short periods of time, the amount of frustration is greater than for each event separately. Suppose you are getting ready for a date. The electricity goes off while you are using your hair dryer. You are frustrated. The electricity comes on shortly afterward, but your hair dryer breaks down. Then you stub your toe while running to borrow one from your sister. After this, you find that buttons are missing from the clothes you had planned to wear. Suddenly, the doorbell rings. Your date is early, and you aren't ready. Any one of these situations by itself would cause you to feel frustrated. But the effect of having them occur one after the other increases the frustration.

Your emotional stability influences the degree of frustration you feel. Individuals with a history of emotional instability are less able to handle frustrating situations than people with a background of emotional stability. In addition, the person who is emotionally unstable is more likely to feel that almost any situation is frustrating.

The distance from the goal is also related to the intensity of frustration. The closer you are to a goal, the more frustrating the barrier

Suppose you were flying a kite and the string became a tangled mess. How would you react to this situation?

makes you feel. If you are a first-year college student and have to quit college, it isn't as frustrating as if you are beginning your last year. Suppose you are picking up a friend and have a flat tire a short distance from the meeting place. This would be more frustrating than if the flat tire occurred before you left home.

Individual differences in experiencing frustration. We've mentioned some factors related to the intensity of the frustration you might feel. But there are great differences in individual reactions. What is highly frustrating to one person may be only a minor irritation to someone else. Your interpretation of the situation and how you expect to behave will affect how you react. If you see yourself as the kind of person who is *never* late, under any circumstances, having that flat tire could cause you to feel very frustrated. But if you see yourself as someone who is not late except when something unexpected happens that is not your fault, the frustration would be minor.

The next time you begin to feel frustrated, you might like to try the following. As soon as you start to feel emotional arousal in such a situation, stop for a moment. Say to yourself, "I will not become frustrated." If necessary, repeat this several times to yourself, until you feel the emotional arousal begin to lessen. Then look for specific ways in which you can reduce the frustration even further. For example, suppose you get a flat tire. You might start getting out the jack, lug wrench, and spare tire to fix it. The actual act of opening the trunk of the car, taking out the spare tire, and so on, will help reduce the frustration—you will be doing something positive about reaching your goal.

Kinds of Conflicts

Frustration results when you are prevented from doing something. But it can also come from **conflict,** from having to choose between alternatives—between two possibilities. Conflict is often very frustrating. When you are shopping, you often have to decide between the inexpensive and the expensive. Between the flashy article of poor quality and the less stylish article of good quality. The frustration occurs because the purchase of one of the two articles becomes a barrier to purchasing the other.

High school and college students are faced with many other conflicts. They must decide whether or not to go on with formal schooling, whether to get a job or not work right away, whether or not to go along with their crowd's activities, and so on. There are many situations that require decisions.

Let's look at three kinds of conflicting situations: approach-approach, avoidance-avoidance, and approach-avoidance.

Approach-approach conflicts. Suppose you are faced with two attractive choices. Both are very desirable. You are torn between them. You would like to do or have

How do you choose between two desirable items?

both, but you can't. This is called an *approach-approach conflict.* We can diagram such a conflict in this way:

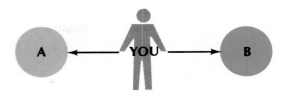

Both choices A and B are equally desirable.

There is the story of the donkey standing halfway between two very attractive bales of hay. In this approach-approach conflict, the donkey starved to death because it couldn't decide which way to go. A girl has been asked to bring a date to a friend's birthday party. She knows two very attractive boys. She would like to have both of them come with her to the party. But two boys with one girl is just not accepted behavior for this event. She can't decide which one to ask. A boy goes to buy a present for a friend. He finds two record albums that his friend would like. The prices are the same. He can't decide which one to buy.

Actually, in everyday life, circumstances often help us make a decision. The donkey probably would have moved around a bit. As it moved nearer one bale of hay, that bale would have seemed more attractive. The donkey would have approached it and feasted instead of starved. The girl might have happened to meet one of the two boys in the hall. She might have stopped to talk a minute and mentioned the party. Her whole problem would have been solved. If he agreed to go with her, the conflict would have been over. If he said no, the conflict would have been over as well. She then could approach the other boy. The boy trying to buy a record album might have been influenced by the salesperson who merely said, "This one is our best seller these days." In many approach-approach conflicts, we do nothing for a short time and then make a decision.

In one experiment, rats were taught to receive food placed at one end of an alley in a maze. The rats were put into a harness. The harness was attached to a spring scale so that the pull on the harness could be measured in grams. The rats could be stopped at any point in the alley—either close to the place of reward or far from it. It was found that the closer the rats came to the place where they had been rewarded (approach behavior), the harder they pulled. This increase in the strength of the pull toward an attractive goal the nearer the subject gets to the goal is called the **approach gradient.** Once an approach has been decided on, the strength of the approach increases in direct relation to the nearness of the goal. Data from this experiment are shown in the graph on the right. The rat was placed at point X.

Avoidance-avoidance conflicts. When you are presented with two alternatives that are equally unattractive, you are facing an **avoidance-avoidance conflict.** We can diagram this kind of conflict in the following way:

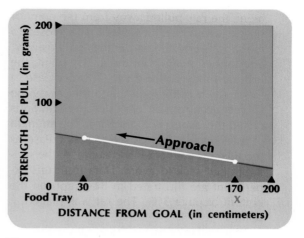

This graph illustrates the approach gradient.

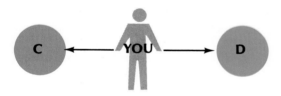

Both choices C and D are equally undesirable.

As a student, you may be faced with the unpleasant thought of having to study for an exam on an evening when there is a special program on television. An equally unpleasant thought is that if you don't study you may fail the exam, fail the course, and fail to graduate. You would like to avoid both situations—studying and failing the exam. Maybe you go to your room and sit down to study. But you can't stop thinking about what you're missing, so you go to the living room and watch the television program. However, you can't enjoy the program because you

keep thinking about the possibility of failing. Back you go to your room and open the book to study—then back to the living room. Such wavering is very unpleasant. You would like to get out of the situation altogether. You decide to take a walk. You drift off into a daydream. You remember a task around the house that needs your attention. You try to avoid both the thought of study and the thought of failing.

In another experiment, rats were put in a harness (so that the strength of their pull could be measured). The rats were given a shock at one end of an alley. In this experi-

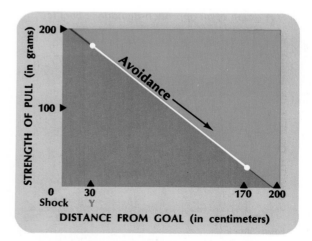

This graph shows the avoidance gradient.

**FACING FRUSTRATION
AND CONFLICT**

ment, the rats pulled away from the point of shock (avoidance behavior). The closer to the shock point, the harder they pulled away. The farther away from the shock point, the less hard they pulled away. This decrease in the strength of the pull the farther away the subject gets from an undesirable situation is called the **avoidance gradient.** The strength of avoidance behavior seems to increase as the subjects get nearer and nearer to the situation they seek to avoid. Data from this experiment are illustrated in the graph on the bottom of page 305. The rat was placed at point Y.

You will note that in the graphs of the two experiments with rats (page 305), the avoidance gradient is much steeper (indicated by the slope of the line) than the approach gradient. What does this indicate?

Approach-avoidance conflicts. Sometimes you are drawn toward certain aspects of a situation and want to turn away from some others. This is an **approach-avoidance conflict.** You would like to approach a particular goal. At the same time, you would like to avoid it. It has both positive and negative value for you. You are pulled in opposite directions, liking and disliking at the same time. We can diagram such a conflict as shown at the top of this page.

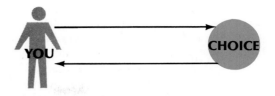

In this conflict, the choice has both desirable and undesirable aspects.

You are at the beach. A swim with your friends seems very attractive. You run down to the water's edge, and a small wave covers your feet. The water is terribly cold. A swim suddenly seems like something to avoid rather than something to approach. You run back up the beach. Your friends call. You approach the water again, but it hasn't warmed up. You run back up the beach, and so on. You are faced with an approach-avoidance conflict.

Perhaps you are trying to decide whether or not to apply for admission to college. You have heard a great deal about the pleasures and advantages of college life. You would like to approach it. But you have also heard of the long hours of study, of difficult examinations, and of the large expense involved. You would like to avoid these unpleasant features.

A rat learns to obtain food from a tray. Then it is given an electrical shock whenever it approaches the tray. It will have an approach-avoidance conflict. Suppose we combine the two previous graphs, placing the approach gradient line and the avoidance gradient line in the same graph, as shown on the left. We find that the point of greatest conflict is where the lines cross. If the rat is placed to the right of the intersection of lines, it will probably pull toward the tray. If placed to the left of the intersection, it is likely to pull away from the tray. Avoidance in this case is stronger than attraction. If the rat is at the point of intersection, it is likely to remain there and waver for some time.

You can see from the graph that the avoidance gradient tends to be steeper than the approach gradient. Evidence for this is

A graph of an approach-avoidance conflict.

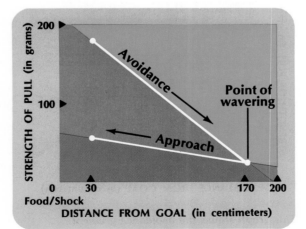

found in studies of skydivers as they approach their first jump from a plane. As they get closer to the first jump, their negative feelings increase. These negative feelings grow from the time they arrive at the airport, put on their gear, board the plane, and take off. At this point, the avoidance feelings are greater than the approach feelings. Then why don't the skydivers back out of making their first jump? For many, the decision to jump is actually made while in the plane. Then avoidance feelings begin to weaken. It seems as if the final decision has committed them to jump. They accept it, and the fear of jumping begins to decrease.

Suppose that you are in an approach-avoidance conflict. Do you usually try harder to avoid an undesirable situation than to approach a desirable one? The answer depends a great deal on how close you are to the situation. But do you reach a point of intersection where you waver back and forth?

Complex approach-avoidance conflicts.

Actually, approach-avoidance conflicts are often more involved than we have described. There is usually more than one aspect of a situation that makes it an approach or avoidance situation. Sometimes there are four or five. Suppose a young woman, Linda, is seriously considering marriage. However, she is in love with two men. One man, Harry, is physically very attractive. But Linda has found that he is also very selfish. He would probably be a self-centered and inconsiderate partner for life. She has an approach-avoidance conflict when she thinks of Harry in terms of marriage. On the other hand, Bill, the other man with whom Linda is in love, is not nearly as physically attractive as Harry. But he is kind and thoughtful and would probably be very considerate as a partner for life. Linda has an approach-avoidance conflict when she thinks of Bill in terms of marriage. We can diagram this situation as shown above.

Linda has a very difficult decision to make. But unlike rats in an experiment, she can have more than two choices. She can begin dating a third man, Jim, with an eye to

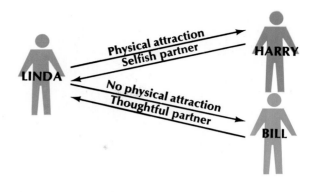

A double approach-avoidance conflict.

marriage. But she may run into an approach-avoidance conflict with Jim. She becomes very fond of him. Then she finds that she dislikes the idea of having his parents as in-laws. She can add several more men friends as possible prospects for marriage. At first she had a simple approach-avoidance conflict. Now she has a complex approach-avoidance conflict.

Which of the three kinds of conflict is easiest to solve? To find out, two psychologists had 70 college students use the maze shown on page 308. The students were led to believe that the maze was simply a technique for measuring speed of movement. They were told to move with a pencil from the starting point (X) to either goal. The goals were to be thought of as cities. At each city, there was a red light and a white light that the experimenter could turn on and off.

The subjects were asked to imagine that whenever the red light was turned on, a bomb would be dropped on that city. So they were to move away from that city as quickly as possible. Whenever the white light was turned on at a city, they would receive a million dollars if they reached the city quickly enough. All areas outside the pathways were regarded as quicksand.

The subjects were given trials with either the red or the white light turned on at only one city. There was no conflict. These situations provided control data for the other parts of the experiment.

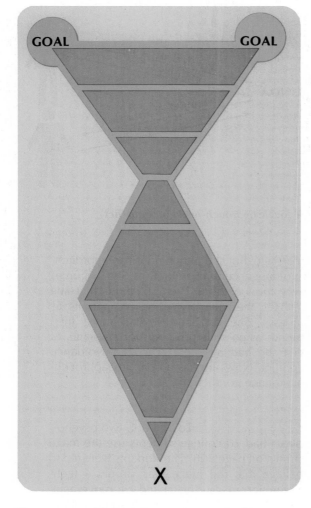

GOAL   **GOAL**

X

The maze used to test the responses of subjects to three types of conflict situations

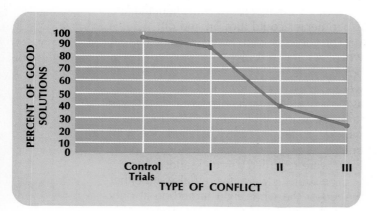

The relationship of good solutions by the subjects to the type of conflict presented

The subjects did not know this in advance, but on the twenty-first, thirty-second, and forty-third trials, one of the following three conflict situations was presented:

Type I.   **Approach-approach:** White lights were turned on in both cities.

Type II.   **Approach-avoidance:** A red light and a white light were turned on in one city.

Type III.   **Avoidance-avoidance:** Red lights were turned on in both cities.

The psychologists then figured out the percentage of good solutions for each type of conflict situation. A good solution was determined by both the quality of the response and the speed of the response. Responses were classified under such headings as going directly and without detour to the goal, stopping at some point along the way, and moving through one or more of the crossways. The results are presented in the graph on this page.

As can be seen from the graph, good solutions were easiest in approach-approach conflict situations. Good solutions were most difficult in avoidance-avoidance conflicts. They were nearly as difficult in approach-avoidance conflicts.

Life is full of conflicting situations. Often people are frustrated for at least a short time. How will they respond to such conflict? By highly emotional and ineffective behavior? Conflicts are unpleasant. But a well-adjusted individual takes them in stride.

Adjustment Mechanisms

We have considered several ways of responding to frustrations and conflicts. Now we will examine other ways of responding to frustrations and conflicts, known as adjustment mechanisms. **Adjustment mechanisms** are ways of behaving that help satisfy needs, reduce anxiety from frustration, and protect the individual's self-esteem. Some of these ways may be either desirable or un-

There are many ways in which people with disabilities can compensate. These men are competing in an Olympic race for the disabled.

desirable, depending on how and to what degree they are used.

Compensation. *Compensation* is an attempt to make up for a lack in one area by putting forth extra effort and energy over an extended period to do well in some other area. A person may purposely set out to compensate for some lack. Or individuals may compensate without being aware that they are doing so.

Compensation can be a very desirable way of meeting frustrations. It may lead toward good social adjustments. It may even result in activities that leave individuals better off than before they experienced frustration. A member of a high school football team was crippled in a car accident. He could never play football or any other active sport again. He might have compensated by becoming a ping-pong player. But even in this relatively mild game, his physical handi-

cap would have meant a very hard uphill fight—a fight he might have found unsatisfying. His interests were in athletics. He didn't want to change his interests just because he could no longer play active games. While still in high school, he became the sports reporter for the school paper. After graduation, he worked his way up as a reporter on a city newspaper. He is now a successful sportscaster on a television program. He has many friends among sports fans. Once in a while, his closest friends hear him say, "Gee, I wish I could get out there and play myself." But he knows that he cannot play. He has compensated for his physical handicap in a desirable way.

Compensation can also be used in an undesirable way. For instance, after his car accident, this same fellow might have decided that since he couldn't play, he would make money out of sports by gambling. He could have gone in for "fixing" games so that the player or team on whom he bet would be sure to win. He would have compensated for his deficiency. But he would have become dishonest, lost friends, and downgraded the activity he was most interested in.

Some students may find that even though they try very hard, they just can't be superior students. They may compensate by becoming superior in some other field in which they do have ability. For example, a girl was just getting by in most subjects in high school in spite of her best efforts. Then she became very interested in her chemistry course when the teacher explained chemical processes involved in photography. In fact, the girl made a B in chemistry for that grading period. And B's were scarce on her record. She began developing and printing pictures at home. She borrowed and studied library books on photography. She joined a local camera club. Several of her pictures were published in the school yearbook. One appeared in the local Sunday newspaper and later won a prize in the paper's photo contest. She had compensated for her lack of general scholastic ability. She had developed an interesting and perhaps profitable hobby.

There are many ways in which a person can compensate. The student who does not do well in vocational subjects may compensate by doing well in the more academic subjects, and vice versa. The person who is unable to travel can compensate by reading books and magazines about travel. What other ways can you suggest in which an individual can compensate for feelings of frustration and inferiority?

Overcompensation. When people go even further than just balancing their feelings of inferiority, guilt, frustration, or inadequacy, *overcompensation* occurs. Shy students may try so hard to compensate for a lack of social life that they study all the time, don't get enough healthful exercise, and drop what little social life they did have. Students may try so hard to compensate for a lack of scholastic ability that they join every available club and social organization. They are

out every night. Their schoolwork drops still lower. Both the student who studies almost all the time and the student who is constantly involved in social activity may be overcompensating for their respective deficiencies.

Did you ever hear a girl say, "I'm the dumbest person in school"? Or hear a boy say "All my friends are better-looking than I am"? Did they expect you to agree with them? Did they want you to say, "I'd hate to see them come any dumber," or "I can't imagine anyone uglier than you"? On the contrary, they probably hoped you would say, "Oh, you're one of the smartest girls in school," or "I think you're the best-looking boy in the class." Putting yourself down often indicates overcompensation.

Identification. The word *identification* refers to the process of copying or associating closely with the behavior of other individuals or groups. Usually, small boys identify with their fathers. Little girls identify with their mothers. Later, they may identify with their teachers or with famous people in films, plays, or television programs. In their imagination, they put themselves in the place of an older and admired person.

As we get older, we tend to identify ourselves with organizations rather than with individuals. Adults may join a club, lodge, or other social group. In this way, they can enjoy the social life and do their part in carrying out the worthwhile objectives of the organization. On the other hand, they may identify with an organization for the feeling of superiority that such membership gives them. Students may join a school club only because it is the largest or most popular club in school. High school graduates may choose a college because it has a very good football team. Then they can say, "We are the strongest team in the league"—even though they may not play themselves and may take physical education only because it is required.

We all do a certain amount of identifying. But some people find themselves absorbing too much glory from the accomplishments of others. Or they find themselves joining organizations solely for the prestige they will get from membership.

Projection. Have you ever seen your own emotions and intentions in someone else? When we perceive our own undesirable traits or motives in other people, we are demonstrating **projection.** We may blame others for our shortcomings or difficulties. Or we may attribute to others our own unacceptable desires. A student cheats on an examination. To reduce the feeling of guilt, the student says, "Everybody else in the class cheats. I even saw Fran and Leslie cheat, and they're on the honor roll." An irritable person may accuse others of being irritable. An impolite person may accuse other people of rudeness. When children are frightened, they are more likely to see other children as frightened.

We may gain a bit of relief from our feelings of frustration and inferiority when we project our traits and motives onto others. But individuals striving to become well-adjusted try to correct their shortcomings rather than to see them in others.

Stereotyped behavior. When faced with frustrating or conflicting situations, some individuals respond simply by continuing in a blind way with their past behavior patterns. They make no attempt to adjust to new conditions. A student has difficulty with a particular kind of algebra problem. Instead of trying to work out a new plan of attack, the student keeps trying the same incorrect approach time after time. Behavior that is not changed by circumstances is called **stereotyped behavior.**

A classic experiment that shows this behavior was performed on white rats. The rats

Text continues on page 314.

When members of a group, such as this band, dress alike, it helps each individual identify with the group as a whole.

After months of captivity, the prisoners were finally released from the concentration camp. You would expect them to rejoice. Yet many just stared emptily into space. Why did they not celebrate their regained freedom? The answer lies in a phenomenon known as learned helplessness.

Learned helplessness can be defined as passive acceptance of an undesirable situation, which results from previous experiences. For example, a child who is judged uneducable by teachers has difficulty learning to read and write. In actuality, the child may be capable of learning. However, after being called stupid time and again, the child accepts the label. Rather than try to prove the teacher wrong, the child has learned to be helpless. Learned helplessness is an unfortunate way in which people sometimes cope with frustration and conflict.

Psychologist Martin Seligman has conducted several experiments on learned helplessness. In one experiment a dog was strapped to a harness similar to that used by Pavlov in his conditioning experiments. The dog received a series of shocks, from which it could not escape. The next day the dog was placed in a box with two compartments separated by a barrier. The dog had freedom of movement and could jump from one compartment to the other.

During this part of the experiment the lights in the box were dimmed, signalling the administering of several shocks. The dog could avoid the shocks completely by jumping when the light was lowered. Or it could escape the shocks by jumping over the barrier when the shocks began. But rather than try to run away, the dog accepted the consequences. As Seligman noted:

> [First] the dog ran around frantically for about thirty seconds. But then it stopped moving; to our surprise, it lay down and quietly whined. After one minute of this we turned the shock off. . . . On all succeeding trials, the dog failed to escape.

All in all, Seligman repeated the experiment with several dogs. Each was given ten trials to clear the barrier. However, very few did. Most just stayed where they were, passively accepting the shocks.

At the same time, Seligman conducted the experiment on a control group of dogs. On the first day these dogs received the same number of shocks as the others, but

A person may learn through experience to be helpless in school. After being labeled "stupid" by teachers and other students, the person may accept the label and simply give up.

were able to turn them off. These dogs quickly learned to escape the shocks on the second day.

What had happened? Why did the dogs in the control group learn to escape the shocks, while those in the experimental group did not? Seligman hypothesized that the dogs in the experimental group had learned to be helpless. They could do nothing about the first series of shocks they had received. Thus, when exposed to a situation where they *could* do something, they responded passively. They had no reason to believe they could escape these shocks either. They had no incentive to try to escape.

A number of additional experiments tended to confirm Seligman's hypothesis. A control group of dogs that had not received prior shocks quickly learned how to jump the barrier and avoid the unpleasant experience. Dogs that were able to avoid the first set of shocks by pushing a panel with their noses were also able to learn the jumping technique. Similar results were obtained from rats, cats, and monkeys.

The phenomenon of learned helplessness was also induced in human subjects. In one experiment students were exposed to unpleasant noise levels that they could not control. Later, when placed in a situation where they could control the noise level, the students tended to be passive. They put up with the noise until the experimenter turned it off. In contrast, students in a control group refused to tolerate the harsh sounds.

An important sidelight that these experiments point out is the effect that punishment can have on behavior. Children who are continually punished for unacceptable behavior might indeed acquire learned helplessness. This is because they quickly learn that there is no way they can avoid the punishment. As a general rule, psychologists believe it is better to reward proper behavior than to rely on punishment as a teaching tool.

Fortunately, though, most healthy individuals do not respond to all uncontrollable events by becoming helpless. The main reason is that most of us have already experienced many events that we *could* control. For example, a student faced with algebra for the first time is motivated to learn the subject if he or she has already been able to learn Spanish. In the same way, difficulties are easier to bear if we have coped successfully with disappointments in the past.

SOURCE: M. E. P. Seligman, *Helplessness,* San Francisco: W. H. Freeman, 1975.

Although these concentration camp victims were finally set free after horrifying experiences, they could not accept this reality.

were rewarded for jumping toward a card with a square printed on it. They were punished when they jumped toward a card with a circle on it. Soon the rats jumped only toward the card with the square. Next, the experimenter frustrated the rats. The corners of the card with the square were cut off so that it looked like the card with the circle. The rats couldn't tell the difference between them.

How do you think the rats reacted? Some of the rats continually jumped to the left, regardless of which card was on the left. Other rats always jumped to the right. Still others always jumped halfway between the cards! Then the experimenters wanted to find out what would happen when the original situation was presented again. Would the rats react as before, always jumping to the card with the square and never to the card with the circle on it? In the experiment, they did not. They continued with the same stereotyped behavior they had developed when they became frustrated. The rats that jumped to the left continued to jump to the left. The rats that jumped to the right, and those that jumped in between the cards, continued to do so. Only after long and difficult training was the experimenter able to break this stereotyped behavior. The experimenter believed that the same may be true of people. When their responses fail to solve a problem, frustrated people may become focused on a particular type of behavior, which is then difficult to change.

Repression. One way of getting around frustrations and conflicts is to "forget" them. We do forget many things. But when we forget because the original thoughts are painful to us, this is *repression* rather than true forgetting. Psychologists often define the term in a more technical way. For our purposes, however, we can say that repression is selective forgetting. We "forget" what we don't want to remember.

Perhaps you have had some very embarrassing experience in the classroom. For weeks you were teased about the incident. Life became rather unhappy. You might say

to yourself, "I'll just forget about it." Perhaps you meant that you were going to try to think of other things and take the kidding good-naturedly. Then you were making a good adjustment. Or perhaps, without realizing it, you began to avoid situations that reminded you of the bad experience. Then you were repressing your thoughts of the experience.

We all repress some unpleasant thoughts. But with some people, such "forgetting" becomes extreme. They repress whole areas —perhaps many years—of their earlier lives because of certain painful experiences that happened to them then.

Regression. Sometimes, when faced with personal problems, individuals try to escape from unpleasant facts or responsibilities. They try to run away from the situation. They may regress, or return to earlier ways of behaving, to avoid present problems. **Regression** is the escaping of present problems by returning to earlier known ways of meeting frustrations. Older children sometimes become babyish in their behavior when they find problems too difficult to face. Adolescents may turn to childish temper tantrums and fights rather than dealing with and solving their problems.

Occasional regressions are normal. But sometimes people run away from their frustrations to the point of showing regressive behavior all the time. They may need to receive psychological or psychiatric care.

Procrastination. Another very common way of escaping problems is by delay, or *procrastination.* By putting off a task, individuals get away from a distressful situation. They escape an unpleasant task for a while.

People are especially likely to procrastinate if they have very high ambitions but feel inferior. They are not willing to test their strength because of fear of failure. For example, Jack, a high school senior, says that he wants very much to go to a certain college. This college is a "must" on his list of ambitions. The college provides a very helpful scholarship. Several seniors are applying for it. Jack says, "I just have to win that scholarship." But he also realizes that someone else might win it. He puts off filling out the necessary application form. Finally, he fills out the form and sends it in — two days after the deadline. Of course, he doesn't win the scholarship. But he can say, "I probably could have received the scholarship if I'd sent in the application on time." Instead of facing a possible failure, he ran away from any possibility of success.

Students who put off doing an assignment, such as writing a paper, briefly escape what seems to be an unpleasant task. But the longer the task is put off, the more unpleasant it becomes. In the meantime, they rush from one activity to another. They say, "I just don't have time to write that paper." Finally, and at the last minute, they hurriedly gather some material and write the paper. Of course, the grade on the paper is poor. They claim, "I wouldn't have had the poorest grade in the class if I'd had enough time to work on the paper." They ignore the fact that they chose to do many other things instead of writing the paper. They kid themselves into believing they would have had a good paper if they had had more time. But in reality, they ran away from the task so that they would have an excuse for not doing well.

Procrastination has been described as "the art of keeping up with yesterday." We all probably get behind in some of our work at times. And it isn't always our fault. But people who are behind in their work most of the time should ask themselves, "Why do I procrastinate? What am I trying to run away from?" An honest answer to these questions may help them overcome this behavior.

Displaced aggression. Perhaps you've run into some difficulty at school. You were not prepared for class, so the teacher gave you an extra assignment to complete. You had planned to go to a movie. Now your plans have been upset. As you come home, your dog runs out to meet you, wagging its tail. Instead of patting the dog, you yell at it. You were angry at the teacher. But you couldn't directly express your anger in the classroom. So you got mad at your poor dog instead.

This boy is frustrated because he put off writing his report, which is due tomorrow.

Joe, an employee, is bawled out by his boss in front of others. Joe feels like hitting the boss. But that direct aggressive behavior might mean the loss of his job. He goes home and snaps at his wife and children instead. The children are playing happily with their toys. Suddenly they are told to put them away and go to bed. They are frustrated. But what can they do to their parents? They kick the toys all over the floor and may even break some of them.

These situations are examples of **displaced aggression**, or the transfer of anger from the source of the frustration to some innocent person or object. Popularly, displaced aggression is spoken of as "blowing off steam."

Letting someone else decide for you. Making a decision is often difficult and even painful. To avoid such difficulty, you can ask a friend for the answer to your problem. You

This cartoon illustrates the concept of rationalization.

"I didn't catch it 'cause you didn't hit it where I was standing."

might say, "What would you do if you were in my place?" But how do friends know what they would do if they were in your place? Both their heredity and their environment are different from yours. Their hopes and goals are different. A friend can give you information and even make recommendations. But all too often when you ask for advice, you are really asking for a ready-made solution to your problem. You are not facing your own problem. You are escaping. Sometimes, instead of asking a friend to solve your problem, you may put the burden on mere chance. You flip a coin, refusing to face the problem yourself.

Rationalization. You may neither actively attack nor run away from your problems. Instead, you may try to "explain" what you've done. You may rationalize. ***Rationalization***

refers to the kind of thinking people do when they use socially approved reasons instead of real reasons to explain their behavior. In projection, individuals place blame for their shortcomings on another person or persons. Rationalization does not necessarily involve another person. Individuals often rationalize their behavior by blaming an object or a set of circumstances.

Rationalizing is not the same as lying. Those who do the rationalizing fool themselves first. They may fool others afterward. They aren't willing to admit that they are wrong. Instead, they accept some explanation for their behavior that will save "face," or pride.

Students who don't do their work find they are getting failing or poor grades. They feel they will have to explain these low grades to parents and friends. The real reason is not a good one. It will not be approved by parents and friends. So they come up with more acceptable explanations for the low grades. They say, "I did the work all right, but the questions on the test were very unfair." Or, "My classes are so dull that I can't possibly pay attention." By such excuses as these, they save their pride in their own eyes. They may even fool a few friends. But others may recognize that they are rationalizing and are unwilling to face the truth.

Gail may stress the importance of honesty to her children. Then, in her business, she has a chance to make a profitable deal if she gives misleading information about the merchandise she is selling. She goes through with the dishonest transaction. Later, a friend may accuse her of not living up to her principles. She is not willing to admit to herself or others that she has been dishonest. She may rationalize by saying, "Business is business. Anyone else would have done the same thing. Customers know, or should know, what they're buying. Anyway, I gave no written guarantee."

But we must be careful not to be too hard on the person we know to be rationalizing. We all rationalize. Often, rationalization takes one of two forms—"sour grapes" or "sweet lemon."

The sour grapes rationalization.

The term *sour grapes rationalization* refers to the kind of rationalization in which we say that we don't want something that we can't have. By finding fault with an object we can't get, we make it seem less appealing. The term comes from the tale of the fox and the grapes. The fox, unable to reach the grapes it wanted, declared that they were sour.

Jack tries out for the school play. Everyone knows that he wants the lead. But someone else gets the part. Jack's pride is hurt. Some friends hear about it and tease him about not getting the lead. He could admit his situation and perhaps try for another part. Instead, he says, "I didn't really want to be in that play anyway. The plot is boring. The play probably won't be a success."

The sweet lemon rationalization.

The term *sweet lemon rationalization* refers to the process of saying that what we have (but don't really want) is just what we want. The lemon is sour. But if we put sugar on it, we may be able to make it taste better. If we add enough sugar, we may be able to make it appear to others and to ourselves that a lemon is exactly what we want.

Carol goes out with Stephen for the first time. She finds that she does not particularly like him. She may say to a friend, "He may *appear* to talk only about himself, but actually he is a very thoughtful and considerate person." By putting enough "sugar" on her disappointment, she is able to accept it a bit more easily. Just possibly she is able to fool some of her friends.

The person who drives an old car says, "I wouldn't trade this old bus for any of the new models. I wouldn't accept a new model as a gift." In spite of this statement, the person enters a contest in which the prize is a new car. Suppose this individual wins the contest. Would he or she refuse to accept the car?

Rationalization can be helpful in providing some relief from disappointment. The sweet lemon rationalization is probably more desirable than the sour grapes rationalization. But people tire of listening to both kinds. It is often best to face reality, even though that reality is sometimes unpleasant.

Groups and nations also rationalize.

Social groups as well as individuals develop rationalized explanations for their behavior. They may rationalize, for instance, that a problem or mistake was caused by someone else. This is called scapegoating.

The term scapegoating comes from a ritual practiced during ancient times. Under the ancient law of Moses, a goat was selected. The high priest confessed the people's sins over the head of this goat. Then the "scapegoat" was driven into the wilderness. The goat was to take with it all those sins. Today we refer to any individual or group blamed for the misdeeds or mistakes of others as a **scapegoat.** People in authority who can't

Part of the ceremony on the Day of Atonement involved placing the sins of the people on the head of a goat. The "scapegoat" was then driven into the desert.

cope with certain problems don't like to admit it. They may find it easier to blame some powerless person or group—the scapegoat.

Wartime produces many instances of group rationalization. Most people don't believe in killing other people. Therefore, to get people to fight, they must be taught to rationalize killing others and destroying property.

When national leaders can't deal successfully with economic and social problems, they may not dare to admit their failure. They rationalize. And they influence the public to rationalize with them.

How useful are adjustment mechanisms? Adjustment mechanisms can help people function. Suppose you are very anxious about something. This feeling of anxiety can hinder your everyday living. It can make it difficult for you to think or make decisions. You would be able to perform more adequately if the anxiety could in some way be reduced. The use of adjustment mechanisms can reduce anxiety for a short period of time. You can then look for better ways of behaving and thinking.

Most people use most of the mechanisms at one time or another. If you have friends who use, say, rationalization quite often, don't assume that they are poorly adjusted. We all make use of certain adjustment mechanisms to some extent.

However, it is true that the use of such mechanisms does not really solve your problems. In fact, they can eventually do more harm than good. Adjustment mechanisms may become the individual's most important behavior. In that case, they do indicate poor personality adjustment.

318

Summary

Frustration occurs whenever people's goal-directed activities are slowed up, made difficult, or become impossible. Among the frustrating situations we face are those resulting from our physical environment, social regulations, and personal limitations.

Several factors determine the intensity of our frustration. These include the motive behind our behavior, the barrier blocking the goal, the number of ways of reaching the goal, the frequency of frustrating events, our emotional stability, and our distance from the goal.

Conflict occurs when we have to choose between two or more alternatives. Three kinds of conflicting situations are approach-approach, avoidance-avoidance, and approach-avoidance. In approach-approach conflicts, we are faced with two attractive choices. In avoidance-avoidance conflicts, both choices are equally unattractive. And in approach-avoidance conflicts, both options have favorable and unfavorable aspects. Researchers have found that approach-approach situations are easiest to solve.

Adjustment mechanisms are a way of responding to frustration and conflicts. They may be desirable or undesirable, depending on how they are used. Some common adjustment mechanisms include compensation, overcompensation, identification, projection, stereotyped behavior, repression, regression, procrastination, displaced aggression, letting someone else decide for you, and rationalization.

INTERPRETING SOURCES

Psychologist C. R. Snyder thinks that excuse-making is a common self-protecting reaction to the frustrations that accompany failures to perform or behave in acceptable ways. As you read this excerpt from "Excuses, Excuses" (*Psychology Today,* September 1984), try to think of times when your own excuse-making prevented you from accepting responsibility for your actions.

In the cartoon strip *Peanuts,* Lucy has blamed her missed fly balls on the sun, the moon . . . and even toxic substances in her baseball glove. We laugh at this light side of excuse-making, thereby preserving the point of view that excuses are . . . weak ploys that other people use. . . .

We all make mistakes of one kind or another and find ourselves in predicaments in which we don't perform well. Something has to be done with these disappointing outcomes so that they don't restrict and intimidate us; that something often takes the form of excuses. . . .

Excuse-making takes three general routes: "I didn't do it," "It's not so bad" and "Yes, but. . . ." Wide-eyed children frequently use simple denial (Who, me?), the most rudimentary form of excuse-making, and even adults occasionally revert to it. . . .

If excuse-makers . . . must admit, "I did it," then they must somehow make it seem "not so bad." Here we see what I have called "reframing maneuvers. . . ."

The simplest reframing strategy is to . . . hide from yourself the undesirable consequences of your actions. . . . In daily life . . . this self-deception leads to such excuses as . . . "I didn't know you needed help cleaning the bathroom."

If excuse-makers accept responsibility ("I did it") and concede further, "It was bad," they then need excuses of the "Yes, but" variety. . . . "Yes, but" excuses tell the audience that the excuse-maker shouldn't be held totally accountable. . . . For example, one way we can diminish responsibility for failure is by showing that other people would perform just as poorly as we did under the same circumstances. . . .

Projection . . . is another way we explain away our failures. . . . The teenager notes, "Well, everyone was doing it. . . ."

Certain styles of excuse-making can be . . . counterproductive. Some people . . . offer excuses so elaborate and so frequent that they cause problems. . . .

The concept of self-handicapping . . . applies here. This is the practice of embracing a "handicap" to maintain a view of oneself as competent, intelligent, and generally worthy. . . . People admit to a . . . problem or weakness (the self-handicap) as an explanation for their failures. . . .

Symptoms [like] hypochondriacal complaints and shyness may have a self-handicapping function as excuses. . . . I have also found that people emphasize their difficult life histories as excuses for a potential failure ("What do you expect out of me, I've had a hard life!").

The best way to deal with pathological excuse-making . . . is first to point out the excuses when they are offered. . . .

Once excuse-makers are aware of their habit, they can begin developing skills in areas that are important to their self-esteem, thereby lessening the chance of a poor performance and the need for excuses. Finally . . . [when] chronic excuse-makers . . . realize that poor performances in life are quite common and do not reflect on one's character, then the continual explanations become unnecessary.

Source Review

1. What types of events lead people to make excuses?

2. How can you help someone to overcome the habit of excuse-making?

CHAPTER 14

REVIEWING TERMS

frustration
frustration tolerance
conflict
approach-approach
  conflict
approach gradient
avoidance-avoidance
  conflict
avoidance gradient

approach-avoidance
  conflict
adjustment mechanism
compensation
overcompensation
identification
projection
stereotyped behavior
repression

regression
procrastination
displaced aggression
rationalization
sour grapes
  rationalization
sweet lemon
  rationalization
scapegoat

CHECKING FACTS

1. Describe some of the different kinds of frustrating situations we face.

2. Discuss the factors that help determine the strength of frustration.

3. Describe and give an example of each of the following kinds of conflict situations: approach-approach, avoidance-avoidance, and approach-avoidance.

4. Describe and give an example of an approach gradient and an avoidance gradient.

5. How does compensation enable us to deal with frustration? How does it differ from overcompensation?

6. Give examples of projection and stereotyped behavior.

7. Is repression true forgetting? Explain.

8. Is regression always abnormal? Explain.

9. Why do people use procrastination? Give an example of this adjustment mechanism.

10. Define and give an example of displaced aggression.

11. Differentiate between the sour grapes rationalization and the sweet lemon rationalization.

APPLYING YOUR KNOWLEDGE

1. Read the following passage:
   As you go down the first corner on the third street, make a left-hand turn onto the next street. If the third street comes before the first street, make a right-hand turn down the block onto the second street. If the second street is past the fourth street, go straight up the first street until the intersection with the third street.

   What were your reactions to this paragraph? How would you have coped with the situation if you were given these directions to a friend's party?

2. Write down an approach-approach, an approach-avoidance, and an avoidance-avoidance conflict that is common among teen-agers. Then note the positive and negative aspects of each alter-

native that a person might consider before reaching a decision. You might wish to do this in front of the class or in small groups so that other students can offer different options.

3. Bring the Sunday funnies section to class and clip out the comics that illustrate adjustment mechanisms described in this chapter. Use your clippings to create a poster or a bulletin board display.

4. Television programs often provide a good opportunity to examine many of life's frustrations. Watch one or two shows and notice how the characters react to various situations. Identify all frustrating circumstances, conflicts, and adjustment mechanisms. Were these

mechanisms desirable or undesirable? How else do you think the characters could have coped?

5. For one week, listen for and jot down rationalizations that you hear. (Be sure not to identify anyone by name.) Some rationalizations may be given by your friends or relatives. Some may be overheard in conversations of strangers. Some may be found in your own conversations. As far as you can judge, which ones are sour grapes? Which ones are sweet lemon? Are there more sour grapes than sweet lemon rationalizations, or the other way around? How can you explain your findings?

THINKING CRITICALLY ABOUT PSYCHOLOGY

1. **Forming Opinions** What might the world be like if frustration did not exist? Do you think that such a world might be possible?

2. **Classifying Ideas** Suppose you were a police officer in a large city with a high crime rate. You had to face many tense and frustrating situations. Under what circumstances do you think you would find it most difficult to control your emotions? What methods would you use to maintain your self-control?

3. **Evaluating Ideas** What might be some

of the benefits of conflicts? Which kind of conflict might be the most beneficial?

4. **Analyzing Ideas** Do you think the adjustment mechanisms we use change with age? In other words, are we more likely to use certain mechanisms as children, others as teen-agers, and still others as adults? Explain your answer.

5. **Defining Ideas** Is putting off a task always considered procrastination? Try to think of situations in which you would not be procrastinating if you postponed doing something.

DEVELOPING SKILLS IN PSYCHOLOGY

Content Analysis of Literary Materials

The study of psychology provides insight that helps an individual to understand his or her own behavior and the behavior of other people to a greater degree. Content analysis is a

procedure that allows social scientists to analyze the psychological content of literary materials and other forms of communication (such as advertisements and television programs). Content analysis may provide a better understanding of the behavior of a real person or of a fictional character.

It may be useful and interesting, for example, to apply content analysis to the behavior of historical figures, or characters in a play. The following skill lesson will help you to use content analysis and apply it to the adjustment mechanisms described in Chapter 14.

Find a book, play, or a short story that includes a character you would like to analyze. As you read, look for passages that illustrate adjustment mechanisms such as compensation, overcompensation, identification, or projection. Keep a record of the passages and the number of the page where each appears. Then classify each passage as an example of a particular adjustment mechanism and summarize the behavior illustrating that particular mechanism. Do the passages represent isolated incidences of specific behaviors, or can you identify patterns of behavior? How might you apply knowledge of this skill to your own behavior? For example, if you have an important test you are not prepared for, do you become irritable and impatient with other people? How can you recognize and change undesirable behavior?

READING FURTHER ABOUT PSYCHOLOGY

Briggs, Dorothy, *Embracing Life: Growing Through Love and Loss,* Doubleday, New York, 1985. Discusses such topics as death, relocation, divorce, and remarriage and offers advice on how to cope with them.

DeRosis, Helen, *Women and Anxiety,* Dell, New York, 1981. Offers a sensible method for understanding and relieving anxiety.

Gilbert, Sara D., *Trouble at Home,* Lothrop, New York, 1981. A book of coping strategies aimed at young people whose families are caught up in the throes of illness, divorce, financial trouble, or the death of a relative.

Harris, Amy B., and Harris, Thomas A., *Staying OK,* Harper & Row, New York, 1985. Presents a practical system for understanding and resolving inner conflicts.

Tavris, Carol, *Anger: The Misunderstood Emotion,* Simon and Schuster, New York, 1984. Deals with the emotion of anger, including the cultural rules of anger, the anatomy of anger, anger and illness, and the myths of expressed anger.

Wiesel, Elie, *Night,* Bantam, New York, 1982. Originally published just after World War II, this novel is the story of a young boy's imprisonment in a Nazi concentration camp and the conflicting feelings he has toward his father.

Chapter 15

COPING WITH STRESS

Chapter Focus

This chapter presents:

- **a description of stress and the stress reaction**
- **some factors that determine stress**
- **the effects of change on our health**
- **various stressors through the life cycle**
- **ways of controlling stress**

Every October signals the arrival of one of America's favorite pastimes. Hearts pound and tensions mount as millions of Americans root for their favorite baseball team during the World Series.

Every May or June signals the arrival of an event dreaded by many American students. Hearts pound and tensions mount as the students prepare for final exams.

It may seem strange to equate the World Series with final exams. Yet watching this annual sports classic and struggling through finals can produce the same symptoms of stress. In this chapter, we will examine the concept of stress—what it is, what causes it, and some of the stresses we face in our daily lives. We will also look at ways of controlling stress to make our lives more manageable.

The Nature of Stress

All of us have some idea of what stress is. We might say that being stuck in a traffic jam is stressful or that going on a job interview produces stress. We might even say

that having a birthday is stressful. While these examples identify possible instances of stress, they do not define it. There are several definitions we can use, but psychologists generally define **stress** as the body's reactions to perceived pressures and threats from the environment.

Various symptoms might indicate the presence of stress. Some common symptoms include increased heartbeat rate and blood pressure, a shortness of breath, trembling, indigestion, headache, loss of appetite or excessive appetite, and general anxiety. However, not all of these symptoms are present in all people experiencing stress.

Stress is a normal part of life. Stress helps you to handle unfamiliar situations and to cope with events that seem threatening. However, just as too much ice cream might give a person an upset stomach, too much stress can cause various problems. On the physical level, an excess of stress can cause ulcers, high blood pressure, a heart attack, or certain other health disorders. On the behavioral level, it can result in such nervous behavior as smoking, nail biting, and trembling. And on the psychological level it can bring about mental illness.

Any number of events can produce stress. Such causes of stress are known as **stressors.** Stressors can be either positive or negative—for example, a high school graduation or the death of a close friend. Stressors can also be either physical—such as air pollution—or psychological—such as an upcoming test. In addition, they might be either short term or long term. A short-term stressor might be a flat tire. A long-term stressor might be constant pressure at work.

Regardless of the source, there are common ways in which stressors affect the body. Let's take a look at what happens when we encounter a stressor.

The **"fight or flight" reaction.** In the 1920's, physiologist Walter B. Cannon identified what he called the ***"fight or flight" reaction.*** According to Cannon, whenever any living creature is faced with what it perceives as an emergency, its body prepares for one of two alternatives. These are a direct confrontation—"fight"—or a hasty retreat—"flight." For either alternative, and regardless of the emergency, the body reacts in the same manner. Blood circulation increases, additional glucose (sugar) is released into the blood, and the breathing rate speeds up. In short, the organism mobilizes its energy and physiological resources to deal with the situation. After it has handled the situation completely, the organism returns to its original state.

For example, suppose a fierce wind has almost knocked you over. Your body perceives this as an emergency situation. As a result, your heartbeat rate accelerates, your blood sugar level rises, and your breathing rate increases. When the danger passes—after you have either regained your balance and prepared for the next gust or run for shelter far enough away—your body returns to normal.

There is a major problem with this theory, however. Not all stressors go away this easily. Some stressors, such as job difficulties, might seem to last indefinitely. Consequently, the body might not always go

This long-awaited reunion of Russian immigrants in Israel is likely to be stressful for both the immigrants and their families. Although all experience joy, all must now face problems of adjustment.

back to its original state. Physiologist Hans Selye recognized this problem. Building on Cannon's work, he proposed a theory that explains the presence of continuing stress. Selye labeled his theory the General Adaptation Syndrome.

The General Adaptation Syndrome. The *General Adaptation Syndrome* (GAS) is a three-stage reaction to stress. The first stage—*alarm*—parallels Cannon's "fight or flight" reaction. During this stage the body mobilizes to deal with the stressor. All of the physiological processes mentioned earlier take place.

The second stage is known as *resistance.* During this stage the body actively tries to resist the stressor, and may appear to be adapting to it. Outwardly, resistance often resembles adaptation. For example, rats that had been exposed to extremely cold temperatures for an extended period seemed to be "holding their own" during this phase. A robbery victim may appear to be coping well with the situation, rationalizing that it will be over soon.

However, this holding pattern does not and cannot last indefinitely. If the stressor disappears, the body returns to its original state. If the stressor continues, the body proceeds to stage three.

The third stage is known as *exhaustion.* At this point, all of the body's coping mechanisms are no longer sufficient to fight the stressor. Consequently, the body seems to break down. The result is often illness or disease. In extreme cases death occurs. The rats in the above example met such a fate. Some robbery victims have suffered fatal heart attacks after their ordeals. Yet organisms may have the ability to tolerate a tremendous amount of stress. Some concentration camp victims and victims of hostage situations, for example, have survived with few stress-related symptoms.

People react to stress in different ways. One person may develop asthma, another might develop diabetes, and another might have a heart attack. Part of the reason may stem from people's biological makeup. Each person has a weak area that a stressor may attack. It might be the heart, the liver, the throat, or any other part of the body.

Yet some people do not seem to suffer any of the unpleasant effects of stress. Why are these people free from such problems? The answer may lie partly in their psychological makeup. They might not find some situations stressful. In the next section we will explore this idea as well as some other related concepts.

What Determines Stress?

Events alone do not necessarily produce stress. Rather, several factors usually help determine whether an event is stressful. These factors include the personality of an individual, a person's expectations, how much control a person has over a situation, the amount of responsibility a person has, and how informed a person is. Let's look at each of these factors.

Personality of the individual. The differences in people's personality may cause them to appraise similar situations differently. Consider this fictitious business executive. Such a person might dictate letters while driving to work, conduct business meetings over lunch, and read a newspaper while standing in line at the bank. On the other hand, another executive might find such a routine unbearable.

Similarly, a standard laboratory stressor often used is the cold pressor test. In this test, a person's hand or foot is placed in a mixture of ice and water for about two minutes. In many people this would produce stress. Yet in many northern cities, groups such as the Polar Bear Club go swimming in the middle of winter in icy oceans or lakes. For these people, an ice water swim is not stressful. Perhaps the cold pressor test would not be either.

Crowding, too, may or may not be stressful, depending on how people view

Charlie Chaplin was a comic yet tragic figure in many oldtime movies. In this classic photo from the film Modern Times, *Chaplin is suffering from the stresses of industrialization, despite his comic pose.*

it. Riding to work on a crowded bus might be stressful to some commuters. But for teen-agers jammed into the back seat of a car on their way to a movie or a concert, the crowding would probably not be stressful at all.

Our appraisal of a situation also depends on the consequences we attach to it. For example, suppose two students receive a "B" on a test. One has an "A" average and the other has a "B" average. Which one would probably find the grade more stressful? Most likely the "A" student, especially if he or she thinks the test grade might affect the student's chances of getting into a good college. The "B" student might expect less-than-perfect grades and might take the score in stride.

People's expectations. The expectations that a person has also may affect the stressfulness of a situation. Have you ever feared giving an oral presentation in front of your classmates? Before you even got up from your chair, you probably showed signs of stress. Then, after it was all over, you realized that your fears were unjustified. You experienced more stress before the speech than during it!

Predictability is a major component of expectations. When events are predictable, people know when they will occur. As a result, people may experience little stress when these events take place.

The New York City subway system provides an example of predictability. This system has large stretches in which trains run above ground. Some of these trains run very close to residential apartment buildings and cause high levels of noise, which you might think would be stressful. Some residents however, are not bothered by regularly scheduled trains. It is only when the city closes down some of the train runs that the residents may be upset by the unexpected silence.

In a study involving animals, two groups of rats were given electrical shocks of equal

Text continues on page 330.

327
COPING WITH
STRESS

Case Study: Focus on Research

TYPE A BEHAVIOR AND YOUR HEALTH

Do you lose your temper easily? Do you stay up half the night perfecting a term paper? Do you become involved more with winning than with enjoying a game? If your answers to these questions are "Yes," then you might be a Type A person.

Who are Type A people? Don't many people lose their tempers, strive for perfect term papers, and try to win? The answer is "Yes, to a degree." But Type A people are compulsive. They go all out to achieve a goal. Their bodies are *always* in a state of stress. In fact, they are so agitated that very often they become physically ill.

Scientists have been studying the relationship between behavior patterns and illness for years. Two pioneers in this field are

Never stopping even to catch their breath, Type A people are always on the go. Research has shown that such a behavior pattern is connected to heart disease.

heart specialists Ray Rosenman and Meyer Friedman.

In the early 1950's these two doctors began investigating factors that might contribute to the alarming increase in the rate of heart disease in this country. At first they examined standard risk factors, including family history of heart disease, cigarette smoking, obesity, lack of exercise, poor eating habits, and the amount of serum cholesterol (a chemical) in the blood. They were particularly interested in serum cholesterol, because over time it can build up in arteries and prevent blood from flowing to the heart. When this happens, a person suffers a heart attack.

Then one day an upholsterer came to the doctors' office to redo the waiting room furniture. He noted that the chairs were worn only on the front edge of the seat. He pointed this out to Dr. Friedman, who thought this was significant. To the doctor this indicated that most of his patients were showing signs of stress in their lives. This key observation was the first step toward uncovering the relationship between stress and heart attacks.

Friedman and Rosenman decided to investigate. In one of their well-known studies, they measured serum cholesterol levels in two groups of accountants. The first group of accountants was heavily involved in preparing income tax returns. They felt pressured to meet an important deadline. The second group was made up of accountants who had no particular deadlines to meet during the course of this study.

When compared on the amount of serum cholesterol in their blood, the two groups differed considerably. The accountants under deadline constraints showed sharp increases in their serum cholesterol level during the six weeks before the tax deadline. After the deadline had passed, their serum cholesterol levels dropped drastically. The second group showed no difference in their level of serum cholesterol throughout the study.

The researchers were fascinated with this finding and began considering the role of stress in heart disease. They speculated that some people experience more stress than others, perhaps because of differences in temperament and personality. Those who experience great amounts of stress were called "Type A" people. Those who are re-laxed and easy-going were labeled "Type B."

What are Type A and Type B people like? Take Paul, for instance, a typical Type A. The manager of a manufacturing com-pany, he is always in a hurry. He talks quickly, eats fast, and detests waiting. He drinks alcohol both before lunch and dinner, and smokes two packs of cigarettes a day. In his impatience to compete for business suc-cess, he rarely takes time off to enjoy sports, hobbies, or the pleasures of friendship.

At the other end of the scale is Ralph, a Type B. Although a busy bank president, he is a patient, mild-mannered man who takes his time and allows others to do the same. His drinking and eating habits are moderate, and he doesn't smoke. He enjoys hobbies, exercises regularly, and keeps in close touch with his friends.

According to Friedman and Rosenman, the Type A behavior pattern is related to the frequency and severity of heart disease. In fact, they argue that Type A behavior is a better predictor of whether or not someone will develop heart disease than such factors as cigarette smoking or obesity. These re-searchers believe that Paul's chances of contracting heart disease are twenty times greater than those of Ralph.

Are you a Type A or a Type B? You may have trouble deciding, for many people are mixtures of the two. In any case, the signs of stressful living—excessive competition, haste, and impatience—are danger signals. The next time you lose your temper over a delay, remember that the tortoise beat the hare in the race to the finish line!

SOURCE: Meyer Friedman and Ray H. Rosenman, *Type A Be-havior and Your Heart*, New York: Alfred A. Knopf, 1974.

The ability to relax is characteristic of Type B people. Exercising regularly may be an effective way to combat stress.

CASE STUDY: FOCUS ON RESEARCH

The amount of responsibility held by the controllers at NASA in Houston makes their job highly stressful. Many of these professionals experience more stress than the astronauts carrying out the space missions.

strength and frequency. One group heard a beeping sound ten seconds before each shock and could then expect a shock. The other group heard the sound at random intervals so the shocks were not predictable. The "random" group developed six times more ulcers than the "predictable" group.

Stress is also related to frustration. As we discussed in Chapter 14, frustration occurs whenever people are prevented from achieving their goals. In frustrating situations, people expect to accomplish something but are blocked, for one reason or another, from doing so. The greater the amount of frustration present, the more stress people experience. For example, being stuck in a traffic jam when you have an appointment would probably be more stressful than when you were out for a leisurely drive.

Degree of control. The amount of control a person has over a situation affects the degree of stress present. In one experiment, two groups of people were subjected to noise. One group was given a "panic" button to push if the noise got too overwhelming.

Pushing the button could stop the experiment. The other group was not given any control over the situation. The researchers found that the people with the panic button showed much less stress than the other group, even when they did not use the button. Just thinking that they could control the situation helped the group eliminate any potential stress.

In another experiment, researchers studied the effects of stress on two groups of commuters in Sweden. One group of subjects boarded the train at the first stop and had a 79-minute ride. The other group got on about midway and had only a 43-minute ride. Which group do you think experienced more stress?

The group with the shorter commute felt a greater degree of stress. Why? Those in the first group were able to choose their seats, sit with their friends, and store their bags and coats on the luggage racks. Those in the second group had little choice in these matters. In short, those in the first group perceived that they had control over their environment. Those in the second group did not. It appears that the perception of control made the ride less stressful. In fact, many authorities believe that our *perception* of lack of control in our fast-paced society is the most important cause of stress.

Amount of responsibility. Another factor that helps determine whether an event is stressful is the amount of responsibility a person has. In a work situation, those with more responsibility tend to experience more stress than those with less responsibility. Air traffic controllers, for example, have a tremendous degree of responsibility. At any given time the fate of hundreds of individuals rests in their hands. One study showed that the controllers experienced two or three times more hypertension (high blood pressure) than others in their age group.

In studies of the Korean and Vietnam conflicts, research has shown that high-ranking officers experienced a different type of stress than troops in actual combat. These officers felt responsible for the lives of the troops they supervised. As a result, they experienced various physical signs of stress.

Amount of information. A lack of reliable information can increase the stressfulness of a situation. Conversely, an ample amount of reliable information can decrease the effects of a potential stressor. Studies conducted after the 1979 nuclear accident at Three Mile Island in Pennsylvania support these views. In these studies, researchers found that discomfort and physical symptoms experienced by the residents of the area were caused by confusing information given by the news media and public officials, as well as by concern and worry about the future. The actual harm caused by radiation leakage appears to be minimal.

In another study, a psychologist found that patients who are given little information before surgery suffer the most stress afterward. Those who are well-informed prepare themselves in advance for their discomforts. They may mentally rehearse all possible consequences of the surgery. As a result,

when discomforts do occur, they take them in stride. However, those who spend *too* much time worrying and preparing seem to suffer greater aftereffects. It seems that a little anxiety but not too much is necessary for proper adjustment after surgery.

In a sense, all of these factors are interrelated. Having ample information leads to predictability. Predictability, in turn, leads to more control. Responsibility also is tied to predictability and control. People with tremendous responsibility might experience less stress if events are predictable and they have control over situations. And none of these factors may cause stressful reactions if an individual has a certain kind of personality.

Change as a Stressor

Among the greatest causes of stress in our lives is change, since change may be unpredictable and may result in less control, more responsibility, and less information. For example, natural disasters such as earthquakes are highly stressful. In the early history of our nation, when life seemed simpler, change was limited. Most people remained in the same communities in which they were born. Men's and women's roles remained fixed, and family life was stable.

When change did occur—often in the form of problems—people were able to tackle it directly. That is, because problems were relatively simple—a bad crop, for instance—people understood how to solve them. They might have planted a different crop or shared with neighbors until the crisis passed. In this way, people maintained control over their lives. As a result, stress-related illnesses rarely occurred.

As our society modernized, however, change became an ever-present part of our lives. We now move more frequently than ever before. In just one year, over 36 million Americans changed their addresses. People also change jobs several times in their lives. In addition, the structure of the family and our life-styles have changed dramatically. Problems now are more complex, unpredictable, and abstract.

The changes we experience are numerous and varied. It is possible, though, to divide these changes into two categories—major life changes and daily hassles.

Major life changes. In the 1960's two researchers, Thomas Holmes and Richard Rahe, proposed a link between our health and the major life changes that we all experience. They hypothesized that our chances of becoming seriously ill were closely related to the major changes that we experience in our lives. The more changes we have in our lives, the greater our chances of becoming seriously ill.

As the basis for their study, Holmes and Rahe devised a scale consisting of over 40 major events in people's lives. These events ranged from such serious occurrences as the death of a spouse to a seemingly minor event such as Christmas. In their scheme, getting married was arbitrarily assigned a numerical value of 50 points. The researchers then asked hundreds of people to rate the other

events in relation to getting married. Based on these interviews, each event was given a value from 11 to 100. For example, the death of a spouse—which was considered twice as stressful as getting married—was given the value of 100.

According to the research of Holmes and Rahe, those people who accumulate less than 150 points during the course of a year have about a one chance in three of becoming seriously ill during the next two years. Those who score between 150 and 300 points increase their chances to about 50-50. And those who exceed 300 points boost their chances to almost 90 percent.

In addition, Holmes and Rahe noted that the changes people experience do not have to be negative to affect their health. Such events as a vacation, a change in schools, and the birth of a baby all might be awaited eagerly. Yet they, too, might increase a person's chances of becoming ill. Let's consider the story of John to understand how this theory works. The numbers in parentheses correspond to the values of events on the Holmes/Rahe scale on the opposite page.

A wedding—a joyous occasion but stressful nonetheless.

John, a recent high school graduate (26) finds a job as an office assistant for a small company (38). No longer able to dress casually, he now must choose his daily wardrobe carefully (24). But choosing his clothes takes time, and he finds he must get up ten minutes earlier each day (16).

John is also very careful in his work and within two months is given more responsibilities (29). To keep up with his duties, he often just eats a sandwich at his desk (15) and stays late at work a few evenings a week (20). His efforts do not go unnoticed. Six months after his starting date, he receives a well-deserved promotion (28).

John's good fortunes are cause for celebration, but they are also cause for worry. Tallying up his score, we find that he has accumulated 196 points in a half year's time. This means, according to Holmes and Rahe, that he has about a 50-50 chance of becoming seriously ill within the next two years. If we consider the changes that he may experience during the rest of the current year, his chances might be even greater. Thus, according to Holmes and Rahe, a seemingly ordinary chain of events might have extraordinary consequences.

Criticisms of the life change approach.

Not all researchers agree with the findings of Holmes and Rahe. For one thing, some argue, what one person considers stressful might have a limited effect on someone else. For example, one person might find retirement to be traumatic, while another might think of it as an expected outcome of turning age seventy.

Also, certain elements of the Holmes/Rahe scale may have limited relevance for certain groups of people. The entries concerning the death of a spouse, a son or daughter leaving home, foreclosure of a mortgage or loan, or retirement, for example, do not apply to most high school or college students.

THE SOCIAL READJUSTMENT RATING SCALE

Life Event	Point Value
Death of spouse	100
Divorce	73
Marital separation	65
Jail term	63
Death of close family member	63
Personal injury or illness	53
Marriage	50
Fired at work	47
Marital reconciliation	45
Retirement	45
Change in health of family member	44
Pregnancy	40
Gain of new family member	39
Business readjustment	39
Change in financial state	38
Death of close friend	37
Change to different line of work	36
Change in number of arguments with spouse	35
Mortgage over $10,000	31
Foreclosure of mortgage or loan	30
Change in responsibilities at work	29
Son or daughter leaving home	29
Trouble with in-laws	29
Outstanding personal achievement	28
Wife begin or stop work	26
Begin or end school	26
Change in living conditions	25
Revision of personal habits	24
Trouble with boss	23
Change in work hours or conditions	20
Change in residence	20
Change in schools	20
Change in recreation	19
Change in church activities	19
Change in social activities	18
Mortgage or loan less than $10,000	17
Change in sleeping habits	16
Change in number of family get-togethers	15
Change in eating habits	15
Vacation	13
Christmas	12
Minor violations of the law	11

From Table 3, "The Social Readjustment Rating Scale" by T. H. Holmes and R. H. Rahe, in *Journal of Psychosomatic Research*, Vol. 11, No. 2, 1967. © 1967 by Pergamon Press. Reprinted by permission of Pergamon Press.

The Social Readjustment Rating Scale ranks some major life events in terms of how much change each requires. The more points people accumulate, the more likely it is that they will experience health problems.

The inconvenience of commuting is a daily hassle faced by many Americans. Some researchers believe that such hassles are more stressful than major life changes.

Moreover, times have changed since this study took place and the ranking of events might not be the same as it was 20 years ago. For example, a $10,000 mortgage in the 1960's was far more stressful for many people than it would be today. Similarly, the increase in the number of working wives in recent years might lessen the stress of a wife who is beginning a job.

Furthermore, it does not take into account a person's health. A score of 200 stress points might mean extra colds or headaches for a healthy individual. In a person in poorer health, however, such a score might lead to ulcers or heart failure.

In addition, the major life change approach does not explain the relationship between major changes and the stresses in our daily lives. How might moving to a new house affect a person's ability to get along with his or her parents? Or how might an upcoming vacation be related to a change in a person's performance at school? The Holmes/Rahe scale does not consider these questions.

Daily hassles. Because of these unexplained relationships, a group of researchers have proposed a new approach to stress. They hypothesize that the minor annoyances, or hassles, in our daily lives—a missed bus, a broken shoelace, a cold classroom—can have a greater impact on our overall health than major life changes.

To test their theory, the researchers asked 100 people in California to fill out various questionnaires during the course of a year. These questionnaires consisted of lists of hassles, lists of symptoms and illnesses (headaches and hypertension, for example), and lists of emotions. The participants also filled out a life events scale similar to that used by Holmes and Rahe.

When the data were analyzed, the researchers found that major life changes were not a great predictor of people's health. Rather, it was the daily hassles in people's lives that were directly related to health and well-being. The researchers found that the more hassles people experienced, the poorer their mental and physical health. They noted, however, that the hassles in and of themselves did not cause people's conditions. It was the intensity of the hassles and the way people reacted to them that were responsible for the impact the hassles had on people's health.

The researchers also noted that people's reactions varied depending on their mood. What may have been overlooked one day may have a much greater impact another day. For example, on a "good" day, a small stain on a shirt might be completely ignored. On a day when everything seems to go wrong, however, the stain may be considered a disaster.

Criticisms of the hassles theory. The major shortcoming of the hassles theory seems to be its newness. So far, the researchers have been able to test their theory only on a small, middle-aged, well-educated group of people from one county in California. Also, if hassles cause illness, then pleasant experiences should be able to counter such negative effects. The researchers did not find this to be the case. Perhaps as the researchers continue their work, they will learn more about the effects on our health of our daily ups and downs.

Stress Through the Life Cycle

Change is an ever-present part of our lives. Therefore stress, too, is always present. Yet the changes we experience vary depending on our stage of development. Young children have different experiences than teen-agers. Teen-agers confront different problems than adults. What are the different stress-producing changes that take place in our lives?

Stresses of infancy and childhood. For all of us, stress occurs the moment we are born. An empty stomach, a wet diaper, a lack of sleep are all stressful to the newborn child. Some infants are also often faced with boredom, or a lack of stimulation in their environments. No matter what the source of stress, though, the reaction to its presence is usually the same. A piercing cry often signals the infant's discomfort.

As children get older, they can express themselves in more eloquent ways. Yet they still are faced with serious stressors. School, particularly the first day, is often one of the most important stressors to the young child. As the child takes leave of the parents on this momentous occasion, several questions may flash through his or her mind. "Will Mommy or Daddy come to pick me up?" "How will the teacher treat me?" "Will the other children be my friends?"

In school the child also has to adjust to competition. No longer the center of attention, as may occur between parent and child, the child must compete with others for the teacher's attention. In addition, children compete with one another for grades.

Stresses of adolescence. If childhood is stressful, adolescence may be even more so. In fact, some people might argue that adolescence is the most stressful period of life.

During adolescence, the body changes dramatically. Males develop facial hair, a deeper voice, and a mature body. Females acquire fuller figures and an awareness of no longer being little girls. In short, boys and girls become men and women. Not all teenagers, however, are immediately able to accept these changes. For those who mature physically either much earlier or much later than their friends, this time is particularly stressful.

Partly because of these physical changes, adolescents experience other stresses as well. In our society, adolescents have an undefined status. On the one hand, they are able to live on their own. On the other, they are often sheltered and treated like children. In addition, they strongly desire social independence, while at the same time having to rely on adults financially. The conflicts that arise because of these contradictions can be quite stressful.

In addition, during this period teen-agers may be faced with decisions that can affect their entire lives. "Should I date only one person, or should I date several?" "Should I go to college?" "What career would be best for me?" "What do I really want out of life?" All these decisions produce stress.

Stresses of adulthood. Many of the decisions made in adolescence carry through into adulthood. The decision to date only one special person often results in marriage. The decision to go on to college outlines a person's career goals. The decision to leave home sets the pattern for independence.

Each of these decisions, though, often comes equipped with a ready-made package of problems. Marriage implies increased responsibilities, with both partners no longer able to think only in terms of their own single lives. Marriage also may result in children.

Although children bring great pleasure, they also bring increased responsibilities and may at times cause tensions between husband and wife. In addition, children may place an increased financial burden on the family, since a larger home, more food, and ample clothing become necessities.

A major source of stress in adulthood centers around the world of work. Very often, people gain their identities through what they do for a living. As a result, they devote much of their energies to their jobs. In fact, sometimes family relationships suffer in the process.

Some jobs are more stressful than others. On-the-job decisions, an overabundance or a shortage of work, and difficulties with co-workers may all cause problems for the worker. In addition, poor working conditions, frequent travel, heavy responsibilities, and a promotion or lack of advancement might all be stressful as well. But as stressful as a job may be, a period of unemployment can be even more upsetting. During times of economic hardship, many people face this prospect. Unemployment causes stress not only for the individual involved but often for the whole family.

Stresses of later adulthood. Growing old is a gift of our modern society. Before the 1900's most people died before reaching their "golden years." Today, however, because of great medical advances, many diseases no longer pose a threat to people. Yet for many who today live to be seventy or eighty, later adulthood is anything but a blessing. To them, the stresses of this period outweigh the pleasures.

For many, later adulthood is a time of tremendous readjustment. People who have worked for much of their lives now must face the prospect of retirement. People who were used to always being around others now must come home to a quiet house. In addition, there may be a loss of energy, a loss of health, and the loss of a spouse.

Because of these changes, later adulthood is sometimes a period of isolation and loneliness. Some people feel that they are useless and that nobody cares about them. As a result, they spend many hours alone. Of course, many people successfully adjust to the aging process. In fact, one researcher notes that individuals with "integrated" personalities seem to make the transition successfully. These people are socially mature, flexible, and happy. But for others, the transition is much more difficult.

In later adulthood, as well as in other periods, the better we can cope with stress, the easier our lives can be. Let's look at some of the ways we can control stress.

Controlling Stress

There are several methods that can be used to control stress. Some involve mostly common sense, whereas others involve more complex procedures. Some might seem right for some people, but impractical for others. Also, some might seem to have drawbacks that outweigh their benefits. However, all have been used at one time or another.

Getting away from the stressor. A logical way of controlling stress is to get away from the stressor. If a late-night movie is making you tense, turn off the TV. If there is too much traffic on the main road, try a different route. If your younger sister or brother is getting on your nerves, take a bicycle ride through the neighborhood. Of course, such a solution is not always possible. For example, it is difficult to walk away from an upset stomach. But, when possible, a temporary escape might be just what is necessary.

Exercise. Exercising helps us to control stress in several ways. The first way is related to the method of control mentioned above. Exercising helps people separate themselves from a problem. By going for a walk, for example, a person can gain some distance from a difficult decision. Upon returning, the person might have some fresh approaches to the problem.

Exercising also helps people forget their problems, at least temporarily. A good game

Loss of a spouse, ill health, and inactivity are stressors sometimes faced by older people.

of tennis, for example, might take an executive's mind off a troubling business decision. After the game, the person might no longer consider the problem as difficult to solve.

In addition, exercising helps keep people's muscles in shape. If muscles aren't working properly, various bodily processes can be affected. This, in turn, might influence how the body handles stress. Put another way, a person in good physical condition can usually deal with stress better than someone who is not.

Relaxation. Relaxation is a technique somewhat opposite to exercising. While exercising, a person gets all "worked up." During relaxation a person tries to "slow down."

Relaxation can be accomplished by doing a few simple things such as closing one's eyes, breathing deeply, or repeating a single word over and over. For example, before giving a speech, a person might take a few minutes to sit back and think of a favorite vacation retreat. When carried out properly,

relaxation causes certain changes to occur in the body. For example, the heartbeat rate slows down, the amount of sugar in the blood decreases, and breathing gets slower. Relaxation enables the body to return to its normal state.

Biofeedback. As you learned in Chapter 9, biofeedback is a way of learning to regulate bodily processes voluntarily. By regulating such processes as heartbeat rate, finger temperature, and muscle tension, a person can control some of the harmful effects of stress.

During biofeedback sessions, small electrodes are placed on the surface of a person's skin. These electrodes are also connected to an electronic device, which might measure a process such as heartbeat rate. Through beeping tones or flashes of light, the device tells the person how fast his or her heart is beating. The person can then learn to relax certain muscles to control the heartbeat rate. The device provides instant feedback on how successful the person is.

Of course, biofeedback will not make a stressor go away. But it will take away some of its harmful effects.

Social support. The friends or family a person has, the various organizations to which a person belongs, and the religious groups that offer assistance all can lessen the effects of a stressor. After the accident at Three Mile Island, for example, researchers found that the people with the most social support showed the least amount of stress. In contrast, those who had to face the threat alone suffered the most stress. These people did not have anyone to turn to for encouragement, support, and understanding.

Drugs. One of the most controversial ways of coping with stress is through the use of drugs. Drugs, including alcohol, alter the body's chemical makeup. Therefore the user sometimes feels more relaxed.

However, there are many problems associated with drug use. The most serious is a physical, as well as a psychological, dependency on drugs. As a result, drugs should be used only as a last resort, and then only under the supervision of a physician.

Preventing stress. When we talk about preventing stress, what we really mean is avoiding some of its harmful effects. As a student, you can accomplish this in several ways. Each of these methods will help you prevent stress in later stages of life, too. Here are some tips.

For one thing, you can budget your time wisely. If you know your homework will take you two hours, you should not expect to do your homework, watch a movie on

Just knowing that someone is nearby to share their grief is comforting to many people. Here a priest attends the injured at a makeshift hospital in Guatemala City after a major earthquake.

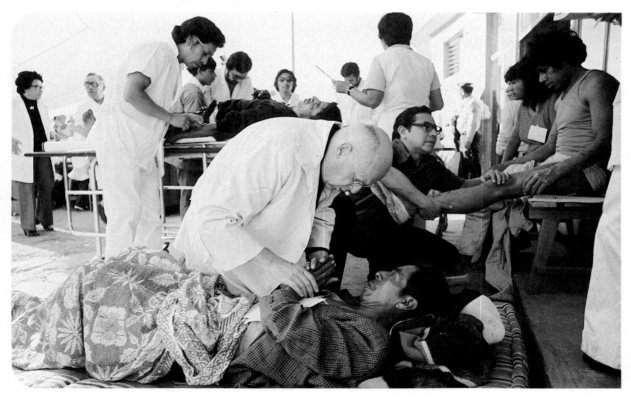

television, and go out with some friends all in the same evening. You should set priorities and follow the guidelines you establish.

You also can learn to say "no." This will prevent you from winding up with more ventures than you can handle. Just thinking about how you will be able to meet all your commitments is enough to cause stress. And this does not include all the stress that will result from carrying out each task.

In addition, you might practice expressing your feelings. When things are bottled up inside you, you begin to feel as if you are about to explode. By talking over your problems, you allow some of the "pressure" to escape. This provides for a calmer and more realistic approach to serious problems.

Another way of preventing stress is to attack a problem in steps. Sometimes by breaking a situation into smaller components, you can make the situation seem more manageable. For example, suppose you have to write a term paper. You might first choose your topic. You might then go to the library to see how much material is available. Next, you might prepare an outline, organizing your thoughts carefully and clearly. Finally, you can begin writing.

One further suggestion is to think positively. Don't say, "I'll never finish the assignment on time." Rather, take the positive approach: "If I work at a steady pace, I'll meet my deadline." Similarly, look at what can still be done instead of dwelling on past failures.

These are only a few ideas for making your life more manageable. With these guidelines in mind, you might be able to control some stressful situations. It won't be an easy task, but it's a goal worth pursuing.

Summary

Stress is the body's reactions to perceived pressures and threats in the environment. It is a normal part of life, but too much stress can cause illness or disease, nervous behavior, and mental illness. Any event that causes stress is known as a stressor. Stressors can be positive or negative, physical or psychological, and short term or long term.

Two attempts to explain the body's reactions to stress are theories concerning the "fight or flight" reaction and the General Adaptation Syndrome. The "fight or flight" theory states that whenever the body confronts a perceived emergency, it prepares either to attack it directly or to flee. The General Adaptation theory states that the body goes through three stages to deal with lingering stressors. These are alarm, resistance, and exhaustion.

Events alone do not necessarily produce stress. Other contributing factors include the personality of an individual, people's expectations, the degree of control people have over a situation, the amount of responsibility they have, and the amount of information they are given.

Change is one of the greatest causes of stress in our society. Two important kinds of change that people experience are major life changes and daily hassles. Various theories argue that both kinds of change can result in illness.

People encounter different stressors at different stages of the life cycle. Infants experience various physical discomforts. An important childhood stressor is school. Adolescents experience rapid bodily changes, an undefined status, and major decision making. Adults are faced with such stressors as marriage, child rearing, and their jobs. Older adults must cope with a tremendous amount of readjustment.

There are several ways of controlling stress. These include getting away from the stressor, exercise, relaxation, biofeedback, social support, and prescribed drugs.

INTERPRETING SOURCES

An all too common source of stress among students is test anxiety. In this excerpt from *Cognitive and Affective Learning Strategies,* Charles Spielberger, Hector Gonzalez, and Tucker Fletcher describe the negative effects that test anxiety has on students' grades and the situations in which test-anxious students are most affected by their test anxiety.

The research of Seymour Sarason and George Mandler . . . at Yale University in the early 1950s is generally regarded as the pioneering work on test anxiety. These investigators conducted a series of studies that demonstrated that test anxiety leads to [lower test grades]. They also developed the first widely used measure of individual differences in test anxiety, the Test Anxiety Questionnaire. . . .

In the Yale studies, . . . Sarason, Mandler, and their colleagues . . . observed that evaluative situations have differential effects on the examination performance of high and low test-anxious students. These investigators demonstrated that failure feedback and other stressful instructions interfered with the performance of high test-anxious students compared with students low in test anxiety, and that high test-anxious subjects did better under conditions in which evaluative stress was minimized. . . .

On the basis of his research, Sarason concludes that test-anxious persons are more self-centered and self-critical than individuals low in test anxiety, and are more likely in examination situations to emit . . . self-critical worry responses that interfere with attention and test performance.

Most of the research literature on test anxiety has been concerned with the conditions under which test-anxious persons show performance decrements. There is also a more recent but substantial literature on the treatment of test anxiety. . . .

A variety of therapeutic procedures have been employed in the treatment of test anxiety, including individual and group counseling, systematic desensitization, . . . and study-skills training. Of these approaches, systematic desensitization has been used more often than any other procedure, and positive evidence of the reduction of test anxiety was found in 27 of 31 desensitization studies evaluated in a recent review of the test anxiety literature. . . .

The research literature on the treatment of test-anxious students demonstrates that desensitization and other behavioral treatments are effective in reducing test anxiety, but there is little evidence that behavioral treatments alone can facilitate academic achievement. On the other hand, improvement in grade point average was reported in six of seven studies in which desensitization or relaxation training was combined with some form of study counseling. The success of these combined treatment approaches has been attributed to their effectiveness in both reducing test anxiety and improving study habits. . . .

Since students with test anxiety generally have poor study habits . . . and devote less time to studying than low anxious students, . . . it would seem important to provide study skills training in combination with desensitization in the treatment of test-anxious students.

Source Review

1. What effect does test anxiety have on test performance?

2. Why does high test anxiety generally cause someone to do more poorly on a test than someone with lower test anxiety?

3. What treatment for test anxiety has been shown to be most effective?

4. Why is it recommended that students who receive treatment for test anxiety also receive study skills counseling?

CHAPTER 15

REVIEWING TERMS

stress

stressor

"fight or flight" reaction

General Adaptation
    Syndrome (GAS)

alarm

resistance

exhaustion

CHECKING FACTS

1. What are some common symptoms of stress?

2. List some of the problems that stress can cause.

3. Give some examples of the different kinds of stressors.

4. Why don't all researchers agree with the theory of "fight or flight" reaction?

5. Describe what happens to the body in each stage of the General Adaptation Syndrome.

6. How does the personality of an individual help determine if an event is stressful? What effect do people's expectations have?

7. How do the degree of control, the amount of responsibility, and the amount of information people have af-

fect the stressfulness of a situation? Give some examples to explain your answer.

8. Why is change considered a stressor in modern society?

9. Describe the theory on major life changes proposed by Holmes and Rahe. What are some criticisms of this approach?

10. How does the hassles theory attempt to explain the relationship between stress and health? Give some examples of daily hassles. What are the shortcomings of this theory?

11. Discuss some of the stresses that affect people at various stages in the life cycle.

12. What are some of the ways in which stress can be controlled? How can stress be prevented?

APPLYING YOUR KNOWLEDGE

1. One of the ways that people can prevent the harmful effects of excess stress is through relaxation exercises. Try practicing the following exercise and see how you feel afterward. Repeat the exercise every day—it will become an enjoyable part of your daily routine.

   (a) Set aside fifteen minutes when you are alone and when you will not be disturbed.

   (b) Select a comfortable spot in a room where you can lie down with the lights dimmed and the noise level reduced.

   (c) Breathe deeply ten times, inhaling and exhaling more slowly and deeply each time.

   (d) As you slowly count to ten, relax the muscles in each of the following areas of your body simply by think-

341

CHAPTER
REVIEW

ing about those muscles: feet, calves, thighs, abdomen, chest, arms, fingertips, shoulders, neck, and face. Repeat this procedure ten times.

(e) When you have completed this exercise, gradually return to your daily routine.

Do you feel any different? In what ways?

2. Sometimes you may think you are under a great deal of stress without knowing the exact reasons why. Before you can cope with a stressful situation, it is necessary to identify the cause of the stress. For about one or two weeks, keep a journal of the daily events that you find are most stressful. See if there are any common patterns. For example, does the stress typically occur at school—when you take tests or meet new people? Or does it occur when you are with friends? Once you have identified the exact cause of the stress, you can develop your own method for coping with it.

3. By using your imagination, you may be able to reduce the stress and anxiety associated with certain situations. The key is to imagine yourself in a stressful situation, calmly and successfully coping with it. Try the following procedure for a few days to see how this works:

(a) Identify a particularly stressful situation you wish to work on.

(b) Find a quiet place where you will not be disturbed.

(c) Close your eyes and relax by inhaling and exhaling slowly ten times.

(d) Create a detailed image of yourself calmly and successfully coping with the situation. For example, if giving an oral report in front of the class is

stressful, imagine yourself presenting your report in a calm and confident manner. After you have finished the report, imagine yourself returning to your desk feeling relaxed and proud.

Whenever you are about to encounter a stressful situation, follow the above four steps. They should help you overcome several anxiety-producing situations.

4. Organize into small groups and have members of each group take turns completing the following sentence: "You know you are under stress when. . . ." Students can give serious or humorous answers. Some students may prefer just to listen. After everyone has had several opportunities to respond, return to your original seating arrangement and discuss some of the unusual or thought-provoking answers. As a variation, the class may wish to write their answers on slips of paper and place them in a box anonymously. The teacher can then read each answer aloud, followed by a class discussion in which students can share their views.

5. Cartoonists often portray many of life's stressors in a humorous and exaggerated fashion. Choose your favorite comic strip from the newspaper and follow it closely for one week. Make a list of each of the characters presented during the one-week period. Next to each name, note what common stressors the character faces and how he or she copes with the stressors. How effective are their coping strategies? If these stressors occurred in real life, what would be the most effective ways of dealing with them?

THINKING CRITICALLY ABOUT PSYCHOLOGY

1. **Forming Opinions** Suppose you could create a world that is completely free of stress. What do you think this world would be like? Would you like to live in such a world? Why or why not?

2. **Evaluating Ideas** Why might the "fight or flight" response be an inappropriate way to deal with some of the stressors in today's world? In what ways do the stressors of today differ from those our ancestors faced?

3. **Analyzing Ideas** Sometimes you hear about a calm, passive person who has suffered a heart attack or other stress-related illness. How would you explain this occurrence? What other factors might have contributed to this person's condition?

4. **Creating Ideas** If you were asked to design a program that would minimize the amount of stress in people's lives, what kind of program would you suggest? Describe the program's features in detail.

5. **Interpreting Ideas** Explain how a lack of change might be just as stressful as change. Support your opinions with specific examples.

DEVELOPING SKILLS IN PSYCHOLOGY

Creating a Stress Scale

Science is cumulative. All scientists build on the work of their predecessors. Familiarity with the contributions of others is important to this process. The informed use of logic and a thoughtful analysis of problems is also useful. As you become familiar with the concepts of psychology, you will find areas in which you can use your own critical thinking skills to build on previous work.

For example, consider the Social Readjustment Rating Scale (SRRS) on page 333. Holmes and Rahe developed the scale as a way of assessing the stressfulness of events in the lives of Navy recruits.

In order to make this concept more applicable to your life, revise the SRRS to make it more appropriate for high school students. With your teacher's supervision, keep the same number of items, but eliminate ones that do not apply to most high school students, and add new items that appear to represent the kinds of stressful events with which high school students must deal. For example, owing a $10,000 mortgage may be replaced with having problems at home or a disagreement with your best friend. Using the SRRS as a guide, assign stress units to each item you add. However, since your scale has not been scientifically tested, do not use it to actually predict the likelihood of serious illness.

READING FURTHER ABOUT PSYCHOLOGY

Brown, Barbara B., *The Biofeedback Syllabus: A Handbook for the Psychophysiologic Study of Biofeedback,* C. C. Thomas, Springfield, Ill., 1975. Summarizes research on biofeedback in the areas of the electrodermal, cardiovascular, skeletal, muscle, and central nervous systems, as well as other physiologic systems.

Charlesworth, Edward A., and Nathan, Ronald G., *Stress Management,* Ballantine, New York, 1985. A guide designed to help the reader identify specific areas of stress and deal effectively with them.

Eliot, Robert, and Breo, Dennis, *Is It Worth Dying For?* Bantam, New York, 1984. Already adopted as a manual by organizations with high-stress occupations, including several metropolitan police departments, this book is an exceptionally clear and reliable effort to explain stress. Techniques are suggested for effective prevention, relief, and management of stress.

Elkind, David, *All Grown Up and No Place to Go,* Addison-Wesley, Reading, Mass., 1984. Presents compelling reasons why American teen-agers today are under stress for which they are neither psychologically nor physiologically prepared.

Lifton, Robert J., *Death in Life: Survivors of Hiroshima,* Basic Books, New York, 1982. A moving report of the short-term and long-term effects of the atomic bomb blast at Hiroshima on survivors.

Paine, Whiton S., editor, *Job Stress and Burnout: Research, Theory, and Intervention Series,* Sage, Beverly Hills, Calif., 1982. An easy-to-read book that offers a comprehensive look at what is known, what is thought, and what is being done about job stress and job burnout.

Raphael, Beverly, *When Disaster Strikes: How Communities and Individuals Cope with Catastrophe,* Basic Books, New York, 1986. A readable book based on human reactions to a wide range of catastrophes.

Selye, Hans, *The Stress of Life,* McGraw-Hill, New York, 1978. Offers an interesting look at stress as a positive force in life.

PSYCHOLOGICAL DISTURBANCES

Chapter Focus

This chapter presents:

- **a general discussion of psychological disturbances in our society**
- **a description of some psychological disorders**
- **some approaches that have been taken to explain psychological disturbances**

In the late 1970's a popular young singer walked on stage and announced his retirement from show business. Upset and grieving over the suicide death of a good friend, the performer decided that the best course of action would be to end his own singing career. Shortly thereafter he checked into a mental hospital, where he was diagnosed by doctors as having a psychological disorder.

Fortunately, the story has a happy ending. After extensive treatment singer Tony Orlando was on the road to recovery. Soon he was once again entertaining thousands of people all over the country.

Psychological disorders can affect people from all walks of life. However, the percentage of people affected is relatively small. Just as most people are generally in good health, most people are in good mental health as well.

But when psychological disturbances do occur, it is important that they are diagnosed properly. In this chapter we will examine some of these psychological disorders. As you read about the various psychological disturbances, you may imagine that you have some of the characteristics described. You will probably be alarming yourself without cause. Everyone shows some of these characteristics to a degree. It is common to occasionally feel sad or anxious or de-

pressed. It is only when these feelings interfere with the ability to function that they become severe enough to require help. And help for severe psychological distress should only be given by qualified individuals.

Psychological Disturbances in Our Society

Even qualified individuals sometimes have difficulty in correctly diagnosing those who have psychological disturbances. In one study examining this topic, a researcher and seven other people pretended to be mentally ill. They applied for admission to different psychiatric hospitals. When they were interviewed for admission, they all claimed they "heard voices." Otherwise, they did not change their usual behavior.

All eight researchers were admitted to the hospitals. No one in any of the hospitals was told that they were only pretending to hear voices. All eight were diagnosed as being mentally disturbed.

After being admitted to the hospitals, the "patients" stopped pretending to have any abnormal symptoms. They behaved in their usual manner. They talked with other patients and staff members. They read and

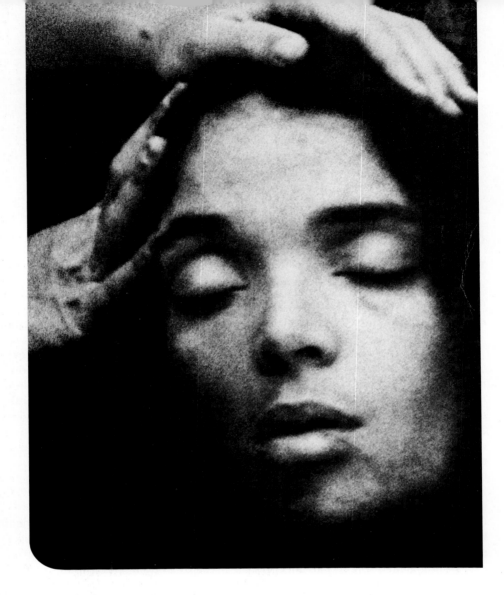

People with chronic psychological disturbances can benefit from the help of professionals.

watched television. When they were given medicine, they put it in their pockets or down the drain when staff members weren't looking.

During their stay in the hospitals, they took notes on their experiences. The staff paid little, if any, attention to their note taking. The only people in the hospitals who suspected that they were researchers and not patients were some of the real patients. Eventually, all of the "patients" were released from the hospitals. (See the Interpreting Sources feature on page 367 for a more ex-

panded description of this study and its implications.)

In another study, a researcher told the staff of a hospital that one or more "normal" subjects would apply for admission to the facility within the next three months. During this period, each staff member was asked to rate all persons who applied as to whether or not they were actually researchers. The staff rated 41 persons as not being real patients. However, no "normal" subjects actually did apply for admission to the hospital during the three months!

As these studies indicate, it is not always easy for someone, even a qualified professional, to correctly diagnose a person as being psychologically disturbed. And it is not always easy to distinguish between normal and abnormal behavior.

What is abnormal behavior? There is no sharp line that divides abnormal behavior from normal behavior. The term "abnormal" simply means "away from the norm." When we look at characteristics such as intelligence or weight or shoe size, for example, we see that there are wide variations in the population as a whole. Most people will fall into a middle range of values on any trait, the "norm," but some people will fall into the highest and lowest values on that trait. This is a statistical definition of abnormality. Any deviation from the statistical norm would be labeled abnormal. But using statistical frequency as a guidepost, people with unusually large feet would be considered abnormal. People with unusually high IQ's would be considered abnormal, too. When considering abnormal behavior, then, factors other than statistical norms must be examined.

Another way to look at abnormal behavior is to examine social norms. These are the rules and regulations that societies establish to determine acceptable standards of behavior. These rules may be highly formalized into codes and laws or they may be informal, such as always allowing dad to have the largest piece of cake at dinner. Behavior that deviates from socially established norms may be labeled abnormal. However, even this definition of abnormal behavior is not clear cut. The norms of any one society may change over time. For example, in Victorian times it was considered indecent for women to show their legs. So it was the norm for women to wear long dresses, heavy stockings, and layers of petticoats to hide their legs from view. This norm was so strong, in fact, that it was the custom also to cover the legs of pianos! We might laugh at this norm today, but it once defined behavior for a large segment of the population.

Norms of behavior also may vary from society to society. For example, people in the United States are allowed to marry only one person at a time. However, in many parts of the world it is customary for one man to be married to several wives at the same time. In fact, in some places around the world the more wives a man can support, the higher is his status and prestige.

As you can see, it is important to keep in mind that definitions of normal and abnormal behavior may vary over time and from place to place. Psychologists today tend to look at behavior in terms of how well a person is able to function within his or her own environment. A person's behavior may be considered abnormal if it interferes with healthy functioning or if it is harmful to the person or others. If the behavior is severe enough, it may indicate a psychological disturbance.

How widespread are psychological disturbances? It is difficult to determine the exact number of disturbed persons in the United States. But it is estimated that at least 15 percent of the population in the United States will experience serious psychological problems during any given year. Some people even estimate that the figure might be as high as 20 percent.

Where are people with psychological disorders being cared for today? Some people with psychological disorders are being cared for in psychiatric hospitals. The number of patients living in psychiatric hospitals is decreasing, however, due to improved forms of treatment. New and more effective types of drugs are helping more people than ever could be helped before. A large number of people are being treated in community mental health clinics and half-way houses. Some disturbed persons are being cared for in their own homes or in the homes of relatives. Some people are being cared for in various institutions, such as prisons, infirmaries, and nursing homes. And some people with psychological disturbances are living on the streets. They often have no place else to turn for help.

Mental illness occurs at all ages and among all races and socioeconomic groups. It is also a very expensive illness to treat. Each year tens of billions of dollars are spent on building facilities to house the mentally ill, caring for patients confined to institutions, maintaining private treatment programs, and providing public assistance. The amount of money lost on absenteeism from work is sizable as well. In addition, the money spent on medical bills amounts to a substantial sum.

How are psychological disturbances classified? You probably are familiar with the terms *neuroses* and *psychoses*. These terms were once used as broad classifications for a number of different psychological problems. The problems labeled neuroses included such disturbances as anxiety, depression, and other mild forms of disturbed behavior that rarely required hospital treatment. The disturbances grouped under the classification of psychoses were more severe and usually indicated an inability to cope with or distinguish reality. Persons suffering from psychoses usually required hospitalization and long-term treatment.

The costs involved in treating psychological disturbances in the United States amount to billions of dollars each year.

Psychologists today no longer use these terms to classify psychological disturbances. Because the categories are very broad, they each contain a number of disorders that have very different symptoms. This sometimes made it difficult for doctors to make an accurate and precise diagnosis. It also was sometimes difficult for doctors to agree on the diagnosis of a problem.

Psychologists today use the *Diagnostic and Statistical Manual of Mental Disorders* (3rd edition), known as the **DSM-III**. The DSM-III was developed by the American Psychiatric Association and lists 18 major diagnostic categories of mental disorders, the subcategories within each major category, and a description of the symptoms that accompany each disorder. The first two editions of the DSM emphasized the causes of disorders or the symptoms of disorders as the basis for classification. The DSM-III, however, places its emphasis on describing the disordered behaviors without theorizing about their causes. Using the DSM-III, with its expanded number of categories, has allowed doctors to make much more precise diagnoses of psychological disturbances.

Psychological Disorders

We will discuss a number of the psychological disorder categories here. These include somatoform disorders, dissociative disorders, anxiety disorders, affective disorders, schizophrenic disorders, paranoid disorders, personality disorders, organic mental disorders, developmental disorders, and substance use disorders.

Somatoform disorders. *Somatoform disorders* include disorders in which physical symptoms appear without any known organic cause. In other words, psychological factors cause the physical symptoms. One type of somatoform disorder is **hypochondria,** a disorder in which the person affected constantly focuses on bodily ailments and worries about every possible symptom. For example, people who get headaches and are convinced that they have a brain tumor might be labeled hypochondriacs. Hypochondriacs usually spend a lot of time visiting doctors and hospitals, only to find out that they have nothing physically wrong with them. They also tend to read a lot of medical material on different ailments and diseases, and to identify their own imagined symptoms with what they've read. Every time they read about something new, they may think that they have that illness or disease. These beliefs continue even after extensive medical tests show that they are healthy.

Another example of a somatoform disorder is *conversion disorder,* a disturbance in which the individual's psychological problems are "converted" into bodily disturbances. This interesting form of behavior is not very common today. It is important to remember that the person's physical symptoms are not under conscious control. It is the mind that is actually producing the physical symptoms. For example, some soldiers in a war became paralyzed in their right hand. Being paralyzed, they of course could not shoot their guns. So they had to leave the battlefront. When they were out of danger, the paralysis in their hands soon disappeared. Had these soldiers pretended to be paralyzed? In most cases, probably not. They were faced with a tremendous conflict. They wanted to be brave soldiers and fight alongside their friends. At the same time, however, they did not want to die in battle. Soldiers who are paralyzed cannot go into battle. Nor can they be considered cowards. So the conflict was solved.

Conversion disorder may take many forms. It may include the jerking of various parts of the body, blindness, pain in various parts of the body, and loss of speech.

Conversion disorder is probably learned behavior. Suppose you are faced with an unpleasant task that you really do not want to undertake. You happen to develop a stomachache. Thus, you avoid having to do the task. Having the stomachache is rewarded by avoiding something unpleasant. This may

An author's psychological fear of writing causes paralysis in her arm. This conversion disorder, however, has no real physical cause.

occur several times. Soon you develop a stomachache whenever you are faced with an unpleasant task—although you are not aware that the learning process has taken place. The pain of the stomachache feels real, even though it has no real cause.

Dissociative disorders. *Dissociative disorders* are a group of disturbances in which individuals view parts of their personalities as separate from their own personality. These psychological disorders represent extreme forms of repression.

One dissociative disorder is *amnesia,* or loss of memory. In general, such memory lapses concern the personal aspects of an individual's life. Individuals may forget that they are married, have children, own a home, and have a job. They usually do not forget how to use a knife and fork, make change for a dollar, or correctly identify colors. Most cases of amnesia follow some kind of traumatic experience. In brain-damage cases, however, amnesia may indicate actual permanent loss of memory.

A second dissociative disorder is *fugue,* or flight. Fugue occurs when individuals not only have amnesia but also take flight away

Text continues on page 352.

349

PSYCHOLOGICAL DISTURBANCES

Case Study: Focus on Research

SIXTEEN PEOPLE ALL IN ONE

The usually gentle schoolteacher burst into a hysterical tirade. Her fists clenched with rage, the teacher began shouting wildly, "Men are all alike. You just can't trust 'em. You really can't."

The other woman in the room watched with amazement. Cornelia Wilbur, a psychoanalyst, had been treating Sybil Dorsett for three months. Never had she seen this quiet young woman in such a state. Gripped by an eerie feeling, the doctor suddenly asked, "Who are you?"

"Can't you tell the difference?" was the reply. "I'm Peggy."

It was during this exchange that Dr. Wilbur first learned that Sybil Dorsett had more than one personality. Cases of multiple personality were not unknown. The three personalities of Chris Sizemore had already been well documented and used as the subject for a movie (*The Three Faces of Eve*). But nothing in medical history prepared the therapist for the revelations that came in the months ahead. Her patient was not simply a dual personality, part Sybil and part Peggy. As time passed, more and more selves emerged, until there were finally an astounding 16.

Sybil, herself often shy and withdrawn, alternated with aggressive Peggy and sophisticated Vicky. Mary was a plump, motherly type, while Vanessa had the flair of an actress. Among the others were baby Ruthie and even two energetic young men, Mike and Sid.

Sometimes Sybil's other selves emerged in the midst of a session, as when Peggy first appeared. Often one would come to take Sybil's place for an appointment. On more than one occasion, two would show up at once; Mike and Sid were usually together.

About a third of Sybil's life was spent in the guise of other personalities. Of these periods Sybil had no recollection—"blank spells," she called them. But during such blank spells, some remarkable events took place. Sybil had actually met with Dr. Wilbur but could not remember such meetings taking place. Sometimes she would wake up in strange places without any idea of how she got there. While in fifth grade, she was completely unaware of ever having left the third grade.

And although Sybil was unaware of her other selves, they were quite aware of Sybil's presence. Peggy claimed that Sybil never got angry. Vicky thought it was appalling the way Sybil worried all the time and did not enjoy life. Mary took care of practical matters for Sybil. And all complained that Sybil didn't feed them enough.

The incidence of multiple personalities is relatively rare. In Sybil's case such a disorder occurred after she experienced numerous childhood abuses.

Dr. Wilbur decided that she had to treat each of Sybil's selves as a separate person. Then she had to bring them into her patient's consciousness if Sybil was to become whole. Together—the doctor, Sybil, and the multiple selves—delved into the past.

What emerged was a childhood of terrible suffering. Sybil's mother had a breakdown shortly after her child's birth and remained in a depression for four months afterward. This depressed state soon increased her anxiety. Sybil, in turn, felt that something was wrong in her life. Moreover, Sybil's mother had physically tortured her only child for years. A washcloth stuffed down her throat and a broom handle to her back were commonplace occurrences to the young child.

Her father, distant and busy with his work, accepted his wife's explanations for Sybil's bruises, her dislocated shoulder, her fractured larynx. There was no one to whom Sybil could turn. And there was nobody who turned to her. Her grandfather who lived upstairs, her teachers, her doctor, and others never tried to discover what was really being done to this child.

Repressing her anger and fear, Sybil created other personalities as defenses and outlets. Peggy, for instance, was an assertive self who denied that Mrs. Dorsett was her mother (enabling Peggy to hate her). Vicky was the confident personality who had the courage to be adventurous. But none of Sybil's selves ever became closely involved with anyone. The danger was too great.

It took a long time for Sybil to face and accept all her personalities. Doing so involved dredging up many painful memories, such as of her beatings and the death of her grandmother. She had to let herself feel many repressed emotions. After eleven years of caring and intensive therapy, Peggy and Vicky and all the others were gone. Instead, one whole Sybil was able to face the future with joy and confidence.

SOURCE: Flora Schreiber, *Sybil,* New York, Warner Books, 1974.

Chris Sizemore, the subject of The Three Faces of Eve, is shown beside a drawing she did to represent her three selves.

Panic disorder is a severe form of anxiety. During a panic attack, the person experiences extreme terror accompanied by frightening physiological reactions.

from their usual geographic location. This condition applies to individuals who suddenly wake up in a strange place. They do not know who they are or how they came to be there. Usually, the person does not remember what has happened during this fugue, or flight away from home.

A third dissociative disorder is **multiple personality,** a disturbance that involves the development of two or more usually independent and separate personalities within the same person. Multiple-personality disorder occurs rarely. One famous case is presented in the film *The Three Faces of Eve.* A more recent example, described in the book

Sybil, is of a young woman who had 16 separate and distinct personalities. In the multiple-personality disorder, a person may attempt to satisfy opposite desires by developing separate personalities. This could enable the person to avoid the guilt and confusion that would be present if only one personality existed.

Anxiety disorders. *Anxiety disorders* are a group of disturbances characterized by feelings of frequent and prolonged anxiety that are out of proportion to the situation at hand. Everyone experiences twinges of anxiety from time to time and this is normal. How-

352

ever, a person with an anxiety disorder experiences anxiety and reacts to it in such a way that it interferes with daily living.

Generalized anxiety disorder is characterized by frequent and generalized anxiety. The anxiety is usually "free-floating"—not attached to any specific object, event, or situation. Persons with this psychological disturbance live in a constant state of fear and dread. They may be unable to eat, sleep, or concentrate on their work. The constant agitation and anxiety they experience may cause physiological reactions, such as feelings of faintness, rapid heartbeat, high blood pressure, and clammy skin.

A severe form of free-floating anxiety is ***panic disorder,*** which is characterized by acute attacks of overwhelming terror and dread. During a panic attack, the person may gasp for breath and believe that he or she is going to die. The heart may pound so hard that it literally may feel like it will burst. Sometimes the person will make an association between a particular location and the panic attacks and begin to avoid that location. For example, a person who experiences a panic attack while in a movie theater might get up and run out of the theater. An association is made between the theater and having the attack. The person may avoid going back to a movie theater for fear that an attack will happen again, even though the theater is not the real cause. Generalized anxiety and panic attacks are particularly distressing to the afflicted person because the feelings of dread are not tied to any specific cause.

While the fears involved in generalized anxiety and panic disorders are general and free-floating, other anxiety disorders involve fears that are more specific. For example, a ***phobic disorder*** involves a strong and unreasonable fear of a specific object or situation. The list of possible phobias is very long. Some interesting phobias are *xenophobia,* fear of strangers; *nyctophobia,* fear of darkness; *lalophobia,* fear of public speaking; and *astraphobia,* fear of thunder and lightning.

People who have phobias usually realize that their fears are irrational, but they also believe that the only way to reduce the fear is to avoid the object or situation causing the fear. This belief can keep them from doing things or going places. For example, a person who suffers from *claustrophobia,* a fear of closed-in spaces or confinement, may avoid using elevators. People who have a fear of heights, known as *acrophobia,* may be unable to climb ladders or to fly in airplanes.

The phobia that interferes the most with daily life probably is *agoraphobia,* or a fear of open places. The feelings of dread and terror involved in agoraphobia are so severe that some sufferers do not set foot outside of their homes for years. In some cases panic disorder will accompany the agoraphobia. For example, the agitation and terror involved in just thinking about leaving the house may be so severe that the person has a panic attack. The experience of the panic attack reinforces the fear of leaving the home. Eventually, the person will stop even thinking about going outside. The home becomes both a safe haven and a prison.

Another form of anxiety disorder is ***obsessive-compulsive disorder.*** This psychological disorder is characterized by constant unpleasant thoughts or images, called *obsessions,* and *compulsions*, the overwhelming need to repeat certain acts over and over again. The obsessive-compulsive person is usually aware that the thoughts are irrational, but is unable to control them. Any attempt to stop or interfere with the behavior brings overwhelming anxiety. These thoughts and actions occupy so much time that they seriously interfere with daily life.

For example, most people have had an experience in which they go to bed, lie there for a few minutes, and worry about whether they remembered to lock the front door of the house. Normally they will get up from bed, check the front door, and then go back to bed. The obsessive-compulsive person, however, will repeat this process over and over, perhaps even hundreds of times a night. The person is never convinced that the door is really locked and must check it over and over again in order to feel safe. Or a person may be obsessed with germs and spend hours ritually washing his or her hands over and over again, never believing that they are clean enough.

Affective disorders. *Affective disorders* are a group of psychological disorders that involve disturbances in mood. The term "mood" refers to a long-term emotion that characterizes the entire psychological makeup of an individual. One of the most frequently found affective disorders is **depression,** which involves a depressed mood all or most of the time. Most people feel sad or tired or depressed from time to time. These are very normal reactions to a number of real-life situations and events. It is only when these depressed feelings are out of proportion to the event and continue long after the event has passed that they become a disorder.

In the depressive phase of bipolar disorder, the person feels utterly helpless and dejected. Just moving is an effort.

The depressed individual may feel hopeless, may cry for long periods of time, and may even consider suicide. The people and things that once brought pleasure are forgotten. The person may lose interest in friends and family members. Nothing is fun anymore. No food tastes good anymore. The future appears to be bleak and the person feels powerless to change it.

People who suffer from this disorder often find it difficult to hold jobs or participate in social activities. They may be unable to eat or sleep, and often feel exhausted and run down. Some depressed people will sleep for days at a time. Others will simply sit and stare at nothing. The episodes of depression may last for a few weeks or they may continue for a year or longer. Most people who suffer from depression eventually recover, with or without treatment. However, the depression is likely to recur without treatment.

Bipolar disorder is an affective disorder characterized by periods of excitement and depression. The term "bipolar" means that the person's behaviors are at the two extremes of excitement or depression at different times.

The term used for this disorder in the past was "manic-depression." *Manic* refers to the excited and overly active periods. People suffering from this disorder go back and forth between feeling overly excited and feeling depressed.

In the excitement phase, people may sing at the top of their lungs, shout, or move about rapidly. They may talk almost continuously. They may make plans to do great things that they cannot possibly do. Their energy seems endless. Sometimes they become so excited and active that they may destroy furniture or injure themselves or others unless they are restrained.

The manic phase eventually passes. The behavior of these individuals may be quite normal for a while. Then they become very depressed. During this phase, which usually lasts longer, they become very sad, tired, and "low." They may feel that they are just about the most unhappy people on earth.

They may refuse food because they believe that they are too unworthy to live. They may stop sleeping or they may sleep too much. Nothing in life brings them pleasure anymore. They may even attempt suicide.

In time, people who suffer from bipolar disorder become quite normal again. Later they may have another manic phase, and still later another depressive phase. However, these periods do not necessarily occur at regular intervals. Nor do they always follow the same pattern. Actually, only 15 to 25 percent of people with this disorder show definite cycles of manic and depressive behavior. The majority of afflicted people are either manic or depressive most of the time.

The exact cause of bipolar disorder is not known. The cycles of the disorder may be related to the person's physiological cycles. Some scientists believe that this disorder is genetically caused, since it tends to run in families. Some cases may have been inherited through a genetic defect. The disorder responds very well to drug therapy, and tends to recur unless it is treated. Psychological theories suggest that people who suffer from this disorder usually have a background of high achievement standards. They often experience extreme feelings of guilt and worthlessness if they fail to reach their goals or believe that they have disappointed other people. They often have a strict conscience that keeps them from expressing anger and hostility. As a result, these strong emotions are turned inward.

Schizophrenic disorders. *Schizophrenic disorders* involve distortions of reality, disturbances in emotions and thought, strange behavior, and confusion as to identity or time. The schizophrenic person may suffer from *hallucinations,* which are faulty, sense-like perceptions for which there are no outside stimuli. The most common type of hallucination is an auditory hallucination. The person hears voices speaking, even though no real voices or other sounds are present. Another hallucination may involve visions of people long since dead. Or, individuals may feel the touch of someone's

This drawing was done by an adult schizophrenic. The blank stare, the lack of hands, and the misshapen body all are tied to this woman's loss of contact with reality.

hand on their shoulder, even though no one is standing near them. Schizophrenics also experience **delusions,** which are false beliefs that the person strongly defends, despite evidence that these beliefs cannot be true.

Schizophrenics also tend to speak and write sentences that are irrational and meaningless. They may string words together that by themselves are understandable, but when put together they reflect a great disorganization of thought. Psychologists call this a "word salad," or a jumble of words thrown together. Schizophrenics are unable to filter out stimuli they encounter and are unable to focus their attention on particular thoughts. Their words and writing reflect this inability to distinguish between relevant and irrelevant thoughts.

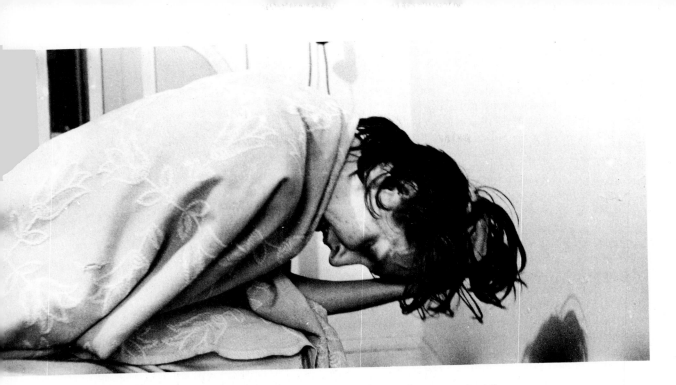

Paranoid people are convinced that other people are plotting against them. Their delusions take over their lives.

Schizophrenics also suffer from disturbances in perception. Often they report that sounds are louder than they really are or that objects are larger than they really are. They may not recognize themselves in a mirror or may see multiple images of themselves. During severe episodes, their perceptions may become "fragmented"—they may see only parts of people, such as an eye or a leg. The world does not look the same to schizophrenics during these episodes as it does to other people.

The emotions of schizophrenics often are dulled or inappropriate to the situation. They may show no emotion in situations that would make other people either very happy or very sad. At times they may burst into uncontrollable sobs or display unexplained anger and hostility. These bizarre emotional reactions result from the disrupted thought processes characteristic of schizophrenics.

Schizophrenia may be linked to hereditary factors because it is often found in members of the same family. However, this may be due to environmental factors as well as heredity. A home environment in which either of the parents is schizophrenic may cause the child to become confused and to withdraw from reality. Yet, a growing number of scientists have linked schizophrenia to a chemical imbalance in the brain. This imbalance affects messages to the brain and results in sensory disturbances. Drug treatment to correct the imbalance often reduces the hallucinations and delusions resulting in bizarre behavior, and allows schizophrenics to function more effectively.

Paranoid disorders. *Paranoid disorders* are characterized by continuing, well-developed delusions. Although many schizophrenics suffer from delusions, people with paranoid disorders are different because they describe, act on, and justify their delusions at great length and without end. The delusions are so severe that they usually interfere with normal daily functioning.

These delusions may take the form of

delusions of grandeur. Individuals with paranoid disorders may believe that they are successful authors, multimillionaires, world-famous doctors, great inventors, members of a royal family, and so on. They may introduce themselves to other people as Napoleon Bonaparte or Abraham Lincoln. The delusions continue even after they have been shown evidence that these beliefs cannot possibly be true.

The delusions of grandeur often are accompanied by delusions of persecution. Paranoid people may talk about how their enemies are plotting against them. Or they may talk about how scheming people are trying to steal their money or have copied their ideas for inventions. Those people who are hospitalized often claim that their enemies have succeeded in keeping them unjustly in the hospital.

People with paranoid disorder also may have delusions of reference. Even the smallest incidents take on a personal reference. Whenever they see two people talking, they are sure that the two are talking about them. A doctor or nurse may happen to make a small gesture. Paranoid patients, however, insist that this hand movement is a signal to their enemies. If their place at the table has been changed, it is because they irrationally believe that the food being served at the new place is poisoned. Such people, however, often give some very logical-sounding explanations. They may be well-read and talk in an interesting manner. Nevertheless, their lives are governed by their delusions.

Personality disorders. *Personality disorders* are a group of disorders that involve firmly established behavior patterns that are unacceptable more from society's standpoint than from the individual's standpoint. People with personality disorders are different from people with psychological disorders in that they experience little anxiety, conflict, or stress. The main problem is that they develop personality traits that differ greatly from accepted social behavior. People with personality disorders show *maladapted,* or poorly adapted, behavior patterns.

Most children learn at a very young age that there are certain things that they are not allowed to do. They are taught by their parents and by society that there are acceptable and unacceptable ways of behaving. Soon they learn to control their own behavior without anyone telling them what is right or wrong. People with personality disorders, however, ignore these rules or do not learn them well. They act only on their impulses. They think only about what they want and do not consider the wants or feelings of other people. When they feel a need, they must satisfy it immediately. If anything or anyone interferes with satisfying that need, they experience a great deal of frustration and anger.

The **antisocial personality** is characterized by violating the rules, laws, and mores of the society. The antisocial person has no conscience. Some young people who have antisocial personalities satisfy their impulses by joining street gangs. Quite a few criminals have antisocial personalities. They have little or no feelings of guilt or sorrow over their behavior. They are usually very good at explaining their actions. And they are convinced that their behavior is completely justified and correct. The "con man" is an example of someone with this type of disorder. Such a person is usually a good talker and is very convincing. Other aspects of the antisocial personality include impulsive behavior, irresponsibility toward others, and sometimes even acts of violence and murder.

Organic mental disorders. *Organic mental disorders* are a group of disorders in which the disturbances stem directly from injury to the brain or from an abnormality in the brain's biochemical environment. Older people who become forgetful, who get lost in familiar locations, and who no longer can remember the names of friends and family used to be called *senile.* Senility once was thought to be an unavoidable outcome of the aging process. We know today, however, that only about 5 to 10 percent of the elderly will suffer severe mental impairment. Most of these cases are linked to an organic mental

The effects of Alzheimer's disease can be devastating. Fortunately, only a small percentage of the population will develop it.

disorder called **Alzheimer's disease,** a deteriorating disease that involves the progressive destruction of brain cells. The brains of Alzheimer's disease patients that have been examined following death have shown brain lesions, tangles of nerve fibers, and loss of nerve cells. There is at present no cure for this disease.

One of the first symptoms of Alzheimer's disease is a loss of memory about current events, even though events from the far past can be recalled quite clearly. The person may not be able to remember the name of the president of the United States or what day it is. A woman may forget where she has put her handbag or a man may forget where he has put his keys. At first, this loss of memory may simply be laughed off as a sign of age.

The memory loss gradually worsens, however, and the person may not remember how to do things that once were done easily. For example, a businessperson who has written hundreds of reports in the past may not be able to finish a single one. The person may forget how to drive an automobile and may inappropriately speed up or slow down, go through stop signs and signal lights, or collide with another vehicle. The severe memory loss may be accompanied by disorientation, hostility, and deterioration of speech, eyesight, and muscle coordination. The person's body may become subject to a number of different infections.

In the most severe stage of the disease, the person regresses to a childlike state and often cannot control bodily functions. He or she may have to be fed, bathed, and clothed by other people. Self-care becomes impossible. Speech, movement, and even the ability to smile eventually stop.

The effects of Alzheimer's disease on the family members of the patient can be devastating. Family members may not understand that the memory loss involved in the disease is not under the conscious control of the patient. Husbands or wives may become angry when they find that they must take on all of the responsibilities of running a home. As the disease progresses, patients may no longer be able to work at a job and provide income to the home. They become incapable of remembering appointments or when bills must be paid. In the later stages of the disease, a spouse who chooses to care for the patient at home finds that this care is a full-time job. It is particularly difficult for the spouses and children of Alzheimer's disease patients to see the steady decline of their loved ones. Often psychological counseling helps family members cope with the jumble of feelings they experience.

The exact cause of Alzheimer's disease is still unknown. Some scientists suspect that the transmission of nerve impulses between the brain cells is blocked by a slow virus that can take years to result in noticeable effects. Other researchers are investigating the possibility that Alzheimer's disease results from a genetic defect. Apparently people with the genetic disorder of Down's syndrome develop symptoms identical to Alzheimer's disease if they survive to middle age. There may be a genetic link between Down's syndrome and Alzheimer's disease. Some scientists are examining the possibility that the disease is caused by deposits of aluminum in the brain. These aluminum traces are thought to be absorbed from various sources in the environment.

There is presently no treatment for Alzheimer's disease, although work is underway to develop drugs that will slow the progress of the devastating memory loss. Alzheimer's disease has been studied for only a very few years and it is difficult to make an accurate diagnosis of the disease while it is still in its early stages.

Developmental disorders. *Developmental disorders* are disturbances that begin in infancy, childhood, or adolescence. *Eating disorders,* psychologically caused disruptions in normal eating patterns, are one type of developmental disorder. *Anorexia nervosa,* an eating disorder, is a chronic aversion to food and an obsession with thinness. Anorexia nervosa most usually afflicts adolescent females. In pursuing thinness, the person literally refuses to eat, and in severe cases may consciously starve to death. The most obvious symptom of anorexia nervosa is a gaunt, emaciated appearance. Anorexics may lose up to 35 percent of their pre-illness weight, but continue to believe that they look fat. One of the characteristics of anorexia nervosa is a disturbance in body image. The body will continue to look too large to the person even when the bones are showing through the skin. This belief can take on delusional proportions.

Another characteristic of people with anorexia nervosa is that they tend to engage in a great deal of physical activity, even though their bodies are starving for nourishment. They may become obsessed with sports or exercise programs that would exhaust even well-nourished people. It may seem as though they never slow down or rest at all. They often exercise until late into the night and may weigh themselves many times during a session to see if they have lost more weight.

Anorexics usually are reluctant to discuss their symptoms and may deny that anything is wrong. They may become experts at avoiding food. When they are encouraged to eat by their parents or friends, they may say that they are not hungry or that they do not feel well enough to eat anything. They may slip food under the table to the dog or hide food in their napkins during meals. Later they will throw the food in the garbage or dispose of it in some other way. If they are forced to take in some food, they may later rid it from the body by vomiting.

Anorexia nervosa is a life-threatening disorder that has many physical complications. The starvation may cause dry, cracking skin due to loss of body fat and water content. The fingernails and toenails may become brittle and the hair may become dull. Anorexics may develop heart irregularities that can cause dizziness and even blackouts. The bowel may shut down and menstrual periods may cease. The starving body may begin to feed on its own muscle tissue, destroying this tissue. The bone development of anorexics may also be retarded.

Another eating disorder is called **bulimia,** which is characterized by a cycle of binge-eating and purging. The anorexic is obsessed with losing weight. The bulimic is obsessed with eating without gaining weight. The bulimic has episodes of compulsive eating, sometimes taking in thousands of calories during one binge. The food eaten usually consists of high-calorie, fattening foods, such as ice cream, cake, candy, and so on. The binge phase of this cycle may continue for

359

hours. The eating is usually done in secret and is followed by strong feelings of guilt and depression. These feelings lead the person to purge the body through vomiting or the use of laxatives and weight-reducing drugs. The cycle of eating and vomiting may also continue for hours. When it is finally over, the person may feel exhausted. Bulimics usually are aware that their eating patterns are abnormal, but they feel unable to stop their behavior. They are terrified of gaining weight.

An episode of binge-eating and purging is usually triggered by some kind of intense emotional experience. Stress, depression, loneliness, or rage may lead the person to try to soothe these feelings with food. Bulimic episodes are not the result of hunger or a strong appetite. Bulimia usually begins as a voluntary diet, but if it continues the person loses control over the behavior.

Bulimia has many medical complications. Chronic vomiting may erode tooth enamel and cause a large number of cavities. Vomiting also may block or enlarge the salivary glands and tear the esophagus. A rup-

tured esophagus may cause death. Long-term use of laxatives and weight-reducing drugs may cause the bowel to shut down. Bulimia also may affect the chemical balance of the body, leading to chronic dizziness, heart irregularities, muscle weakness, and convulsions.

The exact cause of eating disorders is unknown. People who have eating disorders tend to be perfectionists and high achievers. They tend to be very successful in their school work or in their jobs. They are very concerned with what other people think and go out of their way to please others. Part of their picture of perfection may focus on body image.

In our culture, being thin is considered attractive. To achieve this goal, many people diet. Some experts believe that anorexia nervosa results from an obsession to achieve this ideal. They attribute psychological and environmental factors as the cause. Bulimics, on the other hand, are obsessed by the fear of losing control. They are afraid that once they begin to eat they will not be able to stop. So

Feelings of depression and loneliness sometimes lead to a bulimic episode, but binge-eating and purging only make these feelings worse.

they purge their bodies of all food. Bulimics have low self-esteem and soothe their unhappiness with food.

Therapy for severe anorexics usually is undertaken in the hospital. What is most important is to make sure that the person is taking in nutrients. This nutrient therapy is accompanied by individual therapy sessions and group therapy sessions with other sufferers of the disorder. Family therapy often is used to help the sufferer and the entire family understand the environmental factors causing the disorder. Drug therapy often is used to lessen the feelings of depression that usually accompany eating disorders. Individual therapy, group therapy, and drug treatment are helpful for the bulimic, too.

Substance use disorders. Substance use disorders are characterized by the excessive use of alcohol or other drugs that alter behavior. A **drug** is any substance that changes mood, behavior, or consciousness. Substance use disorder is indicated by either a physical or psychological dependence on alcohol or other drugs.

Addiction, or physical dependence, involves both *tolerance,* the need to take more of the substance to produce the same effect, and *withdrawal,* unpleasant physical symptoms that occur when substance use is discontinued. These physical symptoms can range from mild discomfort to trembling and nausea, and possibly death.

Psychological dependence on a substance occurs when the nonuse of it causes the person to have severe feelings of distress. Psychological dependency becomes a problem when the person uses the substance to escape from the problems of living. (Individuals also can become psychologically dependent on such things as movies, television, gambling, books, and hobbies.) A psychological dependency involves making something into such a habit or source of comfort that it interferes with daily living.

We can divide commonly abused substances into five categories. (1) **Hallucinogens** produce sensory perceptions that have no basis in reality. These include LSD and mescaline. The effects of hallucinogens include nausea, headache, increased heartbeat rate and blood pressure, and altered perceptions and behavior sometimes leading to mental illness, suicide, and even murder.

(2) **Stimulants** ("ups" or "uppers") cause increased activity. The most commonly abused stimulants are cocaine and amphetamines. Stimulants act on the sympathetic nervous system. They cause reactions similar to those involved in fear and anger. Cocaine is a particularly addictive drug and one form of it, "crack" cocaine, may cause death with a single usage.

(3) **Depressants** ("downs" or "downers") decrease bodily functions. These include alcohol, barbiturates, and tranquilizers. Depressants cause a slight decrease in respiration, blood pressure, and heart rate. With large doses, a coma may result, sometimes resulting in death. It is particularly dangerous to mix alcohol with barbiturates or tranquilizers. The respiratory system may shut down and result in death.

(4) **Narcotics** cause physical dependence and result in withdrawal symptoms when they are withdrawn abruptly. These include drugs derived from opium, such as morphine, codeine, and heroin. Narcotics slow the central nervous system, reduce reaction to pain, and produce sleep, nausea, and narrowing of the pupils. An overdose can cause death.

Drug addicts who inject narcotics directly into their bloodstreams with hypodermic needles are called *intravenous drug users.* These people are in danger of contracting **AIDS,** or *acquired immune deficiency syndrome.* AIDS is a viral disease that destroys the body's immune system. Without the immune system, the body cannot resist disease and the AIDS victim soon dies from cancer, pneumonia, or other major illness. One way in which AIDS is transmitted is through the blood. Intravenous drug users who share needles may also be injecting the blood of AIDS-infected people into their bodies. They run a very high risk of contracting this deadly disease, for which there is no cure.

(5) **Cannabis** produces sensory and per-

ceptual changes and reduces inhibitions. Marijuana and hashish are derived from cannabis. These drugs produce reddened eyes, headache, dry mouth, cognitive deficits, and possible abnormal behavior and respiratory and cardiovascular damage.

Why do people take drugs? The "pusher" or seller of illegal drugs usually is not the one who introduces individuals to their first drug experience. In the large majority of instances, individuals are first introduced to alcohol or other drugs by a "friend" or member of their peer group.

In one study, students who used marijuana reported that curiosity was the main reason for trying it. Other students reported that they took their first drug because of social pressures from their "friends." Still other students did so because of the supposed thrills or kicks connected with alcohol and other drugs.

Another reason that some individuals turn to substance use is the social attitudes toward alcohol and other substances. We live in a drug-oriented society. We are constantly faced with advertisements showing how pills can be taken for gaining weight or losing it, for headaches and sore throats, for going to sleep or staying awake. Advertisements for alcohol usually feature people who are young and beautiful and having a lot of fun. These advertisements do not show the social, psychological, and physical complications that come with alcohol abuse. When use of a substance becomes a habit, when people must have it or suffer withdrawal symptoms, such people are said to be addicted to the substance.

Helping those who abuse substances. Perhaps the best plan for dealing with the substance abuse problem is a total educational program for students, parents, and school officials that is designed to *prevent* substance abuse. Many sources are available to inform individuals about alcohol and other drugs, including local medical doctors, pharmacists, and public health officials.

One of the older methods of treating individuals who are physically addicted to drugs is to have them withdraw from the substances suddenly and completely. Another method is to decrease the amount of the drug given to the addict over a period of about ten days.

A newer method involves giving a substitute drug to the addict. One such substitute is methadone. Although it is a narcotic itself, methadone does not produce the "high" associated with heroin. However, methadone does not work satisfactorily with all heroin addicts. And some people believe that methadone itself might produce additional addicts, because it is physically addicting.

Some alcoholics have been successfully treated with emetine, a nausea-producing drug. After taking emetine, people get sick when they drink alcohol. Eventually they get sick whenever they see or smell alcohol, even though they have stopped taking the drug.

One of the most promising of the present-day methods of treating drug abuse is therapy at self-help centers. Addicts who come for help are required to live at the center. Many of the centers are set up and run by ex-addicts, who are personally familiar with the addicts' problems.

One organization designed to help alcoholics is Alcoholics Anonymous (AA). It was first started by two men who had helped themselves and each other to recover from alcoholism. Regular meetings focus on the ways in which individuals can have a social life and entertainment without dependence on alcohol. At these meetings the problems of the alcoholic are discussed in a friendly, nonthreatening atmosphere. People tell of their experiences and how they have been helped. Alcoholics are made to feel that they are not alone with their problems. They learn that they will be more successful if they attack their problems rather than if they run away from them. Reports indicate that treatment by Alcoholics Anonymous is effective in about three-fourths of the cases who come for help. There are even special programs for the children and spouses of alcoholics.

Some large businesses have psychiatric

Addiction to alcohol and other drugs is a serious problem in the United States, resulting in the loss of thousands of human lives each year. Fortunately, a number of programs now exist that can help people recover from substance abuse.

programs to help their employees who are abusing alcohol or other drugs. The amount of production and income lost to absenteeism and the inability to work effectively is quite sizable. And more and more clinics are being set up where substance use is treated as a medical problem. Many large companies have insurance programs that will pay all or part of the costs involved in drug abuse treatment. With substance abuse, as with many other problems, prevention is better than cure.

Any treatment of the physical aspects of substance abuse also should include social-psychological treatment. That is, it should include helping the person readjust to a productive life in society.

Various Approaches to Psychological Disturbances

There are a number of major viewpoints, or models, regarding the causes of psychological disturbances. We will discuss the medical model, the psychoanalytic model, the behavioral model, and the sociocultural model.

The medical model. The *medical model* links genetic or biological factors as the causes of psychological disorders. This is the oldest model. It began from observations that behavioral disturbances were the result of brain damage. It replaced earlier ideas that psychological disturbances were caused by demons or were punishments for immoral behavior. The medical model resulted in much more humane treatment of the mentally ill. Disturbed persons were no longer beaten, burned at the stake, or put in prison. They were treated as people with medical problems and put in hospitals.

Some psychologists today find fault with the medical model. First of all, many psychological disorders do not seem to be related to any known genetic or physical cause. For example, there is no evidence that people

The various models of psychological thought view disturbed behavior in different ways.

with conversion disorders have any real underlying physical problem. And hypochondriacs only believe that they have illnesses or diseases.

Another fault with the medical model is that it assumes there is a sharp dividing line between normal and abnormal behavior. As we know, however, behavior considered normal in one setting may be considered abnormal in another. For example, suppose you see several people walking down the street. They start yelling and screaming, for no obvious reason. You would probably think their behavior was somewhat abnormal. But if you saw the same behavior at a football game, you would consider it appropriate to that situation. Another example is the behavior of soldiers during combat. We all know that physically harming someone is wrong. But when a war occurs, it is the duty of soldiers to fight for their country.

Finally, the medical model places the responsibility of providing a cure on the person who makes the diagnosis. Despite these criticisms, however, the medical model has recently gained in popularity.

The psychoanalytic model. The *psychoanalytic model* views psychological disturbances as the result of childhood experiences and of repressed, or hidden, desires and needs. In the case of multiple personality, for example, the person overuses adjustment mechanisms. In the case of schizophrenia, the adjustment mechanisms break down. The basic treatment for individuals, according to this model, is to uncover their repressed desires and learn how the experiences of their childhood have affected their development. They will then be able to handle their wants and desires at a conscious level.

The psychoanalytic model has been criticized because it is very difficult to "prove" a connection between the events of childhood and current psychological illness. While some cases of abnormal behavior may have their roots in early childhood experiences, it is very difficult to establish cause-and-effect relationships.

The behavioral model. The *behavioral model* emphasizes the learning of inappropriate or undesirable behavior. According to this viewpoint, disturbed behavior is learned behavior. People learn to behave largely through operant conditioning and through classical conditioning. They also learn by observing and imitating other people. According to this model any behavior that is learned can be unlearned. For example, George is afraid of high places. When he was very young, he had an unpleasant experience in a high place. Now this experience has become associated with all high places. Every time he is around a high cliff or bridge, he has just about the same feelings he had during the original experience. To change this reaction, George will have to unlearn the association. Or consider the case of Tina, who has received little reinforcement in the past from other people. She has therefore not learned to associate with or be around other people. The treatment for Tina might consist of having many different people reward her. In this way, she will learn to want to be around people. She will unlearn past behavior and learn new ways of behaving.

The sociocultural model. The *sociocultural model* emphasizes the role of environmental factors in causing psychological disturbances. It also emphasizes environmental factors as part of the treatment of such disorders. It notes, for example, that there are more disorders among the lower socioeconomic classes and in urban areas. This model stresses improving environmental conditions to lessen mental illness in society. The idea is to create a healthy society in which each person can "grow" psychologically. Individuals will then have a much better chance of reaching full development.

Each of these models presents a somewhat different approach toward psychological disturbances. In actual treatment, however, various combinations of models are used. For example, a schizophrenic might be treated with drugs, receive psychoanalytic care, and be helped to become a contributing member of society through the use of learning techniques.

How patients view their psychological disturbances. In one study completed in Canada, a group of patients who had been released from mental hospitals were asked what factors might have prevented their psychological disturbances. They also were asked which factors—such as parents, city living, and money—had been harmful or helpful to their disorders. Only a small percentage said that personality factors may have been responsible for their disturbances. Three times as many listed interpersonal relations, such as social isolation. Out of 20 items, a lack of money was listed most often (44 percent as hindering their psychological development). Weather was listed as the second most important factor. In general, the patients agreed on what might have prevented their psychological disturbances. Most of them listed environmental factors and interpersonal relations.

Another study indicates the influence of culture on how patients view their psychological illnesses. Several hundred patients in similar mental hospitals in the United States and Germany were interviewed. The results showed that the patients from Germany saw psychological disturbances as being more of a biological illness and less curable than did the patients from the United States. The German patients more often stated that they were admitted to the hospital in the first place to improve their health. Also, the Germans thought it was the doctors who should decide who was well enough to leave the hospital. The American patients believed that their own efforts were more likely to improve their chances for release from the hospital. Individual effort would make an important difference in how long they stayed in the hospital. The Americans took more responsibility for their behavior in certain areas. The German patients, at least in some ways, took a more biological and deterministic viewpoint. They saw more things happening independently of themselves.

Summary

Psychological disturbances affect a relatively small percentage of people. It often is difficult, however, even for qualified people to diagnose such disorders.

The DSM-III outlines a number of psychological disorders. Somatoform disorders include disturbances in which psychological symptoms appear without any known cause. Dissociative disorders are those in which people view some of their activities as separate from their personalities. Amnesia, fugue, and multiple personality are all dissociative disorders. Anxiety disorders are characterized by frequent and prolonged anxiety. Generalized anxiety disorder, panic disorder, and phobic disorder are three types of anxiety disorders. Affective disorders are distinguished by changes in mood. Depression and bipolar disorder are affective disorders. Schizophrenic disorders involve withdrawal from reality and faulty thought and perceptual processes. Paranoid disorders are characterized by continuing, well-developed delusions.

Personality disorders involve a poor adjustment to society's standards of behavior. One type of personality disorder is the antisocial personality. Organic mental disorders are caused by injury to the brain or its surrounding environment. Alzheimer's disease is one type of organic brain disorder. Developmental disorders usually occur among younger people and include eating disorders. Anorexia nervosa and bulimia are included among the eating disorders. Substance use disorders involve dependence on alcohol or other drugs that alter mood, consciousness, or behavior. Five categories of substances that can be abused are hallucinogens, stimulants, depressants, narcotics, and cannabis.

Various approaches are used to explain and treat psychological disturbances. These include the medical model, the psychoanalytic model, the behavioral model, and the sociocultural model. In actuality, combinations of a number of models are used when treating psychological disorders.

INTERPRETING SOURCES

In this excerpt from "On Being Sane in Insane Places" (*Science*, January 19, 1973), psychologist D. L. Rosenhan makes the point that labels used in diagnosing abnormal behavior may distort our perceptions of those who have been labeled. Once individuals have been labeled as abnormal, we tend to see them as abnormal regardless of their actual behavior.

What is viewed as normal in one culture may be seen as quite aberrant in another. Thus, notions of normality and abnormality may not be quite as accurate as people believe they are....

At its heart, the question of whether the sane can be distinguished from the insane . . . is a simple matter. . . . The belief has been strong that patients present symptoms, that those symptoms can be categorized, and . . . that the sane are distinguishable from the insane. More recently, however, this belief has been questioned.... The view has grown that psychological categorization of mental illness is useless at best and downright harmful . . . at worst. . . .

Gains can be made in deciding [if this] is . . . accurate by getting normal people . . . admitted to psychiatric hospitals and then determining whether they were discovered to be sane and, if so, how. . . . If, on the other hand, the sanity of such pseudopatients were never discovered, serious difficulties would arise for those who support traditional modes of psychiatric diagnosis. . . .

This article describes such an experiment. Eight sane people gained secret admission to 12 different hospitals. . . .

The pseudopatient arrived at the admissions office complaining that he had been hearing voices. Asked what the voices said, he replied that they were often unclear, but as far as he could tell they said "empty," "hollow," and "thud." Immediately upon admission to the psychiatric ward, the pseudopatient ceased simulating any symptoms of abnormality....

The pseudopatient behaved on the ward as he "normally" behaved. . . . When asked by staff how he was feeling, he indicated that he was fine, that he no longer experienced symptoms....

Despite their public "show" of sanity, the pseudopatients were never detected. Admitted, except in one case, with a diagnosis of schizophrenia, . . . each was discharged with a diagnosis of schizophrenia "in remission...." At no time during any hospitalization had any question been raised about any pseudopatient's simulation. . . . The evidence is strong that, once labeled schizophrenic, the pseudopatient was stuck with that label....

Once a person is designated abnormal, all of his other behaviors and characteristics are colored by that label. Indeed, that label is so powerful that many of the pseudopatients' normal behaviors were overlooked entirely or profoundly misinterpreted....

A psychiatric label has a life and an influence of its own. Once the impression has been formed that the patient is schizophrenic, the expectation is that he will continue to be schizophrenic. When a sufficient amount of time has passed, during which the patient has done nothing bizarre, he is considered to be in remission.... But the label endures beyond discharge, with the unconfirmed expectation that he will behave as a schizophrenic again....

Source Review

1. Why might notions of normality and abnormality not be quite as accurate as people believe they are?

2. What makes Dr. Rosenhan believe that the "pseudopatients" in his study were victims of psychological categorization once they had been admitted to the hospital?

3. How can a psychiatric label be harmful?

CHAPTER 16

REVIEWING TERMS

DSM-III
somatoform disorder
hypochondria
conversion disorder
dissociative disorder
amnesia
fugue
multiple personality
anxiety disorder
generalized anxiety
   disorder
panic disorder
phobic disorder
obsessive-compulsive
   disorder

affective disorder
depression
bipolar disorder
schizophrenic disorder
hallucination
delusion
paranoid disorder
personality disorder
antisocial personality
organic mental disorder
Alzheimer's disease
developmental disorder
eating disorder
anorexia nervosa
bulimia

substance use disorder
drug
addiction
psychological
   dependence
hallucinogen
stimulant
depressant
narcotic
AIDS
cannabis
medical model
psychoanalytic model
behavioral model
sociocultural model

CHECKING FACTS

1. What factors must be taken into account when distinguishing between normal and abnormal behavior?

2. How widespread are psychological disturbances in our country? What kinds of people are affected?

3. How does fugue differ from amnesia? Why is amnesia called a dissociative disorder?

4. Describe the components of obsessive-compulsive disorder. How does the behavior involved in this disorder differ from normal behavior?

5. Discuss the reasons why bipolar disorder is thought to have a genetic cause.

6. Describe some of the symptoms of schizophrenic disorder. What kind of treatment helps to reduce these symptoms?

7. How does a person with a paranoid disorder differ from a person with schizophrenia? Describe the behavior of a paranoid person.

8. How does a person with a personality disorder differ from a person with a psychological disorder?

9. How widespread is severe mental impairment among the elderly? Discuss how the symptoms of Alzheimer's disease progress.

10. What is the difference between anorexia nervosa and bulimia? What are some medical complications of bulimia?

11. Describe some of the physical effects of hallucinogens, stimulants, depressants, narcotics, and cannabis.

12. What are the four major approaches to psychological disturbances? How do they differ?

APPLYING YOUR KNOWLEDGE

1. On the board, list several unusual or "crazy" behaviors of famous people (rock and film stars, athletes, artists, writers, and so on). Discuss why these behaviors may be signs of individuality or creativity rather than mental illness.

2. Each student should write down on a piece of scrap paper a behavior that is considered "normal" in some circumstances but "abnormal" in others. For example, jumping up and down is acceptable at a football game but unusual during a school assembly. With the approval of your teacher, collect the papers and redistribute them randomly. One student at a time should then tell the class what behavior appears on his or her paper. The rest of the students should suggest all possible scenarios for the behavior—both "normal" and "abnormal."

3. Label a box "All the things you wanted to know about mental illness, but were afraid to ask." Each student should anonymously jot down questions on this topic and place them in the box. The

psychology teacher, or perhaps a guest psychologist, can then lead a discussion of the questions.

4. Spend some time in the library preparing five-to-ten minute oral presentations on one of the following topics:
   (a) Adolescent suicide—a growing concern
   (b) Drug abuse by athletes
   (c) Ways of identifying and preventing depression
   (d) Coping with growing up

   Also prepare an outline or summary to be distributed to the class.

5. Form a debate team on the issue "Substance abuse is a crime vs. substance abuse is an illness." Include in the debate any differences between the two viewpoints in how substance abuse might be treated. You might also ask a representative from a community treatment program or another organization to speak with your class on the problem of substance abuse in our society.

THINKING CRITICALLY ABOUT PSYCHOLOGY

1. **Forming an Opinion** Which of the four models of psychological disturbances (medical, psychoanalytic, behavioral, and sociocultural) do you agree with most? Why? Or would you combine some of them? If so, how?

2. **Developing Ideas** To what extent do symptoms of psychological disturbances result from the culture in which individuals are reared?

3. **Analyzing Ideas** Do you think that reducing the tensions and fast pace of

life in our society would help reduce the amount of abnormal behavior? Why or why not?

4. **Understanding Ideas** As a child, did you ever believe that you just had to step on every crack in the sidewalk or touch every telephone pole? Did other children make a game of this kind of activity? What is the difference between this kind of activity and obsessive-compulsive behavior?

5. **Proposing Ideas** Suppose you were

asked to set up a program to prevent drug abuse or alcoholism in your community. Which experts would you contact? What guidelines would you establish?

6. **Interpreting Ideas** What do you believe are the most important factors that cause psychological disturbances? Give evidence to support your beliefs.

DEVELOPING SKILLS IN PSYCHOLOGY

Generating Alternative Interpretations

A major controversy within psychology is the nature-nurture, or heredity versus environment, debate. Some psychologists argue that much of human behavior, normal and abnormal, can be attributed to heredity—to the individual's genetically based, biological makeup. Other psychologists insist that aspects of the environment such as learning and experience (nature) are responsible for most of the things that people do.

Consider the problem of alcoholism. Some experts argue that a tendency toward alcoholism is inherited. They point out that alcoholism seems to "run in families." For

example, it appears that individuals are more likely to develop alcohol problems if their parents are alcoholic.

Evaluate the argument that if alcoholism can run in families, then it must have a genetic basis. Try to think of other characteristics that can be found common to family members but clearly do not have a biological basis, such as regional accents. Generate an alternative interpretation for the finding that alcohol abuse may be found in more than one member of the same family. For example, think of the learning and experience factors that could help account for this finding.

READING FURTHER ABOUT PSYCHOLOGY

Crenshaw, Mary Ann, *End of the Rainbow,* Macmillan, New York, 1981. The story of a woman with a seemingly perfect life who becomes addicted to drugs and watches as everything begins to go out of control. She eventually rebuilds her life and learns healthy ways to cope.

Gilman, Charlotte Perkins, *The Yellow Wallpaper,* Feminist Press, New York, 1973. A largely autobiographical study of a brilliant young woman's descent into insanity. Originally published in 1892.

Guest, Judith, *Ordinary People,* Ballantine, New York, 1982. A gripping novel about a young man who returns home after a suicide attempt and subsequently sees the devastating collapse of his family.

Kline, Nathan, *From Sad to Glad,* Ballantine, New York, 1981. Discusses the nature and symptoms of depression and presents various therapies used to treat it.

Levenkron, Steven, *The Best Little Girl in the World,* Warner, New York 1979. An accurate portrayal of anorexia nervosa, a serious eating disorder among teen-age girls.

O'Neill, Cherry Boone, *Starving for Attention,* Dell, New York, 1983. The autobiography of a young woman (the daughter of celebrity Pat Boone) who struggled for ten years to overcome anorexia nervosa.

Peck, Richard, *Remembering the Good Times*, Delacorte, New York, 1985. A novel that deals with the suicide of a 16-year-old boy who turned inward from a seemingly alienating and violent society.

Schreiber, Flora R., *Sybil*, Warner, New York, 1974. True story of a young woman with multiple personalities and the ultimate integration of those personalities through therapy.

Seixas, Judith, and Youcha, Geraldine, *Children of Alcoholism*, Crown, New York, 1985. The authors interview 200 adults who had alcoholic parents to uncover the effects of growing up with parents who drink.

Sheehan, Susan, *Is There No Place on Earth for Me?* Houghton Mifflin, Boston, 1983. A real-life account of a young woman's struggle as a schizophrenic.

Wholey, Dennis, *The Courage to Change: Hope and Help for Alcoholics and Their Families*, Houghton Mifflin, Boston, 1986. Answers questions about the disease of alcoholism. Offers practical advice as well as hope, and may give alcoholics or their families the motivation needed to seek help.

Chapter 17

TREATMENT OF PSYCHOLOGICAL DISTURBANCES

Chapter Focus

This chapter presents:

- **a description of each of the various therapies that are used to treat psychological disturbances**
- **an evaluation of the effectiveness of the different therapies**

"Tell me what you dreamed, and I'll tell you what it meant." So boasts Golde, the wife of Tevye the Milkman, in the play *Fiddler on the Roof*. Actually, Tevye concocted the dream to explain something important to his wife. He wished to explain why their daughter should not be forced to marry the man who had been selected for her by the matchmaker. At a time when matchmakers replaced Cupid in pairing young people, this was a serious issue.

Fortunately, Golde interprets the dream as Tevye had predicted, and the story has a happy ending. The daughter is allowed to marry the young man of her choice.

Although treated lightly here, dream interpretation has played an important role in treating psychological disturbances. Psychoanalysts who take this approach believe that dreams reveal important unconscious conflicts. By helping patients understand their dreams, psychoanalysts help patients deal with their problems.

Dream interpretation is only one of many forms of ***therapy,*** or methods of treating psychological disturbances. In this chapter, we will discuss the various options available to people seeking help. Of course, the best

treatment is prevention, but that is not always possible. Consequently, we must turn to these other methods.

Medical Therapy

Medical therapy involves physical treatment through medicine. Such therapy is given to patients by psychiatrists (who are medical doctors) and by physicians. Although treatment often occurs in mental hospitals, there is an increase in the number of patients who receive medical therapy outside of hospitals. Two forms of this treatment are ***drug therapy*** and ***electroconvulsive shock therapy.***

Drug therapy. The use of tranquilizers and other drugs has been a major factor in reducing the number of patients in mental hospitals. Drugs do not usually *cure* a psychological disturbance, as an antibiotic cures a sore throat. Instead, they help to change people's behavior, which makes other forms of treatment more effective. For example, the drug lithium has been very useful in treating bipolar disorder. The patient often returns to normal mood states a week or so after taking the drug. Then other forms of treatment can be given, such as psychotherapy.

Antipsychotic drugs are used with major psychological disorders, such as schizophrenia. How do these drugs work? No one knows for certain at the present time, although there are many theories. One interesting theory is that schizophrenia results from the abnormal metabolism of a chemical (dopamine) found in the brain. The theory suggests that antipsychotic drugs act to block the effects of this chemical.

Electroconvulsive shock therapy. This method of treatment is used less often than drug therapy. The main reason is that with electroconvulsive shock therapy there is the possibility of brain damage to the patient. However, sometimes drug therapy is not successful, and electroconvulsive shock therapy is employed.

In electroconvulsive shock therapy an electric current is sent through certain areas of the brain for a fraction of a second. The length and severeness of the current can be controlled so that the patient feels no pain. The shock causes temporary unconsciousness and a convulsion. Soon after, though, the patient awakens. There is some memory loss and confusion, but these symptoms disappear after a few hours. (With repeated treatment, however, the brain may be damaged and memory loss occurs.)

Electroconvulsive shock therapy is considered effective as a treatment for severely depressed patients, although no one as yet knows why. However, because of the controversy surrounding its use, electroconvulsive shock therapy is used only as a last resort.

Psychotherapy

The term **psychotherapy** covers a wide variety of procedures and concepts. All of them, however, involve helping emotionally disturbed people to understand their problems and to change their behavior so they can lead a more well-adjusted life. Regardless of the specific form that psychotherapy may take, the goals are usually the same. They include working toward self-understanding, finding more effective techniques for dealing with conflicts, improving interpersonal relationships, and developing satisfying patterns of behavior. Psychotherapy is usually provided by psychologists and psychiatrists either in private practice or at mental health centers.

Psychoanalysis. One of the most familiar types of psychotherapy is **psychoanalysis.** It is based on the theories of Sigmund Freud. The therapist who practices this approach is called a psychoanalyst. The psychoanalyst helps the patient remember forgotten motives and experiences that occurred earlier in life, but are still influencing the person's behavior. After the patient remembers such experiences or motives, the psychoanalyst tries to help the person adjust to them.

There are four basic techniques used in psychoanalysis. **Free association** encourages patients to say anything they wish during a treatment session, regardless of how painful, personal, or disconnected it may seem. The task of the psychoanalyst is to identify repressed ideas, thoughts, or impulses that come to the surface through free association. The psychoanalyst then interprets the meanings of these ideas.

In **dream interpretation,** another therapy technique, the psychoanalyst analyzes the hidden, symbolic content of the patient's dreams. It is thought that during sleep, the mechanisms that keep unconscious ideas from becoming conscious are weakened. Repressed feelings and desires are often expressed in symbolic form during dreams. The psychoanalyst helps patients understand their problems by interpreting the symbolic content of their dreams.

A third technique involves overcoming **resistance** on the part of the patient. The thoughts that patients repress are kept at the unconscious level because they are unacceptable to the patient. Trying to bring these thoughts to the conscious level produces a

high level of anxiety in patients. So patients resist. For instance, a patient may be late for an appointment, or just "forget" an appointment. Since resistance prevents unconscious desires from becoming conscious, it must be broken down. Otherwise patients can't realize their problems and conflicts. This process is necessary if therapy is to progress.

The last technique of psychoanalysis is one of the most difficult to define and understand. It is called ***transference***. As a patient interacts with the psychoanalyst, feelings and emotions come out. Patients often transfer their feelings toward one of their parents or another significant person onto the psychoanalyst. This gives the patient a chance to reexperience these feelings under different conditions. The psychoanalyst can help the patient "work through" feelings, such as anger and hostility, that the patient may have had difficulty in expressing to the parent.

A psychoanalyst uses all these techniques to help patients become aware of their emotional difficulties and thus be able to deal with them.

Play therapy. This is really an extension of psychotherapy that has been especially adapted for young children. *Play therapy* is based on the idea that a child may reveal true emotions or feelings during play. For example, if a child resents a parent, this may come out. In one form of this therapy, the therapist lets the child play with dolls. The dolls might represent various persons in the child's family, such as the mother, father, brother, or sister. How the child plays with the dolls in various settings gives the therapist some ideas as to what the child thinks of the parents or other family members.

The specific form of play therapy used depends on the therapist and the problem being treated. In any case, the child is encouraged to express feelings that might be otherwise difficult to describe.

Client-centered therapy. This form of therapy was developed by Carl Rogers. It is based on the view that human nature is essentially good and that people have a need for positive growth. According to Rogers, our conflicts come about when something in the environment interferes with the growth of our self-concept. *Client-centered therapy* tries to provide conditions under which positive growth can again take place. The therapy is client-centered because it is not the therapist but the clients who must gain insight into their own problems and help themselves.

Rogers believed that unconscious needs and impulses can influence behavior. But his methods for finding out about such desires are quite different from those of psychoanalysis. His basic technique is to create a warm, free, open atmosphere during therapy sessions. The therapist doesn't judge or interpret the client's behavior. In this way the therapist creates an emotional situation in which clients feel psychologically safe to talk or act without fear of being evaluated.

Another technique used by client-centered therapists is known as *reflection of feelings.* This means that the therapist restates the meaning of the client's words. For example, the client may say, "I'm really angry at my boss!" The therapist may restate this as, "You feel a great deal of anger toward your boss?" The therapist uses this procedure to help clients reflect on their feelings and be clear about what they are.

In client-centered therapy, the therapist does not tell the clients what their problems are or what to do about them. But the therapist does decide what to restate and when to move on to other issues. Through these methods, the therapist helps clients to help themselves.

Transactional analysis (TA). According to this form of psychotherapy, psychological disturbances are the result of disorders in interpersonal relationships. In *transactional analysis,* relationships are based on three basic processes that make up personality. One is the *Parent,* which represents judging and restricting behavior and which is learned from our own parents. Another is the *Child,* which represents basic, spontaneous, and dependent behavior. The Child is a carryover of feelings we had when we were children. The third process is the *Adult,* which represents mature, life-oriented behavior. The Adult is the part of our personality that is rational and appropriate for a given set of circumstances.

Transactional analysis often puts people in groups of five to fifteen. The people are asked to communicate with one another using their usual levels of communication. The therapist then helps them develop an awareness of the type of communication they are having. For example, a wife may say to her husband: "Wear your coat when you go outside. It's cold!" In this case, the wife is communicating as a Parent to a Child. The husband might respond as an Adult: "I don't think it's cold enough to wear my coat tonight." Or he might reply as a Child: "No! You can't tell me what to do!"

Transactional analysis is a method of

showing people how they communicate with one another. When people are using inappropriate methods or levels of communication, TA attempts to get them to adopt more appropriate and workable ways of communicating.

Behavior Therapy

As you know, psychoanalysis emphasizes the effect of past experiences on present behavior. Both client-centered therapy and transactional analysis focus on the present situation. **Behavior therapy** does not look for internal conflicts, but emphasizes the behavior itself. Behavior therapy views the maladjusted person as differing from the normal person only in (1) having learned inadequate ways of behaving, or (2) never having learned how to cope with problems involved in everyday living. This form of therapy stresses the role of learning in treatment. It assumes that any learned behavior can be unlearned (except in cases of brain damage). Therefore, behavior therapists point out to patients which behavior shows poor adjustment and what adaptive behavior they need to learn. Behavior therapists reward desirable behavior and may punish undesirable behavior to help patients change their psychological disturbances.

There are various types of behavior therapy (sometimes also called behavior modification). These include aversive therapy, desensitization, implosive therapy, simple extinction therapy, and modeling.

Aversive therapy. *Aversive therapy* consists of changing undesirable behavior by pairing the behavior with some form of punishment, such as an electric shock. Suppose, for example, you wanted to change the habit of biting your nails. You might be given a weak electric shock every time you began to bite your nails. Soon you would associate biting your nails with the electric shock. And you would avoid nail biting.

Desensitization. This procedure is based on the belief that two opposite responses cannot exist at the same time. Can you feel

In desensitization you replace the anxiety attached to a particular situation with relaxing, peaceful thoughts, such as thoughts of a quiet lake.

relaxed and afraid simultaneously? Suppose you are afraid of snakes, and you are taught to relax when you see or are near a snake. Would you still be afraid? **Desensitization** involves getting rid of an undesirable response by strengthening the opposite response.

Treatment involves teaching patients how to relax. At the same time, the therapist makes a list of what kinds of situations cause the patient anxiety. The therapist then arranges these situations in order, or in a hierarchy, from least anxiety-producing to most anxiety-producing. When the patient has learned to relax, the therapist selects the least anxiety-producing situation in the hierarchy and describes it to the patient. If the patient is still relaxed, a slightly more anxiety-producing situation is described. Any time the patient begins to become tense, the therapist describes a scene that is both peaceful and relaxing. As soon as the patient is again relaxed, the therapist describes another situation in the hierarchy. This process continues until the patient can feel relaxed when the therapist describes the most anxiety-producing situation.

The following is an example of how desensitization works. A man became very anxious when he had a pain in the middle of his chest. He imagined that he was having a heart attack. Nothing that medical doctors said to him could reduce the anxiety. Then he was placed in a desensitization program and was taught to relax. He was asked to imagine a pain in the lower right part of his abdomen. This produced much less anxiety than when he imagined pain in the middle of his chest. Gradually, he was asked to imagine pain closer and closer to the middle of his chest, each time relaxing his muscles. Eventually, he could imagine heart pain with no anxiety.

Implosive therapy. This type of therapy does not try to banish anxiety from the treatment process. Instead, the therapist attempts to "flood" the patient with anxiety. However, patients experience this anxiety in a safe environment, where no harm can come to them. The idea behind **implosive therapy**

is that the patient experiences the anxiety-provoking situation with no harmful effects. The situation then loses its power to bring about the anxiety. For example, a person who is afraid of riding in elevators is asked to take a short ride on one with the therapist. Conditions are such that no harm can come to the patient. And the therapist constantly reassures the patient while they are actually riding on the elevator. As a result of experiencing anxiety with no ill effects, the patient begins to overcome the fear of riding in elevators.

Simple extinction therapy. The **simple extinction therapy** method of treatment assumes that maladjusted behavior continues only because it is in some way rewarded. It also assumes that the lack of a reward reduces the chances that particular behavior will occur again. For instance, what do you think would happen if an alcoholic did not get some benefit from drinking alcohol?

In one study, nurses on a ward of a mental hospital were instructed to ignore statements by disturbed patients that were not normal and to reward statements considered normal. There was a marked drop in abnormal statements by patients and an increase in normal statements.

Modeling. One other technique of behavior therapy, which also involves learning, is called **modeling.** It consists of changing behavior as a result of watching and imitating the behavior of a model.

For example, modeling can be used if you are afraid of snakes and want to change that behavior. In one experiment, a group of young adults who were afraid of snakes was divided into several groups. One group watched a film in which child and adult models handled live but harmless snakes. The models clearly enjoyed handling the snakes. Subjects in this group were trained in relaxing techniques. They were told to have the film stopped whenever they felt tense, reverse the film to the beginning, and then relax. A second group imitated the models'

This man is attempting to overcome his fear of flying by sitting in an airplane seat. He may eventually even come to enjoy flying.

behavior. They actually handled the snakes in a series of situations that went from less fearful to more fearful. For example, they handled the snakes first with gloves, then with bare hands. Another group was used as the control group and received no special treatment. The results showed that fear of snakes was reduced in the first two groups. The second group, which handled the snakes, had the greatest reduction in fear. A follow-up study later revealed that the fear of snakes had not returned.

Group Therapy

Another type of therapy, **group therapy,** deals with groups of individuals at the same time. It is used especially with people who have developed unsuccessful ways of interacting with others. Sometimes group therapy is used in addition to individual treatment in psychotherapy. Other times it is used as the sole method of treatment. It has the advantage of being less expensive than individual therapy. And it provides a more social setting in which to work out problems.

Encounter groups. *Encounter groups* are also known as T-groups (training groups) or sensitivity groups. There are usually around ten to fifteen people in such groups. A group leader encourages each person to explore his or her own feelings and motives, as well as those of the other group members. This is done in an atmosphere of love and understanding on the part of everyone in the group. Members are asked to be aware of feelings they usually don't express in public because of fear of punishment or guilt. In this way, they learn to express their true feelings and to develop better social relationships.

Family therapy. This is a special form of group therapy that involves one or two therapists and all members of a family group, including the patient. The entire family participates in this therapy because the patient's problems are thought to be part of a general maladjustment of the family group. *Family therapy* is an attempt to help family members better understand their relationships with one another and to work out common problems. Parents may observe their children under controlled conditions. Children may observe the interactions of their parents. Videotapes may be used to show behavior to all family members. And each member of the family may interact with one or both therapists (usually one male and one female).

Psychodrama. This is another type of therapy that may involve small groups of individuals. *Psychodrama* permits patients to act out their problems by playing roles in realistic situations. It provides the therapist with information about the patient. And it allows patients to act out their emotions instead of talking about them. They may play the part of a disturbed father, a child, or any other of a variety of roles that are related to their emotional problems.

Mental Hospitals and Community Centers

In the earlier days of our country, conditions in "insane asylums" were very bad. Pioneer work in improving conditions was done between 1840 and 1881 by a brave schoolteacher, Dorothea Dix. She visited jails, asylums, and poorhouses and taught a Sunday school class in a women's prison. Shocked at the conditions she found, she began to campaign for improvement. Through her efforts, public interest was aroused. Millions of dollars were raised to build suitable hospitals. A resolution presented by Congress in 1901 described her as "among the noblest examples of humanity in all history."

Another important figure was Clifford Beers, a man who experienced mental illness himself. After his recovery, he decided to help others. In a famous book, *A Mind That Found Itself*, he described his own behavior disorder and the undesirable treatment he received in three typical institutions of that day. In 1909, Clifford Beers founded the National Committee for Mental Hygiene, an organization that did much to promote mental health in the United States.

Treatment in mental hospitals today. Since then, there have been tremendous improvements in the handling of emotionally disturbed people. Some mental hospitals have increased their facilities to meet the recreational, educational, vocational, and therapeutic needs of patients. They now provide a

Community clinics and mental hospitals can make use of the latest research in treating patients with personality disturbances.

TREATMENT OF
PSYCHOLOGICAL DISTURBANCES

larger variety of recreational activities. They offer course work, which can be applied toward obtaining a high school or college diploma. They also use many of the types of therapy described here.

More and more such hospitals are attempting to operate like a community. They are bringing all the programs of the hospital together into a total treatment program. The hospital environment becomes an important part of the treatment. Open wards permit patients to move about the hospital freely. Patients are encouraged to help themselves and to participate voluntarily in treatment programs. The idea is to create a social situation in the hospital that is similar to the one in which patients will live when they are released from the hospital.

Eventually, most hospitalized patients will return to life outside the hospital. So hospital staffs try to learn as much as they can about the lives the patients will lead when released. This involves getting to know the patients' family and friends, possible employers, conditions of employment, and other social aspects of the patients' future life. Staff members encourage patients to leave the hospital and not to use it as an escape from society.

Community facilities for treatment. In addition to mental hospitals, there are many other facilities designed to help people in need of treatment. Community mental health centers provide outpatient care—the patient visits the center for treatment but lives at home. Such centers also provide consultation and educational programs. If needed, emergency care and partial hospitalization are also available. Personnel at mental health centers include psychologists, psychiatrists, social workers, and nurses.

Another type of program involves bringing mental health services to the people, rather than having people come to the centers. A community official may go to the lower socioeconomic areas of a city, explaining the various mental health programs available to community members. Local community service centers are often set up.

In one large midwestern city, a new type of treatment clinic shows promise. Psychiatric patients can walk into the Continuing Care Clinic there and receive therapy, even without an appointment. The same patient sees different therapists. Patients are therefore less likely to develop a dependency on one particular therapist. In addition, the waiting room of this clinic has a pleasant atmosphere in which patients can establish social relationships in an informal setting. Considerably fewer of these patients have had to be readmitted to mental hospitals since the clinic began.

So far we have discussed many types of therapy for treating psychological disturbances. There are, however, a number of others. For example, there is occupational therapy, dance therapy, and art therapy. Although they vary in their specific techniques, they are all aimed at helping people make better adjustments.

The Effectiveness of Different Therapies

Trying to evaluate how well any one type of therapy works is a very difficult task. The effectiveness of therapy depends on many factors. These factors include the particular type of psychological disturbance, the length of time the individual has had the disorder, and what forms of treatment the person may have had. But in general, the majority of patients are improved by the treatment procedures they receive.

Medical therapy. The most effective type of therapy for reducing the symptoms of psychotic disorders is drug therapy. The use of antipsychotic drugs often calms very excited schizophrenic or manic patients within two days, to the point where they can benefit from psychotherapy. Unfortunately, some types of drugs have side effects. They may produce sleepiness and withdrawal (when stopped after lengthy usage). Antidepressant drugs that act very rapidly have caused some

Dance therapy is a form of treatment that involves bodily movement in expressing and working through emotional disturbances.

side effects, such as excitement and increased anxiety.

Some individuals also object to the use of drugs because they treat the symptoms of disorders rather than the causes. But regardless of these arguments, drugs have been one of the most helpful aids to the recovery of individuals with personality disturbances.

Electroconvulsive shock therapy has proven effective mainly in treating depressive individuals. The improvement rate has been as high as 90 percent. However, as the use of antidepressant drugs has increased, the use of this method has declined.

Psychotherapy. Psychotherapy does not work for everyone. It is most successful with people who are able to express their feelings, are above average in ability, voluntarily seek help, and are not too withdrawn. Its success has also been related to a person's socioeconomic status. A larger percentage of people in the lower socioeconomic classes drop out of psychotherapy sooner than middle-class or upper-class people. Some psychotherapists believe this is due partly to the difficulty such persons have in developing future goals. But it also may be due to the fact that a larger percentage of lower-class people are assigned to less experienced therapists. In addition, many people in the lower socioeconomic classes may stop psychotherapy because they can't afford to pay for lengthy treatment.

There are both advantages and disadvantages to specific psychotherapy techniques.

Text continues on page 384.

Case Study: Focus on Research

YOU ARE WHAT YOU EAT

It was a typical school day for seven-year-old Eric. He constantly interrupted his teacher and shouted out several wrong answers to arithmetic problems. He also ran up and down the aisles, spending more time out of his seat than in it.

Many children display some of these behaviors at various times. Eric's case, though, is different. Whereas most children can control their behavior, Eric cannot because he is suffering from hyperkinesis.

Hyperkinesis affects a considerable number of children today. It is a behavior pattern that is characterized by excessive activity. A hyperkinetic, or hyperactive, child is constantly on the go—excitable, impulsive, and irritable. Such a child is easily distracted, and thus has a very short attention span. For these reasons, hyperkinetic children usually

Dr. Feingold might argue not only that an apple a day keeps the doctor away, but that the consumption of only wholesome foods might prevent hyperkinesis as well.

do poorly in school, although their intelligence is often above normal.

It is not known just how many hyperkinetic children there are in the United States. One estimate has placed the total at 5 million. Nor do experts know what causes this behavior pattern. The first physician who described it in the early 1900's linked this pattern to brain tumors, epilepsy, and injury to the brain. (Such conditions can lead to hyperactivity, but many hyperkinetic children show no brain damage at all.)

Another suggested cause includes emotional disturbance. Still other researchers believe that the condition results from a chemical imbalance. The chief evidence for this conclusion is that over half the hyperactive children treated with drugs show dramatic improvement.

In the past, drugs had been the major way of treating hyperkinesis. Drug therapy, however, has many shortcomings. For one thing, the expense can be considerable. In addition, often the drugs have undesirable side effects, ranging from sleepiness and headaches to muscle spasms and hallucinations. Worst of all is the possibility of drug dependency. Will a hyperactive child be hooked on drugs for the rest of his or her life?

One physician, Ben Feingold, came up with a very different treatment, although accidentally. A specialist in allergies, he had developed a restricted diet for his allergic patients that involved a dramatic change in eating habits. Among other things, his patients were required to eliminate from their diets all foods and beverages containing artificial flavorings and colorings. But the results were worthwhile—Feingold's patients seemed to improve markedly.

The diet seemed to have other beneficial effects as well. Some of the allergic children that Feingold treated were also hyperkinetic. The diet seemed to help their behavior problems, too.

Many families with hyperactive children adopted what came to be called the Feingold diet. The change was not easy, since artificial colors and flavors are added to so much American food. Most breakfast cereals, baked goods, cheeses, ice cream, luncheon meats, and soft drinks all contain additives. Mothers found themselves making everything from mayonnaise to candy. But the records they kept showed a great improvement in their children's behavior.

Feingold was convinced that he had found a solution to the problem of hyperkinesis. And his solution seemed to make sense. Hyperkinesis had become a serious problem only after World War II—when food additives also became much more common than they had been earlier.

The Feingold hypothesis has many critics, though. These researchers argue that Feingold's methods were not as scientific as they should have been.

In one test researchers went to great lengths to ensure unbiased results. They alternated between the Feingold diet and a control diet. They put whole families on the diets, without telling them which one they were on. They cleared out kitchens and delivered a family's food supplies each week.

In evaluating the subjects, they used not only parents' reports, but also teachers' observations and a series of laboratory tests. After studying 36 school-age children, they concluded that the Feingold diet had had no effect. However, there was some improvement among the 10 pre-schoolers they tested.

At present, it would seem that diet therapy, at least in treating hyperkinesis, is an interesting but unproven approach. For many families, however, following the Feingold plan had positive results. Its emphasis on fresh meats, fruits, and vegetables helped them break the "junk food" habit and learn to enjoy good, nutritious meals.

SOURCE: B. Feingold, *Why Your Child Is Hyperactive,* New York: Random House, 1975; J. Preston Harley et al., "Hyperkinesis and Food Additives: Testing the Feingold Hypothesis," *Pediatrics,* 1978, 61, 818–827.

Activity in children is normal. It is only extreme overactivity that is considered hyperkinesis.

During group therapy sessions, individuals share their thoughts and feelings about themselves and about other members of the group.

Psychoanalysis is most effective with people of high ability who do not suffer from a severe psychological disturbance, who are highly motivated to improve, and who can easily express themselves verbally. But it is a long and expensive form of therapy. It has been criticized for being based on a negative view of people and for lacking scientific evidence to support its effectiveness. In psychoanalysis, the possibility of a patient having to return when future problems arise is higher than in client-centered therapy. In client-centered therapy, patients learn to solve their own problems. So when problems come up in the future, client-centered patients are more likely to be able to solve them. However, the most serious cases are usually not seen in client-centered therapies or by psychoanalysts.

One criticism of transactional analysis (TA) is that there is no evidence at present that people undergoing TA actually change their behavior. Studies indicate that insight takes place. But there is no proof that insight produces a change in behavior.

Behavior therapy. This type of therapy has three distinct advantages. First, it treats a specific behavior, which can be measured. As a result, it is easier to conduct research on the success or failure of this approach. A second advantage is that it requires a shorter period of time than psychotherapy. Finally, it is easier to train people to use this approach than to use most psychotherapy techniques.

Treating people by behavior therapy results in a success rate of from 50 to 90 percent, depending on the particular behavior pattern being treated. Certain forms of behavior therapy are especially successful with certain kinds of problems. For instance, desensitization is useful in treating avoidance behavior. And aversive techniques are useful in learning to control unruly impulses.

A common criticism of behavior therapy is that, when used alone, it treats the symptoms but not the actual causes of psychological disturbances. Some individuals object to behavior therapy techniques because they believe that such procedures violate human rights. They see them as a social regulation of behavior by computers, data banks, news media, industry, and government. They fear that someday these techniques may be used by a few select people to control the behavior of others in the society.

Group therapy. One difficulty in evaluating the effectiveness of group therapy is that, in many cases, the people who participate are not interviewed enough beforehand. No one really knows the extent of their psychological disturbances. So it is hard to judge how effective group therapy is in changing them.

Encounter groups have been criticized for sometimes using nonprofessional leaders who lack the training to deal with many types of emotionally disturbed people. Others claim that group therapy has only short-term effects. They say that when participants leave the group and go back to the world of reality, they act in the same old ways. In one study, college students participated in encounter groups with trained leaders. One-third of the students had positive growth, one-third had no growth, and one-third developed more negative feelings toward themselves and others. In addition, several studies have found that some group members have actually shown an increase in emotional disturbance after participating in group therapy. But we might ask: "Would these individuals have shown greater emotional disturbance if they had not participated in group therapy?"

If we consider the kinds of treatment given for psychological disturbances only twenty years ago, and the conditions found in mental hospitals today, we can see that great strides have been made. But we have much further to go. In the future, more and better treatment will be possible.

Summary

Various kinds of therapy are available for people seeking treatment for psychological disturbances. Medical therapy involves treating the body through medicine. Drug therapy and electroconvulsive shock therapy are two aspects of this approach.

Psychotherapy consists of different approaches to help people understand their problems and change their behavior. By adjusting their behavior, people can then lead more well-adjusted lives. Psychoanalysis, play therapy, client-centered therapy, and transactional analysis are all forms of psychotherapy.

In behavior therapy, people are taught to unlearn certain behaviors that are causing them problems. Behavior therapists rely on rewards and punishments to bring about desired changes in their patients. Among the approaches they might take are aversive therapy, desensitization, implosive therapy, simple extinction therapy, and modeling.

Group therapy deals with groups of people at the same time. Some common forms of group therapy include encounter groups, family therapy, and psychodrama.

Some emotionally disturbed people are treated in mental hospitals. In addition to mental hospitals, today there are often other community facilities for treatment.

Each of the therapeutical approaches has its advantages and disadvantages. The effectiveness of each therapy depends on many factors, including the kind of psychological disturbance a person has had, the length of time the disorder has been present, and the other forms of treatment the person already has had.

It has such a bad image in the public mind that mental health professionals call it "electroconvulsive therapy," or "ECT," leaving the word "shock" unspoken. Many people believe that ECT is no longer used in psychiatry, yet as many as 100,000 patients receive the procedure every year. In "The Case for ECT" (*Psychology Today,* June 1985), psychologist Harold Sackeim explains what ECT actually involves, and why it is so controversial.

Electroconvulsive therapy (ECT) is the most controversial treatment today for psychological disorders, the subject of frequent, impassioned debate among mental-health professionals, the public and the press. . . .

Many people believe that ECT is barbaric and repugnant. In movies, such as *One Flew over the Cuckoo's Nest,* the treatment is shown as physically and emotionally brutal, imposed on unwilling patients to keep them quiet, to make zombies of malcontents. Despite this image, ECT has been used continuously for more than 40 years, longer than any other physical treatment available for mental illness. It has achieved this longevity because when administered properly, for the right illness (primarily major depression), it can help as much or more than any other treatment.

The aim of ECT is to produce a seizure in the brain, much like the one that occurs spontaneously in some types of epilepsy. A small electric current, typically lasting one second or less, passes through two electrodes placed on the patient's head. Only a fraction of this current reaches the brain because most of it is deflected by the skull. The current excites neural tissue, triggering a seizure that typically lasts about one minute. Experience has shown that without a seizure, ECT proves ineffective. Why this is true remains uncertain. . . .

Since seizures cause the body to convulse intensely, patients receive general anesthesia and muscle relaxants before the current is applied. This allows them to sleep through the procedure and minimizes convulsions, which might otherwise cause broken bones. . . .

Patients with major depression generally receive ECT three times a week for two to four weeks. Given the treatment's brevity and the fact patients sleep through it, it is not surprising that when psychiatrists surveyed 166 former patients in Scotland, 82 percent rated ECT equally or less upsetting than going to the dentist. . . .

If ECT is so effective in treating depression—at times life saving—and if the negative effects are limited, why is there such an intense controversy about the treatment? The fact that the treatment is used for psychological disorders is surely important. Would there be as much outcry, for example, if ECT were used primarily for a life-threatening neurological illness, such as Parkinson's disease?

The fact that ECT is done to, rather than by, patients may also contribute to the controversy. When doctors prescribe medication, people typically take it themselves, with subtle and largely unseen effects. In ECT one human passes electricity into the brain of another. Some of the effects, such as seizure and temporary confusion, are clear and immediately apparent.

The concept of applying electricity to the brain, no doubt calling up images of electrocution, must frighten many. And the fact that such a radical treatment is used to alter something as intimate as mood may threaten our sense of being the masters of our psychological destiny.

Source Review

1. What type of illness is ECT most commonly used to treat?

2. How painful and terrifying is ECT to those who have actually experienced it?

3. Why is ECT treatment controversial?

CHAPTER 17

REVIEWING TERMS

therapy
medical therapy
drug therapy
electroconvulsive shock
   therapy
psychotherapy
psychoanalysis
free association
dream interpretation

resistance
transference
play therapy
client-centered therapy
reflection of feelings
transactional analysis (TA)
behavior therapy
aversive therapy
desensitization

implosive therapy
simple extinction therapy
modeling
group therapy
encounter group
family therapy
psychodrama

CHECKING FACTS

1. Describe the different forms of medical therapy.

2. Describe some different techniques that psychoanalysts use to treat patients.

3. How does client-centered therapy attempt to treat psychological disturbances?

4. What principle underlies transactional analysis? Describe a transactional analysis session.

5. What approach do behavior therapists take in treating psychological disturbances? Describe five forms of behavior therapy.

6. When using implosive therapy, why do therapists "flood" the patients with anxiety?

7. When is group therapy used? Describe three different forms of group therapy.

8. How have the conditions in mental hospitals changed over the years?

9. Discuss some of the alternatives to mental hospitals.

10. What are some advantages and disadvantages of medical therapy? Of psychotherapy?

11. What are the advantages of behavior therapy? What is a common criticism?

APPLYING YOUR KNOWLEDGE

1. With the supervision of your teacher, create a therapy situation with another student that the two of you (one as the therapist and one as the patient) will perform in front of the class. The mock therapy session might involve such things as fear of heights or closed-in places. During the therapy session, and by pre-arrangement, stop the session five times, for about one minute each time, and have students write down what they would do next if they were the therapist.

After the session is completed, have class members compare notes on what they wrote down. Discuss points on which a large number of class members disagree. This activity gives you a chance to consider some of the procedures used in therapy sessions. However, remember that you are not a therapist and that this is only an exercise.

2. Hold a panel discussion that focuses on some of the ethical and legal questions involved in the use of drug therapy, electroconvulsive shock therapy, and aversive therapy. Complete library research beforehand, and make sure to explore all arguments for and against the use of each form of treatment.

3. To understand how desensitization works, make a list of related situations that cause you to feel a bit overanxious. Arrange the list from the least anxiety-provoking situation to the most anxiety-provoking situation. Then, beginning with the first entry, try to relax while imagining yourself in each circumstance. Eventually, you should feel very comfortable when thinking about all entries. By practicing this procedure, you might feel more at ease when you encounter these situations in real life.

4. Suppose you are a therapist who is assigned the following case. An institutionalized patient, although capable of doing so, refuses to walk to the cafeteria and feed herself at mealtime. If the nurses neglect to hand-feed her, she turns to self-starvation, which will eventually result in death. How might you use extinction therapy or modeling to bring about normal mealtime behavior?

5. Read a book, either fiction or nonfiction, about a person who suffered from mental illness. Prepare a written report describing the method of therapy that was used and the person's reactions to the treatment.

6. In order to clarify how free association works, you might try this activity. Have a friend give you a sealed list of ten emotion-invoking words, such as "parent," "accident," "knife," and "love." Do not look at the list until you are in a place where you are completely alone and cannot be overheard. Then open the list of words. As you read each word, say aloud the first thing you think of. Are you able to let yourself respond freely to each word, regardless of whether or not your reactions seem logical?

THINKING CRITICALLY ABOUT PSYCHOLOGY

1. **Interpreting Ideas** Imagine an individual with a particular psychological disturbance who is undergoing some form of treatment for that disturbance. What changes in behavior would you look for to show that the person has improved, even slightly?

2. **Classifying Ideas** Suppose you were going to pursue a career in treating psychological disturbances. Would you be more interested in a medical approach, researching chemical imbalances in the body and using drug therapy? Or would you emphasize a psychoanalytical approach, investigating the unconscious as the basis of psychological disturbances? What are your reasons for preferring this approach?

3. **Formulating Ideas** What procedures could be devised to help protect the rights of patients before, during, and after treatment?

4. **Forming Opinions** Assume that you

have all the money you need to spend. What programs would you recommend to improve the mental health facilities in your community?

5. **Identifying Ideas** What do you consider to be the most important problems involved in the treatment of individuals with psychological disturbances? Explain your answer.

DEVELOPING SKILLS IN PSYCHOLOGY

Using the *Citation Index*

Psychology students—like psychologists—may be especially interested in the work of a particular theorist, therapist, or researcher. They want to know as much as possible about that psychologist's contributions and the extent to which other psychologists have worked with his or her ideas. In the following exercise, you will learn how they proceed.

Assume that you are particularly interested in Carl Rogers. You could use the card catalog in the library to locate books on or about Carl Rogers, but that would not help you identify current journal articles on his work. You could also look up Carl Rogers's name in the *Psychological Abstracts*, but that approach could be very time-consuming.

The most effective approach would be to use the *Citation Index*, which is available in some public libraries and many college and university libraries. This reference journal lists information on sources citing Carl Rogers. Full reference information is given about each source citing the published articles of psychologists in major professional journals.

If possible, examine the *Citation Index* for the last several years and note if journal articles are still citing Carl Rogers. If you find any citations, read the original article to learn more about Carl Rogers's work.

READING FURTHER ABOUT PSYCHOLOGY

Axline, Virginia, *Play Therapy,* Revised Edition, Ballantine, New York, 1974. Through the use of case histories, the author discusses play therapy, a technique in which disturbed children "play out" their feelings in order to learn about and accept themselves.

Corsini, Raymond J., editor, *Current Psychotherapies,* Third Edition, F. E. Peacock, Itasca, Ill., 1984. A detailed survey of 13 major types of psychotherapy, written by leading practitioners in the field.

Gilbert, Sara D., *What Happens in Therapy,* Lothrop, New York, 1982. Examines common misconceptions about various kinds of psychological therapy through the use of simply written sample situations that involve young adults.

Kovel, Joel, *A Complete Guide to Therapy: From Psychotherapy to Behavior Modification,* Pantheon, New York, 1977. Provides answers to many of the questions people ask about psychotherapy.

Kushner, Harold, *When Bad Things Happen to Good People,* Avon Books, New York, 1983. Written by a man whose son died after a ten-year bout with a rare disease, this book discusses a valuable therapeutic perspective for dealing with tragedy.

Rogers, Carl R., *On Becoming a Person: A Therapist's View of Psychotherapy,* Houghton Mifflin, Boston, 1961. In this classic book, Rogers presents the main ideas of his humanistic personality theory and of psychotherapy.

Szasz, Thomas S., *The Myth of Mental Illness: Foundations of a Theory of Personal Conduct,* Harper & Row, New York, 1984. Challenges the traditional ways of diagnosing and treating psychological disorders.

Valenstein, Elliot S., *Great and Desperate Cures: The Rise and Decline of Psychosurgery and Other Radical Treatments for Mental Illness,* Basic Books, New York, 1986. In the past, one of the major treatments for mental illness was the surgical removal of parts of the brain. These operations left thousands of men and women seriously brain damaged. The author explains how and why these crude operations became an acceptable form of treatment.

Using the Skills of a Psychologist

Unit 6 Learning How Values Affect Behavior

As you learned in Chapter 16, norms can affect behavior. Norms, it will be recalled, are the rules that societies establish to determine acceptable standards of behavior. Behavior can also be affected by a society's "values." Values are the beliefs of a particular culture about what is good or bad, desirable or undesirable. For example, people in the United States value hard work, honesty, democracy, and achievement, among other things. People often act in ways that express and uphold their values. We say the Pledge of Allegiance and stand when our national anthem is being sung to show that we value loyalty to the United States. We tell the truth because we value honesty and integrity. These are positive ways of adapting to and expressing values.

However, trying to achieve the values of a society can also affect behavior in a negative way. For example, people in the United States value success. One way in which success is measured is through the possession of money and things. People normally work very hard to earn money and buy what they want. Some people, though, use deviant behavior to acquire money and things. They may break the law and steal money from other people. Even though they may achieve the goal of success (as measured by possessions), they use deviant, or abnormal behavior to do so.

Recall what you have learned about eating disorders from Chapter 16. People who suffer from anorexia nervosa are obsessed with thinness and use many means to avoid eating food. Some scientists believe that young people try to achieve the goal of thinness because it is highly valued in our society. As you learned from your reading, people who suffer from this disorder tend to be perfectionists. Because thinness is valued in our society, these people may come to think that the thinner they are, the closer they come to being perfect. The goal of thinness then becomes an obsession and the person is unable to stop the behavior. Trying to achieve this value affects behavior in a negative, and life-threatening, way.

What evidence do we have that thinness is valued in our society and that this value affects behavior? We can point to the number of weight-reducing products available and the number of diet books in print. We can examine statistics on the number of people involved in weight-reducing programs. We can look to advertisements that show only thin people having fun. We can examine medical evidence on the number of young people who are suffering from anorexia nervosa. If a researcher from the future could look back on this evidence in order to understand the values of our present-day society, he or she would conclude that thinness was desirable during this time period.

Thinness is valued in our society because it is considered to be one aspect of beauty. Beauty has been highly valued throughout time. However, like norms, values change over time. The definition of what is beautiful has changed from century to century, even from decade to decade. Values, like norms, also vary from society to society. What is considered beautiful in our society may be considered ugly in another society.

To learn how values can affect behavior, each student should choose a different present-day society or some society from the past. With the direction of your teacher, research the definition of beauty within that society. Write a report that outlines your evidence for concluding that the society defines beauty in a particular way. Also include in your report the ways in which people now seek, or sought in the past, to achieve beauty.

REVIEWING THE UNIT

1. According to the study discussed in Chapter 14, how did frustration affect the behavior of preschool children?

2. Is a person's frustration tolerance the same in every situation? Explain.

3. How might compensation be used in an undesirable way? Cite a specific example from the text.

4. What determines stress?

5. Why is the DSM-III classification system useful for doctors?

6. Why are intravenous drug users in particular danger?

7. How was public awareness of the need for mental hospitals and community centers aroused?

8. On what factors does the effectiveness of therapy depend?

CONNECTING IDEAS

1. **Contrasting Ideas** How does frustration differ from stress?

2. **Summarizing Ideas** What are some characteristics of type A behavior?

3. **Identifying Ideas** What are some of the current treatments being used for substance abuse?

4. **Understanding Ideas** How can phobias interfere with daily life? Cite some specific examples from the text.

PRACTICING RESEARCH SKILLS

Review the text material concerning the conditions in jails, asylums, and poorhouses in the early days in our country. Then conduct library research on the history of mental illness in the United States. Note the changes that have occurred in perceptions of the mentally ill over time. Discover also how and why changes in the treatment of mental illness have occurred. Pay special attention to the development of modern-day mental hospitals and community centers.

Summarize your findings in a report that focuses on the contrast between how mental illness was perceived in the past and how it is perceived today. Try to think of ways in which the treatment of mentally ill people could be improved even more in the future.

FINDING OUT MORE

You may wish to contact the following organization for additional information about the material in this unit.

American Council for Drug Education (ACDE)
5820 Hubbard Dr.
Rockville, MD 20852

Unit 7

SOCIAL BEHAVIOR

Chapter 18 BEHAVIOR IN SMALL GROUPS
Chapter 19 SOCIAL INFLUENCE
Chapter 20 SOCIAL INTERACTION

Chapter 18

BEHAVIOR IN SMALL GROUPS

Chapter Focus

This chapter presents:

- **the influence that small groups have**
- **various kinds of small groups**
- **the effectiveness, advantages, and disadvantages of small groups**
- **roles and communication patterns within small groups**

Remember the game of telephone? Somebody whispered a message into your ear. You then whispered what you heard to the next person, and so on down the line. By the time the message got to the last person, very often it was quite distorted.

The number of people in the group usually affected the results. If just three or four people were passing along messages, the messages may have survived intact. But if there were many people playing the game, the original messages usually underwent transformation.

Small groups play a valuable role in our society. Because our society is so complex, it is often very difficult for researchers to study it as a whole. As a result, they often focus on small groups.

What do we mean by a small group? Psychologically speaking, a **small group** may be defined as a gathering or unit of individuals who have face-to-face communication with one another, who have a feeling of belonging to the group, and who share a common goal. The group may be as small as only two people or as large as perhaps 15 or 20 people.

In this chapter we will examine behavior in small groups. We will be concerned with such topics as kinds of small groups, the effectiveness of small groups, group roles, and group communication patterns.

The Influence of Small Groups

The family is a small group. Many high school classes can be described as small groups. So can camera, athletic, foreign language, mathematics, and music groups. Sometimes churches, too, qualify as small groups. But usually religious memberships are too large to qualify as small groups. However, within any given church or synagogue, there are usually small-group organizations for certain age levels or special interests.

Small groups have existed throughout history. In some cases, they have developed into established organizations. Our early American history provides one example. In the New England colonies, the functions of local government were often carried out in a small group—the town meeting. All the citizens of the town met to discuss and vote on

When talking to someone, the amount of distance between you will be influenced by the sex of the person, how well you know that person, and where you are.

local matters. As our country has increased in population, we have had to turn to small representative groups to perform many of our government functions. Small groups such as committees, councils, and panels have now replaced the town meeting in many places. They have become an essential part of our government.

Influence in a two-person group. The smallest possible group is a two-person group, or *dyad.* Even a group of this size may influence our behavior. Suppose you are walking along a sidewalk with a friend or acquaintance. Would you walk faster or more slowly than if you were walking alone? Of course, many factors enter into our speed of walking. The time of day. The temperature. The width of the sidewalk. In one research study, factors such as these were controlled. The subjects consisted of 24 males and 24 females who walked alone. There were also 24

pairs of male walkers and 24 pairs of female walkers. The results showed that on the average, a man walking with another man walked more slowly than when alone. And a woman walking with another woman walked more slowly than when walking alone. This is a very simple situation. But it does illustrate how even the smallest possible group—a two-person group—can have an influence on the behavior of a member of the group.

The influence of distance between people. If you are talking with someone, do you feel more comfortable when you are quite close to the person? Or do you prefer to be at a considerable distance? Your answer may depend on a number of factors. On how well you know the person. On whether you approach the person or whether the person approaches you. And probably on whether the person is the same sex as you. Location, too, seems to be an important factor, as the following study illustrates.

In one experiment, 96 college students were asked to meet and talk with another student about a topic of interest to both. The subjects didn't know the true nature of the experiment. Two locations for the meetings were used. One location was an enclosed area, a room. The other location was in the open—a sidewalk that crossed an open area on a college campus. Assistants hidden nearby were able to estimate fairly accurately how far apart the members of each dyad stood while talking. In the open location, the subject was told that the other person would be standing near a yellow cross that had been chalked on the sidewalk. In the enclosed location, the other person was standing near the far end of the room. The subjects who met in the open environment stood and talked at a closer distance (about 61 centimeters, or 24 inches) than those in the enclosed environment (about 132 centimeters, or 52 inches). The experimenters concluded that such enclosed areas as offices, clinic rooms, and doctors' examining rooms may be too small to allow comfortable interaction to take place in such person-to-person situations.

What is the effect of putting objects between people? When you are engaged in conversation with someone, does it make any difference if there is an object, such as a table, between you? Consider the following experiment. The subjects were 120 unmarried male college students. They were divided into dyads on the basis of similar attitudes. Then the dyads were assigned to one of four conversation groups. Each group had a different seating arrangement. One was a close seating distance (86 centimeters, or 34 inches from chair back to chair back). A second was a close seating distance with a 76-centimeter (30-inch) table between them. A third was a far seating distance (163 centimeters, or 64 inches) without a table between them. The fourth was a far seating distance with a 152-centimeter (60-inch) table between them.

Each subject was given a list of 25 topics, varying in intimacy. He was to select seven of them to discuss with his partner for 20 minutes. The conversations were taped. Later they were analyzed for degree of intimacy. In addition, each subject answered a questionnaire concerning his reaction to his partner. The results indicated little difference between the close seating and far seating distances. Nor was there much difference in reactions based on the two sizes of tables. But having a table between the students did make a difference in their conversation and in their reactions to each other. The table served as a psychological barrier between the individuals. They felt more distant from each other when there was a table between them.

How does the size and makeup of the group affect behavior? In many restaurants, it is expected behavior to tip the waiter or waitress—usually about 15 percent of the amount of the food bill. Who do you think leave larger tips—people who dine alone, or people who dine in groups?

In one study, 11 waiters were asked to keep a record of the amount of each tip they received and how many people were at the table in each case. They received tips from 396 people. The number of people at each table ranged from one to six. The results are summed up in the graph on page 397. Individuals dining alone tipped an average of almost 19 percent. Groups of six people tipped less than 14 percent. It may be that individuals in a group feel less responsibility for tipping than individuals dining alone, and so leave a smaller percentage. Another finding of the study was that groups of all women tipped the most (16.3 percent). Mixed groups with fewer men than women tipped the least (12.8 percent). It appears that the makeup of a group as well as its size is important.

Do small groups affect whether you lie or tell the truth? How often have you heard someone say, "Everybody else is doing it, so why shouldn't I?" Of course, by "everybody" the person usually means everyone in a small group of which he or she is a member. Even at that, probably everyone in the group is not doing whatever it is. We often try to get rid of our feelings of guilt for wrongdoing by saying that everyone else is acting the same way.

One study compared the emotional reactions of telling a lie along with everyone in the group to telling a lie when some members of the group told the truth. The subjects were 94 male college students. They were told that some of them would play the role of a spy. Others would play the role of an innocent person accused of being a spy. Each person was given a list of 24 commonly used words. The spies were required to memorize six of these words as code words to be kept secret. The innocent people did not learn any code words.

Each subject in both groups was asked, "Do any of the following words have special meaning to you?" The subjects were told that if they were caught lying, they would be given an electrical shock. The more lies they told, the greater the shock. All were blindfolded. They gave their "yes" or "no" responses by nodding or shaking their heads. To know if the spies were lying about whether any of the six code words had a special meaning for them, the experimenter used a device that measured physiological changes in the body.

Subjects were tested in small groups of five to seven. Some groups consisted entirely of spies, or people who were required to lie about the code words. Some groups were composed entirely of innocent persons. Since the innocent people didn't know which words were code words, they couldn't lie. Still other groups were composed of both spies and innocent persons. Subjects were told which group they were assigned to. It was found that people in mixed groups showed a much greater physiological reaction to code words than did people in groups of either all spies or all innocents. Individuals showed less physiological reaction when they believed that all other members of the group were giving the same answers as theirs.

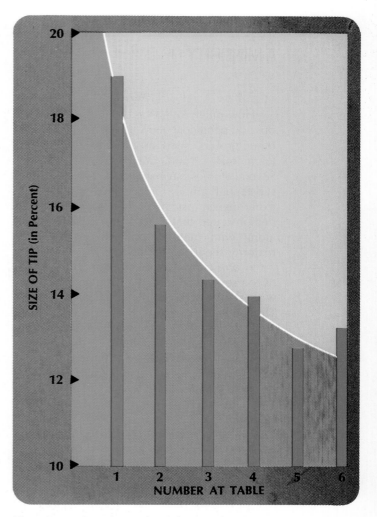

This shows the relationship between the number of people sitting together at a restaurant and the amount of tip they left.

Kinds of Small Groups

There are a number of ways to classify small groups. We will consider only three basic categories. One stresses the reason for forming the group. The second focuses on how membership is determined. The third centers around the group's organization.

Task-oriented and interaction-oriented groups. Small groups that are classified by the purpose for which the individuals have

Text continues on page 400.

Case Study: Focus on Research

A MINORITY OF ONE

How much influence do our friends have on our behavior? How much influence do other groups, such as our classmates, our team mates, and our co-workers have? Several studies have shown that they have a substantial amount indeed. In a series of experiments psychologist Solomon Asch demonstrated that there is a tendency to go along with majority opinion, even if the majority seems to be wrong.

In one classic experiment, groups of between seven and nine male college students were shown 36 big cards, displayed in pairs. The left card in each pair had a single black vertical line. The right one had three lines of different lengths, labeled 1, 2, and 3. The students were asked to call out the number of the line on the right that seemed to match the single line on the left.

The tendency to conform is a strong one. Asch found that this tendency was so strong that people agreed with the majority's opinion even when the majority was obviously wrong.

In actuality, the experiment was rigged. All but one of the students in each group were assisting the experimenter. Thus, when the cards were held up and group members were asked for their choice, all but one knew what response was expected. When the other group members seemed to match the line correctly, the single unsuspecting subject had no problem. He also chose the correct response.

However, sometimes he was faced with a conflict. After a pair of cards was held up and one by one the other subjects called out their responses, he noted a discrepancy. For example, the others all thought that line 1 matched the line on the left card; he, on the other hand, thought that line 3 was the correct choice (and in reality it was). Should he voice his opinion or go along with the majority?

All in all, 123 subjects were tested. In each experiment there was a discrepancy between the majority's answer and the correct answer 12 out of 18 times. How do you think the unsuspecting subjects responded?

The results showed that these subjects gave the same incorrect answers as the rest of the group almost 37 percent of the time. That is, they conformed with the rest of the group, despite their own opinions, in over a third of all trials. Of course, it could be argued that a subject really might have made a mistake in judging the correct line. This, though, was unlikely. Members of a control group who were asked to make similar judgments were correct in 99 percent of their trials.

Individuals—both those who conformed and those who disagreed with the majority—varied a great deal in their responses. About a fourth of the subjects stuck to their guns throughout the test. "I had to call them as I saw them," one young man commented. At the other extreme were those who went along with the group almost all the time. "I'm wrong, they're right," reasoned one. Another subject explained that he yielded to the majority so that he wouldn't "spoil the results." In between were subjects who answered correctly part of the time and incorrectly the rest of the time.

Other experiments conducted by Asch confirmed the powerful influence of group pressure. In the original test, no comparison lines were more than 5 centimeters (2 inches) shorter or longer than the sample line. Yet even when the discrepancy was more glaring —as much as 17.5 centimeters (7 inches)— some subjects still adjusted their answers to match that of the majority.

Under certain circumstances subjects were less likely to yield to group pressure. Studies have shown that a subject was more apt to answer independently if there were fewer people in the group. A subject was also more likely to give the correct response if one of the experimenter's assistants sided with the subject.

This last finding was shown in the following experiment. This time around several men (one at a time) were once again asked to match two lines. Someone was selected from among the group members to act as the subject's partner. (Of course, the subject was unaware of this situation.) Whenever a choice had to be made, the "partner" was instructed to select the correct line. Even though the rest of the group still insisted on an incorrect answer, most of the subjects usually resisted the social pressure to conform with the majority.

Later, as previously arranged, the "partners" switched over to agreeing with the incorrect answers of the majority. The result was an immediate increase in the subjects' errors.

These studies and others like them have shown that the tendency to conform is a strong one. Even those who resisted were upset by the experience. As one person put it: "I felt disturbed, puzzled, separated, like an outcast from the group." It seems no wonder, then, that many people go along with the majority at least some of the time. This is especially true if no one else supports their opinions.

SOURCE: Solomon Asch, "Opinions and Social Pressure," *Scientific American*, 1955, *193*, 31–35.

"I have to call them as I seem them," explains this subject. He was one of the few who stuck to his opinion throughout the study.

come together may be either task-oriented or interaction-oriented. A **task-oriented group** is a group whose main purpose is to perform a specific job or task. One example is a small production unit in an industrial plant. The unit's job is to turn out a specific product that meets the required standards for quality and quantity. The men and women in the small group are there to put out a product. They are generally not involved in the larger problems of the plant's management, design, or sales promotion. Their focus is on their production task.

In a high school, a small committee may be formed to put together the yearbook. The

Which kind of group is illustrated here—task-oriented or interaction-oriented?

members of this small group are not particularly concerned with the larger problems of how to teach journalism or of school administration. They are a task-oriented group. Their purpose is the specific job of getting out the yearbook.

An **interaction-oriented group** is a group whose main purpose is to provide opportunity for social contacts or interaction. For example, the small production group in a plant may form a bowling team. The bowling team has nothing to do with production. Its purpose is to provide pleasant social recreation for its members. In other words, it is an interaction-oriented group. Or, to take another example, high school students may form a small rock group because they want to play music together and talk with one another about music.

Of course, many small groups are task-oriented and interaction-oriented. The men and women in the plant production unit may work together more efficiently because of their interaction as a bowling team. And their bowling team may be better as a result of their work contacts. The high school yearbook committee may provide the school with a yearbook and have a very enjoyable social experience as well. Similarly, a group with the task of helping underprivileged children in the community could make their plans at a supper meeting. Or they could enjoy social contact at a fund-raising dance.

Inclusive and exclusive groups. Another way of classifying groups is in terms of how the group's membership is determined. An **inclusive group** is a group whose members get satisfaction from increasing their activities and trying to include more people. The group generally emphasizes the individual equality of its members.

Take the high school group whose original aim was to put out the yearbook. They may decide to expand their activities and publish a school newspaper. Along with such an increase in the group's activities, there is usually a tendency to increase the size of the group. As a result, some of the new members may be more interested in other aspects of the school than the newspaper. The basis of the group may begin to change. Inclusive small groups have a tendency to grow into larger groups. They then lose some of the purpose and closeness of a small group.

An **exclusive group** is a group whose members get satisfaction from a feeling of being important. Exclusive groups do not permit everyone to join. Or else they permit people to join only if they meet certain requirements. Fraternities, sororities, and certain high school clubs are examples of exclusive groups. So are community groups such as literary societies, business executives clubs, garden clubs, and music organizations. Members of exclusive groups usually get a great deal of satisfaction from the feeling that they belong to a special group.

Exclusive groups frequently emphasize initiations and other ceremonies. At such ceremonies, the members may go through established rituals in special dress. Before initiation, candidates for membership may also have to pay a fee or prove their qualifications.

Exclusive groups can serve the useful purpose of preserving valuable traditions and maintaining some long-established, desirable forms of social behavior. But they can also present serious problems in a democratic society. Exclusive groups are sometimes based on dictatorial standards and biased attitudes. In some cases, these groups assume that certain individuals are better than others simply through birth. They stress only their own achievements, even if these are minor. Often they ignore the many achievements of non-members.

Informal and formal groups. Groups may also be classified by the way they are organized. Small groups may be casual or rigid. A group that is casual with no official structure or deliberately formed organization is an **informal group.** Your group of friends would probably be thought of as an informal group. There are no set rules for group members to follow. Moreover, group members were not forced to become friends.

Instead, they liked one another and the group just "happened to form." In addition, members of the group have no formal functions and interact with one another on a personal level.

In contrast, a **formal group** is a group formed deliberately and with a rigid structure. There are certain rules and established procedures. In addition, people interact on a more limited level. For example, the Social Studies department in your school might be a small formal group. The department may consist of fewer than 15 members with one person in charge and each teacher responsible for certain subject areas. At departmental meetings, the teachers discuss matters that pertain to the whole department.

Within formal groups, however, informal groups may form. The chairperson may play tennis with another member of the department. Or two teachers might become close friends. When this happens, the individuals interact on a personal level and leave behind the roles they played in the formal group setting.

The Effectiveness of Small Groups

How does the size of a small group affect how much it gets done? Does production increase as the size of the group increases?

The size of work groups. You might think that the more members there are in a group, the greater the background of information and the larger the number of ideas that can be presented. And that in a big group, there will be more people to carry out the jobs that the group undertakes. So you might expect that the larger the membership, the more the group can accomplish. But idea production and work output do not necessarily increase with an increase in group size. Idea productivity often gains more slowly as the size of the group grows. That is, with each increase in the size of the group, there is a smaller increase in the number of ideas presented and the amount of work accomplished.

This relationship between size of the group and production of ideas is linked to problems of communication. In very small groups, there is usually enough time for each member to express ideas and to provide the group with whatever special information he or she may have. As the size of the group increases, the time available for each member's participation decreases. In large groups, much of the talking is done by relatively few people. The other members of the group spend much of their time in silence.

Should a small work group have an odd or even number of members? Take the smallest possible group, the dyad. Each member usually has an opportunity to express his or her ideas. In fact, the two members will probably try to avoid any major disagreement. Agreement between two members has some advantages. But it can limit the growth of new ideas. One member of the two-member group may tend to be dominant and the other submissive. The submissive member may give up his or her good ideas and work efforts rather than disagree with the dominant member. Also, the submissive member cannot get support from anyone else.

In a group of three, the members tend to break up into a majority of two and a minority of one. The members of the pair support each other. But the single member has no one for support. Single members may have very good ideas and be willing to work hard. But they are often dominated by the pair. As a result, they may begin to keep their ideas to themselves and to lose interest in the group work.

What happens in groups larger than two or three members? In groups of an even number, there is always the possibility that exactly half the group will disagree with the other half. If neither subgroup is willing to back down on its original position, any votes taken are likely to end in a tie. In odd-numbered groups, a disagreement will cause members to divide into a majority subgroup and a minority subgroup (or single individual). This means that votes cannot end in ties.

The minority members may not like the majority decision. But in groups based on democratic ideals, the minority will nevertheless accept the decision.

Many psychologists believe that the best size for a work committee or work group is usually five. A group of five allows members to know each other personally. It usually allows each member a chance to express ideas. All of the members can feel that they are doing their part in the group. And the group is large enough to be stimulating. Suppose there is a three-to-two difference of opinion. Then the two members of the minority group have the satisfaction of knowing that one other person supported their contribution to the group's work.

However, several factors influence the ideal size of a work group or committee. Under some circumstances, small work groups of seven, nine, eleven, or more members can be very effective. They might actually be more effective than five-person groups. But as the size of the group increases, certain factors must be kept in mind. Most important, each member has more personal relationships to maintain in the group. Less of the total time can be devoted to each of these relationships.

How can you increase the efficiency of group work? There are ways to conduct a group meeting that increase its effectiveness, regardless of the group's size. With skill and planning, groups larger than five can also operate very efficiently.

A common difficulty with small-group meetings is how to control the discussion so that members can join in without taking over. Just trying to begin the meeting can be a problem. Did you ever attend a meeting in which most of the discussion was about everything except the subject matter for which the meeting was called? Before all the members of the group arrived, perhaps those present were talking about jazz musicians or a party they were at recently. Such conversation often serves the useful purpose of establishing warm, friendly relationships. But it may cause the leader of the group some problems in getting the meeting underway. When the leader finally says, "Let's get down to the business of the meeting," someone may respond, "That's a good idea because I have to leave early. But first, what did you think of that mystery on TV last night?"

One way to increase the effectiveness of a meeting is to prepare an agenda and pass it out to members beforehand. The members will then know what work needs to be done in the meeting. An agenda helps to keep the meeting moving forward. It also helps prevent a few members from taking the group's time with their pet ideas.

Another way in which the leader of the group can increase the effectiveness of the meeting is to have all needed materials and information on hand before the meeting begins. Some meetings start off with, "Brian and Maria, will you go find some more chairs," and "David, will you get some paper and a pencil so you can take notes." This shows a lack of planning.

Another technique for small groups is to seat members around a table or even in an open circle. Such seating arrangements permit face-to-face relationships among members. This is an important part of any small group.

Even good small-group meetings can become boring if they go on for a long period of time. It is often a good idea to set a time limit. If the group cannot finish its work in a reasonably short amount of time, it should take a brief break or two. This might include some refreshments. Members who have disagreed with each other during a meeting may come to terms when they relax over juice and a doughnut. Admittedly, it takes a good leader to get the group back to work following a break.

In a small group, there is a tendency to criticize whoever is leading the group. Sometimes giving each person a turn to be the leader increases the efficiency of a small group. Members are more likely to be in-

A small group functions best when all the members have a chance to communicate their ideas and suggestions.

volved in the group if they know that at some point it will be their turn to run it. And during their term as leader, they will work better with the other members because they know what it is like to be in their position.

Belonging to Small Groups

A society is made up of many groups. Individuals join some groups and do not join other groups. What factors determine which groups they will join? The following are several reasons that individuals join certain small groups.

1. Pleasure from activities. Suppose you enjoy such activities as collecting stamps, going camping, or helping people in need. You can join groups whose members like doing the same thing. People can often enjoy their activities more, and accomplish more, in groups than they can acting alone.

2. A feeling of security. There is often security in numbers. People frequently feel more sure of themselves and can protect themselves better if they have other people to back them up. Soldiers on combat duty get some feeling of security from having other members of their unit near them. Players on a basketball team get some feeling of security by knowing that other members of the team will help them try to make winning points.

3. Gaining status. By joining a group whose members have similar interests, an individual may also gain social status. *Status* is a person's standing in a group. A citizen of limited formal education who knows about the historical events of the community may gain status by becoming active in a local historical society. In this group, the individual may meet with history teachers and other well-educated people on an equal or even superior basis.

4. Business purposes. Membership in such organizations as bridge clubs, country clubs, business associations, or civic improvement groups can enable individuals to make social contacts that often turn into business contacts. The insurance salesperson can say, "That was quite a game of golf we had this afternoon. By the way, did I understand you to say that you had very little theft insurance? Perhaps I can help you." Some people join social groups for business purposes. After all, business can also be a social activity.

Some disadvantages of belonging to small groups. Probably our most interesting, pleasurable, and valuable activities are carried on in small groups. But there can be some disadvantages to small-group membership. As we've said, small groups can be very slow in reaching decisions and carrying out work projects. Many good ideas that are suggested in a small group are lost because they are referred to a committee that never gets around to acting on them. In this last case, there are two disadvantages. The member who made the proposal may feel frustrated at what happened to the idea. And the group members lose the benefit of the good idea.

Small groups have other disadvantages related to getting their work done. Sometimes small groups spend too much time discussing minor problems. Then they carelessly rush through major decisions. Or, if the group performs both a social and a work function, some members may be so interested in the social activity that they slow up the work activity. Another disadvantage is that in a small close group, members with differing opinions may give in just to keep the peace. They agree to questionable suggestions rather than risk hurting someone's feelings.

Belonging to small groups can also have the disadvantage of encouraging people to be too one-sided. Individuals become so wrapped up in the activity of a group that their other interests suffer. They may actively take part in only this one small group. For example, Richard is a coin collector. He talks about collecting rare coins all day long—at breakfast, lunch, and dinner. At coffee breaks on the job. Even when he plays bridge, his casual conversation during the evening is

In a small group, sometimes one person is left out. This may be a disadvantage both to the person and the group.

mostly about his coin collection. He generally greets his friends with news of a rare coin he has just acquired. In short, he is not only a coin collector. He is also a bore.

Keeping Small Groups Together

Small groups have certain characteristics that help keep them together and functioning as a unit. We will consider four such characteristics: group cohesiveness, morale, atmosphere, and climate.

Group cohesiveness. *Group cohesiveness* is the mutual, overall attraction that each member feels toward other members of the group. This attraction depends partly on whether the members have common goals.

It also depends on how strongly the members believe that they share a common fate. Small military units often show great cohesiveness because the members have the common goal of specific missions. And they believe that they all share a common fate.

How can cohesiveness be measured? Techniques have been developed for measuring group cohesiveness. One such technique is *sociometry,* which is a research method that measures how individuals perceive, feel, and think about the other members of their group. For example, the members of a group may be asked to indicate which of the members they would prefer to work with or attend a social event with. From such data, a diagram or chart illustrating group relationships, called a *sociogram,* can be constructed.

Suppose we ask the members of a six-person group to indicate secretly which individual they would most prefer to work with on a particular group task. Each circle represents a member of the group. Each arrow indicates the individual's choice of a work partner. A sociogram of this information might look like the following diagram:

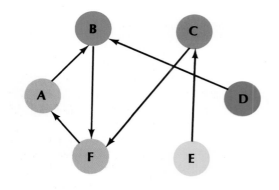

A two-way arrow indicates a mutual choice. That is, both individuals prefer to work with each other. Consider the sociogram that appears below. Which of the two groups do you think is more cohesive? Is there any indication of cliques (close-knit subgroups) within either group?

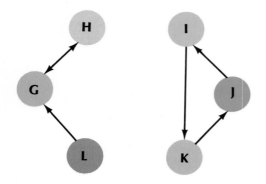

Instead of asking for just one preference, we might have asked members for their first, second, and third choices of partners for a group task. We can also make sociograms that include additional information about the group. For example, a square and a circle can be used to represent the two sexes.

Sociograms do have certain limitations. The relationships indicated may change within a few days, a few weeks, or a few months. Suppose a group of teen-agers are asked to name their best friends. If there is a fight within the group, their choices a few days later might be quite different. Also, in constructing a sociogram, care must be taken in how questions are stated and interpreted. For example, suppose you want to determine the most popular person in your class. You might ask your classmates to indicate on a slip of paper the one person with whom they would most like to study. You are assuming that the most popular person will be selected by the majority of students. But this may not be the case. Your classmates may select the person they believe to be the best student. That person may not necessarily be greatly liked as an individual.

Besides sociometry, there are other ways to measure group cohesiveness. Psychologists have measured group cohesiveness by counting the number of times members use the word "we" rather than "I." Group cohesiveness has also been measured by checking on the number of members who regularly attend group meetings. Or even the number who pay their dues regularly. Still another way is to see how easily group members can identify who are the leaders and who are the isolated members in their group.

Group morale. *Group morale* refers to the attitudes of the individuals in a group, their loyalty to the group, and their willingness to do the group's work. Group morale is somewhat similar to group cohesiveness. But morale usually emphasizes the task orientation of the group. The morale of military units refers to their willingness to work together on an assignment, regardless of how unpleasant or dangerous it may be. The morale of a student body means the willingness of the students to work together on the tasks assigned to them, even though these tasks may be unpleasant.

Group morale is determined to a large extent by the morale of each individual in the group. When the morale of the individuals is high, they are willing to fulfill their particular role in the group. If you believe that your efforts in a school club will not produce worthwhile results, your morale is low. If morale is low among many of the individuals in a group, the group morale is likely to be low.

Group atmosphere. *Group atmosphere* is the general emotional state of a group at any given time. The atmosphere of a student group may be "up" at a party. It may be "down" after losing an important game to a rival school. It may be angry if school authorities decide to cancel a vacation. A classroom may have a happy atmosphere on a day when there is a lively discussion. It may have an unhappy atmosphere on the day of a difficult examination.

Group climate. When a certain kind of atmosphere remains in a group over a considerable period of time, we speak of **group climate.** There is one climate in a classroom of students of superior ability and high ambition. It will differ from the climate in a classroom of students of lesser ability who are in-different about their schoolwork. Sometimes the climates of early-morning classes are quite different from the climates of classes meeting late in the afternoon.

Leaders can be an important factor in the development of group climates. For instance, there are differences of climate and behavior in groups under democratic and dictatorial leadership.

How Group Roles Vary

Think about your behavior in the various groups to which you belong. Do you act the same in each group? Or do you play a different role in different groups?

To understand more about roles, remember that different actors play different roles in the theater. Part of an actor's role is determined by the script. Part of the role is determined by the personality of the actor.

What is an individual's role in a small group? The term **role** has two meanings when applied to behavior in groups: it refers

On a hiking trip the members usually assume different roles. For instance, one person acts as leader and the others are followers.

to the function of the individual in a group and it refers to the individual's expected behavior based on personality. For example, one member of the group, Helen, might be elected or appointed to keep a record of the group's finances. Her role in the group would be that of treasurer. Helen is also a very friendly girl. On her own, she might assume the role of seeing that each person in the group gets to know every other member of the group.

The number of roles that people play depends on the number of groups to which they belong. Although in most cases individuals can adjust to their various roles without difficulty, occasionally there is conflict. A teen-ager may find it difficult to assume the role of a growing child in the family and the role of a young adult outside the home. Even if no conflict exists between two roles, a person may be successful in one role and not in another. For example, a man may be unsuccessful in his role as a businessman and very successful in his role as a father. A woman may be superior at her job and perform poorly as a homemaker.

Roles change with age. At one time your role was that of a small child in the family group. Then your role changed to that of a preadolescent. Now your role is that of an adolescent. Before long you will assume the various roles of an adult.

There are two periods in life in which it is very difficult for people to adjust to their roles in groups. Adolescence is one such period. During this stage, teen-agers find that their roles in one group may conflict with their roles in another. For example, your parents (part of your family group) might say that you cannot stay out past midnight. But within your peer group such behavior might be accepted.

Old age is the second period of difficulty. There are certain problems that individuals face as they change from the role of active adult to the role of older adult. For example, elderly people must adjust to performing physical activities more slowly than they did when they were younger.

Communication Within a Group

Communication involves the passing on of information from one organism to another by means of gestures, words, or other symbols. For communication to occur, the individuals must be able to understand what is passed on, or transmitted.

Communication is not limited to words and sentences. Nonverbal communication is of great importance to humans in their social relations. People can signal to one another by such means as posture, the direction of their gaze, physical closeness, nods of the head, pats on the back, and slaps.

One example of communication is the special vocabulary that a small group of friends may develop. Clubs and other social groups often have their own secret language. They may also have "high signs" and special handshakes. All such behavior serves as communication.

Does the number of people in a group affect communication? Most people find it easier to communicate with one other person than with a small group of people. Many people have an easier time talking to a small group than to a large group.

The same individual may even say one thing in a face-to-face situation with only one person, and another thing in a group situation. It is not unusual for a leader to sound out the individuals on a committee. Later, in a group meeting, the leader may discover that their opinions are quite different from the views they expressed during face-to-face communication.

The importance of feedback. As we discussed in Chapter 10, an individual's learning is helped if there is feedback — if the person is told how well he or she is doing. Such feedback is given easily in small groups. For instance, when you communicate your ideas to group members, you can get reactions to your thoughts. Feedback can help you know more precisely what you think. There is also

The flags and symbols on this windmill illustrate a nonverbal form of communication.

group feedback, which informs the members of a group how well they are doing as a whole.

Studies have been made to determine which is more effective, individual feedback or group feedback. One investigation, using groups of seven men, provided feedback under two different conditions. In one case, each member was informed of the success or failure of the group as a whole. In the other case, each member was informed of his own success or failure as well as the success or failure of each other person and of the group as a whole. This second condition brought about the greater improvement in perfor-

mance. In this case, individual feedback was very effective, and group feedback was relatively ineffective. Under some conditions, however, group feedback has proved to be more effective than individual feedback. Further research is needed on the relative value of group and individual reinforcement. But the evidence clearly indicates that some kind of feedback is very important in small-group communications.

How do psychologists study communication? One of the techniques that psychologists use is a one-way laboratory for observing group behavior. Part of the laboratory is a room containing what appear to be mirrors. Actually, these mirrors are one-way-vision glass. There is also a dimly lighted area on the other side of the "mirrors." From it, psychologists and students can observe what goes on in the room. They themselves cannot be seen. In the lighted room, microphones carry the sound to the observation area. They are usually hidden. And they can be connected to recording devices. Observers behind the one-way glass make notes on the group members in the lighted room. The observers may make sociograms, with arrows indicating all the communication of any person with any other person.

It should be noted, however, that problems are involved in such research. There is the danger of invading people's privacy. To control for this, certain steps should be taken. After the observation has been completed, the subjects should be told that they were observed. Researchers should also get permission to use any of the material obtained during the observation.

The communication in a three-person group. Using a one-way laboratory, psychologists can study communication in a three-person group and diagram the directions of communication. In a group of two persons, the line of communication is very simple, A ↔ B. Adding even one person complicates the situation, as the diagrams on this page show. The arrows show the direction of communication from talker to listener.

The following experiment used five three-person groups. All five groups were given the task of putting together the words from three lists into one list. Each of the three individuals in a group had one of the three lists. So each had to communicate with the others to form the combined list. Members of the groups could speak whenever they wished. But their speech would be carried by headphones only in the direction indicated by the arrows.

In Group 1, communication in all directions was perfectly free. In Group 2, there was a difficulty not found in either Group 1

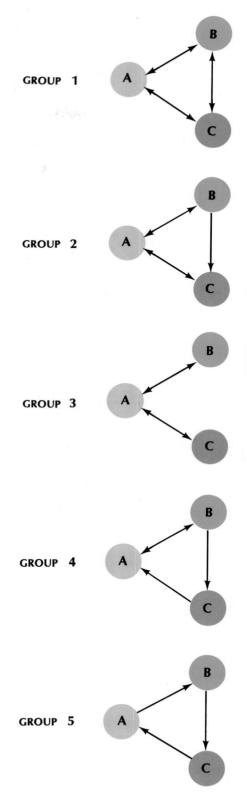

or Group 3. B had a choice. B could communicate with either A or C, or with both. But when B chose C instead of A, C had to waste time because C could not communicate directly with B. If B spoke to A and C at the same time, C had to tell A to tell B to keep quiet. Group 2 was slower in its work than either Group 1 or Group 3.

In Group 5, there was no direct communication between any two members. If B wished to check on what C said, B had to go through A. This had the disadvantage of possible misunderstandings, as well as loss of time. Group 5 was the least efficient of all the groups. Group 4 was the next least efficient. In general, it was found that when two members of a group could not communicate directly, their communication through a third party was likely to act as a disturbance rather than as a help.

Communication in a four-person group.
A group of four persons can communicate in more different patterns than three-person groups. There can be a completely open communication system. In this case, each person can communicate with every other person, as shown in the figure given below. There can also be various combinations of partly closed channels, in which some persons cannot communicate with certain other persons.

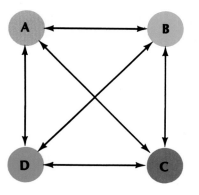

Communication in a five-person group.
Open, or all-channel, communication in a group of five individuals is much more complex than in a three-person group. It is also

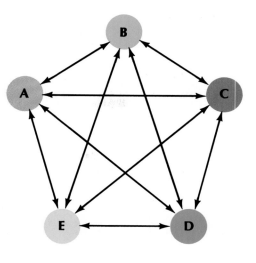

more complicated than in a four-person group, as you can see from the diagram presented above.

To study different patterns of communication, a psychologist divided 100 male college students into 20 groups of five men each. These groups of five students were seated in the four different arrangements shown on page 412. The students were seated in separate cubicles. Each student could communicate only with someone in a connecting cubicle. In the circle arrangement, for instance, A could communicate with both B and E. In the chain pattern, A could communicate only with B, although B could communicate with both A and C. Messages were passed through slots in the cubicle walls.

Each subject in a group was given a card on which appeared five out of a possible six symbols. A different symbol was missing from each subject's card. Thus, in any set of five cards, there was only one symbol that appeared on all the cards. The subjects had to discover which symbol that was. They did this by passing messages back and forth.

Each group was given 15 trials on each pattern of communication. It was found that the wheel pattern was the most efficient. This was determined by the number of errors and by the time needed to find the symbol. Next in efficiency was the Y pattern. Then the chain pattern. Least efficient was the circle.

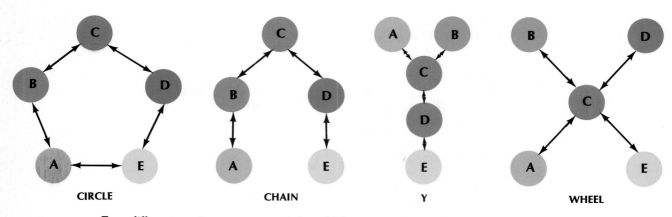

Four different seating arrangements by which groups can communicate

After finishing this part of the experiment, all subjects were given a questionnaire. One of the questions asked was, "Did your group have a leader? If so, who?" Only about half of the students in the circle arrangement were able to identify any leader. Those they did name as leaders were scattered among the five positions in the circle. On the other hand, almost all of the students in the wheel pattern of communication were able to identify a leader. They selected the person at the center of the group (C). The chain and the Y groups fell between the circle and the wheel patterns in ability to select a leader. It seems that the individual whose position in a group gives the most opportunity to communicate with others may be seen as a leader, regardless of the individual's personality.

Another question the subjects were asked was, "How did you like your job in the group?" The order for enjoyment was: circle, chain, Y, wheel. Some of the differences in enjoyment were not great. However, the circle members enjoyed their job to a much greater degree than the wheel members. Thus, efficiency in the various communication patterns did not agree with the enjoyment patterns.

Communication in larger groups. You might try diagramming channels of communication for groups of six, seven, or ten persons. You can keep the four basic patterns of communication—circle, chain, Y, and wheel

—but add more subjects. For example, you could use a group of eight subjects, but limit the lines of communication for three of them, as shown on page 413. Note that three members of each group are on the fringes of the group. They are part of the group, but not part of the main pattern of communication. They may be persons of lesser social status than those in the main pattern. Or they may be persons with special knowledge or skills who are called in as consultants to members in the main pattern. These additional members are often part of the functioning of committees or of business organizations. Scientists, executives, and others may be called in to provide special knowledge to committee members or business leaders.

Groups of more than five persons can also have all-channel patterns of communication. For example, the members of a congressional committee may consult with specialists at a meeting in which every member is free to speak out.

Which small-group pattern of communication is best? In the experiment involving the six symbols, the wheel was found to be the most efficient pattern. But the task was fairly simple. For more complex problems, the circle may be more efficient than the wheel. In the wheel pattern, the central person (C) has to do most of the work. C either has to produce the solution to the problem or relay information. C may tire of the task. It may be too much work. Someone else may have to become the leader, which would be less efficient.

There is another reason that the circle is more efficient than the wheel for complex problems. In the circle pattern, each member receives information from two different sources. In the wheel pattern, each member —except C—receives information directly from only one person. Individuals receiving information from two people are more likely to discover errors than if they receive information from only one person. And they have a better chance to get information from others.

Another factor to consider in deciding which pattern of communication is best is the amount of restriction on the members. All-channel communication is the least restricted. And circle communication is less restricted than wheel communication. In our society, most people seem to like to have some degree of independence. In the wheel pattern, it may be that the central person (C) is thought of as having too much control. The other individuals in the group may resent the limitations put on them by the central person.

One other factor that affects which small-group pattern is best is the size of the group. The efficiency of small groups depends a good deal on how many members there are in the group.

Pseudogroup effects. A ***pseudogroup effect*** refers to the incorrect assumption that certain results are due to group influence, when no group communication actually took place. A true group influence is present only if there is communication between the group members.

For example, suppose you have an object whose exact weight you know. Suppose the object is quite heavy. But it is in a small box.

These are modified seating arrangements of the four basic patterns of communication shown on page 412. Here three of the eight subjects in each pattern have limited communication.

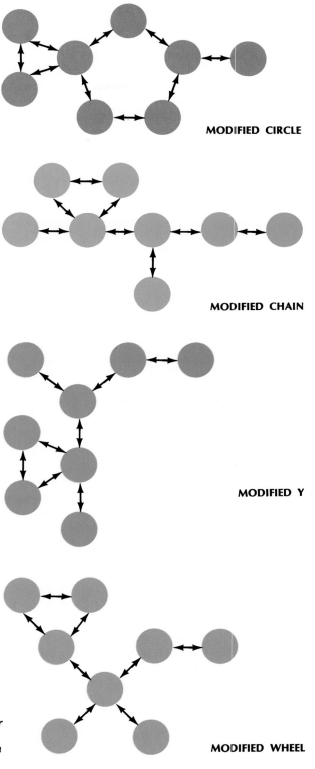

MODIFIED CIRCLE

MODIFIED CHAIN

MODIFIED Y

MODIFIED WHEEL

BEHAVIOR IN
SMALL GROUPS

You call the members of a group into the room one by one and ask each person to lift the box. You have each person estimate how much the box weighs. And you make sure that the individuals who leave the room can't communicate with the members of the group who have not yet lifted the box. Some individuals will overestimate and some will underestimate the box's weight. But you will probably find that the average estimated weight is not very far from the actual weight. And if you increase the size of the group, the average will probably come even closer to the actual weight.

In this case, however, the improvement in average estimates would be a pseudogroup effect. There had been no opportunity for group communication. If you had selected just one individual to repeat his or her estimates of the weight of the box at different times, you would have gotten about the same results.

Consider another example. Suppose you present a small group from your school with a technical problem of some kind — perhaps a problem involving electrical circuits. There may be an individual in the group who knows a great deal about electrical circuits. That person might be able to explain the basic principles to other members of the group in a short time. The group would then come up with a solution in far less time than the average time for individual solutions.

You might be tempted to conclude that group behavior is more effective in solving this problem than individuals would be acting on their own. However, you do not have a true group effect. When presented with a group solution, you need to know whether the solution is really the result of communication between group members, or whether it is based on the behavior of one individual. If it is based on information provided by one individual, it is a pseudogroup effect.

From the studies described in this chapter, you can get some idea of how much influence small groups have on people's behavior. Do small groups have a great deal of influence on your behavior?

Summary

Small groups play a valuable role in our society. The smallest possible group is a dyad, and a small group usually consists of no more than 15 to 20 individuals. Some factors that influence behavior in small groups are the distance between group members, the presence of an object between people, and the size and makeup of the group.

Small groups may be classified in various ways. They may be task-oriented or interaction-oriented, inclusive or exclusive, and formal or informal.

The effectiveness of small groups is influenced by the size of the group and whether the group has an odd or an even number of members. The efficiency of a meeting can be increased by preparing and distributing an agenda, having necessary materials on hand before the meeting, limiting the duration, and alternating leaders.

There are various advantages and disadvantages to joining a small group. We get pleasure from many small-group activities, but small groups may result in frustration, inefficiency, and limited viewpoints.

Among the characteristics that keep small groups functioning as a unit are group cohesiveness, morale, atmosphere, and climate. An individual's role in a small group also affects the group.

Communication involves the passing on of information within group members. Feedback is a very important element in small-group communications. The effectiveness of communication also depends on the size of the group and the pattern of communication taking place within the group.

INTERPRETING SOURCES

Marvin E. Shaw is one of this country's most noted researchers and writers in the field of social psychology. In this excerpt from *Contemporary Topics in Social Psychology*, Shaw has attempted to define what a small group is and how it differs from a crowd or a mob. As you study this reading, consider how scientists benefit by studying the psychology of the group as something different from the psychology of the individual.

A major characteristic of any society is that it is divided into many smaller social units. Indeed, if more than a few people are to join together in common cause it is essential that the larger group be structured in a manner that permits effective social interaction. The division of the larger social unit into smaller groups and subgroups is a natural consequence of this need for social units of manageable size. In fact, it has been estimated that the ideal size for effective group action is between five and seven persons.

In our society it is easy to find examples of the tendency to form small groups—the family unit, work groups, athletic teams, committees, and social groups such as fraternities and sororities provide ready examples. Every person in our society, with the possible exception of hermits and other seclusive persons, participates in many groups throughout his [or her] lifetime and usually in several different groups at any one time. Most of these groups are small groups. For example, ... the average person belongs to five or six groups at any given time, and ... approximately 92 percent of all group memberships are in groups of five persons or less. ...

A group may be defined as two or more persons engaged in social interaction. This definition implies that each member of the group is aware of the existence of, and is influenced by, each of the other members of the group. ...

Groups as social phenomena have been observed and studied for centuries, but even so there has been little agreement concerning the nature of groups. Around the turn of the century, groups were conceived as being something more than the sum of individual members, and it was popular to speak of the group mind. ... Today, the notion of the group mind is entirely discredited; however, there is still lack of agreement about the determinants of group behavior. Some students of groups argue that if all the principles governing individual behavior were known it would be possible to predict group behavior. Others insist that no amount of knowledge concerning individual psychology would permit the prediction of group behavior that occurs at a different level of abstraction.

Both points of view have some merit. It seems evident that there can be no group behavior apart from the behavior of the individuals who compose the group. It also seems evident that an individual's behavior is determined by stimuli which impinge upon him [or her]. But here is a critical point: the stimuli that are present in the group situation can never be duplicated exactly in the individual situation, because other group members—their responses, attitudes, opinions, and so forth—are powerful stimuli which influence the individual group members. The group is not more than the sum of its parts, but rather it is *different* from the sum of its parts. An individual behaves differently in the group situation because he [or she] is experiencing a different set of stimuli.

Source Review

1. According to the author, what is the ideal size for effective group action?

2. How can a "group" be defined?

3. What is meant by "the group is not more than the sum of its parts, but rather it is *different* from the sum of its parts"?

CHAPTER 18

REVIEW

REVIEWING TERMS

small group
dyad
task-oriented group
interaction-oriented group
inclusive group
exclusive group
informal group

formal group
status
group cohesiveness
sociometry
sociogram
group morale
group atmosphere

group climate
role
communication
group feedback
pseudogroup effect

CHECKING FACTS

1. How does the physical distance between people influence behavior in a small group? How does placing an object between people affect behavior?

2. How does the size and makeup of a group influence behavior? What effect do small groups have on whether people lie or tell the truth?

3. How do task-oriented groups differ from interaction-oriented groups? Give an example of each group.

4. Distinguish between inclusive and exclusive groups. Between formal and informal groups.

5. What effect does size have on the effectiveness of small groups?

6. Describe some of the ways to increase the efficiency of small groups.

7. What are the advantages of belonging to small groups? What are the disadvantages of belonging to such groups?

8. How is group cohesiveness measured?

9. How is group morale determined?

10. How does group atmosphere differ from group climate?

11. What are the two meanings of "role" when applied to groups? In which periods do people have particular difficulty adjusting to their group roles? Why?

12. Which pattern of communication was most efficient in a five-person group? Which provided the most enjoyment?

APPLYING YOUR KNOWLEDGE

1. With your teacher's permission, rearrange the desks in your classroom into different formations during one week of instruction. One day you might choose clusters of four desks, another day you might make one large circle. At the end of the week, discuss how the various arrangements influenced student relationships with one another and with the teacher. Did one arrangement seem more effective for interaction? For learning?

2. The next time you and a friend sit down together—at lunch, at home, or in class—vary the distance between you. For

example, skip a seat in the school cafeteria. Or sit down so your chairs are almost touching. What is the reaction of the other person? What do you think is an acceptable "social distance"?

3. Listen to some enjoyable music or watch your favorite TV programs, first alone and later with a group of friends. How did your mood and behavior compare when alone and with the group? How did the other group members act and feel when together?

4. Look through your wallet or purse for various cards or symbols that indicate your membership in a group or organization. Or you might make a list of all the groups to which you belong. List whether each group is task-oriented or interaction-oriented, inclusive or exclusive, and formal or informal.

5. Organize the class into four groups. Two of the groups should each have three members and the other two each should contain half of the remaining students. Each group is to take five minutes to devise a plan for transporting a cup of water from one side of the room to the other without spilling a drop. At the end of the allotted time, have each group put its plan into action while the other groups watch. Which plan seemed most effective? Discuss how the size of each group affected the amount of cooperation, pattern of leadership, and degree of interaction in the group.

6. Ask two student volunteers in your class to leave the room for a few minutes while the rest of the class thinks up a simple task. (For example, have the students guess a number from 1 to 100.) Ask the students to return one at a time to perform the task. While the first student is carrying out the assignment, the class should frequently provide feedback (such as "too high," "too low," or "getting close"). The other student should receive no feedback at all. Which student successfully completed the task first? What effect does feedback have on student performance?

7. To illustrate communication with gestures, have one student try to communicate specific ideas to the class using only gestures.

THINKING CRITICALLY ABOUT PSYCHOLOGY

1. **Evaluating Ideas** Where do you think your ideas about social distance originated? Do you think all societies hold similar ideas? Explain your answer.

2. **Classifying Ideas** How might you reorganize your classes to make learning more efficient? What other factors would you take into account when carrying out this assignment?

3. **Forming an Opinion** If the leader of a group is popular, intelligent, and good at getting things done, then the size of the group has no bearing on the group's productivity. Do you agree or disagree with this statement? Explain.

4. **Applying Ideas** If you were the manager of a large industrial plant, what procedures would you introduce so that all personnel in the plant would be more highly motivated? Would you organize departments into large groups or small groups? Would you emphasize group feedback? What would you do to improve group atmosphere?

5. **Interpreting Ideas** In election years, to what extent do candidates running for office try to communicate with the voters? Do you think communication increases or decreases after the election? Why?

DEVELOPING SKILLS IN PSYCHOLOGY

Achieving Reliability

One important criterion for the adequacy of psychological research is reliability. All measuring devices are expected to be *reliable*—to produce consistent, reproducible results. If you were to get on and off your scale four times in the morning, and it reported four different weights, it would not be reliable.

One important type of reliability is interobserver reliability. In the experiment on the influence of distance between people (described in this chapter), it was important that observers become reliable with each other in their estimates of how far apart members of dyads were standing when they talked. If one observer said that A was 20 inches from B and C was 40 inches from D, while a second observer said that A was 30 inches from B and C was 35 inches from D, then there would be inadequate interobserver reliability. The results of the study would be very different depending on whether we used the first observer's judgments or the second observer's judgments.

Try working with a friend to see how reliable the two of you can become in making judgments of distance between people. It will be useful to measure some actual distances first for practice. Then you should both make judgments of distance within the same 10 dyads and see how reliable (consistent) with each other you are.

READING FURTHER ABOUT PSYCHOLOGY

Babad, Elisha Y., Birnbaum, Max, and Beene, Kenneth D., *The Social Self: Group Influences on Personal Identity,* Sage, Beverly Hills, Calif., 1983. A readable book that examines group influences on personal identity. Includes exercises to encourage an analysis of one's own attitudes, perceptions, and values.

Berne, Eric, *Games People Play,* Ballantine, New York, 1978. A popular look at how individuals interact with one another.

Frankl, Viktor, *Man's Search for Meaning,* Pocket Books, New York, 1984. Describes a psychiatrist's experiences as a prisoner in a World War II prison camp and gives his conclusions about the need for meaning in life.

Golding, William, *Lord of the Flies,* Putnam, New York, 1964. A novel about a group of boys stranded on a remote island and the conflicts that arise among them in their competition for leadership.

Peters, Thomas, and Waterman, Robert, Jr., *In Search of Excellence: Lessons from America's Best Run Companies,* Harper & Row, New York, 1982. Presents interesting information on the basic characteristics of successfully managed companies.

Chapter 19

SOCIAL INFLUENCE

Chapter Focus

This chapter presents:
- **a discussion of attitudes and propaganda**
- **a description of attribution**
- **the role of leaders and leadership**
- **the influence of authority, peer groups, and male and female roles**

An athlete promoting a soft drink? A singer endorsing a car? No doubt, you've seen such familiar images on TV and in magazines.

Why do such advertisements fill the media? The most important reason is because they work. You may laugh at the thought of buying a car recommended by someone who probably rides around town in a chauffeured limousine. Yet such advertisements do influence your attitudes. Studies have shown that people are more likely to buy a product endorsed by someone they like and trust than by an unfamiliar source.

Attitudes are only one of the many influences that affect the way we interact with members of our society. In this chapter we will examine various social influences.

Social Attitudes

Much of our behavior is influenced by our attitudes. An *attitude* may be defined as a readiness to respond favorably or unfavorably to a person, object, situation, or event. When individuals express an opinion, they are revealing an attitude. But an attitude can be made known in other ways besides expressing an opinion. For example, the way we treat others reveals our attitude toward them. People have attitudes toward everything from their pets to world problems. In this chapter, we will focus on attitudes that relate to social situations, problems, and questions. We call these *social attitudes.*

Attitudes can be very emotional in nature. People may become quite upset when they find that someone has a very different attitude from their own toward some social problem. People often defend their own attitudes despite strong opposing arguments.

When does an attitude become a prejudice? Any attitude that prevents us from objectively considering and evaluating new evidence is a *prejudice.* The attitude may be either for or against a given issue or group.

Suppose we say that all politicians are corrupt because we know a few who are corrupt. We are merely expressing an attitude. Then we meet a politician who very clearly is not corrupt. If we refuse to recognize his or her honesty and don't change our statement concerning all politicians, our attitude is one of prejudice.

When this person decides she doesn't like certain foods just because they are unfamiliar, she is expressing a prejudiced attitude.

How are social attitudes measured? One technique for measuring attitudes is to give individuals a list of statements about a particular social problem. Then they are asked to indicate which statements they agree with and which ones they disagree with. For example, in one study of attitudes toward ecology, people were asked to indicate by "True" or "False" their reactions to certain statements. There were statements such as, "I'd be willing to ride a bicycle or take the bus to work in order to reduce air pollution." "I would not be willing to pay a pollution tax, even if it would considerably decrease the smog problem." "I have never joined a cleanup drive."

A somewhat similar technique for measuring attitudes presents statements about a social problem. But it doesn't ask individuals whether or not they agree with each statement. Instead, it asks them to indicate the degree to which they agree or disagree according to a rating scale.

Attitudes may also be measured by asking individuals to complete statements like the following: "If a mentally retarded person were to come to my home, I would . . ." Or, "If a mentally retarded person were to come to their homes, most people would . . ."

Changing Attitudes

Attitudes, once formed, tend not to change. Under some conditions, however, they will change. For example, one study found that 80 percent of the children in elementary school tend to favor the same political party as their parents. Somewhat fewer high school students agree with their parents on political parties, although the students still live at home. With the varied social contacts of college life, only 55 percent of college students have the same attitudes toward political parties as their parents.

Propaganda and changing attitudes. Sometimes we change our attitudes because of propaganda. On occasion, the term "propaganda" has been used to mean any attempt to influence the people of one nation against another nation during wartime. Actually, *propaganda* refers to any organized attempt to influence social attitudes. The word has been defined as "the art of making up the other person's mind." Propaganda may even be highly desirable.

Propaganda is not a twentieth-century invention. In the ancient Italian city of Pompeii (buried under volcanic ash in 79 A.D.), the walls were covered with election appeals. There had been an organized attempt back then to influence citizens to vote in a particular way. In our day, politicians use newspapers, radio, and television for propaganda as well as the traditional means of signs and public meetings.

Advertising is a good example of propaganda. Manufacturers make an organized attempt to get us to drive certain models of cars, to wash with certain brands of soap, to eat certain kinds of breakfast cereal, and so on. In other words, they try to influence our attitudes.

What determines the effectiveness of propaganda? Being first is one factor in determining how effective propaganda is. Advertisers who are first to call the attention of the public to their products usually have an advantage in sales. The reason is that, once having been influenced by a given bit of propaganda, many individuals are no longer interested in, and do not expose themselves to, another point of view.

Another factor is repeated exposure. An unfamiliar object or situation causes conflicting responses and uncertainty. This may produce negative feelings. But repeated exposure produces familiarity. This makes the person feel comfortable and makes the object or situation seem attractive. Individuals trying to decide which brand of soap or breakfast cereal to buy will usually select the brand to which they've had repeated exposure—the one they're most familiar with. A great deal of advertising is based on the effects of repeated exposure.

Propaganda, including advertising, seems to be a constant part of our social life. Certainly it is a force in national and international affairs. Our problem is to recognize it. We should consider propaganda from both sides. Then and only then do we make our own decisions.

Cognitive dissonance and changing attitudes. In *cognitive dissonance,* individuals are faced with a lack of agreement between two ideas, attitudes, or beliefs. They feel tense, uncomfortable, or frustrated. So they try to alter their thoughts or actions to reduce this dissonance.

You may be familiar with the word "dissonance" as it applies to music. We say that dissonant sounds are harsh, that they jar us. And we may find them unpleasant. Similarly, our thinking may become harsh, jarring, and

Ads are a form of propaganda. They attempt to influence people to develop a favorable attitude toward a particular product, such as a car.

CHARIOT
STYLED FOR NOW!

From NATIONAL MOTORS

unpleasant to us. We feel uncomfortable when our thinking or behavior doesn't agree with information we have about ourselves and our environment. In cognitive dissonance, individuals realize that their thinking is inconsistent. They try to do something about it. They may change their thinking so that it is more consistent and pleasant. Or they may change their behavior.

In one study, college students serving as subjects were asked to a do a very boring task. On the table in front of them were rows of blocks. They were to go through the rows of blocks, giving each block a quarter-turn. As soon as they had turned all of the blocks, they were to begin again, giving every block another quarter-turn. After completing their task, feeling very tired and bored, they were asked to tell the next subject in the waiting room that the experiment was fun and very interesting. That is, they were to present to the next subject a favorable attitude toward the task.

Some of the students were paid a dollar for lying about the task being enjoyable and interesting. Others were paid $20 for telling the same lie. Then all students who told the lie were asked to rate the task on a scale ranging from extremely dull and boring to extremely interesting and enjoyable.

Which students would be most likely to change their attitudes toward the dull and boring task? Would it be the group that was paid $20? Or the group that was paid only $1.00? The $20 group rated the task as slightly dull and boring. But the $1.00 group rated it as quite interesting and enjoyable. Why did the $1.00 students change their attitudes? For the $1.00 students, the payment was not high enough to justify telling a lie. So to reduce their cognitive dissonance, they actually came to believe that the experiment was interesting and enjoyable. For the students who were paid $20, the financial reward was apparently high enough to justify their inconsistent thinking. They weren't that disturbed by cognitive dissonance. So they didn't feel that they had to change their attitudes.

Often factors other than cognitive dissonance influence our change of attitudes. But do you ever find yourself accepting ideas that are inconsistent with what you believe, and then changing your beliefs? Or have you ever done something that you didn't really approve of and then were uncomfortable because your behavior was inconsistent with your beliefs? Did you reduce your cognitive dissonance by changing your attitude toward the behavior?

Attribution

One topic that is related to attitudes is attribution. **Attribution** is a process by which we attempt to interpret and explain the behavior of others. For example, suppose you are waiting in line for a bus and someone bumps into you. How will you react? Will you get angry? Or will you just brush the incident off as an accident? Your answer depends on *why* you think the person behaved in that manner. Or, put another way, your answer depends on to what you attributed the behavior.

Dispositional versus situational behavior. If you thought that the person deliberately tried to hurt you, you would say that the behavior was a **dispositional factor.** This means that the behavior is attributed to the personality of the individual. As a result, you might get angry.

Perhaps, though, you might blame the behavior on the situation. The bus stop was crowded and the person may have lost balance. In this case the behavior was a **situational factor.** This means that it is attributed to the situation or environment. Your reaction, then, might be to forget the incident.

By attributing people's behavior to different causes, we assign meaning to various events. This meaning, in turn, helps determine our reactions and attitudes.

Which is the stronger force? In analyzing people's behavior, which way do we tend to lean? Do we place more emphasis on dispositional factors or situational factors?

You think you should have all of the records by your favorite performer. Yet you feel that you can't afford all of them. Faced with such cognitive dissonance, what would you do?

Studies have shown that we tend to attribute the behavior of others to dispositional forces. For example, a salesperson might tell us to have a nice day. We attribute the behavior to the warm personality of the individual rather than to the fact that the supervisor is standing nearby. However, when analyzing our own behavior, we tend to favor situational factors. If, for instance, we do poorly on a test, we tend to blame the teacher for making the test too difficult. We rarely blame ourselves for not studying hard enough.

Leadership

A leader is an individual who exerts great influence on a group. The leader suggests, organizes, and directs group activity. Leaders guide the thinking of their group. They play a major role in establishing goals and inspiring members to work toward these goals. They influence the development of social attitudes within the group.

An ideal leader is responsible both to those within the group and those outside it. Leaders must direct the members of their group toward goals that are in line with their own welfare. But they must also see that the group's goals and activities don't interfere with the welfare of those outside the group. For example, a leader in school athletics strives to produce a winning team. But such a leader does not suggest dishonest practices that might bring victory but would also bring dishonor to the school.

Why do some persons wish to be leaders? People become leaders for a variety of reasons. Individuals who lead because they have the characteristics of leadership behavior are probably enjoying good social adjustment. But some individuals strive to achieve a position of leadership because, whether they realize it or not, they feel inferior. They want to be a leader to increase their self-esteem. They want to acquire followers so that they will feel less unsure of themselves. These individuals are probably not well-adjusted.

Different kinds of leaders. One psychologist has suggested that there are two basic kinds of leaders. (1) Some individuals lead a group in getting done whatever tasks it has set for itself or in solving whatever problems are at hand. They are able to guide the group's thinking because of their superior ideas, carefully thought-out plans, and willingness to work. (2) Other individuals have charisma. They handle the social and emotional problems of a group with relative ease. They tend to have pleasing personalities and to be popular with members of the group. They are able to settle arguments between members of the group or between subgroups within the group. At times they may even be

able to prevent the group from breaking up. In rare cases, an individual may be a leader in both task accomplishment and in handling social-emotional problems.

Another way of classifying leaders is in terms of how they achieve their positions of leadership. In some groups, a leader comes out of the group itself, either informally or by election. For other groups, a leader is appointed or placed over the group by those higher in authority.

The personalities of leaders. Leadership depends partly on the characteristics of the individual. Research indicates that the following aspects of personality are related to leadership: (1) Intellectual ability. (2) Good personal adjustment. (3) Outgoingness. (4) Dominance. (5) A tendency to understand role relations. And (6) sensitivity to interpersonal relationships.

There is also the characteristic of verbal activity. People who talk quite freely in a group are more likely to be chosen as leaders

An individual may be a leader in some types of settings, such as in this tennis club, and a follower in other types of settings.

than those who are fairly quiet. Communication is essential for effective group behavior. Individuals who communicate freely are likely to be chosen as leaders, even though their ideas may not be the best in the group.

Leadership always depends on the situation. A leader in one society may be labeled a terrorist by another society. Also, it is not uncommon for an individual to be a leader in one social group and a follower in another social group. Or, as group goals change, an individual may switch between the role of leader and that of follower in the same group. Nevertheless, one research study reported high leadership ratings for the same person when placed in different groups with different tasks. People who are used to being leaders in one group often show leadership tendencies in other groups.

Techniques of leadership. Leaders can be classified by the way in which they work with the group. We can identify three kinds of leaders on this basis. How do their techniques differ? *Democratic leaders* work with their group. At times they may have special guidance responsibilities. They generally join in as members of the group. They may suggest certain policies. Yet they welcome and appreciate contributions by others.

Autocratic leaders, on the other hand, direct the operation of their group with a firm hand. They establish policies and give detailed and frequent directions. They are essentially outside the group. They do not ask for or welcome suggestions from other members.

Laissez-faire ("layssay-fair") *leaders* are not really a moving force in their group. *Laissez-faire* is French for "let do," or "let people do as they please." These leaders tend to stand by passively without exerting much influence on their group. But they are willing to give information or help if asked.

In one well-known investigation, the behavior of boys was studied in three kinds of social climates. The boys organized into clubs. Those in the various clubs were matched so that they were as nearly alike as possible. They worked under adult leaders who played the roles of democratic, autocratic, and laissez-faire leaders.

Under democratic leadership, the boys offered ideas in making plans. They worked happily and energetically. They used their time to good advantage. They were friendly toward one another and toward the leader. And they worked well even when the leader left the room.

Under autocratic leadership, there was much hostility. Certain boys became scapegoats. All the boys worked. But the work was done with little enthusiasm. Whenever the leader left the room, work stopped and the boys became aggressive.

Under laissez-faire leadership, group interest lagged. Individuals tended to work for themselves rather than for the group.

Are some people "born leaders"? Do we inherit the qualities of leadership? No. Techniques of leadership are learned. This learning may begin very early in life. It may continue for many years without a conscious effort by the individual. Suppose, however, that a person is not a leader but wants to be one. Such persons can undertake to develop qualities of leadership. They can set themselves the task of developing skills that win them the deserved respect of others.

Two psychologists asked themselves this question: "Can social leadership be improved by instruction in its technique?" To find out, they had students in a high school rate one another on leadership. Next, they divided the students into two groups. The groups were selected so that they were equal in leadership qualities as indicated by the ratings. In a series of 11 conferences over seven months, the students in one group were instructed in the qualities and techniques of leadership. Students in the other group were not given such training. At the end of the seven months, the students again rated one another on leadership. This time the average rating of the students who had had training in qualities and techniques of leadership was noticeably higher than the average rating of those who did not have this training.

One of the techniques that has proved effective in training for leadership is role playing. A situation is outlined. Then individuals take on the roles of the people who would be involved. Without a script, the role players act as people do in real-life situations, assuming their feelings, attitudes, and characteristics. For example, one way of training supervisors for business is to have the trainees act out certain situations involving interpersonal relationships. One trainee assumes the part of a supervisor. The others play the parts of workers under the supervisor. The individual playing the role of a supervisor learns how to handle the problems of those being supervised. And those playing the worker roles learn to understand some of the feelings and attitudes of the employees they will be supervising.

Teachers are in positions of leadership. Sometimes part of the training for teaching includes acting out the role of a teacher while others assume the roles of students. Such role playing is very likely to give future teachers a new insight into problems of student-teacher relationships and thus make them better leaders.

Leaders are needed. There is evidence that people can be trained for positions of leadership. But don't forget that everyone is a follower in many situations. Being a good follower is also important. Psychologists need to study the characteristics of good followers as well as those of good leaders.

The Power of Authority

We have seen how important leaders are as a social influence. Sometimes they have the power of authority, and their followers are expected to obey them. If someone in authority ordered you to injure another person, would you obey? If so, under what circumstances?

There are many examples of individuals harming and even killing other human beings because someone in authority told them to do so. For instance, there is the Nazi torturing and killing of Jews in World War II.

Such an example of blind obedience to authority raises the question, "Under what circumstances will individuals obey the commands of persons in authority to harm other human beings?" Psychologists have investigated this question.

Would you harm another person in a laboratory experiment? One psychologist, Stanley Milgram, advertised in a local newspaper for people to serve as subjects in an experiment. He selected men from twenty to fifty years in age. Their occupational levels ranged from unskilled labor to professional work. They were asked to report to a laboratory at Yale University.

Each man was to serve as a "teacher." His task was to push a button that would give an electric shock to a "student" whenever the "student" gave an incorrect answer to certain test questions. There were 30 levels of shock, ranging from 15 volts to 450 volts. The "teacher" was told to increase the shock to the next higher level whenever the "student" made an error.

The "student" was actually an assistant of the psychologist. He was placed in another room. His responses were on tape (unknown to the "teacher"). Each "teacher" heard the same responses at various shock levels. For example, at 75 volts the "student" moaned or grunted. At 125 volts he said, "Hey, that really hurts." At 180 volts, "I can't stand the pain, don't do that." At 195 volts he complained of heart trouble. At 285 volts he gave an agonized scream. At 315 volts and higher, there was silence.

Sometimes the "teacher" protested and wanted to stop giving the shock. Then he was told, "You have no other choice, you must go on." Or, "The experiment requires that you go on." Actually, the button used by the "teacher" was not connected to a source of electricity. So no shocks were given. But the "teacher" didn't know this.

How much do you think the "teachers" would be willing to shock the "students"? Unbelievably, no "teacher" stopped giving shocks at less than 300 volts. The average maximum shock for all 40 "teachers" was

The uniform of a police officer is a visual symbol of authority.

368 volts. And 65 percent of them kept giving the shocks up to the limit of 450 volts. An authority, the experimenter, had commanded them to do so. And they obeyed.

It should be noted that when some conditions of this experiment were changed, the results changed. For example, if the experimenter was in another room rather than next to the "teacher," and if he telephoned his orders, the obedience dropped from 65 percent to 22 percent. And some "teachers" gave shocks of lower intensity than the conditions of the experiment required without telling the experimenter that they had cheated.

Remember that this experiment was conducted in a leading university. Would the "teachers" have responded differently in a less impressive environment? Milgram repeated the experiment under different conditions. He moved his laboratory equipment to a rundown office building and used the name "Research Associates." Even under these changed conditions, 48 percent of the "teachers" supposedly gave shocks of 450 volts. They were willing to cause pain and possibly even death because someone in authority had told them to do so, even though the authority of Research Associates was less than that of the university.

Would you or your classmates administer 450 volts just because someone in authority told you to do so? In a study similar to the ones just described, 35 percent of a group of high school seniors gave what they believed to be this amount of voltage.

Deceiving subjects in an experiment. Should an experimenter be allowed to mislead subjects by making them think that they are actually harming another person? Psychologists are quite concerned over the ethics of such experimentation. Milgram was very aware of this problem. After the experiment, he carefully explained to the "teachers" the real purpose of the experiment and just what had been done. He told them that

Text continues on page 430.

Case Study: Focus on Research

THE POWER OF POWER

"I don't know what's gotten into him. He's usually so quiet and passive."

You've probably heard comments like this before. A normally gentle and shy individual starts acting aggressive. Or a leader suddenly becomes passive. One factor that has been shown to have a dramatic effect on people's behavior is power—both the granting of it and the removal of it. Let's consider the following experiment.

In this well-known study, psychologist Philip Zimbardo and three colleagues paid student volunteers to participate in an experiment concerned with prison life. From about 70 applicants, the psychologists selected 24 male college students as subjects. Through interviews and questionnaires the researchers determined that the subjects were all

Clutching a nightstick in his hands, this "guard" is prepared to do his job. Most "guards" acted in a similar fashion, casting a harsh reality on their roles.

stable and mature adults. None had any criminal record, and they seemed to be typical of their age group.

The experiment was to last two weeks. During this period the researchers would try to find out what it meant psychologically to be a prisoner and to be a prison guard. To carry out their study they prepared a "prison" in the basement of a university building housing the psychology department. It had all the appearances of an actual prison, including barred cells.

By the flip of a coin the subjects were randomly divided into two groups, "prisoners" and "guards." The guards were briefed about the seriousness of the situation and were given an opportunity to create rules. They also were free to create new regulations as the experiment progressed.

For the "prisoners" the situation was completely different. With sirens blaring, police cars abruptly picked them up at their homes. Frisked, handcuffed, and blindfolded, the men were taken to a police station, where they were fingerprinted and booked. Then the "prisoners" were taken to the "prison" in the university building. Here they were given prison outfits and a number, had a chain and lock put around one ankle, and were "deloused." For all this humiliation, the "prisoners" were to be paid $15 a day—their incentive to take part in the experiment.

After only a few days, both the "guards" and the "prisoners" had difficulty separating their roles from reality. The "guards," wearing uniforms and sunglasses, and carrying nightsticks, began to use their power and authority. They ordered the "prisoners" to do pushups, used abusive language, and even refused requests for permission to use the toilet facilities. While making life miserable for the "prisoners," they seemed to enjoy the abuse and hardship they were inflicting.

The "prisoners," like actual prisoners, resented such treatment. They tried to organize an escape, but were unsuccessful. They then became depressed and passive. After just four days, three of the prisoners had to be released because of their depressed mental state. Others asked to be paroled, offering to give up the $15 a day that they were earning. However, parole was denied, and they returned passively to their cells.

By the end of the sixth day, the situation had gotten so frightening that the researchers decided to stop the experiment. Zimbardo noted that in just a short period of time—less than a week—the worst side of human nature surfaced. People no longer held any regard for one another or for themselves. It seemed that this brief experience caused people to forget everything they ever learned about treating others. He wrote:

> We were horrified because we saw some boys (guards) treat others as if they were despicable animals,

taking pleasure in cruelty, while other boys (prisoners) became servile, dehumanized robots who thought only of escape, of their own individual survival, and of their mounting hatred for the guards.

To ensure that the subjects would not be emotionally scarred by their experience, the researchers conducted therapy sessions with them immediately after the experiment. They also kept in touch with them for a year to try to make sure that any harmful effects had been eliminated. (However, there is no assurance that some subjects did not suffer irreversible harm. This highlights the need for research standards that protect the rights and health of subjects who take part in an experiment.)

The implications of Zimbardo's experiment are alarming. It seems that a group of ordinary individuals given just a little unchecked power could be radically transformed, at least temporarily, by an experimental situation.

SOURCE: Philip Zimbardo, Craig Haney, and W. Curtis Banks, "A Pirandellian Prison," *The New York Times Magazine,* April 8, 1973.

Blindfolded and wearing a prisoner's smock, this male "prisoner" is being processed by two "guards."

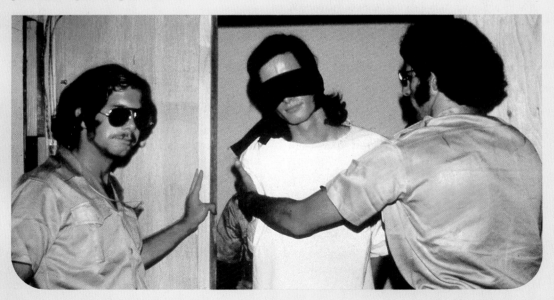

they had not made any "student" suffer. Nevertheless, many of the "teachers" were quite emotionally upset. They could not understand why they might have done such a terrible thing. What do you think the effect of such an experience might be on subjects? Could such an experience bother an individual for years to come?

Are you more likely to harm a person who can't recognize you? To find out, a psychologist had four women subjects dress so they could not be recognized. They were given baggy clothing. They wore hoods that covered their faces, except for small holes permitting them to see and breathe. They were seated in a dark room. Their names were never mentioned. There was no way that their "victims" could tell who they were. Another group of four women could clearly be identified. Their faces were exposed. They wore name tags and were frequently spoken to by name. Their victims could easily tell who they were.

The four women in each of the groups were told to give a series of 20 painful electric shocks to each of two women victims. They thought that they were participating in an experiment on empathy. The women in both groups could see their victims jump and squirm as they were supposedly given the shocks. As you may have guessed, however, shocks were not actually given. The two victims were assistants of the psychologist.

The results showed that the women who could not be recognized gave more shocks than the women who could be identified. The unrecognizable women more often increased the amount of shock they gave to the victims over the period of 20 trials.

This experiment also found that both identifiable and unrecognizable subjects gave more shocks to an unpleasant person — someone who "deserves to be punished" — than to a nice, sweet, loving person — someone who does not deserve to be hurt. But the subjects who could be identified gave only about half as much shock as the unrecognizable subjects gave to the unpleasant person.

Laboratory experiments on the power of authority help us understand behavior outside a laboratory. For example, they may help us understand why soldiers kill when commanded to do so by their officers. Soldiers are in uniform, which makes them less easy to identify as individuals. They may not be able to see the people they are killing. And they have been told how unpleasant and dangerous the people in the enemy army are. In states where capital punishment is legal, prison officials execute convicted prisoners because they are ordered to do so by the authority of the courts.

We have discussed only the power of authority to produce pain and death. What about the other side of the picture? Do individuals ever use their power of authority to be kind? Are there acts of kindness by people who arrange not to be identified?

Peer-Group Influence

Another source of influence on our behavior is the peer group. **Peers** are those persons who are considered to be our equals. They are usually of about the same age and ability. As we progress from infancy to adulthood, the peer group becomes more and more of a social influence on us.

The peer group and young people. The peer group is a great influence on young people for many reasons. First of all, it permits a young person to find secure relationships with others of the same age. The support of peers helps the individual move from parental control to more self-control. To some extent, the peer group takes over the control of behavior. It sets limits on what behavior is allowed and what is unacceptable.

Another reason that the influence of peers is so important is that the peers help individuals obtain an accurate picture of themselves. For example, children with a higher than average mechanical ability may have brothers and sisters who have even more ability in this area. When they compare themselves to their brothers and sisters, they

The peer group can influence the style of clothing we wear.

may develop the belief that their mechanical ability is inferior. But when they later compare their ability to those in their peer group, some of whom have less than average ability, they can arrive at a more accurate assessment. Individuals need to evaluate themselves and their abilities in different areas with people of their own age and sex.

A third reason for the influence of the peer group is the opportunity it gives an individual to identify with role models. **Role models** are persons who provide examples for behavior that another individual might copy. Some peers command more respect than others. Some achieve positions of leadership. The individual who needs a model to develop certain behavior can usually find one in the peer group.

Peers also provide a social setting in which social behavior can be developed. The family unit begins the process of social development. This process is carried further by the peer group. It is within the peer group that individuals develop certain roles, such as clown, athlete, leader, or rebel. Individuals cast in a role tend to play out the behavior expected of them. It gives them acceptance and special recognition.

Another reason for the importance of peer influence is that in the peer group an individual can express feelings about personal or controversial matters. Individuals often feel secure in discussing feelings of hostility, lack of trust in authority, and other topics with their peers. Perhaps people are comforted when they discover that their peers share similar feelings.

The influence of peer-group attitudes and values. The peer group is very influential in helping the individual form attitudes. For example, boys from lower socioeconomic levels are sometimes less interested in school than boys from middle socioeconomic groups. Yet the influence of the peer group is such that boys from lower socioeconomic groups who associate with a peer group of boys from middle socioeconomic groups usually show a favorable attitude toward school.

What are some values among members of a peer group? In one research study, American adolescents were asked to rank certain values according to their importance in their peer groups. Here are the percentages of individuals who had ranked the following

431
SOCIAL
INFLUENCE

peer-group values as "extremely important":

Having a good reputation	78%
Earning money	56%
Being well-liked	54%
Being popular in school	46%
Going out on dates	40%
Participating in sports	31%
Being a leader in activities	20%
Being accepted by other students	18%

Do you consider these peer-group values extremely important? Would you rank them in the same order?

How strong is conformity to peer standards? All of us are influenced in one way or another by what our peers say and do. The contacts that members of a group have with one another usually result in establishing group standards of behavior. Individuals may conform to the group standards rather than risk having others disapprove of them or even disagree with them. This tendency to conform is shown in the following laboratory experiment.

This experiment involved the autokinetic illusion and conformity. The **autokinetic illusion** or autokinetic effect is the apparent movement of a small fixed spot of light in an otherwise dark room. You can produce an autokinetic effect with a member of your family or a friend. First you have to have a completely darkened room. It has to be so dark that nothing in the room can be seen. Then arrange a light source to show a very small point of light in a fixed position. You can cover the source of light with heavy black paper. Then punch a pinhole in the paper. The idea is that your subject can see nothing else except the point of light. Tell your subject that you will turn on the tiny spot of light. In a few seconds, the light will appear to move. As soon as the subject reports that the light has moved, turn off the light. Ask your subject to tell you as accurately as possible — to at least the nearest centimeter (or else the nearest half-inch) — how far the light has moved. Since the source of light is in a fixed position, your subject will be reporting an illusion.

In the laboratory experiment, three subjects separately gave 100 judgments on the amount of apparent movement they saw. At first the judgments of each subject tended to vary. After a time, however, their judgments of length of movements tended to become fairly stable. It is true that the subjects' judgments differed from each other. One subject said the light generally moved a little over a centimeter (or a half-inch). Another said it moved about 5 centimeters (2 inches). The third said the light generally moved about 19 centimeters (7½ inches). Nevertheless, average judgments for each individual subject were established.

Next, the experiment was set up to study group influence. The subjects were placed together in a dark room. Each could hear the judgments made by the others. As a result, judgments tended to come together. By the end of the group session, the average judgments for the three subjects were between 5 and 6 centimeters (2 and 2½ inches). Two subjects had raised their estimates, and one had lowered his estimate, until all their judgments were quite close together. And when the subjects gave judgments alone after the group situations, they still tended to give group estimates. The conformity to group judgments stayed with them.

The influence of peer groups in making decisions involving risks. Are decisions involving the taking of risks best made by individuals or by a group? Some early research suggested that a group tends to come up with more risk-taking decisions than the same individuals do when acting alone. This is known as **risky shift.** Some psychologists believe that group decisions are riskier than those of individuals because responsibility for the results of a decision is spread out among the members of the group. Other psychologists believe that those members of a group who are quite willing to take risks have more of an influence on a group decision. There are still other psychologists who believe the greater amount of risk-taking by groups is due to our general cultural values that favor risk-taking. Many people consider it socially acceptable to take risks such as betting, gambling, and "playing" the stock market.

More recent research suggests that sometimes the risk-taking of groups is no greater than decisions made by individuals. For instance, does a jury make a riskier decision than a judge? In making financial investments, is a group decision of bankers better than the decision of an experienced financier? More research is needed on the taking of risks by groups versus the risks taken by individuals. Meanwhile, some psychologists have suggested that decision making be left to groups rather than to individuals only when the risk-taking is socially desirable.

Male and Female Roles

One great influence on the behavior and social attitudes of individuals is the fact that people are classified either as male or female. We tend to behave according to what we think is the appropriate role for our own sex. Here the word "role" refers to the kind of behavior that is expected of us in a social situation.

What determines the male and female roles in a society? The roles that women and men are expected to assume in a society are determined by biological differences and by the culture. In the past, men have tended to do work requiring muscular strength. Women have tended to do work related to the home and the care of children. This division of roles reflected assumptions about biological differences.

Cultural influences are especially important in determining the roles of each of the sexes. Parents begin to teach their children sex roles very early in life. One experiment has shown that the reaction of a mother differs according to the sex of the infant. Mothers were given a chance to hand a toy fish, a doll, or a toy train to a six-month-old infant. It was found that they more often handed the doll to the female and the train to the male infant. Thus, these mothers had already begun to direct children into traditional sex roles at the age of six months.

In early childhood, there is some tendency for both boys and girls to choose what are considered "masculine" toys. Even in kindergarten, girls are apt to prefer "masculine" toys more than boys prefer "feminine"

Male and female roles are learned very early in life.

The Prince   Fantasyland   Cinderella

toys. As children of both sexes grow older, they tend to choose toys considered appropriate to their own sex, although boys are more likely to do so than girls.

One way that children learn about sex roles in our society is through TV programs. In the past, children's programs have often stressed different roles for males and females. Males were portrayed as being more successful, dominating, aggressive, and active than females. Females were more yielding in their opinions and judgments than males. Some programs still portray these traditional sex stereotypes. Recently, however, some efforts have been made to show males and females in more varied roles. You might watch some children's programs on Saturday mornings to see how male and female roles are being presented now.

It is important to remember that appropriate male and female behavior differs from one culture to another. In a well-known anthropological study of tribes in New Guinea in the 1930's, three quite different sex roles were found. In one tribe, the behavior of men and women was much more similar than in our culture. Both sexes were gentle, mild, passive, and very interested in family life. In another tribe, the behavior of both men and women was also similar. But both sexes often showed violent and aggressive behavior. In a third tribe, the sexes played different roles. But it was the men who usually cared for the children and were submissive. The women were quite aggressive and usually handled the business affairs.

Are male and female roles changing in our society? Traditionally, our language has placed emphasis on the male. We referred to "mankind" rather than to "womankind" or even "humankind." We spoke of the chairman of a committee, even though that person was a woman. Today we often use the word "chairwoman" if the office is held by a woman. Or we speak of a chairperson to avoid relating the duties of the position to the sex of the individual holding the office.

In the past, we have used the title "Miss" to refer to an unmarried woman, and the title "Mrs." to refer to a married woman. Today we also have the title "Ms.," which refers to both married and unmarried women. But we have no separate title that indicates if a man is married.

There is some evidence that the titles "Miss" and "Mrs." still have traditional values attached to them. Consider the following study, which involved 160 male high school seniors. The seniors were told that a group of American colleges wanted to know about the interests of students who planned to attend college. They were asked to read descriptions of courses and then answer some questions. The courses described were introductory courses for first-year college students. One course was technical. The other was nontechnical. The seniors indicated whether they thought each course would be enjoyable and whether they thought it would be intellectually stimulating. The course description included the name and the title—"Miss," "Mrs.," "Ms.," or "Mr."—of the instructor. There was also a course with no title given, and only the initials and last name of the instructor. The seniors rated the nontechnical course lower in both enjoyment and intellectual stimulation when the instructor was listed as "Miss" and "Mrs." than when listed as "Ms.," "Mr.," or no title. There were little differences in the ratings for the technical course.

The same experiment was carried out with 88 male and two female university students. These students were told that the university might offer two new courses, one more technical than the other. They were also to rate the proposed courses for enjoyment and intellectual stimulation. Again, the titles of "Miss," "Mrs.," "Ms.," and "Mr." were used, as well as some names with no title. The results were the same. The students rated the nontechnical course as probably less enjoyable and less intellectually stimulating when they thought it was to be taught by a "Miss" or "Mrs." It is true that almost all the students in both studies were male. Perhaps high school and university female students would have reacted differently.

More and more women are now entering occupations that once were held almost exclusively by men.

In spite of some traditional expectations of women and men in our society, many changes have taken place in what is considered male and female behavior within the past generation. The roles of the two sexes are tending to be less different. Many schools now offer courses in cooking and child care for boys. They have courses in home and car repair for girls. Husbands often help with such household duties as dishwashing and housecleaning, especially if their wives hold jobs outside the home. Many women have organized to gain equal recognition and equal pay with men in the job market.

Are family roles changing? In our society, people used to assume that women would either marry and probably have children, or would not marry and would have a career. But the number of women who combine career and family roles has been rising steadily for more than a quarter of a century. This change is reflected in the increase in higher education now being received by women as compared to men. For example, in the past thirty-five years, the percentage of female high school graduates who have gone on to complete at least some college work has more than doubled. And today a higher percentage of women are preparing for occupations that in the past were held almost entirely by men. These occupations include law, medicine, architecture, and engineering.

Women are also playing a bigger role in the field of psychology and in business. However, this picture is far from complete.

With the increased cost of living in the 1980's, it has become increasingly difficult for single-income families to maintain the standard of living they are accustomed to. Because of this, there has been an enormous increase in the number of dual-career families in the United States. For many women, this means that it is necessary to combine a number of roles: wife, mother, and worker.

In two-parent families during the 1980's, men have been more involved with household tasks and child care than in previous decades. However, the average number of hours devoted to care of the home and children is still considerably higher for women than for men. Women have made great strides toward equality in the workplace, but many wives are still looking toward greater participation by their husbands in the home and family.

Summary

Attitudes may be an important influence on our behavior. When attitudes interfere with our ability to evaluate new material objectively they become prejudices. Attitudes can be measured by various techniques. Some of the simple techniques include asking people whether they agree with a list of statements, asking them to complete a rating scale, and asking them to complete statements.

Propaganda is often used to change our attitudes. The effectiveness of propaganda is determined by such factors as being first and repeated exposure. When we experience cognitive dissonance we also try to change our attitudes to coincide with or fit our experiences.

Attribution is a process by which we attempt to interpret and explain the behavior of others. We tend to attribute the behavior of other people to dispositional forces, although we attribute our own behavior to situational factors.

Leaders exert great influence on a group. People become leaders for a variety of reasons. Sometimes leaders are classified as democratic leaders, autocratic leaders, and laissez-faire leaders. These categories describe the way in which leaders work with a group.

The power of authority sometimes causes people to inflict harm on others. Milgram's experiment showed that ordinary subjects were willing to administer potentially dangerous levels of shocks under the influence of an authority figure. Other studies have shown that people are more likely to harm someone who won't recognize them and someone who is unpleasant.

The peer group is another influence on our behavior, especially in the case of young people. The peer group influences the formation of attitudes and also sets group standards of conformity.

The fact that we are classified as males or females also influences our behavior. Cultural factors are particularly important in determining our sex roles. There is evidence that our male and female roles are changing in our society, especially in the case of females.

INTERPRETING SOURCES

Some critics of studies of conformity and obedience have suggested that the findings reported were unrealistic because they were "artificial" laboratory experiments. In the following excerpt from "Making Sense of the Nonsensical: An Analysis of Jonestown" (*Reading About the Social Animal*, 1984), Neal Osherow suggests otherwise. As you study the reading think about the words on a placard at Jonestown—"Those who do not remember the past are condemned to repeat it." Also consider whether future Jonestowns can be prevented.

Close to one thousand people died at Jonestown. The members of the Peoples Temple settlement in Guyana, under the direction of the Reverend Jim Jones, fed a poison-laced drink to their children, administered the potion to their infants, and drank it themselves. Their bodies were found lying together, arm in arm; over 900 perished.

How could such a tragedy occur? The image of an entire community destroying itself, of parents killing their own children, appears incredible. The media stories about the event and full-color pictures of the scene documented some of its horror but did little to illuminate the causes or to explain the processes that led to the deaths. . . .

Social psychological concepts can facilitate our understanding: The killings themselves, and many of the occurrences leading up to them, can be viewed in terms of obedience and compliance. The processes that induced people to join and to believe in the Peoples Temple made use of strategies involved in propaganda and persuasion. . . .

In the Peoples Temple, whatever Jim Jones commanded, the members did. When he gathered the community at the pavilion and the poison was brought out, the populace was surrounded by armed guards who were trusted lieutenants of Jones. There are reports that some people did not drink voluntarily but had the poison forced down their throats or injected. . . .

While there were isolated acts of resistance and suggestion of opposition to the suicides . . . such dissent was quickly dismissed or shouted down. . . .

Jim Jones utilized the threat of severe punishment to impose the strict discipline and absolute devotion that he demanded, and he also took measures to eliminate those factors that might encourage resistance or rebellion among his followers. . . . In the Peoples Temple, Jones tolerated no dissent, made sure that members had no allegiance more powerful than to himself, and tried to make the alternative of leaving the Temple an unthinkable option. . . .

Thus, expressing any doubts or criticisms of Jones—even to a friend, child, or partner—became risky for the individual. As a consequence, such thoughts were kept to oneself, and with the resulting impression that nobody else shared them. . . .

Defecting became quite a risky enterprise, and, for most members, the potential benefits were very uncertain. They had little to hope for outside of the Peoples Temple; what they had, they had committed to the church. . . . Finally, in Guyana, Jonestown was surrounded by dense jungle, the few trails patrolled by armed security guards. . . . Escape was not a viable option. Resistance was too costly. With no other alternatives apparent, compliance became the most reasonable course of action.

Source Review

1. What social psychological concepts can explain the tragedy at Jonestown?

2. How did Jim Jones discourage disobedience among members of the Temple?

REVIEW

REVIEWING TERMS

attitude
social attitude
prejudice
propaganda
cognitive dissonance

attribution
dispositional factor
situational factor
democratic leader
autocratic leader

laissez-faire leader
peer
role model
autokinetic illusion
risky shift

CHECKING FACTS

1. When does an attitude become a prejudice?

2. What are some of the techniques that researchers use to measure attitudes?

3. What two factors influence the effectiveness of propaganda?

4. How do people deal with cognitive dissonance?

5. Describe the difference between situational and dispositional forces. To which do we tend to attribute the behavior of others? Our own behavior?

6. What are some characteristics of leaders?

7. Discuss the difference between democratic leaders, autocratic leaders, and laissez-faire leaders. Under which kind of leader do people work best? Explain.

8. Are people "born leaders"? Explain.

9. How does the power of authority influence our behavior? Give an example.

10. Are people more likely to harm people who can't recognize them? Explain through an example.

11. Why is the peer group such a great influence on young people?

12. Explain what is meant by the "risky shift" in making decisions. How do psychologists explain this phenomenon?

13. How are male and female roles determined in a society? Are such roles changing? Explain.

APPLYING YOUR KNOWLEDGE

1. Bring to class a magazine or newspaper advertisement or the summary of a television or radio commercial that shows how propaganda is used to shape public attitudes. You may wish to create a display with these items. Or perhaps you might use them in a class discussion on how the ads work and how shoppers can avoid their powerful influence.

2. Using propaganda techniques, set up a taste test for two soft drinks in your classroom. In actuality, both drinks should be identical—ice water with some fruit juice added. However, your displays should differ greatly. For the first, give the product a neutral name and construct a plain "no frills" set up. For the second, create a catchy name and slogan, along with attractive posters and positive images. Then ask several students not taking the course to sample the

products. Which display attracts more students? If students tasted both products, question them as to their preferences. Did they like one better than the other? Which one? Why? What conclusions can you draw about the influence of propaganda?

3. Organize the class into two groups. Students in each group should place their desks in identical configurations (for example, two rows each with five desks). Then the teacher should ask both groups to seat themselves in alphabetical order. In the first group, however, the teacher will appoint one student to act as leader. The second group will be asked to work on its own. See how long it takes both groups to accomplish the task. Did any leaders emerge in the "leaderless" group? Why do you think this happened?

4. To understand the difference between being a leader and being a follower, spend one 24-hour period in each role. As a leader, assert yourself and attempt to shape as many group decisions as possible, at home and at school. As a follower, avoid any involvement in group decisions, and allow others to assume the leadership role. At the end of each day write down your reactions and details of your experiences.

5. Obedience to authority is important, but at times there may be dangers if obedience is excessive. Using historical accounts from newspapers, magazines, and school textbooks, compile a list of the dangers associated with excessive obedience to authority. Take examples from war, politics, and situations of social discontent. Can you think of current examples of excessive obedience to authority? Give several examples in our country and others.

6. Read the following passage: A man and his son were in a car accident. The man was killed and the son was critically injured. The boy was rushed by ambulance to a nearby hospital and prepared for surgery. All was going smoothly until the surgeon appeared. After taking one look at the patient, the doctor exclaimed, "I can't operate—that's my son!" How can this be? Who is the surgeon? You might also ask several other people not taking this course to read the passage. Did you realize that the surgeon was the boy's mother? What does this activity tell you about people's views on male and female roles?

THINKING CRITICALLY ABOUT PSYCHOLOGY

1. **Evaluating Ideas** How would big business and our economic well-being be affected if there were no such thing as the propaganda of advertising? How would the absence of advertising affect your life personally?

2. **Expressing Opinions** Should psychologists be permitted to lie to subjects about the true nature of an experiment? On the other hand, if subjects are told about the real purpose of the experiment, will their reactions be the same? Do you have suggestions for ways to avoid misleading subjects and still be able to obtain valid data?

3. **Analyzing Ideas** If you had absolute, unlimited power, what would you do? How would your present behavior change? How do you think the behavior of others would change toward you?

4. **Applying Ideas** If you had to change roles with people of the opposite sex, which aspects of the other role would you like the most? Which ones would you like the least?

5. **Forming Opinions** Do you think the day will come when most married men will stay home and take care of the children while their wives work outside the home to support the family? Would you prefer this arrangement or not? Why?

DEVELOPING SKILLS IN PSYCHOLOGY

Understanding Attitudes and Behavior

Another important skill of the psychologist is understanding the relationship between attitudes and behavior. When answering questions on a survey, for example, people sometimes give the answers they think are the most socially acceptable. Their answers, then, may not always reflect their true behavior. As you learned in Chapter 7, that is why it is important to determine attitudes and behavior by phrasing questions in different ways and checking for consistency. For example, most people would answer "no" to the question "Are you a prejudiced person?" But asking questions about specific situations in which prejudice could play a part might uncover a lot more prejudice. In several of his studies, Stanley Milgram asked college students how likely they would be to administer potentially lethal shocks to an anonymous stranger in a psychological experiment. Almost all subjects replied that they would administer no shocks or only very low-level shocks.

Turn to page 426 of the text and read again about what Milgram actually found when he looked at the "shocking behavior" of his subjects. Which do you think is the most valid measure of people's tendency to submit to authority and obey orders—their self-reports or their actual behavior? Why?

READING FURTHER ABOUT PSYCHOLOGY

Aronson, Elliott, *The Social Animal,* Third Edition, W. H. Freeman, San Francisco, Calif., 1980. Discusses such human traits as aggression, prejudice, attraction, and communication.

Bennis, Warren, and Nanus, Burt, *Leaders: The Strategies of Taking Charge,* Fourth Edition, Harper & Row, New York, 1985. Based on interviews with leaders in the business world, this book presents the traits that successful individuals have in common.

Carnegie, Dale, *How to Win Friends and Influence People,* Revised and Updated Edition, Simon & Schuster, New York, 1983. The classic book that teaches the art of dealing with people. Using principles that have been tested over time, the author demonstrates how one person may affect the actions and reactions of others.

Elkin, Frederick, and Handel, Gerald, *The Child and Society: The Process of Socialization,* Fourth Edition, Random House, New York, 1984. Discusses the socialization process in modern society, including the influences of the family, the peer group, and the school.

Evans, Richard I., editor, *The Making of Social Psychology: Discussions with Creative Contributors,* John Wiley & Sons, New York, 1980. Presents a series of interviews with 19 prominent social psychologists.

Nixon, Richard, *Leaders,* Warner, New York, 1982. Presents an engrossing study of a dozen powerful leaders who have shaped the world.

Orwell, George, *Animal Farm,* New American Library, New York, 1983. A satire that explores the implications of various political systems, the evils of totalitarianism, and the origins of prejudice.

Toffler, Alvin, *The Third Wave,* William Morrow, New York, 1980. Describes the increasingly impersonal civilization that is emerging in today's technologically oriented society.

Yablonsky, Lewis, *Fathers and Sons,* Simon & Schuster, New York, 1984. The author, a noted sociologist, examines male roles and how they develop.

Chapter 20

SOCIAL INTERACTION

Chapter Focus

This chapter presents:
- **some conditions under which people are likely to help others**
- **a discussion of social facilitation**
- **the concepts of social competition and social cooperation**

If you saw someone across the street who obviously needed help, would you cross over and provide aid? Would you stop for only a moment and then continue on your way? Or would you try to ignore the situation completely and continue walking on your side of the street? Social interaction includes helping or not helping others. It includes working with and assisting others. It also often includes competing with as well as cooperating with other people. These are some of the aspects of social relationships that we will consider in this chapter.

Helping Others

Sometimes people are motivated to help other people. Offering to help or giving help to other people is called *altruistic behavior*. In recent years, many social psychologists and other researchers have been investigating when and why altruistic helping behavior takes place.

Some cases of failure to help. Returning home from work at three in the morning, a woman was attacked on the street in front of her home in New York City. She screamed and made desperate pleas for help. Thirty-eight of her neighbors came to their windows and watched for over half an hour as she was attacked and murdered. Not one of the neighbors made any attempt to come to her aid. Not one of them even called the police.

A seventeen-year-old boy was stabbed on a subway. There were 11 other passengers in the car. None came to his assistance, although the attackers were no longer around.

Suppose the 38 neighbors or the 11 passengers had been given a social attitude questionnaire. Suppose they were asked, "If you saw a defenseless person being attacked, would you do anything to help?" How do you think they would have answered? Yet when they had a chance to act on their attitude in such a situation, they did nothing.

An experiment with an abandoned car. The cases just described were social incidents, not experiments. But there have been experiments indicating that people sometimes fail to help those in need.

In one experiment, a car was parked on a New York City street where it could be observed. The hood was raised. Might the owner have gone for help? Within ten minutes after being parked, the car was discovered by a man, a woman, and a boy about eight years old. They searched the trunk and glove compartment. Then they removed the battery and radiator. Within three days there was nothing left of the car but a battered, useless wreck. There were 23 incidents of looting, most during daylight hours. They were usually observed by one or more passersby, some of whom stopped to chat with the looters.

However, the results of the experiment were not all negative. Of the people who came in contact with the car, twice as many did no damage as did some damage. Also, a car was parked under the same conditions on a street in a smaller city—Palo Alto, California. The car remained undamaged. When it began to rain, one passerby even stopped and lowered the hood—apparently so the engine would not get wet and become more difficult for the owner to start.

Helping by mailing a letter. If you saw a letter on the sidewalk, would you pick it up and mail it? Would you do a simple act of helping? Or would it depend on whether the envelope had a stamp on it? And whether you were on a crowded sidewalk or one that was not crowded?

In one experiment, 200 letters were dropped during daylight in New York City. Three hundred others were dropped in small towns in central New Jersey. All locations were at least one block from the nearest letter box or post office. In each setting, half of the letters were stamped and half were not. All were addressed to a Pennsylvania location. But the name on half the letters was "Fight Calories." The name on the other half was "Fight Inflation." It was thought that the "Inflation" name would suggest a more important message than the "Calories" name. All envelopes were sealed. All contained a note asking for more information about the organization.

Abandoned cars are more likely to be looted by passersby in large cities, where most people don't know one another.

An experimenter walked along dropping letters. An assistant acted as an observer. The observer made sure that the letters fell with the address facing up. The observer also recorded the number of people who passed by the dropped letter and whether each person noticed the letter. Two weeks were allowed for the letters to arrive at the Pennsylvania address.

In small towns, 17 percent of the passersby noticed the letters. Only 7 percent of the city passersby noticed them. Of those in the small towns who noticed the letters, 24 percent picked them up, compared to only 15 percent in the city.

Once the letter was picked up, the finder had to decide whether or not to mail it. There was little difference in return rate between the "Inflation" and the "Calories" names. But stamped letters were returned in considerably greater numbers than letters without stamps. For example, in small towns 71 percent of the stamped "Inflation" letters that

were picked up were mailed. Only 21 percent were mailed when they had no stamps.

Those conducting the experiment concluded that helping was not determined by something in the person, but by something in the situation. They felt that life in the city may involve circumstances that make it less likely that people will give help.

At the time of this experiment, the post office would deliver unstamped mail if the addressee paid the postage. Today such mail may not be delivered. If this experiment were repeated today, how do you think the results might differ?

The influence of your mood on helping behavior. In general, are you more likely to help others if you are in a good mood than if you are in a bad mood? Suppose you just found some money. Are you more likely to display helpful behavior immediately afterward? If you've just had a minor accident of some kind, are you less likely to provide help?

In one experiment, stamped and addressed envelopes were left in a telephone booth by the researcher, who pretended to be making a call. The researcher then left the booth under four different conditions: (1) taking the dime from the coin return; (2) pretending to take the dime from the coin return; (3) taking the dime and spraying graphite into the coin return; (4) pretending to take the dime and spraying graphite into the coin return. Presumably, subjects would be in a good mood if they found money. They would be in a bad mood if they got their hands dirty in the coin return. How would their mood affect whether or not they helped by mailing the letters?

There were 32 male and 32 female subjects in the experiment. None of them knew that the phone booth was part of an experiment. Of the subjects who found a dime in a clean coin return, 38 percent mailed the letters. Of the subjects who found no coin and got dirty on the graphite, only 6 percent mailed the letters. What other conclusions can you draw from looking at the data given in the table on page 445?

If you were walking by, would you pick up this letter and mail it? Why or why not?

444

	FOUND DIME		DID NOT FIND DIME		FOUND GRAPHITE		FOUND GRAPHITE AND DIME		TOTALS
	Male	Female	Male	Female	Male	Female	Male	Female	
MAILED LETTERS	2	4	2	0	0	1	2	1	12
DID NOT MAIL LETTERS	5	5	5	9	7	8	9	4	52
TOTALS	7	9	7	9	7	9	11	5	64

The results of an experiment in which people found letters in a phone booth under four different conditions

This experiment throws some light on conditions under which individuals are likely to be helpful. Remember, however, that the number of subjects under each condition is small. In other words, the conclusions are based on limited data.

In another study, 30 university students served as subjects. They were divided into three groups, with each listening to a different tape recording. In the first group the recording asked the subjects to imagine that they had just been given a free trip to Hawaii. In the second group the subjects were asked to imagine that their best friend would be going to Hawaii instead. In the third group the recording merely suggested an unemotional activity.

The experimenter then asked all subjects to complete a boring and difficult questionnaire for a "friend of the experimenter." Can you predict the results? If you said that those in the first group answered more questions than did members of either of the other two groups, you would be correct. The psychologists concluded that joy brings about helping behavior, but only when the joy is your own. When joy is experienced for another person, you would be less likely to help.

The effect of physical attractiveness on helping behavior. Are you more likely to help an attractive person than an unattractive person? This question was examined in another experiment using the lost-letter tech-

nique. Experimenters left unsealed but stamped and addressed letters in telephone booths at a large airport. Each envelope contained a completed application form and a photograph. Some of the photographs were of men and some were of women. Some photographs in each classification showed attractive individuals. Others showed unattractive individuals. Of the total of 604 "lost" letters, 442 contained pictures of men, and 162 contained pictures of women. These letters would be important to the people who lost the letters, since they were trying to get a job. Would finders help by mailing the letters or turning them in to someone who handles lost material?

On the whole, finders mailed or turned in the letters more for attractive than for unattractive applicants. In most cases, the majority of finders did not mail the letters. But more than half of the male finders of attractive female pictures mailed them. And over half of the female finders mailed the attractive male pictures.

In a different experiment on the effect of physical attractiveness on helping, a young woman left a dime on the shelf in various telephone cubicles. She left the booth after making a call and waited where she could not be seen. Shortly after someone entered the cubicle, the young woman returned and said, "Excuse me, I think I might have left a dime in this booth. Did you find it?"

Half of the time the young woman was attractive. Cosmetics were used to emphasize

Would you help this person collect his groceries? Would you be more likely to help if the person were a woman?

her natural good looks. The other half of the time the same young woman was made to appear unattractive. She had dark circles under her eyes and blemishes on her face. Her hair was uncombed and messy. She wore unattractive glasses. Through practice she was able to use the same behavior—such as smiling or frowning, certain posture, and different tones in the voice—for both the attractive and unattractive conditions.

The subjects were 90 people who happened to use the phone cubicles. They consisted of 51 males and 39 females. When the young woman looked attractive, 87 percent of the subjects returned her dime. When she looked unattractive, only 64 percent returned her dime. Thus, most people were helpful and honest, although more often with an attractive person than with an unattractive person. Interestingly, the attractiveness of the woman had no more effect on male subjects than on female subjects. Nor was their age related to whether they returned the dime.

In another experiment, researchers asked people to solicit donations for worthy causes. There were two distinct groups of solicitors, both women. One group had an average age of thirty-eight years and was made up of members of the League of Women Voters. Members of this group usu-

ally wore dresses and looked well-kept. The other group averaged nineteen years of age and generally wore jeans. The researchers found that people were more likely to give money when approached by members of the first group. In addition, their contributions tended to be higher. Thus, it seems that appearance plays an important role in whether people will contribute to worthy causes.

Would you help a person who has had a minor mishap? Suppose you saw a woman drop a bag of groceries. Would you help her pick them up?

In one experiment, two young female college students dropped their groceries just outside a supermarket. They were about the same age, height, and weight. They were dressed alike. They had on little makeup and wore no jewelry. Each woman was about 6 meters (20 feet) in front of the main exit of the supermarket. Most of the customers had to pass her on the way to their cars.

In addition to the two young women, there was a "spotter" and an "observer." The spotter and observer were also college students, both men. The spotter stood to one side of the exit within view of the grocery dropper. The observer took a position in the parking lot where he could see exactly what was happening.

Twelve supermarkets were used in the experiment. The markets were similar in prices, size of store, and amount of business. For the most part, the supermarkets attracted shoppers of the middle and lower socioeconomic levels.

The 176 subjects for the experiment were men and women shoppers who were selected as they left the store exit. They ranged in age from about twenty to sixty. Each subject had to be alone. The subjects could not be so loaded down with groceries that they couldn't help.

When the spotter saw a suitable shopper leave the supermarket, he would turn quickly and walk away. This was the signal for the dropper to turn away from the subject, tear open the bottom of her bag of groceries, and drop them when the subject was about 3 meters (10 feet) away from her. The dropper made gestures of surprise, displeasure, and dismay. She slowly circled around the dropped groceries for about five to ten seconds. This gave the subject time to come to her aid.

The behavior of the subjects fell into one of the following four categories: (1) Subject ignores the dropper and walks by. (2) Subject hesitates and shows surprise but does not help. (3) Subject helps dropper with a few of her groceries, then hurries on. (4) Subject helps the dropper with all of her groceries, offers to get her a new grocery bag, and so on. After each trial the observer, the dropper, and other students in the experiment decided on the rating of the subject's behavior.

Data from the ratings revealed that nearly 20 percent of all the subjects gave complete help (category 4). Thirty-three percent ignored the situation (category 1). Twenty-one percent offered some help (category 3). And 26 percent reacted without helping (category 2). Also, there was a sex difference in help given—men helped more than women. It would be interesting to know whether the same results would be obtained if the droppers had been men.

Of the 104 subjects who did not help the dropper, 46 percent did so in full view of another shopper. Would these other shoppers help the dropper? In fact, of these other shoppers, 77 percent of the men and 46 percent of the women did help the dropper, even though they had seen someone else fail to help.

Suppose you saw another student drop an armful of papers or books. Would you offer assistance? Would it make any difference whether the student were male or female?

Do you help someone because it makes you feel good? You probably have opportunities to help those who are handicapped. Perhaps at one time you've helped a blind person cross the street. Suppose you help such people and they show their appreciation by thanking you. Does it make you feel good? Does it make you feel more like help-

When you help someone it can make you feel good and make the person you help feel good, too.

ing the next needy person you meet?

One experiment determined if having been reinforced or punished for helping in the past affects helping behavior. Subjects for the experiment were 160 women. They were asked for assistance while walking on a university campus. An assistant would approach and ask for directions to the university library. The subjects could not just point to the library—they had to go to a bit of trouble to give directions. The assistant would then either reinforce or punish the subject. For reinforcement, the assistant would smile and say, "Thank you very much, I really appreciate this." For punishment, the assistant would interrupt the subject's attempt to give directions with, "I can't understand what you're saying. Never mind, I'll ask someone else." And then quickly walk away.

After walking about 23 meters (75 feet) from this assistant, the subject would meet someone who clearly needed help. The person would drop a small paperback book and walk on, seemingly unaware of having dropped anything. Half of the time it was a person walking in a normal manner. The other half of the time it was a person walking with two crutches.

The subject had three choices of behavior: (1) to pick up the book and return it to

Text continues on page 450.

Case Study: Focus on Research

HELPING THE HELPLESS

Consider the distressed motorist by the side of the road, the woman whose purse has been stolen, and the man who has just fallen on the ice. Obviously all these people need help, although they may not ask for it in so many words. But what about someone who *does* ask? And what if that someone is a lost child? How do you think most people would respond?

Three psychologists based in New York City—Harold Takooshian, Sandra Haber, and David J. Lucido—believed that the answers to these questions depended on the

Large cities tend to encourage anonymity. In this study, people were more likely to help a lost child in a small town than they were in a large city.

size of the community in which the situation occurred. The larger the town, they hypothesized, the less willing people would be to lend a helping hand.

To test their hypothesis, the researchers set up the following situation. A young child, aged six to ten, stood on a busy street. The child approached the first stranger who passed by and said, "I'm lost. Can you call my house?" If the stranger responded positively, the child told a story of having become separated from his or her mother. The stranger was then shown an identification card with the family phone number. An observer stood nearby to ensure the child's safety. The observer also noted data about those questioned, as well as the number of people in the vicinity. The mother, also close at hand, intervened if the stranger did act to help. She quickly ran up to the child, warmly thanked the person for offering to help, and took the child briskly on his or her way.

The role of the lost child was played by a total of 14 children. Black children, white children, boys, and girls all played the part. They asked 127 people for help in big cities. Midtown Manhattan, the Boston Common, Philadelphia's City Hall area, and the Chicago Loop were all designated sites. Researchers also selected 12 different small towns, where the total number asked was 57.

When the study was over, the results were clear. The size of the community was indeed related to helping behavior. In big cities, 46 percent of those asked offered to help. In small towns, the proportion of helpers was 72 percent.

The behavior of helpers varied considerably. A few city people offered to buy the

448

child lunch and even to take him or her home in a taxi. Others, especially Chicagoans, turned to the police for aid. In one case a helper asked the advice of another passerby. He then turned for assistance to a third passerby. This helper did the same until the child was eventually surrounded by a nine-person rescue committee. Although clearly concerned, the group was indecisive.

The psychologists felt that their sample was too small for a reliable generalization about cities. They noted, however, that in Boston and Philadelphia, two-thirds of those who were asked refused to help. In New York, the split was about fifty-fifty. Chicagoans responded positively two-thirds of the time.

The nonhelpers also differed in their responses. Most city people hurried on without stopping, although some offered a dime. One woman snapped, "So what's your problem, kid? I'm lost too." An elderly man, who spoke with the child but refused to do anything else, crossed the street and hid behind a lamppost as the child asked other passersby for help. Not until someone finally responded, after 15 minutes or so, did the man go on his way. Another nonhelper breezily advised: "Go into that restaurant. Your mother's waiting for you there." In small towns, even those who did not help were sympathetic, frequently offering advice or at least excuses.

Interestingly enough, the number of people nearby during the experiment did not make any difference in the results. (Nor did the time of day or the child's or stranger's age, race, or sex.) The researchers concluded that the size of the community as a whole was the determining factor. In large cities, they believed, people adjust to the constant demands on their attention by ignoring requests as much as possible. The nervous pace, the quick sideways glance, and the refusal to help a lost child are ways of avoiding others.

SOURCE: Harold Takooshian, Sandra Haber, and David J. Lucido, "Who Wouldn't Help a Lost Child? You, Maybe." *Psychology Today*, February 1977, pp. 67–68, 88.

The thought of this small child lost in a large city would arouse compassion in many people. Yet others would refuse to help him.

CASE STUDY:
FOCUS ON RESEARCH

TREATMENT OF EARLIER HELP	HELP TO NORMAL WALKER	HELP TO WALKER ON CRUTCHES	OVERALL
REINFORCED	74%	95%	84%
PUNISHED	41%	73%	58%
OVERALL	60%	85%	

A comparison of the treatment of helping behavior in the past with whether the subject helps someone in a new situation

the person; (2) to call the person's attention to the dropped book; and (3) to offer no help. The results showed that the subjects were much more likely to pick up the book than merely to call the person's attention to it. They were also much more likely to help the person on crutches than the person who was walking normally (96 percent versus 71 percent). Subjects who had been reinforced for giving directions to the library helped the person — either by picking up the book or calling attention to it — in 84 percent of the cases. Subjects who had been punished for giving directions helped in only 58 percent of the cases. The data are presented in the table above. In general, a great deal of help was given, as you can see.

Diffusion of responsibility. Are you more likely to help a person when you are alone or when you are in a group? Psychologists have found that people by themselves are more likely to offer assistance. In fact, there is some evidence that the more people there are in a group, the less likely it is that anybody would give help. Psychologists refer to this phenomenon as *diffusion of responsibility,* which means that people in a group do not feel as responsible for offering aid as when they are alone. They feel that they can pass on the responsibility to somebody else.

In one research study, subjects waited in a room to fill out a questionnaire. In some cases the subjects were alone. In others there were two subjects in the room. The experimenter, a young woman, went out of the room after talking with the subjects. Almost immediately, the subjects heard the crash of a chair and the woman's screams. Seventy percent of the subjects who were alone went to the aid of the experimenter. But in the other group only 40 percent offered to help.

In another experiment, college students were asked to participate in a group discussion of personal problems. The students were placed in individual booths and spoke through an intercom system. The discussion seemed to be going smoothly until one student suddenly began having a seizure.

Actually, all voices were on tape, except for that of the subject. The seizure, too, was faked. Nevertheless, for the subject in the study, all events seemed real.

Some of the subjects thought they alone were in contact with the person having the seizure. Some students thought they were part of a three-person group, and others thought they were part of a six-person group. Of the subjects who thought they were alone with the victim, 85 percent reported the seizure. This figure dropped to 62 percent in three-person groups and 31 percent in six-person groups. The researchers concluded that people in a group assume that someone else will offer assistance.

Under certain circumstances, however, people in groups will tend to offer assistance.

If group members can see the person in distress, they may realize that the situation really is an emergency. As a result, they may come to the aid of the victim. In the studies just mentioned, the group members *heard* the victims' screams but were unable to *see* the person.

In addition, if the group members could see one another, they are more likely to take action. They can no longer assume that someone else will help, as may have happened in the studies mentioned earlier.

In a study conducted on a subway in New York City, researchers found that groups of seven or more were more likely to help than smaller groups if they saw both the victim and each other. In this study, a male "victim" of between twenty-five and thirty-five suddenly collapsed as a train began to move. The scene was repeated several times, with different numbers of bystanders, and with the man looking either drunk or ill.

The average time it took to help the "ill" victim was 9 seconds for groups of seven or more. The time was 15 seconds for groups of 1-3, and 18 seconds for groups of 4-6. The time it took to help the "drunk" was 97 seconds for the group of seven or more, compared to 309 seconds and 149 seconds for the other two groups. Thus, even when the victim appeared to be drunk, the larger group was the most likely to offer assistance in this study.

An interesting sidenote is that when a victim appeared to be bleeding, all bystanders were less likely to help. In a later study, the same researchers staged the collapse with the victim sometimes bleeding from the mouth. When this occurred, bystanders were slower to offer assistance than if there was no blood. Perhaps they felt less competent to help in what appeared to be a more serious situation. Or perhaps the bystanders felt uneasy about the sight of blood.

Several factors may affect whether or not people decide to help this heart attack victim. These include the number of people present and how ill they perceive the victim to be.

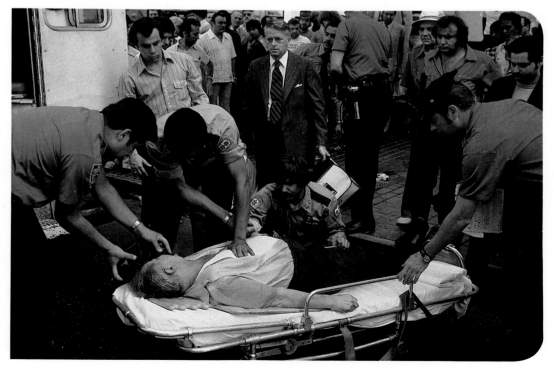

Social Facilitation

Sometimes business executives complain that work production goes down because their employees spend time arguing about social situations and problems. Maybe you've said to yourself, "If only I could get away from my family, or my classmates, I would get some work done." Could the opposite be true?

Actually, the presence of other persons can cause an individual's work output to increase. *Social facilitation* is said to occur whenever an individual does better in a group situation than when working alone because of the presence of other persons. The group situation increases motivation. The individual gets more done because of the stimulation provided by other people. However, individuals are not necessarily more efficient in a group situation. In fact, they may make more errors than when they are working alone. Social facilitation also does not refer to individuals assisting one another in performing a specific task. It refers only to the increase of an individual's work output due to the influence of other people's presence.

Social facilitation among animals. As is so often the case, we can learn much about human behavior by studying the behavior of other organisms. For many years, psychologists and biologists have known that fish eat more when they are with other fish than when eating alone. Ants dig more dirt in a given length of time when working in the presence of other ants than when digging alone. Rats eat and drink more when in group situations than when feeding alone. This is especially true if the food supply is limited or if they have to take turns at a water spout.

Social facilitation among human beings. Research with both children and adults indicates that subjects doing the same tasks achieve more when working near one an-

other than when working alone. In one classic experiment, adult subjects were given several tasks. They had to cross out certain letters of the alphabet from a page of scrambled letters. They were given multiplication problems to work. And they were asked to write arguments to disprove a given statement. The subjects first worked on these tasks in separate rooms. At another time, they worked on similar tasks while seated around a common table. Although seated close to one another, they were asked not to compete or cooperate with one another. The data revealed that a majority speeded up their performance when working at the same table as others doing the same kind of work. However, along with the increase in amount of work, there was some loss in the quality of work.

Another psychologist had subjects work in separate rooms. But all of their working times were controlled by the same starting and stopping signals. Even though the subjects were in separate rooms, the common signals served to provide some social facilitation.

There is evidence that greater production in group situations may be due to rivalry. Many times the individuals in the group don't realize that they are competing. One psychologist had individuals work near one another, but told them that their work records would not be compared to the work records of others. Social facilitation was not indicated by the data. The same psychologist then had some individuals work in rooms by themselves. But they were told that their work record would be compared with the results of others working in other rooms. Their scores were very similar to the work scores of individuals working in group situations. The increase in their work output seemed to be due to rivalry.

Can you study more efficiently when others are around you? Some students find that they can study better in a library or study hall than in a room by themselves. Just the fact that other students are around them, even though there is no communication, results in social facilitation.

One first-year college student was close to being dismissed because of very poor grades. She changed from studying alone to studying in the college library. In just a few weeks, her grades improved and were above average. She had been raised in a large family. All through elementary and high school, she had studied with her brothers and sisters in the same room. Her room at college was in a private home where there were no other students. For her, it was "just too quiet to study there."

On the other hand, students with different home backgrounds may find it very difficult to study efficiently in group situations, or even with a roommate around. And some college dormitories are not well-designed for studying alone.

Social Competition

As we have seen, social facilitation is sometimes related to rivalry or competition. We find competition in many areas of American society. For instance, we thoroughly enjoy such athletic competitions as basketball, hockey, and softball. Both players and spectators want to have their teams win. Such

Is it easier for you to study in a place where other people are also studying? Or do you find it easier to study alone?

sports as track and swimming may be thought of as competition between individuals. Yet there are many track and swimming meets that involve group competition. We enjoy both individual and group competition in such fields as music and debating.

Of course, we accept competition in business. For example, car manufacturers compete with one another for sales. So do electronics firms, book publishers, steel companies, and clothing manufacturers, to name but a few. In many schools, students compete for high grades and scholastic honors, although some schools try to encourage group effort and cooperation rather than competition.

What can experiments tell us about competition?

The pecking order in hens. In some species, when two or more animals desire the same objective, such as food or a mate, competition develops. A hierarchy of dominance or authority, called a *pecking order,* is established. Such social competition occurs, for example, among barnyard hens.

After several hens have been together for some time, a pecking order develops. The most dominant hen in the social competition pecks all other hens in the group and is pecked by none. The next most dominant hen pecks all other hens except the dominant one. This order continues down to one hen that is pecked by all the other hens but does not peck any hen. The order becomes relatively fixed. It can be illustrated by the diagram here for five hens — A, B, C, D, and E.

What happens if a new hen is put in the pen with a group of hens that has already established a pecking order? In that case, a new hierarchy develops. The new hen learns its position in the group.

There are several factors that determine the pecking order among hens. For example, the most dominant hen — the A hen in our diagram — tends to be the largest and fastest hen in the group. And it tends to be the "smartest" one. It learns quickly in experimental learning situations.

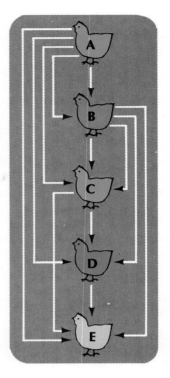

The pecking order in human beings. Can you think of examples of a pecking order in human social situations? What about the chain of command in military life? What about the seating of guests at formal dinners? If you attend a college commencement ceremony, you may find that faculty members enter in the order of their academic rank and tenure.

If you have a chance, watch a group of children at play. Does one child tend to boss and perhaps win fights over all the others? Is one child always picked on by the others? Does there seem to be a pecking order for the other children?

Studying competition between human beings in the laboratory. One psychologist has studied social competition by having two subjects compete in a business situation. Both of the players in this competitive game operate toy trucks. Each player tries to drive a truck over the shorter of two roads to make as much profit as possible. To be sure that they are motivated, both drivers are actually paid money, although the amount of money for each trip is small. It might be 60 cents, minus 1 cent for each second used in travel time. The road situation is shown in the figure on this page. One firm is called Acme. The other is Bolt. Trucks for both firms travel at the same speed. They can be made to go either forward or backward.

If a player takes the alternate route, the player will lose money on each trip. If both players try to use their shorter route, they will meet on a one-lane section of the road, where they cannot pass. If one of them backs up so that the other can go through on the one-lane section of the road, that player will lose money. And the other player will make a profit, or at least suffer less of a loss. If neither driver gives in and allows the other to use the one-lane road, time costs will build up and both players will lose heavily. On the other hand, if the drivers learn to take turns in letting each other go through on the one-lane road, both will be better off financially.

The use of a threat by one person. The psychologist conducting the experiment introduced the possibility of a threat. One driver—Acme, for example—was given a gate that Acme could close. After Acme had entered the one-lane road, the gate could be shut. In that case, Bolt could not get through and would be forced to back up the one-lane road. This would let Acme get to the destination and make a profit, or at least reduce any loss. After Acme had left the one-lane road, the gate would open. Bolt could proceed. But Bolt would have wasted time and money. Of course, Bolt, knowing of Acme's threat of closing the gate, could take the alternate route from the start. But Bolt would be certain to lose some money by doing so.

In this one-gate situation, data from the experiment indicated that the driver with a gate did better financially than the other driver. This was especially true on the first few trips. Interestingly enough, the driver with the gate gradually gave up the advantage of a threat, and the two players began cooperating. The psychologist concluded this part of the experiment by saying, "If one member of a bargaining pair has a weapon,

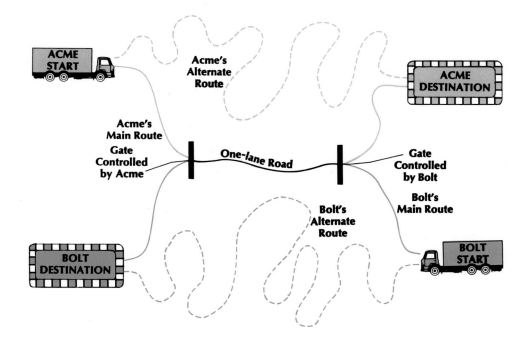

This is a painting of a World War II sea battle. When competition occurs between nations and both sides begin to use threats, communication may break down, compromises are harder to achieve, and the result may be war.

you are better off if you are the one who has it. But you may be even better off if neither of you has a weapon."

The use of threats by two persons. What happens if both drivers are given gates? It was found that both drivers lost more money than in the one-gate situation.

The two drivers were given intercoms so that they could talk to each other. Presumably, this should have given them a great advantage. But such was not the case. Their conversations, which were held under the strain of competition and threats, were not helpful. They said things that worked against them rather than for them.

Could there be similar situations in social groups? One great world power threatens another great world power, which in turn produces a threat of its own. A minority group threatens a majority group, which then produces a threat of its own. Workers threaten management, and management threatens

workers. In such situations, communication is attempted, as it should be. But will it be successful? When competition and threats are involved, communication often turns into conversations that are not helpful. For a time they may even seem to work against settling differences. At conferences between diplomats of opposing nations, communications often seem to break down. No solutions may be found, at least for a considerable period.

Playing "chicken." In another experiment using the same trucking apparatus, high school students were used as subjects. The game was changed to introduce the idea of "chicken."

The students were told that if their two trucks met at any place along the one-lane road, it would be considered a collision. This would cost each player at least 10 cents. Instead of a gate as a threat, a player could use a "lock." This device enabled a player to lock the truck so that it could move in only

456

one direction—forward. A signal informed the other driver that the competitor's truck was locked into a forward-only commitment. Data indicated that the driver who had the commitment device made considerably more money than the driver without a lock.

If both drivers could lock their trucks into a forward-only position, both would lose all of their profits. The psychologists found that the high school students playing the game tended to avoid locking themselves into a position from which they could not compromise. This was especially true if they knew they were going to have repeated encounters with another player who could use the same threat. If they knew in advance that there was to be only a single encounter with another driver, they became less careful. They also lost money.

Minority groups and social competition. These experiments suggest some of the problems of competition between social groups in our society. Consider, for example, two ethnic or religious groups. Both are striving to reach certain economic and social goals. Will they cooperate on the "one-lane road" that both must travel? Or will both groups try to threaten each other so that eventually one group will have to "chicken out"? Will they lock themselves into positions from which they cannot retreat?

National groups and social competition. What about two nations that have separate goals but face some conflicts in achieving those goals? They can agree to alternate in negotiating the one-lane road of international relationships. Or one nation can build up military and economic power. It can force the other nation to let it win all or most of the international disputes. Or else both nations can build up military and economic might. This can make any solution to their problems very difficult. One or both nations can lock themselves into a commitment situation so that they cannot back down or compromise. They can play the international game of "chicken." But in this game, millions of lives are at stake.

The Effects of Competition

Competition often improves the quality and quantity of work. Sometimes, however, competition has disadvantages. The disadvantages include confusion due to the pressure, the effects of winning at any price, the effects of losing, and the aggression that may result.

Confusion and inefficiency. Some individuals do more and better work when they are not under the pressure of individual or group competition. One classic experiment used a horse race to study the effect of competition. Wooden horses were attached to a string. They could be pulled along a track by winding the string onto a fishing reel. Working alone, without any element of competition, individuals could usually pull their horses along the track quite efficiently. But when they competed against others in a horse race, they would often tangle their lines. They even reversed their reels. They became excited and confused. They were less efficient than when running their horses alone.

Winning at any price. When competition is keen, some individuals may become dishonest in order to win. Some children will cheat at party games to win a desired prize. A student may turn to cheating to get top grades if public recognition, a college scholarship, or parental praise is at stake. There are examples throughout history of elections being rigged by political candidates who wanted to win at any price. Can you think of other examples of winning at any price?

The effects of losing. Whether in beauty contests, musical competitions, athletic events, or debates, all too often we glorify the winner. We don't consider the effects of competition on those who don't win top prizes. It is true that some people who lose in a contest try all the harder to win the next time. But it seems that such individuals are often the exception rather than the rule.

What about the effects of frequently being a loser? Will such a loser become discouraged and stop even trying to win?

These questions were considered in a research study involving school grades. The members of a college class were asked to indicate what grade they expected to receive on an important examination to be given the next day. Half of the students did as well as or better than they expected. They had been successful. The other half of the students could be thought of as being unsuccessful. They did not achieve their goals.

Just before the next important examination, all students were again asked to indicate what grade they expected to achieve. Of the successful group, 62 percent expected to achieve the same grade as they had indicated on the first exam. Of the unsuccessful group, 66 percent gave the same response. There was not much difference. But only 2 percent of the successful group lowered their expectations. And 36 percent of them raised their expectations for the second exam. On the other hand, 34 percent of the unsuccessful group lowered their expectations. And none of them raised their expectations. Do you try harder in courses in which you've been successful than in courses in which you feel you've been unsuccessful?

Hostile aggression. If competition between individuals or groups becomes intense, hostile aggression may result. **Hostile aggression** means responding to a situation in ways that are intentionally harmful to another person or group and are not for purposes of self-defense.

Athletic contests are generally conducted in a fair way. But athletes have been known to try to injure a particularly threatening rival. After a game, fans of the losing team may start a brawl. They may try to injure fans of the opposing team. Or they may destroy property belonging to the rival team.

Suppose leaders and their followers in some nations come to believe that they cannot compete successfully in world trade. They become hostile. They may even threaten to kill or actually kill people in rival nations. They destroy as much of the material wealth of the other nations as possible. We call such a situation war.

Can we reduce the disadvantages of competition? We may be swinging somewhat away from the very competitive way of life that characterized the early days of America. But our society still stresses competition and puts up with its undesirable effects. Can anything be done to lessen the undesirable aspects without ending competition?

One possibility is to improve communication between competitors. We have seen that under conditions of competition, effective communication between competitors may break down. Suppose, however, that two competing individuals or groups can talk or otherwise communicate without using threats or furthering the competition. They may be able to resolve some of their differences and work together in a helpful way.

Another possibility is to stress competition with the individual's own record rather than with the performance of others. In competing with others, some individuals are bound to succeed and others are bound to lose. In the case of school grades, for example, a few students will receive high grades. A few will receive low grades. And most students will receive average grades. But if students compete against their own scores, every student has an opportunity to succeed. For example, suppose at the beginning of a semester students take a standardized test in some subject area. Suppose near the end of the semester the same test, or an equivalent test, is repeated. Even the students with the lowest scores on the earlier test will probably find that they've improved. They will have succeeded in this competition with themselves.

Another way to reduce the disadvantages of competition for those who do not win is by sharing the disappointment of failure. An athletic team may lose all, or nearly all, of its games in a given season. Each member of the team may be quite unhappy about the season. But there is some comfort in being able to share the disappointment. Some businesses have sales teams that compete with one another. One team is bound to lose, or at best tie for last place. The individual salespeople on this team may find comfort in knowing that others in the group also tried and still did not succeed.

Competition seems to be a basic part of our social life. But perhaps it would be worthwhile for our society to place more emphasis on cooperation.

Social Cooperation

With certain insects, such as ants and bees, social cooperative behavior is biologically determined. However, we will devote our attention here to learned social cooperation. We will examine some situations in which animals and humans learn to cooperate to achieve various goals.

Social cooperation in animals. A number of experiments have shown that rats can learn to cooperate with one another. One such experiment used a box with an electrified floor. A rat could be given a shock through the floor as it ate from a dish of food. But the shock could be avoided if another rat would cooperate. At one end of the box, and away from the food, was a platform that turned off the current if a rat climbed on it. Alone in the box, each rat learned two things: (1) to eat from the dish of food, and (2) to turn off the electrical current by stepping on the platform. Then two such trained rats were placed in the box together. At first, the pair of rats showed uncooperative behavior. They both put up with the electrical shock to eat at the same time. Or they both climbed on the platform to avoid being shocked.

In time, some pairs of rats did learn to cooperate. One rat ate while the other stayed on the platform. This was a pleasant situation for the rat that was eating. It was not a pleasant situation for the hungry rat on the platform. The rat on the platform began pulling on the tail of the rat that was eating. Apparently, it was trying to get the eating rat to come to the platform. Eventually, the rats learned to shuttle back and forth so that each could eat without receiving a shock.

Social cooperation has also been ob-

Social cooperation can be found among animals. These musk oxen huddle together to protect one another from the cold.

served in chimpanzees. Two chimpanzees were placed in separate cages. One cage contained a green and a blue panel. The other contained a red and a yellow panel. Food was given only if the chimpanzees pushed on their panels in a certain order. For example, one chimpanzee had to push its yellow panel and then wait for the other chimpanzee to push its green panel. Next, the first chimpanzee had to push its red panel. Then the second animal had to push its blue panel. If the pair cooperated and pushed their panels in the correct order, food became available to both. In some pairs, one chimpanzee's partner was slow in pushing its panels. The first chimpanzee would reach through the bars of its cage and give the other chimpanzee a push. It might even try to turn it in the direction of its panels. The chimpanzees learned to cooperate.

There are even examples of social cooperation between two species that are usually hostile to each other. A young rat and a young kitten were kept in the same cage. They learned to live together. Then a screen was placed between the animals and their food. If the rat pressed one lever at the same time that the kitten pressed another lever, the screen would open. They could both eat. Neither of the animals could open the screen by itself. They had to learn to cooperate. Once, when the kitten was playing with the rat's tail, they both happened to press their levers. The screen opened. They both got food. With repeated trials, learning took place. Before too long, the kitten and rat were cooperating whenever they wanted food.

Animals, even those that are usually hostile to each other, can learn to work together for a common good. What about the human species?

Social cooperation among people. In one experiment, 20 children, seven to twelve years old, were divided into ten teams of two each. The two children on each team were seated on opposite sides of a table. Each child was given a pen with an electrical connection. In front of the child were three holes. If the two children happened to place their pens in holes opposite each other, a red light would flash on, and a single jelly bean was delivered. If the two children placed their pens in holes that were not opposite, no reinforcement was given. All ten teams learned the cooperative response within ten minutes after the experiment began. No team had been told that cooperation was necessary. Almost immediately, eight of the teams learned to divide the jelly beans in some manner. In the other two teams, one child took all of the jelly beans until the partner refused to cooperate. Then they began talking to each other. They soon reached an agreement, such as, ''The first piece is mine, the next piece is yours.'' After this, members of the two teams began cooperating.

In another experiment, college students solved puzzles and worked out answers to human relations problems under two conditions—cooperation and competition. In the cooperative condition, members of the group were told to work together, although each group would be in competition with other groups. All members of the highest-ranking group would receive an honor mark in the course. In the competitive condition, only those individuals in each group who made the best contributions would receive the honor mark. Data revealed that members of the group working under cooperative conditions solved their puzzles more rapidly and worked out more creative solutions to their human relations problems than members of the group working under competitive conditions.

Of course, there is also evidence of social cooperation outside the laboratory. Perhaps you've heard people say that competition, rather than cooperation, is ''natural'' for humans. Most sociologists and anthropologists, as well as social psychologists, disagree.

Cooperation in the traditional Hopi Indian culture. Among Hopi Indians, social cooperation is considered to be a virtue. Competition is discouraged. As farmers in the Southwest, the Hopi Indians had to rely on irrigation. Irrigation projects involve co-

Members of the Amish sect emphasize cooperation. They work together and help one another in their daily tasks.

operation. The Hopi people learned that co-operation was socially much more desirable than competition.

Yet even in the Hopi culture, children may display competitiveness, although such social behavior is frowned upon by adults. In one study, Hopi children were asked what they would do in certain social situations. For example, they were asked if they would prefer to make the best grades in their class or to make the same grades as most of the other children. Sixty percent of the boys and 79 percent of the girls replied that they would prefer to make the best grades. Another question asked if they would prefer to run a race for a prize or just for fun. Seventy-two percent of the boys and 63 percent of the girls said they would rather run for a prize. It would be interesting to know how their parents would have answered these questions when they were children.

Social cooperation and communication. Communication often fails to achieve its goal. Yet it can make for greater cooperation both among Americans and with other nations. The United States—and also the world—seems smaller when brought together through communication and social contacts. This can increase the chances for social cooperation.

Many national and international problems might be solved or improved if there could be a friendly system of communication among individuals. Suppose each of us could communicate in a friendly way with just a few individuals from different social, economic, ethnic, and national groups. We might become more sensitive to others and overcome some of our prejudices.

When you travel, near or far, do you try to communicate in a friendly way with people who do not have the same socioeconomic, ethnic, or religious background as your own? Or do you limit your social contacts to people much like yourself? Do you try to do your part in increasing social contacts and communication?

You have now come to the end of your course in psychology. Some of you may continue studying psychology. Others will seek a future in some other field. Regardless of the future you choose to pursue, it is hoped that you will make use of what you've learned in psychology. Perhaps you now have a better understanding not only of yourself but of everyone with whom you come in contact. Perhaps, by understanding and helping others, you can make our world a better place in which to live.

Summary

Social psychologists have focused on when and why people help other people. Some influential factors include the size of the city or town in question, people's mood at the time, and attractiveness of the person in need of help. People also tend to help others if they have been reinforced for earlier helping behavior.

An especially influential factor in determining whether people will help others is diffusion of responsibility. We help people more often when we are alone than when we are in a group.

Social facilitation is the increase in effort and motivation that occurs when people are in a group. Research shows that both animals and people often work better in a group than when alone.

Competition exists in many areas of society and may be advantageous. Sometimes it results in a pecking order, which is a hierarchy among those in a group. Studies have also shown that the use of threats by one or both parties may influence the outcome of a competitive situation.

Competition also has some serious disadvantages. These include an increase in confusion, the possibility of dishonesty, lowered expectations, and hostile aggression. These disadvantages can be reduced, however, by improving communication between competitors, competing with oneself instead of others, and sharing the disappointment of failure.

Social cooperation occurs when people help each other achieve various goals. In both animals and people, members have been taught to cooperate with one another. Communication increases the chances for social cooperation.

INTERPRETING SOURCES

In this excerpt from *The Unresponsive Bystander: Why Doesn't He Help?*, Bibb Latané and John Darley discuss some of the reasons that people may hesitate to get involved when emergencies arise. As you read, think about the reasons that people are reluctant to become involved in emergency situations.

Perhaps the most distinctive characteristic of an emergency is that it involves threat of harm or actual harm. Life, well-being, or property are in danger. At worst, an emergency can claim the lives not only of the victims, but of anyone who intervenes. At best, the major result of any intervention is a restoration of the status quo before the emergency, or more normally, a prevention of further damage to an already damaged person or property.

Even if an emergency is successfully dealt with, rarely is anybody better off afterwards than before. Consequently, there are few positive rewards for successful action in an emergency. These high costs and low rewards put pressure on individuals to ignore a potential emergency, to distort their perceptions of it, to underestimate their responsibility for coping with it.

A second important feature of an emergency is that it is an unusual and rare event. Fortunately, although he [or she] may read about them in newspapers or watch fictionalized accounts on television, the average person probably will encounter few real emergencies in his [or her] lifetime. Unfortunately, when [an individual] does encounter one, he [or she] will have had little direct personal experience in handling such a situation. An individual facing an emergency is untrained and unrehearsed.

In addition to being rare, emergencies differ widely one from another, both in cause and in the specific kind of intervention required to cope with them. The one common requirement is action—but the type of action differs from one emergency to another. A fire and a drowning are both emergencies: one requires the addition of water, the other its removal. Each emergency presents a specific problem and each requires a different type of action. Consequently, unlike other rare events, there is no short list of rules for coping with emergencies. . . .

The fourth basic characteristic of emergencies is that they are unforeseen. They "emerge," suddenly and without warning. Being unexpected, emergencies must be handled without the benefit of forethought and planning, and an individual does not have the opportunity to think through in advance what course of action he [or she] should take. [The individual] must [think] in the immediacy of the situation and has no opportunity to consult others as to the best course of action or to alert others who are especially equipped to deal with emergencies. The individual confronted with an emergency is thrown on his [or her] own resources. . . .

A final characteristic of an emergency is that it requires immediate, urgent action. . . . It forces [the individual] to come to a decision before [there is] time to consider . . . alternatives. . . .

The picture is a grim one. Faced with a situation in which [an individual] can gain no benefit, unable to rely on past experiences, on the experiences of others, or on forethought and planning, denied the opportunity to consider carefully his [or her] course of action, the bystander to an emergency is in an unenviable position. It is perhaps surprising that anyone should intervene at all.

Source Review

1. According to the authors, what are the five characteristics of an emergency?

2. In an emergency situation, what reward for helping can a bystander expect?

CHAPTER 20

REVIEWING TERMS

altruistic behavior	social facilitation	hostile aggression
diffusion of responsibility	pecking order	

CHECKING FACTS

1. How can a situation contribute to people's willingness to help others?

2. What is the influence of mood on helping behavior? What role does physical attractiveness play?

3. Do people tend to help others if they have been reinforced in the past? Give some evidence to support your answer.

4. How does diffusion of responsibility affect group behavior? How can diffusion of responsibility be overcome?

5. Does social facilitation increase productivity? Explain using examples.

6. How does the use of threat affect competitive situations?

7. What are some of the disadvantages of competition? How can these disadvantages be reduced?

8. Cite some evidence to show that people can learn to cooperate.

9. How does communication affect cooperation?

APPLYING YOUR KNOWLEDGE

1. With the help of a friend of the opposite sex, arrange to drop an armful of papers or books in front of the school. Have your friend stand nearby and note how many people do and do not offer assistance and the sex of each. Change roles with your friend and repeat the procedure. Did the sex of the person in need have any influence on people's helping behavior? You may have to do the experiment several times at different locations to get a sizable sample.

2. Repeat the above activity but vary the procedure slightly. Plan to drop your papers or books half the time when only one person is walking by, and the other half when small groups of people are passing. In which situation were people more likely to offer assistance? The results of both activities could be written up and presented to your school newspaper.

3. To test whether people work better alone or in groups, prepare several lists of numbers to be totaled. Present your lists to individual students and groups of students in the cafeteria. State that your psychology class has conducted an experiment and needs help tabulating the data. Allow the subjects ten minutes to work on the problems. How did individual performance compare with group performance in terms of speed and accuracy?

4. Look through the newspaper for articles illustrating competition between social groups. The examples may occur at a

local, national, or international level, and may concern politics, religion, economics, or even sports. Note where the groups cooperate, use threats, or have locked themselves into a position from which they cannot retreat.

5. For one week, perform your family chores and duties in your usual manner.

During the next week, however, devise a plan that provides for equal distribution of duties among cooperating family members. At the end of the second week, compare whether working alone or in cooperation with others produced better results.

THINKING CRITICALLY ABOUT PSYCHOLOGY

1. **Classifying Ideas**   In general, are people who live in rural areas and small towns more kind than those who live in large cities? Why do you think this is or is not so? What evidence do you have?

2. **Organizing Ideas**   Would you say that people in other highly industrialized countries are usually more helpful to individuals in distress than are people in the United States? If so, which countries? What is different in their society that influences them to be more helpful or less helpful?

3. **Forming an Opinion**   Do you believe that school grades should be assigned on a competitive basis? If you were the

teacher, on what basis would you assign grades?

4. **Evaluating Ideas**   Should we have a law saying that the first car to come on the scene of any highway accident, or even a car breakdown, must stop and offer assistance or the driver will be fined? What reasons can you give for your answer?

5. **Implementing Ideas**   What can be done to increase social cooperation in this country? What can you do?

6. **Proposing Ideas**   How can large cities be made more "friendly"? What sorts of housing arrangements would you propose?

DEVELOPING SKILLS IN PSYCHOLOGY

Designing an Experiment

This chapter describes a number of social psychological experiments on helping behavior. In these experiments, the independent variables consist of some feature of the situation—whether or not an envelope had a stamp, whether or not a dime was left in the coin return box of a public telephone, whether the photograph in an envelope with an application was of an attractive or unattractive person. In every case, the depen-

dent variable was some sort of helping behavior.

Use what you have learned about psychology and about helping behavior to design an experiment of your own. Obtain a large, empty box. Your question should be "What kinds of variables influence whether or not someone will help a student who is approaching a closed door carrying what appears to be a heavy box?" Choose a safe setting to carry out your experiment. Decide what variables might be important—sex of student, sex of passerby, time of day, location of the incident—and design an experiment to test your hypothesis. Do not put anything in the box, but carry it as though it is very heavy. Develop a form for recording your results. Consider issues of reliability and validity. Decide how best to summarize your results.

READING FURTHER ABOUT PSYCHOLOGY

Argyle, Michael, *The Psychology of Interpersonal Behavior,* Revised Edition, Penguin, New York, 1985. An introductory explanation of the dynamics that control human interactions.

Buscaglia, Leo, *Loving Each Other: The Challenge of Human Relationships,* Holt, Rinehart and Winston, New York, 1984. Suggests ways of replacing emotional detachment with emotional attachment.

Coleman, Daniel, *Vital Lies, Simple Truths: The Psychology of Self-Deception,* Simon & Schuster, New York, 1986. Discusses how people purposely overlook unpleasant experiences and block out painful memories. Examines the impact of this phenomenon on relationships and on society in general.

Frank, Pat, *Alas, Babylon,* Bantam, New York, 1976. This classic novel tells the story of a small group of men and women who found the strength and courage to join together during a global catastrophe.

Ten Boom, Corrie, *The Hiding Place,* Revised Edition, Zondervan, Grand Rapids, Mich., 1984. True story of a devout Christian woman who was sent to a Nazi concentration camp during World War II as punishment for trying to protect Jews.

Using the Skills of a Psychologist

Unit 7 Studying Group Behavior

Social psychologists are very interested in studying group behavior. As you learned in Chapter 18, small groups are characterized by a gathering of people who have face-to-face communication with one another, who share a sense of belonging to the group, and who share a common goal.

Groups are established for many purposes and are organized in many ways. One of the ways in which psychologists study small groups is through natural observation. For example, a psychologist who is interested in exploring the organization and functions of a literary club might become a member of that club. He or she might participate in the literary readings and criticisms, and get to know the members of the club. This would allow the psychologist to observe the activities of the group members in their natural environment.

You can use natural observation to study small group behavior. First, make a list of all the school-related or extracurricular groups and clubs associated with your school. These groups may include, for example, the chess club, the student council, or the high school yearbook committee. Information on school-related groups should be available from a school administrator, guidance counselor, or school psychologist. When the list is complete, use your knowledge of small groups to determine whether each group is task-oriented or interaction-oriented, inclusive or exclusive, and formal or informal.

With the permission of your teacher, choose one group to observe. Speak to the sponsor of the group and ask permission to attend one of the group's meetings as an observer of group behavior for your psychology class. If the sponsor gives you permission, arrange to sit in on one of your chosen group's meetings. Observe the group's activities and make notes on your findings. Be aware that the behavior of some people changes when they know they are being observed, so take notes on the ways in which you think your presence is changing the behavior of the group members.

As you observe the group, refer back to your earlier classification of the group. If you classified the group as a task-oriented one, for example, what behavioral evidence can you gather to verify this? Include in your notes any evidence you can gather to verify whether the group is formal or informal and inclusive or exclusive.

Pay attention to the leadership style of the group. Is one person clearly the leader of the group or is leadership shared by a number of people? If one person is the obvious leader of the group, what is his or her leadership style? Is the leader an autocratic leader, a democratic leader, or a laissez-faire leader? Include in your notes your impressions of the ways in which leadership style influences group behavior.

Also pay attention to the communication patterns of the group. Are the group members effective communicators? Do they work well together to solve problems, generate ideas, and get things done? Is everyone encouraged to participate or do some people dominate the proceedings? Include in your notes your impressions of the way in which the seating arrangement of the group members encourages or inhibits their interaction.

Finally, take notes on your impressions of the following group characteristics: group cohesiveness, group morale, and group atmosphere. Include any behavioral evidence you observe to substantiate your impressions of these group characteristics.

Without identifying the group, prepare a written report on your findings to present to the class. Use your notes as the basis for the report.

REVIEWING THE UNIT

1. Why do researchers focus on the study of behavior in small groups?

2. To what problem is the relationship between size of the group and production of ideas linked?

3. What four characteristics help keep groups together and functioning as a unit?

4. How do psychologists go about studying communication?

CONNECTING IDEAS

1. **Classifying Ideas** In what three ways may small groups be classified?

2. **Summarizing Ideas** What are four reasons that individuals join certain groups?

3. **Contrasting Ideas** What is the distinction between verbal and nonverbal communication?

4. **Identifying Ideas** What are some examples of peer-group values? Cite four examples from the text.

5. **Evaluating Ideas** Are people more efficient in a group situation? Why or why not?

PRACTICING RESEARCH SKILLS

Using library materials, research ways in which people in different societies communicate verbally and nonverbally. In order to make the research project more interesting to the class, each student should select a different society from around the world.

Students should focus on customs within the culture, and freedom to communicate within the political system of the country. For example, are people in democratic countries more likely to communicate in public than people who live under totalitarian governments? How do the laws of the nation protect or prohibit freedom of speech?

Present your findings to the class. Discussion may also focus on the similarities or differences in verbal and nonverbal communication between the United States and other nations. Some students may wish to research particular United States Supreme Court cases that define the freedom of speech.

FINDING OUT MORE

You may wish to contact the following organization for additional information about the material in this unit.

Center for Communication
1133 Ave. of the Americas
New York, NY 10036

468

USING STATISTICS

CAREERS IN PSYCHOLOGY

BIOGRAPHICAL PROFILES

GLOSSARY

INDEX

Suppose you have been asked to carry out a study on the college preferences of seniors at your school. You have conducted interviews and received dozens of completed questionnaires. Now you find yourself almost overwhelmed with data, or information. What do you do next?

Your next step would be to organize and analyze your data. Psychologists would use statistics to help them with these tasks. **Statistics** are simply mathematical procedures for collecting, organizing, analyzing, and interpreting data.

To many students the thought of statistics brings to mind images of Albert Einstein frantically sorting out complex mathematical formulas in his laboratory. Statistics, though, need not be that forbidding or complex. And you don't have to be a genius to use them. With an understanding of only a few basic concepts, you can use statistics to help carry out some research.

Organizing Data

The most important function of statistics is to help psychologists make sense of their findings. In this book you learned about many research studies that psychologists have conducted and about the conclusions they have drawn. But before these researchers could make any concluding statements, they had to sort out their data carefully. One way of doing this is through the use of frequency distributions.

Frequency distributions. Suppose that your teacher gives a short ten-question quiz to the 35 students in your class and the 35 students in another class. After grading the tests, the teacher finds that the students received the following scores:

YOUR CLASS							OTHER CLASS						
5	7	8	9	8	9	7	5	8	6	6	7	7	8
9	8	7	10	7	7	8	10	7	8	7	8	8	6
8	10	7	9	8	8	7	8	5	7	9	6	9	7
8	6	8	6	8	9	10	9	7	7	7	7	8	8
9	6	7	5	7	8	5	7	6	5	8	6	9	7

What does this tell the teacher about how well each class did? The way the scores appear, the teacher would have a difficult time making sense of the findings. However, suppose the teacher arranged the scores in the following manner:

YOUR CLASS			OTHER CLASS		
Score	Tally	Frequency	Score	Tally	Frequency
10	III	3	10	I	1
9	JHT I	6	9	IIII	4
8	JHT JHT I	11	8	JHT IIII	9
7	JHT IIII	9	7	JHT JHT II	12
6	III	3	6	JHT I	6
5	III	3	5	III	3

Notice how much easier the data now are for the teacher to analyze. The teacher can readily see at a glance, for example, how many students received a score of 10, a score of 9, and so forth.

Such an arrangement is known as a *frequency distribution.* It is simply a way of arranging data to find out how often a certain score, age, salary, or other piece of data occurs. To set up a frequency distribution a researcher would arrange the data from high to low and enter a tally mark each time a piece of data occurs. The researcher would then total each group of tally marks to obtain their frequency.

Sometimes there are too many different scores or other data for a researcher to list individually. For example, if the same teacher gave a test in which scores ranged from 37 to 100, the teacher might have over 50 individual listings. When this occurs, the teacher may use *class intervals.* These are specific numerical spans rather than individual scores. As with individual listings, scores are arranged from high to low. A frequency distribution for these scores that uses class intervals might be:

Class interval	Tally	Frequency
91–100	II	2
81–90	IIII	4
71–80	JHT JHT	10
61–70	JHT IIII	9
51–60	JHT I	6
41–50	III	3
31–40	I	1

The size of the class is determined by the number of classes the researcher wants and the span between the highest and lowest scores. Generally, researchers try to limit the number of classes to between 10 and 20.

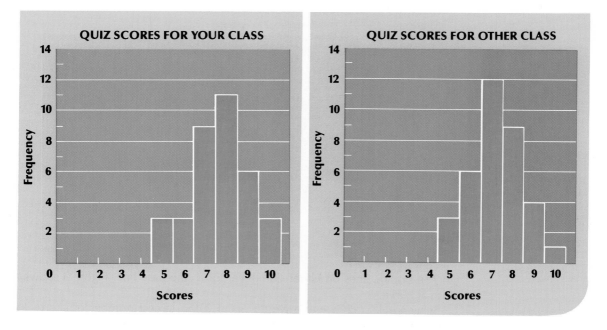

Figure 1   **Figure 2**

Histograms. Many times researchers wish to show their results graphically. This makes it easy for people to interpret their findings. One typical way of doing this is through the use of a histogram. A **histogram** resembles a bar graph, but with two important differences—it is always vertical and there is never any space between the bars. Note the two histograms for the quiz scores (Figures 1 and 2).

Histograms (and frequency distributions in general) provide important information. As you can see in these histograms, most scores for both your class and the other class fall somewhere in the middle. Only a few students in each group made exceptionally high scores. Similarly, relatively few made very low scores.

This is typical of the way many skills and characteristics are distributed. Most people have average athletic ability, although some are extremely good in sports and others are not nearly as coordinated. Most people have average singing voices, although some sing beautifully and others can hardly carry a tune. Most people are of average height, although some are exceptionally tall and others are exceptionally short. In general, the farther you go from the center of a distribution, the fewer entries you will find in each category.

This tendency is closely related to another important concept in statistics. This is known as the normal curve.

The normal curve. The **normal curve** is one of the most useful concepts in statistics. It is a perfectly symmetrical curve that has the following characteristics: (1) It has one high point, from which the line slopes downward smoothly on both sides. (2) One side looks exactly like the other, only in reverse. (3) It is bell-shaped, and therefore is sometimes called a bell curve.

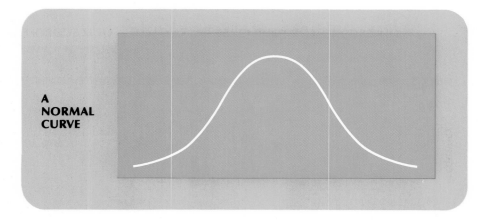

A NORMAL CURVE

Figure 3

(4) The sloping lines on either side never touch the base line. Figure 3 shows a normal curve.

In general, such a curve would occur if the largest number of scores (or other data) fell exactly in the middle of a range of scores. In addition, an equal number of scores would have to fall on either side of the high point. Furthermore, the farther you get from the high point of the curve, the fewer your number of entries.

In actuality, the normal curve is a hypothetical standard against which actual scores can be compared. Most curves do not look exactly like the nor-

Figure 4   **Figure 5**

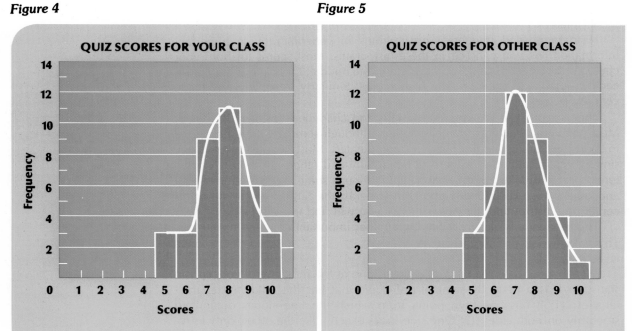

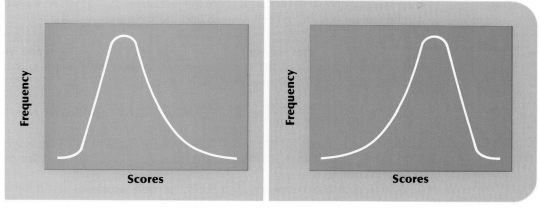

Figure 6   **Figure 7**

mal curve. For example, look at the histograms of the quiz scores. If we connect the midpoints of each bar, we can create curves (Figures 4 and 5). However, these curves do not look exactly like normal curves because the scores are not perfectly symmetrical. Usually, the larger the number of scores you are plotting, the more your graph would look like a normal curve.

Yet researchers often hope that their data will resemble a normal curve when graphed. A comparison with a normal curve will give them an idea of how representative their results are. For example, suppose a researcher gave a test and most students scored at the low end (see Figure 6). The researcher would conclude that the test was too difficult. Similarly, if most students received high scores (see Figure 7), the test would be too easy.

Measures of Central Tendency

Knowing about frequency distribution and the normal curve gives researchers much information about their data. However, they may be interested in finding out other information as well. Another concept that is especially useful when researchers wish to compare data is the idea of central tendency, or central points in a distribution. There are three kinds of central points that are of interest to a researcher. These are the mode, the mean, and the median.

Mode. The *mode* is the score (or other piece of data) that occurs most frequently in any given set of scores. For example, consider the following scores: 72, 83, 89, 89, 91, 91, 91, 94. The mode in this case would be 91 because it occurred more often than any other score.

The mode can usually be found by inspecting any frequency distribution. Let's look again at the frequency distribution of scores cited earlier for your class and the other class. We see that the mode for your class is 8, and for the other class is 7.

In many cases the mode has limited use for researchers. For example, suppose that in a given distribution of 100 scores only one score occurred twice—the rest occurred only once. This would tell researchers very little. The mode is useful only when there is a score that occurs *several* times. As a result, researchers often rely more on the mean and the median.

Mean. The *mean* is what we often think of when we think of an average. We find the mean by adding all the scores together and then dividing the sum by the number of scores. The formula for the mean is:

$$\text{mean} = \frac{\text{sum of the scores}}{\text{number of scores}} \text{ or } \overline{X} = \frac{\Sigma X}{N} \text{ or } \overline{X} \text{ equals } \Sigma X \text{ divided by N.}$$

In this formula, $\overline{X}$ stands for the mean. ΣX stands for the sum of all the scores. (Σ is a Greek symbol that stands for "the sum of.") And N stands for the number of scores.

Let's return to our frequency distribution of quiz scores to see how we determine the mean. In your class, the sum of all the scores is 268. Dividing this by the number of scores (35), we have

$$\overline{X} = \frac{268}{35} = 7.7 \text{ (rounded off).}$$

In the other class, the sum of all scores is 253. Replacing the letters of the formula with numbers, we have

$$\overline{X} = \frac{253}{35} = 7.2 \text{ (rounded off).}$$

Therefore, the mean for your class is higher than the mean for the other class.

One important disadvantage of using the mean is that any extreme scores will distort your results. For example, suppose you are given the salaries of workers in a particular factory. The figures are: $26,000, $14,900, $14,000, $13,400, and $13,200. The mean would be $16,300, although four of the five workers are earning under $15,000. In such a situation it would be better to use the median.

$26,000
14,900
14,000
13,400
13,200
―――――
$81,500

$\dfrac{\$81,500}{5} = \$16,300$

Median. The *median* is the score (or other piece of data) that falls exactly in the middle of all the scores. Exactly half the subjects score above the median, and exactly half score below it. Let's return to the salaries of the factory workers we used in the previous example. The median would be $14,000 since two workers earned more and two workers earned less.

In our quiz frequency distributions, the median is 8 for your class, and 7 for the other class. In each case the median would be the 18th score, since there are 35 students in each class.

Unlike the mean, the median is usually an actual score. One exception would be if you have an even number of scores. For example, suppose you wish to find the median of the following scores: 20, 30, 40, 50, 60, and 70. In this case you would find the two scores that fall in the middle—40 and 50. Then you would take the mean of those scores (40 + 50 = 90; 90 ÷ 2 = 45). The median of this distribution is 45.

One advantage of using the median is that extreme scores will not affect it. For example, consider the following two distributions:

Group A: 3, 4, 5, 6, 7
Group B: 3, 4, 5, 6, 102

The median for each group is 5. However, the mean for Group A is 5 (3 + 4 + 5 + 6 + 7 = 25; 25 ÷ 5 = 5), whereas the mean for Group B is 24 (3 + 4 + 5 + 6 + 102 = 120; 120 ÷ 5 = 24). By just changing one figure to introduce an extreme score, we have changed the mean dramatically. Yet the median remains the same.

A researcher should not always use the median, though. The kind of central point the researcher should use depends on what he or she is trying to find out. In fact, in a normal curve the mode, the mean, and the median are identical!

Variability of Data

If a psychologist knows what the mode, mean, and median are, he or she still doesn't know everything about the data. The psychologist also needs to know how much variability there is between the scores in a group. In other words, the psychologist wishes to find out how spread out the scores are in relation to the mean. Two measures that are often used are the range and the standard deviation.

The range. The *range* is the mathematical difference between the highest and lowest scores in a frequency distribution. In our frequency distributions for the quiz scores, the range for each class of students is 5 since the highest score was 10 and the lowest score was 5 in both cases (10 − 5 = 5).

The range for two groups may differ even if they have the same mean. For example, let's consider the batting averages of the following two teams (the decimal point has been dropped for convenience):

Team A:	210	250	285	300	340
Team B:	270	270	275	285	285

The mean for each team is 277. Yet the range for Team A is 130 points while the range for Team B is 15 points. This tells us that the team members in Team B are much more alike in terms of hitting ability than are the members of Team A.

Therefore, knowing the range of scores tells a psychologist how similar the subjects in each group are to each other in whatever is being measured. The researcher could not get this information from the mode, the mean, or the median alone, since each is just one number.

Yet the range has an important disadvantage. It takes into account only the highest and lowest scores of a frequency distribution. For example, look at the following distributions:

A: 3, 6, 9, 12, 15
B: 3, 4, 5, 6, 7, 15

Each has the same range of 12. But the scores in one group differ greatly from the scores in the other. For this reason researchers often use the standard deviation.

Standard deviation. Psychologists often wish to find out how much any particular score is likely to vary from the mean, or how spread out all scores are

TEAM A
210
250
285
300
340
1385

1385 ÷ 5 = 277

TEAM B
270
270
275
285
285
1385

1385 ÷ 5 = 277

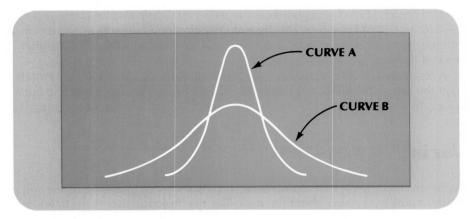

CURVE A

CURVE B

Figure 8

around the mean. To do so they determine the standard deviation. The formula for computing this measure is:

$$SD = \sqrt{\frac{\Sigma(X - \overline{X})^2}{N}}$$

In this formula, X stands for each individual score and $\overline{X}$ stands for the mean. The formula says that the mathematical difference between each score and the mean is squared $(X - \overline{X})^2$. Then these numbers are added together (Σ), because Σ means "the sum of." Next, they are divided by the number of scores (N). Finally, we find the square root.

In our batting average example, the standard deviation for Team A is about 44.2. For Team B the standard deviation is about 6.8. This tells us that the scores for Team A are much more spread out around the mean than are the scores for Team B. Put another way, this tells us that for Team A a typical score will fall within 44.2 points of the mean. For Team B a typical score will fall within 6.8 points of the mean. The quality of hitting is more consistent or similar on Team B than it is on Team A.

In any distribution in which the data form a normal curve, about 68 percent of all scores fall within one standard deviation above and below the mean. Thus, if the mean on an intelligence test is 100 and the standard deviation is 15, about 68 percent of all scores would fall between 85 and 115. Studies have shown that scores on intelligence tests indeed follow this pattern.

Two normal curves can have the same mode, mean, and median but have different standard deviations. For example, both curves in Figure 8 have the same mode, mean, and median. Curve B, however, would have a larger standard deviation than Curve A. You can see this in the graph.

Correlation and Causation

Psychologists often are interested in learning about the relationship between two variables. As you learned in Chapter 2, a **variable** is any condition or behavior that can change in amount or quality. Height, weight, age, and time

TEAM A	Mean = 277	
Scores	$(X - \overline{X})$	$(X - \overline{X})^2$
210	−67	4489
250	−27	729
285	+ 8	64
300	+23	529
340	+63	3969
		9780

$$\frac{9780}{5} = 1956$$

$$\sqrt{1956} = 44.2$$
(rounded off)

TEAM B	Mean = 277	
Scores	$(X - \overline{X})$	$(X - \overline{X})^2$
270	−7	49
270	−7	49
275	−2	4
285	+8	64
285	+8	64
		230

$$\frac{230}{5} = 46$$

$$\sqrt{46} = 6.8$$
(rounded off)

are some of the variables the psychologists may encounter. Two kinds of relationships between variables that psychologists focus on are correlation and causation.

Correlation. Changes in variables often occur together. When two variables are related, they are said to have a **correlation.**

Sometimes an increase or decrease in one variable is accompanied by an increase or decrease in another. For example, as children grow taller, their weight usually increases. A decrease in studying often is accompanied by a drop in grades. Such variables are said to be **positively correlated.**

Sometimes, as one variable increases another variable decreases. Such variables are said to be **negatively correlated.** For example, the more infants walk, the less they crawl. The less time a person spends practicing the piano, the more mistakes the person is likely to make during a recital.

Psychologists often use a term known as the **correlation coefficient** to describe the degree of relationship between variables. This number ranges from +1.00, which signifies a perfect positive correlation, to −1.00, which signifies a perfect negative correlation. A correlation coefficient of 0 indicates there is no correlation between two variables.

As with other concepts, psychologists often show these relationships graphically. Figure 9 is a graph of a correlation coefficient of +1.00. Notice that if the dots were connected, they would form a straight line. Such a graph would result if we were showing the relationship between a particular class's scores on a biology test and on an algebra test. Maria made a score of 100 on both the biology test and the algebra test. Stuart scored 90 on each test. Alfred scored 80 on each, and so on down the line.

A graph such as Figure 10 would occur if there were a perfect negative correlation between the tests. For example, suppose that Maria scored 100 on

Figure 9   **Figure 10**

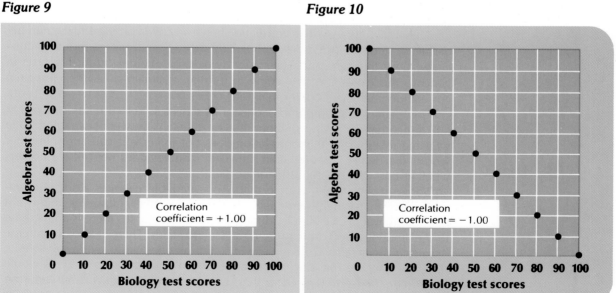

479

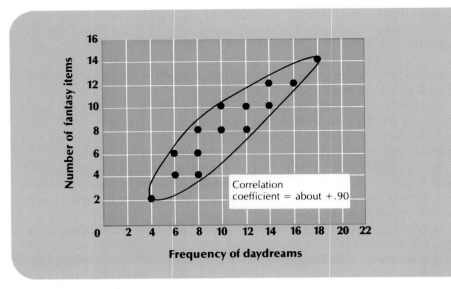

Figure 11

the biology test but got a 0 on the algebra test. Stuart got a 90 on the biology test but got a 10 in algebra. Alfred got an 80 in biology but only a 20 in algebra. The dots in this graph would also form a straight line, but this time in the opposite direction.

Few, if any correlations, however, are perfect. In other words, while one variable may increase or decrease, the other may not increase or decrease to the same degree. For example, Figure 11 shows the relationship in a hypothetical experiment between how often some students daydreamed and the number of fantasy items they reported.

As you can see, these dots do not form a straight line. Yet the dot pattern goes in the same direction as in Figure 9. Therefore, researchers would conclude that there is a positive correlation between daydreaming and the number of fantasy items that students report. Although we shall not go into the actual calculation, the correlation coefficient would be about +.90 in this case. In general, the closer the dots come to forming a straight line, the closer the correlation coefficient comes to +1.00 or −1.00.

Correlation is an important concept in statistics. Yet correlation does not tell researchers everything about the relationship between variables. One valuable relationship that correlation does not indicate is causation. In other words, the degree of correlation between variables does not tell researchers whether one variable *causes* another.

Some people might assume that if one variable changes along with another, then that variable produces change in the other. However, this is not necessarily true. For example, during the summer months there is an increase in the amount of soft drink sales in the United States. There is also an increase in sales of swimwear. Does the rise in soft drink sales cause swimwear sales to rise? We can see that this would be a foolish conclusion to draw. It would make more sense to say that a third variable—the change in temperature—caused the changes in the other two variables.

480

The most valuable usage of correlation is prediction. Knowing that two variables are correlated allows us to predict the value of one variable when we know the value of another. For example, there is a high correlation between college entrance examination scores and college grades, so we can predict how well college freshmen are likely to do in their first year. Similarly, pediatricians (children's doctors) know that a child's height at any particular age is correlated with his or her height at a later age. This knowledge enables them to predict how tall a person is likely to be as an adult.

Sometimes, though, researchers are more interested in causation. We will now examine this relationship.

Causation. How do researchers determine if one variable causes another? We have seen that they cannot rely on correlation. Instead they compare the differences between an experimental group and a control group, after the experimental group has experienced the independent variable. (In Chapter 2 we defined an *experimental group* as the group in which the condition under study is present. A *control group* was defined as the group in which the condition is not present. And the *independent variable* was defined as the variable manipulated by the experimenter.) If an experimental group reacted differently from a control group in an experiment, researchers are likely to conclude that the independent variable *caused* changes in the other variable (the *dependent variable*).

For example, suppose that researchers want to show that watching violence on television—the independent variable—will cause an increase in the number of aggressive acts that people commit—the dependent variable. They might assemble two groups that are as similar as possible, except that only one is shown programs with violence. If only that group—the experimental group—committed a significant number of aggressive acts afterwards, the researchers would probably conclude that televised violence *causes* an increase in aggressive behavior.

Similarly, studies have been done to show that there is a cause-and-effect relationship between cigarette smoking and lung cancer. An experimental group of laboratory animals that was forced to inhale cigarette smoke developed lung cancer while a control group did not.

How do researchers know, however, if the differences between the two groups were real or the result of coincidence? In general, most experimenters have adopted a probability standard of 5 percent, which is computed by certain tests. This means that if there is only a 5 percent (or lower) probability that the results of an experiment had occurred because of chance alone, it is probably safe to conclude that the differences between the experimental group and the control group are real. Researchers can then say with some degree of certainty that one variable caused changes in another.

A Word of Caution

Now that you have had an overview of the role of statistics in psychology, you may become more aware of how people use statistics in your everyday lives. Newspaper and magazine advertisements, television and radio commercials, and sporting events are just a few of the instances in which you will encounter statistics daily. But beware—used incorrectly, statistics can be misleading and will tend to create false impressions. Consider the following examples, all similar to those you may come across.

- An advertiser claims that Brand X laundry detergent causes clothes to come out 30 percent cleaner. Does this mean 30 percent cleaner than using no detergent at all? Or 30 percent cleaner than using a different brand? Or 30 percent cleaner than if you didn't wash your clothes?
- You read that the average annual salary for secretaries is $15,000. Is this figure the mean, the median, or the mode?
- The newspaper reports that there is a 10 percent increase in automobile accidents during the summer months. Does this imply that people who drive during the summer months are less cautious? Or are there more cars on the road during this period, thus increasing the likelihood of an accident?
- An article reports that 50 percent of the women employed by a certain company marry before age thirty. How does your impression change when you find out that there are only two female employees at that firm?

Clearly, statistics are an important tool when used properly. But when used incorrectly, they can be misleading and dangerous. With a little caution you can make statistics work for you. You should be aware, though, that we have only touched on this broad topic. There are many procedures and ideas that have not been mentioned. Before you draw any conclusions from the results of statistical studies, it is best to check with someone who has a solid background in the field.

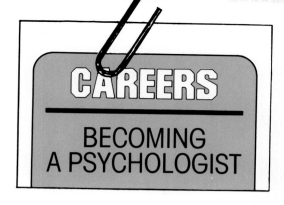

CAREERS
BECOMING A PSYCHOLOGIST

Training in psychology opens up a number of career possibilities.

The study of human behavior is a fascinating one. It is so fascinating, indeed, that many people choose a career in psychology. What career options might be open to you? How do you become a psychologist?

There are many exciting career opportunities for people with a background in psychology. If you would like to work in a laboratory setting, conducting experiments on behavior and biological processes, you might consider a career in experimental psychology. Or perhaps you might like to work for a large corporation, promoting good relations between workers and management. Then a career in industrial psychology might be a good career choice.

If you would like to work with children or teen-agers, several options are available. School psychologists work in school systems, testing students and advising them about their educational plans. They may also help students with their personal problems. Counseling psychologists perform similar tasks, although they are more likely to work with older teen-agers and even adults.

Developmental psychologists also work with young people. They study different processes such as language development and the development of intellectual abilities. However, since development is a lifelong process, these psychologists may focus on adults—both young and old—as well.

Clinical psychologists, too, might work with children and teen-agers. These professionals devote their time to helping people who have disturbing personal problems. But, like developmental psychologists, they also work with adults.

There are still other careers in psychology. One of the newest and fastest growing areas relates to computers. Psychologists with a background in computer science can design computer programs for research. Many people with backgrounds in psychology are going into government service, where they may serve as consultants.

One career that might seem related to psychology is a career in psychiatry. However, psychiatrists are *not* psychologists. Psychiatrists are medical doctors who specialize in the prevention, diagnosis, and treatment of psychological disturbances. In contrast, psychologists rarely hold a medical degree and are not licensed to practice medicine or prescribe drugs. Instead, psychologists usually have a Ph.D., a Psy.D., or an Ed.D. degree. All are doctorate-level degrees.

The doctoral degree is often the final step to becoming a psychologist. It comes after four years of college and about four to six years of study at the graduate level. Most important, it involves hard work and determination.

This does not mean, however, that all psychological work requires a doctorate. A bachelor's degree in psychology, which comes after four years of college, opens up opportunities in personnel administration, management training, sales, advertising, government, and social services. With a master's degree in psychology, which takes about two years of graduate work, you may work with children who are having problems in school, do testing or other work in a psychological clinic, or teach psychology. At any level, there are challenging and rewarding opportunities awaiting dedicated individuals.

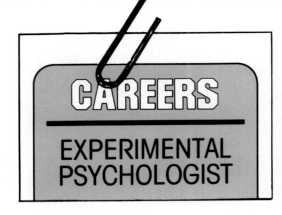

CAREERS

EXPERIMENTAL PSYCHOLOGIST

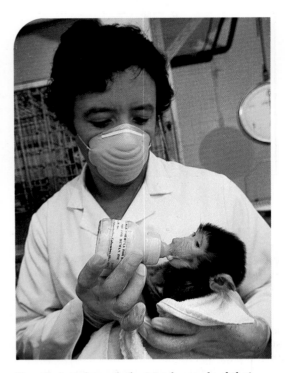

Experimental psychologists do much of their work with animals. Even so, they try to ensure that the animals receive humane treatment. This baby chimp is being fed a special milk formula.

Do students study better at home or in the library? Is there a relationship between school performance and eating a well-balanced diet? If you were an experimental psychologist, you might wish to explore questions like these.

Experimental psychologists follow a set of strictly controlled scientific procedures to learn about the relationship between two or more variables. Although most psychologists do some experimental work in connection with their careers, experimental psychologists conduct most of their work in a laboratory setting. Their topics of concern—sensation and perception, learning and remembering, emotional behavior, and motivation—can all be subjected to rigorous laboratory methods. In a sense, these psychologists are what we think of as "true scientists" because of the procedures they follow.

Experimental psychologists conduct what is called basic research in an attempt to understand behavior. They do not necessarily try to apply the knowledge they acquire. That is, they do not necessarily try to use their research to solve practical problems, such as "Are small groups of people more efficient than large groups?" Such problems are the domain of psychologists in other areas.

In conducting their research, experimental psychologists often work with animals. This is because certain experiments cannot be performed on human beings. (See the discussion that begins on page 25 for other reasons for using animals as subjects.) By studying animal behavior, these psychologists hope to learn more about the behavior of human beings. They may also compare the behavior of one species with that of another. Some typical laboratory animals include rats, pigeons, chickens, dogs, cats, and chimpanzees. If larger animals such as gorillas are used, for obvious reasons they are often studied in zoo environments.

Sometimes experimental psychologists use people as subjects. When they do, though, they follow certain research guidelines. (Some of these are described on page 28.) Protection of the subjects' physical and emotional well-being is an overriding concern of the psychologist.

An important requirement for becoming an experimental psychologist includes proficiency in mathematics. Statistical procedures play an important part in this field. It is true that modern computers take over much of the drudgery formerly found in statistical work. However, experimenters must know how and why data are fed into a computer. They must also be prepared to understand and interpret the data provided by the machine.

Most experimental psychologists hold a Ph. D., or other doctoral degree. As a requirement for this degree, graduate students must prepare a thesis based on their own research, and usually publish this material. They must be able to defend their research before members of the faculty, and demonstrate that they are competent. The road to this career is long and difficult, but the final outcome is rewarding.

484

CAREERS

DEVELOPMENTAL PSYCHOLOGIST

No longer concerned only with children, developmental psychologists study behaviors in people from infancy through old age.

How do children learn language? At what age do intellectual abilities begin to develop? Which emotions do newborn infants first express? If you are interested in these and similar questions, then perhaps you might like to become a developmental psychologist.

Developmental psychologists study the behavioral changes that occur in people at various stages of life. Until recently, these psychologists focused mostly on children. (These professionals were often referred to as "child psychologists.") However, today most developmental psychologists take a lifespan approach. As a result, they study the changes that take place in people from birth until death—including the periods of infancy, childhood, adolescence, adulthood, and old age. (In fact, the study of old age is currently one of the most important fields.)

In the United States today, about 4 percent of all psychologists classify themselves as developmental psychologists. These individuals study such topics as the development of language, intellectual abilities, social attachments, emotions, creativity, physical skills, thinking, and perception. In fact, any aspect of behavior that may change or bring about change in people over a period of years is of concern to a developmental psychologist.

There are many contemporary issues that are currently under investigation by developmental psychologists. Such psychologists may study how our ability to perform certain tasks changes through the life cycle. For example, recent evidence suggests that our intellectual ability does not decline in later adulthood. Rather, older people continue to be able to think abstractly, make judgments, and reason until nearly the end of life. Similarly, older adults can perform motor tasks throughout their later years.

Or, developmental psychologists may study the effects of retirement on a person's psychological adjustment. What adjustments, for example, are the most difficult for a retired person to make? What activities would be of most value to retired people?

Another topic that holds interest for developmental psychologists concerns the changing roles of males and females in our society. Today more and more females, especially young girls, are participating actively in sports. How might this new role affect the emotional development of females? What other areas of development might be affected? How might these changes influence development in years to come?

The field of developmental psychology covers an infinitely large number of topics for study. Therefore, developmental psychologists specialize. For example, a developmental psychologist may concentrate on language development, emotional problems of childhood, or the development of thinking. Even these are general areas, and so such psychologists may study only one specific sub-area. For instance, a developmental psychologist might focus on the development of abstract thinking in children from six to eleven years of age. Or a developmental psychologist might be interested in studying how children first acquire language.

As our society changes, new and more exciting issues will be raised. It will fall to developmental psychologists to seek answers, for the more we learn, the more we can understand about human behavior.

CAREERS

REHABILITATION COUNSELOR

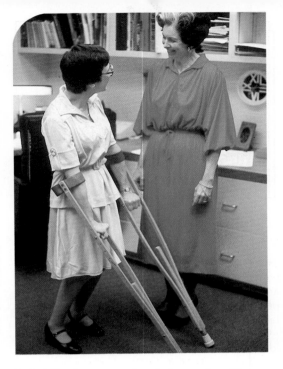

Rehabilitation counselors help people with various disabilities get the most out of life. Their efforts may make all the difference to handicapped people.

At one time, many handicapped persons were destined to lead useless and unproductive lives. Those unable to support themselves remained dependent on others even for their most basic needs. This is not so today, thanks to changing attitudes and the persistent efforts of rehabilitation counselors.

The rehabilitation counselor works with handicapped people to help them fulfill their potential. Usually this involves getting them to be self-supporting, at least partially. To reach this overriding goal, the counselor first explores with the person the type of job he or she is interested in. Both also discuss any jobs that might be difficult because of the person's handicap. The counselor tries to present as realistic a picture as possible to prevent the person from creating false hopes. Yet, at the same time, the counselor tries to build a positive self-image and maintain the person's morale.

Next, the counselor makes available any information about potential jobs. Sometimes the handicapped person may require special training before being considered for a position. If this is so, the counselor helps the person obtain appropriate schooling.

When the training has been completed, the rehabilitation counselor helps the handicapped person secure a job. Sometimes there aren't any openings, but because of extensive contacts with local employers the counselor can often place the person. The counselor's job, though, is still not complete. For a long follow-up period, the counselor checks on the person's progress.

Sometimes people are uncertain about which career might best suit their abilities or interests. When this occurs, often the counselor will request that a series of intelligence and aptitude tests be administered. By carefully interpreting test scores, the counselor gives the individuals a better idea of their vocational possibilities.

There are also other important aspects of a rehabilitation counselor's job. Rehabilitation counselors are concerned with the physical and emotional well-being of the people under their care. Consequently, they work with various outside agencies to make sure all physical and emotional needs are met. For example, if a person needs a hearing device, the counselor contacts the proper agencies.

A master's degree is usually required for becoming a rehabilitation counselor. Usually this degree is in rehabilitative counseling, but a degree in psychology may be an acceptable substitute. If you wish to consider this career, you can start to prepare while in high school. Courses in English and speech, psychology, mathematics, and social studies all will be valuable. English will be extremely helpful, since much of the job involves communication—with the handicapped, with outside agencies, and with employers.

On the nonacademic side, you will need a great deal of patience. The job can be frustrating if you get shuttled back and forth between agencies. Yet, at the same time, you must be persistent—a lot of people will depend on you for help. And helping others can be extremely satisfying.

CAREERS

SPECIAL EDUCATION TEACHER

Special education teachers are very dedicated people. This Down's syndrome child will benefit from the skills and patience such teachers share.

A special education teacher, as the title implies, is a person who teaches "special" students. These students may be gifted, mentally retarded, or have physical, emotional, or learning disabilities that may make it difficult for them to learn in an ordinary classroom setting. For example, a child may be dyslexic. Such children tend to read backwards or to confuse certain letters. Or some of these children may be autistic. Autistic children display extreme withdrawal and often do not speak or respond to human contact.

Special education students, for part of the school day, may be taught in a regular classroom. This policy is known as mainstreaming. During most of the day, however, they are taught in their own classroom or resource room, by a teacher especially trained to meet their needs. In most cases classes are small, so students can receive individual instruction and attention.

Special education teachers are qualified to teach regular subjects, such as reading or math. Very often, though, they may also teach certain "life skills," such as how to tell time, how to keep neat and clean, and how to tie shoelaces.

The amount of patience needed for this job cannot be overemphasized. Special education teachers may have to repeat an exercise over and over again before students will catch on. And even if students do master a concept, it may be forgotten the next week.

Special education teachers may also have to deal with behavior problems. For example, some children may have a limited attention span and will need constant motivation. Others may disrupt the rest of the class with periodic outbursts. For these reasons, these teachers often work as a team with other professionals—social workers, psychologists, and therapists.

There are problems at other levels as well. A lack of funds has sometimes caused an increase in the size of classes. Run-down classrooms, out-moded equipment, and limited supplies can also make the job difficult.

Yet, despite these problems, the rewards can be tremendous. The smile on a child's face upon mastery of a new activity can make it all worthwhile. A hug or a kiss can make you forget that just an hour earlier you were discouraged.

There are certain academic prerequisites for becoming a special education teacher. Prospective teachers must take all the required courses in college for becoming a teacher. In addition, they should take courses that focus on the causes and control of learning disabilities, as well as the rehabilitation of special education students. Necessary psychology courses usually include General Psychology, Educational Psychology, Developmental or Child Psychology, and Psychological/Educational Testing and Measurement. This last course helps teachers determine the educational strengths and weaknesses of their students. Prospective teachers also must do substantial field work before getting their degree.

As with other careers, though, no amount of formal education can bring about the patience and personality needed for the job. Some of the greatest achievements result from a warm word of praise and an encouraging smile.

487

CAREERS IN PSYCHOLOGY

CAREERS
WRITER/EDITOR

Writers often go through many drafts, or versions, of a manuscript before producing satisfactory copy. A willingness to evaluate one's own work critically is an important part of a writer's job.

One of the most valued skills in our society today is the ability to communicate effectively. And writing is an important form of communication, especially when you wish to influence people. One of your first contacts with a prospective employer, for example, might be through a letter you write to the company.

If you enjoy putting your thoughts on paper, and have the ability to express them well, you might consider a career as a writer. Writing, combined with a background in psychology, can offer numerous possibilities. You might work for a psychology magazine, preparing articles on contemporary issues. Or you might work for a corporation, writing pamphlets for the general public or preparing technical reports. You might even work for a textbook publisher, preparing a book similar to the one you are now reading.

Writing often involves careful research, and that's where your psychology training comes in handy. The ability to gather information and interpret it correctly, the skill of organizing facts, and the knack for deciding what's important all are essential to a writer.

A closely related career is that of editor. (We will consider only book and magazine editors here, since a psychology background is especially applicable in editing such materials.) Editors usually don't prepare original manuscript, although they may supply outlines. Rather, they work closely with authors, guiding them from an idea to a finished product.

At the idea stage, editors offer suggestions based on their familiarity with a subject and their knowledge about the needs of the potential market. For example, an editor for a psychology textbook might ask an author to provide more material on a new research study or on a topic of special interest to students. The editor often bases judgments on market research and past experience.

Once a manuscript is written, the actual editing process begins. An editor reads the material closely for accuracy, style, organization, clarity, and appropriateness, as well as for grammar and punctuation. Because an editor may not always be an expert in a subject area, he or she often has the manuscript reviewed by outside consultants. Sometimes the editor rewrites some passages to give the author a clearer idea of what is needed.

The next stage involves turning the manuscript into a printed book or magazine. This involves many tasks, including choosing the type, deciding how the book or magazine should look, and selecting photographs. There are also such tasks as proofreading and writing or rewriting captions. Editors usually work with several other people during the production process.

There are no set requirements for becoming a writer or an editor. However, because of stiff competition, a college degree (with plenty of English courses) is usually necessary. Many employers prefer workers with a liberal arts background, including courses in history, sociology, political science, and psychology. Your psychology courses will also be useful if you are asked to work on psychology manuscripts.

Requirements on the nonacademic side include a good memory, a fondness for detail, and the ability to work well with others. The work may be hard, but your finished product makes it all worthwhile.

CAREERS
PERSONNEL MANAGER

An applicant's appearance, facial expressions, and gestures are often as important to a well-trained personnel manager as what the applicant says.

Suppose you answered a Help Wanted ad and have been asked to come for an interview. One of the people with whom you might speak is a personnel manager.

A personnel manager is often responsible for the hiring of employees. However, the work of a personnel manager involves much more. Personnel managers also set up training programs for new employees, assign persons to specific areas of work, oversee the promotion of individuals, help to determine job satisfaction and productivity, develop wage and salary scales, and administer benefits programs.

Personnel managers are, in a very real sense, also public relations officers. They not only help to promote employee morale within the company but try to promote the company in the eyes of the general public. Very often people's impressions of a firm stem from the efforts of an effective personnel department.

Personnel managers constantly work with people in different capacities. As a result, they must have tact, patience, and be sensitive to the feelings of others. Excellent communications skills—both written and oral—are also a must to carry out the job effectively. Such skills are essential because a major part of the job involves interviewing candidates and preparing follow-up reports.

Although an advanced degree in psychology is not a requirement of the job, a knowledge of psychology can be very beneficial. For example, in contract disputes between labor and management, personnel managers trained in human relations skills could act as mediators. Their position in the company might enable them to better understand and present management's side of an issue. Yet their contact with employees might give them insight into labor's side of the dispute. As a result, they might be able to present both sides of a controversial issue.

In addition, some knowledge of abnormal psychology would help personnel managers in recognizing possible psychological disturbances in employees. They could then refer the workers to a person qualified to handle the problem, such as a clinical psychologist.

Along with courses in psychology, personnel managers often take courses in business administration, economics, statistics, public speaking, and English. Some companies also want their managers to have a background in the area in which the firm specializes. For example, if the company deals with computers, prospective managers should have a degree in computer science.

In any case, a college degree is almost always required for the position of personnel manager. Large companies tend to require a bachelor's degree, whereas some smaller companies will consider candidates with two years of college. Many personnel managers also have advanced degrees from graduate schools.

The most important qualification, however, is a candidate's personality. The ability to get along with and gain the confidence of others signals a possible future in personnel management.

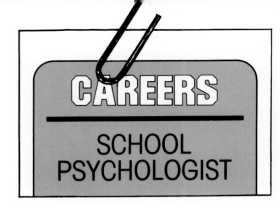

CAREERS

SCHOOL PSYCHOLOGIST

This school psychologist is giving a manual dexterity test. Such a test measures a person's ability to work well with his or her hands.

Perhaps you are considering a career in education—teaching or becoming a guidance counselor. There is another career that might be equally fascinating. Why not consider becoming a school psychologist?

School psychologists work with students, teachers, and administrators to make the school the best possible environment for learning. This involves numerous tasks.

A routine part of a school psychologist's job is to administer and score standardized tests. More important, though, the school psychologist interprets test results. This interpretation is used as part of an overall program for helping students with special needs. For example, perhaps a student has difficulty learning to read and scores poorly on reading tests. The school psychologist might suggest that the child be placed in a remedial reading program.

This process of interpretation, however, is not used only on "special" students. By studying the test strengths and weaknesses of all students, the school psychologist may advise average as well as exceptional students about their educational plans.

Sometimes a school psychologist is called in by a teacher when a student frequently disrupts the class. The teacher has been unable to handle the situation and asks the school psychologist for assistance. Because of special training, the psychologist may be able to diagnose the difficulty and offer a solution. This often involves working with the parents, the teacher, and the student. Such treatment, however, is successful only on youngsters with mild adjustment problems. More serious cases are referred to clinical psychologists or other specialists.

School psychologists work with teachers in other ways, too. They may set up training programs that help teachers relate better to students and to one another. Or they may set up workshops in an attempt to improve teacher morale.

School psychologists might also be consulted in cases of parent/student conflicts. The psychologist will listen to both parties and try to offer a mutually acceptable solution. Most important, the psychologist provides opportunities for both sides to air their views.

On the administrative level, the school psychologist is sometimes asked to help evaluate textbooks, curricula, and teaching methods. The school psychologist might also conduct studies on practical matters—the effect of classroom size or the effectiveness of textbooks, for example—in an effort to improve the quality of education that goes on in a school.

As with other careers in psychology, a bachelor's degree is taken for granted and a master's degree is almost always required. In fact, now that the school psychologist plays such a large part in the educational setting, many school psychologists are getting doctoral degrees. This means four to six years of further study after graduating from a four-year college.

On the nonacademic side, a great deal of patience, the ability to get along with people, and a desire to help others are all requirements of the job. If you have all these qualifications, you might consider this rewarding career.

Why might one student excel in math while another is superior in history? Do smaller classes provide a better learning environment? What role do computers serve in the classroom? In short, how do we learn?

Learning is the primary concern of educational psychologists. They perform research both in and out of the classroom, investigating various methods of teaching, different curricula, and other factors that influence the learning process. Their basic goal is to improve education and make learning easier and more efficient.

Educational psychologists may work in school systems but most often are employed by a college or university. There they conduct research on learning and teaching methods, help train teachers, and assist in the training of school psychologists. They may also work in other settings, such as the military or a large corporation.

The work of an educational psychologist is related to that of a school psychologist, although the educational psychologist is involved less in the day-to-day problems in a school system. For example, both kinds of psychologists might be concerned with the low reading scores in a school. However, the educational psychologist might focus on how to improve scores in general, whereas the school psychologist might want to find out if a student's home environment may have affected his or her test performance.

Because much of the work of educational psychologists involves research, they spend much of their time evaluating and interpreting data. An important requirement of the job, therefore, is proficiency in mathematics and statistics. Another requirement is the ability to take measurements in a careful and precise manner.

Several steps should be taken to pursue a career in educational psychology. You will first need a bachelor's degree from a four-year college, usually with a major in either educational psychology or psychology. Some people then secure a master's degree, although this is not always necessary. The next step should be to gain a few years of teaching experience in an elementary, middle, or high school. This will help you understand classroom problems and talk about them with teachers and administrators. Finally you should obtain a doctoral degree—a Doctor of Philosophy degree (Ph.D.) or a Doctor of Education degree (Ed.D.)—from a graduate school. The process is long, but the career is interesting, as you make inroads into the complex process of learning.

The ability to program computers and interpret the results is an important part of an educational psychologist's job.

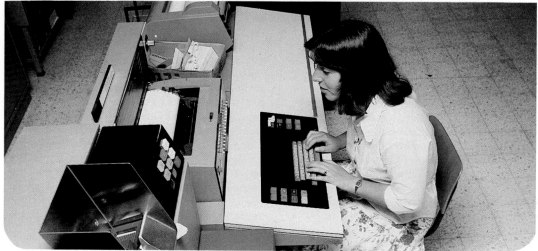

CAREERS
TEACHER

Teachers teach more than just "reading, writing, and arithmetic," especially to younger students. They teach children important social skills, such as leadership and getting along with one another.

Have you ever admired a favorite teacher and tried to pattern your life after that person? Or have you ever wanted to share an interest—such as music or history—with other people? In either case, you may have thought of becoming a teacher.

To some people, a teacher works only a few hours a day teaching four or five classes. And to those same people, a teacher does little more than talking to a group of kids. In reality, though, nothing is farther from the truth. A teacher's job involves more complex tasks, with each being a vital part of the job.

Most important, a teacher instructs students in the skills necessary to become good citizens and productive members of their society. Through our teachers we learn to read, add and subtract, and write. We also learn certain job skills, such as how to conduct research or write a business letter. The amount of information imparted by teachers is tremendous. If you think about everything you learned since starting school, you will appreciate the role your teachers have played.

Even more remarkable is that much of this information is conveyed in an interesting and pleasant way. Most teachers do not just read aloud from a book day after day. Rather they motivate students through real-life experiences, the media, and thought-provoking questions. A teacher must be an actor or actress, sometimes performing the same lesson with undampened enthusiasm to five different classes.

A teacher also often serves as a parent figure, especially to young children. Teachers help children tie their shoes, put on their boots, and button their coats. Moreover, they often help students handle certain problems of both a school-related and a personal nature.

When the school bell rings in the afternoon, a teacher's day is far from over. Many teachers are involved in extracurricular activities, such as coaching the soccer team, heading the French club, or supervising the yearbook staff. Some teachers may also devote several hours to giving students extra help in certain subject areas. In addition, teachers often are required to attend faculty meetings and parent/teacher conferences, both held after the school day has ended.

After returning home, a teacher is often faced with still more school-related chores. There are papers to grade, tests to mark, and lessons to plan. There also may be library research to provide students with up-to-date information on a recent development. Or perhaps a teacher will have to take a special course related to the subject he or she teaches.

The requirements for becoming a teacher are as numerous as the job's responsibilities. On the academic side, all teachers must be certified by the state that employs them. In all states at least a bachelor's degree is needed to obtain such certification. The actual courses that lead to the degree may vary depending on the college, the state, and the level at which you plan to teach. On the nonacademic side, patience, the ability to motivate students, and care and concern are all needed for the job.

CAREERS

COLLEGE PROFESSOR

College students often benefit from the additional help professors provide.

There are many stories and jokes about absent-minded college professors. Professor Chandler's wife calls him at his office to remind him that he was to meet her for dinner an hour ago. He'll be right there, just as soon as he finishes the last two pages of his journal article.

And what about Professor Kirk? Sitting in her office going over the data in her latest research project, she hears a group of students pass by her door. Suddenly she notes that her watch says 10:20. Because students can leave if a teacher is more than 15 minutes late for class, her 10:00 class gets an unexpected holiday.

Yes, college professors are absent-minded at times, but no more so than anyone else. Part of this myth stems from the nature of the job. Professors are constantly striving to expand their knowledge and to make great strides in their field. They are often involved in new and exciting discoveries—those made by others and those they themselves make.

The work of a college professor is for the most part interesting and varied. On the most visible level, professors teach college students—in large lecture classes, small seminars, or perhaps laboratories. In addition, they may conduct research and write articles for professional journals. Or they may publish books—for students, professors, or a general audience. Professors also may act as consultants for corporations or government agencies.

Most professors are active in professional organizations. This often means attending meetings at which they can present papers on their research. Such meetings also provide an opportunity for them to hear papers prepared by their colleagues and to discuss new developments.

Not all aspects of a professor's job are this exciting, however. Professors often spend several hours of preparation for each hour spent in the classroom. They may also spend time advising students, helping them to work out their programs and to select their majors. Finally, they may have to perform the task of reading term papers and grading examinations.

Teaching at the college level is a popular career choice for psychologists. Over 40 percent of all psychologists belonging to the American Psychological Association are employed in colleges and universities. They are usually employed at one of four levels, depending on their education and amount of teaching experience: instructor, assistant professor, associate professor, and full professor.

Instructors usually have at least a master's degree in their field of specialization. For the most part, they are inexperienced teachers, who are hired by a college on a trial basis. If they prove themselves worthy, they are often promoted to the level of *assistant professor*.

After teaching at the assistant level for three or more years, and possibly gaining a doctoral degree, a teacher may become an *associate professor*. From there, a college teacher can move on to become a *full professor*. Before reaching this level, however, a teacher must have extensive teaching experience at the college level, and perhaps have published several articles and/or books related to his or her field.

If you are interested in pursuing this career, you might visit a nearby college campus and talk to one or more professors. They may be more than happy to share with you the joys and frustrations of their jobs.

CAREERS

OCCUPATIONAL THERAPIST

Occupational therapists help both young and old to become as independent as possible.

Most of us take our daily routines for granted. We shower, brush our teeth, eat our meals, and take the bus to work or school almost without thinking about it. But for the person who has suddenly become paralyzed because of a stroke or who has suffered a mental breakdown, such activities become tremendous tasks. Through the help of an occupational therapist, however, disabled people can learn to become as self-sufficient as possible.

One part of an occupational therapist's job is to help physically or mentally disabled people adjust to their handicaps and perform the activities of daily living. They try to restore a person's confidence and sense of independence. For example, an occupational therapist might teach a disabled homemaker how to cook and clean from a wheelchair. Or, perhaps a patient has recently lost a leg and is afraid to travel alone. The therapist might accompany the person until he or she gains a sense of security.

Sometimes an occupational therapist helps design devices to accommodate a person's needs. A person who has limited use of his or her arms will need a special device to turn the pages of a book. A person who is in a wheelchair might need special ramps to get around the house. A person who has trouble sitting might need a special chair. The occupational therapist evaluates each person's disabilities and tries to come up with devices that will make life more manageable.

An important part of an occupational therapist's work is to teach skills that will make the person employable. By working closely with the person to learn about his or her likes and dislikes, as well as strengths and weaknesses, the occupational therapist can outline a program that would have the most value. For example, a person who is now confined to a wheelchair might learn skills needed for watch repair or computer programming. Although occupational therapists might not

be able to teach all these skills themselves, they can get the program started.

As implied in the preceding paragraph, occupational therapists often work as part of a rehabilitation team. They may work with physicians, nurses, social workers, clinical psychologists, and speech therapists to help a patient once again become a productive member of society.

To become an occupational therapist, a person must get a bachelor's degree in occupational therapy. Necessary courses include biology and anatomy, which deal with the human body; psychology and sociology, which deal with human behavior; and skills and crafts, which deal with human activities. In addition, there is a six- to nine-month clinical training period in which the person gains actual field experience.

You also may wish to consider a career as an occupational therapy assistant (OTA). The requirements for this career are an associate degree or a certificate. Both are usually obtained after satisfactorily completing a program at a technical school or a two-year college.

The requirements are many in occupational therapy. The rewards, though, are equally extensive. Occupational therapists gain the satisfaction of helping discouraged people develop skills and interests that they may never have known they had.

494

CAREERS

MARRIAGE/FAMILY COUNSELOR

If a child is in trouble, family counselors often talk with other family members, as well as the child, to gain helpful background information about the child's problems.

Cynthia and Tony have been married for five years. They had a "storybook" marriage until about eight months ago, when Cynthia received a promotion. Before then, Tony was the major wage earner. But with Cynthia's promotion the situation has changed—Cynthia's paycheck is now larger than Tony's. Although the couple can now afford many luxuries, their relationship has deteriorated.

Barbara's parents also seem to be having problems. They have been arguing a lot lately, spending increasing amounts of time away from the house, and drinking excessively. They have even talked about getting a divorce—a prospect that is very upsetting to Barbara.

Fortunately, both couples have decided to consult a marriage counselor before taking any drastic steps. Marriage counselors advise couples who are having difficulties. They try to help the partners gain a better understanding of themselves and of one another. Most important, they try to get the partners to sit down and talk with one another openly and objectively. This isn't always easy, since the partners may have bitter feelings toward one another. Through strong efforts, however, marriage counselors try to help the couple build stronger and more loving relationships.

Sometimes a relationship may have deteriorated so much that it seems impossible to repair it. When this occurs, a marriage counselor may suggest a trial separation. This gives the partners a chance to gain some distance—both actual and psychological—from their situation. In any case, the marriage counselor helps the couple thoroughly explore all possible options before they permanently end a marriage.

The job of family counselors is similar to that of marriage counselors. These professionals, however, work with entire families or individual family members. Sometimes they try to get all family members to work through their differences or solve a problem that affects the whole family. For example, if a teen-ager uses drugs, the whole family may suffer.

When counselors work only with individuals, they also focus on repairing damaged relationships with the family. For example, a family counselor may be called in to work with a teen-age runaway. The teen-ager may have left home believing that he or she could not follow in a parent's footsteps. The counselor might help the teen-ager realize that both the teen-ager and the parents might be satisfied if the youngster chose a different path.

Both marriage and family counselors can work in various settings. Some might work in private practice. Others might work in social agencies. Still others might work in hospitals or clinics. Some might even hold two jobs, combining a private practice with a part-time job with a social agency.

The professional requirements for marriage and family counselors vary from state to state. Some counselors have only a bachelor's degree, whereas others might have at least a master's degree. Most, though, have a background in psychology, as well as courses in sociology and social work.

Other requirements include patience, the ability to think clearly, and the desire to help people. A person must also be flexible since he or she may have to work evenings or weekends. In return, though, the counselor gets the satisfaction of helping others. This can be a good feeling.

CAREERS
GUIDANCE COUNSELOR

Not all students are referred to guidance counselors by teachers or deans. Many students often turn to guidance counselors voluntarily for advice and encouragement.

Maria can't decide whether to go to college or get a job after graduating. Robert is upset because his family is moving and he will have to change schools. Joanne feels her parents don't understand her need for independence.

All of these students are facing problems that are affecting their daily lives. How can their situations be remedied? To whom can they turn for help?

One person to whom students can turn is the school guidance counselor. A guidance counselor works in the school to help students with their problems—whether school-related or of a personal nature. Because of their understanding of human behavior and their rational approach to difficult situations, guidance counselors try to help students solve their problems.

For example, suppose a student has trouble with schoolwork and considers dropping out of school. The counselor may try to make the student aware of alternative, more positive solutions. The counselor might suggest that the student give up an after-school job that takes up valuable study time. Or perhaps the student may be advised to take a different course of study. Such counseling gives students a basis for making decisions that will help them in the future.

The duties of guidance counselors vary greatly. Counselors may become involved in a standardized testing program to assess the abilities of students in the school. Or they may help students plan their courses or help them select colleges. In addition, they may advise students how to budget their time more wisely or study more effectively. Sometimes guidance counselors hold discussion groups on topics that concern teen-agers, such as the dangers of drugs, alcohol, and cigarette smoking.

Guidance counselors also may help students obtain part-time jobs. This may involve giving students material to read, writing letters of recom-

mendation, or contacting business leaders about job opportunities in the community.

There are certain things, however, that guidance counselors should not do. They should not impose their ideas or values on others. Rather they should listen, give support when necessary, and suggest alternatives. Moreover, the guidance counselor should not discipline students. If a discipline problem arises, the counselor should call in persons qualified to handle the situation. Similarly, the guidance counselor should not perform therapy. If a student shows signs of serious emotional disturbances, the counselor should refer the person to a therapist.

The requirements for becoming a guidance counselor differ from state to state. The basic requirement in many states is a bachelor's degree plus certain graduate-level courses. A counselor should also have a background in psychology. This understanding of human behavior better enables the counselor to recognize problems and identify possible solutions. Teaching experience is often necessary as well, and this experience ranges from one to five years. In addition, certain courses are often helpful, though not required. Courses in mathematics and statistics prepare prospective counselors for interpreting test results. English courses help future counselors develop good communications skills.

Above all, though, a person must have the desire to help other people and the ability to work well with others. The last requirement is extremely important because a guidance counselor does not work alone.

CAREERS

INDUSTRIAL PSYCHOLOGIST

Many industrial psychologists work very closely with advertising and marketing personnel to develop new products for the public.

An industrial psychologist is just what the name implies—a psychologist who works in a business setting. This person applies the principles of psychology to a work environment.

Industrial psychology is a broad field and includes a number of sub-areas. Organizational psychology may be considered one important sub-area of industrial psychology. Organizational psychologists are concerned with human problems in the work world. They might, for example, try to maintain good relations between labor and management in a large corporation. They might work with a sales force to help them develop more productive selling strategies. Or they might recommend ways to improve employee morale.

Consumer psychology is another branch of industrial psychology. A consumer psychologist might conduct research to determine people's buying habits and then test certain products on the market. Are people more likely to buy ketchup in a tall, slim jar or a short, wide one? Do they prefer a see-through glass jar or an opaque plastic container? Which size do people buy most often? Although these questions may seem trivial, consumer psychologists have found that such factors affect what a person buys.

Engineering psychology, another important branch, is concerned with the design of machinery and the effects of equipment on people. Engineering psychologists perform a variety of tasks that range from designing artificial limbs for the handicapped to helping design space capsules for astronauts. The overriding concern of these psychologists is to come up with a product that is within the limitations of the people who must use it. An instrument panel, for example, should not require an operator to make decisions more quickly than the average operator can make. In addition, the product should provide maximum comfort for the people using it.

A large number of industrial psychologists are involved in testing programs. These psychologists develop tests that predict how well job applicants would perform if they were hired. Companies then use these tests to screen potential candidates. These industrial psychologists also make sure that the tests do not discriminate against various groups of people.

In carrying out their jobs, industrial psychologists work with many people. They may assist advertisers and market researchers in developing new products. They may advise industrial and electrical engineers in the design of new equipment. They may work with different groups of employees to improve worker morale. They may even work with other psychologists. For example, they may work alongside environmental psychologists to solve problems of toxic agents, overcrowding, and noise, air, and water pollution.

Industrial psychology provides varied career opportunities to qualified individuals. In fact, many business people are taking courses in industrial psychology even if they do not plan to become professional psychologists. If, however, you do plan on making industrial psychology your career, you should get a doctoral degree in that area. Some states also require industrial psychologists to pass an examination and be licensed.

CAREERS

PSYCHIATRIC NURSE

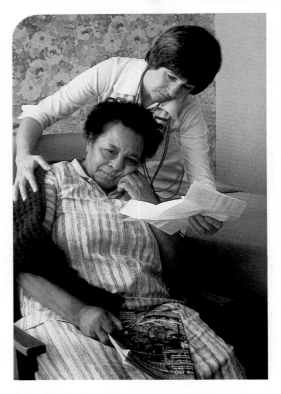

A tender gesture often means more to a depressed patient than words. Psychiatric nurses often rely on such gestures to help patients under their care.

When people think of a nurse, they often think of a woman in a white uniform and cap taking someone's temperature or blood pressure in a hospital. Of course, some female—and male—nurses do fill this role, but others are concerned more with psychiatric patients than with patients suffering from illness or recovering from the effects of surgery. And some of these nurses to not even work in hospitals. We are referring to psychiatric nurses.

Psychiatric nurses help mentally ill patients learn to adapt to their environments. They may also help these patients learn to change their surroundings so that the patients can cope more successfully with life. For example, a person who has difficulty living with others might be taught to live alone.

Because of the kinds of patients under their care, the psychiatric nurse must be able to communicate effectively both through words and through actions. In fact, sometimes actions are the more important form of communication. A tender gesture is sometimes more important than a daily "hello." A hug may mean more than a comment about what a nice day it is.

In addition, the psychiatric nurse must have patience, understanding, and a willingness to give emotional support whenever necessary. The nurse must also be able to overcome any personal biases against the mentally ill and accept the patients as they are. This often involves ignoring displays of unusual behavior.

Psychiatric nursing is different from ordinary nursing in one important respect. Whereas nurses in other capacities usually help a patient directly, psychiatric nurses perform an additional function—they teach patients to help themselves. They help their patients gain enough self-assurance to deal with day-to-day problems on their own.

Very often psychiatric nurses are considered an equal part of a patient's psychiatric team. As such, they may take part in group therapy sessions and conduct individual psychotherapy. Because of their extensive training, they might even be asked to advise on a patient's diet or medical treatment.

Although many psychiatric nurses do work in hospitals or mental institutions, some work in outpatient clinics. They help patients who are well enough to spend much of their time in the outside world but who must return to a clinic periodically. Some psychiatric nurses might even make home visits in special situations.

The requirements for becoming a psychiatric nurse are usually at least a bachelor's degree in nursing. Many credits in biology and chemistry are needed for these degrees. Some necessary psychology courses include General Psychology, Developmental Psychology, and Abnormal Psychology. At one time, before psychiatric nurses played such a large role in patient care, only a degree from a two-year school or a bachelor's degree was needed. But with the increased demands on the psychiatric nurse, an advanced degree is almost a necessity.

498

CAREERS

CLINICAL PSYCHOLOGIST

Clinical psychologists sometimes work in casual settings to make their patients feel more relaxed.

Sometimes people have problems that they find difficult to face—a divorce in the family, the loss of a job, or pressure at school. They may also feel that there is no one they can turn to for help. They don't feel comfortable talking about the problems to teachers or religious advisors, friends have their own difficulties, and parents may not understand. What, then, is the next step? Perhaps they can contact a clinical psychologist.

Clinical psychologists try to help people with emotional or adjustment problems. To do so, they administer and interpret psychological tests, conduct psychotherapy, and sometimes carry out research. In the course of their work they may deal with problems of mental illness, juvenile delinquency, drug addiction, criminal behavior, mental retardation, or marital difficulties.

People often confuse clinical psychologists with psychiatrists and psychoanalysts, since all are concerned with helping people cope with problems. Clinical psychologists have a doctoral degree from a graduate school, but are not licensed to prescribe medicine. In contrast, a psychiatrist is a physician who has attended medical school. A psychiatrist has the legal right and responsibility to prescribe medicine. A psychoanalyst is a person whose training and experience are based on the theories of Sigmund Freud. Psychoanalysts often use such methods as dream interpretation and free association to help clients. They may or may not be psychiatrists or clinical psychologists.

Clinical psychology is the most popular branch of psychology in terms of the number of psychologists involved. These psychologists work in many settings, depending on their interests and job availability. Some engage in private practices, where they might work independently or in cooperation with other professionals such as pediatricians (children's doctors) or social workers. These psychologists have their own offices, and see patients on a voluntary basis. Other clinical psychologists may work in mental hospitals, veterans hospitals, hospitals or schools for the mentally retarded, prisons, or mental health clinics. In these settings most psychologists are assigned a certain number of patients for whom they are responsible. Still other clinical psychologists may teach in colleges, universities, or medical schools, where they pass on their knowledge rather than apply it directly.

As indicated above, the requirements for becoming a clinical psychologist include a graduate school degree. Most clinical psychologists have earned a Ph.D. at a university and have served an internship in the fields of testing, diagnosis, psychotherapy, and research. An internship is a period of work that is carried out under the close supervision of professionals in a particular field.

Some prospective clinical psychologists choose to attend a graduate school of professional psychology and earn a Doctor of Psychology degree (Psy.D.). This degree emphasizes applied clinical skills. It requires four or five years of academic course work and clinical experience.

There are also state licensing requirements for those wishing to enter private practice. These vary from state to state but all require an individual to pass an exam. The requirements are rigid, but they protect the public from people who are not qualified to practice as psychologists.

CAREERS
SALESPERSON

A career in sales is one of the most varied careers in terms of setting, products, and requirements. Selling by telephone offers much opportunity and a flexible schedule.

"Would you ever buy a used car from _____?" Sound familiar? Clearly, we judge the salesperson as much as we judge the product. Perhaps this is because we look for certain qualities in someone who sells us a product.

A career in sales is a good possibility for someone with a background in psychology. Psychology will provide you with knowledge about human behavior. It also may give you insight into the art of persuasion. That is, it may tell you how to convince people to buy what you are selling.

A sales career covers many different areas. You might be interested in selling directly to people door-to-door. This will enable you to be your own boss and to organize your time as you wish. Or you might wish to pursue a career as a manufacturer's representative. This involves demonstrating and selling a line of products to wholesale and retail firms. You still would have personal contact with customers, but your clients would be business firms. Still another possibility would be telephone sales. In this case you would rely solely on the telephone to contact potential customers.

The products you sell might also vary greatly. You might sell anything from a shirt to a life insurance policy. Products such as encyclopedias or cosmetics are often sold door-to-door. Subscriptions to newspapers and magazines are frequently sold over the telephone. Most products that are sold to business concerns—whether machinery, sporting goods, or books—are sold through catalogues or in-person visits by manufacturers' representatives.

People in sales careers deal with customers on a daily basis. Therefore, as in many other careers, you would have to enjoy being around people. In addition, because of the nature of the job, you would have to "sell" yourself as much as your product.

Actually, there are two different sales approaches that can be taken: the "hard-sell" approach and the "soft-sell" approach. In the "hard-sell" approach the salesperson creates the need for a product or service. Such individuals try to be very persuasive, convincing the potential customer to make a purchase. If the first attempt is unsuccessful, they may call again and again in an effort to make the sale. In the "soft-sell" approach the product or service is so good that it almost sells itself. But the salesperson still must guide the customer and answer questions correctly. In either approach, the personality of the salesperson may either make or break a sale.

A sales career is one of the most flexible careers in terms of requirements. For some jobs, a high school diploma is sufficient. For others, you will need a college degree from either a two-year or a four-year school. For still others, you will need a more advanced degree, often related to the product you are selling. For example, if you are selling computer software, you might need an advanced degree in computer science.

In general, the more technical and specialized the product is that you are selling, the more likely it is that you will need a specialized education. It is not too early, however, for you to start preparing now for a sales career. Such high school courses as English, public speaking, and psychology might start you on your way to an interesting and exciting future.

500

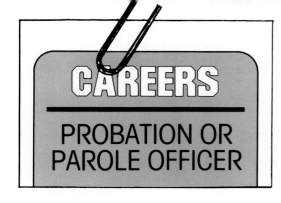

CAREERS

PROBATION OR PAROLE OFFICER

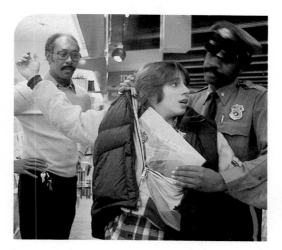

Because shoplifting is a serious crime, this youth will most likely be assigned a probation officer after a court hearing.

Bart, a sixteen-year-old male, has been caught breaking into a local store. Because this was his first offense, the court decided to place him on probation for three years. This means that if he does not commit another crime, or violate the rules of his probation during this period, he will not have to go to prison.

Janet, a twenty-four-year-old female who was convicted of armed robbery, has served part of her prison sentence. However, because she has been a model prisoner, she is being paroled, or released ahead of schedule. During the next two years, she must follow the rules of her parole, or she will have to return to prison to serve the remainder of her sentence.

One of the procedures that both Bart and Janet must follow is to report to their case workers immediately. Bart will have to check in with his probation officer, Janet with her parole officer. (Probation officers work with juvenile delinquents or first offenders who are released by the courts. Parole officers work with former offenders.) The probation or parole officer will have a cumulative record of their crimes, plus a case history consisting of medical, school, psychological, and other personal data.

One of the primary responsibilities of a probation or parole officer is to try and assist people like Bart and Janet in making psychological readjustments to life. This involves numerous tasks. For example, her parole officer will help Janet find a job, unless she already has one lined up. Both case workers will counsel these offenders, providing positive support and helping them solve personal problems. Among other things, they will advise Bart and Janet to stay away from known criminals. This will lessen the likelihood that they will commit other crimes.

The life of a probation or parole officer can be highly rewarding. Probation or parole officers may, after years of trying, believe they are getting nowhere with a former offender. Then the person suddenly changes, never again getting into trouble with the law. The officers take pride in their accomplishment.

In many cases, a close personal relationship develops between the probation or parole officer and the offender. At times, such personal relationships will make offenders and officers feel like members of the same family.

At other times, however, the job can be frustrating. Officers may work with a person for years, encouraged that everything is going fine. Then one morning the officer finds out that the person has committed another, more serious crime. In these cases, a return to jail is almost inevitable for the offender.

There are other frustrations as well. In some cities or regions, there is a shortage of funds and an abundance of cases. Thus instead of having to handle a caseload of 30, each officer may be responsible for as many as 100 cases. The officer must cope with the emotional strain that results from having to carry out the job with limited resources. Probation or parole officers also may have to work long hours, often giving up time with their own families.

Yet the rewards often outweigh the drawbacks, and many people choose to enter this field. The educational requirements for becoming a probation or parole officer often include a bachelor's degree, with courses in psychology, sociology, criminology, and law. The most important prerequisites, however, are patience and the ability to establish a rapport with others.

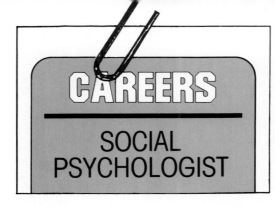

CAREERS

SOCIAL PSYCHOLOGIST

Not even the rain can dampen the spirits of these sports enthusiasts. Social psychologists study the behavior of such groups of people.

A social psychologist is a scientist who studies the effects of group membership on individual behavior. Social psychologists focus on such topics as attitudes, influence, interaction, social relationships, and social perception. For example, social psychologists may wish to explore the effects of television commercials on our attitudes. All in all, they study how behavior in social situations affects individuals.

Social psychologists, however, are not the only ones to focus on social behavior. Social workers also are interested in people, but their work is more practical and less research oriented. They tend to apply their knowledge of social phenomena to help people overcome personal and social handicaps.

Anthropologists, too, study social behavior, but they are concerned with the customs, distribution, and social relationships of various groups of people. They often restrict their work to studies of primitive peoples, such as the aborigines of Australia.

The subject area of social psychologists is often closely related to that of sociologists. However, a distinction can be made. Social psychologists are interested primarily in how individual behavior is influenced by group membership. Sometimes they study how an individual can influence a group, as in studies of leadership. The sociologist, on the other hand, is much more concerned with the group as a whole—its structure and formal characteristics. For example, sociologists might study why certain groups of people have a high divorce rate or how propaganda influences voting behavior.

The work of social psychologists is often highly visible, although we may not realize it. News stories in newspapers and magazines, as well as on radio and television, often reflect research by social psychologists. Articles about the causes and possible prevention of riots, the effects of segregation and racial prejudice, and changing life-styles might all be attributed to social psychological sources. Subjects studied by social psychologists often capture public interest.

Much of the research carried out by social psychologists is done in college and university laboratories. Here conditions can be controlled fairly well. Such control, however, may limit the value of the study. Just knowing that they are participating in some kind of experiment might cause subjects to alter their behavior. In addition, psychologists sometimes find it necessary to withhold information from subjects about the true nature of the research. This may influence subjects in any later research in which they take part.

Because of these drawbacks, some social psychologists prefer to conduct field research. They go out into various settings—schools, recreation areas, and neighborhoods—to learn how individuals behave in groups and how groups behave as a whole. Their controls may not be as precise as in a laboratory setting but their findings are based on "real-life" social situations.

Most social psychologists hold academic positions. They may be college or university professors, or may teach at the high school level. In order to be called a social psychologist, a person must have a doctoral degree.

BIOGRAPHICAL PROFILES

The following pages contain short biographical sketches of a number of outstanding researchers and scholars in the field of psychology. This listing includes both historical and contemporary contributors to the science of human behavior.

ADLER, ALFRED (1870–1937)
Alfred Adler was a German-born psychologist who was a contemporary of Freud. He established the branch of psychology known as individual psychology. Adler believed that individuals are motivated mainly by social interests and that the creative self is what makes them strive toward complete fulfillment.

ALLPORT, GORDON (1897–1967)
Gordon Allport was an American psychologist who is best known for his studies of personality. He focused especially on prejudice.

ANASTASI, ANNE (1908–   )
Anne Anastasi is a psychologist who specializes in intelligence testing and measurement.

BANDURA, ALBERT (1925–   )
Albert Bandura is a behavioral psychologist who has been influential in demonstrating the importance of observation and imitation in learning.

BINET, ALFRED (1857–1911)
Alfred Binet focused on human intelligence and, with Theodore Simon, developed tests to measure the mental abilities of human beings. Binet is considered to be the most important French psychologist of his time.

CATTELL, RAYMOND B. (1905–   )
Raymond B. Cattell is a British-born psychologist who is best known for studying the traits that make up and predict personality.

CLARK, KENNETH B. (1914–   )
Kenneth B. Clark is a psychologist and educator who studies prejudice and racial problems.

EBBINGHAUS, HERMANN (1850–1909)
Hermann Ebbinghaus was a German-born psychologist who studied memory processes. He introduced the use of nonsense syllables as a way to test learning, relearning, and memory.

ELLIS, HAVELOCK (1859–1939)
Havelock Ellis was a psychologist who is best remembered for his research into the psychology of human sexuality.

ERIKSON, ERIK (1902–1982)
Erik Erikson was a German-born psychoanalyst who believed that individuals must successfully pass through certain developmental stages in order to reach the next stage of personality development.

FREUD, SIGMUND (1856–1939)
Sigmund Freud is considered to be the father of psychoanalysis. He believed that the unconscious portion of the mind plays

a large part in determining human behavior. Freud introduced the concepts of id, ego, and superego, and used free association and dream analysis to uncover people's hidden needs and desires.

FROMM, ERICH (1900–1980)
Erich Fromm was a psychoanalyst who believed that personality is shaped by the interaction between needs and the opportunities in the society for fulfilling these needs. He identified five specific needs.

GIBSON, ELEANOR (1910–   )
Eleanor Gibson is a psychologist who researches mainly in the area of children's perceptual development and perceptual learning. She has conducted studies on depth perception using the visual cliff.

HALL, G. STANLEY (1846–1924)
G. Stanley Hall was the first president of the American Psychological Association and established one of the first experimental psychology laboratories in the United States. He also is well-known for his studies of childhood and adolescence.

HARLOW, HARRY F. (1905–1981)
Harry F. Harlow was an American psychologist who is best known for researching the effects of surrogate mothers on monkeys. He focused especially on motivation, love, and affection.

HORNEY, KAREN (1885–1952)
Karen Horney was a German-born psychoanalyst who focused on problems in the parent-child relationship to find the causes of psychological problems.

HULL, CLARK (1884–1953)
Clark Hull was an American psychologist whose best-known work was in the area of learning theory.

JAMES, WILLIAM (1842–1910)
William James was an American psychologist, philosopher, and educator who founded the branch of psychology known

as functionalism. He also established the first psychology laboratory in the United States.

JUNG, CARL (1875–1961)
Carl Jung was a Swiss psychologist and psychiatrist who was a contemporary of Freud. He believed that behavior is largely determined by goals toward which human beings strive. Jung introduced the terms personal unconscious, collective unconscious, introversion, and extraversion.

KOFFA, KURT (1886–1941)
Kurt Koffa was an American psychologist and researcher who was one of the founders of Gestalt psychology.

KOHLBERG, LAWRENCE (1927–   )
Lawrence Kohlberg is a psychologist who is best known for his studies of moral reasoning and moral development. He proposed the theory that moral reasoning develops in stages.

KOHLER, WOLFGANG (1887–1967)
Wolfgang Kohler was a Gestalt psychologist who was especially interested in animal behavior and how animal learning processes influence behavior.

LAING, R. D. (1927–   )
R. D. Laing is a humanistic psychologist who believes that mental illness arises in individuals as a defense against bizarre stresses in the environment. According to Laing's view, mental illness is not necessarily abnormal.

LEWIN, KURT (1890–1947)
Kurt Lewin was a German-born social psychologist who tried to explain human behavior in terms of the total influences affecting individuals.

LORENZ, KONRAD (1903–   )
Konrad Lorenz is an animal behaviorist who has studied animals in their natural environments. He is best known for his finding that there is a critical period in the

development of ducklings during which they learn to follow behind their mother or any other moving object. Lorenz was awarded the Nobel Prize in 1973 in physiology and medicine.

MACCOBY, ELEANOR (1917–)
Eleanor Maccoby is a psychologist who has studied child development, methods and techniques of child rearing, and sex-role differences among children.

MASLOW, ABRAHAM (1908–1970)
Abraham Maslow was a humanistic psychologist who believed that individuals act the way they do because they are motivated by certain needs. He developed a theory that proposes that individuals must successfully move through a hierarchy of needs before they can achieve self-actualization.

MAY, ROLLO (1909–)
Rollo May is a psychologist who has been very influential in bringing European existential psychology to the United States.

MILGRAM, STANLEY (1933–1984)
Stanley Milgram was a psychologist who is best known for his studies on conformity and obedience to authority.

PAVLOV, IVAN (1849–1936)
Ivan Pavlov was a Russian-born scientist who developed and tested the concepts surrounding classical conditioning. One of his best-known studies involved conditioning a salivation response in dogs.

PIAGET, JEAN (1896–1980)
Jean Piaget was a Swiss-born psychologist who focused on the development of intelligence, reasoning, and thinking in children. He developed a theory that proposes that there are four stages of intellectual development through which children progress as they grow: sensory-motor period, preoperational period, concrete-operational period, and formal-operational period.

PINEL, PHILIPPE (1745–1826)
Philippe Pinel was the first person in modern times to suggest that the mentally ill are sick people rather than criminals or people possessed by demons. He ordered that the mentally ill individuals being treated in his asylums be unchained and treated with kindness.

ROGERS, CARL (1902–1987)
Carl Rogers was a humanistic psychologist who introduced the treatment technique of client-centered therapy. He believed that an important part of the human personality is the development of an individual's self-concept.

RORSCHACH, HERMANN (1884–1922)
Hermann Rorschach was a Swiss-born psychiatrist who developed the inkblot test still used today in studying the personality.

SCHACHTER, STANLEY (1922–)
Stanley Schachter is a social psychologist who is best known for his studies of group behavior and social influence.

SIMON, THEODORE (1878–1961)
Theodore Simon worked with Alfred Binet to develop the first test designed to directly measure intelligence.

SKINNER, B. F. (1904–)
B. F. Skinner is a behavioral psychologist who has studied how reward, reinforcement, and punishment influence learning. He focuses on the ways in which conditions external to the individual influence behavior.

SPERRY, ROGER W. (1913–)
Roger W. Sperry is an American researcher who has studied patients in whom the brain's corpus callosum has been severed. His work has led to a great deal of research and speculation on the split-brain phenomenon.

SULLIVAN, HARRY STACK (1892–1949)
Harry Stack Sullivan was a psychologist

who believed that the individual's personality must be studied in terms of interpersonal relationships. He introduced the concepts of dynamism, personification, and cognitive processes.

TERMAN, LEWIS (1877–1952)

Lewis Terman was a psychologist who revised Binet's intelligence test to make it compatible with American culture. He believed that intelligence is inherited, and conducted a longitudinal study of gifted children.

THORNDIKE, EDWARD LEE (1874–1949)

Edward Lee Thorndike was an educational psychologist who studied learning, teaching, and intelligence.

TOLMAN, EDWARD C. (1886–1959)

Edward C. Tolman was a cognitive psychologist who focused on mental constructs and purposeful behavior. He developed the concept of a cognitive map, which consists of past experiences and current behavior, knowledge, and meanings.

WATSON, JOHN B. (1878–1958)

John B. Watson developed the branch of psychology known as behaviorism, in the belief that observable behavior is the most important subject matter of psychology. According to Watson's view, behavior is determined completely by environmental factors.

WERTHEIMER, MAX (1880–1943)

Max Wertheimer was a German-born psychologist who founded the Gestalt branch of psychology. He believed that experience must be examined in its totality.

WUNDT, WILHELM (1832–1920)

Wilhelm Wundt was a German-born psychologist who is called the father of modern psychology. He developed the branch of psychology known as structuralism and established the first psychology laboratory in Germany. Wundt's carefully controlled experimental procedures greatly contributed to the development of experimental psychology as a science.

A

absolute threshold: minimum amount of stimulus that a subject can detect. (p. 253)

accommodation: in Piaget's theory of development, the adjustment of the cognitive structure to adapt to new experiences in the environment. (p. 230)

achievement test: series of questions that measure the amount of knowledge an individual has acquired in a particular area, such as in biology, history, or psychology. (p. 144)

acquired immune deficiency syndrome: see **AIDS.** (p. 361)

addiction: physical dependency on the use of a drug, so that larger and larger doses are required to obtain the same effect. When an individual stops taking the drug, withdrawal symptoms occur. (p. 361)

adjustment mechanism: any form of behavior that helps individuals adapt to their environment, reduce anxiety from frustration, and satisfy needs. (p. 308)

adrenal gland: ductless gland located above each kidney. Produces hormone called adrenalin. (p. 94)

affective disorder: disorder characterized by a disturbance in mood. (p. 354)

AIDS: (acquired immune deficiency syndrome) viral disease that destroys the body's immune system. (p. 361)

alarm: see **General Adaptation Syndrome (GAS).** (p. 326)

altruistic behavior: offering help or giving help to other people. (p. 442)

Alzheimer's disease: disease characterized by the progressive destruction of brain cells. (p. 358)

amnesia: loss of memory as a result of physical or psychological factors. (p. 349)

anorexia nervosa: chronic aversion to food and an obsession with thinness. (p. 359)

anthropology: study of the culture, or way of life, of people in all parts of the world. (p. 6)

anthropomorphism: attribution of human characteristics to animals. (p. 28)

antisocial personality: disorder characterized by the violation of the rules, laws, and mores of a society in which a person lives. (p. 357)

anxiety disorder: disturbance characterized by frequent general anxiety and uneasiness that is out of proportion to the situation at hand. (p. 352).

approach-approach conflict: see **conflict.** (p. 304)

approach-avoidance conflict: see **conflict.** (p. 306)

approach gradient: increase in the tendency of an organism to move toward a desired goal the closer it gets to the goal. (p. 305)

aptitude: ability to acquire some knowledge or skill, or the likelihood of acquiring it with training. An **aptitude test** measures what an individual is likely to be able to accomplish with training rather than what the person has accomplished already. (p. 144)

aptitude test: see **aptitude.** (p. 144)

assimilation: in Piaget's theory of development, the process of organizing new experiences into the existing cognitive structure. (p. 230)

atmospheric perspective: difference in visual clarity between objects close by and objects far away. Objects that appear to be hazy are perceived as being distant. Well-defined objects are perceived as being near. (p. 261)

attention: focusing of perception on a limited number of stimuli at a given moment. (p. 254)

attitude: readiness to respond favorably or unfavorably to a person, object, situation, or event. **Social attitude** refers to readiness to respond to social situations, problems, or questions. (p. 419)

attribution: process in which an attempt is made to interpret and explain the behavior of others. If the behavior is explained in terms of personality, the attribution is said to be a **dispositional factor.** If it is explained in terms of the environment, it is said to be a **situational factor.** (p. 422)

autocratic leader: directs the operation of a group with a firm hand. Does not ask for or welcome suggestions from other members. (p. 425)

autokinetic illusion: apparent movement of a small, fixed spot of light in a dark room. (p. 432)

autonomic nervous system: classification for those parts of the central and peripheral nervous systems that regulate the activity of the vital organs. (p. 86)

aversive therapy: method of treatment in which the person is conditioned to avoid a previously desired object or goal. (p. 376)

avoidance-avoidance conflict: see **conflict.** (p. 305)

avoidance conditioning: process of learning to avoid some unpleasant stimulus, such as learning not to place your hand on a hot stove. (p. 182)

avoidance gradient: increase in the tendency of an organism to avoid an undesirable goal the closer it gets to the goal. (p. 306)

axon: see **neuron.** (p. 86)

B

behavior: those activities of people or animals that can be observed directly or measured by special techniques. (p. 3)

behaviorism: approach to psychology that focuses on overt behavior and is based on the belief that personality is determined by rewards and punishments. (p. 10)

behavior sampling: method of measuring certain specific traits of personality by creating a situation in which the individual displays the behavior being studied. (p. 141)

behavior therapy: form of treatment that stresses that misbehavior is learned and can therefore be unlearned. (p. 376)

behavioral model: emphasizes the learning of inappropriate or undesirable behavior. (p. 365)

biofeedback: regulation, through training, of involuntary bodily responses, such as blood pressure or heartbeat. (p. 196)

bipolar disorder: disorder characterized by periods of extreme excitement and depression; formerly known as a *manic-depressive psychosis.* (p. 354)

brain lesion: destruction of a specific area of the brain through surgery, accident, or disease. (p. 87)

brainstorming: method of thinking in which all ideas that seem to have any bearing on a problem are noted but are not critically evaluated until some later time. (p. 233)

branching program: form of instruction that progresses step by step but also provides alternative, or branching, supplementary information if the subject makes incorrect responses. (p. 194)

brightness: sensation of lightness or darkness of any color or gray. (p. 257)

bulimia: disorder characterized by a cycle of binge eating and purging. (p. 359)

C

cannabis: substance that produces sensory and perceptual changes and reduces inhibitions. (p. 361–62)

Cannon-Bard theory: states that the awareness of an emotion and bodily changes occur at the same time. (p. 288)

cell body: see **neuron.** (p. 86)

central nervous system: part of the nervous system composed of the brain and spinal cord. (p. 84)

cerebral cortex: surface or outer layer of the brain in humans and higher animals. (p. 89)

chromosome: tiny rodlike body in the cell nucleus. A human cell normally has 46 chromosomes, arranged in 23 pairs. (p. 65) See **gene.**

chronological age (CA): number of years, months, and days a person has lived from birth to the present. (p. 161)

chunking: combining or grouping of information into related units to make the information easier to learn. (p. 212)

class interval: specific numerical span rather than an individual score. (p. 472)

classical (or Pavlovian) conditioning: repeated pairing of an unconditioned stimulus, which originally elicited a given response, with another stimulus until this conditioned stimulus elicits the given response. (p. 181)

client-centered therapy: form of treatment, originated by Carl Rogers, that stresses placing the client in a psychologically secure environment, finding out more about the client's feelings, and not judging the client's behavior. It is based on the idea that all people have a need for positive growth. (p. 375)

closure: factor that influences perception. Occurs when the brain fills in the gaps to make an object seem complete. (p. 264)

cognitive dissonance: occurs when individuals are faced with a lack of agreement between two ideas, attitudes, or beliefs. (p. 421)

cognitive learning: active process that involves organizing information, making comparisons, and forming new associations, and that is guided by past and present experiences. (p. 197)

cognitive map: mental map that helps people get from one point to another without losing their way. (p. 197)

cognitive process: Sullivan's term for how people think and experience things. An important part of his theory of personality. (p. 116)

cognitive psychology: approach to psychology that focuses on how people perceive, store, and interpret information. (p. 14)

cognitive theory of emotion: emphasizes the mental processes involved in emotional experiences. (p. 288)

collective unconscious: according to Jung, the most important and influential system within the personality. It contains the memories passed on to us by our ancestors. (p. 113)

colorblindness (color weakness): inability to discriminate certain hues. In the most common form, red and green are seen as alike and are confused with a faded yellow. (p. 258)

communication: process of transmitting or exchanging symbols, such as words or gestures, that are understood by the two or more members engaged in the interaction. (p. 408)

compensation: attempt by an individual to make up for a deficiency in one area by expending extra time, effort, and energy in order to excel in some other area. (p. 309)

complementary colors: colors whose light waves, when mixed together, are seen as gray. (p. 258)

concept: meaning, expressed in words or other symbols, that an individual attaches to the common property of a variety of objects, situations, or events. (p. 229)

concrete-operational period: third stage in Piaget's theory of cognitive development, in which children can classify objects in a variety of groupings, based mainly on observing concrete events. This stage occurs from about ages seven to eleven. (p. 57)

conditioned response (CR): new or acquired response elicited by a stimulus not originally capable of arousing it. (p. 181)

conditioned stimulus (CS): new stimulus, in a conditioning process, that was originally ineffective in eliciting a given response but has become capable of doing so. (p. 181)

conflict: state of tension or stress involved when an individual is faced simultaneously with either opposing or mutually exclusive impulses, tendencies, or desires. An **approach-approach conflict** is a conflict in which both choices are desirable. In an **avoidance-avoidance conflict** both choices are undesirable. In an **approach-avoidance conflict** both choices have positive and negative aspects. (p. 303)

conscious: awareness of something, such as a feeling of pressure during a handshake or the sound of someone talking. (p. 112)

control group: comparison group of subjects in an experiment usually matched to an experimental group but with whom the independent variable (condition being studied) is not present or is controlled. (pp. 25, 481)

convergence: movement of eye muscles that causes our pupils to come closer together as an object is brought closer than about 6 meters (20 feet) to our eyes. It provides a cue to distance. (p. 260)

conversion disorder: disturbance in which the individual's psychological problems are changed or converted into bodily disturbances, such as the paralysis of an arm or the inability to speak. (p. 349)

correlation: consistent relationship between two sets of events or variables. (pp. 29, 479) When two variables are related, they are said to be **correlated.** Measures that move in similar directions are said to be **positively corre-**

lated. (pp. 29, 479) Measures that move in opposite directions are said to be **negatively correlated.** (pp. 30, 479)

correlation coefficient: statistical measure that indicates the degree of relationship between two variables. (p. 479)

counter-conditioning: replacing one conditioned response to a stimulus with another (usually incompatible) response. The process is often used to get rid of undesirable behavior. (p. 182)

creative self: Adler's idea that people constantly strive to be fulfilled. They create goals and search for ways of reaching these goals. The creative self is what makes each individual unique. (p. 114)

creative thinking: nonroutine directed thinking in which the individual seeks new solutions to problems or new forms of artistic expression. (p. 232)

critical period: time period during which an individual can learn specific behaviors most easily. (p. 43)

cross-sectional method: means of studying human behavior by observing groups of individuals of different age levels at the same time. (p. 44)

crystallized intelligence: those parts of intelligence that are acquired mostly through interaction with the environment. (p. 162)

D

deductive reasoning: process of reasoning from general principles or rules to particular cases or consequences. (p. 242)

delusion: false belief that persists in spite of evidence or proof to the contrary. (pp. 231, 355)

democratic leader: works within the group and appreciates contributions made by other members. (p. 425)

dendrite: see **neuron.** (p. 86)

dependent variable: factor whose changed condition is considered to result from, or to depend on, the independent variable in an experiment. (pp. 25, 481)

depressant: see **drug.** (p. 361)

depression: an affective disorder characterized by a depressed mood all or most of the time. (p. 354)

desensitization: therapeutic technique based on classical conditioning principles used to reduce severe anxiety. The anxious situation is associated with pleasant stimuli to make it less threatening. (p. 377)

developmental disorder: disorder that begins in infancy, childhood, or adolescence. (p. 359)

deviation IQ: method for computing an intelligence quotient (IQ) by comparing the test score of an individual to the average score of a large number of persons of the same chronological age. (p. 162)

Diagnostic and Statistical Manual of Mental Disorders: see **DSM-III.** (p. 348)

difference threshold: amount of change necessary for a subject to detect a difference in stimulation 50 percent of the time. **Just-noticeable difference** is the minimum amount of change necessary for a subject to be able to detect the difference in a stimulus. (p. 253)

diffusion of responsibility: tendency of individuals in a group not to take action in an emergency because other people are present. (p. 450)

discrimination: tendency to respond to a certain stimulus in one way and to respond to similar stimuli in another way. (p. 187)

displaced aggression: adjustment mechanism in which individuals transfer their hostility from the original source of frustration to an object or person not directly associated with it. (p. 315)

dispositional factor: see **attribution.** (p. 422)

dissociative disorder: disturbance in which certain parts of an individual's personality are in disagreement with, and separate from, the remaining parts of the personality—as in amnesia. (p. 349)

distributed practice: kind of practice in which the sessions are separated by rest periods. (p. 208)

divergent thinking: flexibility in thinking; many ideas or solutions to a problem are considered before a conclusion is reached. (p. 241)

DNA (deoxyribonucleic acid): chemical substance in the cell nucleus that is largely responsible for genetic inheritance. (p. 66)

dominant gene: gene that determines if an individual will show a particular characteristic or trait controlled by that gene. (p. 66)

dream interpretation: technique used by psychoanalysts to analyze the hidden and symbolic content of dreams. (p. 373)

drive: physiological condition that activates behavior toward a goal. (p. 277)

drug: any chemical substance that changes

mood, perception, or awareness and can harm the individual or society if misused. **Hallucinogens** are drugs that produce sensory perceptions that have no basis in reality. **Stimulants** are drugs that cause increased functional behaviors. **Depressants** are drugs that decrease bodily activity. **Narcotics** are addictive drugs that slow the central nervous system, relieve pain, and induce sleep. Forms of **cannabis** reduce inhibitions. (p. 361)

drug therapy: treatment of individuals with psychological disturbances through the use of drugs, such as tranquilizers. Often used in combination with other forms of therapy. (p. 372)

DSM-III: (Diagnostic and Statistical Manual of Mental Disorders, Third Edition) lists 18 major diagnostic categories of mental disorders, the subcategories within each major category, and a description of the symptoms that accompany each disorder. (p. 348)

duct gland (exocrine gland): gland that discharges its secretions through an outlet onto an external or internal surface of the body. (p. 92)

ductless gland (endocrine gland): gland having no duct (outlet). Its secretions are released into the bloodstream. (p. 93)

dyad: group of two people—the smallest possible group. (p. 395)

dynamism: according to Sullivan, the smallest unit of behavior that can be studied. It is a pattern of behavior that occurs over and over, similar to a habit. (p. 116)

E

eating disorder: psychologically caused disruption in normal eating pattern. (p. 359)

educable: mildly retarded individuals who can profit to some extent from schooling. As adults they can work in unskilled or semi-skilled jobs under supervision. (p. 169)

ego: psychoanalytic term referring to the rational aspect of the personality and the learned ways of behaving. (p. 112)

eidetic image: exceedingly vivid image (usually visual) that is popularly spoken of as a ''photographic mind.'' It is much more common in children than in adults. (p. 236)

electroconvulsive shock therapy: form of therapy in which an electric current is passed through the brain for a very brief period of time, producing temporary loss of awareness. It is used in the treatment of psychological disturbances. (p. 372)

electroencephalograph (EEG): instrument that records the tiny electrical variations, or brain waves, that accompany the activity of the brain. (p. 87)

emotion: complex state of awareness that involves bodily activity, a response to an external or internal event, and some change in behavior. (p. 285)

emotional development: increase in awareness and expression of affective experiences, whether pleasant or unpleasant. (p. 52)

encoding: process of transferring information from one communication system to another, such as changing words printed in a book into some form that can be stored in the memory system. (p. 217)

encounter group (training group): usually consists of ten to fifteen individuals. A group leader encourages each person to explore his or her own feelings and motives, as well as those of the other group members. (p. 378)

environment: all the surrounding forces that affect your life. (p. 65)

equilibrium: sense used to help a person maintain position of the body in space. It is governed by the inner ear. (p. 270)

exclusive group: group whose members place restrictions and limitations on the opportunity for others to participate. (p. 401)

exhaustion: see **General Adaptation Syndrome (GAS).** (p. 326)

existential psychology: an approach to psychology that stresses the importance of individual choice in determining human behavior. (p. 15)

experimental group: group of subjects in an experimental situation with whom the independent variable (condition being studied) is present in variable degrees. (pp. 25, 481)

extinction: dying out of an established conditioned response as a result of presenting the conditioned stimulus without the usual reinforcement. (p. 183)

extrasensory perception (ESP): area of parapsychology that investigates experiences in which knowledge appears to be gained independently of the known senses. (p. 33)

extraversion: tendency for individuals to center their interests in their external environment and in social life. (p. 114)

extrinsic motivation: activating force that comes mainly from outside rather than from inside the individual. (p. 285)

F

family therapy: participation of an entire family in treatment. It is based on the belief that the problems of the patient are part of a general maladjustment of the family group. (p. 378)

feedback: knowledge of results, or the process of providing individuals with information on the correctness of previous responses so they can make adjustments in their behavior. (p. 208)

"fight or flight" reaction: physical response to an emergency situation in which the body prepares to defend itself or to retreat. (p. 325)

fixed-interval schedule: see **interval schedule.** (p. 192)

fixed-ratio schedule: see **ratio schedule.** (p. 192)

fluid intelligence: those aspects of intelligence that are mostly inherited. (p. 162)

formal group: deliberately formed group with a rigid structure. (p. 401)

formal-operational period: fourth stage in Piaget's theory of cognitive development, in which individuals can think logically, can try all possible combinations systematically, and can experiment with cause-and-effect relationships. This stage usually begins around age eleven. (p. 58)

frame: single unit displayed at each step in programmed learning. (p. 194)

fraternal twins: twins developing from two ova (eggs) fertilized by two sperm. They may be of the same sex or different sexes. (p. 70)

free association: technique involving the open expression of whatever thoughts occur to an individual. It is used in psychoanalysis to explore the patient's unconscious thoughts and ideas. (pp. 113, 373)

frequency distribution: arrangement for summarizing data that is based on a count of how often scores or other data appear. (p. 472)

frustration: thwarting or blocking of motivated, goal-directed behavior. (p. 300)

frustration tolerance: ability of an individual to withstand frustration without developing undesirable ways of responding, such as becoming very emotionally upset. (p. 302)

fugue: amnesia with flight, in which a person with amnesia runs away from the area in which he or she usually resides. (p. 349)

functional fixedness: process of believing that some tool or object has only one use or function, rather than seeing how such things might be used in new or different ways. (p. 241)

functionalism: approach to psychology that focused on how the mind works rather than on the structure of mental processes. (p. 8)

G

galvanic skin response (GSR): change in electrical resistance of the skin, especially as such change accompanies an emotional state. (p. 290)

gene: factor in a cell that determines the transmission and development of inherited characteristics. Tiny parts within chromosomes. See **dominant gene** and **recessive gene.** (p. 66)

General Adaptation Syndrome (GAS): three-stage reaction to prolonged periods of stress. During the **alarm** stage, the body mobilizes to deal with the stressor. During **resistance** the body appears to hold its own completely. During **exhaustion** the body appears to break down. (p. 326)

generalization: in conditioning, after a conditioned response has been established to a certain stimulus, an organism's tendency to respond to other similar stimuli in the same way. Also, the reaching of a general conclusion or judgment based on specific facts or observations. (p. 186)

generalized anxiety disorder: characterized by frequent and generalized anxiety that is not attached to any specific object, event, or situation. (p. 353)

Gestalt psychology: approach to psychology that stresses the importance of the whole, as opposed to small parts. (p. 10)

gifted: describes persons with exceptional or special abilities or persons of high intellectual ability— IQ's of about 140 or higher. (p. 170)

gonads: sex glands that provide the sperm or egg cells for reproduction, and produce hormones that determine secondary sex characteristics and influence sexual behavior. (p. 95)

graphic rating scale: psychological scaling method that allows someone to rate an object, event, situation, or person on a trait by checking an appropriate description, such as "poor," "average," or "excellent." (p. 133)

group atmosphere: general emotional state of a group at any given time. (p. 407)

group climate: kind of atmosphere that prevails in a group over a considerable period of time. (p. 407)

group cohesiveness: mutual, overall attraction that each member feels toward other members of the group. (p. 405)

group feedback: communication within a group that provides members with information on their progress or lack of progress. (p. 409)

group morale: attitude of individuals in a group, their loyalty to the group, and their willingness to do the group's work. (p. 406)

group therapy: psychotherapeutic treatment in which a small group of people meet to discuss their problems and to interact. (p. 378)

H

hallucination: faulty, senselike perception for which there is no appropriate external stimulus, as in the case of a person who hears voices although there are no voices present. (p. 355)

hallucinogen: see **drug.** (p. 361)

halo effect: tendency, when one person is rating another, to be influenced by an estimate of some other trait or by a general impression of the individual being rated. (p. 134)

heredity: all the characteristics transmitted from parent to child by means of genes in the chromosomes. (p. 65)

histogram: graph that resembles a bar graph, but in which the bars touch. (p. 473)

hostile aggression: responding to a situation primarily for the purpose of inflicting harm on others and not in self-defense. (p. 458)

hue: quality of redness, blueness, yellowness, or greenness that differentiates one color from another. (p. 257)

humanistic psychology: study of how people try to achieve their maximum potential, or ''self-actualization,'' through health and self-growth. (p. 15)

hypnosis: artificially induced state characterized chiefly by extreme suggestibility. It usually, though not always, resembles sleep but is physiologically different from it. (p. 98)

hypochondria: somatoform disorder characterized by a preoccupation with health and bodily ailments, and a tendency to exaggerate or imagine numerous symptoms. (p. 348–49)

hypothesis: assumption adopted as a tentative explanation of observed facts and as the basis for further reasoning or investigation. (p. 24)

I

id: psychoanalytic term referring to the original system of personality. (p. 112)

identical twins: twins developing from a single fertilized ovum (egg), thus having the same heredity. Always of the same sex. (p. 68)

identification: adjustment mechanism in which an individual imitates, or closely associates with, the behavior of some other person or group. (p. 310)

imagination: reproduction and reorganization of past experiences to form ideas in the present. (p. 236)

implosive therapy: form of treatment that encourages the patient to undergo anxiety but in a safe, controlled environment, so that the anxiety-producing situation loses its power over the person. (p. 377)

inclusive group: group whose members get satisfaction from increasing their activities and including more people. (p. 400)

independent variable: the factor whose effects are being examined in an experiment. It is selected and then manipulated by the experimenter in some systematic and predetermined manner while all, or as many as possible, other variables are held constant. (pp. 25, 481)

inductive reasoning: process of reasoning from particular facts or cases to general conclusions. (p. 241)

informal group: group that is casual with no official structure or deliberately formed organization. (p. 401)

insight: rather sudden grasp of the relationships involved in problem solving. (p. 198)

intellectual development: development of an individual's mental abilities. (p. 56)

intelligence: ability of a complex organism to adapt adequately to both new and old situations in the environment. (p. 154)

intelligence quotient (IQ): ratio of mental age to chronological age times 100. (p. 161)

$$IQ = \frac{MA}{CA} \times 100 \text{ (see } \textbf{deviation IQ.)}$$

interaction-oriented group: group whose main purpose is to provide opportunity for social contacts and interaction. (p. 400)

intermittent reinforcement: rewarding some, but not all, correct responses. (p. 186)

interval schedule: reinforcement schedule in which the reward is given after a specified amount of time. In a **fixed-interval sched-**

513

ule, the organism is rewarded for the first correct response after a fixed time limit. In a **variable-interval schedule,** the organism is rewarded at the end of time limits that change from one reinforcement to the next. (p. 192)

interviewing: method of evaluating a person in a relatively short time by means of a standardized or an informal conversational situation. (p. 139)

intrinsic motivation: motivation that comes from within the individual rather than from the environment. (p. 285)

introversion: tendency for individuals to center their interests in themselves and their own experiences. (p. 114)

J

James-Lange theory: states that a stimulus first leads to bodily responses, and that the awareness of these responses constitutes an emotion. (p. 286)

just-noticeable difference: see **difference threshold.** (p. 253)

K

kinesthetic sense: muscle, tendon, and joint sense that is important in determining body movement and position. (p. 269)

L

laissez-faire leader: tends to stand by passively without exerting much influence on the group. (p. 425)

language development: learning to use symbols, such as spoken words, to communicate with others. (p. 48)

leader: individual in a group who exerts the greatest influence on the members of the group. He or she guides the thinking of the group and initiates, directs, or organizes the group's activities. A **democratic leader** works within the group and appreciates contributions made by other members; an **autocratic leader** determines regulations and does not welcome suggestions made by other group members; a **laissez-faire leader** does not exert much influence on the group and makes little effort to lead. (p. 425)

learning: acquiring the ability to respond adequately to a situation. The modification of behavior through experience, involving rather lasting changes. (p. 180)

linear perspective: perception of objects as smaller and closer together the more distant they are from the observer. (p. 261)

linear program: form of instruction that contains a series of statements arranged in a step-by-step progression to which the subject responds and then learns immediately whether or not the answer is correct. (p. 194)

loci method: mnemonic device to help remember items by associating what is to be remembered with a series of familiar locations. (p. 210)

long-term memory (LTM): storage and retention of information that has been situated briefly in short-term memory. (p. 220)

longitudinal method: means of studying human behavior by observing the development of the same individual or group over a considerable period of time. (p. 44)

loudness: intensity of a sound, determined primarily by the amplitude, or height, of the sound waves. (p. 265)

M

massed practice: running together of practice sessions during which material is being learned. (p. 208)

maturation: bodily growth or development and the accompanying behavioral changes that occur automatically. (p. 70)

mean: average in a distribution that is found by adding all the values and then dividing by the number of values. (p. 476)

median: score (or other data) that falls exactly in the middle of a distribution. (p. 476)

medical model: links genetic or biological factors as the causes of psychological disorders. (p. 363)

medical therapy: treatment, by psychiatrists and other medical doctors, of individuals through the use of medicine. (p. 372)

memory trace: assumed changes that occur in the nervous system between the time learning takes place and the time it is recalled. It is hypothesized that these changes explain the process of retention. (p. 220)

mental age (MA): measure of mental development in terms of the ability of average individuals of a particular chronological age. (p. 161)

mental retardation: term used to refer to the condition of individuals of subnormal intellectual ability. **Mildly retarded** individuals have IQ's of between 50 and 69 and can learn basic school skills. **Moderately retarded**

people have IQ's of between 35 and 49 and can learn to take care of themselves somewhat. **Severely retarded** people have the intellectual ability of a three-year-old child (IQ's of between 20 and 34). **Profoundly retarded** individuals have IQ's of below 20 and show almost no response to environmental stimulation. (p. 167)

mnemonic device: catchword or formula used to help in the process of learning. (p. 210)

mode: score (or other data) that occurs most frequently in a distribution. (p. 475)

model: person whose behavior is imitated. **Modeling** is learning in which the behavior of another person is observed and imitated. (pp. 119, 377)

molar approach: way of studying behavior in large general units, such as studying how someone makes friends. (p. 111)

molecular approach: way of studying behavior in small specific units, such as how specific parts of the brain function. (p. 111)

moral development: individual's development of the knowledge of the difference between right and wrong. (p. 58)

motivation: activating of behavior that satisfies an individual's needs and enables the person to work toward his or her goals. (p. 276)

motive: expected outcome that causes individuals to strive toward a goal. (p. 276)

motor development: increase in control over the muscles of the body. (p. 46)

motor neuron: nerve cell that conducts impulses from the brain or spinal cord to muscles and glands. Motor neurons are involved in such activities as running, jumping, and riding a bicycle. (p. 86)

multiple personality: dissociative disorder involving the development of two or more usually separate personalities within the same individual. (p. 352)

N

narcotic: see **drug.** (p. 361)

negative reinforcement: see **reinforcement.** (pp. 119, 186, 190)

negative transfer: see **transfer.** (p. 206)

neuron: nerve cell over which impulses travel, carrying messages. A neuron consists of a cell body, dendrites, and an axon. The **cell body** is the mass that surrounds the cell's nucleus and contains the chromosomes and genes. At one end of the neuron are the **dendrites,** which receive impulses from other neurons. The impulses then travel the length of the **axon,** the long, thin portion of the cell. The **synapse** is the space between the axon ending of one neuron and the dendrite of another. (p. 86)

norm group: group of people who provide a set of scores on a standardized test against which the scores of people who take the test later on can be compared. (p. 131)

normal curve: perfectly symmetrical bell-shaped curve that has one high point, from which the line slopes downward smoothly on both sides. (p. 473)

O

obsessive-compulsive disorder: characterized by preoccupation with unwanted ideas and persistent impulses to repeat certain acts over and over. (p. 353)

operant conditioning: strengthening of a given stimulus-response relationship by following the response with a reinforcement. (p. 188)

optical illusion: false visual perception. (p. 261)

organic mental disorder: disorder in which the disturbance stems directly from injury to the brain or from an abnormality in the brain's biochemical environment. (p. 357)

organism: any living person or animal. (p. 4)

overcompensation: extreme effort by an individual to overcome feelings of weakness, guilt, or inferiority in some area. (p. 310)

overlearning: learning in which practice goes beyond the point of just required mastery. (p. 211)

overrating: tendency of people to give overly high ratings to most persons on most traits. (p. 134)

P

panic disorder: disorder characterized by accute attacks of overwhelming terror and dread. (p. 353)

paradoxical sleep: stage of sleep in which an individual is only slightly asleep according to electroencephalograph (EEG) records and yet is difficult to arouse when having rapid eye movements (REMs). (p. 97)

paranoid disorder: disorder characterized by persistent, systematized delusions of grandeur, persecution, and reference. (p. 356)

parapsychology: branch of study concerned with psychological phenomena that are gen-

515

erally considered very unusual, fantastic, and outside the range of "normal" events. They include trances, telepathy, and apparitions. (p. 31)

pecking order: accepted order of dominance in a small group, as established through aggression and intimidation. (p. 454)

peer: person considered to be one's equal, or a companion or associate of about the same age or ability. (p. 430)

perception: process of interpreting sensations. (p. 252)

performance test: specialized test in which verbal directions play a minimum role. (p. 158)

peripheral nervous system: classification for the nerves that branch out from the spinal cord and brain. (p. 85)

personal unconscious: according to Jung, experiences that were once conscious but have since been forgotten. (p. 113)

personality: sum total of an individual's relatively consistent, organized, and unique thoughts and reactions to the environment. (p. 108)

personality disorder: disorder characterized by behavior patterns that are unacceptable to society but that cause the individual little anxiety or stress. (p. 357)

personality inventory: standardized questionnaire or self-rating scale in which individuals give information about their attitudes and behavior, which can then be evaluated in terms of norms. (p. 135)

personification: according to Sullivan, the image that people have of themselves or of another person. It is a kind of "mental picture" that we carry around with us. (p. 116)

phobic disorder: strong and unreasonable fear of a specific object or situation. (p. 353)

physical development: growth of an individual's body. (p. 45)

pigeonhole error: tendency to place people into a category because they share some common characteristic, such as being the "blond" type. (p. 134)

pitch: highness or lowness of a sound. It is determined chiefly by the vibration frequency of the sound wave. (p. 264)

pituitary gland: ductless gland located on the underside of the brain. Secretes several hormones that influence growth, sex development, and metabolism. (p. 94)

plateau: in a learning graph, an intermediate period of little or no apparent progress preceded and followed by periods of measurable progress. (p. 213)

play therapy: form of therapy most often used with children, in which individuals express their feelings during such processes as playing with dolls or puppets or drawing pictures. (p. 375)

pleasure principle: Freudian concept regarding how the id functions to keep the level of tension low by obtaining pleasure. (p. 112)

polygraph: apparatus that simultaneously records a number of physiological changes such as blood pressure, pulse rate, breathing, and galvanic skin response. (p. 290)

positive reinforcement: see **reinforcement.** (pp. 119, 186, 190)

positive transfer: see **transfer.** (p. 206)

positron-emission tomography (PET): technique that enables scientists to measure brain activity by means of radioactive glucose that has been given to a subject. (p. 92)

prejudice: attitude, either for or against something, that prevents the person from objectively considering and evaluating new evidence. (p. 419)

prenatal development: development that takes place before birth. (p. 44)

preoperational period: Piaget's second stage of cognitive development, in which children have mental images and the beginnings of language development take place, but the child's thinking lacks organization. This stage usually runs approximately from ages two to seven. (p. 57)

proactive inhibition: tendency for present learning to interfere with the recall of material learned later. See **retroactive inhibition.** (p. 220)

procrastination: escape or withdrawal mechanism that gives an individual temporary relief from a distressful situation by putting off doing the activity or task. (p. 314)

prodigy: person who displays a very high degree of mastery in a particular area, usually at an early age. (p. 170)

programmed learning: learning from material arranged in a series of steps that enable the learner to proceed with a minimum of error and receive a maximum of reinforcement. (p. 194)

projection: adjustment mechanism in which individuals attribute to others their own unacceptable motives or thoughts, or place the blame for their difficulties on others. (pp. 141, 311)

propaganda: organized attempt to influence attitudes. (p. 420)

proximity: factor in perception based on the nearness of different objects. (p. 264)

pseudogroup effect: incorrect assumption that certain results are due to group influence. (p. 413)

psychoanalysis: process of bringing unconscious feelings to the surface. (pp. 9, 373)

psychoanalytic model: views psychological disturbances as the result of childhood experiences and of repressed, or hidden, desires and needs. (p. 364)

psychodrama: form of treatment in which individuals act out situations related to their personal problems. (p. 378)

psychokinesis: study of experiences in which the thought of an individual is said to influence the performance of some physical object or event. (p. 31)

psychological dependence: situation in which the removal of something or someone on which the person depends causes the person to have severe feelings of distress. (p. 361)

psychology: science that deals with the behavior and thinking of organisms. (p. 2)

psychotherapy: treatment of psychological disturbances by psychologists, psychiatrists, and psychoanalysts, involving increased self-understanding, improved relationships, and more satisfying patterns of behavior. (p. 373)

punishment: any form of unpleasant or painful stimulation applied after the performance of undesirable behavior. (pp. 119, 193)

R

random: having an equal chance of being assigned to a group taking part in a study or experiment. (p. 25)

range: mathematical difference between the high and low scores in a frequency distribution. (p. 477)

ranking method: psychological scaling method in which someone ranks objects, events, or persons from lowest to highest, such as from least beautiful to most beautiful. (p. 133)

rapid eye movement (REM): movement of the eyes during sleep. Usually indicates that an individual is dreaming. (p. 97)

rating: assigning a rank or score to an individual. Also, an individual's position in a scale of values. A rating scale provides a uniform method of securing evaluations of an individual's personality traits. (p. 133)

ratio schedule: reinforcement schedule in which the organism is rewarded according to the number of correct responses. In a **fixed-ratio schedule,** the organism is rewarded after a set number of correct responses. In a **variable-ratio schedule,** the number of responses between reinforcements is varied or changed from one reinforcement to the next. (p. 192)

rationalization: process of justifying conduct or opinions by inventing socially acceptable reasons. People who rationalize may not realize that they are explaining their behavior in terms of socially approved and high-sounding reasons instead of real reasons. (p. 316)

reality principle: Freudian concept regarding how the ego uses realistic thinking and adjusts to real-life situations, such as delaying satisfaction until a suitable object is found. (p. 112)

reasoning: form of thinking in which one attempts to solve a present problem on the basis of general principles derived from elements in two or more previous experiences. (p. 241)

recall: way of estimating how much has been remembered by asking the individual to reproduce from memory what has been learned. (p. 215)

recessive gene: gene that determines a characteristic or trait only if the gene on the matching chromosome is also recessive. (p. 66)

recognition: method of estimating memory by presenting material and having the individual identify what has been learned. (p. 215)

reflection of feelings: technique used by client-centered therapists in which the therapist restates the meaning of a client's words but in somewhat different terms, thus helping the client to reflect on and clarify his or her feelings. (p. 375)

reflex: relatively simple, unlearned, involuntary response to a stimulus. (p. 181)

regression: adjustment mechanism by which a frustrated individual retreats to an earlier known, less mature, and usually less adequate way of meeting problems. (p. 314)

rehearsal: repeating or practicing information for learning purposes. (p. 217)

reinforcement: in classical or Pavlovian conditioning, presentation of the unconditioned stimulus immediately following the conditioned stimulus, such as giving an animal an electric shock immediately following the sounding of a bell. In operant or instrumental conditioning, the strengthening of a response when it leads to satisfaction, typically a reward of some kind. Reinforcement is said to be **positive** if its presentation strengthens a response and **negative** if its removal strengthens a response. (pp. 119, 186, 190)

relearning: method of estimating how much has been remembered by having the individual learn the same material again. (p. 214)

reliability: degree to which a test score will have the same, or about the same, position or rank each time an individual takes a test. (p. 132)

repression: unconscious process by which an individual selectively ''forgets'' unpleasant or undesirable situations. (pp. 222, 314)

resistance: term used by psychoanalysts to refer to the blocking of a patient's thoughts by anxiety and/or repression. (p. 373) Also see **General Adaptation Syndrome (GAS).** (p. 326)

retention: remembering or holding onto what has been learned. (p. 214)

retrieval: process of obtaining information or data that have been stored in short-term or long-term memory. (p. 217)

retroactive inhibition: tendency of later learned material to interfere with the recall of previously learned material. See **proactive inhibition.** (p. 220)

risky shift: tendency of a group to make more risk-taking decisions than each individual in the group would make alone. (p. 432)

role: function of the individual in a group and the kind of behavior expected of an individual in a specific situation. (p. 407)

role model: person who provides examples for behavior that another individual might copy. (p. 431)

S

saturation: degree to which any color differs from a gray of the same brightness. Pure colors are highly saturated. Colors such as maroon and pink are low in saturation. (p. 258)

scapegoat: individual (or group) that is blamed for the misdeeds or mistakes of others. (p. 317)

schizophrenic disorder: disorder characterized by distortions of reality, disturbances in emotions and thought, strange behavior, and confusion as to identity or time. (p. 355)

science: branch of study that is based on systematically conducted research. (p. 3)

secondary reinforcement: when, as a result of being associated with a primary reinforcement, some object or event becomes itself a reinforcer. (p. 192)

self-actualization: belief that individuals innately strive to make their potential abilities develop into actual or real abilities. (p. 123)

self-concept: system of attitudes that individuals have toward themselves. (p. 123)

sensation: physiological arousal of a sense organ by something in the environment. (p. 252)

sensitive period: term used by some psychologists to refer to a time during development that is important, but not critical, for the learning of certain behaviors. (p. 43)

sensory-motor period: first stage in Piaget's theory of cognitive development, in which children focus on the present, respond to stimuli, acquire skills, but do not plan actions very far ahead. This stage occurs from birth to about two years of age. (p. 56)

sensory neuron: nerve that conducts impulses from our sense organs, such as our eyes and ears, to the brain or spinal cord. (p. 86)

sensory register: kind of memory in which information is stored only momentarily. (p. 217)

shaping: procedure in which the experimenter rewards the organism each time it makes a response that approximates the desired response. (p. 189)

short-term memory (STM): process of initial and brief storage of sensory information, which is available for immediate recall. (p. 217)

similarity: factor in perception based on the degree of resemblance in objects. (p. 264)

simple extinction therapy: method of treatment in which a maladjusted behavior is reduced by not reinforcing the behavior. (p. 377)

situational factor: see **attribution.** (p. 422)

small group: gathering or unit of individuals who have face-to-face communication with one another, who have feelings of belonging to the group, and who share a common goal. Usually consists of no more than fifteen or twenty persons. (p. 394)

social attitude: see **attitude.** (p. 419)

social development: learning to act and live in a society as a member of that society. (p. 54)

social facilitation: increase in motivation and effort that arises from the stimulus provided by the presence of other people. (p. 452)

social psychology: branch of psychology that is concerned with the effects of groups on the individual and with how individuals think about other people. (p. 6)

society: large group of people who share common traits, customs, or ways of behaving. (p. 110)

sociocultural model: emphasizes the role of environmental factors in causing psychological disturbances. (p. 365)

sociogram: diagram of the interaction among group members. (p. 405)

sociology: study of human groups. (p. 6)

sociometry: research method that measures how individuals perceive, feel, and think about the other members of the group. (p. 405)

somatoform disorder: disorder in which physical symptoms appear without any known organic cause. (p. 348)

sour grapes rationalization: form of rationalization in which people say that they do not want what they cannot have or achieve. (p. 317)

spontaneous recovery: reappearance of a conditioned response after a period of rest following extinction but without further reinforcement. (p. 183)

standardized test: test that can be given, scored, and interpreted the same way by different people. (p. 131)

statistic: mathematical procedure for collecting, organizing, analyzing, and interpreting data or information. (p. 471)

status: person's standing in a group. (p. 404)

stereotype: preconceived idea of the appearance or behavior of individuals of a given group, such as racial, political, or occupational. (p. 134)

stereotyped behavior: adjustment mechanism in which an individual displays inflexible behavior; behavior that is not altered by circumstances. (p. 311)

stimulant: see **drug.** (p. 361)

storage: retention of information or data in the memory system. (p. 217)

stress: body's reactions to perceived pressures and threats from the environment. (p. 324)

stressor: any cause of stress. (p. 325)

structuralism: approach to psychology that focused on the structure of human consciousness. (p. 8)

subject: person or animal participating in an experiment and whose behavior is then observed and measured. (p. 25)

subliminal perception: perception of stimuli so weak that the individual is not aware of their influence on his or her behavior. (p. 254)

substance use disorder: disorder characterized by the excessive use of alcohol or drugs that alter behavior. (p. 361)

superego: psychoanalytic term for the ethical or moral aspects of personality. It involves moralistic goals of the society learned by the individual. (p. 113)

sweet lemon rationalization: form of rationalization in which individuals have something they don't want, but say that what they have is just what they want. (p. 317)

symbol: object, act, or sound that becomes a representative substitute for something else. (p. 229)

synapse: see **neuron.** (p. 86)

T

task-oriented group: group whose primary purpose is to perform a specific job or task. (p. 400)

taste buds: receptors on the tongue for the sensation of taste. (p. 268)

telepathy: apparent communication of thought from one person to another by other than the usual means of sensory stimulation. (p. 33)

texture gradient: amount of detail perceived in an object. (p. 261)

theory: general principle, based on information, to explain what has been learned. (p. 25)

therapy: treatment of behavior disorders to bring about psychological and social adjustment. (p. 372)

thinking: unobservable activity by which a person or animal reorganizes past experiences through the use of symbols and concepts. (pp. 4, 228)

thyroid gland: ductless gland, located in the front of the neck close to the upper part of the windpipe, that produces the hormone that regulates the speed of chemical reactions and the rate of growth. (p. 93)

timbre: quality of a sound as determined by the complexity and pattern of the sound waves. (p. 265)

tone: sound whose stimulus consists of a regular wave. (p. 264)

trainable: term used by schools to refer to severely retarded individuals who can be taught some self-care under constant supervision. (p. 169)

transactional analysis (TA): form of psychotherapy that considers psychological disturbances to be the result of disorders in interpersonal relationships, and therefore stresses the development of interpersonal skills. (p. 375)

transfer: in psychology, the effect of previous learning on later learning. If the earlier learning improves later learning, there is said to be **positive transfer.** If the earlier learning interferes with later learning, there is said to be **negative transfer.** (p. 206)

transference: in Freudian analysis, the patient's experiencing of feelings and reacting toward the therapist as if the therapist were some other person in the patient's life, such as a parent. (p. 374)

U

unconditioned response (UCR): response that occurs normally, with no learning necessary. (p. 181)

unconditioned stimulus (UCS): original stimulus that elicits the desired response before the conditioning process begins. (p. 181)

unconscious: lack of awareness of some desires, experiences, concepts, and information under ordinary circumstances. (p. 112)

V

validity: degree to which a test or some other instrument measures what it is supposed to measure. (p. 132)

variable: condition in a research study that can change in amount or quality. (pp. 24, 478)

variable-interval schedule: see **interval schedule.** (p. 192)

variable-ratio schedule: see **ratio schedule.** (p. 192)

visible spectrum: complete arrangement of hues that can be seen by the human eye. (p. 257)

vocational interest inventory: written form designed to help individuals determine their vocational interests by comparing their interests to those of people in an occupation. (p. 145)

Page numbers in *italics* that have *c*, *f*, or *p* written before them refer to charts or tables (*c*), features (*f*), or pictures (*p*). Page numbers in **boldface** show that the word's meaning is given on that page. (In addition, many words are defined in the Glossary.)

Absolute threshold, 253

Accommodation, 230

Achievement, intelligence tests and, 166–67

Achievement motive, 279–83, *p279;* in women, 282–83, *p282*

Achievement test, 143–**44,** 145

Addiction, 361–63

Adjustment mechanisms, 308–18; avoidance of decision making, 315–16; compensation, **309–**10, *p309;* displaced aggression, **315;** identification, **310–**11, *p311;* overcompensation, **310;** procrastination, **314–**15; projection, **310;** rationalization, **316–**18, *p318;* regression, **314,** *p315;* repression, **314;** stereotyped behavior, **311–**14; usefulness of, 318

Adler, Alfred, 114, *p114,* 503

Adolescence: dreams in, 97–98; mental retardation in, 169–70; motor development in, 46; peer-group influence in, *p117,* 431–32; physical development in, 45; social behavior in, 54–55; stress in, 335

Adrenal glands, *p93,* 94–95

Adrenalin, 94–95

Advertising: optical illusions and, 264; as propaganda, 420–21, *p420;* subliminal perception and, 254

Affection, *p4,* 53, *p115;* in personality development, 109. *See also* Love

Affective disorders, 354–55; bipolar disorder, **354–**55; depression, **355;** manic-depression, 354–55

Age: chronological, **161;** dreams and, 97–98; emotions and, 52–53, *c52,* 54; intellectual development and, 56–58, *f485;* mental, **161;** motor development and, 46; physical development and, 45; social development and, 54–56; social roles and, 408; stress and, 335–36

Aggression, 53, *f120–21, f239;* displaced, **315;** hostile, **458**

AIDS (acquired immune deficiency syndrome), **361**

Alarm, 326

Alcohol, effects of, 362–63, *p363*

Alcoholics Anonymous (AA), 362

Alcoholism, 362–63, *p363;* counter-conditioning and, 182; pregnancy and, 74; treatment of, 182, 362–63

"All-or-nothing" thinking, 231

Allport, Gordon, 503

Altruistic behavior, 442

Alzheimer's disease, 358–59; stages of, 358

American Psychological Association (APA), 28, 33

Amish, social cooperation and, *p461*

Amnesia, 349

Anastasi, Anne, 503

Anger, 53

Animals: biofeedback and, 196; chromosomes of, **65;** classical conditioning of, 181, *p181,* 182, 183, 187; conflicts of, 304, 305–06; dreams of, 98; emotions of, 286; environmental influences on, 75–76, *c76;* experiments on, 4, *f12–13, p24,* 25, 28, *f484,* 46–47, 68, 75–76, 181, *p181,* 183, 198, *p198, p199, f280–*81, 283, 286, 305–06, *f312–13,* 327, 330; in heredity studies, 67–68, 75–76; insight in, 198, *p198, p199;* language of, 47–48, *p48;* learned helplessness in, *f312–13;* loving relationships as need of, *f280–81;* maturation and learning in, 70; motivation in, 277–78, 283; operant conditioning of, 188–90, 191–93, *p193,* 196; perception in, *f262–63;* selective breeding in, 67–68; social cooperation in, 449–60, *p459;* social facilitation among, 452; stress in, 327, 330

Anorexia nervosa, 359–61; treatment of, 361

Anthropology, 6

Anthropomorphism, 28

Antipsychotic drugs, 373

Antisocial personality, 357

Anxiety, 4, 115, 182; **352–**54, *p376,* 377; resistance and, 374; stranger, 53; treatment of, *p376,* 377

Anxiety disorders, 352–54; generalized anxiety disorder, **353;** panic disorder, **353;** phobic disorder, **353**

Approach-approach conflict. See Conflicts

Approach-avoidance conflict. *See* Conflicts

Approach gradient, 305, *c305,* 306–07, *c306*

Approval motive, 283–84, *p284*

Aptitude test, 143, **144–**45

Aristotle, 7

Army, U.S.: intelligence testing in, 159, *p159,* 162; inventories used in, 135

Asch, Solomon, *f398–99*

Assimilation, 230

Atmosphere, group, 407

Atmospheric perspective, 261

Attention, 254–55, *p255,* 264; condition of individual and, 255; forgetting and, 220; maintaining of, 255;

stimulus and, 254–55

Attitude, 419; transfer of learning and, 207–08. *See also* Social attitudes

Attribution, 422

Authority, power of, 426–30, *p427, f428–29*

Autocratic leader. *See* Leaders

Autokinetic illusion (autokinetic effect), **432**

Autonomic nervous system, 86–87, 196–97

Aversive therapy, 376, 385

Avoidance-avoidance conflict. *See* Conflicts

Avoidance conditioning, 182

Avoidance gradient, *c305,* **306–07,** *c306*

Axon, 86, *p86,* 88

Bandura, Albert, *p10,* 119–22, *p119, f120–21,* 503

Barnum effect, *f137*

Basic research, *f484*

Beers, Clifford, 379

Behavior, 3–4; abnormal, 347; aggressive, 53, *f120–21, f239,* 315, 458; brain and, 87–92; conditioning and (*see* Classical conditioning; Operant conditioning); disorders (*see* Psychological disturbances); dispositional vs. situational, **422–23;** emotional, 52–54; environmental influences on, 10, 65, 69, 71, 74–78; everyday, 4–5, *p5;* human development and, 42–61; learned vs. inborn, *f262–63;* power of authority and, 426–30; scientific study of 21–29; sleep and, 95–98; in small groups (*see also* Groups, small), 394–414; social, 54–56, 394–462; stereotyped, **311,** 314; theories of, 6–15; Type A, *f328–29;* unlearned, 181; voluntary vs. involuntary, 196. *See also* Personality

Behavioral model, 365

Behaviorism, 10, 14; criticism of, 125; personality theories and, 118–22, *p119, f120–21, p122,* 125

Behavior sampling, 141

Behavior therapy (behavior modification), 376–78; aversive, **376,** 385; desensitization, 376–77, *p376,* 384–85; effectiveness of, 384–85; implosive, 377; modeling, 377–78, *p378;* simple extinction, 377

Belongingness, as need, 115, 122–23

Binet, Alfred, 156–57, *p156,* 173, 503

Biofeedback, 196; operant conditioning and, 196–97, *p196;* practical uses of, 196–97, 337–38

Biology: biofeedback and, **196–**97, *p196,* 337–38; drives and, **277–**79, *p278;* emotions and, 285–86, 287–91, *p287, c290;* glands and, 85, 86, 92–95, *p93,* 286; nervous system (*see also* Brain), 74, 84–92, *p85,* 196–97; psychology and, 5; stress and, 324, 325, 326, 334, 337–38. *See also specific topics*

Bipolar disorder, 354–55, *p354;* treatment of, 372–73

Birth order, personality and, 109–10

Blake, Eubie, *p47*

Blindness, 47, *f239;* colorblindness, **258–**60; sense of pressure and, 269

Books, programmed, 195–96, *p195*

Bouchard, Thomas, *f72–73*

Brain, 5, 84, *p85,* 87–92, 93; behavior and, 87–92; biochemical analysis of, 87; biofeedback and, *p196;* cerebellum, *p88;* cerebral cortex, **89,** *p89, f90–91,* 286; cerebrum, *p88, p89;* computer compared to, 87–88; development of, 66; EEG and, 87; electrical stimulation of, 87; electroconvulsive shock therapy and, **372–**73; emotions and, 286; "faculties" of, 8; hypothalamus, *p88,* 277, 286; information processing in, 88–89; lesion, **87;** major parts of, *p88;* memory trace and, **220;** PET scans of, 92; pituitary gland in, *p88, p93,* 94, *p94;* prenatal malnutrition and, 74; split, *f90–91;* surgery, 87, 89, *f90–91,* 92; techniques for study of, 87

Brainstorming, 233–34, *p234*

Branching program, 194

Breeding, selective, 67–68

Brightness, 257

Buckhout, Robert, *f218*

Bulimia, 359–61; treatment of, 361

California Test of Mental Maturity (CTMM), 159

Cannabis, 361–62

Cannon, Walter B., 325–26

Cannon-Bard theory of emotion, 288

Case-study method, 22

Cattell, Raymond B., 503

Causation, 29–30, 481; and relationship with correlation, 481, *c479,* 480, *c480*

Cell body, 86, *p86*

Central nervous system, 84, 85–86, *p85,* 196. *See also* Brain

Central tendency, measures of, 475–77; mean, **476;** median, **476–**77; mode, **475–**76

Cerebral cortex. *See* Brain

Chagall, Marc, *p237*

Chaplin, Charlie, *p327*

Chemistry: of brain, 87; mental retardation and, 169; psychology and, 5, 7

Chromosomes, 65–66, 69, 86

Chronological age, 161

Chunking, 212–13

Clark, Kenneth B., 503

Classical conditioning, 181–88, *f184–85;* of animals, 181, *p181,* 182, 183, 187; avoidance conditioning and, **182;** conditioned response in, **181,** 182, *p182,* 183–87, 188; conditioned stimulus in, **181,** 182, *p182,* 183–86, 187, 188, 190; counter-conditioning and, **182–**83, *p183;* demonstration of, 181–82; discrimination in, **187,** *p187;* extinction in, **183–**86, *c186,* 190; generalization in, **186–**87; operant conditioning compared to, 188, 189, *c189;* Pavlov's experiments on, 181, *p181,* 183, *f184;* practical applications of, 182–83; reinforcement in, **186,** 187–88; spontaneous recovery in, 183–86; unconditioned response in, **181,** 182, *p182,* 188; unconditioned stimulus in, **181,** 182, *p182,* 183–86, 188, 190; workings of, 181

Class intervals, 472

Client-centered therapy, 375, 384; reflection of feelings in, **375**

Climate, group, 407

Clinical psychologists, *f483, f499*

Clinics and community centers, mental health, 362–63, *p379,* 380

Closure, 264
Cognitive dissonance, **421**–22, *p423*
Cognitive learning, **197**–99; characteristics of, 197–98; insight in, 197–99, *p198, p199*
Cognitive map, **197**
Cognitive process, **116**
Cognitive psychology, **14**–15, *p14*
Cognitive theory of emotion, **288**–89
Collective unconscious, **113**–14
College professors, *f493*
Color, 256–60; brightness of, **257**–58, *p257;* combinations of, 258, *p259;* complementary, *p256,* **258;** hues and, **257**–58; physical nature of, 257–58; saturation of, **258;** solid, 257–58, *p257;* visible spectrum of, *p256,* 257; wheel, *p256,* 258
Colorblindness, **258**–60
Communication, **408**–14; group size and, 408; importance of feedback to, 408–09; nonverbal, 408, *p409;* pseudogroup effects and, **413**–14; social cooperation and, 461–62; study of, 409–14; *c410–13. See also* Language; Language development
Compensation, **309**–310, *p309;* overcompensation, **310**
Competition, social. *See* Social competition
Complementary colors. *See* Colors
Computers: brain compared to, 87–88; psychologists' use of, *f483, f485;* as teaching machines, 194
Concepts, **229;** formation of, 229–30, *p229*
Concrete-operational period, **57;** of intellectual development, 57
Conditioned response (CR), **181,** 182, *p182,* 183–87, 188
Conditioned stimulus (CS), **181,** 182, *p182,* 183–86, 187, 188, 190
Conditioning, **181**–97; autonomic nervous system and, 196–97; classical (*see also* Classical conditioning), **181**–88; insight compared to, 199; operant (*see also* Operant conditioning), **188**–93, 194–95; punishment and, **183**–94
Conflicts, **303**–18; adjustment mechanisms and, 308–18; approach-approach, **304**–05, *p304, c305,* 307–08, *c308;* approach-avoidance, **306**–08, *c306, p306, p307, c308;* approach gradient, **305,** *c305,* 306–07, *c306;* avoidance-avoidance, **305**–06, *p305, c305,* 307–08, *c308;* avoidance gradient, *c305,* **306**–07, *c306;* kinds of, 303–08; stress and, 331. *See also* Adjustment mechanisms
Conformity, peer groups and, 432, 437
Conscious level of mind, **112,** 373–74
Consumer psychology, *f497*
Control group, **25,** 481
Convergence, **260**
Conversion disorder, **349;** *p349*
Cooperation. *See* Social cooperation
Correlation, **29**–30, 479–81; and causation, 479, 480; coefficient, **479**–80; negative, **30, 479,** *c479,* 480; positive, **29, 479,** *c479,* 480, *c480*
Cortisone, 95
Counseling, genetic, 69–70
Counseling psychologists, *f483*
Counselors: guidance, *f496;* marriage and family, *f495;*

rehabilitation, *f486*
Counter-conditioning, **182**–83, *p183*
Creative self, **114**
Creative thinking. *See* Thinking
Creativity, 155, *c155,* 171; brainstorming and, **233**–34, *p234;* characteristics of, 234–35; development of, 235, *p235;* inspiration and, 233; measure of, 235–36; preparation and, 232–33; "sitting on" problem and, 233; steps of, 232–34, *p234;* thinking and, 232–36, *p232, p234, p235;* verification and revision and, 233
Cretinism, **93,** 94, 170
Critical periods, **43,** *f50–51*
Cross-sectional method, **44**
Crystallized intelligence, **162**
Culture: intelligence tests and, 77; roles and, 433–34. *See also* Environment; Society
Curie, Marie, *p171*

Dance therapy, **380,** *p381*
Daydreaming, *f238–39*
Deafness, 49, **266**–67
Decision making, **109;** avoidance of, 315–16; peer-group influence on, 432–33
Deductive reasoning, **242**
Delusion, **231**–32, **355,** 356–57
Democratic leader. *See* Leaders
Dendrite, **86,** *p86,* 88
Deoxyribonucleic acid (DNA), **66**
Dependent variables, **25,** 481
Depressants, **361**
Depression, **354,** *p354;* treatment of, 373, 381
Deprivation experiments, 4
Depth, perception of, **260**–61, *f262–63*
Descartes, René, 7
Desensitization, **376**–77, *p376,* 384–85
Development, human, **42**–60; of creativity, 235, *p235;* critical periods of, **43,** *f50–51;* emotional, **52**–54, *c52;* environmental influences on, 65, 69, 71, 74–78, *f79,* 93; general principles of, 42–43; heredity influences on, **65**–73, 75–78, *f79;* intellectual, **56**–58, *f485;* of language, 43, 47–49, *p48,* 163; methods for studying, 43–44; moral, **58**–59; motor, **46**–47; patterns of, 42–45, *p44;* of personality, 108–11; physical, **45,** 181; prenatal, **44**–45; sensitive period of, **41;** social, **54**–56, *p55;* "stages of," 43, *p43;* of thinking in children, 230
Developmental disorders, **359**–61; anorexia nervosa, **359**–61; bulimia, **359**–61; eating disorders, **359**–61
Developmental psychologists, *f483, f485*
Deviation IQ, **162**
Diabetes, 78
Diagnostic Interest Blank (DIB), *f136–37*
Diet, hyperkinesis and, *f382–83*
Difference threshold, **253**
Diffusion of responsibility. *See* Responsibility
Digestion, effects of emotions on, 286
Discrimination, **187;** in classical conditioning, 187, *p187;* in operant conditioning, 193
Disorders, physical: biofeedback in control of, 196–97, 337–38; brain and, 92, *f382;* environment and, 74–

75, 77–78; glands and, 93–95, *p94;* heredity and, 65–66, 77–78

Displaced aggression. *See* Aggression

Dispositional factor, 422

Dissociative disorders, 349–52; amnesia, **349;** fugue, **349,** 352; multiple personality, 350–**52,** *p350*–51

Distance, perception of, 260–61, *p260*

Distributed practice. *See* Practice

Divergent thinking. *See* Thinking

Divorce, 231, *f495*

Dix, Dorothea, 379

Dominant gene, 66

Dorsett, Sybil, *f350*–51

"Dove Counterbalance General Intelligence Test," 77

Down's syndrome, 66–67, 169

Dream interpretation. *See* Dreams

Dreams: age and, 97–98; length of, 96, 97; necessity of, 98; psychoanalytic interpretation of, 9, 113, 372, **373;** REMs and, 96, 97, *c97,* 98

Drives, 277–79; hunger, 277, *p278;* thirst, 277–79

Drugs, 361–63; addiction to, **361**–63; classification of, 361–62; in control of stress, 338; counter-conditioning with, 182; emotions and, 288–89; physical symptoms of abuse of, 361–62; pregnancy and, 74; psychological dependence on, **361**–63; reasons for use of, 362; treatment of addiction to, 362–63

Drug therapy, 372–73, *f382;* for alcoholism, 362; effectiveness of, 380–81

DSM-III, 348

Duct glands (exocrine glands), 92–93

Ductless glands (endocrine glands), 93–95, *p93*

Dwarfs, 94

Dyads, 395, 396

Dynamism, 116

Eating disorders, 359–61; anorexia nervosa, **359**–61; bulimia, **359**–61, *p360*

Ebbinghaus, Hermann, 214, *p215,* 503

Eclectic psychology, 15

Editors, careers as, *f488*

Educable, 169

Educational psychologists, *f491*

Edwards Personal Preference Schedule, 138

Ego, 112–13, *p112*

Egyptians, ancient, behavior as viewed by, 6

Eidetic images, 236

Einstein, Albert, 232

Electroconvulsive shock therapy, 372–73, 381

Electroencephalograph (EEG), 87, 96, 97

Ellis, Havelock, 503

Emetine, 362

Emotional development. *See* Emotions

Emotions, *p4, p53,* 276, **285**–91; age and, 52–53, *c52,* 54; bodily changes and, 285–86, 287–91, *p287, c290;* common, 53–54; development of, **52**–54; digestion affected by, 286; disorders of (*see* Psychological disturbances); frustration influenced by, 302, 303; labeling and interpretation of, 288–89; measurement of, 4, 289–91, *p289;* theories of, 286–89

Encoding and memory, 209, *p217,* 220

Encounter groups, 378, 385

End branches, *p86*

Endocrine glands (ductless glands), 93–95, *p93*

Environment, 65; accommodation and, **230;** animal experiments and, 75–77, *c76;* assimilation and, **230;** behavior influenced by, 10, 14, 65, 69, 71, 74–78; creativity and, 235; extrinsic motivation and, **285;** and schizophrenia, 69; frustration and, 301; glands and, 95; hunger drive and, 277; intelligence affected by, 74, 75, 76–77, 78, 162, *f164*–65, 171; interaction of heredity with, 75–78; mental retardation and, 168–70; personality and, 108–09, *p109,* 114–18, *p115,* 125; pregnancy and, 74–75, *p74*

Equilibrium, sense of, **270**

Erikson, Erik, 116–18, *p116,* 503

Evil spirits, belief in, 6, *p7*

Exclusive group. *See* Group

Exercise, in control of stress, 336–37

Exhaustion, 326

Existential psychology, 15

Exocrine glands (duct glands), 92–93

Experimental group, 25, 481

Experimental psychologists, *f485*

Experiments, 8, 24–28; on animals (*see* Animals, experiments on); conducting of, 25; problems of, 28; setting up, 24–25; subjects in, *p24,* 25–28, *f26*–27, *f485,* 426–30

Exploratory motive, 283

Extinction, 183; in classical conditioning, 183–86, *c186,* 190; in operant conditioning, 190; simple, in behavior therapy, 377

Extrasensory perception (ESP), 33–34; telepathy, *p32,* **33**

Extraversion, 114

Extrinsic motivation. *See* Motivation

Eysenck, Hans, 173

Family: birth order in, 109–10; intelligence and, 171; personality and, 109–10, *p109,* 115; stress and, 335–39; women's careers and, 435

Family counselors, *f495*

Family therapy, 378

Fear, 53, 54, 182, 288; James-Lange theory of emotion and, **286**–87; of success, 282

Feedback, 208; communication and, 408–09; in control of stress, 337–38; group, **409;** learning and, 196–97, *p196,* 208

Feingold, Ben, *f382*–83

"Fight or flight" reaction, 325–26

Fixed-interval schedule, 192

Fixed-ratio schedule, 192

Fluid intelligence, 162

Forer, Bertram, *f136*–37

Forgetting, 220–22, *p221,* 373; elapse of time and, 220; inattention and, 220; motivated, 220–22; proactive inhibition and, **220;** retroactive inhibition and, **220.** *See also* Memory; Retention

Formal group. *See* Group

Formal-operational period, 58; of intellectual development, 57

Frame of reference, need for, 115

Frames, in programmed learning, **194,** 195, p195
Fraternal twins, 70, p71
Free association, 9, **113, 373**
Free will, 10, 15
Frequency distributions, 471–72, c472; class intervals in, **472,** c472; histograms used to show, **473,** c473; information provided by, 473
Freud, Sigmund, 9, p9, 14, 111–13, p112, 114, 115, 122, 129, f239, 503
Friedman, Meyer, f328–29
Fromm, Erich, 114–15, p114, 503
Frustration, 300–19, p301, p303; causes of, 301–02; conflict and, **303–308;** individual differences in experiencing of, 303; reactions to (see also Adjustment mechanisms), 300–01, 308–18; strength of, 302–03, 320; stress and, 330; tolerance, **304**
Frustration tolerance. See Frustration
Fugue, 349, 352
Functional fixedness, 241
Functionalism, 8, 14

Galileo, 170
Galvanic skin response (GSR), 290, c290
Geller, Uri, p31
General Adaptation Syndrome (GAS), 326
Generalization, 28, **186;** in classical conditioning, 186–87; in operant conditioning, 193
Generalized anxiety disorder, 353
Genes, 66–67, p66, p67, 86; dominant, **66;** recessive, **66**
Genetic counseling, 69–70
Genetic defects, 65–66, 69–70
Gestalt psychology, 10–11, 14, 15
Gibson, Eleanor, f262–63, 504
Giantism, 94
Gifted people, 170–71, p171
Glands, 85, 86, 92–95; duct, 92–93; ductless, **93–95,** p93; emotions and, 286; environmental effects on, 95
Goiter, 93
Gonads, p93, 95
Graphic rating scale, 133–34, c134
Greeks, ancient, behavior as viewed by, 6–7
Group atmosphere. See Atmosphere
Group climate. See Climate
Group cohesiveness. See Groups
Group feedback. See Feedback
Group morale. See Morale
Groups, 6; control, **25, 481;** experimental, **25, 481;** intelligence tests for, 158–160, p159, p160, p161; minority, social competition and, 457; national, social competition and, p456, 457; norm, **131**–32; personality influenced by, 110–11; rationalization by, 317–18; social facilitation and, **452**–53. See also Family; Peer-group influence
Groups, small, 394–414, c397; advantages of membership in, 404; atmosphere of, **407;** belonging to, 404–05, p405; business purposes of, 404; climate of, **407;** cohesiveness of, 405–06, c406; communication in, **408**–14; control of discussion in, 402–03; disadvantages of belonging to, 402–05, p405; distance between people in, 395–96, p375; effectiveness of,

401–04, 415; efficiency increased in, 402–04, p403; exclusive, **401;** formal, **401;** inclusive, **400**–01; influence of, 394–97, f398–99; informal, **401;** interaction-oriented, **400,** p400; kinds of, 397–401; leadership in, 403–04, 407; lying vs. truth telling in, 396–97; morale of, **406**–07; objects between people in, 396; odd vs. even number of members in, 402; pseudogroup effects and, **413**–14; roles in, 407–08, p407; seating arrangements in, 403, p403, 410–13, c410–13; security and, 404; size and makeup of, 396, 401–02, 408; status and, **404;** task-oriented, 397–**400,** p400; two-person (dyad), **395,** 396
Group therapy, 378–79, p384; effectiveness of, 385; encounter groups, 378, 385; family therapy, **378;** psychodrama, **378**–79
Guidance counselors, f496
Guilford, J. P., 155

Haber, Sandra, f448–49
Habits, personality inventories and, 139
Hall, Stanley G., 504
Halley, Edmund, 170
Hallucination, 355
Hallucinogens, 361
Halo effect, 134
Hand-eye coordination, 46–47
Handicapped people, f486, f494; programmed learning and, 195–96
Harlow, Harry and Margaret, f280–81, 504
Hassles theory of stress, 334–35
Hawthorne effect, f27–28
Hearing, 264–67; audible sound range and, 264–65; deafness and, 266–67; loudness and, **265,** c265; noise problem and, 265–66, c266; pitch and, **264,** c265; space perception and, 265; timbre and, **265,** c265; tone and, **264**–65, c266
Height, p44, 45, 94, p94
Helping behavior, 442–53, p447, f448-49, 450, 463; diffusion of responsibility and, **450;** effects of reinforcement or punishment on, 447–50; failures of, 442; minor mishaps and, 446–47; mood as influence on, 444–47; physical attractiveness as influence on, 445–46, p446; previous experience and, 447–50, c450; urban experiments on, 442–45, p443, p444, c445
Helplessness, learned, f312–13
Heredity, 5, **65**–73; animal experiments and, 67–68, 75–76; colorblindness and, 260; family studies and, 68–69; inherited characteristics and, 65–67, p66, p67; intelligence and, 66, 68, 76; interaction of environment with, 75–78; maturation and, **70**–71; mental retardation and, 66, 169; schizophrenia and, 68–69, 356; studies of, 67–70
Heroin, 361
Hippocrates, 7
Histograms, 473, c473
Holmes, Thomas, 332–34
Holtzman Inkblot Test, 142
Hopi Indians, 70–71, 111, 460–61
Hormones, 286; adrenal, 94–95; mental retardation and, 170

INDEX

Horner, Matina, 282–83
Horney, Karen, 115–16, *p115,* 504
Hospitals, mental, 345–47, 357, 361, 379–80, *p379*
Hostile aggression. *See* Aggression
Hue, 257
Hull, Clark, 504
Humanistic psychology, 15; criticism of, 125; personality theories and, 122–25, *c123, p124*
Humors, bodily, 7, 14
Hunger drive, 277, *p278*
Hydrocephalus, 170
Hyperkinesis, *f382–83*
Hypnosis, 9, 98–99, 113; methods of, 99; practical uses of, 99; reactions under, 99; repression and, **222**
Hypochondria, 348–49
Hypothesis, 24–25; 484

Id, 112, *p112,* 113
Identical twins, 66, **68**, *p69,* 70, *f72–73;* diabetes in, 78; in intelligence studies, 76; schizophrenia in, 68–69
Identification, 310–11, *p311*
Identity, as basic need, 115
Illusions, optical, 260
Images, eidetic, 236
Imagination, 155, **236–37**, *p237*
Implosive therapy, 377
Inclusive group. *See* Group
Independent variables, 25, 481
Individual Psychology, 114
Inductive reasoning, 241–42
Industrial psychologists, *f483, f497*
Infant development, 4, *p43;* emotions and, 52–53; general vs. specific responses in, 42–43; head-to-foot control in, 42, 46; language and, 48–49; malnutrition and, 74–75; motor development in, 46; perception and, *f263;* personality and, 108–09; social development and, 54; stress and, 335
Infant-mother bonding, 4, 43
Informal group. *See* Group
Information processing, 271
Inhibition: proactive, **220**; retroactive, **220**
Inkblot tests, 141–42, *p142,* 143
Insight, 115; in animals, 198, *p198, p199;* causes of, 198–99; in cognitive learning, 197–99, *p198, p199;* in humans, 198
Inspiration, creative thinking and, 233
Intellectual development, **56**–58, *f485;* concrete-operational period of, 57; formal-operational period of, 58; preoperational period of, 56–**57;** sensory-motor period of, **56**
Intelligence, **154**–73; brain size and, 92; creativity and, 235; crystallized, **162;** environmental factors in, 74, 75, 76–77, 78, 162, *f164–65,* 171; factor theories of, 154–56; fluid, **162;** heredity and, 66, 68, 76, 173; measurement of (*see also* Intelligence tests), 154–73; nature of, 154–56; superior, 170–71, *p171*
Intelligence quotient (IQ), 161–62; changes in, 162–63; of children vs. adults, 162; deviation, **162;** meaning of, 161–62; mental retardation and, 162, 167, 168; problems in determining stability of, 162–63;

ranges of, 163–66, *p163;* school grades and, 166–67; superior intelligence and, 170, 171
Intelligence tests, 56, 156–67; American modifications of, 157–58; brain surgery and, 89; culture-fair, 158; environmental influences and, 75, 76–77, 78, 162, *f164–65,* group, 158–60, *p159, p160, p161;* of identical twins, 76; individual, 156–58, *p157;* IQ and, 161–66; malnutrition and, 75; origin of, 156–57; performance (nonverbal), 158; use of in schools, 160, *p160, p161,* 166–67
Interaction-oriented group. *See* Group
Interests: changes in, 146, *p147;* vocational, inventories of, 145–46
Intermittent reinforcement. *See* Reinforcement
Interval schedule, 192
Interviewing, 22–23, **139**–140; improvement of, 140; validity of, 139
Intrinsic motivation. *See* Motivation
Introspection, 8–9
Introversion, 114
Inventories, personality, **135**–39, *c138;* cautions about use of, *f136–37,* 138–39; making up and scoring of, 135–38; vocational interest, **145–46**

Jackson, Reggie, *p3*
Jacobson, Lenore, *f164–65*
James, William, 8, *p9,* 14, 504
James-Lange theory of emotion, 286–88
Jenson, Dylana, 170
Jones, Mary Cover, *f185*
Jung, Carl, 113–114, *p113,* 504
Just-noticeable difference, 253

Ka, 6, 14
Kinesthetic sense, 269
Koffa, Kurt, 504
Kohlberg, Lawrence, 58–59, 504
Kohler, Wolfgang, 504
Kuder Preference Record—Vocational, 145–46

Laing, R. D., 504
Laissez-faire leader. *See* Leaders
Language: brain hemispheres and, *f90–91;* foreign, 210, 215; intelligence tests and, 159
Language development, 48, .47–49, 169; animals and, 47–48, *p48;* common features of, 47; critical period in, 43, *f50–51;* stages of, in humans, 48–49; theories of, 49, 52
Leaders, 423–30; authority of, 426–30, *p427;* autocratic, **425;** democratic, **425;** kinds of, 424; laissez-faire, **425;** motives of, 423–24; personality of, 424–25, *p424;* in small groups, 403–04, 407; techniques of, 425; training of, 425–26
Learned helplessness, *f312–13*
Learning, **180**–220; behaviorist views on, 10, 14, 118–22, *f120–21;* behavior therapy and, 376–78; chunking and, 212–13; classical conditioning and (*see also* Classical conditioning), **181–88;** cognitive, **197–99,** 340; curve, 213, *c213;* efficient, 206–213; feedback and, 196–97, *p196,* 208; graphs of, 213, *c213;* by insight,

526

197–99, p198; of language (see also Language development), 43, 49, 210, 215; leadership and, 425–26; massed vs. distributed practice and, **208**–09, p209; maturation and, 70–71; meaningfulness and, 208; mental retardation and, 167–70, p168; mnemonic devices and, **210**–11, p211; models and, 119–22, p119, f120–21, p122; operant conditioning and (see also Operant conditioning), 188–97; overlearning, **211**–12, c212; plateaus, **213**–14, p214; principles of, 180–99; process of, 213–14; programmed, 194–96, p195; punishment and, 10, 119, 122, 125, **193**–94, 447, 450; reinforcement and (see Reinforcement); remembering and, 210–11, p211, 214–20; during sleep, 216; strategies, 340; transfer of, **206**–08, p207; whole vs. part, 209–10

Lewin, Kurt, 504
Life change approach to stress, 332–34; criticism of, 333–34
Lincoln, Abraham, p279
Linear perspective, p260, **261**
Linear programs, 194
Lithium, 372–73
Loci method of remembering, 210–11, p211
Loftus, Elizabeth, f218–19
Longitudinal method, 44
Long-term memory. See Memory
Lorenz, Konrad, 504
Loudness, 265
Love, 115, p115, 288; animal behavior and, f280–81; developmental stages of, 55; in hierarchy of needs, 122–23, c123
Lucido, David J., f448–49

Maccoby, Eleanor, 504
Malnutrition, 74–75; mental retardation and, 169, 170
Manic-depression. See Bipolar disorder
Marijuana, 362
Marriage, 56, 231; careers vs., 435–36; stress and, 335–36
Marriage counselors, f495
Maslow, Abraham, 122–23, p123, 125, 505
Massed practice. See Practice
Maturation, 70; heredity and, 70–71
May, Rollo, 505
Mayo, Elton, f27
Mead, Margaret, 6
Mean, 476, 477; range and, 477
Meaningfulness, learning and, 208
Measurement techniques, 23–24, 131–73; behavior sampling, **141;** direct observation, 3, 10, 22; for emotions, 4, 289–91, p289; group cohesiveness and, 405–06, c406; intelligence and, 154–73; interviews, 139–40; inventories, **135**–39, f136–37, c132, 145–46; personality and, 131–47; projective, 141–43, p142, p143; ratings, 133–35, c134, 140; social attitudes and, 404; standardized tests, **131**–133, 143–145, p144
Mechanical aptitude tests, 145
Median, 476–77
Medical model of psychological disturbances, 363–64

Medical therapy, 372–73; drug, 372–73, 380–81, f382; effectiveness of, 380–81; electroconvulsive shock therapy, **372**–73, 381
Memory, 74, 155, 169, 217–20, f218–19, 223; auditory, 157, 158; encoding and, **217,** p217, 220; long-term (LTM), p217, **220;** short-term (STM), **217**–20, p217; trace, **220;** visual, 158. See also Forgetting; Recall; Retention
Memory trace. See Memory
Mental age, 162
Mental retardation, 66, 92, **167**–70, f487; causes of, 169; cure of, 169–70; educable vs. trainable, **169;** education and, 168–69, p168, 170; heredity and, 66, 169; IQ and, 162, 167, 168; mild, **167**–69, p169; moderate, **167**–69; profound, **167**–68, 169; severe, **167**–68, 69
Methadone, 362
Methods, psychological, 21–34; case-study, 22; cross-sectional, **44;** in developmental studies, 43–44; experiments, 24–28; in hypnosis, 99; interviews, 22–23; longitudinal, **44;** measurement techniques (see also Measurement techniques), 23–24; observation, 3, 10, 22; questionnaires, 23, c23
Middle Ages, behavior as viewed in, 6, 7
Midgets, 94
Mild retardation. See Mental retardation
Milgram, Stanley, 426–30, 505
Mind: conscious, **112,** 373–74; structure vs. function of, 8, 14. See also Unconscious
Minnesota Multiphasic Personality Inventory (MMPI), 138, c138
Minnesota Study of Twins Reared Apart, f72–73
Minority groups: intelligence testing and, 77, f165; social competition and, 457
Mnemonic device, 210–11, p211
Mode, 475–76
Modeling, as behavior therapy, **377**–78, p378
Model, in learning theory, **119**–22, p119, f120–21, p122
Moderate retardation. See Mental retardation
Molar vs. molecular theories of personality, 111
Moral development, 58–59; measuring of, 58; stages of, 58–59, 61
Morale, group, 406–07
Motivation, 276–85; achievement, 279–83, p279, p282; approval, 283–84, p284; biological drives as, 277–79, p278; concept of, 276; creativity and, 235; exploratory, 283; forgetting and, 220–22; frustration and, 302; intrinsic vs. extrinsic, **285;** IQ changes and, 162; of leaders, 423–24; personality theories and, 122–23; social, 279–84, p279, p282, p284
Motives, 276
Motor development, 46–47
Motor neuron, 86
Multiple personality, f350–51, 352
Muscles, 85, 86; stress and, 337

Narcotics, 361
National Committee for Mental Hygiene, 379
Nations: rationalization and, 318; social competition and, p456, 457

Needs: Maslow's hierarchy of, 122–23, *c123,* 125; personality theories and, 115, 122–23, *c123,* 125
Negative reinforcement. *See* Reinforcement
Negative transfer. *See* Transfer
Nerve impulses, 85–86, *p85,* 88–89
Nervous systems, 74, 84–92; autonomic, **86**–87, 196–97; central, **84,** 85–86, *p85,* 196; nerve impulse transmission in, 85–86, *p85,* 88–89; peripheral, 85–86, *p85. See also* Brain
Neuron, 86, 88
Newton, Isaac, *p232*
Noise problem, 265–66, *c266*
Nonsense syllables, retention of, 214, *p215*
Nonverbal behavior, 292
Normal curve, 473–75, *c474*
Norm group, 131–32
Numerical ability, 155, 158
Nurses, psychiatric, *f498*
Nutrition, development and, 74–75

Observation: direct, 3, 10, 22; directed, 22; 484; natural, 22
Obsessive-compulsive disorder, 353–54
Occupational therapists, *f494*
Operant conditioning, 188–93, 194–97; of animals, 188–90, 191–93, *p193,* 196; biofeedback and, 196–97, *p196;* classical conditioning compared to, 188, 189, *c189;* discrimination in, 193; extinction in, 190; generalization in, 193; programmed learning and, 194–96, *p195;* reinforcement in, 188, 189, 190–92, *p191,* 201; spontaneous recovery in, 190
Optical illusions, 261–64, *p261;* practical use of, 264
Organic mental disorders, 357–59; Alzheimer's disease, **357**–59, *p358*
Organism, 4
Organizational psychology, *f497*
Orlando, Tony, 345
Otis-Lennon Mental Ability Test, 159–60
Overcompensation, 310
Overlearning, 211–12, *c212*
Overrating, 134

Pain, hypnosis and, 99
Panic disorder, *p352,* **353**
Paradoxical sleep. *See* Sleep
Paralysis, 9, 349, *p349*
Paranoid disorders, 356–57, *p356*
Parapsychology, 31–34
Pavlov, Ivan, 181, *p181,* 183, *f184,* 505
Pecking order, 454
Peer-group influence, 430–33, *p431;* animals and, *f281;* attitudes and values, 431–32; conformity and, 432; risky shift and, **432**–33; role models, **431;** young people and, 430–31
Peers, 430
Perception, 155, 169, **252**–70; attention and, 254–55, *p255;* closure and, **264;** of distance and depth, 260–61, *p260,* f262–63; optical illusions and, **261**–64, *p261;* proximity and, **264;** psychological disorders and, 356–57; relationship of sensation to, 252, 253,

p253; sense of taste and, 268; similarity and, **264;** subliminal, 253–**54**
Peripheral nervous system, 85–86, *p85*
Personality, 108–49; antisocial, **357;** behavioristic theories of, 118–22, *p119, p122,* 125; behavior sampling in measurement of, **141;** birth order and, 109–110; creativity and, 235; criticisms of theories of, 125; development of, 108–11; in early childhood, 108–09; effects of physical development on, 45; environmental influences on, 108–09, *p109,* 114–18, *p115, c118,* 125; factor theory of intelligence and, 156; humanistic theories of, 122–25, *c123, p124;* humors theory of, 7, 14; interviews in measurement of, 139–40; inventories, **135**–39, *f136–37, p138,* 139–40; of leaders, 424–25, *p424;* measurement of, 131–48, *p132;* molecular vs. molar theories of, **111;** new approach to measurement of, 146–47; projection and, **141;** projective techniques in measurement of, 141–43, *p142, p143;* psychoanalytic theories of, 111–14, *p112,* 125; ratings, **133**–35, *c134, p135,* 140; social influences on, 110–11, *p110,* 114–18; social psychoanalytic theories of, 114–18, *p115, p118,* 125; standardized tests in measurement of, 131–35, 143–45; stress determined by, 326–27, 336; theories of, 111–25
Personality disorders, 357; antisocial personality, **357**
Personality inventory, 135–39, *f136–37, c138*
Personal unconscious, 113
Person-centered psychology, 147
Personification, 116
Personnel managers, *f489*
Phobic disorder, 353
Phrenology, 7–8, *c8,* 14, 31
Physical development, 45; disorders (see Disorders, physical); learning vs., 181; malnutrition and, 74–75; personality and, 45
Physics, psychology and, 5
Piaget, Jean, 56–58, 230, 505
Pigeonhole error, 134
Pinel, Philippe, 505
Pitch, 264
Pituitary gland, *p88, p93,* **94**
Plateau, 213
Plato, 6–7
Play therapy, 375
Pleasure principle, 112
Polygraph, emotional states and, 290–91
Positive reinforcement. *See* Reinforcement
Positive transfer. *See* Transfer
Positron-emission tomography (PET), 92
Practice, massed vs. distributed, **208**–09, *p209*
Pregnancy, environmental influences and, 74–75, *p74*
Prejudice, 419, *p420*
Prenatal development, 44–45; environmental influences on, 74–75, *p74*
Preoperational period, of intellectual development, 56–57, *p57*
Proactive inhibition. *See* Inhibition
Probation or parole officers, *f501*
Problem solving, 237–42; creativity and, 233–34;

divergent thinking and, *p240,* **241,** *p241;* factors affecting, 240–41; functional fixedness and, **241;** reasoning and, **241**–42; study of, 240

Procrastination, 314–15

Prodigies, 170

Professors, college, *f493*

Profound retardation. *See* Mental retardation

Programmed learning, 194–96, *p195;* advantages of, 195–96; presentation of, 194

Projection, 141, 311

Projective techniques, 141–43; cautions in use of, 143; drawing or filling in pictures, 142–43; inkblot tests, 141–42, *p142,* 143; picture interpretation, 142, *p143;* playing with toys, 142; sentence completion, 143

Propaganda, 420; changing attitudes and, 420–21; determinants of effectiveness of, 421

Proximity, 264

Pseudogroup effects, 413–14

Psychiatrists, *f483*

Psychoanalysis, 9, 14; criticism of, 125; dream interpretation in, 9, 113, 372, **373;** free association in, 9, **113, 373;** Freudian, 9, 14, 111–13, *p112,* 114, 115, 122, 125; id, ego, and superego in, 122–23, *p112;* introversion vs. extraversion in, **124;** Jungian, 123–24; personality theories and, 111–14, 125; pleasure principle in, 112; reality principle in, 112–13; resistance in, **373**–74; as therapy, 170, 373–76, *p374,* 381, 384; transference in, **374;** unconscious in, 9, 14, 112–14, 373–75. *See also* Social psychoanalysis

Psychoanalytic model, 364

Psychodrama, 376–77

Psychokinesis (PK), 31–33

Psychological dependence, 361

Psychological disturbances, 345–65; behavioral model of, **365;** difficulties in diagnosing of, 345–46; environment and, 69; heredity and, 68–69, 356; Horney's views on, 115–16; labeling of, 345–46; medical model of, **363**–64; psychoanalytic model of, **364;** sociocultural model of, **364**

Psychological disturbances, treatment of, 347–48, 372–85; aversive therapy, **376,** 376–78, *p376, p378,* 384–85; client-centered therapy, **375,** 384; in clinics and community centers, 347, *p379,* 380; dance therapy, 380, *p381;* desensitization, 376–**77,** *p376,* 384–85; drug therapy, 362–63, **372**–73, 380–81, *f382;* effectiveness of, 380–85; electroconvulsive shock therapy, **372,** 381; encounter groups, **378,** 385; family therapy, **378;** group therapy, **378**–79, *p384,* 385; hospitalization, 345–46, 361, 379–80, *p379;* hyperkinesis, *f382*–83; hypnosis, 9, 98–99; implosive therapy, **377;** medical therapy, 363–64, **372**–73, 380–81; modeling, **377**–78, *p378;* play therapy, **375;** psychodrama, **378**–79; psychotherapy, 170, **373**–376, *p374,* 381–84; simple extinction therapy, **377;** transactional analysis, **375**–76, 384

Psychological methods. *See* Methods, psychological

Psychologists: clinical, *f483, f499;* counseling, *f483;* developmental, *f483, f485;* educational, *f491;* evaluation of, 31; experimental, *f483, f484;* industrial, *f483,*

f497; school, *f483, f490, f491;* social, *f502;* types of, *f483*

Psychology, 2–4; activities studied in, 4–5, *p5;* approaches to psychological thought, 11–15, *c483;* early history of, 6–8, 17; introduction to, 2–16; later developments in, 8–11, 17; in relation to other sciences, 5–6

Psychotherapy, 170, 373–76, *p374;* client-centered, 375, 384; effectiveness of, 381, 384; play, 375; psychoanalysis, 373–75, 384; transactional analysis, 375–76, 384

Punishment, 10, 119, 122, 125, **193**–95; helping behavior and, 447–48

Questionnaire method, 23, *c23*

Race, intelligence tests and, 77, *f165,* 173

Rahe, Richard, 332–34

Random selection, 25

Range, 477

Ranking method of rating, 133

Rapid eye movements (REMs), 96–97, *c97,* 98

Ratings, personality, 133–35, 140; dangers of, 134–35, *p139;* graphic scales of, **133**–34, *c134;* ranking method of, **133**

Rationalization, 316–18, *p318;* scapegoating, **317**–18, *p318;* sour grapes, **317;** sweet lemon, **317**

Ratio schedule, 192

Rayner, Rosalie, *f184*

Reality principle, 112–13

Reasoning, 155, 157, **241;** deductive, **242;** inductive, **241**–42; in problem solving, **241**–42

Recall, 215, 222; mnemonic devices and, **210**–11, *p211*

Recessive genes, 66

Recognition, retention and, 215

Reflection of feelings, 375

Reflex, 181

Regression, 314

Rehabilitation counselors, *f486*

Rehearsal, 217, *p217*

Reinforcement, 119; in classical conditioning, **186,** 187–88; helping behavior and, 447–48; intermittent, **186,** 191–92, *p191;* interval schedules of, **192;** negative, **190;** in operant conditioning, 188, 189, 190–92, *p191;* positive, **190;** ratio schedules of, **192;** secondary, **192**–93, *p193. See also* Rewards

Relatedness, as basic need, 115

Relaxation, in control of stress, 337

Relearning, 214–15, *p215*

Reliability. *See* Tests

Repression, 222, 314

Resistance, 326, 373–74

Response: conditioned, **181,** 182, *p182,* 183–87, 188; discrimination and, **187;** extinction and, **183**–86, *c186;* generalization and, **186**–87; spontaneous recovery and, 183–86, *c186;* unconditioned, **181,** 182, *p182,* 188

Responsibility: diffusion of, **450;** stress and, 331, 335–36

Retardation. *See* Mental retardation
Retention, 214–16; of ideas vs. exact words, 216, *p216*; recall method and, 215; recognition and, 215; relearning method and, 214–15, *p215*; sleep and, 216
Retrieval, 217, *p217*
Retroactive inhibition. *See* Inhibition
Revised Stanford-Binet, 157–58, 162
Rewards, 10, 119, 125; achievement motive and, 283; in language learning, 49; in simple extinction therapy, 377
Risky shift, 432–33
Rogers, Carl, 123–25, *p123*, 375, 505
Role. *See* Roles, social
Role model. *See* Roles
Roles, social: changes in, 434–35; cultural influences on, 433–34; models, **431**; sex and, 433–36, *p433*, *p435*; in small groups, 407–08, *p407*
Rorschach, Hermann, 142, 505
Rorschach test, 142, *p142,* 143
Rosenman, Ray, *f328*–29
Rosenthal, Robert, *f164*–65

Salespeople, *f500*
Sampling, behavior, 141
Saturation, 258
Scapegoats, 317–18, *p318*
Schacter, Stanley, 505
Schizophrenia, 68–69, 92, **355**–56; treatment of, 373, 380
Scholastic Aptitude Test (SAT), 145
School psychologists, *f483, f490, f491*
Science, 3; psychology and, 5–6
Secondary reinforcement. *See* Reinforcement
Self-actualization, 15, **123,** *c123*
Self-concept, 123–25, *p124*
Self-esteem, 122–23, *c123,* 284
Seligman, Martin, *f312–313*
Selye, Hans, 326
Sensation, 252–70; attention and, 254–55, *p255*; relationship of perception to, 252, 253, *p253*
Senses, 252–53, 257–70; equilibrium, **270**; hearing, 264–67, *c265, c266, p267*; kinesthetic, **269**; skin, 268–69, *p269*; smell, 267–68; taste, 268, *p268*; thresholds and, 253; vision, 257–64, *p256, p257, p259, p260, p261,* 269
Sensitive period, 43
Sensory-motor period, of intellectual development, **56**
Sensory neuron, 86
Sensory register, 217, *c217*
Severe retardation. *See* Mental retardation
Sex: achievement motive and, 282–83; brain size and, 92; differences in development rates and, 45; dream differences and, 97; helping behavior and, 447; intelligence tests and, 77; social roles and, 433–36, *p433, p435*
Sex glands, 95
Shaping, 189
Sheldon, William H., 149
Short-term memory (STM). *See* Memory

Similarity, 264
Simon, Theodore, 156–57, 505
Simple extinction therapy, 377
Singer, Jerome L., *f238–39*
Situational factor, 422
Sizemore, Chris, *f351*
Skin: galvanic response (GSR), **290,** *p290*; senses, 268–69, *p269*
Skinner, B. F., 10, *p10, f12–13,* 118–19, *p118,* 125, 188, *p188,* 189, 505
Sleep, 87, 95–98; hypnosis compared to, 99; importance of, 95–97; learning during, 216; paradoxical, **97;** REM, 96–97, *c97,* 98; schedule, changes of, 96; stages of, 96. *See also* Dreams
Small groups. *See* Group
Smell, sense of, 267–68
Smoking, 74; counter–conditioning and, *p183*; intermittent reinforcement and, 192
Social attitudes, 419–36; attribution and, **422**–23; authority and, 426–30, *p427, f428–29*; changes in, 420–22; cognitive dissonance and, **421**–22, *p423*; leadership and, 423–26, *p424*; measurement of, 420; peer-group influence and, 430–33, *p431*; prejudice, **419,** *p420*; roles and, 433–36, *p433, p435*
Social behavior, 394–462
Social class: superior intelligence and, 171; test taking and, 77
Social competition, 453–59; confusion and inefficiency and, 457; effects of, 457–59; effects of losing and, 457–58; experiments on, 454–53, *p455, p456*; hostile aggression and, **458;** minority groups and, 457; national groups and, *p456,* 457; pecking order and, 454, *p454*; playing "chicken" and, 456–57; reduction in disadvantages of, 458–59; threats and, 455–56, *p455, p456*; winning at any price and, 457
Social cooperation, 459–62; in animals, 459–60, *p459*; communication and, 461–62; of Hopi Indians, 460–61
Social development, 54–56, *p55*
Social facilitation, 452–53; studying and, 452–53, *p453*
Social interaction, 442–62; competition and, 453–54; cooperation and, 454–56; facilitation and, 452–53; helping others and (*see also* Helping behavior), 442–53
Social motives, 279–84, *p279, p282, p284*
Social psychoanalysis: basic needs theory in, 115; creative self and, **114;** criticism of, 125; dynamism, personification, and cognitive processes in, **116;** Individual Psychology in, 114; parent-child relationships and, 115, *p115*; personality theories and, 114–18, 125; stage theory and, 116–18, *c118*
Social psychologists, *f502*
Social psychology, 6
Society, 110; personality influenced by, 110–11, *p110,* 114–18
Sociocultural model, 365
Sociograms, 405–06, *c406, c410–13*
Sociology, 6
Sociometry, 405–06

Somatoform disorders, 348–49, *p349;* conversion disorder, **349;** hypochondria, **348**–49
Sound. *See* Hearing
Sour grapes rationalization, 317
Spatial perception, 155, 260–61, *p260;* atmospheric perspective and, **261;** convergence and, **260;** hearing and, 265; linear perspective and, *p260,* **261;** texture gradient and, **261**
Special education teachers, *f487*
Sperry, Roger, *f90,* 505
Spinal cord, 84, *p85, p88*
Spontaneous recovery, **183;** in classical conditioning, 183–86; in operant conditioning, 190
Standard deviation, 477–**78**
Standardized test. *See* Tests
Stanford-Binet Intelligence Test, 157–58, *p157*
Statistical procedures, *f484*
Statistics, **471**–82; causation in, 479, 480, 481; correlation in, **479**–81, *c479, c480;* defined, **471;** frequency distributions in, 471–**72,** *c472;* histograms, **473,** *c473;* measures of central tendency, 475–77; the normal curve in, **473**–75, *c474;* precautions when using, 481–82; the range in, **477;** standard deviation in, 477–78, *c478*
Status, 404
Stereotype, **134,** *p135,* 243
Stereotyped behavior, 311–**14**
Stimulants, 361
Stimulus: absolute threshold and, **253;** attention and, **254**–55; avoidance conditioning and, **182;** conditioned, **181,** 182, *p182,* 183–86, 187, 188, 190; counter-conditioning and, **182**–83; difference threshold and, **253;** discrimination and, **187;** generalization and, **186**–87; just-noticeable difference and, **253;** reinforcement and, **186;** subliminal, 253–54; unconditioned, **181,** 182, *p182,* 183–86, 188, 190
Stone Age, views on behavior in, 6, *p7*
Storage, 217–20, *c217*
Stranger anxiety, in infants, 53
Stress, 324–39; alarm and, **326;** biofeedback in control of, 337–38; change and, 331–36; control of, 336–39; control as factor in, 330–31; determination of, 326–31; drugs in control of, 338; exercise in control of, 336–37; exhaustion and, **326;** expectations and, 327–30; "fight or flight" reaction to, 325–26; General Adaptation Syndrome and, 326; hassles theory of, 334–39, *p334;* information as factor in, 331; life change approach to, 332–34, *p332;* through life cycle, 335–36, *p337;* nature of, 324–26; personality and, 324–25, *p327,* 335; physiological responses to, 324, 325, *p325,* 326, 334, 337; prevention of, 338–39; relaxation in control of, 337; resistance to, **326;** responsibility as factor in, 331; social support in control of, 338; Type A behavior and, *f328*–29
Stressors, 325–26, *p325*
Strong-Campbell Interest Inventory, 146
Structuralism, **8,** 14
Subjects in experiments, *p24,* **25**–28, *f26*–27, *f484,* 426–30; protection of, 28; selection of, 28
Subliminal perception, 253–54

Substance-use disorders, 361–63
Success, women's fear of, 282
Sullivan, Harry Stack, 116, *p116,* 505
Superego, *p112,* 113
Surgery, brain, 20, 87, 89, 286; hypnosis and, 99; stress and, 331
Sweet lemon rationalization, 317
Symbol, 229
Synapse, 86, *p86,* 88

Takooshian, Harold, *f448*–49
Task-oriented groups. *See* Group
Taste, sense of, 268, *p268*
Taste buds, 268, *p268*
Teachers, *f487, f492*
Teaching machines, 194, 195–96
Telepathy, *p32,* **33;** coincidence vs., 33
Terman, Lewis M., 157, 171, 173, 506
Tests, 23–24; achievement, 143–**44,** 145; aptitude, 143, **144**–45, *p144;* inkblot, 141–42, *p142,* 143; norm group for comparison of, 131–32; projective, 141–43, *p142, p143;* reliability and validity of, **132**–33; standardized, **131**–33, 143–45, *p144. See also* Intelligence tests
Texture gradient, 261
Thalidomide, 74
Theory, 25
Therapy, 372–85. *See also* Psychological disturbances, treatment of
Thinking, 4, **228**–42; accommodation and, **230;** "all-or-nothing," 231; assimilation and, **230;** cerebral cortex and, 89; concepts and, **229**–30; confusion of coincidence with cause and, 231; creative, 232–36, *p232, p234, p235;* daydreaming; *f238*–39; delusions and, **231**–32; development of, 230; divergent, **241,** *c241;* emotions and, 276; imagination and, **236**–37, *p237;* problem solving and, 233–34, 237–42; symbols and, **229;** uncritical, 230–32, *p231*
Thirst drive, 277–79
Thorndike, Edward Lee, 506
Thurstone, L. L., 155
Thyroid gland, 93, *p93,* 95
Thyroxin, 170
Timbre, 265
Tolman, Edward C., 197, 506
Tone, 264
Trainable, 169
Tranquilizers, 372, 373
Transactional analysis (TA), 375–76, 384
Transcendence, as basic need, 115
Transfer: increasing, 207–08; of learning, **206**–08, *p207;* negative, **206**–07; positive, **206,** 207, *p207,* 208
Transference, 373
Twins: fraternal, **70,** *p71;* identical, 66, **68**–69, *p69,* 70, *f72*–73, 76, 78; maturation and learning in, 70

Unconditioned response (UCR), **181,** 182, *p182,* 188
Unconditioned stimulus (UCS), **181,** 182, *p182,* 183–86, 188, 190

Unconscious, 9, 14, **112**–14; collective, **113**–14; personal, **113;** repression and, **222, 314;** techniques for studying of, 113, 373–75

Validity. *See* Tests
Variable-interval schedule, 192
Variable-ratio schedule, 192
Variables, 24–25, 478–79
Verbal ability, 155, 157, 158
Verhave, Thom, *f13*
Veterinary Aptitude Test, 145
Visible spectrum, *p256,* **257**
Vision, 257–64; color and, *p256,* 257–60, *p257, p259;* distance and depth perception and, 260–61, *p260;* distortion and, 261; optical illusions and, **261**–64, *p261;* perception patterns and, 264; sense of pressure and, 269
Visual cliff, *f262–63*
Vitamins, 75, 170
Vocabulary, 47, 49, 157

Vocations: intelligence and, 156, 167; vocational interest inventory and, **145**–46

Walk, Richard, *f262–63*
Walking, as maturation vs. learned process, 70–71
Watson, John B., 10, *p10,* 14, *f184,* 506
Wechsler Adult Intelligence Scale–Revised (WAIS-R), 158, 162
Wechsler descriptive classification of IQ, 163
Wechsler Intelligence Scale for Children–Revised (WISC-R), 158, 162
Weight, 45; counter-conditioning and, 183
Wertheimer, Max, 506
Western Electric Company, experiments at, *f26–27*
Wilbur, Cornelia, *f350–51*
Work, stress caused by, 336
Writers, careers as, *f488*
Wundt, Wilhelm, 8, *p9,* 14, 506

Zimbardo, Philip, *f428–29*

ACKNOWLEDGMENTS (continued)

Addison-Wesley Publishing Co., Reading, MA: From pp. 13–36 in *Conceptual Blockbusting: A Guide to Better Ideas,* Second Edition, by James L. Adams. Copyright © 1974, 1976, 1979 by James L. Adams.

American Association for the Advancement of Science and D. L. Rosenhan: From "On Being Sane in Insane Places" by D. L. Rosenhan in *Science,* Vol. 179, January 19, 1973, pp. 250–258. Copyright 1973 by the AAAS.

American Psychological Association: From "Born to be Shy?" by Jules Asher in *Psychology Today,* April 1987. From "Detecting Deception from the Body or Face" by Paul Ekman and Wallace V. Friesen in *Journal of Personality and Social Psychology,* Vol. 29, No. 3, 1974. From "Little Brother Is Changing You" by Farnum Gray with Paul S. Graubard and Harry Rosenberg in *Psychology Today,* March 1974. From "Male Brain, Female Brain: The Hidden Difference" by Doreen Kimura in *Psychology Today,* November 1985. From "The Case for ECT" by Harold A. Sackeim in *Psychology Today,* June 1985. From "Excuses, Excuses" by C. R. Snyder in *Psychology Today,* September 1984.

Discover Magazine: From "Intelligence: New Ways to Measure the Wisdom of Man" by Kevin McKean in *Discover Magazine,* October 1985. © 1987 by Family Media, Inc.

W. H. Freeman and Company: From *HUMAN MEMORY: Structures and Processes,* Second Edition, by Roberta Klatzky. Copyright © 1975, 1980 by W. H. Freeman and Company. From "Making Sense of the Nonsensical: An Analysis of Jonestown" by Neal Osherow in *Readings About the Social Animal,* Fourth Edition, edited by Elliot Aronson. Copyright © 1973, 1977, 1981, 1984 by W. H. Freeman and Company.

Harcourt Brace Jovanovich, Inc.: Adapted from p. 115 in *Introduction to Psychology,* Ninth Edition, by Atkinson et al. Copyright © 1987 by Harcourt Brace Jovanovich, Inc. Abridged from pp. 274–282 in *Human Information Processing,* Second Edition, by Peter H. Lindsay and Donald A. Norman. Copyright © 1977 by Harcourt Brace Jovanovich, Inc.

Holt, Rinehart and Winston, Inc.: From *Modes of Thinking in Young Children* by Michael A. Wallach and Nathan Kogan. Copyright © 1965 by Holt, Rinehart & Winston, Inc.

Thomas Lickona: From "Moral Stages and Moralization" by Lawrence Kohlberg in *Moral Development and Behavior: Theory, Research, and Social Issues,* edited by Thomas Lickona. Published by Holt, Rinehart and Winston, 1976.

McGraw-Hill Book Company: From "Toward the Articulation of Psychology as a Coherent Discipline" by Amedeo Giorgi in *A Century of Psychology as Science,* edited by Sigmund Koch and David E. Leary. Published by McGraw-Hill, Inc., 1985. From pp. 388–392 in *Systems and Theories in Psychology,* Second Edition, by Melvin H. Marx and William A. Hillix. Published by McGraw-Hill, Inc., 1973.

Prentice-Hall, Inc., Englewood Cliffs, NJ: From pp. 29–31 in *THE UNRESPONSIVE BYSTANDER: Why Doesn't He Help?* by Bibb Latané and John M. Darley. © 1970. From pp. 27–29 in *EXPERIMENTAL PSYCHOLOGY: Methods of Research,* Fourth Edition, by F. J. McGuigan. © 1983.

Marvin E. Shaw: From "An Overview of Small Group Behavior" by Marvin E. Shaw in *Contemporary Topics in Social Psychology,* edited by John W. Thibaut, Janet T. Spence, and Robert C. Carson. Copyright © 1976 by Scott, Foresman and Company.

PICTURE CREDITS
Key: (t) top; (c) center; (b) bottom; (l)left; (r)right

COVER
The Marketing Connection Florida

TITLE PAGE
The Marketing Connection Florida

TABLE OF CONTENTS
v, HBJ Photo/Earl Kogler; vi, HBJ Photo/Earl Kogler, vii, Alexander Tsiaras/Science Source/Photo Researchers; viii, John Ficara/Woodfin Camp & Associates; ix, Douglas B. Nelson/Peter Arnold, Inc.; x, HBJ Photo/Earl Kogler; xi, Wally McNamee/Woodfin Camp & Associates.

UNIT 1
1, HBJ Photo/Earl Kogler; 3, Focus on Sports; 4, Ira Stanley; 5, HBJ Photo/Earl Kogler; 7, Julius Kirschner, American Museum of Natural History; 8, The Granger Collection; 9(l), The Granger Collection; 9(c), Culver Pictures; 9(r), The Granger Collection; 10(l), The Granger Collection; 10(c), Wide World; 10(r), Courtesy Dr. Bandura, Stanford University; 11, Judi Benuenuti; 12, T. McHugh/Photo Researchers; 13, Joel Yale/*Life Magazine,* Time, Inc.; 14, J. Alex Langley/D.P.I.; 15, Sybil Shackman/Monkmeyer; 24, Dr. Nicholas Pastore; 26, Photograph

courtesy of Western Electric; 27, James Karales/Peter Arnold; 29, HBJ photo; 30, HBJ Photo; 31, Syndication International; 32, Reprinted from *Psychology Today Magazine;* copyright © 1976 American Psychological Association; 34, Drawing by W. Miller, © 1977, *The New Yorker Magazine.*

UNIT 2

41, HBJ Photo/Earl Kogler; 44, HBJ Photo/Sam Joosten; 47, George Walker/Liason; 48, Reprinted from *Psychology Today Magazine,* copyright © 1973, American Psychological Association; 50, The Museum of Modern Art/Film Stills Archive; 51, Ken Karp/Omni Photo Communications; 53, Photo Researchers; 55(l), C. H. Brinton; 55(r), H. T. Keller/Shostal Associates; 57, (t, c, b) Marcia Weinstein; 61, Timothy Eagan/Woodfin Camp & Associates; 66, Courtesy HBJ Picture Library; 69, Phil Huber/Black Star; 71, Mimi Cotter/ International Stock Photo; 72, Wide World Photos; 73, Alvis Upitis/Black Star; 74, Robin Forbes; 85, Mike Quon; 86, Mike Quon; 88, Mike Quon; 89, Mike Quon; 90, Roger Sperry, Cal Tech Biology Department; 91, Roger Sperry, Cal Tech Biology Department; 93, Mike Quon; 94, Bettina Cirone/Photo Researchers; 97, (t, c, b) HBJ Photo.

UNIT 3

107, Alexander Tsiaras/Science Source/Photo Researchers; 109, John Blaustein/Woodfin Camp & Associates; 110, Dominique Buisson/Photo Researchers; 112, Culver Inc.; 113, The Bettmann Archive; 114(t), Culver, Inc.; 114(b), © 1983 Jill Krementz; 115(t), Culver, Inc.; 115(b), Molly Dean/Shostal Associates; 116(t), Courtesy William Alanson White Psychiatric Foundation; 116(b), Ted Streshinsky; 117, Richard Hutchings; 118, Ken Heyman; 119(t), HBJ Photo; 119(b), Courtesy, Holt, Rinehart, and Winston, Inc.; 120, (l, r) Albert Bandura; 121, (l, r) Albert Bandura; 122(t), Drawing by Garrett Price © 1944, 1972 *The New Yorker Magazine,* Inc.; 122(b), Marcia Roltner; 123(t), Michael Roughier/*Life Magazine* © 1966, Time Inc.; 123(b), HBJ Photo; 124, James Woodward/Shostal Associates; 126, HBJ Photo/Earl Kogler; 132, Robin Gorbes; 135, Karl Kummels/Shostal Associates; 136, H. Armstrong Roberts; 137(l), William U. Harris; 137(r), Lizabeth Corlett/D. P. I.; 138, Reproduced from the Minnesota Multiphasic Personality Inventory, © copyright 1943, Renewed 1970 by the University of Minnesota. Reproduced by special permission of the publisher.; 140, Jim Pickerell/Click/Chicago; 142, HBJ Photo; 143, Dan McCoy/Rainbow; 144, HBJ Photo; 147, Rhoda Sidney/DeWys Inc.; 156, Culver, Inc.; 157, HBJ Photo/Earl Kogler; 159, U. S. Signal Corp.; 160, Reproduced by special permission of the publisher from the Otis-Lennon Mental Ability Test, copyright © 1967 by Harcourt Brace Jovanovich, Inc. All rights reserved.; 161, Marcia Weinstein; 163(l), Ken Karp; 163(r), Bill Gillette/Stock Boston; 164, Wil Blanche/D. P. I.; 165, Paul Conklin/Monkmeyer; 168, Robert J. Capece/Monkmeyer; 171, The Bettmann Archive.

UNIT 4

179, John Ficaro/Woodfin Camp & Associates; 183, The American Cancer Society; 184, Richard Hutchings; 185, N. Wayne Hanson; 187, Marcia Weinstein; 191, Richard Hutchings; 193, Yerkes Laboratory of Primate Biology; 196, Bob West/Photo Trends; 198, Three Lions, Inc.; 199, (l, c, r) Three Lions, Inc.; 207, Robin Forbes; 209, Mimi Forsyth/Monkmeyer; 211, Sal Murdocca; 214, Ann Hagen Griffiths/Omni Photo Communications; 218, H. Armstrong Roberts; 219, Tom Pantages; 221, © 1959 United Features Syndicate Inc.; 231, Robin Forbes; 232, Sal Murdocca; 234, Dick Durrance II/Woodfin Camp & Associates; 235, Joshua Tree/Editorial Photocolor Archives; 237, Collection, The Solomon R. Guggenheim Museum, New York. Gift of Solomon R. Guggenheim, 1937. Photo by Robert E. Mates and Susan Lazurus; 238, Rob Chabot/D. P. I.; 239, Luis Villota/The Stock Market.

UNIT 5

251, Douglas B. Nelson/Peter Arnold, Inc.; 255, Lambert/Frederic Lewis, Inc.; 260, Peter Vadnai/Editorial Photocolor Archives; 262, William Vandivert; 263, Nicholas Foster/The Image Bank; 267, Photo Trends; 268, Lester V. Bergman & Associates, Inc.; 269, Ken Heyman; 278, Shostal Associates; 279, Culver, Inc.; 280, CBS-TV; 281, Harry F. Harlow, University of Wisconsin Primate Laboratory; 282(tl), D. Fineman/Sygma; 282(tr), Claudio Edinger/Gamma Liaison; 282(bl), Kevin Horan/Picture Group; 282(br), Gamma Liaison; 284, Beth Ullman/Taurus Photos; 287(tl), Dan McCoy/Rainbow; 287, (tc, tr) James Kittle; 287(bl), Etyan Ribner/Editorial Photocolor Archives; 287(bc), Eric Carle/Shostal Associates; 287(br), DeWys, Inc.; 288, HBJ Photo; 289, Erik Anderson/Stock Boston.

UNIT 6

299, HBJ Photo/Earl Kogler; 301, Drawing by S. Gross; © 1974, *The New Yorker Magazine,* Inc.; 303, Robin Forbes; 304, Ted Russell; 309, United Press International; 311, Joe McNally/Wheeler Pictures; 312, Richard Hutchings/Photo Researchers; 313, The Bettman Archive; 315, HBJ Photo/Earl Kogler; 316, Bil Keane, Family Circus/© King Features; 318, Culver, Inc.; 325, Marvin E. Newman/Woodfin Camp & Associates; 327, The Bettman Archive; 328, Alfred Gescheidt/The Image Bank; 329, William U. Harris; 330, Tom Carroll/Alpha; 332, Zimmerman/Alpha; 334, Peter Gridley/FPG; 337, Michael Heron/Woodfin Camp & Associates; 338, Ricardo Ferro/Black Star; 346, Laima Druskis/Editorial Photocolor Archives; 348, Dominick Micholupo; 349, Robin Forbes; 350, J. Baker/Alpha; 351, Gerald Martineau, *The Washington Post;* 352, HBJ Photo; 354, HBJ Photo; 355, The Lafayette Center of the Brooklyn Psychological Rehabilitation Institute; 356, Archie Lieberman/Black Star; 358, C. H. Brinton; 360, HBJ Photo; 363, Robin Forbes; 364, HBJ Photo; 374, © 1965 United Features Syndicate Inc.; 376, Esther Henderson/Frederic Lewis, Inc.; 378, Rick Friedman/Black Star; 379, Rhoda Sidney/DeWys Inc.; 381, (l, r) Ken Karp; 382, William U. Harris; 383, Sepp Seitz/Woodfin Camp & Associates; 384, Jim Pickerell/Click/Chicago.

UNIT 7

393, Wally McNamee/Woodfin Camp & Associates; 395, Mike Yamashaita/Woodfin Camp & Associates; 398, T. Molenouk/The Image Bank; 399, William Vandivert, *Scientific American;* 400, Shostal Associates; 403, HBJ Photo/Earl Kogler; 405, HBJ Photo/Earl Kogler; 407, Clyde H. Smith/Peter Arnold, Inc.; 409, Courtesy KLM Airlines; 420, Ken Karp; 423, Sybil Shelton/Monkmeyer; 424, HBJ Photo/Earl Kogler; 427, Laimute Druskis/Taurus Photos; 428, Phillip G. Zimbardo, Stanford University; 429, Phillip G. Zimbardo, Stanford University; 431, HBJ Photo/Earl Kogler; 433, C. H. Brinton; 435, Catherine Ursillo/Leo DeWys; 443, Rhoda Galyn; 444, HBJ Photo; 446, Robin Forbes; 447, Rhoda Sidney/DeWys, Inc.; 448, Wil Blanche/D. P. I.; 449, Bill Stanton/Magnum Photo Inc.; 451, Paul Katz/The Image Bank; 453, Everett C. Johnson/Dewys, Inc.; 456, *The Battle for Fox Green Beach* by Shepler, U. S. Navy; 459, Jerry Hout/Bruce Coleman, Inc.; 461, Shostal Associates.

CAREERS IN PSYCHOLOGY

483, Cliff Moore/Taurus Photos; 484, David Hiser/The Image Bank; 485, FPG; 486, T. McNee/FPG; 487, Mark Sherman/Bruce Coleman, Inc.; 488, Richard Howard/Black Star; 489, Mike Kagan/Monkmeyer; 490, Sepp Seitz/Woodfin Camp & Associates; 491, Isian Marlinsky/Alpha; 492, Jeffry W. Myers/Alpha; 493, Jim Pickerell/Black Star; 494, Steve Liss/Liaison Agency; 495, Leo Choplin/Black Star; 496, William U. Harris; 497, Charles Harbutt/Archive Pictures; 498, Gabe Palmer/The Image Bank; 499, Robin Forbes/The Image Bank; 500, Larry Mulvehill/Photo Researchers; 501, Richard Hutchings/Photo Researchers; 502, FPG.

C 0
D 1
E 2
F 3
G 4
H 5
I 6
J 7